THE DORLING KINDERSLEY
GEOGRAPHY
OF THE
WORLD

The Friday Mosque at Mopti in Mali.

Street scene in Tokyo, Japan.

Chinese boy writing characters.

Traditional house built by the Tswana people from Botswana.

Black pepper plant and peppercorns from the Pacific Islands.

High, windswept plains, called the altiplano, in Bolivia.

Aymará Indians from the altiplano in Bolivia.

A variety of different crops grown on small farms in Italy.

Copper from Namibia.

Street market in Lausanne, Switzerland.

Wine and cheeses from Germany.

UNITED KINGDOM

 JAPAN

 BHUTAN

 ITALY

 SWEDEN

 GHANA

 IVORY COAST

 BRAZIL

 MEXICO

 NORWAY

 INDIA

 SAUDI ARABIA

 GERMANY

 FRANCE

 SOUTH AFRICA

 SENEGAL

 AUSTRALIA

 AZERBAIJAN

 TUVALU

 PHILIPPINES

 ARGENTINA

 NEW ZEALAND

 CANADA

 BRUNEI

 PARAGUAY

 KAZAKHSTAN

 BAHAMAS

 SUDAN

 UNITED STATES OF AMERICA

THE DORLING KINDERSLEY
GEOGRAPHY
OF THE
WORLD

 CHINA

 RUSSIAN FEDERATION

 VENEZUELA

 PANAMA

 PORTUGAL

 BELGIUM

 KENYA

 SPAIN

 IRAQ

 CHILE

 NETHERLANDS

 JAMAICA

 GREECE

 INDONESIA

 THAILAND

DORLING KINDERSLEY

London • New York • Stuttgart • Moscow

 KIRIBATI

 MALAYSIA

 MONGOLIA

A DORLING KINDERSLEY BOOK

Senior Art Editor
Rachael Foster

Senior Editor
Susan Peach

Art Editors
Marcus James, Tina Robinson,
Jane Tetzlaff

Editors
Marie Greenwood, Fran Jones,
Veronica Pennycook

Deputy Art Director Miranda Kennedy
Deputy Editorial Director Sophie Mitchell

Senior DTP designer Mathew Birch
DTP designer Almudena Díaz

Cartography Jan Clark, Robin Giddings
Picture research Rachel Leach
Research Robert Graham
Special photography Andy Crawford
Production Catherine Semark, Louise Barratt

Chief consultant Dr David Green

Consultants
Dr Kathy Baker, Professor Mark Blacksell, Dr Tanya Bowyer-Bower, Dr Robert Bradnock,
Dr Edward Brown, Dr Brian Chalkley, Professor Roman Cybriwsky, Professor Dennis Dwyer,
Professor Alan Gilbert, St John Gould, Professor Ian Hamilton, Robert Headland, Dr Michael Heffernan,
Professor Eleanore Kofman, Keith Lye, Professor Robert Mason, Professor Bill Mead, Professor William
Morgan, Susan Murrell, Jenny Nemko, Dr Rewi Newnham, Professor Robert Potter, Dr Jonathan Rigg,
Dr David Simon, Dr David Turnock, John Wright and Nicholas Awde, Dr Ted Yates

Authors Simon Adams, Anita Ganeri, Ann Kay
Additional text by Ann Kramer, Claire Watts

First published in Great Britain in 1996
by Dorling Kindersley Limited,
9 Henrietta Street, London WC2E 8PS
Visit us on the World Wide Web at http://www.dk.com

A CIP catalogue record for this book is available from the British Library.

ISBN 07513 5430 9

Colour reproduction by Colourscan, Singapore
Printed and bound in Italy by A. Mondadori Editore, Verona

CONTENTS

132 ASIA

HOW TO USE THIS BOOK

THIS BOOK IS DIVIDED INTO six continental sections – North America, Central and South America, Europe, Asia, Africa, and Australasia and Oceania. At the start of each section there is a map showing the whole area, as well as pages that describe the peoples who live there. Each country, or group of countries, then has an individual map that shows its cities, towns, and main geographical features. This is followed by the country pages that go into detail about life in that country. The reference section can be used to find out more about subjects of general interest, such as world religions or political systems. There is also a glossary, a gazetteer, and an index. The pages here explain the information and symbols that you will come across in the book.

COUNTRY PAGES

The country pages, like this one for Japan, have been designed to give you as much information as possible about the way of life in a country – its people, their traditions, politics, and the economy. All the countries of the world are featured in the book.

COLOUR BORDERS

Each continental section has a different colour border to help you locate that section easily. This page on Japan has the colour used for all the countries in Asia.

HEADING

Every page in the book ha a heading that tells you th name of the section follo by the name of the count featured on that page.

FACT BOXES

Each country page has a box with important statistics about that country, such as its area, the size of its population, the capital city, and the currency. The notes below explain some other entries that appear in most fact boxes.

Locator map
This shows the position of a country, or countries, in relation to its neighbours. This locator map shows where Japan lies off the coast of mainland Asia.

JAPAN

Capital city:	Tokyo
Area:	377,800 sq km (145,869 sq miles)
Population:	123,611,167
Official language:	Japanese
Major religions:	Shinto and Buddhist 92%, other 8%
Government:	Multi-party democracy
Currency:	Yen
Adult literacy rate:	99%
Life expectancy:	79 years
People per doctor:	610
Televisions:	620 per 1,000 people

Major religions
The figures provide a breakdown of the religious beliefs of the people. All the main religions are explained in detail on pages 274–275.

Government
This describes how a country is ruled, or governed. The main types of government are explained on pages 270–271.

Adult literacy rate
This is the percentage of people who can read and write. Literacy rates are based on the ability of people aged 15 or over to read and write a simple sentence. Find out more about literacy rates on page 277.

People per doctor
This figure shows how many people there are for every one doctor. It gives a rough guide about whether people have easy access to medical attention. Find out more on page 276.

Life expectancy
The number shows how long the average person in a country can expect to live. Figures are a combination of the average life expectancy of men and women. There is more about life expectancy on page 276.

Abbreviations used in the book:

Metric

m	metres
mm	millimetres
cm	centimetres
km	kilometres
sq km	square kilometres
km/h	kilometres per hour
°C	degrees Centigrade

Imperial

ft	feet
in	inches
sq miles	square miles
mph	miles per hour
°F	degrees Fahrenheit

Other abbreviations

BC	Before Christ
AD	Anno Domini
USA	United States of America
UK	United Kingdom

Find out more

EARTHQUAKES: *13*
GROWING CITIES: *17, 136*
LIFE EXPECTANCY: *276*
PACIFIC RIM ECONOMIES: *137*

FIND OUT MORE BOXES

At the end of each country entry there is a Find out more box. This directs you to other pages in the book where you can discover more about a particular subject. For example, one of the pages on Japan explains how the country suffers from hundreds of earthquakes a year. You can then find out more about earthquakes and why they occur by turning to page 13 in the book.

MAP PAGES

Each country appears on one of the regional maps, like the one of Southern Africa shown below. These maps show many geographical features, such as mountain ranges, deserts, rivers, and lakes, along with capital cities and other major towns. The key on the far right shows you what these features look like on the maps. A compass point fixes the direction of the region in relation to North (N).

This figure is the page number.

This figure gives the grid reference on the map.

Durango *Town* Mexico 39 E5
Durban *Town* South Africa 247 I10
Dushanbe *Town* Tajikistan 161 G8
Düsseldorf *Town* Germany 95 D6
Dvina (Northern, Western) *River* Russian Federation 78 I8, L6, 109 G6, J8, 138 E5
Dzhugdzhur Range *Mountain range* Russian Federation 133 O6, 139 Q8

E

East China Sea China 10 K6, 133 L10, 265 A3
East Frisian Islands Germany 95 E3

USING THE GRID

The grid around the outside of the page helps you to find places on the map. For example, to find the city of Durban, look up its name in the gazetteer on pages 284–295. Next to the word Durban are the reference numbers 247 I10. The first number shows that Durban is on page 247. The second number shows it is in square I10 of the grid. Turn to page 247. Trace down from the letter I on the grid and then across from the number 10. You will find Durban situated in the square where the number and the letter meet.

Key to features on the maps

International border

Disputed border

State or province border

River

Wadi

Lake

Seasonal lake

Waterfall

Dam

Capital city

Major town

Special feature

Volcanic mountain

Mountain

SCALE

0   100 200 300 400 500 km
0   100   200   300 miles

Each map features a scale which shows how distances on the map relate to kilometres and miles. The scale can be used to see how big a country is, or how far it is from one place to another. Not all maps in the book are drawn to the same scale.

LOCATOR MAP

This map shows the position of the country, or countries, within the continental section. It also shows how near the country is to the Equator, the Tropics of Cancer and Capricorn, or the Arctic or Antarctic Circle. This gives an indication of how hot or cold a country is. Find out more about climate on pages 14–15.

Angola   Namibia

COUNTRY FLAGS

The national flag for each country or territory appears around the edge of the map. The designs often reflect the culture or religion of the country.

WEATHER FACTS

The average temperature and amount of rainfall recorded in January and July are shown around the main map. Weather facts are given for several places on the map to show how temperature and rainfall can vary within an area. The weather inland, for example, will generally be hotter than it is near the coast.

The sun symbol represents the average temperature.

Francistown, Botswana

 Jan 25°C (77°F)
July 15°C (58°F)

 Jan 107 mm (4.2 in)
July 0 mm (0 in)

The cloud symbol represents the average rainfall.

AFRICA • SOUTHERN AFRICA

THINGS TO LOOK FOR ON THE MAP
Longest river: Zambezi, Mozambique/Zimbabwe/Zambia/Namibia/Angola, 2,700 km (1,678 miles) *Map J5*
Highest point: Mt. Thabana-Ntlenyana, Lesotho, 3,482 m (11,424 ft) *Map H10*
Largest lake: L. Nyasa, Mozambique/Malawi/Tanzania 28,490 sq km (11,000 sq miles) *Map J4*

0 100 200 300 400 500 km
0   100   200   300 miles

Francistown, Botswana
Jan 25°C (77°F)
July 15°C (58°F)
Jan 107 mm (4.2 in)
July 0 mm (0 in)

Port Elizabeth, South Africa
Jan 21°C (70°F)
July 13°C (56°F)
Jan 31 mm (1.2 in)
July 48 mm (1.9 in)

247

CITY GROWTH

Across southern Africa, people are leaving the countryside and moving to the cities in search of work. The urban area surrounding Johannesburg in South Africa now houses a population of more than 9 million, making it the second biggest African city, after Cairo. Maputo, the capital of Mozambique (right), doubled in size between 1975 and 1983, and now contains more than 1.5 million people.

WOMEN'S ROLE

In traditional African society, women generally acted as wives and mothers and were responsible for routine household tasks and growing crops. Today, many African men work away from home in the mines and cities for one or two years at a time, leaving women to form the majority in their villages. This means that women are now taking on more responsibility in the households.

Abbreviations used on maps

L.	Lake
I.or Is.	Island (s)
R.	River
Mt. or Mts.	Mountain(s)
St	Saint
C.	Cape
Res.	Reservoir

THE PHYSICAL WORLD

THE EARTH, OUR HOME in the universe, is one of the nine planets that circles around the Sun. It is the only place scientists know that can support life because it has oxygen in its atmosphere and water in its oceans – both essential for life. More than two-thirds of the Earth is covered with water in the form of oceans, seas, rivers, and lakes. The remainder is made up of seven vast expanses of land, called continents, whose physical features are remarkably varied. Among the most notable features are the mountain ranges, rivers, and deserts, which can be found on this world map.

CONTINENTS

The seven continents that make up the world's land mass are, from largest to smallest: Asia, Africa, North America, South America, Antarctica, Europe, and Australia. The Polar regions, not completely visible on the flat map, surround the North and South Poles and are shown on the globes, left and below.

Only 29 per cent of the Earth's surface is land. The percentage area of each continent is shown here

Earth's surface
Water: 71%
Land: 29%

Australia: 5%
Europe: 7%

Asia: 30%
Africa: 20%
North America: 16.5%
South America: 12%
Antarctica: 9.5%

ARCTIC CIRCLE
TROPIC OF CANCER
EQUATOR

Ellesmere I.
Melville I.
Devon I.
Greenland
Banks I.
CHUKCHI SEA
BEAUFORT SEA
Victoria I.
Baffin Bay
GREENLAND SEA
ARCTIC CIRCLE
Great Bear L.
Baffin I.
Yukon
Mackenzie
Great Slave L.
Davis Strait
Bering Strait
BERING SEA
Great Bear L.
Hudson Bay
LABRADOR SEA
Aleutian Is.
Gulf of Alaska
ROCKY MOUNTAINS
COAST MTS.
NORTH AMERICA
Newfoundland
COAST RANGES
GREAT PLAINS
Missouri
Great Lakes
ATLANTIC
Midway Is.
SONORAN DESERT
Mississippi
APPALACHIAN MTS.
OCEAN
Azores
Bermuda Is.
Hawaiian Is.
SIERRA MADRE
Rio Grande
Gulf of Mexico
Bahamas
TROPIC OF CANCER
PACIFIC
Greater Antilles
OCEAN
CENTRAL
CARIBBEAN SEA
Lesser Antilles
Line Is.
AMERICA
Gibert Is.
Phoenix Is.
Galápagos Is.
Marquesas Is.
ANDES
LLANOS
Amazon
AMAZONIA
EQUATOR
Samoa
Tuamotu
SOUTH
Tuvalu
Fiji
Society Is.
Tahiti
AMERICA
São Francisco
Vanuatu
Cook Is.
Tubuai Is.
L. Titicaca
ANDES
PLATEAU OF MATO GROSSO
TROPIC OF CAPRICORN
Juan Fernández Is.
ATACAMA DESERT
PAMPAS
Paraná
New Zealand
Chatham Is.
PATAGONIA
ATLANTIC
Bounty Is.
Antipodes Is.
Auckland Is.
OCEAN
Falkland Is.
Cape Horn

THINGS TO LOOK FOR ON THE MAP

Highest point on Earth: Mt. Everest, China/Nepal, 8,848 m (29,029 ft) *Map H6*

Lowest point on Earth: Mariana Trench, Pacific Ocean, 10,924 m (35,840 ft) below sea level *Map L8*

Longest river: Nile, Egypt/Sudan/Uganda, 6,738 km (4,187 miles) *Map E7*

Largest lake: Caspian Sea, Azerbaijan/Iran/Turkmenistan/Kazakhstan/Russian Federation, 378,400 sq km (146,101 sq miles) *Map F5*

Largest ocean: Pacific Ocean, 165,241,000 sq km (63,804,540 sq miles) *Map Q7*

1
2
3
5
6
7
9
10
11
12
13

N O P Q R S T U V W X Y A

MOVING CONTINENTS

THE CONTINENTS THAT MAKE UP most of the Earth's land surface are always on the move, shifted around by forces deep inside the Earth. This is known as continental drift. Movement, or drift, takes place because the inside of the planet is hot and turbulent. The intense heat generated within the Earth is carried upwards where it disturbs the cool, rocky surface and forces the plates of crust that make up the continents to move. Each year the continents drift about a centimetre (nearly half an inch), some getting closer together, others moving further apart, some grinding past each other. When this happens, many of the Earth's natural features are created or changed.

IN THE BEGINNING

Scientists believe that, some 300 million years ago, all the land on Earth was joined together in one "supercontinent", called Pangaea. It was surrounded by a giant ocean, Panthalassa. About 200 million years ago, as the plates moved, Pangaea began to split into two great landmasses, Laurasia in the north, and Gondwanaland in the south. These were separated by the Tethys Sea. As the plates continued to move, the two landmasses split and moved further apart, eventually forming the continents on the map below.

200 million years ago

PANTHALASSA PANGAEA PANTHALASSA

180 million years ago

LAURASIA TETHYS SEA GONDWANALAND

65 million years ago

NORTH AMERICA EUROPE ASIA AFRICA SOUTH AMERICA INDIA AUSTRALIA ANTARCTICA

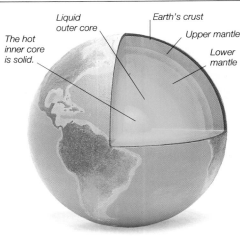

The hot inner core is solid.
Liquid outer core
Earth's crust
Upper mantle
Lower mantle

INSIDE THE EARTH

The Earth is not a solid ball, but is made up of many different layers. The crust that forms the continents and the ocean floor is a thin layer of rock that covers the Earth like a shell. The mantle beneath is 3,000 km (1,864 miles) thick and made of hot rock, some of which is molten (liquid). At the centre is the core, the hot metallic centre of the Earth. This is liquid on the outside and solid on the inside.

EURASIAN PLATE

JUAN DE FUCA PLATE

NORTH AMERICAN PLATE

IRANIAN PLATE

ARABIAN PLATE

PHILIPPINE PLATE

MID-ATLANTIC RIDGE

CARIBBEAN PLATE

COCOS PLATE

PACIFIC PLATE

AFRICAN PLATE

MID-INDIAN RIDGE

SOUTH AMERICAN PLATE

INDO-AUSTRALIAN PLATE

EAST PACIFIC RISE

NAZCA PLATE

SOUTHWEST INDIAN RIDGE

SOUTHEAST INDIAN RIDGE

ANTARCTIC PLATE

MID-ATLANTIC RIDGE

SCOTIA PLATE

PACIFIC-ANTARCTIC RIDGE

KEY TO MAP
— Subduction zone
— Mid-ocean ridge and faults
— Collision zone
- - - Uncertain plate boundary
➤ Movement of plate
▲ Volcano

RESTLESS EARTH

Because the Earth appears to stand still, it is difficult to imagine that the crust is moving. However, there are three main ways in which plates move, and these are known as spreading ridges, subduction zones, and transform faults, all shown on the artwork below. It is possible to see the effect this activity has had on the landscape. The Rocky Mountains in North America were formed when two plates collided, while the Great Rift Valley in Africa is the result of plates pulling apart. Volcanoes and earthquakes are also dramatic reminders that the plates are still moving.

At Thingvellir, Iceland, the spreading ridge between the North American and Eurasian plates appears as a long gash in the landscape.

SPREADING RIDGES

A spreading ridge occurs where two plates start to pull apart and molten rocks from the Earth's mantle well up to fill the gap. If this happens along the ocean floor, it creates an underwater mountain chain such as the Mid-Atlantic Ridge. Sometimes the peaks of these mountains break the surface as volcanic islands, as happened with Iceland. When a spreading ridge occurs on land it creates a steep-sided rift valley.

Chains of volcanoes are often found along subduction zones.

A mid-ocean ridge where two plates are pulling apart.

Plates slide past each other along a transform fault.

At a subduction zone, the crust is forced down into the mantle, where it melts.

When plates collide the crust buckles and folds and may be pushed up to form mountains.

TRANSFORM FAULT

A transform fault is where two plates grind past each other in opposite directions, or in the same direction but at different speeds. No crust is made or destroyed in the process, but the movement creates deep cracks in the ground. The sliding movement often occurs in short bursts which are felt on the surface as earthquakes. The San Andreas fault in California, USA, is an active earthquake zone.

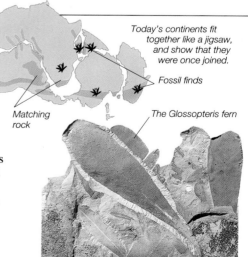

The San Andreas fault is the point where the Pacific and North American plates meet.

SUBDUCTION ZONE

When two plates meet, the edge of one can be pushed down (subducted) under the other and into the mantle below. The rocks from the crust melt in the mantle. Often these molten rocks force their way to the surface as a volcano. The many volcanoes around the edge of the Pacific plate, such as Mt Mihara, Japan, were formed this way. Sometimes when plates collide, rocks are forced up to form great mountain ranges.

LOOKING AT THE EVIDENCE

When the German scientist Alfred Wegener first put forward his theory of moving plates in 1923, people dismissed his ideas as nonsense. Since then, evidence had proved him correct. Fossils of the fern, *Glossopteris*, for example, have been found in rocks as far apart as India, Australia, and Africa. All these places were once joined together as Gondwanaland. Further proof comes from matching types of rock that have been found in Australia, Antartica, and South America.

Today's continents fit together like a jigsaw, and show that they were once joined.

Fossil finds

The Glossopteris fern

Matching rock

CLIMATE AND VEGETATION

CLIMATE IS THE AVERAGE PATTERN of weather and temperature in a particular area over a long period of time. Similar types of climate are found in different places around the world. For example, there are regions of hot, dry desert in Africa and North America, as well as across central Australia. It is a region's climate, together with its physical landscape, that determines the sort of vegetation, or plant life, which is usually found there. Cold areas near the Poles, or icy mountain peaks, will support little, or no, vegetation. Hot, wet rainforests near the Equator, however, will encourage the fast growth of a variety of plants.

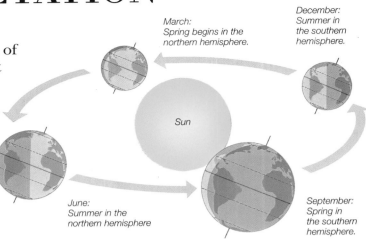

March:
Spring begins in the northern hemisphere.

December:
Summer in the southern hemisphere.

Sun

June:
Summer in the northern hemisphere

September:
Spring in the southern hemisphere.

SEASONS OF THE YEAR

As the Earth travels around the Sun, the tilt on its axis means that each place leans gradually nearer the Sun, and then farther away from it. This causes the seasons. When the northern hemisphere leans towards the Sun it has summer. When it tilts away it has winter. In the southern hemisphere this is reversed. In between the warm days of summer and the cold of winter come spring and autumn. The Earth also spins on its axis, turning once every 24 hours to give us day and night. The side facing the Sun has day, while the other side has night.

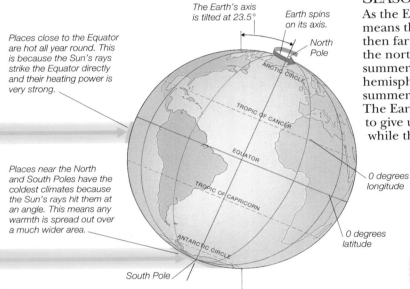

The Earth's axis is tilted at 23.5°

Earth spins on its axis.

North Pole

Places close to the Equator are hot all year round. This is because the Sun's rays strike the Equator directly and their heating power is very strong.

ARCTIC CIRCLE

TROPIC OF CANCER

EQUATOR

0 degrees longitude

Places near the North and South Poles have the coldest climates because the Sun's rays hit them at an angle. This means any warmth is spread out over a much wider area.

TROPIC OF CAPRICORN

ANTARCTIC CIRCLE

0 degrees latitude

South Pole

LATITUDE AND LONGITUDE

A region's climate is influenced by how far to the north or south of the Equator it lies. This is called its latitude. The Equator, an imaginary line running round the Earth, lies at 0 degrees latitude. Other lines of latitude include the Tropics of Cancer and Capricorn. Regions around the Equator are the hottest in the world, while the closer to the Poles you go, the colder it gets. There are also lines which run from north to south, known as longitude.

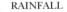

RAINFALL
The amount of rainfall a place receives during the year greatly affects its vegetation as well as its climate. Plants need water to make their own food and will thrive in the warm, wet climate of a tropical rainforest, as shown here in Costa Rica. Where rainfall is very low, in deserts or Polar regions, only a few plants manage to survive. In other places, the amount of rainfall varies with the seasons.

LAND AND SEA
The climate of a region is affected by altitude – how high a place is above sea-level. The higher a place, the colder its climate, even if it lies near the Equator or the Tropics like these Atlas Mountains in Morocco. Another important influence is how close a place is to the sea. The sea warms and cools slower than land, so coastal areas usually have fewer extremes of temperature.

CHANGES IN WORLD CLIMATE
The world's climate can be changed by both natural as well as human events. When Mt Pinatubo, a volcano in the Philippines, erupted in 1991, it threw ash and dust high into the atmosphere. Locally, this caused dark skies, heavy rainfall, and high winds. The distance the ash was carried can be seen from this satellite photo. Equally, events such as the massive oil fires in Kuwait, started during the Gulf War, can have a long-term effect on climate.

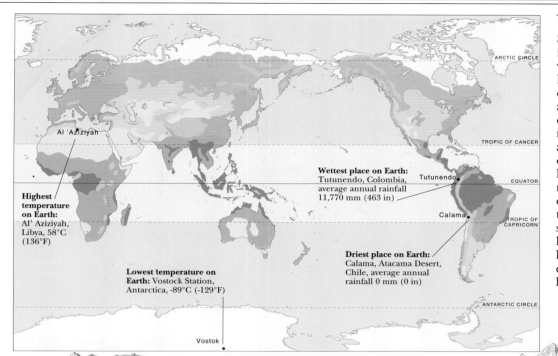

Highest temperature on Earth: Al' Aziziyah, Libya, 58°C (136°F)

Wettest place on Earth: Tutunendo, Colombia, average annual rainfall 11,770 mm (463 in)

Driest place on Earth: Calama, Atacama Desert, Chile, average annual rainfall 0 mm (0 in)

Lowest temperature on Earth: Vostock Station, Antarctica, -89°C (-129°F)

Vostok

ARCTIC CIRCLE

TROPIC OF CANCER

EQUATOR

Tutunendo

Calama

TROPIC OF CAPRICORN

ANTARCTIC CIRCLE

VEGETATION ZONES

Scientists divide the Earth into a number of different vegetation zones, also known as "biomes", shown on the map left. The plant and animal life found in each zone depends on the region's climate, landscape, and latitude. Over millions of years, plants and animals have adapted to life in this range of climates, often developing special features that have helped them to survive. The map also highlights how similar landscapes, such as taiga or deserts, occur at the same latitude across the world.

POLAR AND TUNDRA

The areas around the North and South Poles are freezing cold and covered in ice. South of the North Pole lies a region called the tundra, where the lower layers of soil are permanently frozen. Hardy mosses, lichens, and shrubs are the only plants that can survive here.

TAIGA

In Russian, the word taiga means "cold forest". It describes the vast evergreen forests that stretch across northern Canada, Scandinavia, and the Russian Federation. Evergreen trees, such as fir, spruce, and pine, are well-adapted to the long, snowy winters.

MOUNTAIN REGIONS

The higher up a mountain you go, the colder it gets. Trees and plants grow on the lower slopes of many mountains. But, above a certain level, called the tree line, it is too cold and windy for plants to survive. High mountain peaks are often covered in snow all year round.

TEMPERATE FOREST

Much of the land in northern Europe and North America was once covered by deciduous forests (trees that lose their leaves in winter). Most of these have now been cut down. Deciduous trees grow well in temperate climates where it is never very hot or very cold.

MEDITERRANEAN

Areas with a Mediterranean climate have hot, dry summers and cool, wet winters. They include land around the Mediterranean Sea and other similar places, such as California in the USA. Plants and trees, such as olives, have adapted to survive the lack of water in summer.

DRY GRASSLAND

Vast grasslands cover the centre of some of the continents. They include the South American pampas and the North American prairies. They have hot, dry summers and very cold winters. Large parts of these grasslands are now ploughed for wheat or used to raise cattle.

TROPICAL RAINFOREST

Around the Equator, the climate is hot and wet all year round, and provides ideal conditions for lush, green tropical forests to thrive. The world's rainforests may contain 50,000 different types of tree, as well as millions of other species of plants and animals.

HOT DESERT

Deserts are the hottest, driest places on Earth. Temperatures are often very hot during the day but may plunge below freezing at night. Some deserts have no rain for several years. Deserts often contain sandy soil that can only support plants such as cacti.

TROPICAL GRASSLAND

Between the hot deserts and tropical rainforests lie tropical grasslands, such as the African savanna. The climate here is always hot, but the year is divided into a wet and a dry season. Tall grasses, as well as low trees and shrubs, grow in these hot areas.

WORLD POPULATION

PEOPLE HAVE LIVED ON EARTH for at least 2 million years. For most of that time, the population remained small, because the number of people born was roughly the same as the number who died. Disease and famine ensured that the size of the population did not overtake the supplies of food and other resources. However, as farming methods became more efficient and medical knowledge improved, the population rapidly began to grow. It now stands in excess of 5.5 billion people, with more than one million babies born every four days. In many parts of the world, rapid population growth can create serious problems, such as shortage of food or overcrowding in cities.

WHERE PEOPLE LIVE

People are not evenly distributed among the world's continents. The fact that a continent is large, such as North America, does not necessarily mean that it has a large population. Some regions cannot support more than a few people whilst others, with fertile soils and good communication, can support many. The world map below shows the average number of people who live in a square kilometre, or mile, in each country. This is known as population density.

Asia: 63%

Africa: 12.5%

Australasia and Oceania: 0.5%

Europe: 10.4%

North America: 6.9%

Antarctica: 0%

South America: 6.7%

This chart shows the size of each continent or region, together with the percentage of the world's population who live there. Far more people live in Asia than anywhere else on Earth.

World map showing the population density of each country

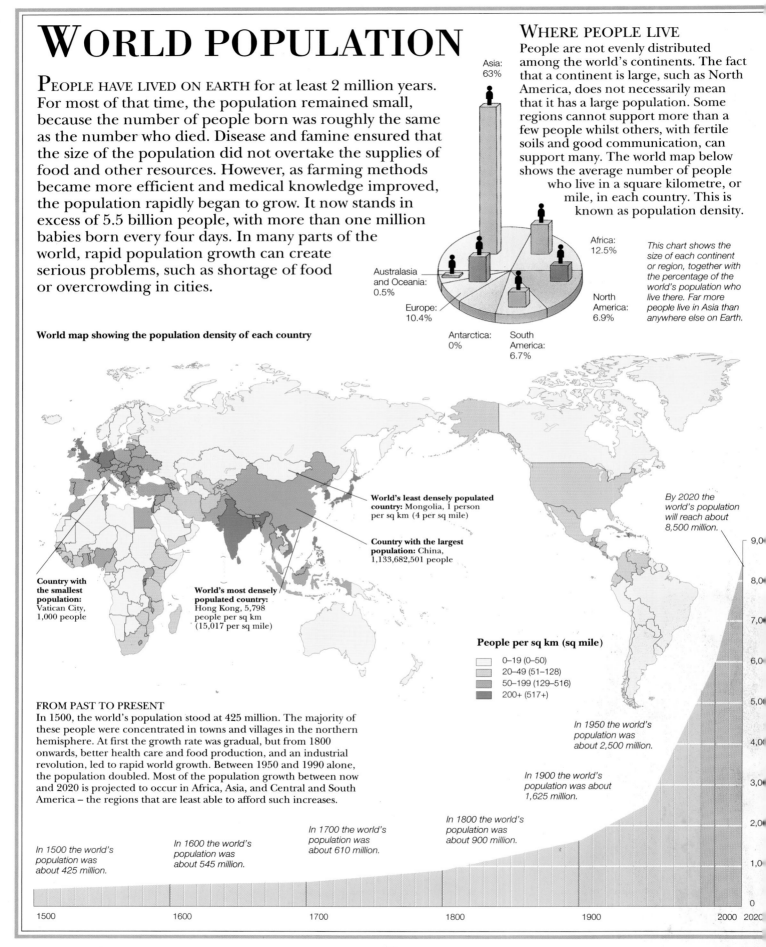

World's least densely populated country: Mongolia, 1 person per sq km (4 per sq mile)

Country with the largest population: China, 1,133,682,501 people

Country with the smallest population: Vatican City, 1,000 people

World's most densely populated country: Hong Kong, 5,798 people per sq km (15,017 per sq mile)

People per sq km (sq mile)

- 0–19 (0–50)
- 20–49 (51–128)
- 50–199 (129–516)
- 200+ (517+)

By 2020 the world's population will reach about 8,500 million.

In 1950 the world's population was about 2,500 million.

In 1900 the world's population was about 1,625 million.

FROM PAST TO PRESENT

In 1500, the world's population stood at 425 million. The majority of these people were concentrated in towns and villages in the northern hemisphere. At first the growth rate was gradual, but from 1800 onwards, better health care and food production, and an industrial revolution, led to rapid world growth. Between 1950 and 1990 alone, the population doubled. Most of the population growth between now and 2020 is projected to occur in Africa, Asia, and Central and South America – the regions that are least able to afford such increases.

In 1500 the world's population was about 425 million.

In 1600 the world's population was about 545 million.

In 1700 the world's population was about 610 million.

In 1800 the world's population was about 900 million.

1500   1600   1700   1800   1900   2000 2020

9,0
8,0
7,0
6,0
5,0
4,0
3,0
2,0
1,0
0

Percentage growth of city dwellers

People living in the cities (urban)　　People living in the countryside (rural)

Asia　16% 23% 34% 43%

North America　64% 74% 75% 77%

South America　43% 60% 75% 80%

1950　1970　1990　Estimate for year 2000　Rural areas

Highest and lowest fertility rates within each continent

Rwanda: 8.3
Yemen: 7.3
Guatemala: 4.9
Papua New Guinea: 4.8
Mexico: 3.3
Albania: 2.9
Tunisia: 3
San Marino: 1.5
Canada: 1.8
Uruguay: 2.5
Australia: 1.8
Hong Kong: 1.3

BIRTH AND DEATH

The number of babies a woman has varies from one country to another. In Sudan, above, the fertility rate is high with an average of 5.7 babies per mother. Better health care, even in the poorer countries of the world, means that less babies now die of hunger or disease, and fewer women die in childbirth. In wealthy countries, such as Canada, the birth rate is low because people can choose to have small families. Advances in medical knowledge also mean that people are living longer.

URBAN GROWTH

Even at the start of this century, only one in ten people lived in a city. The vast majority lived in villages in rural areas, and worked on the land. Today, about half the population are city dwellers. There are various reasons for this growth. In South America, for example, people have been pushed out of the countryside by poverty and loss of land. They are drawn to the cities in search of work. By 2020, if the growth continues, about two out of three people will live in a city.

WORLD'S BIGGEST CITIES IN 1950	
New York, USA	12,300,000
London, UK	8,700,000
Tokyo, Japan	6,700,000
Paris, France	5,400,000
Shanghai, China	5,300,000

WORLD'S BIGGEST CITIES IN 1990	
Mexico City, Mexico	20,200,000
Tokyo, Japan	18,100,000
São Paulo, Brazil	17,400,000
New York, USA	16,200,000
Shanghai, China	13,400,000

CITY SLUMS

One effect of the move of large numbers of people from the countryside to the cities is overcrowding. There are simply not enough houses and resources to go round. In many large cities, such as Bombay, India, this has led to the growth of sprawling shanty towns on the edges of cities. Conditions in these city slums are often unhygienic. Families survive in crowded homes made of make-shift materials, often with no electricity or running water.

SUPER CITIES

Before the 19th century, cities with more than a million people were rare. In the last 100 years, however, the number of large cities has grown dramatically. Today, several cities, such as Tokyo, already have populations approaching 20 million. This means that some cities have more people than the population of countries such as New Zealand or Sweden. Large cities often suffer from pollution caused by car exhausts, factory emissions, and domestic waste.

LOOKING TO THE FUTURE

Slowing down the growth of the population is one of the most serious issues facing the world in the future. To encourage people to have fewer children, programmes have now been set up to teach women about family planning and health care so that they have more choice about the size and health of their families. Today, more than half the married women in the developing world report that they or their partner use birth control, compared with less than a quarter in 1980.

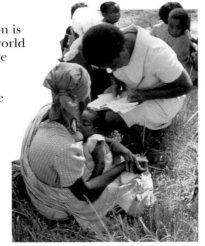

This doctor is writing out a prescription for contraceptives, now used by 43 per cent of the women in Zimbabwe.

THE POLITICAL WORLD

AS WELL AS BEING DIVIDED into physical land masses, the world is also split into countries. These countries are separated from one another by language, government, and culture, and this creates the political world. As recently as 1950, there were only 82 countries. Today there are more than twice that many – some vast, others tiny. New countries are created when people want freedom from their past colonial rulers or when separate peoples living within one country seek independence. The break-up of Yugoslavia, for example, has recently created more countries.

KEY
1 NETHERLANDS
2 BELGIUM
3 LUXEMBOURG
4 SWITZERLAND
5 LIECHTENSTEIN
6 MOLDAVIA
7 ANDORRA
8 MONACO
9 SAN MARINO
10 VATICAN CITY
11 SLOVENIA
12 CROATIA
13 BOSNIA & HERZEGOVINA
14 YUGOSLAVIA
15 ALBANIA
16 MACEDONIA

Running between the USA and Canada is the longest undefended border in the world. The border is shown here as it cuts through a forested area in the east of both countries.

COUNTRY BORDERS

The line that separates one country from another is called a border. Sometimes these follow a natural feature, such as a mountain range, or a river. On other occasions they follow a straight line, ignoring physical features. When countries are on friendly terms, borders can be little more than lines on a map which can be easily crossed. If there is conflict, however, borders may be heavily defended, and it is often difficult to move from one country to another.

1

Greenland
(Den)

ARCTIC OCEAN

2

Alaska
(USA)

3

CANADA

4

PACIFIC
OCEAN

UNITED STATES

St Pierre &
Miquelon
(Fr)

5

OF AMERICA

Azores
(Port)

Bermuda
(UK)

ATLANTIC
OCEAN

6

Midway Is. (USA)

MEXICO

BAHAMAS

7

Hawaii
(USA)

CUBA
DOMINICAN
REPUBLIC
HAITI

Revillagigedo Is.
(Mex)

BELIZE
JAMAICA

ANTIGUA & BARBUDA
DOMINICA
ST LUCIA
BARBADOS
GRENADA
TRINIDAD AND TOBAGO

ke I.
(SA)

Johnston
Atoll
(USA)

GUATEMALA
HONDURAS
EL SALVADOR
NICARAGUA

ST KITTS & NEVIS
ST VINCENT &
THE GRENADINES

8

RSHALL
ANDS

Kingman Reef
(USA) *Palmyra Atoll*
(USA)

Clipperton I.
(Fr)

COSTA
RICA PANAMA

VENEZUELA
COLOMBIA

GUYANA
SURINAM
FRENCH
GUIANA
(Fr)

Howland I. (USA)
Baker I. (USA)

Jarvis I.
(USA)

Galapagos Is.
(Ec)

ECUADOR

9

KIRIBATI

BRAZIL

Fernando
de Noronha
(Br)

TUVALU

Tokelau
(NZ)

PERU

MON
NDS

Wallis &
Futuna
(Fr) WESTERN
SAMOA

American
Samoa
(USA)

Cook Is.

10

UATU

FIJI

TONGA

Niue

French
Polynesia (Fr)

BOLIVIA

Trindade
(Br)

nia (Fr)

San
Felix I.
(Ch) *San*
Ambrosio I.
(Ch)

PARAGUAY

11

Norfolk I.
(Aus)

Kermadec Is.
(NZ)

Pitcairn Is.
(UK)

URUGUAY

THINGS TO LOOK FOR ON THE MAP

World's largest country: Russian Federation, 173,750,400 sq km (6,592,800 sq miles) *Map I3*

World's smallest country: Vatican City, 0.44 sq km (0.17 sq miles) *Map C5*

World's longest frontier: between USA and Canada 6,416 km (3,987 miles) *Map T4*

Country with the most neighbours: China has borders with 16 other countries *Map I6*

I.

Juan
Fernandez
Is. (Ch)

ARGENTINA

CHILE

ATLANTIC
OCEAN

12

NEW
LAND

PACIFIC
OCEAN

13

Chatham I.
(NZ)

Bounty I.
(NZ) Antipodes Is.
(NZ)

Falkland Is.
(UK)

npbell I. (NZ)

O   P   Q   R   S   T   U   V   W   X   Y   Z

NORTH AMERICA

NORTH AMERICA INCLUDES THE COUNTRIES of Canada, the United States, and Mexico, as well as the world's largest island, Greenland. During the last Ice Age, a great sheet of ice flowed across the continent, scouring the landscape, deepening the depressions that now hold the Great Lakes, and dumping fertile soil onto the central plains. The Rocky Mountains form the backbone of the continent, running from Alaska to New Mexico. In the east are the Appalachian Mountains, flanked by coastal lowlands to the east and south. In eastern Canada lies the Canadian Shield, a huge basin of ancient eroded rocks now covered with thin soils. Deserts stretch from the southwestern United States down into northern Mexico.

Section across the USA

San Francisco — Rocky Mountains — Great Plains — Great Lakes — Appalachian Mountains — Washington DC

MOUNTAIN RANGES

The main mountain ranges of North America, the snow-capped Rockies, and the forested Appalachians, vary greatly in appearance (see above cross-section). The difference can be explained by their age. The Rockies, shown right, are relatively young mountains that have not yet been worn down. The Appalachians, however, are among the world's oldest mountains and have been gradually eroded by the scouring action of wind, water, and the movement of glaciers.

This view shows the Rockies in Canada.

THE GRAND CANYON

The Grand Canyon was formed over millions of years as the waters of the Colorado River and its tributaries carved their way through the solid rock. At some points the canyon is 1.6 km (1 mile) deep, and cuts through rocks that are 2,000 million years old. Different types of fossils found in the canyon walls reveal the dates of its changing history.

THE GREAT LAKES

Estimated to contain one-fifth of the world's fresh water, the five Great Lakes straddle the border between Canada and the USA. Only Lake Michigan, shown left, lies entirely within the USA. The lakes are linked by waterways, and drained by the St Lawrence River, which empties into the Atlantic Ocean. The Niagara River, which joins lakes Erie and Ontario, passes over the famous Niagara Falls.

THE GREAT PLAINS

Across the centre of Canada and the USA lie the Great Plains, also called the prairies. This huge area has hot summers and cold snowy winters. Trees are rare except along rivers and lakeshores, but the region was once covered with grasses and grazed by millions of buffalo. Today, little natural prairie survives, and in its place farmers cultivate vast fields of maize and wheat.

Lowest temperature:
Northice, Greenland,
-66°C (-87°F)

| 0 | 250 | 500 | 750 | 1000 | 1250 km |
| 0 | 250 | | 500 | | 750 miles |

THINGS TO LOOK FOR ON THE MAP

Area: 23,482,844 sq km
(9,066,726 sq miles)

Highest point: Mt. McKinley
(Denali), Alaska, USA,
6,194 m (20,320 ft) *Map E5*

Longest river system:
Mississippi–Missouri, USA,
5,971 km (3,710 miles)
Map L10

Largest lake: L. Superior,
Canada/USA, 82,414 sq km
(31,820 sq miles) *Map L8*

Largest island: Greenland,
2,175,219 sq km
(839,852 sq miles) *Map R3*

The water hyacinth grows fast and can choke the waterways.

Highest temperature:
Death Valley,
California, USA,
57°C (135°F)

THE MISSISSIPPI RIVER
The great Mississippi flows from Minnesota to the Gulf of Mexico. At the turn of the century, the destruction of forest and the ploughing of prairies around the river basin caused severe soil erosion. Soil washed into the river, raised the water level, and caused floods. Replanting forests and building dams has helped control the flow, but exceptionally heavy rains still cause floods.

THE EVERGLADES
Florida's Everglades is a protected wetland habitat, home to many rare plants and animals. Originally covering a much larger area, part of the Everglades has been drained and used for the cultivation of sugarcane. The northern part of the surviving wetland is now a sawgrass prairie, covered by shallow water with islands of higher land. In the south, fresh water mixes with water from the sea, creating saltmarshes fringed by mangrove swamps.

PEOPLES OF NORTH AMERICA

ONCE POPULATED BY GROUPS of native peoples who lived off the land, the vast majority of North America's population has arrived as immigrants over the last 400 years. Today, in terms of both population and economic wealth, the continent is dominated by the USA, the richest country in the world. To the north, Canada covers a vast area, much of it cold and inhospitable, and so has a much smaller population. Both of these countries were once British colonies and are still mostly English speaking. In contrast, Mexico is Spanish speaking, reflecting its past as a Spanish colony. Mexico is a relatively poor country, despite its vast oil and gas reserves.

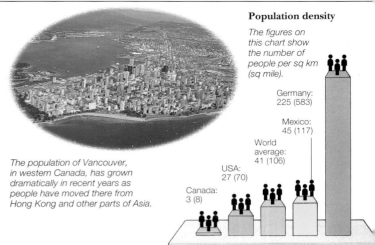

The population of Vancouver, in western Canada, has grown dramatically in recent years as people have moved there from Hong Kong and other parts of Asia.

Population density

The figures on this chart show the number of people per sq km (sq mile).

Germany: 225 (583)
Mexico: 45 (117)
World average: 41 (106)
USA: 27 (70)
Canada: 3 (8)

POPULATION DISTRIBUTION

In general, North America is one of the most sparsely populated continents. Over two-thirds of the population live in the USA. Mexico has the next largest population, followed by Canada. Historically, the east of the USA was the most densely populated area, but in the past few decades, many people have moved to the warmer southern and western states. In Canada, people have also left the east coast for the Great Lakes and cities such as Toronto, or for west coast cities, such as Vancouver.

Population: approximately 378,261,000 people
Number of countries: 3

Largest country: Canada, 9,976,140 sq km (3,851,788 sq miles)

Greenland (Den)

Alaska (USA)

CANADA

These people in New York reflect the many different ethnic groups that make up the population of the USA.

Least densely populated country: Canada, 3 people per sq km (8 per sq mile)

Most densely populated country: Mexico, 45 people per sq km (116 per sq mile)

Smallest country: Mexico, 1,958,200 sq km (756,061 sq miles)

St Pierre & Miquelon (Fr)

UNITED STATES OF AMERICA

MEXICO

Population of the USA

Others: 1%
Asian: 3%
Native Americans: 1%
Black: 12%
White: 83%

PEOPLE OF THE USA

The USA is often known as a cultural "melting pot" because of all the different peoples who make up its population. The main groups are whites (people of European descent and Hispanics), blacks, Asians, and native peoples.

A CONTINENT OF IMMIGRANTS

There have been many waves of immigrants to North America, mostly from Europe, but from South America and Asia too. Not everyone chose to go. Today's black Americans are descended from African slaves, who were forced to the USA between 1619–1808 to work on the plantations. Slavery was not abolished there until 1865. Today, increasing numbers of African-Americans are playing important roles in American life.

CANADIAN CULTURE

About fifteen years ago, many Canadian rooftops were dominated by huge television aerials, high enough to receive signals from the USA. Thanks to cable television, the aerials are gone, but the issue of the dominance of US culture remains. Television and radio broadcasts, music, and books from the USA flood into Canada. To encourage people to recognize and maintain Canada's own national identity, the government has given grants to the arts, broadcasting, publishing, and film industries.

This Canadian "patriotic workshop" is painted in the colours of the country's flag.

This Mayan family are cooking tortillas.

NATIVE PEOPLES

Native Americans are the descendants of people who migrated from Asia via a land bridge across the Bering Strait about 50,000 years ago. Today, native peoples form only a small proportion of the population of the USA and Canada. In the USA, many native Americans were moved into special reservations in the 19th century as settlers took over their lands. In Mexico, native peoples, like these Maya, form about 30 per cent of the population and are spread throughout the country.

This building in the city of Sacramento is home to the government of the state of California, USA.

GOOD NEIGHBOURS

There has not been a war between the countries of North America for nearly 150 years. Recently, Canada, the USA, and Mexico agreed to abolish trade barriers and open their markets to each other's exports. The full effects of this agreement are yet to be discovered, but Mexican workers like these farmers have already lost out, as cheaper US food and goods have flooded into Mexico. By contrast, cheaper food can benefit the poor.

EUROPEAN SETTLERS

Europeans have been settling in the USA and Canada since the 16th century, but in the 19th century, immigrants began to flood in. They were often driven from Europe by economic hardship, political unrest, and religious persecution. North America was seen as a land of opportunity, where there was plenty of cheap land and people were promised their freedom. The first immigrants settled on the east coast, but began to move northeast in the 1800s as industry began to grow.

State government		Federal government	
📖	Education	💰	Foreign policy
🚌	Highways	$	Currency
🏠	Housing	➕	Health care
🚓	State police	🌲	National parks

In the USA, local matters, such as the police, running hospitals, and maintaining the highways, are decided by individual states. Matters which affect all the states, such as foreign policy, defence, and issuing currency, are dealt with centrally.

FEDERAL GOVERNMENTS

All three countries in North America have federal systems of government. This means that the country is divided into a number of states. The states make their own local laws and also send representatives to the national government, so that they all have a say in how the country is run. Tension sometimes develops between the interests of the individual states and the interests of the country as a whole. In Canada, for example, a strong independence movement has grown up in French-speaking Québec.

CANADA

THE SECOND LARGEST COUNTRY in the world,
Canada occupies two-fifths of the North American
continent, stretches across five time zones, and is
divided into 10 provinces and two territories. It was
once inhabited only by Native Americans and Inuit
peoples. The French were the first Europeans
to settle in Canada, but after years of fighting the
British gained control in 1763. Gradually they took
over the rest of the country, as pioneers and
settlers moved west and north. Today,
Canada is an important industrial
nation and one of the world's
richest countries. Most of its
manufacturing is based on
natural resources of wood,
metals, and
mineral fuels.

CANADA

Capital city: Ottawa

Area: 9,976,140 sq km
(3,851,788 sq miles)

Population: 27,400,000

Official languages:
English, French

Major religions: Christian
72%, other 28%

Government: Multi-party
democracy

Currency: Canadian
dollar

Adult literacy rate: 99%

Life expectancy: 77 years

People per doctor: 450

Televisions: 640 per 1,000
people

OTTAWA
Ottawa, which is named after the Native
American people on whose land it sits,
was chosen as Canada's capital city in
1855. Today, the city boasts many
magnificent copper-roofed government
buildings, museums, and art galleries,
and a park-lined canal that turns into
the world's longest skating rink once
the winter freeze sets in.

Canadian vegetation zones

- Tundra and polar
- Mountain
- Taiga
- Temperate forest
- Grassland

THE CHANGING LANDSCAPE

About one-third of Canada lies within
the Arctic Circle and can remain frozen
for up to nine months of the year. In
these cold northern areas, known as the
tundra, any vegetation is limited to
lichens, grasses, and small shrubs and
trees. Further south, large areas of land
are covered by dense coniferous forests,
known as taiga. Towards the border with
the USA lie the mixed, temperate forests
and the grasslands of the Prairies.

WHERE PEOPLE LIVE

Canada is such a large country, much of it
uninhabitable, that on average there are only
three people living in each square kilometre
(eight per square mile). Almost 75 per cent
of the population lives near the US border,
in towns and cities around the shores of the
Great Lakes, and along the St Lawrence
River. The rest live in fishing villages along
the coasts or on farms and villages inland.

PEOPLE OF CANADA

Until recently, most Canadians were
descendants of British or French settlers.
Most of the French, like those at this winter
carnival, live in Québec province. Italians
make up the next largest group, with
Toronto the world's fifth largest Italian
city. Recently people have come from
eastern Europe, southeast Asia, and
South America. Native peoples make
up only 4 per cent of the population.

CALGARY STAMPEDE
Every year since 1923, thousands
of people have flocked to Calgary
for the famous Calgary Stampede.
People dress up in cowboy style to
celebrate the old Wild West and
Alberta's origins as a cattle trading
centre. Attractions include a rodeo,
complete with bucking broncos.

THE FIRST CANADIANS

Indians and Inuit, such as the children here, are sometimes called Canada's "First Nations", because they lived in Canada long before European settlers arrived. Gradually, the settlers took over their lands, leaving the original people to live in poverty. Since 1970, the government has tried to draw these peoples into Canadian society, but many prefer their own culture and traditions. Recently, Indians and Inuit have begun to win battles for their rights to ancestral lands. In 1999, the Nunavut area in the Northwest Territories will become a self-governing territory, the first part of Canada to be governed by Native Canadians in modern history.

The Inuit live in such cold conditions that they depend on warm clothing for survival.

Caribou fur is used by the Inuit as it traps hot air between each of the hairs.

Traditional Inuit jacket, called a parka.

Insulated boots keep feet warm in freezing winter weather.

JAMES BAY
In 1971, construction began on a vast hydroelectric project to dam the rivers that flow into James Bay and Hudson Bay, and generate electricity for use in Canada and the USA. However, the project will displace thousands of Cree Indians who live in this region. There has been strong opposition from the Cree as well as from environmental groups, and the future of the project is uncertain.

CANADIAN PACIFIC RAILROAD

The last spike of the transcontinental rail link of the Canadian Pacific Railroad was pounded in at Eagle Pass, British Columbia, on November 7, 1885. It was the start of a new era for Canada, opening up the west for trade and settlement, and finally making the vast country seem like one nation. One of the railway's most amazing engineering feats is a spiral tunnel drilled into the Rocky Mountains. Curving steadily round, the tunnel rises for more than 914 m (3,000 ft). In spite of quicker alternatives, tourists often take the spectacular trip across Canada by train, although the railroad is mostly used for cargo.

MINERAL WEALTH
Most of Canada's wealth comes from its abundance of natural resources, many of them mineral. It is the world's largest producer of uranium, zinc, and nickel, and also has reserves of aluminium, gold, copper, and silver. Underground work has also begun on what are thought to be the world's richest diamond deposits in an area near Yellowknife in the Northwest Territories.

Zinc can be galvanized onto steel to prevent it from rusting.

Nickel can be mixed with other metals to to make jet engines.

Main cargo loads

Containers and trailers: 19%
Forest products: 11%
Cars and other products: 26%
Grain: 22%
Coal: 12%
Fertilizers: 10%

AGRICULTURE

Wheat and cattle farming dominate Canada's main farming area, the Prairies. Elsewhere, a wide variety of fruit and vegetables is grown. Apples, shown growing here in British Columbia, are the country's most important fruit crop. Between Lakes Ontario and Erie lies the Niagara fruit belt. The lakes protect this area from the worst of Canada's weather, making it the ideal place for growing tender fruits such as pears, plums, peaches, and cherries.

COPING WITH THE COLD
Winters are long and cold throughout Canada but when the first snow falls, snow ploughs and grit lorries are out making sure the roads are safe. Next to some parking places there are even electric outlets where motorists can plug in heaters to keep their car's engine warm. Winter is fun for children who can play ice-hockey on temporary rinks in the streets as well as on frozen lakes and ponds.

Snow ploughs clear the roads to make them safe.

Find out more
DIAMONDS: *150, 226, 248*
EARLY SETTLERS: *23, 31*
INUIT: *266*
VEGETATION ZONES: *15*

WESTERN CANADA

A WEALTH OF NATURAL RESOURCES first attracted European settlers to the wilds of western Canada. Fur trappers, gold prospectors, and loggers all hoped to make their fortune from the land. Today, natural resources are still the basis of the economy. The fertile soils of the prairie provinces of Alberta, Manitoba, and Saskatchewan make up four-fifths of Canada's farmland. Fishing is a major industry along the Pacific coast, where the main catch is salmon, most of which is canned for export. By contrast, the desolate Northwest and Yukon territories have important reserves of gold, zinc, and lead. These territories are also the only part of Canada where the native peoples form the majority of the population.

VANCOUVER

Situated between the mountains and the sea, Vancouver is an attractive city as well as a rapidly growing industrial centre, and a busy port. Its ice-free harbour provides Canada with year-round access for trade with Asian countries across the Pacific Ocean. Many Chinese families are settling here rather than staying in Hong Kong when it reverts to China in 1997.

The most used softwood trees are spruce, shown left, then pine and fir.

The most used hardwood trees are poplar, then birch, shown right, and maple.

TIMBER INDUSTRY

Moist winds from the Pacific Ocean deposit rain on the western slopes of the Rocky Mountains, making ideal conditions for trees to grow to enormous sizes. Canada is the world's largest exporter of forest products, and British Columbia produces almost half of Canada's timber. Some logs are floated to the sawmills, but today they are often transported by road or helicopter. Most of the timber is softwood, used for building materials as well as to make chopsticks for Japan. Hardwoods can be used for furniture.

At the sawmill the timber is cut into planks or pulped for papermaking.

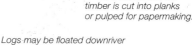

Logs may be floated downriver from the forests to the sawmills in the form of huge rafts.

Logs are sawn when they are still "green", or full of sap. The method shown here produces boards with a decorative grain.

TOTEM POLES

For generations, native peoples of the northwest coast carved wooden totem poles to record their family trees. Part of the pole shows which of the main clans the family belongs to, such as the raven or the wolf clan. Totem poles often guarded doorways to village homes.

The animals carved on the totem pole are symbols of the family's ancestors.

LIVING IN THE WILD

Large parts of Canada, such as the Northwest Territories and the Yukon, are home to more animals than people. Although part of the area is forested, and home to grizzly bears, most of it is icy wilderness. Animals that live here are adapted to the cold, and waterproof fur helps them to survive the snow and ice. Food is hard to find and grizzlies will kill large animals such as caribou. Caribou, or reindeer, live on the tundra but migrate to the forests further south in winter to escape the cold.

COAL, OIL, AND GAS WEALTH

Once grain and beef processing centres for the prairies, Edmonton and Calgary grew rich during the 1970s from the coal, oil, and gas found in the prairies and nearby Rocky Mountains. Now Edmonton boasts a gigantic shopping mall with an ice-hockey rink, a swimming pool, a rollercoaster ride, and even a hotel where people can stay while they shop.

CANADA

THINGS TO LOOK FOR ON THE MAP

Longest river: Mackenzie, 1,120 km (696 miles) *Map D9*

Highest point: Mt. Logan, 6,050 m (19,850 ft) *Map A9*

Largest lake: Great Bear Lake, 31,080 sq km (12,000 sq miles) *Map D8*

Arctic Bay, Northwest Terr.

☀ Jan -30°C (-21°F)
July 7°C (44°F)

🌧 Jan 8 mm (0.3 in)
July 18 mm (0.7 in)

Churchill, Manitoba

☀ Jan -28°C (-19°F)
July 12°C (54°F)

🌧 Jan 13 mm (0.5 in)
July 56 mm (2.2 in)

Edmonton, Alberta

☀ Jan -14°C (6°F)
July 17°C (63°F)

🌧 Jan 23 mm (0.9 in)
July 84 mm (3.3 in)

A R C T I C   O C E A N

BEAUFORT SEA

Ellesmere Island

Nares Strait

Axel Heiberg I.

Queen Elizabeth Islands

Parry Islands

Mackenzie King I.

Bathurst I.

Cornwallis I.

Devon Island

Baffin Bay

Melville I.

Resolute

Lancaster Sound

McClure Strait

Viscount Melville Sound

Banks Island

Somerset I.

Prince of Wales I.

McClintock Channel

Gulf of Boothia

Arctic Bay

Davis Strait

Baffin Island

Pangnirtung

Cumberland Sound

Mackenzie Bay

Amundsen Gulf

Victoria Island

Prince Charles I.

Foxe Basin

Iqaluit

Frobisher Bay

Tuktoyaktuk

King William I.

Old Crow

Inuvik

Fort McPherson

Coppermine

Hudson Strait

ALASKA (U.S.A)

N O R T H W E S T   T E R R I T O R I E S

Dawson

YUKON TERRITORY

Norman Wells

Great Bear L.

Contwoyto L.

Garry L.

Southampton Island

Coats I.

Yukon

MACKENZIE MTS.

Mackenzie

Coppermine

Kluane L.

Faro

Mt. Logan

Haines Junction

WHITEHORSE

Lac la Martre

C A N A D A

Fort Simpson

Great Slave L.

YELLOWKNIFE

Nonacho L.

Dubawnt L.

Chesterfield Inlet

Rankin Inlet

Eskimo Pt.

Teslin L.

Watson Lake

Fort Resolution

Hay River

Slave

Fort Smith

Hudson Bay

Churchill

ROCKY MOUNTAINS

Fort Nelson

Uranium City

Seal

Peace

L. Athabasca

Wollaston L.

Alexander Archipelago

Fort Vermilion

Athabasca

Cree L.

M A N I T O B A

Churchill

Nelson

Fort St John

Fort McMurray

Frobisher L.

Reindeer L.

Lynn Lake

Hayes

O N T A R I O

Queen Charlotte Is.

Prince Rupert

Kitimat

Dawson Creek

Lesser Slave L.

Thompson

Prince George

Nechako

Grande Prairie

S A S K A T C H E W A N

Flin Flon

The Pas

BRITISH COLUMBIA

A L B E R T A

Athabasca

Saskatchewan

L. Winnipeg

Queen Charlotte Sound

Fraser

Columbia

EDMONTON

Jasper

Leduc

Wetaskiwin

Lloydminster

North Battleford

Prince Albert

Saskatoon

L. Winnipegosis

Port Alice

Red Deer

L. Louise

Drumheller

Yorkton

Melville

Selkirk

Campbell River

Kamloops

Calgary

Moose Jaw

REGINA

Vancouver I.

Squamish

Vernon

Penticton

Medicine Hat

Swift Current

Weyburn

Brandon

WINNIPEG

Vancouver

Cranbrook

Lethbridge

Estevan

VICTORIA

P A C I F I C   O C E A N

U N I T E D   S T A T E S   O F   A M E R I C A

Sunflower oil is made from the seeds of the tiny central flowers.

THE PRAIRIES

Wheat, the most important crop in Canada, is grown on the fertile grasslands known as the prairies. The province of Saskatchewan is the major producer. Sunflowers and rapeseed are also important crops which are grown to make cooking and industrial oils as well as animal feed.

EASTERN CANADA

SOME OF THE RICHEST AND POOREST areas of Canada are found within the eastern part of the country. The provinces of Ontario and Québec that lie around the Great Lakes and the St Lawrence River form Canada's wealthy industrial region, and contain most of the population. The Atlantic, or Maritime, provinces along the stormy east coast have few natural resources and are suffering from a decline in the fishing industry. The harsh climate and thin soil means there is no major agriculture, except in the farmland of southern Ontario and in the milder parts of the Maritimes. At the end of Lake Erie, on the border with the United States, is Niagara Falls, one of the main attractions that draws tourists to the region.

ICE HOCKEY
Canadians take advantage of long winters by playing ice hockey on temporary rinks in city streets, as well as on frozen lakes and ponds. Ice hockey is the world's fastest team game, with the puck moving at speeds of up to 190 km (118 miles) per hour. It is a violent sport, and the action stops frequently, when players are sent to sit out penalties in the "sin bin".

TORONTO
On the north shore of Lake Ontario lies Toronto, Canada's leading industrial city, financial capital, and fastest growing urban area. The city has a reputation for being safe, with the lowest crime rate of any major city in North America. It also boasts SkyDome, the world's first stadium with a moving roof, and the Canadian National (CN) Tower, the tallest free-standing structure in the world.

ST LAWRENCE SEAWAY
Completed in 1959, the Great Lakes–St Lawrence Seaway system made it possible for ships to travel 3,769 km (2,342 miles) from the industrial centre of North America to the Atlantic Ocean. Ships carrying cargoes of grain, timber, iron ore, and coal descend 183 m (600 ft) from Lake Ontario to sea level through a system of locks. Tolls are charged for ships that use the system. The Seaway is closed because of ice for four months during the winter.

Golden Horseshoe

Oshawa

Toronto

Brampton

Mississauga

Oakville

Lake Ontario

Niagara-on-the-Lake

St Catherine's

Hamilton

Queen Elizabeth Way

GOLDEN HORSESHOE
Canada's leading industrial region, known as the Golden Horseshoe, curves around the western end of Lake Ontario, from the car-industry centre of Oshawa, through Toronto and Hamilton and on to Niagara. Its location makes it easy to move products by water, by rail, and by road via the Queen Elizabeth Way (QEW). There has been little concern for the environment, and the "golden" only refers to the fact that people here earn some of the highest incomes in Canada.

🚗 Car assembly   🏭 Steelworks   🚢 Shipbuilding
✈ Aircraft assembly   💻 Finance   Fruit canning

QUÉBEC
In 1608, Frenchman Samuel de Champlain set up a fur trading post on the St Lawrence River at a place the native peoples called Kébec. By 1700, there were 25,000 French people living in Québec. Under British control, this French province grew into a major commercial centre. Today, 90 per cent of Canadians whose native language is French live in the province of Québec. Although laws guarantee the right of French Canadians to their own language, laws, and culture, many Québecois want to be separate from the rest of Canada.

Cranberries are used to make sauces and syrups.

CRANBERRIES
Along the coast of New Brunswick the land is marshy and ideal for growing cranberries. The plants are grown in bogs and the ripe berries are collected by hand or by special machines that scoop the fruit from the water. Berries are ready to pick in September or October.

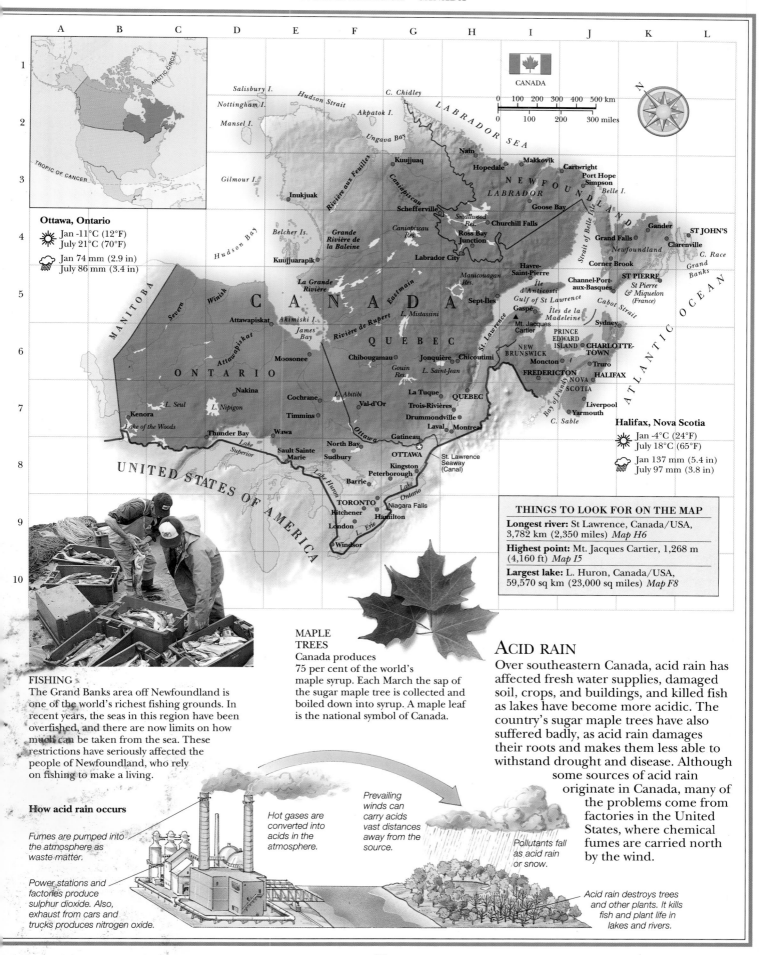

Ottawa, Ontario
☀ Jan -11°C (12°F)
July 21°C (70°F)
🌧 Jan 74 mm (2.9 in)
July 86 mm (3.4 in)

Halifax, Nova Scotia
☀ Jan -4°C (24°F)
July 18°C (65°F)
🌧 Jan 137 mm (5.4 in)
July 97 mm (3.8 in)

THINGS TO LOOK FOR ON THE MAP
Longest river: St Lawrence, Canada/USA, 3,782 km (2,350 miles) *Map H6*
Highest point: Mt. Jacques Cartier, 1,268 m (4,160 ft) *Map I5*
Largest lake: L. Huron, Canada/USA, 59,570 sq km (23,000 sq miles) *Map F8*

FISHING
The Grand Banks area off Newfoundland is one of the world's richest fishing grounds. In recent years, the seas in this region have been overfished, and there are now limits on how much can be taken from the sea. These restrictions have seriously affected the people of Newfoundland, who rely on fishing to make a living.

MAPLE TREES
Canada produces 75 per cent of the world's maple syrup. Each March the sap of the sugar maple tree is collected and boiled down into syrup. A maple leaf is the national symbol of Canada.

ACID RAIN
Over southeastern Canada, acid rain has affected fresh water supplies, damaged soil, crops, and buildings, and killed fish as lakes have become more acidic. The country's sugar maple trees have also suffered badly, as acid rain damages their roots and makes them less able to withstand drought and disease. Although some sources of acid rain originate in Canada, many of the problems come from factories in the United States, where chemical fumes are carried north by the wind.

How acid rain occurs

Fumes are pumped into the atmosphere as waste matter.

Power stations and factories produce sulphur dioxide. Also, exhaust from cars and trucks produces nitrogen oxide.

Hot gases are converted into acids in the atmosphere.

Prevailing winds can carry acids vast distances away from the source.

Pollutants fall as acid rain or snow.

Acid rain destroys trees and other plants. It kills fish and plant life in lakes and rivers.

UNITED STATES OF AMERICA

IN LESS THAN 400 YEARS, the United States of America (USA) has grown from wild countryside inhabited by native peoples to the world's most powerful industrial nation. The country is made up of 50 states, including Alaska in the far north and Hawaii in the Pacific Ocean. There are two major mountain ranges, the Appalachians to the east and the Rockies in the west, while much of its centre is covered by the gently sloping Great Plains. Vast supplies of coal, oil, and minerals, together with mass immigration in the 19th and early 20th centuries, helped business and industry to grow fast. Today, American products and culture are recognized throughout the world.

UNITED STATES OF AMERICA

Capital city:
Washington, DC

Area: 9,372,610 sq km
(3,618,760 sq miles)

Population: 255,200,000

Official language:
English

Major religions: Christian 84%, Jewish 2%, other 14%

Government: Multi-party democracy

Currency: Dollar

Adult literacy rate: 99%

Life expectancy: 76 years

People per doctor: 420

Televisions: 810 per 1,000 people

STARS AND STRIPES
On the US flag, the stars stand for the 50 modern states, while the stripes represent the original 13 states on the East Coast. Until independence in 1776, these were governed by Britain. Today, each state has its own laws but is ruled by the national government in Washington, District of Columbia.

PEOPLE OF AMERICA

People in the USA belong to a wide range of different groups and races. Most are descended from immigrants – people who moved there from other parts of the world, such as Europe and Asia. Many African-Americans are descendants of slaves forced to the USA in the 17th, 18th, and early 19th centuries. Today the population is increasingly Hispanic (Spanish speaking), Asian, and African-American. By 2050, these groups will make up more than half the population.

This girl has a mother who is part Hawaiian and part Korean.

This child has Japanese parents who moved to the US during the 1970s.

African-Americans now make up 12 per cent of the population.

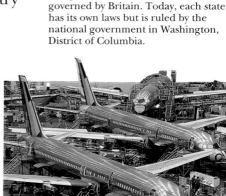

WORLD LEADER
The USA is the world's richest country, and its leading products include iron and steel, timber and paper products, electronic equipment, cars, and aircraft, shown above. These industries create many jobs, and women now make up almost half of the country's total workforce.

LIVING IN THE CITY

More than 75 per cent of Americans live in cities or the surrounding suburbs. Most people who live in the suburbs own their own homes and travel to work by car. New York is the biggest city, with almost 8 million inhabitants, followed by Los Angeles, and then Chicago. People from different backgrounds mingle in most cities. Often they have their own neighbourhoods, with names such as Little Italy or Chinatown. This view shows the island of Manhattan, New York.

As cities became more crowded, and land more expensive, architects began to design taller and taller buildings where people could live and work.

Every day, half a million people use Grand Central Station to get to work.

Many US cities are laid out on a simple grid system where main roads, or avenues, run north to south and streets run east to west.

Americans live in a variety of homes – detached houses, townhouses, and high-rise apartment buildings.

Skyscrapers, such as the Empire State Building, now dominate the skyline of most cities in the US.

Places of worship like the Holy Family Church, can be found in every city.

MOVING WEST

The people of America have always been quite mobile, often moving to a new state in search of work or a better lifestyle. Major events, such as the Great Depression in the 1930s, also forced people to move in the hope of finding work. The general pattern of movement since settlers first arrived is shown on this map. Over the past 30 years or so, more and more people have moved to the "Sunbelt" states of the south and west. These include California, Arizona, Texas, and Florida.

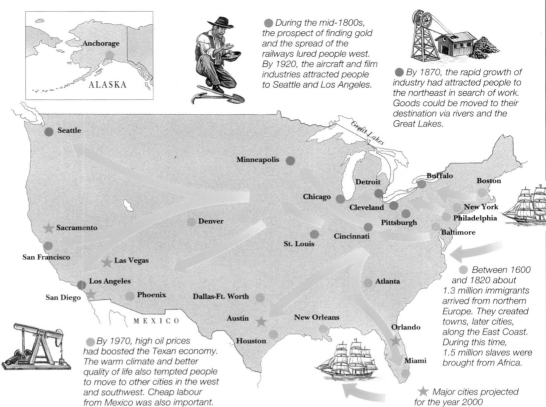

Anchorage

ALASKA

● During the mid-1800s, the prospect of finding gold and the spread of the railways lured people west. By 1920, the aircraft and film industries attracted people to Seattle and Los Angeles.

● By 1870, the rapid growth of industry had attracted people to the northeast in search of work. Goods could be moved to their destination via rivers and the Great Lakes.

Seattle

Minneapolis

Detroit

Buffalo

Boston

Chicago

Cleveland

New York

Pittsburgh

Philadelphia

Sacramento

Denver

Cincinnati

Baltimore

San Francisco

St. Louis

Atlanta

Las Vegas

Los Angeles

San Diego

Phoenix

Dallas-Ft. Worth

Austin

New Orleans

Orlando

Houston

Miami

M E X I C O

● Between 1600 and 1820 about 1.3 million immigrants arrived from northern Europe. They created towns, later cities, along the East Coast. During this time, 1.5 million slaves were brought from Africa.

● By 1970, high oil prices had boosted the Texan economy. The warm climate and better quality of life also tempted people to move to other cities in the west and southwest. Cheap labour from Mexico was also important.

★ Major cities projected for the year 2000

Kauai

Oahu

Maui

HAWAII

Hawaii

NATIONAL PARKS

Large areas of America's most spectacular countryside are protected in more than 350 national parks. Yellowstone National Park, above, in Wyoming and Montana, was the first park to open, in 1872. Yellowstone provides a safe environment for animals including bison, elk, antelope, grizzly bear, moose, and deer.

THE FIRST AMERICANS

Native Americans, the first inhabitants of the USA, make up less than 1 per cent of the population. Since Europeans arrived in the 1500s, the Native American tribes have had to fight long and hard to keep their homelands. Despite these struggles, they have held on to many tribal traditions and languages. Today, about one-fifth live on reservations – land returned to them by the American government.

This Zuni artist, a member of the Pueblo tribe, makes and sells silver and turquoise jewellery.

LARGEST TRIBES	
Cherokee	308,000
Navajo	219,000
Chippewa	104,000
Sioux	103,000
Choctaw	82,000
Pueblo	53,000

BASEBALL

Baseball is the country's national sport. The first game played between two organized teams took place in New Jersey in 1846. The National League was formed in 1876 and today baseball is the most popular spectator sport. It is traditional for the President to pitch the first ball at the start of each new baseball season. The batter shown in action here plays for the Minnesota Twins.

AMERICAN CULTURE

The influence of US culture can be seen all over the world. Fast foods, such as hamburgers, hot dogs, and soft drinks, as well as characters from films and TV shows, are recognized in cities from Berlin to Beijing. This "selling of America" is a billion-dollar industry and plays a vital part in the US economy.

Strawberry milkshake

Double hamburger

Find out more

NATIVE PEOPLES: 22–23
SETTLING THE CONTINENT: 23, 24–25
US GOVERNMENT: 23, 270

USA: WESTERN STATES

FROM THE ICY LANDSCAPE OF ALASKA, through the deserts of Nevada and Arizona, to the semi-tropical islands of Hawaii, the western states cover a dramatic range of scenery. Down the Pacific Coast, large cities such as Seattle, Portland, and San Francisco ship timber, fish, and fruit all over the world. The West is also home to Hollywood, capital of the multi-million dollar film industry, and Silicon Valley, a stretch of northern California which lies at the heart of the high-tech computer business. Sun Valley in Idaho ranks as one of the country's leading ski and summer resorts.

THE NORTHERN FORESTS

Great forests of pine, cedar, and fir trees thrive in the wet climate near the coasts of Oregon and Washington. These states are the country's major suppliers of timber and wood pulp. The trees are cut into logs and transported by road to the coast. Environmental groups are now trying to protect the trees, many of which are more than 200 years old.

EARTHQUAKE COUNTRY

People in California have to live with the constant threat of earthquakes. The area lies on the boundary, or fault line, between two plates of the Earth's crust. When these plates push and slide against each other, it causes earthquakes which can destroy roads and homes. It is difficult to predict an earthquake, so most people keep a survival kit in case they are trapped or left without supplies. Some of the items included in such a kit are displayed here.

Lightweight bag of emergency items, including first-aid supplies (not shown)

Bar of dried food with vitamins

Heavy-duty torch

Mini rolls of toilet tissue

Towelette

Disposable toothbrush with toothpaste

Packet of pure drinking water

FAULT LINES

The San Andreas fault runs for 1,207 km (750 miles) across California, passing through the cities of San Francisco and Los Angeles. There are also hundreds of other smaller faults that constantly cause minor tremors.

— Major fault
— Minor faults

OREGON

PACIFIC OCEAN

San Francisco

NEVADA

CALIFORNIA

San Andreas Fault

Los Angeles

MEXICO

Light sticks work for 12 hours and do not need batteries.

Emergency blanket designed to reflect body heat

FIELDS OF PLENTY

Fertile soil, plenty of sunshine, and water diverted from rivers that flow from the Sierra Nevada Mountains, make California the leading agricultural state. The land is used to grow more than 40 per cent of the fresh fruit and vegetables eaten in the USA, including peaches, oranges, strawberries, artichokes, and brussels sprouts. The Napa Valley, north of San Francisco, is an important grape-growing and wine-producing area. Mexicans often cross into California illegally to find work on the fruit farms.

SOUTH OF THE BORDER

The majority of immigrants living in the western states come from nearby Mexico. They are called Hispanics because their ancestors came from Spain and they speak Spanish. Many still follow the religion and festivals of Mexico. Hispanics also arrive from Cuba, Puerto Rico, and El Salvador.

CAR CULTURE

When Henry Ford introduced the first cheap car in 1910, it promised freedom on the open road. Today, there are more cars on the road in the USA than in any other country. Networks of 6-lane freeways weave across cities such as Los Angeles, shown above. Fumes from the cars contribute to the city's smog problem.

CARS PER 100 PEOPLE		
USA		74
France		48
Denmark		37
Brazil		8.5
India		0.7

BEAUFORT SEA

Prudhoe Bay

BROOKS RANGE

RUSSIAN FEDERATION

ALASKA

Bering Strait

Nome

Fairbanks

Denali (Mt. McKinley)

Yukon

CANADA

ALASKA RANGE

Anchorage

BERING SEA

ALASKA PENINSULA

Valdez

Gulf of Alaska

JUNEAU

Kodiak I.

PACIFIC OCEAN

0   150 km

0   50   100 miles

Aleutian Islands

UNITED STATES OF AMERICA

Fairbanks, Alaska
Jan -24°C (-11°F)
July 16°C (60°F)

Jan 23 mm (0.9 in)
July 48 mm (1.9 in)

ARCTIC CIRCLE

TROPIC OF CANCER

THINGS TO LOOK FOR ON THE MAP

Longest river: Colorado, USA/Mexico, 2,253 km (1,400 miles) *Map I12*

Highest point: Denali (Mt. McKinley), 6,194 m (20,320 ft) *Map C2*

Largest lake: Great Salt Lake, 3,525 sq km (1,361 sq miles) *Map J8*

World's largest land gorge: Grand Canyon, 349 km (217 miles) long, 1,900 m (6,234 ft) deep *Map J10*

Boise, Idaho
Jan -1°C (30°F)
July 23°C (74°F)

Jan 48 mm (1.9 in)
July 5 mm (0.2 in)

CANADA

WASHINGTON

Everett
Bellevue
Tacoma   Seattle   Spokane   Coeur d'Alene
OLYMPIA   MONTANA
Snake
ROCKY MOUNTAINS
Columbia   Lewiston

Portland
SALEM   CASCADE RANGE   John Day   BLUE MTS.   IDAHO   WYOMING
Corvalis
Eugene   OREGON   BOISE
Burns   Nampa   Sun Valley   Idaho Falls
Medford   Snake   Pocatello
Goose L.   Twin Falls

LIVING IN THE DESERT

The Sonoran Desert was once home only to creatures adapted to the heat. Today, Phoenix, Arizona, is one of the fastest-growing US cities, despite its location in the middle of the desert. Between 1960–1990, its population grew by more than 300 per cent. Part of the reason why the Colorado River fails to reach the ocean is because of demands for water from Phoenix.

Alturas   BLACK ROCK DESERT   Ogden   Great Salt L.
Winnemucca   GREAT SALT LAKE DESERT   SALT LAKE CITY   COLORADO
Eureka   GREAT BASIN   Orem Provo
PACIFIC OCEAN   Pyramid L.   Salina
Reno   UTAH
CARSON CITY   Ely
Santa Rosa   L. Tahoe   NEVADA   Green River
SACRAMENTO   ABAJO MTS.
Concord   Stockton   San Juan
San Francisco   Oakland   L. Powell
San Jose   CALIFORNIA   Grand Canyon   NEW MEXICO
Fresno   COLORADO PLATEAU
L. Mead   PAINTED DESERT
Las Vegas   ARIZONA

Cactus plants can survive the desert heat.

Bakersfield   MOJAVE DESERT
Oxnard   San Bernardino   PHOENIX   Mesa
Los Angeles   Santa Ana   Colorado
Long Beach   SONORAN DESERT   Tucson
Oceanside   Salton Sea
San Diego

The collared lizard of the southwestern deserts hides under a rock at night and comes out in the morning to warm up in the sun.

MEXICO

PACIFIC OCEAN

Niihau   Kauai
Oahu   HONOLULU
Lanai   Maui
HAWAII   Hilo
Hawaii

0   100   200   300 km
0   100   200 miles

Honolulu, Hawaii
Jan 22°C (72°F)
July 25°C (77°F)

Jan 104 mm (4.1 in)
July 23 mm (0.9 in)

This extraordinary road runner rarely flies, but can run very fast. It uses its long tail as a brake or as a rudder to change direction.

0   100   200   300 km
0   50   100   150   200 miles

N

USA: CENTRAL STATES

FAMOUS FOR COWBOYS AND CATTLE RANCHES, the central states of the USA are also the country's cereal bowl and oil refinery. This vast region includes high mountains, fertile plains, and the Mississippi River system. Texas and Oklahoma have major oil and gas fields, while coal is mined in Wyoming and Montana. The Rocky Mountains contain important national parks, such as Yellowstone and Glacier, and are rich in mineral resources. Hot summers and cold winters, as well as violent hailstorms and tornadoes, make the region's climate one of extremes.

Ears of the type of wheat used for making bread.

Grains of wheat

THE GREAT PLAINS

Once home to millions of buffalo, the vast open plains between the Rocky Mountains and the Mississippi River are now planted with cereals. Farmers on the Great Plains produce more wheat and maize than anywhere else on Earth. Farming is highly mechanized, with huge machines to harvest the grain. In the drier parts, the land can be farmed only if it is irrigated using water taken from a natural underground reservoir, known as an aquifer.

TORNADO ALLEY

Several hundred tornadoes a year strike "Tornado Alley", an area that runs through Kansas, Oklahoma, and Missouri. They occur when hot air from the Gulf of Mexico hits cold dry air from Canada. The violent storms, known as "twisters", cut through the towns and countryside, destroying everything in their path.

A twisting column of rising air forms beneath a thunder cloud.

The air spirals up the column and sucks up dirt and objects in its way.

Tornadoes can travel at 180 km/h (112 mph).

RURAL AMERICA

Today, most Americans live in cities and towns, but at the start of this century, two out of every five adults lived on farms. There are still many small towns with populations of less than 10,000 people. These towns are often in farming country, and are where people go for supplies, and attend school or church. This fair is taking place in Montana.

Hats keep off the sun and the rain, and were once used to carry water.

Leather cuffs

COWBOY COUNTRY

Cattle are raised on the Great Plains and foothills of the Rocky Mountains. In summer, cowboys on horseback used to drive the cattle to fresh pastures; in winter, they herd them back to the ranch to be sold at auction for food. Hollywood films turned cowboys into heroes, but life in the saddle was not easy. Pay was poor and men often spent 15 hours a day on horseback in scorching heat or driving rain. Today, ranches are smaller and cowboys and horses may be ferried from ranch to pasture by truck and trailer.

Chaps protect the rider from cattle horns.

Fringe helps to drain away any rainwater.

Spurs

A lasso is used to rope cattle.

Boots have heels to keep feet firmly in the stirrups.

CITIES OF THE DEAD

Cemeteries in New Orleans are built above ground to protect them when the Mississippi floods. The burial grounds are called Cities of the Dead.

A wreath of flowers

MISSISSIPPI RIVER

From Minnesota in the north to its enormous delta in the Gulf of Mexico, the mighty Mississippi River flows through the central states. It is one of the world's busiest waterways, suitable for cargo boats for almost 2,900 km (1,802 miles). This view of the river shows it flowing through Iowa, where it forms a natural border with Illinois and Wisconsin. In the south, severe flooding often occurs after heavy rains.

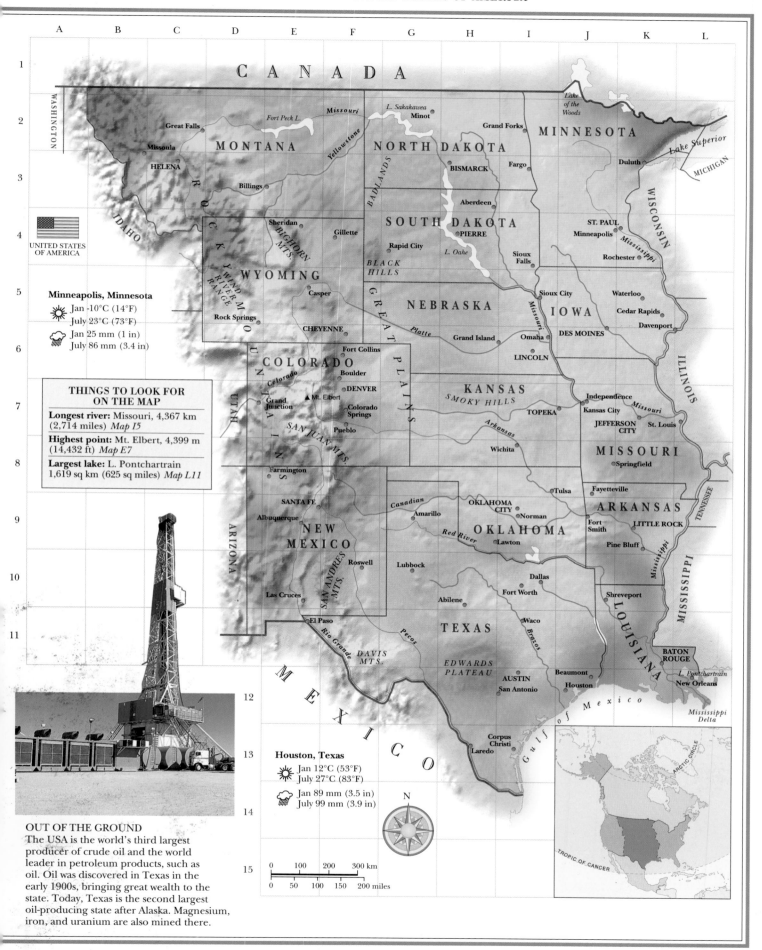

A B C D E F G H I J K L

1

CANADA

WASHINGTON

Great Falls

Missoula

HELENA

Billings

MONTANA

Fort Peck L.

Missouri

Yellowstone

Sheridan

Gillette

BIGHORN MTS.

ROCKY

IDAHO

WYOMING

WIND RIVER RANGE

Casper

Rock Springs

CHEYENNE

L. Sakakawea

Minot

NORTH DAKOTA

BISMARCK

Fargo

Aberdeen

SOUTH DAKOTA

PIERRE

Rapid City

L. Oahe

BLACK HILLS

BADLANDS

GREAT

NEBRASKA

PLAINS

Grand Forks

Duluth

MINNESOTA

Lake of the Woods

Lake Superior

MICHIGAN

ST. PAUL

Minneapolis

Rochester

WISCONSIN

Mississippi

Sioux Falls

Sioux City

IOWA

Waterloo

Cedar Rapids

Davenport

Missouri

Grand Island

Omaha

DES MOINES

LINCOLN

ILLINOIS

Minneapolis, Minnesota
☀ Jan -10°C (14°F)
☀ July 23°C (73°F)
🌧 Jan 25 mm (1 in)
🌧 July 86 mm (3.4 in)

UNITED STATES OF AMERICA

Fort Collins

Boulder

COLORADO

DENVER

Colorado

Grand Junction

▲ Mt. Elbert

Colorado Springs

Pueblo

UTAH

ARIZONA

SAN JUAN MTS.

THINGS TO LOOK FOR ON THE MAP
Longest river: Missouri, 4,367 km (2,714 miles) *Map I5*
Highest point: Mt. Elbert, 4,399 m (14,432 ft) *Map E7*
Largest lake: L. Pontchartrain 1,619 sq km (625 sq miles) *Map L11*

Farmington

SANTA FE

Albuquerque

NEW MEXICO

Roswell

Platte

Missouri

KANSAS

SMOKY HILLS

TOPEKA

Arkansas

Wichita

Independence

Kansas City

JEFFERSON CITY

St. Louis

MISSOURI

Springfield

Tulsa

Fayetteville

ARKANSAS

TENNESSEE

Canadian

Amarillo

OKLAHOMA CITY

Norman

OKLAHOMA

Red River

Lawton

Fort Smith

LITTLE ROCK

Pine Bluff

Mississippi

Las Cruces

SAN ANDRES MTS.

Lubbock

Dallas

Fort Worth

Abilene

Waco

Brazos

TEXAS

Shreveport

LOUISIANA

MISSISSIPPI

El Paso

Rio Grande

Pecos

DAVIS MTS.

EDWARDS PLATEAU

AUSTIN

San Antonio

Beaumont

Houston

BATON ROUGE

L. Pontchartrain

New Orleans

MEXICO

Corpus Christi

Laredo

Gulf of Mexico

Mississippi Delta

Houston, Texas
☀ Jan 12°C (53°F)
☀ July 27°C (83°F)
🌧 Jan 89 mm (3.5 in)
🌧 July 99 mm (3.9 in)

N

0 100 200 300 km
0 50 100 150 200 miles

ARCTIC CIRCLE

TROPIC OF CANCER

OUT OF THE GROUND
The USA is the world's third largest producer of crude oil and the world leader in petroleum products, such as oil. Oil was discovered in Texas in the early 1900s, bringing great wealth to the state. Today, Texas is the second largest oil-producing state after Alaska. Magnesium, iron, and uranium are also mined there.

USA: EASTERN STATES

EXCELLENT HARBOURS, FERTILE LANDS, and rich mineral resources have made this region one of the most densely populated in the country. It was along the East Coast that the first settlers from Europe arrived in the 16th century. Today the area includes some of the country's largest cities, such as New York and Washington DC, as well as the once-great industrial centres of Chicago, Detroit, and Cleveland on the Great Lakes. Further south, farmers use the land to cultivate cotton, tobacco, and vegetables grown for their oil. Each year, hurricanes are a threat to people living on the Gulf and Atlantic coasts.

The White House has been the home of every US president since 1800.

RULING THE COUNTRY
The USA has a written set of laws, known as a constitution, which sets out how the country should be governed. The centre of government is Washington, DC, where the President and his family live in The White House. The President is the head of state and is chosen in elections which are held once every four years.

BIG BUSINESS IN NEW YORK

Originally a fur-trading post at the mouth of the Hudson River, New York is now the country's financial capital. Wall Street, so called because it marked the line of the old city wall, is the home of the New York Stock Exchange. Financial deals worth billions of dollars are made there every day, and on the trading floor screens display up-to-date information from around the world. New York is known as "the city that never sleeps" and many people are still out at 4 a.m. The city is also famous for its museums, theatres, restaurants, and parks.

THE APPALACHIANS
The Appalachian Mountains run through North Carolina, Virginia, and West Virginia. For many years, coal was mined here and used to power the steel mills. Today, many mines and factories have closed and taken away jobs. Despite a plan to open up the area to tourists, Appalachia remains one of the poorest parts of the USA.

This huge machine picks the cotton bolls from the plant.

Flower buds form on the cotton plants.

The sign on this blues club in Memphis, Tennessee, is shaped like a giant guitar.

Flowers turn pink and then fall off.

THE BIRTH OF THE BLUES
This part of the USA is the birthplace of some of the world's most popular music. Jazz and blues were based on the spirituals and work songs of the black population. Country music began as poor white people's music in Kentucky and Tennessee, and the soul label Motown grew up in Detroit, or Motor Town.

Neon, used to light up so many buildings across America, was first invented in 1898.

After the flower falls off, a tiny seed ripens and grows into a pod, or boll.

The cotton boll opens into a fluffy fibre ready for harvesting.

Cotton is woven into fabric for shirts, trousers, and towels, which are sold at home and abroad.

COTTON – FROM FIELD TO FABRIC

In the mid-1800s, the southern states produced 80 per cent of the world's cotton and grew rich on the profits. Cotton was grown on huge plantations, then hand-picked by black slaves who had been brought by force from Africa. Slavery was finally abolished in the USA in 1865. Cotton is still an important crop, although modern machinery now does the hard work. Soya beans, used mainly for oil, are now the biggest crop in this region.

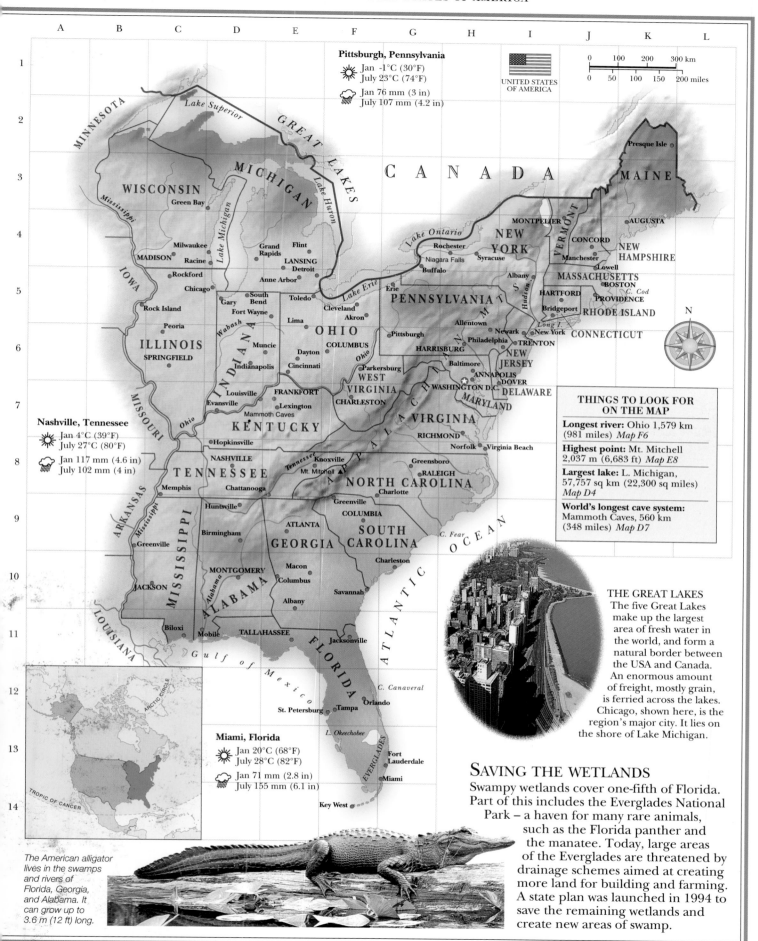

A B C D E F G H I J K L

Pittsburgh, Pennsylvania
☀ Jan -1°C (30°F)
July 23°C (74°F)
🌧 Jan 76 mm (3 in)
July 107 mm (4.2 in)

UNITED STATES
OF AMERICA

0   100   200   300 km
0   50   100   150   200 miles

MINNESOTA

Lake Superior

GREAT LAKES

CANADA

MAINE

Presque Isle

WISCONSIN

MICHIGAN

Mississippi

Green Bay

Lake Huron

MONTPELIER

AUGUSTA

VERMONT

NEW
YORK

CONCORD

NEW
HAMPSHIRE

Milwaukee
MADISON
Racine
Rockford
Chicago

Grand
Rapids
Flint
LANSING
Detroit
Anne Arbor

Lake Michigan

Rochester
Niagara Falls
Buffalo

Lake Ontario

Syracuse
Albany

Manchester
Lowell

MASSACHUSETTS
BOSTON

IOWA

Rock Island

South
Bend
Gary
Fort Wayne

Toledo

Lake Erie

Erie

PENNSYLVANIA

HARTFORD
PROVIDENCE

C. Cod

RHODE ISLAND

Peoria

Lima

Cleveland
Akron

Bridgeport

N

ILLINOIS

Muncie

Dayton

OHIO

COLUMBUS

Pittsburgh

Allentown

Newark

Long I.
New York

CONNECTICUT

SPRINGFIELD

Wabash

Indianapolis

Cincinnati

Ohio

HARRISBURG

Philadelphia
Baltimore

TRENTON

NEW
JERSEY

Nashville, Tennessee
☀ Jan 4°C (39°F)
July 27°C (80°F)
🌧 Jan 117 mm (4.6 in)
July 102 mm (4 in)

INDIANA

Louisville
Evansville

Ohio

FRANKFORT
Lexington

KENTUCKY

Mammoth Caves

WEST
VIRGINIA
CHARLESTON

Parkersburg

WASHINGTON D.C.
MARYLAND

ANNAPOLIS
DOVER

DELAWARE

VIRGINIA

RICHMOND

Missouri

Hopkinsville

NASHVILLE

Tennessee

Knoxville
Mt. Mitchell ▲

Norfolk
Virginia Beach

Memphis

Chattanooga

Greensboro
RALEIGH

Mississippi

ARKANSAS

TENNESSEE

Huntsville

NORTH CAROLINA

Charlotte

Greenville

Charleston

Greenville

COLUMBIA

C. Fear

ATLANTIC

Birmingham

ATLANTA

SOUTH
CAROLINA

MISSISSIPPI

ALABAMA

GEORGIA

OCEAN

JACKSON

MONTGOMERY
Columbus

Macon

Savannah

Albany

Alabama

Biloxi

Mobile

TALLAHASSEE

Jacksonville

LOUISIANA

Gulf of Mexico

FLORIDA

C. Canaveral

**THINGS TO LOOK FOR
ON THE MAP**

Longest river: Ohio 1,579 km
(981 miles) *Map F6*

Highest point: Mt. Mitchell
2,037 m (6,683 ft) *Map E8*

Largest lake: L. Michigan,
57,757 sq km (22,300 sq miles)
Map D4

World's longest cave system:
Mammoth Caves, 560 km
(348 miles) *Map D7*

THE GREAT LAKES
The five Great Lakes
make up the largest
area of fresh water in
the world, and form a
natural border between
the USA and Canada.
An enormous amount
of freight, mostly grain,
is ferried across the lakes.
Chicago, shown here, is the
region's major city. It lies on
the shore of Lake Michigan.

ARCTIC CIRCLE

TROPIC OF CANCER

Miami, Florida
☀ Jan 20°C (68°F)
July 28°C (82°F)
🌧 Jan 71 mm (2.8 in)
July 155 mm (6.1 in)

St. Petersburg

Tampa

Orlando

L. Okeechobee

EVERGLADES

Fort
Lauderdale

Miami

Key West

SAVING THE WETLANDS

Swampy wetlands cover one-fifth of Florida.
Part of this includes the Everglades National
Park – a haven for many rare animals,
such as the Florida panther and
the manatee. Today, large areas
of the Everglades are threatened by
drainage schemes aimed at creating
more land for building and farming.
A state plan was launched in 1994 to
save the remaining wetlands and
create new areas of swamp.

The American alligator
lives in the swamps
and rivers of
Florida, Georgia,
and Alabama. It
can grow up to
3.6 m (12 ft) long.

MEXICO

THE COLOURFUL LAND OF MEXICO was once home to the golden civilizations of the Maya and Aztecs. These ancient empires were destroyed by the Spanish, who invaded in the 1500s and ruled the country until its independence in 1821. Descendants of the native peoples still live in Mexico, but most people are *mestizo*, of mixed Spanish and native Indian descent. About half of all Mexicans are under 19 years old, and the population is growing rapidly, leading to overcrowding in the cities. Mexico has limited farmland, and cannot produce enough food for the growing population.

MEXICO	
Capital city: Mexico City	
Area: 1,958,200 sq km (756,061 sq miles)	
Population: 81,249,645	
Official language: Spanish	
Major religions: Christian 95%, other 5%	
Government: Multi-party democracy	
Currency: Mexican new peso	
Adult literacy rate: 89%	
Life expectancy: 70 years	
People per doctor: 1,850	
Televisions: 146 per 1,000 people	

A LAND OF CONTRASTS
Mexico's landscape ranges from vast deserts in the north, through snow-capped mountains and a central plateau in the centre, to tropical rainforests in the south. The Sonoran Desert, shown here, stretches across the border into the USA. This desert is home to the giant saguaro cactus, and to poisonous animals such as rattlesnakes and scorpions.

SITE SEEING
Tourism is one of Mexico's biggest sources of income. Visitors from all over the world come to see Chichén Itzá, Tenochtitlán, Palenque, and other sites of the ancient Maya and Aztec civilizations. The warm sea and sandy beaches at coastal resorts, such as Acapulco and Cancun, also attract many tourists.

Mexico City's most famous street is the wide Paseo de la Reforma, with its tall buildings, cafés, and theatres.

These buildings at Teotihuacán, near Mexico City, are the remains of an ancient religious centre.

MEXICO CITY
With a population of about 20 million, Mexico City is one of the world's largest cities. But its size and location bring many problems. It lies at high altitude and is ringed by mountains, so pollution from cars and factories cannot escape and poisons the air. Children sometimes do not leave for school until after the rush hour to avoid car fumes. Mexico City is very overcrowded, and the area is also prone to earthquakes; the most recent one devastated the city centre in 1985.

Most Mexicans are Roman Catholic and worship in churches often named after saints.

Women carry decorated baskets of flowers. They wear wrap-around skirts, called enrados, and white blouses.

Men parade with large cotton globes on which the name of their town is written.

A dip called guacamole is made with avocados.

Beer with a slice of lime

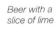

Avocado

Chillies

Tortillas are eaten like bread or made into a snack called a taco.

VILLAGE FESTIVALS
Festivals, or *fiestas*, are a common part of Mexican village life. Each village has its own patron saint and on the saint's day there is a colourful celebration. There are 115 separate saints' days in Mexico. Here the people of a small town near Oaxaca celebrate their *fiesta* with a street procession. Although most people in Mexico are Roman Catholic, native Indian beliefs are also important and many festivals are a mixture of Christian and Indian traditions.

MEXICAN FOOD
Mexicans eat a variety of spicy foods using chillies. Most of their food is based on home-grown produce, such as avocados, beans, tomatoes, and maize. Pancakes, called *tortillas*, are made from maize flour and filled with meat or vegetables, and cheese. Cooks also mix chillies and chocolate to make a spicy sauce called *mole* which is served on chicken.

Map labels (reading grid A–L across top, 1–10 down side):

Mexicali, Tijuana, Sonoran Desert, UNITED STATES OF AMERICA, Colorado, Nogales, Ciudad Juárez, Bravo del Norte, Ángel de la Guarda I., Tiburón I., BAJA CALIFORNIA, Cedros I., Hermosillo, Chihuahua, Conchos, Guaymas, Gulf of California, Delicias, Piedras Negras, Río Grande, SIERRA DE LA GIGANTA, Ciudad Obregón, Hidalgo del Parral, Nuevo Laredo, Monclova, MEXICO, Carmen I., San José I., Los Mochis, Culiacán, Torreón, Monterrey, Saltillo, Matamoros, Reynosa, SIERRA MADRE OCCIDENTAL, SIERRA MADRE ORIENTAL, Cerralvo I., Durango, La Paz, Mazatlán, Zacatecas, Ciudad Victoria, San Luis Potosí, Ciudad Madero, Marías Is., Tepic, Río Grande de Santiago, Aguascalientes, León, Panuco, Tampico, Guadalajara, Irapuato, Querétaro, Poza Rica, L. Chapala, Morelia, Pachuca, Gulf of Mexico, Colima, Teotihuacán, Jalapa, Mérida, Cancún, Uxmal, Chichén Itzá, Cozumel I., Campeche, YUCATAN PENINSULA, Uruapan, MEXICO CITY (Tenochtitlán), L. Texcoco, Puebla, Veracruz, Bay of Campeche, Balsas, Popocatépeti, Citlaltépetl (Orizaba), Chetumal, Lázaro Cárdenas, Coatzacoalcos, Villahermosa, BELIZE, Chilpancingo, Minatitlán, Palenque, SIERRA MADRE DEL SUR, Monte Albán, Oaxaca, Acapulco, Tuxtla Gutiérrez, GUATEMALA, PACIFIC OCEAN, Gulf of Tehuantepec, Tapachula

Monterrey
☀ Jan 14.5°C (58°F)
☀ July 27°C (80.5°F)
🌧 Jan 15 mm (0.6 in)
🌧 July 58 mm (2.3 in)

Mexico City
☀ Jan 12.5°C (54°F)
☀ July 28°C (82.5°F)
🌧 Jan 25 mm (1 in)
🌧 July 122 mm (4.8 in)

Acapulco
☀ Jan 26.5°C (80°F)
☀ July 28.5°C (83.5°F)
🌧 Jan 6 mm (0.2 in)
🌧 July 256 mm (10.1 in)

THINGS TO LOOK FOR ON THE MAP

Longest river: Rio Grande (Río Bravo del Norte), 3,030 km (1,883 miles) *Map G4*

Highest point: Citlaltépetl (Orizaba), 5,700 m (18,700 ft) *Map H8*

Largest lake: L. Chapala, 1,550 sq km (598 sq miles) *Map E7*

World's largest gulf: Gulf of Mexico, 1,813,000 sq km (700,000 sq miles) *Map I7*

MEXICO

Scale: 0 100 200 300 400 km / 0 50 100 150 200 250 miles

N

ARCTIC CIRCLE / TROPIC OF CANCER

OIL FROM THE GULF
Huge reserves of oil were found along the Gulf of Mexico coast in 1976, and today Mexico is the world's fifth largest producer. There are about 3,000 oil platforms in the gulf, extracting oil from the sea bed. Mexico is also rich in other minerals, including iron, zinc, copper, and silver, of which it is the world's biggest producer.

TRADITIONAL CRAFTS
Weaving and embroidery are among the traditional crafts of Mexico's native Indian peoples. Images of gods, birds, and flowers are often used in their designs. Just like their ancestors, women bring brightly decorated clothes into the towns to sell in the markets.

Blue, red, and black are the main colours used in traditional Mexican designs.

MADE IN MEXICO
Clustered along Mexico's border with the USA are some 2,000 factories, called *maquiladoras*. Here, huge numbers of cars, computers, shoes, and other manufactured goods are assembled from parts, ready to be exported. Most of the factories are owned by foreign companies, who are attracted to Mexico by the cheap labour costs. The *maquiladoras* are an important source of income for Mexico, and help to prevent its economy from being too dependent on oil.

Find out more
OIL: *137, 152, 281*
POPULATION GROWTH: *16–17*
ROMAN CATHOLICS: *274*
TRADE (*MAQUILADORAS*): *280*

CENTRAL AND SOUTH AMERICA

CENTRAL AMERICA IS A NARROW BRIDGE of land linking Mexico in the north to South America in the south. A string of mountains runs down its length, capped by volcanoes. The beautiful, palm-fringed islands of the Caribbean Sea lie off the east coast. South America, the fourth largest continent, contains a range of very different landscapes. About 60 per cent of the continent is covered in vast, grassy plains. The towering Andes mountains stretch along the west coast, with the long, thin Atacama Desert sandwiched between the mountains and the sea. Tropical rainforests spread in a lush, green blanket across huge areas of the northeast.

The Andean condor has a wingspan of 3 m (10 ft). Its huge wings help it to soar above the mountain peaks.

THE AMAZON RIVER

The world's largest rainforest grows in the vast basin of the mighty Amazon, the longest river in South America. The Amazon rises high in the snow-capped Andes in Peru, then flows 6,439 km (4,001 miles) across Peru and Brazil to its mouth in the Atlantic Ocean. The Amazon carries more water than any other river. At its mouth, the Amazon is so wide that you cannot see from one bank to the other. The river discharges so much water into the ocean that the water is still brackish 180 km (112 miles) out to sea.

As the winds reach the Andes they cool and rain starts to fall.

Wet winds from the Atlantic.

Rainforest

Fog bank

Pacific Ocean

THE ANDES

Stretching for 7,250 km (4,505 miles) along the entire length of South America, the Andes are the world's longest mountain range. Many peaks rise above 6,000 m (19,685 ft). The mountains were formed when two plates of the Earth's crust collided. The plates are still moving, causing numerous earthquakes and volcanoes along the range. An extinct volcano, Aconcagua, is the highest Andean peak and the highest mountain in South America at 6,960 m (22,835 ft). The world's highest navigable lake, Titicaca, lies in the Andes between Peru and Bolivia.

Very little rain falls on the west side of the Andes, which is mostly desert.

THE ANDES AND CLIMATE

The Andes have a major effect on the weather of South America. Warm, wet winds from the Atlantic rise up the eastern slopes. As they rise, they cool and the water in them falls as rain. On the dry, western slopes, the weather conditions are completely different. Here the winds pass over the cold Humboldt Current as they blow in off the sea. This causes them to cool and form a bank of fog.

Patagonia covers about 700,000 sq km (270,272 sq miles) of southern Argentina and Chile.

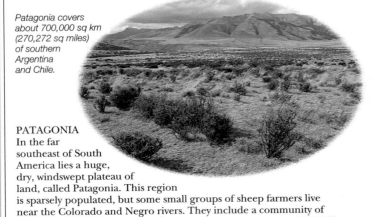

PATAGONIA

In the far southeast of South America lies a huge, dry, windswept plateau of land, called Patagonia. This region is sparsely populated, but some small groups of sheep farmers live near the Colorado and Negro rivers. They include a community of Welsh-speakers whose ancestors settled in the region during the 1860s. Northern Patagonia is semi-desert with some scrubby vegetation. The south is colder, drier, and bleaker with very little plant life.

THE PAMPAS

Rolling grasslands cover the centre of Argentina and extend into neighbouring Paraguay. These are the pampas, vast open plains which stretch across an area of 650,000 sq km (250,967 sq miles). The western pampas are dry, semi-desert, but the eastern part has frequent rainfall. The pampas form the economic heartland of Argentina. Large herds of beef cattle are grazed on the plains. Other areas have been ploughed up to grow huge amounts of wheat, maize, beans, and other crops.

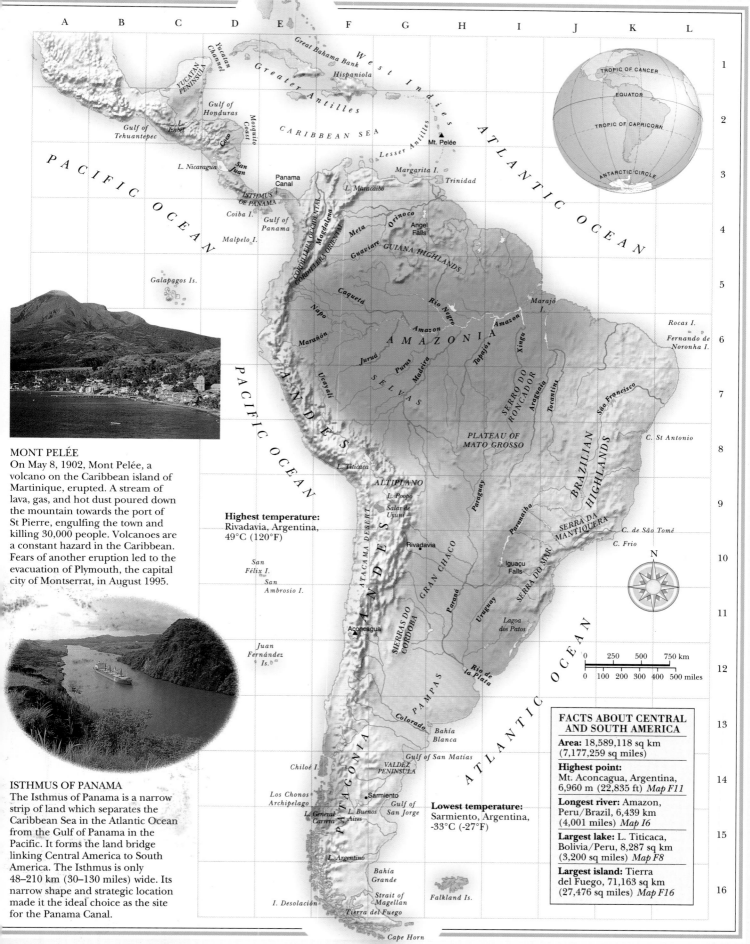

A B C D E F G H I J K L

1 2 3 4 5 6 7 8 9 10 11 12 13 14 15 16

TROPIC OF CANCER
EQUATOR
TROPIC OF CAPRICORN
ANTARCTIC CIRCLE

Yucatan Channel
YUCATAN PENINSULA
Gulf of Honduras
Gulf of Tehuantepec
L. Izabel
Mosquito Coast
Coco
L. Nicaragua
San Juan
ISTHMUS OF PANAMA
Coiba I.
Gulf of Panama
Malpelo I.
Panama Canal

Great Bahama Bank
Hispaniola
Greater Antilles
West Indies
CARIBBEAN SEA
Lesser Antilles
Mt. Pelée
Margarita I.
Trinidad
L. Maracaibo

PACIFIC OCEAN

ATLANTIC OCEAN

Galapagos Is.

CORDILLERA OCCIDENTAL
CORDILLERA ORIENTAL
Magdalena
Meta
Guaviare
Caquetá
Napo
Marañón
Juruá
Ucayali
Purus
Amazon
SELVAS
Rio Negro
Orinoco
Angel Falls
GUIANA HIGHLANDS
AMAZONIA
Madeira
Tapajós
Xingu
Marajó I.
Amazon
Araguaia
Tocantins
SERRO DO RONCADOR
São Francisco
Rocas I.
Fernando de Noronha I.
C. St Antonio
PLATEAU OF MATO GROSSO
BRAZILIAN HIGHLANDS

L. Titicaca
ALTIPLANO
L. Poopó
Salar de Uyuni
ATACAMA DESERT
Rivadavia
Paraguay
GRAN CHACO
Paraná
Parnaíba
SERRA DA MANTIQUEIRA
Iguaçu Falls
SERRA DO MAR
C. de São Tomé
C. Frio

San Félix I.
San Ambrosio I.
A N D E S
Aconcagua
SIERRAS DO CORDOBA
Uruguay
Lagoa dos Patos
Juan Fernández Is.
PAMPAS
Colorado
Rio de la Plata
Bahía Blanca
Gulf of San Matías
VALDÉZ PENINSULA
Chiloé I.
Los Chonos Archipelago
Sarmiento
L. Buenos Aires
Gulf of San Jorge
L. General Carrera
PATAGONIA
L. Argentino
Bahía Grande
I. Desolación
Strait of Magellan
Tierra del Fuego
Falkland Is.
Cape Horn

N

0 250 500 750 km
0 100 200 300 400 500 miles

MONT PELÉE

On May 8, 1902, Mont Pelée, a volcano on the Caribbean island of Martinique, erupted. A stream of lava, gas, and hot dust poured down the mountain towards the port of St Pierre, engulfing the town and killing 30,000 people. Volcanoes are a constant hazard in the Caribbean. Fears of another eruption led to the evacuation of Plymouth, the capital city of Montserrat, in August 1995.

Highest temperature:
Rivadavia, Argentina,
49°C (120°F)

Lowest temperature:
Sarmiento, Argentina,
-33°C (-27°F)

ISTHMUS OF PANAMA

The Isthmus of Panama is a narrow strip of land which separates the Caribbean Sea in the Atlantic Ocean from the Gulf of Panama in the Pacific. It forms the land bridge linking Central America to South America. The Isthmus is only 48–210 km (30–130 miles) wide. Its narrow shape and strategic location made it the ideal choice as the site for the Panama Canal.

FACTS ABOUT CENTRAL AND SOUTH AMERICA

Area: 18,589,118 sq km
(7,177,259 sq miles)

Highest point:
Mt. Aconcagua, Argentina,
6,960 m (22,835 ft) *Map F11*

Longest river: Amazon,
Peru/Brazil, 6,439 km
(4,001 miles) *Map I6*

Largest lake: L. Titicaca,
Bolivia/Peru, 8,287 sq km
(3,200 sq miles) *Map F8*

Largest island: Tierra
del Fuego, 71,163 sq km
(27,476 sq miles) *Map F16*

PEOPLES OF CENTRAL AND SOUTH AMERICA

THE LANGUAGE, HISTORY, and culture of Central and South America have been shaped by colonization. Until 1492, when Christopher Columbus first landed in the Bahamas, the continent had been inhabited by native peoples. After that time, European settlers arrived from Spain and Portugal, and huge numbers of Africans were imported as slaves, especially to the Caribbean and Brazil. The Caribbean also became home to English, French, and Dutch settlers. As a result, the population of the continent today is a combination of these different ethnic groups. Spanish is the main language spoken throughout most of the continent, together with Portuguese in Brazil. English and French are more common in the Caribbean, while Dutch can still be heard in Surinam.

Population: approximately 373,739,000 people

Number of countries: 32

Most densely populated country: Barbados, 601 people per sq km (1,556 per sq mile)

Smallest country: Grenada, 340 sq km (131 sq miles)

Least densely populated country: Surinam, 3 people per sq km (7 per sq mile)

Largest country: Brazil, 8,511,970 sq km (3,286,472 sq miles)

Map labels: BAHAMAS, CUBA, DOMINICAN REPUBLIC, HAITI, JAMAICA, BELIZE, GUATEMALA, HONDURAS, EL SALVADOR, NICARAGUA, COSTA RICA, PANAMA, ANTIGUA & BARBUDA, ST KITTS & NEVIS, DOMINICA, ST LUCIA, ST VINCENT & THE GRENADINES, BARBADOS, GRENADA, TRINIDAD AND TOBAGO, VENEZUELA, COLOMBIA, GUYANA, SURINAM, FRENCH GUIANA (Fr), ECUADOR, Galapagos Is. (Ec), PERU, BRAZIL, BOLIVIA, PARAGUAY, San Felix I. (Ch), San Ambrosio I. (Ch), Juan Fernandez Is. (Ch), CHILE, ARGENTINA, URUGUAY, Falkland Is. (UK)

Magnificent Catholic churches, such as the Church of St Francisco in Brazil, are a lasting reminder of colonial rule.

SPANISH INFLUENCE

From the 16th century, Spain and Portugal began to colonize South America. Both countries also sent missionaries to spread the Roman Catholic religion. Spain colonized much of the continent, but Portuguese-ruled Brazil became the largest and most economically powerful country. Today, the majority of South Americans are still Roman Catholic.

ETHNIC GROUPS

Native Indians, who can trace their history back to people living in Central and South America before the Europeans arrived, make up just two per cent of the continent's population today. The next largest group are people of African descent, the greatest number of whom are today found in Brazil and the Caribbean. In most countries, the largest group of people is of mixed European and native Indian descent, known as *mestizos*.

These young Brazilian men are a mix of ethnic groups.

Ethnic groups

Key
- European
- Native Indian
- African/Mulatto
- Mestizo

Brazil / Ecuador / Guatemala / Uruguay

The peoples of Central and South America can be divided into four distinct ethnic groups. This chart shows what proportion of the population makes up each of the four ethnic groups in four countries.

NATIVE PEOPLES

Within a hundred years of the Spanish arrival in South America, as much as 90 per cent of the native population had died, mainly from diseases brought by Europeans, such as smallpox or measles, against which the native peoples had no natural immunity. Today, native Indians make up a very small minority, except in Guatemala, where Mayan people still inhabit the highlands in large numbers, and in the Andean ranges of Bolivia where descendants of the Incas live.

This map is shaded to show the percentage of native Indian survival in each country across the continent. Some native Indians, such as this Yaminahva Indian woman and child, in Peru, now live in special reservations.

Refugees from the countryside building a squat on the outskirts of Buenos Aires, Argentina.

Nicaragua

$US10,445 million

$US1,371 million

Country earns in one year

Country's foreign debt

Brazil

$US552,698 million

$US132,749 million

FOREIGN DEBT

All governments borrow money. The loans are paid back using the money that the country earns by exporting its goods. However, many countries in Central and South America have huge debts. Brazil has a very large foreign debt, but it is still relatively small compared to Brazil's earnings. Nicaragua has a much smaller debt, but it is eight times the country's earnings.

LARGE SCALE FARMS

Across the region, ranches for cattle and sheep and plantations growing export crops, such as bananas and sugar, often extend over a vast area and are operated as profit-making businesses. These huge farms may be owned by foreign companies or by a handful of rich and powerful families. Cuba is different, for the government controls these large estates.

CROWDED CITIES

Nearly three-quarters of the continent's population live in cities. In some countries, such as Chile and Uruguay, more than a third of the population live in the capital. Many people have been forced to migrate from rural areas to escape widespread poverty, or have been drawn to the cities by the chance of work, and now live in crowded shanty towns that are growing up on the city outskirts.

SMALL SCALE FARMS

Most of the continent's farmers have only enough land to support one or two people. People grow crops, like this Bolivia family does, and keep a few animals such as chickens or pigs to eat rather than to sell. Since the farm cannot provide enough food for all the family, some family members are forced to move elsewhere in search of work.

Birth rate

Kenya: 6.4

Bolivia: 4.7

Peru: 3.3

Argentina: 2.8

Germany: 1.5

POPULATION GROWTH

This century, population growth across the continent has been rapid, particularly in Brazil and the northern countries. In most countries, birth rates are now beginning to fall. However, since so many of the population are young, and improvements in health allow more children to survive into adulthood, the population is still growing. By the year 2000, another 80 million people will live here.

This birth rate chart shows the average number of children per woman in five countries. Birth rates in Central and South America are lower than in Africa, but higher than birth rates in Europe where most families have 1 or 2 children.

CENTRAL AMERICA AND THE CARIBBEAN

THE SEVEN SMALL COUNTRIES OF CENTRAL AMERICA lie within a neck of land that joins North and South America. To the east, hundreds of Caribbean islands stretch from the USA almost to Venezuela. When Christopher Columbus and his Spanish crew dropped anchor in the Caribbean in 1492, they thought it was Asia, and the islands became known as the West Indies. From that time on, Europeans competed for control of the region, bringing slaves from Africa to work on the land. Central America's greatest influence is still Spanish, while the Caribbean retains its African culture. The entire area is affected by natural hazards with volcanoes, earthquakes, and hurricanes.

Havana, Cuba
Jan 22°C (72°F)
July 28°C (82°F)

Jan 71 mm (2.8 in)
July 125 mm (4.9 in)

San José, Costa Rica
Jan 19°C (66°F)
July 21°C (70°F)

Jan 15 mm (0.6 in)
July 211 mm (8.3 in)

FARMING THE LAND
Even before the arrival of Europeans, Central America was an agricultural region. The land divides into three main zones: the fertile Pacific plain, ideal for growing crops such as bananas; the central highlands, with coffee plantations (above) and cattle ranches; and the forested northeast, where the soil is less suitable for farming. Intensive farming has damaged much of the environment.

Arrows indicate the movements of storms and show how they die out once they hit land and "spend" all their energy.

The red line across the map marks the southern limit of the area of hurricane activity.

HURRICANE STRENGTH
Powerful tropical storms, known as hurricanes, affect the Caribbean between May and October. A hurricane starts off as a normal storm over the ocean, but grows in force if the waters are particularly warm. Winds then blow the swirling mass of cloud, wind, and rain westwards, towards the islands, where it can cause massive destruction when it hits land. The word hurricane comes from Huracan, the local name for the god of storms.

BAHAMAS

ISLANDS LARGE AND SMALL

In the centuries after Columbus, Spanish influence remained on the mainland, although Spain, France, Britain, the Netherlands, and later the USA laid claim to many of the islands. St Lucia, for example, changed hands between Britain and France 14 times. Most of the larger islands are now independent countries, while others are still "dependencies". The island of Martinique, with its replica of the Sacré Coeur church in Paris, remains French, while the Netherlands Antilles are controlled by the Dutch.

PEOPLE OF THE CARIBBEAN

The original inhabitants of the Caribbean islands were the Carib and Arawak peoples. Most died from disease and slavery at the hands of the Spanish, although a few descendants of Caribs survive on the island of Dominica. Today, most people in the Caribbean are descendants of the African slaves brought over to work the plantations. Europeans, Asians, Syrians, and Lebanese also form a part of Caribbean culture.

ATLANTIC OCEAN

Little Abaco
Freeport
Grand Bahama
Great Abaco
Berry Is.
NASSAU
New Providence
Eleuthera
Andros I.
Cat I.
San Salvador
Great Exuma
Rum Cay
Long I.
Crooked I.
Acklins I.
Mayaguana

BAHAMAS

Clara
Camagüey
Las Tunas
Holguín
Great Inagua
Caicos Is.
Turks Is.
TURKS & CAICOS ISLANDS (UK)
Gulf of Guacanayabo
Bayamo
Santiago de Cuba
Guantánamo
Guantánamo Bay (USA)
Windward Passage
Port-de-Paix
Cap-Haïtien
Montecristi
Montego Bay
Gonaïves
Santiago
Puerto Plata
JAMAICA
Jérémie
HAITI
San Francisco de Macorís
Spanish Town
PORT-AU-PRINCE
DOMINICAN REPUBLIC
Samaná
KINGSTON
Les Cayes
Jacmel
L. Enriquillo
SANTO DOMINGO
La Romana

ST KITTS & NEVIS

	0	50	100	150	200	250 km
	0		50	100		150 miles

JAMAICA

Antilles
Mona Passage
Mayagüez
Puerto Rico (USA)
SAN JUAN
Ponce
St Croix
Virgin Islands (USA)
British Virgin Islands (UK)
Anguilla (UK)
Leeward Islands
St Martin (France & Neth.)
St Eustatius (Neth.)
Barbuda
ANTIGUA & BARBUDA
BASSETERRE
ST KITTS & NEVIS
ST JOHNS
Montserrat (UK)
Antigua
Basse Terre
Guadeloupe (France)
Grande Terre
Marie Galante
Lesser Antilles
DOMINICA
ROSEAU
Martinique (France)

HAITI

DOMINICAN REPUBLIC

ANTIGUA & BARBUDA

DOMINICA

CARIBBEAN SEA

THINGS TO LOOK FOR ON THE MAP

Longest river: Coco, Honduras/Nicaragua, 483 km (300 miles) *Map F10*

Highest point: Tajumulco, Guatemala, 4,220m (13,845 ft) *Map A8*

Largest lake: L. Nicaragua, Nicaragua, 8,029 sq km (3,100 sq miles) *Map E12*

Port-of-Spain, Trinidad
☀ Jan 26°C (78°F)
July 27°C (80°F)
🌧 Jan 69 mm (2.7 in)
July 218 mm (8.6 in)

ST LUCIA

ST VINCENT & THE GRENADINES

BARBADOS

Aruba
Netherlands Antilles
Curaçao
Bonaire
Lesser Antilles

GRENADA

Windward Islands
St Vincent
KINGSTOWN
St Lucia
CASTRIES
ST LUCIA
ST VINCENT & THE GRENADINES
BRIDGETOWN
The Grenadines
BARBADOS
GRENADA
ST GEORGE'S

COLOMBIA

Isla de Margarita

VENEZUELA
TRINIDAD & TOBAGO
Tobago
PORT OF SPAIN
Trinidad
San Fernando

TRINIDAD & TOBAGO

K L M N O P Q R S T U V W

GUATEMALA

Villagers carry a statue of the Virgin Mary.

FROM THE RUINED CITIES of the ancient Maya civilization to the Catholic churches of the Spanish, Guatemala represents a blend of cultures. Today, more than half the people are direct descendants of the Maya Indians and live mainly in highland villages; the remainder of the population is part Indian and part Spanish. Many Maya work for rich landowners who grow the coffee, sugar, and bananas that are the country's main cash crops. Guatemala also exports fresh cut flowers, mostly roses, which are grown in the valleys around Antigua.

GUATEMALA	
Capital city: Guatemala City	
Area: 108,890 sq km (42,043 sq miles)	
Population: 10,000,000	
Official language: Spanish	
Major religions: Christian 98%, other 2%	
Government: Multi-party democracy	
Currency: Quetzal	
Adult literacy rate: 56%	
Life expectancy: 64 years	
People per doctor: 2,270	
Televisions: 52 per 1,000 people	

BELIZE	
Capital city: Belmopan	
Area: 22,960 sq km (8,865 sq miles)	
Population: 190,792	
Official language: English	
Major religion: Christian 100%	
Government: Multi-party democracy	
Currency: Belizean dollar	
Adult literacy rate: 93%	
Life expectancy: 68 years	
People per doctor: 2,220	
Televisions: 166 per 1,000 people	

HOLY WEEK

Most Guatemalans are Roman Catholic, the religion the Spanish brought with them in the 16th century. However, many people are now becoming Protestant. Guatemalans also practise their own form of worship based on traditional beliefs. This procession in Antigua forms part of their celebration of Holy Week.

MARKET DAY

Markets such as this one in Chichicastenango, in the highlands near Lake Atitlán, are a feature of daily life. Many native Guatemalans farm small plots of land where they grow corn, beans, and squash, as well as fruit. They regularly walk long distances from outlying villages to sell crops, flowers, and handcrafted goods such as pottery and baskets.

People worship Catholic saints and ancient gods at the Church of Santo Tomas.

Lilies and roses, as well as carnations and gladioli, are grown in the valleys. Many are sold to North America.

Goods are weighed in a simple, hand-held balance.

Village women wear brightly coloured ankle-length skirts. Patterns date back hundreds of years.

Maize and other cereals are the main foods.

Maya crafts, such as baskets and handwoven textiles, are popular with tourists.

A basket of fruit, called papayas (pawpaws).

Avocados have grown in Central America for hundreds of years.

WEAVING STYLES

Weaving is a traditional craft. Cloth is made from coloured yarn, using patterns that have been handed down through the generations. There are more than 300 different styles, each with a special historical meaning.

Weavers use a backstrap loom that can be moved from place to place.

CITIES OF THE MAYA

Tourism is one of Guatemala's fastest growing industries. Each year more than 500,000 tourists visit the country to see its ancient sites. Spectacular ruins mark the site of Tikal, one of the great Mayan cities. Tikal was mysteriously abandoned in about AD900. Today its ruined temples lie in a huge area of tropical forest.

REFUGEES

Life for the Maya is a constant struggle for survival, and many have suffered hardship and death in their attempts to avoid being forced into mainstream society. Persecution was particularly bad in the early 1980s when the then military government set out to destroy them. Some 60,000 Maya fled to safety in refugee camps in Mexico. Today, they are returning to Guatemala, but their safety is uncertain, and many of their lands have been seized.

STREET CHILDREN

Guatemala City is home to growing numbers of so-called street children. Forced to leave home because of poverty, children live in small groups and survive through crime, by begging, and by selling whatever they can find. Recently, human rights groups such as Amnesty International have drawn attention to their plight.

BELIZE

LYING ON THE CARIBBEAN COAST, Belize is both an old and a new country. Ancient ruins dot the landscape, reminders of its Maya history, but the country itself only achieved full independence in 1981. For many years, Belize was a British colony, the only one in Central America. English is the official language, but Belizeans are descended from several ethnic groups – Caribs, Africans, Mayas, Asians, and Europeans – and many people speak a Creole or African dialect. Caribbean foods and music are popular, and the country is famous for its wildlife.

CORAL REEF

A chain of coral reefs, dotted with small sandy islands called cayes, runs 290 km (180 miles) along the coastline of Belize. It is the world's second largest barrier reef, after Australia's, and is home to turtles, sea anemones, and spiny lobsters, as well as a wonderful array of tropical fish. The clear, warm water attracts divers from around the world.

Flooding and hurricanes can cause serious problems along the coast of Belize, so a new capital, Belmopan, has been built further inland than Belize City, the old capital.

DEEP IN THE FOREST

Dense tropical rainforest covers half of Belize's land area. Rosewood, mahogany, and other products from the forest such as chicle, used to make chewing gum, and kapok, a silky cotton from the giant Ceiba tree, are important to the economy. So, too, are the increasing number of citrus groves. But cultivation is limited. Much of the rainforest is protected and provides a rich habitat for plants and animals.

BELMOPAN

In 1961, a massive hurricane and tidal wave devastated the coastal capital, Belize City. In 1970, a new capital, Belmopan, was built 80 km (50 miles) inland to protect it from tropical storms. Although people and businesses are gradually moving to the new capital, Belize City remains the country's most populated city.

FOREST WILDLIFE

The forests are filled with an amazing variety of wildlife. Jaguars, tapirs, howler monkeys, and coatimundi are just a few of the world's endangered species still thriving in the forests of Belize. Butterflies and tropical birds fly through the trees. And there are 250 different types of orchids, including the black orchid, Belize's national flower.

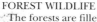

Toucans live in the treetops so they can fly around the open areas.

The howler monkey defends its part of the rainforest with a noisy howl.

Find out more
CORAL REEFS: *255, 258*
HURRICANES: *44*
RAINFORESTS: *15, 69, 204*
RELIGION: *274–275*

HONDURAS

THE HOT, STEAMY CLIMATE of Honduras is ideal for growing fruit, and for many years the banana industry has dominated the life of the country. Today, Honduras has developed other exports such as coffee, sugar, and beef. More than half of Hondurans live in the countryside, in small villages or isolated settlements. Many are poor farmers, growing maize, beans, or rice for their own use. Life is hard, and many people go hungry. Land is unevenly distributed – wealthy families and the fruit companies own 60 per cent of the land.

HONDURAN PEOPLE
Most Hondurans are *mestizos* – mixed descendants of native Indians and the Europeans who arrived in the 16th century. Some are descended from black Africans who were shipped to the Caribbean as slaves. Some are white (European) or Indian.

HONDURAS
Capital city: Tegucigalpa
Area: 112,090 sq km (43,278 sq miles)
Population: 5,600,000
Official language: Spanish
Major religion: Christian 100%
Government: Multi-party democracy
Currency: Lempira
Adult literacy rate: 75%
Life expectancy: 65 years
People per doctor: 3,130
Televisions: 72 per 1,000 people

EL SALVADOR
Capital city: San Salvador
Area: 21,040 sq km (8,124 sq miles)
Population: 5,057,925
Official language: Spanish
Major religion: Christian 100%
Government: Multi-party democracy
Currency: Salvadorean colón
Adult literacy rate: 75%
Life expectancy: 65 years
People per doctor: 1,560
Televisions: 92 per 1,000 people

As the bananas grow, they begin to point upwards.

The stalk has a flower on the end made of thick, purple petals.

Workers cover bananas with bags to protect them from insects and the spray from pesticides.

Coloured tags identify which bunches are ready for picking.

Bananas take between 9 and 13 weeks to ripen.

Workers cut down the bananas when they are still green.

BANANA PLANTATIONS
Banana exports are important to the economy of Honduras. Many are grown on huge plantations, particularly around La Lima in northeastern Honduras. Labourers work long hours and the pay is low. Cutters regularly have to carry loads of bananas weighing about 40 kg (88 lb). Once cut down, the bananas are washed, inspected, and weighed into boxes, ready to be shipped abroad.

EL SALVADOR

THE SMALLEST COUNTRY in Central America, El Salvador has suffered a history of civil war and revolution. Historically, a handful of rich families have controlled the land and wealth while most Salvadoreans have lived in poverty. A line of volcanoes, many still active, dominates the landscape. Forests, once rich with cedar, mahogany, and oak, have been cut down for farmland.

THE FOOTBALL WAR
In 1969 long-standing border disputes erupted when El Salvador played Honduras to qualify for the World Cup. The incident led to the Salvadoran army invading Honduras. More than 3,000 people were killed during the Football War.

SAN SALVADOR
San Salvador was founded by Spanish colonists in 1525. Since then it has been damaged by earthquakes many times. Much of the original Spanish architecture has been replaced with modern buildings. Overcrowded slum areas have developed around the city as thousands of refugees have arrived in search of work.

PEACE ACCORD
Between 1979 and 1991, a bitter civil war raged between the US-backed government and left-wing guerilla forces. Some 75,000 Salvadoreans died. On 16 January 1992, the country celebrated a peace agreement signed by guerilla leader Chano Guevara (left).

Find out more
COFFEE: 50, 62, 66
PEOPLES OF THE CONTINENT: 42
SUGAR: 52
VOLCANOES & EARTHQUAKES: 13

NICARAGUA

SOMETIMES CALLED "the land of lakes and volcanoes", Nicaragua is a beautiful country. It could also be one of the richest in Central America, except that its recent history has been as violent as its earthquakes, and the economy has been thrown into chaos by past political events. The economy is mainly based on agriculture with fishing along the coasts, but Nicaragua also has large deposits of minerals, including copper and gold, which are mined for export. The country has a young population with more than half the people under 15 years of age.

NICARAGUA	
Capital city: Managua	
Area: 130,000 sq km (50,193 sq miles)	
Population: 4,100,000	
Official language: Spanish	
Major religions: Christian 97%, other 3%	
Government: Multi-party democracy	
Currency: New córdoba	
Adult literacy rate: 57%	
Life expectancy: 65 years	
People per doctor: 1,670	
Televisions: 65 per 1,000 people	

SANDINISTA REVOLUTION

For more than 40 years, the Somoza family ruled Nicaragua as a dictatorship. But in 1979, rebel forces took control and formed the left-wing Sandinista government. They provided better health care, and set up a programme of taking land from the rich and giving it to thousands of poor peasants. They were opposed by the Contras, anti-Sandinista forces backed by the USA. The Sandinistas lost the last election, in 1990, and the country remains unstable.

FAMILY LIFE

Extended families are common in Nicaragua. Parents and children often live with their grandparents under one roof. Until 1979, more than half the population could not read or write. Under the Sandinistas, a literacy campaign was set up, and newly trained teachers, many of them women, were sent into rural areas to teach reading and writing. Within just a few months, literacy levels rose to 87 per cent. However, when the Sandinistas lost power, the campaign faded and reading levels dropped again.

Overcrowding is a problem and large families are often crammed into very small living spaces.

LIVING DANGEROUSLY

Most of the population of Nicaragua live on the Pacific coast, where most of the major cities are located. Within this area, there are many active volcanoes, but the most serious danger comes from earthquakes. In 1972, the country's capital, Managua, was nearly destroyed by an earthquake that killed more than 6,000 people and left 300,000 homeless.

FARMING THE LAND

The fertile volcanic soil near the Pacific coast forms the main farming region of Nicaragua. Maize (shown growing here), beans, and sorghum are the main food crops, and are harvested twice a year. Coffee, cotton, and bananas are also important export crops.

The maize ear, or cob, needs plenty of sunshine to grow and ripen.

Maize kernels are ground into flour and used to make tortillas, a type of pancake.

LAKE NICARAGUA

The west of the country is dominated by Lake Nicaragua, the largest lake in Central America. It is also the only freshwater lake in the world to contain sea fish, including sharks and swordfish. Scientists now think that sharks find their way to the lake by swimming up the San Juan River from the Caribbean Sea.

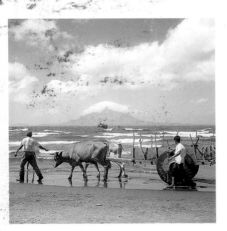

Lake Nicaragua is named after Nicarao, an ancient Indian chief whose people lived by the lake.

Find out more

LITERACY: *277*
POLITICAL SYSTEMS: *270–271*
POPULATION GROWTH: *43*
VOLCANOES & EARTHQUAKES: *13*

COSTA RICA

BORDERED BY SEA on both sides, Costa Rica differs from its Central American neighbours in many ways. It is a peaceful country with a democratically elected government and, since 1949, no army. The country is also relatively wealthy. Schools are free and Costa Rica spends part of its budget on education. There is not much poverty and life expectancy is the highest in Central America. Exports include coffee, bananas, and sugar which grow on the country's fertile volcanic soils. The main port is Limón on the Caribbean coast.

COSTA RICA

Capital city: San José

Area: 51,100 sq km (19,730 sq miles)

Population: 3,300,000

Official language: Spanish

Major religions: Christian 95%, other 5%

Government: Multi-party democracy

Currency: Costa Rican colón

Adult literacy rate: 93%

Life expectancy: 76 years

People per doctor: 1,030

Televisions: 148 per 1,000 people

THE WAY TO SAN JOSÉ
San José lies in the mountainous centre of the country directly on the Pan-American Highway. It is the processing centre for the crops which grow in the nearby valleys. The area developed as a tobacco growing centre under Spanish rule and became the capital in 1823.

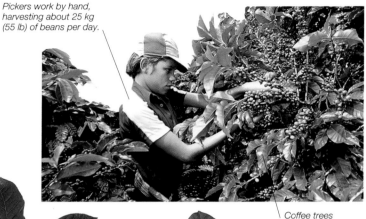

Pickers work by hand, harvesting about 25 kg (55 lb) of beans per day.

COFFEE BEANS

Costa Rica was the first country in Central America to grow coffee, and for more than 100 years this has been its leading export. From time to time this success is affected by falling international prices. Coffee is made from the fruit of the coffee tree, which grows best on well-drained soil. Trees need a warm, but not hot, climate, and are often grown in areas partly shaded with larger trees. They can produce good crops for 15 years.

The coffee fruit is called a cherry.

The sweet-smelling flowers last about 3 to 4 days.

Coffee trees grow to about 3 m (9.8 ft) tall.

Berries turn from dark green to yellow to ripe red.

Coffee is made from the two beans inside the cherry.

TRAIN TO THE COAST
The Atlantic Railway, completed in 1890, was built to take coffee from the plantations to the coast for export. The project was fraught with problems. Thousands of workers lost their lives due to terrible working conditions, and the cost plunged the government into debt.

SAVING THE FORESTS

Costa Rica was once covered with forests that included mahogany and tropical cedar trees. But now its tree cover has been greatly reduced because forests have been cut down for timber and to make room for coffee plantations. However, the government is aware that loss of forest also means loss of valuable plant and animal life, and it is now working to conserve its forests. Today, about 23 per cent of the forest is protected in reserves and national parks.

This tiny violet-ear hummingbird is just 12 cm (4.75 in) long. It hovers in the air and takes nectar from flowers through its long beak.

The hummingbird's wings can beat 55 times per second.

Nectar is a sweet liquid.

Find out more

COFFEE: *62, 66*
DEMOCRACY: *270*
LOGGING: *69, 244*
TRADE (COMMODITIES): *281*

PANAMA

PANAMA

Capital city: Panama City

Area: 77,080 sq km (29,761 sq miles)

Population: 2,329,329

Official language: Spanish

Major religions: Christian 92%, Jewish and other 8%

Government: Multi-party democracy

Currency: Balboa

Adult literacy rate: 90%

Life expectancy: 72 years

People per doctor: 840

Televisions: 165 per 1,000 people

THE COUNTRY OF PANAMA forms a land link between the North and South American continents. The Panama Canal, which cuts through the country and joins the Atlantic and Pacific Oceans, is a vital link in international sea trade. Panama has a hot steamy climate with heavy rainfall, especially on its Caribbean coast. The interior is mountainous and the best farmland is in the lowlands of the Pacific coast where the main cash crops, bananas, coffee, and sugar, are grown. Shrimp, caught in the coastal waters, are also an important export.

FROM OCEAN TO OCEAN
There is a 26 m (85 ft) difference in height between Gatun Lake and the two oceans. From the Atlantic, ships are raised up through the Gatun locks (1, 2, and 3). Then they are lowered via the Pedro Miguel locks (4) and, finally, through the Miraflores locks (5 and 6) into the Pacific.

PANAMA CANAL
Every year some 14,000 ships negotiate the locks of the Panama Canal. First opened in 1914, the canal is 82 km (51 miles) long, with a minimum depth of 12 m (39 ft). Forty thousand workers, mostly from the Caribbean, worked on the canal which took 10 years to build and cost US$380 million. It also cost thousands of lives. After sharing the canal with the USA for many years, Panama will take complete control from the year 2000.

Cross-section of canal

Nine months of tropical rain each year keeps Gatun Lake full. Water from the lake feeds the locks.

Atlantic Ocean · 1 · 2 · 3 · Gatun Lake · 4 · 5 · 6 · Pacific Ocean

Banks and business centres line the canal approach to Panama City.

CANAL AT THE CROSSROADS
The canal puts Panama at the crossroads of international trade. Revenue from the canal, and from the Free Trade Zone around the canal, is vital to the economy. Since 1970, Panama has been one of the world's main financial centres, and its tax-free banking attracts investors from around the world.

Detail of lock chamber

A ship waits in a lock chamber while water is piped in to lift the ship to the next level.

Water is fed through huge pipes, called culverts, down the sides of the lock.

Trains, called mules, help pull the ship through the lock.

Ships travel in the opposite direction along this channel.

A series of smaller pipes feeds water into the lock from the culverts.

CUNA INDIANS
The original inhabitants of Panama were mostly Cuna, Guaymi, and Choco Indians, but their numbers were severely reduced after the arrival of European explorers in the 16th century. The Cuna once held considerable power in the area and traded, mainly by canoe, along the Caribbean coast. Important chiefs were carried by hammock. Today, the Cuna live in small villages and depend on agriculture for a living.

Hammocks are made of woven fibre from plants that grow on the coast.

Embroidered clothing designs, known as molas, are a feature of the Cuna culture.

THE GOOD SOIL
Panama has many rivers. The soil that develops from clays, sand, and silt deposited from these rivers is called alluvial soil, and is good for growing crops such as the vegetables shown here. On poorer soils the land is used for a few years and then left until its natural fertility returns. This system of land use is called *roza*.

Find out more

BANANAS: 48
COFFEE: 50, 62, 66
PEOPLES OF THE CONTINENT: 42

CUBA

MORE THAN 200 RIVERS WIND their way across Cuba, watering the lush green scenery of the Caribbean's largest island. The land is made up of mountains, rolling hills, and flat plains, all covered in a fertile soil that is ideal for growing sugar, tobacco, and a variety of tropical fruits and vegetables. Most Cubans are descended from the early Spanish settlers, or from Africans brought over later to work as slaves on the plantations. Over recent decades, the socialist policies of the long-standing leader, Fidel Castro, have kept Cuba isolated from much of the world.

CUBA	
Capital city: Havana	
Area: 110,860 sq km (42,803 sq miles)	
Population: 10,800,000	
Official language: Spanish	
Major religions: Christian 42%, other 58%	
Government: One-party state	
Currency: Cuban peso	
Adult literacy rate: 96%	
Life expectancy: 76 years	
People per doctor: 270	
Televisions: 207 per 1,000 people	

MUSIC AND DANCE
Cuba's lively music reflects its mix of Spanish and African influences. The Spanish brought their distinctive melodies, along with the guitar and violin, and the Africans brought a very different style, as well as various drums and short wooden sticks called claves. The music has gradually fused to create rhythms such as the mambo and salsa. A thriving Afro-Cuban jazz scene has also developed.

CUBAN POLITICS

In 1959, Fidel Castro and a group of rebels overthrew the ruling dictator, Fulgencio Batista. Since then, Cuba has been a communist state, aided by the Soviet Union until its breakup in the early 1990s. Many of Castro's social policies have been successful. Housing and health care have greatly improved, and most people can now read and write. However, the USA remains hostile to the communist government.

Cigars are stored in boxes made from cedar wood to keep them fresh.

Dark brown sugar has not been refined to remove all the syrup.

Light brown sugar has been part refined.

Sugarcane is a giant grass that needs plenty of rain as well as sunshine.

Rum is made from the distilled juice of sugarcane.

CUBAN CIGARS
Warm days and cool nights are ideal for growing tobacco to make the famous Cuban cigars. Tobacco leaves are picked when pale green and hung up to dry for 40–45 days. They are then sorted and packed for the fermentation process which mellows the flavour of the leaf before it is sent to one of the cigar factories. Cigars are rolled by hand by men and women working at long wooden tables.

A good cigar is made from at least five different types of tobacco.

Sugar is stored inside the stalk, in a firm pulp.

A dark syrup, known as molasses, is a by-product of cane juice.

HAVANA

The largest city in the Caribbean, Cuba's capital, Havana, has a population of more than 2 million. It was founded by the Spanish in 1515 and some areas of the city are extremely old, with cobbled streets and elegant colonial buildings. Today, parts of Havana have become rather run down and in need of improvement. However, housing policies mean there are no shanty towns around the city. Havana is a major port and exports most of Cuba's sugar, tobacco, and tropical fruit.

SUGAR INDUSTRY

Sugar has long been important to Cuba and still makes up 75 per cent of the country's earnings from exports. By the 1800s, the sugar industry was already booming, fuelled by African slaves who worked by hand on the vast colonial plantations. Today the methods are more modern and the cane is usually cut down by machine or bulldozer. However, during the early 1990s, poor weather reduced the sugar harvests and there were also problems with obtaining fuel from the former Soviet Union. To overcome this oil crisis, many of the mills started to use *bagasse*, a by-product of sugarcane, to run their machinery.

Find out more
BREAK-UP OF THE USSR: *136*
CITIES: *17, 14*
PEOPLES OF THE CONTINENT: *42*
POLITICAL SYSTEMS: *270–271*

JAMAICA

JAMICA

THE BEAUTIFUL ISLAND OF JAMAICA is a place of strong contrasts. On one hand, there is the relaxed attitude of people enjoying the national passions – cricket and reggae music. On the other hand, there is tension between the few powerful families and the poor in the violent slums of Kingston. This side of life is rarely seen by the tourists who flock here each year, attracted by the tropical climate. As well as tourism, a mineral ore called bauxite is a valuable source of income. Sadly the landscape is being damaged by the bauxite mines, which leave red mud lakes with an acid content that kills the vegetation.

JAMAICA

Capital city: Kingston

Area: 10,990 sq km (4,243 sq miles)

Population: 2,374,193

Official language: English

Major religions: Christian 60%, other 40%

Government: Multi-party democracy

Currency: Jamaican dollar

Adult literacy rate: 99%

Life expectancy: 73 years

People per doctor: 2,040

Televisions: 130 per 1,000 people

RASTAFARIANISM

The Rastafarian religion began among the poor of Kingston, Jamaica, in the 1930s. Members believe that Haile Selassie, the former Emperor of Ethiopia (Ras Tafari), was a god. They also believe that God (Jah) will lead black people back to Ethiopia, the promised land. Rastafarians do not usually eat pork, they are against violence, and wear their hair in long dreadlocks. Their clothes are often green, yellow, and red because these are the colours of the Ethiopian flag.

REGGAE MUSIC

The driving rhythms of reggae music can be heard everywhere across the island. Its songs often tell of hardship and political struggle, and are linked to Rastafarianism. Reggae developed in Jamaica from ska, which was a blend of African, European, and South American styles. Jamaican singer Bob Marley (1945–81) made reggae music popular around the world.

ISLAND INDUSTRIES

A variety of industries brings money to Jamaica, from oil refining to producing clothes, such as the jeans being made here. Various minerals are mined, with bauxite being the most important. One rapidly growing industry is data processing, which involves typing data into computers and sending it to companies in the USA. Unlike many other Caribbean countries, however, Jamaica's data processing companies are mostly owned by Jamaicans, and not by large foreign organizations.

KINGSTON

Jamaica's capital city and chief port, Kingston, is one of the largest urban centres in the Caribbean. Founded by the British, the city first grew as a major port for shipping cane sugar to Europe. However, an earthquake in 1907 damaged the city. It has now been rebuilt with modern hotels, banks, and financial offices. Crowded shanty towns also exist on the western side of the city. Violence frequently breaks out here, connected either to political unrest or to the long-established trade in illegal drugs.

FARMING THE LAND

Not everyone in Jamaica works in industry or tourism – agriculture is also important. Plantations growing sugar, bananas, coffee, and cocoa employ large numbers of people. Many Jamaicans also fish for a living or farm their own small plots of land, producing food for themselves, as shown here, with a little left over to sell at local markets.

Okra is used in soups and stews or eaten as a vegetable.

Dasheen is grown for its edible root and leaves.

The breadfruit tree produces fruit with a pulp that is eaten as a vegetable.

Find out more

ETHOPIA: *218*

GROWTH OF CITIES: *17*

RELIGION: *274–275*

SUGAR: *52*

THE BAHAMAS

THE BAHAMAS

PUERTO RICO

THIS LONG LINE OF ABOUT 700 coral islands snakes its way across the warm Caribbean Sea. It was on the island of San Salvador that Christopher Columbus first set foot when he arrived in the "New World" of the Americas in 1492. The Spanish, who called the islands *Bajamar*, meaning "shallow seas", were followed by British settlers and the islands remained a British colony until 1973. Today, the islands are a paradise for holiday-makers of every nationality. They are also a major financial centre, because tax laws make it profitable for banks and foreign businesses to have offices here.

THE BAHAMAS

Capital city: Nassau

Area: 13,880 sq km (5,359 sq miles)

Population: 300,000

Official language: English

Major religions: Christian 95%, other 5%

Government: Multi-party democracy

Currency: Bahamian dollar

Adult literacy rate: 98%

Life expectancy: 72 years

People per doctor: 1,060

Televisions: 224 per 1,000 people

PUERTO RICO*

Capital city: San Juan

Area: 8,959 sq km (3,459 sq miles)

Population: 3,500,000

Official language: Spanish

Major religions: Christian 85%, other 15%

Government: Multi-party democracy

Currency: US dollar

* Puerto Rico is not an independent country. It is a self-governing commonwealth state of the USA.

JUNKANOO FESTIVAL
At the end of each year, the streets come alive with the dancing and music of the Junkanoo parades. This festival forms a link with the country's past. It is said that when an African chief, given the name John Canoe (Junkanoo), came here as a slave he was granted the right to celebrate in true African style.

Main overseas tourists (1994)

USA	Canada	UK	Germany	Others
1,254,210	99,025	29,395	28,490	104,915

TOURIST DESTINATION
People from all over the world come to relax on the white sandy beaches and in the warm waters of the Bahamas. Tourism is vital to the economy and at least half the local people work in jobs linked to the tourist trade, such as in hotels, restaurants, and shops. The city of Freeport on Grand Bahama is the largest resort, with a deep-water harbour for cruise ships. However, passengers often eat and sleep on the ships, which does not help the local economy.

PUERTO RICO

ALTHOUGH SPANISH IS THE MAIN language of Puerto Rico, it is strongly American in flavour. Colonized by Spain in the years after Columbus, the Spanish stayed in control until the 1890s, when the USA took over. The cultivation of tobacco, sugar, and tropical fruits remains important despite the increasing number of factories set up here by US companies. Most people have a good standard of living with excellent education and health care schemes.

PEOPLE OF PUERTO RICO
Puerto Ricans are mainly of Spanish and African descent. Most live in the cities, with one-third in the capital of San Juan. Overcrowding forces others into housing projects outside the main cities. Some people choose to move to the USA.

OPERATION BOOTSTRAP
This plan, which began in 1948 with backing from the USA, was set up to tackle the island's economic problems. Attracted by low taxes and cheap labour, many US companies moved here and, over the years, the plan helped raise living standards on the island. The main industries include petrochemicals, textiles, and medicines.

Find out more

CORAL ISLANDS: *202*
EDUCATION: *277*
HEALTH: *276*
PEOPLES OF THE CONTINENT: *42*

HAITI

THE POOREST COUNTRY IN the western world, Haiti shares the island of Hispaniola with the Dominican Republic. A revolution by African slaves in 1791, led by Toussaint Ouverture, broke French rule and Haiti became the first black republic. Recent decades have been dominated by the cruel dictatorship of François Duvalier, known as "Papa Doc" and, until recently, his son "Baby Doc". Political unrest continues and the country suffers from great poverty. Many Haitians practise the religious cult of voodoo which blends traditional African beliefs with Roman Catholicism. Followers believe in powerful spirits, and dancing to the beat of sacred drums is part of the voodoo ritual.

ART AND CULTURE
Many Haitians try to make extra money by selling crafts, such as straw hats and woodcarvings, to visitors as well as acting as unofficial tourist guides. Since the 1930s, artists have been noted for producing simple, bold paintings, in a style derived from the decorations in voodoo temples.

HAITI	
Capital city: Port-au-Prince	
Area: 27,750 sq km (10,714 sq miles)	
Population: 6,800,000	
Official languages: French, French Creole	
Major religions: Christian 96%, other 4%	
Government: Multi-party democracy	
Currency: Gourde	
Adult literacy rate: 56%	
Life expectancy: 55 years	
People per doctor: 7,140	
Televisions: 5 per 1,000 people	

DOMINICAN REPUBLIC	
Capital city: Santo Domingo	
Area: 48,730 sq km (18,815 sq miles)	
Population: 7,500,000	
Official language: Spanish	
Major religions: Christian 95%, other 5%	
Government: Multi-party democracy	
Currency: Dominican Republic peso	
Adult literacy rate: 84%	
Life expectancy: 67 years	
People per doctor: 930	
Televisions: 84 per 1,000 people	

SOIL EROSION
Farming is the main occupation here and most Haitians live on small plots of land, growing food and keeping goats. They make very little money and pressure for more land to farm means that trees are constantly being cut down. Some wood is turned into charcoal, shown here, and used as fuel in rural areas. Goats overgraze on the remaining woodland. The exposed soil has now become so severely eroded that crop yields are poor. It has been estimated that one-third of the land in Haiti is no longer usable.

DOMINICAN REPUBLIC

THE LANDSCAPE OF MOUNTAINS and forests in the Dominican Republic may be similar to that of its island neighbour, but other aspects of life are very different. Spain was the main colonial power here and US influences are also strong. The people and the culture are a mix of Spanish, African, and native peoples. The island is rich in natural resources, with deposits of silver, platinum, uranium, and nickel, and the largest gold mine in the Caribbean. Tourism and sugar are the most important source of foreign earnings.

Island of Hispaniola

HAITI
DOMINICAN REPUBLIC

	HAITI	DOMINICAN REP.
🚗	**4 cars** per 1,000 people	**84 cars** per 1,000 people
☎	**9 telephones** per 1,000 people	**86 telephones** per 1,000 people
📖	**1.7 years** at school	**4.3 years** at school

THE ECONOMY
People in the Dominican Republic have a better standard of living than those who live in Haiti, where most cannot even afford health care. The economy is stronger in the Republic because it is boosted by earnings from tourism and mining and by a government that encourages new industries, such as textiles. In recent years holiday resorts have sprung up across the country, creating jobs. Many Haitians come here in search of work.

SANTO DOMINGO
The capital city of Santo Domingo was founded by Columbus' brother Bartolomé in 1496. The city became the main base from which Spain launched its conquest of the region. The city has many recently restored colonial buildings which date back to the 16th century.

Find out more
DICTATORSHIP: 271
PEOPLES OF THE CONTINENT: 42
RELIGION: 274–275
SOIL EROSION: 55, 244

LESSER ANTILLES

THE ISLANDS OF the Lesser Antilles stretch in a gentle curve from the Greater Antilles island of Puerto Rico in the north down to the coast of South America. Once European colonies, most of the islands are now independent. However, the background of African, European, and Asian influences has resulted in a vibrant and distinctive culture, highlighted in the music and festivals. Bananas, which thrive in the heat and high rainfall, remain a major export, although some producers are at risk from hurricanes which can devastate the land.

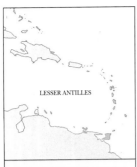

LESSER ANTILLES

ST KITTS AND NEVIS
Capital city: Basseterre
Area: 360 sq km (139 sq miles)
Population: 44,000

ANTIGUA AND BARBUDA
Capital city: St Johns
Area: 440 sq km (170 sq miles)
Population: 63,880

DOMINICA
Capital city: Roseau
Area: 750 sq km (290 sq miles)
Population: 83,000

ST LUCIA
Capital city: Castries
Area: 620 sq km (239 sq miles)
Population: 153,000

ST VINCENT AND THE GRENADINES
Capital city: Kingstown
Area: 340 sq km (131 sq miles)
Population: 117,000

BARBADOS
Capital city: Bridgetown
Area: 430 sq km (166 sq miles)
Population: 300,000

GRENADA
Capital city: St George's
Area: 340 sq km (131 sq miles)
Population: 84,000

TRINIDAD AND TOBAGO
Capital city: Port-of-Spain
Area: 5,130 sq km (1,981 sq miles)
Population: 1,300,000

CRICKET
Cricket is the national game of the English-speaking islands. Children learn to play on sun-dried pitches which allow the ball to be bowled at high speeds. As adults they can play for the West Indies team, drawn from the best players on each island. The team has included many great bowlers and batsmen.

Brian Lara from Trinidad has played for the West Indies cricket team since 1990.

TRANSPORT
In the past, people and goods were transported by boat between the islands. Today ships are still the most economic way to move cargo, and ports, such as Castries in St Lucia, handle the islands' exports. Many islands have no railways and main roads are often confined to the coasts, making the interior difficult to reach. Antigua, Barbados, Martinique, and other islands now have large airports capable of taking jumbo jets.

TOURISM
The main industry in the Caribbean is tourism which provides work for local people in restaurants, hotels, shops, and beach stalls. However the work is mainly seasonal, as most visitors only come when it is cold at home. Also many hotels are owned by foreign companies and money does not always remain on the islands. Some local governments are trying to reduce their dependence on tourism.

SCARLET IBIS
The Caribbean is a haven for colourful birdlife, notably the scarlet ibis of Trinidad and Tobago. The ibis lives in the islands' mangrove swamps, flying off during the day to feed on crabs and other small sea creatures that live in the coastal mudflats.

Curved beak for digging in mud

FOOD FROM THE LAND
Because of the shortage of land, most island farms are small. Farmers grow food for themselves, and sell a wide range of crops in local markets, including yams, sweet potatoes, okra, and salad crops, as well as fruit such as mangoes, limes, coconuts, and bananas. They also grow cash crops for export. The main crop varies from island to island, with nutmeg grown in Grenada, coffee in Trinidad, arrowroot in St Vincent, and sugar and bananas almost everywhere.

INDUSTRY

The most industrialized country in the area is Trinidad and Tobago, which has petrochemical, iron, and steel industries based on its reserves of oil and natural gas. Apart from Barbados, the other islands have few mineral resources and rely on bananas, sugar, cotton, and cocoa for export. In recent years, all the islands have tried to produce a wider range of exports. St Vincent now has a flour mill, and Martinique an oil refinery. Light industrial estates have been set up on a number of islands.

PITCH LAKE
La Brea, in the south of Trinidad, boasts one of the world's most unusual sights. Near to the town is a lake filled not with water but with natural pitch, a black, sticky tar that is mainly used for surfacing roads. The lake, which is 60 m (200 ft) deep, is the world's largest single supply of natural pitch. It is thought to be linked to the underground rocks that supply nearby South America with oil.

LESSER ANTILLES

LESSER ANTILLES

SOUTH AMERICA

LESSER ANTILLES INDUSTRIES
ANTIGUA AND BARBUDA
Cotton production, tourism, rum
ST KITTS AND NEVIS
Sugar, cotton production, tourism
DOMINICA
Bananas, citrus fruits, essential oils
ST LUCIA
Bananas, tourism, electrical parts
ST VINCENT AND THE GRENADINES
Bananas, cement works, food processing
BARBADOS
Sugar, tourism, electrical parts
GRENADA
Bananas, cocoa, tourism
TRINIDAD AND TOBAGO
Oil refining, sugar, chemicals

ISLAND MUSIC

Almost every Caribbean island resounds to the beat of calypso music, which has its origins in the slave songs brought from west Africa. Calypso has a strong beat and lyrics that tell about social and political problems. In recent years soca, a mixture of soul and calypso, has started to become popular with younger people.

Steel band music originated in Trinidad, using pans or drums made from large oil drums.

This steel band is playing music for tourists in Tobago.

The Jinnah Memorial Mosque in Trinidad serves the Muslim community. People are called to prayer from the minarets.

Minaret

PEOPLE OF THE CARIBBEAN
Most people who live on the islands are a mixture of descendants of African slaves, Europeans, and local Carib Indians. The exception are the people of Trinidad, where almost 40 per cent are originally from the Indian subcontinent. Shipped over to work in the plantations, the immigrants brought their religions with them, setting up Hindu temples and Muslim mosques and continuing to observe their own religious customs.

ISLAND SPICES

The island of Grenada is the world's second largest producer of nutmeg, after Indonesia, and grows almost one-quarter of the world's total crop. Nutmeg, a spice used to flavour food, originated in the East Indies, and was introduced to Grenada by the Dutch in the 19th century. The trees flourished in the fertile volcanic soil, warm temperatures, and high annual rainfall. Ginger, cinnamon, pepper, and cloves are also grown on the island.

The single brown nutmeg seed is protected within a green fruit.

Ginger comes from the thick underground stem of this flowering plant.

The oil from nutmeg can be added to perfume and soap.

Ground nutmeg used in cooking

Ginger root can be used fresh or dried.

Find out more
BANANAS: *48*
HURRICANES: *44*
SPICES: *198, 264*
SUGAR: *52*

NORTHERN SOUTH AMERICA

ARCHING AROUND THE RAINFORESTS of the great Amazon River, the countries in northern South America are dominated by the Andes Mountains. Running north to south from Venezuela to Ecuador, and then through Chile, the mountains were once home to the Inca Empire. In search of gold, the Spanish arrived in the 16th century and carved out a huge empire. British, French, and Dutch colonies were also established in the northeast. All but French Guiana are now independent, although not without problems. Extremes of wealth and poverty, overcrowded cities, and the illegal drugs trade are features of most of the countries in this region.

ANIMALS OF THE ANDES
For centuries, the people of the Andes have relied on a group of versatile mammals for food and clothing. The wild guanaco and vicuña, as well as the domesticated llama and alpaca, are all treasured for their wool and meat. Vicuña wool is as fine as silk, while coarse llama wool is used to make blankets, ropes, and other goods.

The llama is used to carry goods.

QUECHUA INDIANS
The Quechua have lived high in the Andes in Bolivia, Peru, and Ecuador for hundreds of years. The Quechua were once farmers who had a system where their work and their land was shared equally between men and women. Today many Quechua have moved to the cities in search of work. Those who remain farm tiny plots of land.

The Andes is the longest unbroken mountain chain over 3,000 m (9,850 ft) in the world.

Lake Titicaca straddles the border between Peru and Bolivia.

The Altiplano, or high plain, is used for growing potatoes and grazing animals.

La Paz

3,000 m (9,850 ft)

Potatoes, wheat, and barley grow in the cool highland areas of the Andes.

Potato plant

2,000 m (6,550 ft)

CULTIVATING THE ANDES
Fertile land is in such short supply in the Andes that every available scrap of soil must be used. Farmers often cut terraces into the hillsides to get maximum use from their land. Crops are grown to suit the temperature, which is hot and humid on the lower slopes near the coast but gets cooler as the mountains rise upwards. On the high plains beyond the Andes only the potato will ripen successfully. To the right is a section of the Andes from Peru to Bolivia.

Sugarcane

Sugarcane, coffee, tobacco, and corn flourish in the temperate zone.

1,000 m (3,280 ft)

Bananas, cocoa, cotton, and rice all grow well in the warm climate of the lowlands.

Sea level

Bananas

USA

To Eastern USA

To Europe

To Mexico

To North Africa

To Western USA and Canada

SOUTH AMERICA

Main growing areas

Main traffic routes

THE DRUG TRADE
For many centuries, people in this region have chewed the leaves of the coca plant to reduce hunger. Today the leaves are processed to make cocaine, an illegal drug much in demand in North America and Europe. Coca bushes thrive on poor soil and need little attention, unlike food crops which need tending. Growing coca is also more profitable than growing food. As a result, large quantities of coca are grown in isolated areas of the Andes. Once refined into cocaine, the drug is smuggled out of the region.

ANGEL FALLS
Angel Falls is the highest waterfall in the world. It was discovered in 1935 by Jimmy Angel, an American pilot who was flying across Venezuela in search of a river he had once prospected for gold. Instead he flew over a vast waterfall, that plunges 980 m (3,215 ft) into the River Churún.

Bogóta, Colombia
☀ Jan 14°C (57°F)
July 14°C (57°F)
🌧 Jan 58 mm (2.3 in)
July 51 mm (2 in)

ECUADOR

Georgetown, Guyana
☀ Jan 26°C (79°F)
July 26.5°C (80°F)
🌧 Jan 203 mm (8 in)
July 254 mm (10 in)

VENEZUELA

GUYANA

SURINAM

COLOMBIA

PERU

THINGS TO LOOK FOR ON THE MAP

Longest river: Orinoco, Colombia/Venezuela, 2,736 km (1,700 miles) *Map G3*

Highest peak: Huascarán, Peru, 6,768 m (22,205 ft) *Map C8*

Largest lake: L.Titicaca, Bolivia/Peru, 8,287 sq km (3,200 sq miles) *Map F10*

World's highest waterfall: Angel Falls, Venezuela, 980 m (3,215 ft) *Map H3*

Lima, Peru
☀ Jan 24°C (74°F)
July 16°C (62°F)
🌧 Jan 3 mm (0.1 in)
July 8 mm (0.3 in)

BOLIVIA

LOST WORLDS
Towering above the rainforests of Venezuela are more than 100 flat-topped sandstone hills, called *tepuis*, some of them 1,000 m (3,300 ft) high. These *tepuis* were once part of a vast plateau that has been eroded by wind and rain over millions of years. Many unique plants and animals have evolved in these "lost worlds".

THE CARIBBEAN COASTLINE
In most of South America, the population is made up of a mixture of European immigrants and the native Indian peoples. But the Caribbean coast and islands are home to a largely black population, like these Colombians. They are the descendants of slaves brought over from Africa to work on the sugar plantations. Many have remained among the poorest members of society.

BORDER DISPUTES
There is not a country in South America that has not fought with its neighbours about its borders, and many frontiers are still disputed today. Wars between Bolivia and Paraguay in the 1930s, and Ecuador and Peru in the 1940s, resulted in thousands of deaths. The checkpoint shown here marks the border between Bolivia and Chile.

VENEZUELA

WHEN THE ITALIAN EXPLORER Amerigo Vespucci first visited the southern shores of the Caribbean Sea in 1499, he named the land Venezuela, or "Little Venice". The lake dwellings of the native Indians reminded him of the houses and canals of the Italian city of Venice. Part of the Spanish Empire for three centuries, Venezuela became independent in 1811. Today it is a country of huge contrasts: the oil industry produces immense wealth, yet many people live in shanty towns. Most people live in cities, yet the tribes of the interior are barely touched by modern life.

HIGH-RISE CARACAS
For most of its 400-year history, Caracas was a sleepy town 900 m (2,950 ft) up in the hills near the Caribbean coastline. With the discovery of oil, the population rapidly rose from a few thousand to more than 4 million. Today Caracas is a modern city, with steel and glass architecture, an extensive motorway, and a subway system.

VENEZUELA	
Capital city: Caracas	
Area: 912,050 sq km (352,143 sq miles)	
Population: 20,200,000	
Official language: Spanish	
Major religions: Christian 98%, other 2%	
Government: Presidential republic	
Currency: Bolívar	
Adult literacy rate: 89%	
Life expectancy: 70 years	
People per doctor: 650	
Televisions: 171 per 1,000 people	

RAINFOREST TRIBES

The few native peoples who still survive in Venezuela live in the remote interior of the country near the border with Brazil. The main group is the Yanomami, who number about 17,000 people. The Yanomami are hunters and gatherers who live in enormous thatched huts, called *yanos*, built in clearings in the forest. Their way of life is threatened both by the timber companies and mineral prospectors anxious to exploit the wealth of the region, and by measles and other diseases against which they have no defence.

Where people live

91% live in cities   9% live in the country

Hammocks are slung between the outer wall and one of the upright poles.

Circular yanos contain between 10 and 20 families, each living in their own section.

Yanos are made from wooden beams covered with palm branches and supported by tall poles; the central part is often open to the sky.

The 2-m (6-ft) long bows are used to fire arrows tipped with poison made from plants.

OIL WEALTH

The discovery of oil in Lake Maracaibo in 1917 transformed Venezuela from one of the poorest countries in South America to one of the richest. The reserves underneath Lake Maracaibo are the biggest outside the Middle East; oil-bearing beds of tar by the Orinoco River add to the country's wealth. Despite these reserves, many people remain poor. Public services and agriculture have been neglected, and the fall in oil prices has affected the economy.

Women tend the gardens as well as bringing up the children.

Yanomani men hunt wild animals for food. Boys are trained to hunt from an early age.

CABLE CAR
Far above the city of Mérida is the world's highest cable car system. It carries passengers from the city up to 4,765 m (15,600 ft) above sea level. The journey is in four stages and takes more than an hour.

YOUNG VENEZUELA
Out of a total population in Venezuela of 20 million, more than 8 million are under the age of 15. The majority of them live in the cities of the north. Many enjoy North American activities such as playing baseball (which was introduced by workers in the oil industry), as well as listening to rock music.

Find out more

NATIVE PEOPLES: *43*
OIL: *137, 152, 281*
POPULATION GROWTH: *43*
RAINFORESTS: *15, 69, 204*

GUYANA	
Capital city: Georgetown	
Area: 214,970 sq km (83,000 sq miles)	
Population: 800,000	
Official language: English	
Major religions: Christian 57%, Hindu 33%, Muslim 9%, other 1%	
Government: Multi-party democracy	
Currency: Guyana dollar	
Adult literacy rate: 97%	
Life expectancy: 65 years	
People per doctor: 6,220	
Televisions: 38 per 1,000 people	

SURINAM	
Capital city: Paramaribo	
Area: 163,270 sq km (63,039 sq miles)	
Population: 425,000	
Official language: Dutch	
Major religions: Christian 48%, Hindu 27%, Muslim 20%, other 5%	
Government: Democratic coalition	
Currency: Surinam guilder	
Adult literacy rate: 96%	
Life expectancy: 70 years	
People per doctor: 1,260	
Televisions: 130 per 1,000 people	

FRENCH GUIANA*	
Capital city: Cayenne	
Area: 91,000 sq km (35,135 sq miles)	
Population: 114,808	
Official language: French	
Major religions: Christian 75%, other 25%	
Government: Ruled from France as part of multi-party democracy	
Currency: French franc	

*French Guiana is not an independent country. It is a French overseas department.

GUYANA

ONLY ABOUT 800,000 PEOPLE live in Guyana, most of them on the coastal plain in and around the capital city of Georgetown. Guyana takes its name from a native Indian word meaning "Land of Many Waters", for the country is crossed by numerous rivers draining north into the Atlantic Ocean. Guyana was once a British colony, but gained independence in 1966. Today the country exports sugar and bauxite, and also possesses vast natural resources, including timber and minerals.

THE POPULATION
Most people in Guyana are descendants of workers or slaves brought into the country to labour on the sugar plantations. Black African slaves were shipped in between the 17th and 19th centuries. After slavery was abolished in the British Empire in 1833, people from the Indian Subcontinent arrived to take their place. The Caribs, the original Indian inhabitants, now number no more than 60,000 people.

SUGAR PLANTATIONS
The Dutch were the first Europeans in Guyana, establishing a settlement on the Essequibo river in 1615. They planted sugar, cocoa, and other tropical crops, importing slaves from West Africa to help them run the plantations. The British took control of the country in 1814, and concentrated on growing sugar. Today sugar, rice, bauxite, and gold are the main exports.

SURINAM

FORMERLY KNOWN AS DUTCH GUIANA, Surinam was originally owned by the British who exchanged it for the Dutch island of Nieuw Amsterdam, now called Manhattan, in 1667. Surinam became independent from the Netherlands in 1975. Because the country is so poor, about 200,000 Surinamese live in the Netherlands, and send money back to support their families at home.

PARAMARIBO
The capital city of Surinam lies just inland from the Atlantic coastline. The Dutch origins of the city can be seen in the Dutch-style architecture and in street names such as Konigstraat. Most of the city is built of wood, including the 19th-century cathedral of St Peter and St Paul with its tall spires. Half the population of Surinam lives in Paramaribo.

FRENCH GUIANA

THE ONLY REMAINING colony in South America is French Guiana. For years the colony was famous for its offshore prison on Devil's Island, but today it is better known for its role in the European space programme. The colony is dependent on France for much of its income, with the result that it now has one of the highest standards of living in South America.

KOUROU
More than 15,000 people live and work at Kourou, the launch site for the European Space Agency. *Ariane* rockets put satellites and probes into space on behalf of European nations.

The ocelot is an endangered animal.

FORESTS
Most people live on the coast and the interior is largely untouched tropical rainforest. Thousands of different species of flora and fauna, including ocelots, jaguars, and pumas, plus a variety of reptiles, inhabit the forests.

Find out more

DEPENDENT TERRITORIES: *271*
NATIVE PEOPLES: *43*
RAINFORESTS: *15, 69, 204*
SUGAR: *52*

COLOMBIA

COLOMBIA	
Capital city: Bogotá	
Area: 1,138,910 sq km (439,733 sq miles)	
Population: 34,000,000	
Official language: Spanish	
Major religions: Christian 95%, other 5%	
Government: Multi-party democracy	
Currency: Colombian peso	
Adult literacy rate: 87%	
Life expectancy: 69 years	
People per doctor: 1,150	
Televisions: 118 per 1,000 people	

CARTAGENA
The bustling port of Cartagena was founded by the Spanish in the 1500s. Great Spanish galleons bound for home set off from here piled high with riches looted from the native peoples. The old city walls, enclosing beautiful mansions and churches, are still there today, along with the many fortifications built by the Spanish to ward off pirates and attacks from other countries.

COLOMBIA

WHEN SPANISH CONQUERORS reached Colombia in 1499 they discovered a civilization that was rich in gold. They spread tales of a mysterious lost city called *El Dorado*, filled with wealth, but it has never been found. Since 1819, when Colombia became an independent country, it has suffered decades of violent political battles and, more recently, bloody rivalry between gangs involved in the drugs trade. Today Colombia is the world's largest producer of cocaine. Large rivers, such as the Orinoco and Amazon, form an important means of transport for goods across the country.

BURIED TREASURE

Mining is becoming very important to the Colombian economy since large deposits of oil have been found northeast of Bogotá. Petrochemical plants, like this one at Barranquilla, convert oil into fuel for cars and planes. New sources of coal, the largest in Latin America, as well as deposits of nickel, are also helping to boost the economy. The USA, Germany, and Japan are Colombia's main trading partners.

The women's skirts look like those worn by Spanish flamenco dancers.

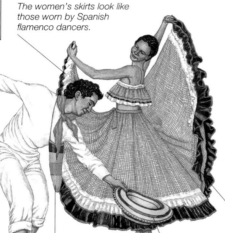

THE CUMBIA
All Colombians know how to dance the *cumbia*, even young children. The dance is a blend of traditions from the black slaves who were brought to Colombia from Africa in the 1800s, together with Spanish and native Indian influences. The men wear white which was the colour of slaves' clothes. Women's clothes are more Spanish in origin.

A small pouch, called a mochila, is traditionally worn to hold coca leaves or rum.

Men wear sombreros – hats which have wide brims to keep off the sun.

Skirts have weights in the hems to keep them from swirling too high.

EMERALDS
Many people consider Colombian emeralds to be the finest in the world. The earliest civilizations to live in this region made beautiful objects from gold and emeralds. Today, Colombia produces more than half of the world's emeralds.

Veins of natural emeralds are found in rocks such as calcite or pyrite.

AGRICULTURE

The variety of climate zones in Colombia means that a wide range of crops can be grown. For many years coffee was the country's main export and Colombia is still the world's second largest producer, after Brazil. Once picked, coffee beans are spread out in trays to dry naturally in the sun. Falling world coffee prices have forced Colombia's farmers to develop other products, such as sugar, bananas, cotton, and cut flowers, which are all grown for export.

SAN AGUSTIN
This small village near the southern mountains is famous for its ancient stone figures. The statues are at least 800 years old, but very little is known about the people who carved them. Some experts believe that the site was a ceremonial centre where the Agustinians buried their dead, placing statues near the tombs.

About 500 statues have been found at San Agustin. Many are shaped like birds or animals.

Find out more

COFFEE: *50, 66*
DRUG TRADE: *58*
GEMSTONES: *172, 191*
OIL: *137, 152, 281*

ECUADOR

CUT THROUGH BY THE EQUATOR, after which it is named, Ecuador is a small country with a varied landscape. A journey of just 200 km (125 miles) takes you from humid coastal lowlands, up into the cold air of the Andes, and down into tropical rainforest. Ecuador also includes the Galápagos Islands, which lie about 1,000 km (620 miles) west in the Pacific Ocean. Ecuador has large reserves of oil and natural gas, and these products account for nearly half of the country's export earnings.

ECUADOR	
Capital city: Quito	
Area: 283,560 sq km (109,483 sq miles)	
Population: 11,100,000	
Official language: Spanish	
Major religions: Christian 95%, other 5%	
Government: Multi-party democracy	
Currency: Sucre	
Adult literacy rate: 87%	
Life expectancy: 66 years	
People per doctor: 960	
Televisions: 83 per 1,000 people	

COTOPAXI
Ecuador is home to the notorious "volcano boulevard" – four rows of volcanic mountains which form part of the Andes chain. At least 10 of them are still active. One of the most famous is Cotopaxi. A towering 5,897 m (19,348 ft) in height, this is one of the world's tallest active volcanoes. It last erupted in the early 1900s.

MANGROVE SWAMPS
Along the coast are swamps filled with trees, called mangroves, that can grow in salt water. This watery habitat is very important: the trees provide firewood and timber, while the fish, crustaceans, and shellfish that live here are an important source of food. Shrimps in particular have become a major export. Large shrimp farms have created thousands of much-needed jobs, but they are gradually destroying the coastal environment on which they depend.

The roots trap silt from the sea and help to prevent erosion of the land.

At high tide, the sea comes in and covers the roots.

Mudskippers are the only fish that can live on land and in the water.

The mangroves' tangled roots spread far and wide, some even emerging above water to trap oxygen.

Swamp water is usually very muddy.

Shrimps are washed in with the tide. They feed on plankton.

Statice

Carnations

AGRICULTURE
Twenty years ago, Ecuador's economy was based on three crops – bananas, coffee, and cocoa. Today, agriculture is less dominant, but about a third of the workforce still makes a living from farming. Fishing is also important, with shrimps, sardines, and tuna among the main catches. A recently introduced crop is cut flowers, such as roses, carnations, and statice, which are exported to North America and Europe.

Panama hats are made from the leaves of the jipijapa plant.

PANAMA HAT
Panama hats have never been made in Panama. They come from Ecuador, where they were originally made for export to Panama – hence the name. A good-quality hat takes three months to make and can be rolled up without being spoiled.

THE OTAVALO INDIANS
The town of Otavalo, high in the Andes, is home to one of the wealthiest groups of Indians in South America. The Otavalo make blankets, ponchos, rugs, and other woven goods, which they sell to tourists and export all over South America, the USA, and Europe. Demand for Otavalo goods is so great that many of them are now mass-produced, using artificial dyes and fibres and machines for weaving. The money raised allows the Otavalo to continue their traditional way of life.

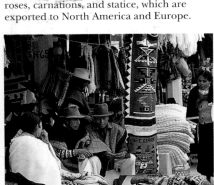

Otavalo market is so popular with tourists that it now occupies all five squares in the centre of town.

Otavalo rug, decorated with llamas.

Find out more	
ANDES:	*40, 58*
GALÁPAGOS ISLANDS:	*265*
NATIVE PEOPLES:	*43*
VOLCANOES:	*13*

PERU

FOUR HUNDRED YEARS AGO, Peru was the centre of the great Inca Empire that stretched the length of South America. Descendants of the Incas still continue their traditional way of life in the Andes Mountains, and make up about half of Peru's population. In recent years, unemployment, poverty, and other social problems have led to much political violence in Peru. This has stopped foreign companies investing in Peru and kept it one of the poorest countries in South America.

PERU	
Capital city: Lima	
Area: 1,285,220 sq km (496,223 sq miles)	
Population: 22,900,000	
Official languages: Spanish, Quechua, and Aymará	
Major religions: Christian 95%, other 5%	
Government: Multi-party democracy	
Currency: New sol	
Adult literacy rate: 86%	
Life expectancy: 64 years	
People per doctor: 970	
Televisions: 97 per 1,000 people	

LIMA

Grey skies and damp mists hang over Lima for much of the year. But the population of Peru's capital city has grown rapidly to more than 6 million as people flock there in search of work. Although the rich live in new apartment buildings or suburban houses, the poor survive in *calampas*, huge, overcrowded shanty towns that have sprung up on the outskirts. Lima was founded in 1535 by the Spaniard, Francisco Pizarro.

PACIFIC FISHING

Peru's cool coastal waters are teeming with plankton, which provide food for huge numbers of anchovies, sardines, pilchards, and mackerel. Anchovies, caught and processed into fishmeal, are a major export. Every nine or 10 years a current of warm water, called *El Niño*, upsets the balance of plankton and the fish move to better feeding areas. It struck in 1992, devastating the fishing industry.

Mackerel

Sardines

The islands are built from layers of reeds which rot away at the bottom and are replaced at the top.

New reeds are cut and stacked ready for use.

Villagers grow potatoes in fields by the lake.

The Urus build their homes and boats from the totora reeds that grow at the edge of the lake.

Remains of the city of Machu Picchu

Women untangling fishing nets.

LAKE TITICACA

Lying 3,810 m (12,500 ft) above sea level, Lake Titicaca is the world's highest navigable lake. It stretches across the border into Bolivia and, for thousands of years, native peoples have fished its waters. One group, the Urus, live by the lake in floating villages built on huge rafts made from reeds. They grow potatoes, one of the few crops that will ripen at such high altitudes, fish, and hunt birds that live by the lake.

Women wear their hair in a single plait which they tuck into their hats.

The Urus build boats from tightly bundled reeds. A well-built boat can last a family up to six months.

THE LOST CITY OF THE INCAS

Perched high in the Andes, Machu Picchu was an important Inca city in the 15th and 16th centuries. This fortress city escaped the notice of the Spanish conquerors who arrived in 1532, and remained a "lost city" until it was rediscovered by American archaeologist, Hiram Bingham, in 1911. The site includes the remains of ceremonial buildings, such as temples, and 143 homes.

SHINING PATH

During the 1980s a guerilla group called the Shining Path conducted a terrorist campaign in Peru. The group wanted to restore a communist government, and proceeded to terrorize the country. They were able to assassinate people and bomb targets in Peru's cities. Their leader, Abimael Guzman, was captured and imprisoned in 1993.

Find out more

ANDES: 40, 58
CITIES: 17, 43
NATIVE PEOPLES: 43
POTATOES: 140

BOLIVIA

THE SMALL, MOUNTAINOUS country of Bolivia has no coastline. In 1883, its coastal region was lost to Chile in the Pacific Wars, and now its main means of export are by roads and railways running through Peru and Chile. Bolivia has many resources, such as silver and tin, but its isolated position and frequent changes of government have kept it poor. About 70 per cent of the population are Aymará or Quechua Indians who live on the high windswept plains, called the *altiplano*, growing barely enough food to feed themselves and their families.

SIMÓN BOLÍVAR
Bolivia is named after Simón Bolívar (1783-1830), the Venezuelan freedom fighter known as "The Liberator". From 1812, Bolívar devoted his life to freeing South America from Spanish control. He liberated New Granada (Colombia), Venezuela, Ecuador, Panama, and finally Bolivia, then known as Upper Peru. Bolívar dreamed of a united South America, but his dream has not come true.

BOLIVIA

Capital city: La Paz	
Area: 1,098,580 sq km (424,162 sq miles)	
Population: 6,344,396	
Official languages: Spanish, Quechua, and Aymará	
Major religions: Christian 95%, other 5%	
Government: Multi-party democracy	
Currency: Boliviano	
Adult literacy rate: 79%	
Life expectancy: 61 years	
People per doctor: 2,080	
Televisions: 105 per 1,000 people	

It is cold living on the high plains of Bolivia. The soil is poor and villagers break up the ground to sow potatoes.

Tin

Silver

MINING
Bolivia is rich in tin, silver, lead, zinc, and other minerals. Tin mining is an important industry and, even though production has fallen, Bolivia still ranks among the world's top five tin producers. Thousands of people work in the mines, but conditions are dangerous and wages are low. Many miners believe that a spirit, called *El Tio*, lives in the mines, and they leave cigarettes as offerings for him.

LIFE ON THE HIGH PLAINS
Life is hard for the Aymará Indians who live in villages without electricity or plumbing. Most are poor farmers who grow potatoes as well as maize and barley stalks to feed their cows, sheep, and chickens. Sometimes they kill an animal for food. Llamas provide wool for warm clothing and llama droppings are used as fuel. Aymará women and girls wear dark green, black or brown hats.

This lamb will later provide milk for the family.

Many Aymará wear plastic shoes, called ojotas.

FESTIVAL IN THE SUN
Although Bolivia is Roman Catholic, many traditional beliefs still survive. The Isla del Sol (Island of the Sun) in Lake Titicaca is thought to be the birthplace of the Sun and is the location for the celebration shown here. Music is important at Bolivian festivals, when pan-pipes, drums, and brass instruments are played.

Traditional pan-pipes are made from reeds.

COCA GROWING
The leaf of the coca plant is used in the production of the illegal drug cocaine. Coca grows well in Bolivia's mountain valleys and provides a much-needed source of income for local people. The government has tried to stop coca production by offering farmers money to destroy their plantations and grow other crops, such as coffee, cocoa, or bananas, instead. However, this policy has not succeeded, and coca is still Bolivia's main crop.

Loose seeds inside the maracas make a noise when they are shaken.

Maracas are pairs of rattles made from dried gourds.

Find out more
DRUG TRADE: *58*
LLAMAS: *58*
NATIVE PEOPLES: *43*
ROMAN CATHOLICS: *274*

BRAZIL

THE LARGEST COUNTRY in South America, Brazil covers almost half the continent. From the 16th–19th centuries it was ruled by the Portuguese who named it after the brazilwood tree. The country contains deserts in the northeast, rainforests in the north and west, and rolling grasslands in the south. Because the climate is so varied, it is possible to grow almost any crop. Brazil also has crowded modern cities and areas which have never been explored. In the south, the forces of the Paraná and Paraguay rivers have been harnessed to form the world's largest hydroelectric project, the Itaipú Dam.

CITY LIFE

About 75 per cent of Brazilians live in cities, most of which have developed near the coast. Over the years many people have moved to the cities from the countryside in search of work and a better standard of living. For many years the cities grew rapidly, although this has now slowed down. The largest city, São Paulo, already has 16 million people – more than the populations of Paris and London put together.

TOP CITIES BY POPULATION	
São Paulo	16,800,000
Rio de Janeiro	11,100,000
Belo Horizonte	3,400,000
Salvador	2,400,000
Fortaleza	2,100,000

PEOPLE OF BRAZIL

The population of Brazil is a mixture of peoples. Some are descended from native Indians who have always lived in Brazil, others from the Portuguese who ruled there for 300 years. Many Brazilians have African ancestors who were brought over in the 17th century to work as slaves on the sugar plantations. At the beginning of this century many Japanese sailed to Brazil to escape crop failures at home. Also during this century, large numbers of European migrants have settled in the south of the country.

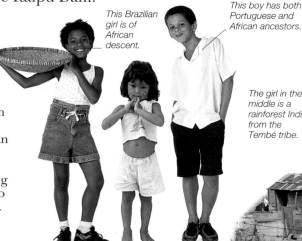

This Brazilian girl is of African descent.

This boy has both Portuguese and African ancestors.

The girl in the middle is a rainforest Indian from the Tembé tribe.

The homes in this shanty town in São Paulo are built from wood and corrugated metal.

World's top coffee producers 1994

(Figures show percentage of world production)

6.7% Indonesia
14.3% Colombia
24.6% Brazil

AGRICULTURE

Brazil is the world's major producer and exporter of coffee which is grown on huge plantations, mostly in the states of Paraná and São Paulo. However, coffee is only one of the country's main crops; soya beans, sugarcane, and cotton are also produced on a large scale. Brazil is also one of the world's main producers of oranges, bananas, and cocoa beans. About one-third of Brazilians work in agriculture, although the size of farms varies from tiny plots of land to vast estates. Many people work in the fields for little pay while a few rich landowners benefit from the huge profits.

SHANTY TOWNS

Housing shortages in Brazil mean that about 25 million people live in sprawling shanty towns, called *favelas*, that surround the cities. Most of the homes are built by the families themselves, sometimes from waste materials but more often from wood, bricks, and cement bought from builder's merchants. Services such as running water and sanitation are poor.

Favela homes (1993)

No running water: 70%

No toilets or drains: 60%

No waste collection: 52%

FOOTBALL

Everyone in Brazil plays or watches football (soccer), and there is a stadium in every city. The huge Maracana stadium in Rio de Janeiro was built for the 1950 World Cup and holds 200,000 spectators. Brazil has won the World Cup more times than any other country, most recently in 1994. Many Brazilian stars play football abroad for teams in England, Spain, and Italy.

Manaus
- ☀ Jan 27°C (82°F)
- ☁ July 27°C (82°F)
- 🌧 Jan 249 mm (9.8 in)
- 🌧 July 58 mm (2.3 in)

BRAZIL

THINGS TO LOOK FOR ON THE MAP

Longest river: Amazon, Brazil/Peru, 6,439 km (4,001 miles) *Map G3*

Highest point: Pico da Neblina, 3,014 m (9,888 ft) *Map C3*

World's largest lagoon: Lagoa dos Patos, 10,145 sq km (3,917 sq miles) *Map G12*

VENEZUELA

GUYANA

SURINAM

FRENCH GUIANA (France)

COLOMBIA

Boa Vista

Pico da Neblina

Negro

Jari

Macapá

Belém

São Luís

Parnaíba

ATLANTIC OCEAN

A M A Z O N I A

Balbina Res.

Manaus

Santarém

Amazon

Amazon

Madeira

Tapajós

Xingu

Tucuruí Res.

Serra dos Carajás

Teresina

Fortaleza

Mossoró

Natal

Juruá

Purus

BRAZIL

Rio das Pires

Carolina

Parnaíba

Picos

Campina Grande

João Pessoa

Recife

Cruzeiro do Sul

Pôrto Velho

PLATEAU OF MATO GROSSO

Serra do Roncador

Araguaia

Tocantins

Palmas

Sobradinho Res.

Juàzeiro

Maceió

Rio Branco

PERU

SERRA DOS PARECIS

Barreiras

Ibotirama

Feira de Santana

Salvador

Aracaju

BOLIVIA

Cuiabá

BRASÍLIA

São Francisco

Corumbá

Goiânia

B R A Z I L I A N   H I G H L A N D S

N

Uberlândia

Ilha Solteira Res.

Belo Horizonte

Ouro Prêto

Vitória

Campo Grande

Ribeirão Prêto

Furnas Res.

Juiz de Fora

PARAGUAY

Paraná

Campinas

São Paulo

Rio de Janeiro

Santos

Porto Alegre
- ☀ Jan 25°C (77°F)
- ☁ July 14°C (57°F)
- 🌧 Jan 89 mm (3.5 in)
- 🌧 July 114 mm (4.5 in)

Itaipú Res.

Londrina

Curitiba

Iguaçu Falls

Iguaçu

Joinville

ARGENTINA

Uruguay

Florianópolis

Passo Fundo

ATLANTIC OCEAN

URUGUAY

Santa Maria

Pôrto Alegre

Lagoa dos Patos

Pelotas

Rio Grande

0 100 200 300 400 500 km
0 250 500 750 miles

TROPIC OF CANCER

EQUATOR

TROPIC OF CAPRICORN

PIRANHA FISH

These vicious fish live in the rivers of the rainforest. They have razor-sharp teeth and when hundreds of them attack together, they can kill and strip a large animal in minutes.

AMAZON

The Amazon River starts life in the Andes Mountains of Peru and flows for 6,439 km (4,001 miles) across South America until it gushes into the Atlantic Ocean. For more than half of its length, the Amazon flows through Brazil. It is the country's most important waterway, and large boats can travel inland as far as the modern city of Manaus, about 1,600 km (994 miles) from the sea. Every year the river floods and deposits fertile silt on the land.

The Amazon, its tributaries, swamps, and lakes, form a vast network of fresh water.

FUN IN THE SUN

Brazil's eastern coastline stretches for 7,400 km (4,598 miles) along the Atlantic Ocean. In Rio de Janeiro, local people and tourists flock to the wide, sandy beaches to meet friends and play volleyball. The most popular beach in Rio de Janeiro is Copacabana, which is overlooked by Sugarloaf Mountain. Only good swimmers brave the waves here because of the strong currents.

BRAZIL

BRAZIL

BRAZIL	
Capital city: Brasília	
Area: 8,511,970 sq km (3,286,472 sq miles)	
Population: 146,154,502	
Official language: Portuguese	
Major religions: Christian 90%, other 10%	
Government: Multi-party democracy	
Currency: Réal	
Adult literacy rate: 82%	
Life expectancy: 66 years	
People per doctor: 670	
Televisions: 215 per 1,000 people	

BOOM AND BUST BEST DESCRIBES the pattern of the economy in Brazil. In the 1960s and 1970s the country enjoyed a period of massive industrial growth. Then the boom ended, Brazil went bust, and the country became the world's greatest debtor. Paying back the loans is now the government's biggest problem. But Brazil has a great supply of natural resources, including gold and iron ore, and mining is one of the country's most important industries. Brazil is both a rich and poor country. Some landowners and business people are extremely wealthy while most of the rural population is very poor. Although there has been a democratic government since 1985, corruption is still a problem in Brazilian politics.

CARNIVAL

For four days and nights before Lent each year (February or March), it is carnival time in Brazil. People come from all over the world to join the celebration in Rio de Janeiro where there are street parties, balls, and a contest for the best costume. Day and night the streets are crammed with people in wonderful costumes moving to the rhythm of the music. A parade of brightly coloured floats, organized by neighbourhood samba schools, is the highlight of the carnival.

FOOD FROM BAHIA
The state of Bahia in northeast Brazil was the first to be colonized by Europeans. Later, black slave cooks created lots of tasty dishes using fish from the sea mixed with spices from their native Africa. Along the beaches of Bahia, women still sell these dishes as well as snacks of coconut sweets and delicious spicy fish patties.

Electrical goods such as refrigerators, washing machines, and food mixers

Leather goods such as bags, shoes, jackets, tennis shoes, and footballs

RELIGION

Almost all Brazilians are Roman Catholic, the religion the Portuguese brought with them, and every town and village has its own patron saint to protect it. Millions of Brazilians also exercise their right to freedom of belief and worship gods and spirits from African religions. In December and January, for example, people leave gifts of flowers, soap, and fruit on the beaches in honour of *Iemanjá*, the African goddess of the sea, who they hope will grant their wishes for the new year. The goddess is linked with the Catholic Virgin Mary.

ECONOMY

Brazil produces most of its own food and manufactured goods but needs money to pay off its enormous debts. The country's major exports, some of which are shown here, include coffee, minerals, and aeroplanes, as well as large numbers of Brazilian cars which are sold in Argentina. Most of Brazil's manufacturing takes place in a rough triangle formed by the industrial cities of Rio de Janeiro, São Paulo, and Belo Horizonte.

Textiles of cotton and silk, and finished goods including towels and sports clothes

Agricultural produce including oranges, tangerines, lemons, and limes

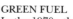

GREEN FUEL
In the 1970s, the rising cost of oil forced Brazil to look for an alternative fuel. Researchers came up with ethanol, a fuel which is made from fermented sugarcane. Ethanol is cheaper than ordinary petrol and produces less carbon monoxide, which is much better for the environment. Today, about one-third of Brazil's cars run on this "green petrol".

AMAZON RAINFOREST

Covering an area the size of Australia, the Amazon rainforest is the largest remaining tropical rainforest anywhere on Earth. It covers about one-third of South America, mostly growing around the Amazon River in Brazil. Many animals, birds, insects, and reptiles rely on the trees for food and shelter, as do the tribes of Amazonian Indians who have lived in the forest for thousands of years. But the rainforest is a fragile environment and both wildlife and people are under serious threat as vast areas of the forest are cut down.

This village chief is from the Tembé tribe.

Native Indian homelands

Brazilian rainforest

B R A Z I L

① Tikuna
② Yanomani
③ Guajajara
④ Xavante
⑤ Sateré Maué

INDIAN TRIBES

At one time there were about 5 million native Indians living in the rainforest; today fewer than 200,000 remain. The largest of these tribes are located on the above map. Most live as shifting cultivators which means they settle for a while to hunt and grow basic food crops and then move on. This way the forest soil can recover its fertility. Since the arrival of people from outside the forest, the Indians are at risk from diseases, such as influenza and measles, to which they have no resistance.

MINING

In the last 20 years large deposits of gold and other minerals have been discovered in the Amazon rainforest. At Carajas, a huge iron mountain was accidentally discovered when a geologist crash-landed his helicopter. The rock contains massive amounts of iron ore as well as manganese and copper. Mining is one of Brazil's major industries, despite the damage it does to the rainforest.

PLANT POWER

Quinine is obtained from the chinchona plant.

Brazil nuts contain vitamins.

Bark

Shelled nut

The forests contain plants that provide the basis for many valuable products such as rubber, varnish, paint, cosmetics, and most importantly medicines. The bark of *chinchona*, for example, supplies the quinine used to treat malaria. Other plants have properties that help fight cancer.

LOSS OF FOREST

Vital areas of forest are lost through logging, cattle ranching, and relocation (moving people). Building roads also opens up the interior to further destruction. If the present rate of deforestation continues, there will be no forest left by the end of the century.

RELOCATION

The Brazilian government recently cleared large areas of forest and encouraged landless people to buy small plots of land there for farming. But the soil is shallow and rapidly loses its fertility.

CATTLE BREEDING

About 30 per cent of Brazil's rainforest has been cut down for cattle ranches. But the land can only support cattle for a few years before all its grazing is used up. Then the ranchers have to move on and clear another site.

LOGGING

Thousands of ebony, teak, and mahogany trees are cut down each year for export. People are now encouraged to buy furniture made of softwoods, such as pine, which take less time to regrow.

Plan of Brasília

Business districts

Government buildings

Residential areas

BRASÍLIA

The city of Brasília was built in the late 1950s as part of a government scheme to encourage people to move into the interior of the country. It became Brazil's capital in 1960, taking over from Rio de Janeiro. The city is laid out in the shape of an aeroplane with the business district in the centre, residential areas in the wings, and the government in the cockpit. Bold architecture, such as the glass cathedral shown here, is a feature of this modern city.

Find out more
CITIES: 17, 43
COFFEE: 50, 62
RAINFORESTS: 15, 204
ROMAN CATHOLICS: 274

SOUTHERN SOUTH AMERICA

FROM THE TROPICAL INTERIOR OF Paraguay, through the warm Mediterranean climate of central Chile, to the freezing conditions around the glaciers of Argentina, southern South America is a region of great contrasts. Four countries – Chile, Argentina, Paraguay, and Uruguay – make up this half of the continent, often called the "southern cone" because of its shape. An important land resource is the pampas, a vast fertile plain that stretches across Argentina and Uruguay, where huge quantities of wheat are grown. During the 1970s, all four countries were known for their brutal military dictatorships. These have since been overturned and the countries are now run as democracies.

ATACAMA DESERT
This desert in northern Chile is the driest place on Earth, often with no rain for years on end. When rain does fall, devastating flash floods are often the result. The Atacama is a barren wilderness of sun-baked rock and shifting sand dunes, where the night-time temperature can fall dramatically in just one hour. The only paved road across this empty desert is the Pan-American Highway.

Main migration routes from 1860–1926

Uruguay
Paraguay
Argentina

MIGRANT GROUPS
Many people from Europe have settled in South America. During the 19th and early 20th centuries, poverty in Italy drove labourers to Argentina for the wheat harvest; many never went home. Workers also left Spain for Argentina and Uruguay. A German religious group, the Mennonites, moved to Paraguay from Canada to find freedom of worship, and the Welsh set up a community in Argentina to escape English rule and preserve their language.

INDIAN PEOPLES
Unlike northern South America, the countries in the south have only a few native Indian groups, with Paraguay home to the largest proportion. Uruguay has no Indian population at all. The main surviving groups include the Kolla of Argentina, shown here, the Mataco and Mapuche of central and southern Chile, and the Ache who live in Paraguay.

WHERE PEOPLE LIVE
In the past 50 years, there has been a great shift as people have moved from the country to the cities in search of work. In Argentina and Uruguay, city populations were already swollen by large numbers of immigrants. In each country, the capital city has grown very quickly while the population in other cities has remained fairly small. One-third of Argentinians, for example, live in the capital city of Buenos Aires, shown here. Since the 1970s, the move to the cities has begun to slow down.

CATTLE BREEDING
In Argentina and Uruguay, cattle breeding for beef exports is a major source of income. Vast herds of cattle graze the pampas, many feeding on alfalfa plants which produce a leaner meat. The main breeds are Aberdeen Angus and Hereford, brought over from Europe during the last century. Sheep are grazed in the cooler area of Patagonia, and both Argentina and Uruguay are among the world's top wool-producing nations.

Growth of cities

The chart shows the percentage of people living in cities in 1950, 1970, and 1990.

37%
35%
48%
58%
86%
75%
86%
78%
65%
89%
78%
82%

Paraguay
Chile
Argentina
Uruguay

About 11 million people now live in Buenos Aires.

1990
1970
1950

A B C D E F G H I J K L

Asunción, Paraguay
Jan 28°C (83°F)
July 17°C (63°F)
Jan 140 mm (5.5 in)
July 56 mm (2.2 in)

PARAGUAY

Buenos Aires, Argentina
Jan 23°C (74°F)
July 10°C (50°F)
Jan 79 mm (3.1 in)
July 56 mm (2.2 in)

TROPIC OF CANCER

EQUATOR

TROPIC OF CAPRICORN

0 100 200 300 km
0 50 100 150 200 miles

CHILE

ITAIPÚ DAM
Huge amounts of earth were cleared to build the
Itaipú Dam on the River Paraná in Paraguay. One
of the world's largest hydroelectric projects, the
dam was built jointly by Paraguay and Brazil, and
can produce massive amounts of electricity.
Unfortunately, the lake made by the dam drowned
a set of waterfalls and created a breeding ground
for malaria-carrying mosquitoes.

MORENO GLACIER
At the southern tip of Argentina lies one of the
region's most dramatic natural spectacles, the vast
Moreno Glacier. Every few years, the glacier
advances across Lake Argentino, creating a dam
of bluish-white ice that can be up to 60 m (197 ft)
high. Eventually, the dammed water in the lake
bursts through the icy barrier. The ice collapses
and cracks, while torrents of water gush over it.

GIANT ANTEATER
The giant anteater is one of South
America's most striking animals.
It spends the day roaming the
pampas in search of ants and
termites. If it finds a nest, the
anteater breaks it open with
its powerful claws and then
laps up the insects with its
long, sticky tongue.

PERU
BOLIVIA

Arica
Iquique
Tocopilla
Calama
Antofagasta
Chañaral
Copiapó
Vallenar
La Serena
Ovalle
San Felipe
Viña del Mar
Valparaíso
SANTIAGO
Rancagua
Curicó
Talca
Chillán
Concepción
Los Ángeles
Temuco
Valdivia
Osorno
Puerto Montt

ATACAMA DESERT
CHILE
ANDES

Mayor Pablo Lagerenza
General Eugenio A. Garay
Fuerte Olimpo
Filadelfia
PARAGUAY
Pedro Juan Caballero
Pozo Colorado
Concepción
Salto del Guairá
Itaipú Dam
ASUNCION
Villarica
Formosa
Pilar
Posadas

GRAN CHACO
Bermejo
Pilcomayo
Paraguay
BRAZIL

San Salvador de Jujuy
Salta
San Miguel de Tucumán
Santiago del Estero
Catamarca
La Rioja
Córdoba
San Juan
Mt. Aconcagua
Mendoza
Godoy Cruz
San Rafael
San Luis
Río Cuarto
Rosario
Mercedes
Junín
BUENOS AIRES
La Plata
Las Flores
Azul
Olavarría
Santa Rosa
Mar del Plata
Necochea
Bahía Blanca
Neuquén
Zapala
San Antonio Oeste
Viedma

Resistencia
Corrientes
Vera
L. Mar Chiquita
Concordia
Santa Fe
Villa María
Salado
ARGENTINA
PAMPAS
Colorado
Negro
Bahía Blanca
Gulf of San Matías

Artigas
Rivera
Tacuarembó
URUGUAY
Fray Bentos
Trinta y Tres
Florida
MONTEVIDEO
Río de la Plata
Melo
Mirim Lagoon
Rocha

Nigro
Uruguay
Paraná

URUGUAY

ARGENTINA

VALDÉZ PENINSULA
Puerto Madryn
Trelew Rawson
Chubut
Chiloé I.
L. Nahuel Huapi
San Carlos de Bariloche
Esquel

Gulf of San Jorge
L. Colhué Huapi
Coihaique
L. General Carrera
L. Buenos Aires
Comodoro Rivadavia
Caleta Olivia
Deseado
Puerto Deseado

PATAGONIA

ATLANTIC OCEAN

PACIFIC OCEAN

Bío-Bío

ANDES
CHILE

L. Viedma
L. Argentino
Puerto Santa Cruz
Bahía Grande
TORRES DEL PAINE
Río Gallegos
Puerto Natales
Punta Arenas
Strait of Magellan
Río Grande
TIERRA DEL FUEGO
Ushuaia
Beagle Channel
Cape Horn

Falkland Islands (UK)

N

THINGS TO LOOK FOR ON THE MAP
Longest river: Paraná,
Argentina/Paraguay/Brazil,
2,940 km (1,827 miles) *Map J7*

Highest point: Mt. Aconcagua,
Argentina, 6,960 m (22,835 ft)
Map F7

Largest lake: L. Buenos
Aires/L. General Carrera,
Argentina/Chile, 2,240 sq km
(865 sq miles) *Map G13*

World's driest place: Atacama
Desert, Chile *Map F4*

URUGUAY

URUGUAY HAS BEEN DESCRIBED as a giant city with a ranch attached. Half the population of 3 million plus live in the capital city of Montevideo, while the rest earn a living on the rich lowland pastures that spread out across the rest of the country. The rearing of livestock has brought great wealth to Uruguay, although in recent years tourism and banking have also contributed to the national income. Apart from a period of brutal military rule in the 1970s, the country enjoys a stable government that has built up an impressive welfare system to look after its people.

Silver straw, called a bombilla

Carved gourd for holding the maté tea

MATÉ TEA
The national drink of Uruguay and other South American nations is a herbal tea called *maté*. The hot drink, which is rich in caffeine, can be mixed with sugar and aromatic herbs. *Maté* is sipped by straw from a dried gourd, a type of fruit with a hard rind.

URUGUAY
Capital city: Montevideo

Area: 177,410 sq km (68,498 sq miles)

Population: 3,100,000

Official language: Spanish

Major religions: Christian 68%, Jewish 2%, other 30%

Government: Multi-party democracy

Currency: New Uruguayan peso

Adult literacy rate: 96%

Life expectancy: 72 years

People per doctor: 350

Televisions: 233 per 1,000 people

PARAGUAY
Capital city: Asunción

Area: 406,750 sq km (157,046 sq miles)

Population: 4,500,000

Official languages: Spanish, Guaraní

Major religions: Christian 100%

Government: Multi-party democracy

Currency: Guaraní

Adult literacy rate: 91%

Life expectancy: 67 years

People per doctor: 1,610

Televisions: 58 per 1,000 people

CATTLE AND SHEEP
Nine million cattle and 25 million sheep live on the grassy plains of Uruguay, easily outnumbering the population. In the 1860s the country's first meat-processing factory was set up in Fray Bentos, a name forever linked with corned beef. The town became the centre of the national meat industry when a huge refrigeration plant opened in 1901. Today, Uruguay exports animal products all over the world, and is the world's second biggest exporter of wool after New Zealand.

PARAGUAY

TUCKED INLAND, LARGELY EMPTY, and with few natural resources, Paraguay is one of the forgotten countries of the world. Once part of the vast Spanish Empire, Paraguay gained its independence in 1811. For most of its history, it has been ruled by a series of military dictators. The most famous of these was General Alfredo Stroessner, who governed for 35 years until he was overthrown in a sudden coup in 1989. Today, Paraguay is struggling to modernize itself. The vast Itaipú Dam generates sufficient electricity to export supplies to neighbouring Brazil. Efforts are also being made to widen the economy so it does not depend on agricultural products.

JESUIT MISSIONS
Almost a century after the occupation of Paraguay by Spain in 1536, Jesuit missionaries began to convert the local people to Christianity. The Jesuits, a Roman Catholic order of priests, set up missions and built huge stone churches, protecting the local Guaraní Indians from attack by their enemies. When the Jesuits were expelled in 1767, many of their buildings fell into disrepair, but are now being restored.

ASUNCIÓN
The capital, and almost only, city of Paraguay is Asunción, home to about 800,000 people. Situated on the eastern bank of the Paraguay River, the city is laid out in a rectangular grid, with wide, tree-lined avenues and beautiful parks. Asunción still retains the atmosphere of the Spanish colonial town it once was.

PEOPLE OF THE CHACO
The north of Paraguay is dominated by the Gran Chaco, a vast stretch of grassland and forest. The only people who live there are the Guaraní and Macá Indians. The Macá sell woven bags to tourists.

Find out more
CATTLE FARMING: *75*
NATIVE PEOPLES: *43*
POLITICAL SYSTEMS: *270–271*
ROMAN CATHOLICS: *274*

CHILE

A NATIVE OF CHILE ONCE SAID that his country had a mad geography, because it is the longest, thinnest country in the world. Protected by the Andes, it was the last country in the Americas to be occupied by the Spanish, but gained its independence in 1818. Since the end of a cruel military dictatorship, which lasted from 1973–1990, the country has enjoyed a more stable political life. Most people live in central Chile around the capital, Santiago, and the main port of Valparaiso. Fruit, cereals, and grapes are cultivated in the valleys which are well-watered by rivers from the Andes. Fishing off the long Pacific coast is also important.

CHILE	
Capital city: Santiago	
Area: 756,950 sq km (292,258 sq miles)	
Population: 13,231,803	
Official language: Spanish	
Major religions: Christian 100%	
Government: Multi-party democracy	
Currency: Chilean peso	
Adult literacy rate: 94%	
Life expectancy: 72 years	
People per doctor: 2,170	
Televisions: 205 per 1,000 people	

CHILEAN WINE
Vines were first brought to Chile by the Spanish to grow for their communion wine. Today, the valleys that surround Santiago contain some of the best vineyards on the American continent. Chilean red and white wines are so good that they are exported around the world.

CHANGING SCENERY
From the dry, barren lands of the Atacama Desert in the north to the icy rocks of Cape Horn in the south, Chile includes almost every type of climate and landscape in the world. The northern desert is one of the driest places on Earth, while the central agricultural valley has a Mediterranean climate similar to California or southern Europe. In the cold and stormy south, 55 volcanoes are currently active, and huge glaciers block the valleys. More than 80 per cent of the country is mountainous, and much of the rest is forested. Not much land is available for growing crops.

COPPER MINING
Chile is the world's largest exporter of copper, and also mines significant quantities of iron ore, coal, gold, silver, and other minerals. High up in the Atacama Desert, in the north of Chile, lies one of the world's largest deposits of copper. The mine at Chuquicamata is 4,115 m (13,500 ft) long and 670 m (2,200 ft) deep. Every week millions of tonnes of rock are blasted out of the ground and taken away to be turned into copper.

MAPUCHE INDIANS
For centuries, the Mapuche Indians have fought for their independence, first against the Incas of Peru, then against invading Spaniards, and most recently against the Chilean government. Today, most of the 800,000 Mapuche live on reservations in the south. One of Chile's main football teams, Colo-Colo, is named after an old Mapuche chief.

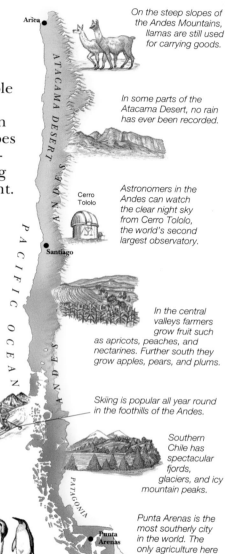

From north to south
Chile is 4,200 km (2,610 miles) long from north to south, the same as the distance from Norway to Nigeria. At no point is the country more than 180 km (112 miles) wide.

Arica

On the steep slopes of the Andes Mountains, llamas are still used for carrying goods.

In some parts of the Atacama Desert, no rain has ever been recorded.

Cerro Tololo

Astronomers in the Andes can watch the clear night sky from Cerro Tololo, the world's second largest observatory.

Santiago

In the central valleys farmers grow fruit such as apricots, peaches, and nectarines. Further south they grow apples, pears, and plums.

Skiing is popular all year round in the foothills of the Andes.

Southern Chile has spectacular fjords, glaciers, and icy mountain peaks.

PATAGONIA

Punta Arenas is the most southerly city in the world. The only agriculture here is sheep grazing.

Punta Arenas

King penguins live on the ice caps of Chilean Patagonia.

Cape Horn

PUNTA ARENAS
The city of Punta Arenas lies on the Straits of Magellan, the route used by ships to avoid stormy Cape Horn. The port is filled with fishing and Antarctic research vessels, and is a base for oil exploration. It lies under the hole in the ozone layer above Antarctica, and people are easily burned by the Sun's rays.

Find out more
ANDES: *40, 58*
COPPER MINING: *237, 245*
NATIVE PEOPLES: *43*
VEGETATION ZONES: *15*

ARGENTINA

STRETCHING FROM THE SUBTROPICAL forests of the north down across the vast central plains of the Pampas to the snow-capped mountains of Patagonia in the south, Argentina occupies most of southern South America. The country is bounded by the Andes Mountains in the west, and slopes gently downhill to the Atlantic Ocean in the east. Today's population is a mixture of native Indians, Spanish settlers, and immigrants from southern Europe who arrived during the past 100 years. The country is relatively wealthy, but has suffered from years of political instability, with periods of army rule alternating with elected governments.

ARGENTINA	
Capital city: Buenos Aires	
Area: 2,766,890 sq km (1,068,296 sq miles)	
Population: 33,100,000	
Official language: Spanish	
Major religions: Christian 92%, Jewish 1%, other 7%	
Government: Multi-party democracy	
Currency: Argentine peso	
Adult literacy rate: 96%	
Life expectancy: 71 years	
People per doctor: 330	
Televisions: 222 per 1,000 people	

DANCING THE TANGO
Tango, the national music of Argentina, began in the slums of Buenos Aires. The music, and the dramatic dance style that goes with it, reflects the hopes of working people and is sometimes happy, but often sad. Tango music is played on a *bandoneon*, a type of concertina, with a piano and violin accompaniment.

BUENOS AIRES

Almost 40 per cent of Argentinians live in or near the capital city of Buenos Aires, making it one of the major cities in the southern half of the world. The city was founded by the Spanish in 1536 as a port on the Río de la Plata, and inhabitants are still called *porteños*, meaning "people of the port". Modern Buenos Aires is highly sophisticated, with grand avenues, a subway system, and expensive shops. It is the trading centre of the country, and most of Argentina's exports are shipped through its docks.

MEDIA AND NEWSPAPERS

Argentinians can choose from a range of 220 daily newspapers, among them *La Prensa*, *La Nación*, and *Clarín*, which has the biggest circulation of any newspaper in South America. Most are published in Spanish, but German, English, and French language papers circulate widely. The constitution of Argentina guarantees freedom of the press, but during the military dictatorship newspapers and television were both heavily censored.

Simple potato pasta is traditionally eaten at the end of the month, just before payday.

ITALIAN IMMIGRANTS
In the years leading up to World War I in 1914, about 2 million people fled the poverty of southern Europe to start a new life in Argentina. More than half came from Italy, finding work on the land or in the expanding cities of Buenos Aires and Rosario. Italian food, such as the potato pasta *ñoquis*, is still served in restaurants throughout Argentina.

FALKLAND ISLANDS
Some 480 km (300 miles) east of Argentina lie the disputed Islas Malvinas. Occupied by Spain in 1767, the islands were invaded by Britain in 1833 and renamed the Falkland Islands. Britain and Argentina have contested ownership ever since. In 1982 an Argentinian invasion was repelled by Britain, which now has a military garrison there.

TIERRA DEL FUEGO
When Ferdinand Magellan and his Spanish crew first saw the rocky islands at the tip of Argentina in 1520, they named them Tierra del Fuego, or Land of Fire, because they saw fires lit by the Fuegian Indians to keep warm. The islands, shared between Argentina and Chile, are wet and windswept, with glaciers carving out huge valleys in the mountains.

THE ECONOMY

With rich, productive farmland and plentiful mineral resources, Argentina is one of South America's wealthier countries. The major exports are the agricultural products from the Pampas: wheat, corn, meat, hides, and wool. Factories turn out steel, chemicals, plastics, and machinery. Argentina is also self-sufficient in energy supplies and has large reserves of oil and gas that have yet to be fully explored. Despite its natural resources, the country has not been well-run and has large overseas debts.

Argentina exports 1993

Agricultural products: 64%
Manufacturing: 18%
Fuels and minerals: 10%
Machinery and transport: 8%

STEAM TRAINS

In 1857 a steam train made its way slowly south from Buenos Aires to the inland town of Las Flores, opening the first railway line in Argentina. Within 40 years, the country was linked by more than 34,000 km (21,000 miles) of track. Largely built by British engineers and using rolling stock constructed in British factories, this vast railway system still runs carriages and freight wagons, although diesel locomotives are now taking over.

The car industry is important to Argentina, and many of the leading manufacturers have factories there. Cars are made in the industrial centres of Buenos Aires, Córdoba, and Rosario.

GOING TO SCHOOL

The literacy level of Argentina is one of the highest in South America. Primary education is compulsory up to the age of 12, although attendance is often low in country areas. In most state primary schools children wear white coats called *guarda polvo*, meaning "dust guard". The coats protect their clothes from chalk dust. About one-third of the students go on to attend one of the free state universities.

GAUCHOS OF THE PAMPAS

As famous as his northern cousin, the American cowboy, the Argentine gaucho has roamed the rolling plains of the Pampas for about 300 years. The name gaucho comes from a South American word for outcast, as gauchos have always chosen to live beyond the law of the cities. The men work on the vast *estancias*, or ranches, fixing fences and corrals (pens for animals), tending the horses, and looking after the large herds of cattle. Tough, self-reliant, and free, the gauchos have become legendary heroes and a national symbol of Argentina.

The gaucho wears a hat with a broad brim to protect him from the hot sun.

A cotton or woollen cape, called a poncho. provides warmth at night.

The gaucho's broad leather belt has a silver buckle and is decorated with silver coins.

Bombachas, or baggy trousers, are worn tucked into boots.

Boleadoras were whirled around and flung at the legs of a running animal to trip it up. Today, a gaucho would use a lasso.

The round stones of a boleadora are covered with horsehide.

Gauchos ride criollos; a breed of wild horse that originally came from Mexico.

Beef cattle feed on pasture, or alfafa mixed with grains of sorghum grass to produce a leaner meat.

Gauchos regularly have to "throw a steer" to check for ticks and fleas.

To throw a steer, one man holds the animal by the horns, while another two men hold on to the tail.

Horse bridle of plaited raw horsehide.

Boots are made of tough leather to withstand wear and tear in the stirrups.

Find out more

DEBT: *280*
EDUCATION: *277*
POLITICAL SYSTEMS: *270–271*
VEGETATION ZONES: *15*

THE ATLANTIC OCEAN

BORDERED BY THE AMERICAS to the west, and Africa and Europe to the east, the Atlantic covers about 82 million sq km (31.7 million sq miles), one-fifth of the Earth's surface. Down the ocean's entire length runs the Mid-Atlantic Ridge, a great underwater mountain chain formed by lava which oozes up from the seabed, cools, and then hardens. Some peaks break the surface to form volcanic islands. The Atlantic contains some of the world's richest fishing grounds, but is also the most polluted ocean because of the industry around its shores.

ICELAND

Capital city: Reykjavik

Area: 103,000 sq km (39,770 sq miles)

Population: 300,000

Official language: Icelandic

Major religions: Christian 96%, other 4%

Government: Multi-party democracy

Currency: New Icelandic krona

Adult literacy rate: 99%

Life expectancy: 78 years

People per doctor: No figures available

Televisions: 320 per 1,000 people

CAPE VERDE

Capital city: Cidade de Praia

Area: 4,030 sq km (1,556 sq miles)

Population: 400,000

Official language: Portuguese

Major religions: Christian 99%, other 1%

Government: Multi-party democracy

Currency: Cape Verde escudo

Adult literacy rate: 67%

Life expectancy: 67 years

People per doctor: 5,130

Televisions: No figures available

Key to currents

Warm currents

Cold currents

ICELAND

The volcanic island of Iceland is part of the Mid-Atlantic Ridge. Intense heat generated deep underground creates bubbling hot springs and mud pools. Iceland has the most *solfataras* (volcanic vents) and hot springs in the world, and many of its towns are heated by underground hot water. Cape Verde, off the west coast of Africa, is also volcanic.

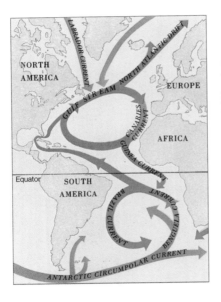

OCEAN CURRENTS

Water in the oceans is never still but moves in huge belts of water known as currents. In the open ocean, surface winds drive these currents in vast, roughly circular patterns. The currents can be as warm as 30°C (86°F) or as cold as -2°C (30°F) and affect the world's weather. Warm water from the Equator moves towards the cooler poles helping to spread the warmth across the globe.

FISHING

About 90 per cent of the world's fish live in the shallow waters of the continental shelves that surround the land, feeding on the plankton that live there. Over the past 20 years, stocks of cod, herring, and other fish in the Atlantic have run low as the number and size of fishing fleets has increased.

ICEBERGS

Icebergs, which are made of frozen fresh water, occur when warmer weather causes icesheets and glaciers on icy coastlines to break up, or calve. At sea, icebergs are moved by the wind and ocean currents and can be a danger to ships. Icebergs vary in size from small Arctic growlers, which are about as big as a grand piano, to much larger Antarctic icebergs, which can be 8 km (5 miles) long.

Only about one-seventh of an iceberg shows above the surface of the ocean. The rest of the ice remains hidden below the waterline.

GULF STREAM

The Gulf Stream is a warm current, only about 100 km (60 miles) wide, that moves across the North Atlantic. It raises the temperature of northern Europe and helps keep its ports ice-free in winter. It also allows tropical plants to grow in normally cool places, such as the west coast of Scotland.

Rio de Janeiro, Brazil
☀ Jan 26°C (78°F)
July 20°C (69°F)
🌧 Jan 125 mm (4.9 in)
July 41 mm (1.6 in)

ICELAND

Reykjavik, Iceland
☀ Jan 0°C (32°F)
July 11°C (52°F)
🌧 Jan 89 mm (3.5 in)
July 50 mm (2 in)

ARCTIC OCEAN

Greenland
(Denmark)

GREENLAND SEA

Murmansk

Baffin Bay

ICELAND

REYKJAVIK

Faeroe Is.
(Denmark)

Bergen

Hudson Bay

Davis Strait

C. Farewell

LABRADOR SEA

Rockall
(UK)

NORTH
SEA

British
Isles

BALTIC SEA

Rotterdam

EUROPE

NORTH AMERICA

Newfoundland

St Lawrence

St John's

Halifax

Grand Banks

Newfoundland
Basin

North-Eastern
Atlantic Basin

Marseille

BLACK SEA

New York City
Baltimore

Bay of
Fundy

Azores
(Portugal)

A Coruña

Porto

Naples

Bermuda
(UK)

Mid-Atlantic Ridge

Madeira
(Portugal)

Gibraltar

ALGIERS

MEDITERRANEAN SEA

Casablanca

Port Said

Mississippi

New Orleans

North American
Basin

SARGASSO SEA

Canary Is.
(Spain)

Nile

Gulf of
Mexico

Puerto Rico
Trench

Canary
Basin

AFRICA

CENTRAL
AMERICA

West Indies

CARIBBEAN SEA

CAPE VERDE

PRAIA

C. Verde

Praia, Cape Verde
☀ Jan 22°C (72°F)
July 26°C (79°F)
🌧 Jan 3 mm (0.1 in)
July 5 mm (0.2 in)

PANAMA CITY

N

Georgetown

Cayenne

Guyana Basin

Niger

Lagos

SOUTH AMERICA

Amazon

Fortaleza

Fernando
de Noronho I.
(Brazil)

Gulf of Guinea

São Tomé
Principe

LIBREVILLE

Congo

CAPE VERDE

Recife

Ascension I.
(UK)

Salvador

ATLANTIC OCEAN

St. Helena
(UK)

Angola Basin

0   500   1000   1500 km
0   250 500 750 1000 miles

THINGS TO LOOK FOR
ON THE MAP

World's largest island:
Greenland, 21,756,600 sq km
(839,780 sq miles) *Map F2*

Deepest Atlantic trench:
Puerto Rico Trench, 8,648 m
(28,372 ft) *Map D6*

World's most remote island:
Bouvet Island, Norway,
1,700 km (1,056 miles) from
nearest land *Map I12*

Rio de
Janeiro

Trindade
(Brazil)

Brazil Basin

Welvis Ridge

BUENOS AIRES

Mid-Atlantic Ridge

Tristan Da Cunha
(UK)

Cape of
Good Hope

CAPE TOWN

Gough I.
(UK)

Cape Basin

Argentine
Basin

Atlantic-Indian Ridge

Falkland Is.
(UK)

South Georgia
(UK)

C. Horn

SCOTIA SEA

Bouvet I.
(Norway)

South Shetland Is.
(UK)

South Orkney Is.
(UK)

South
Sandwich Is.
(UK)

Atlantic-Indian-Antarctic
Basin

WEDDELL SEA

ANTARCTICA

TURTLE TURNAROUND
Green turtles live off the coast of
Brazil, but make their way across the
South Atlantic to Ascension Island to
lay their eggs. Once the young turtles
have hatched, they return to Brazil – a
round trip of 2,800 km (1,740 miles).

WHALE MIGRATION
Humpback whales
can be found in all
the world's seas. Many
spend a large part of the year
feeding on krill and fish in the cold
waters off the coasts of Canada, Greenland,
and Iceland. When it is time to breed,
however, they make their way south to the
tropical waters of the Caribbean Sea.

*An average humpback
whale needs about a
tonne of food per day.*

Find out more
FISHING: *29, 203*
GEYSERS: *255*
MID-OCEAN RIDGES: *13*
OCEAN CURRENTS: *64*

EUROPE

A GREAT CURVE OF mountain ranges, that includes the Pyrenees and the Alps, roughly divides the cooler north of Europe from the warmer south. In the far north, treeless tundra merges into the cool coniferous forests that extend across Scandinavia and into Russia. South of this lies the fertile North European Plain, which supports most of the continent's agriculture and mixed woodland. By contrast, the Mediterranean region to the south is hot and almost desert-like in places. Volcanic activity is confined to Iceland and southern Italy, where Mount Etna is constantly active. The Ural and Caucasus Mountains form Europe's eastern borders.

Bird's Eye primrose

THE ALPS
The mountains that form the Alps run from southeastern France, through Switzerland and Italy, into Austria. In the last 2 million years, ice has moulded the scenery, carving pyramid-shaped peaks, like the Matterhorn, knife-edged ridges, dramatic waterfalls, and armchair-shaped basins filled with lakes. Alpine plants, such as the Bird's Eye primrose, have adapted to growing at high altitudes.

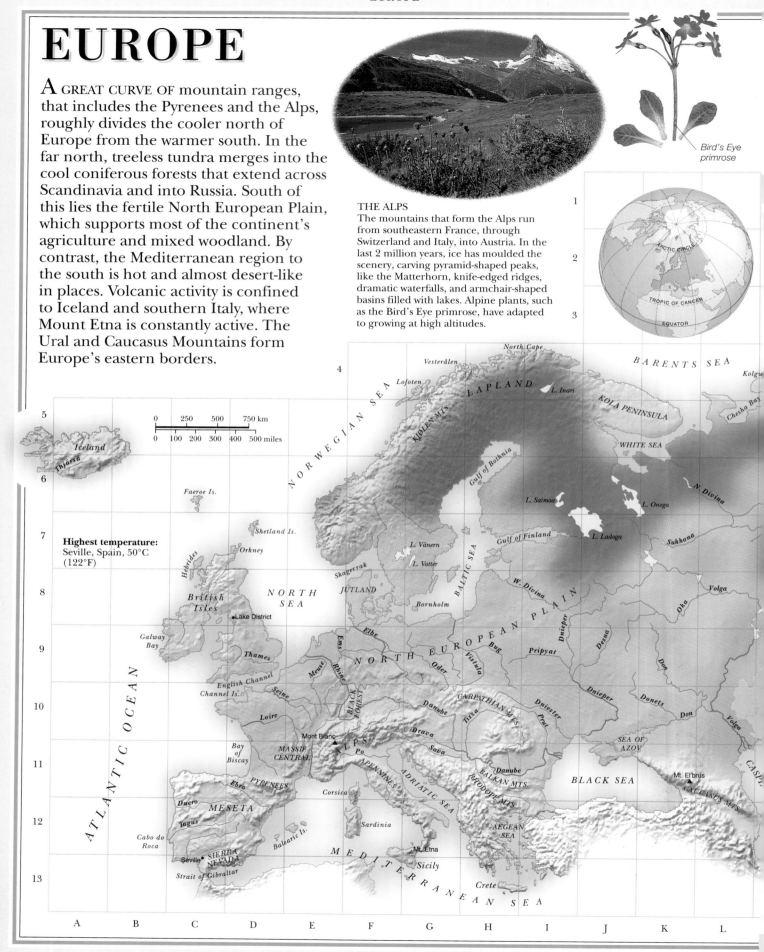

Highest temperature:
Seville, Spain, 50°C
(122°F)

This is a river valley before the arrival of a glacier. Glaciers are huge masses of ice that grind the shape of the land as they move slowly forwards.

THE LAKE DISTRICT

The 15 lakes of the Lake District in northwestern England lie in U-shaped valleys extending outwards like the spokes of a wheel from an uplifted dome of low mountains. Long ago, the valleys contained rivers, but during the Ice Age these were deepened by the movement of glaciers and most were dammed by eroded rock left behind when the glaciers melted. The erosion of the main valleys has cut off tributary valleys and left them "hanging" above the main valleys, often with waterfalls cascading from them.

When glaciers retreat, at the end of an Ice Age for example, they leave behind U-shaped valleys.

A hanging valley on the side of the main valley.

Ullswater is a lake that lies in a U-shaped valley.

NORTHERN FORESTS

A thick band of dense coniferous forest, known as taiga, covers northern Europe. Conifers (trees that have cones), such as spruce and pine, keep their leaves all year round and can withstand heavy snow. They also provide winter food and shelter for many animals.

KARA SEA

vaya Zemlya

Vaygach I.

URAL MOUNTAINS

N O P

N

Lowest temperature: Ust'Shchugor, Russian Federation, -55°C (-67°F)

Kama Res.

NORTHERN PLAINS

The North European Plain stretches from southern England across France and Germany as far as Russia, ending at the Ural Mountains. Most of the Plain is low-lying, and in the Netherlands it even lies partly below sea level. Some of the world's most fertile farmland is found here, as well as important deposits of coal, oil, and natural gas. This is Europe's most densely populated area and contains many major cities.

Wheat, sugarbeet, and apples are grown on the plains of northern France.

Foxes are often found in the fields and woodlands of Europe, although many now live in towns. They eat almost anything from rabbits to apples or worms.

THINGS TO LOOK FOR ON THE MAP

Area: 10,400,000 sq km (4,000,000, sq miles)

Highest point: Mt. El'brus, Russian Federation, 5,642 m (18,510 ft) *Map K11*

Longest river: Volga, Russian Federation, 3,530 km (2,194 miles) *Map L8*

Largest lake: L. Ladoga, Russian Federation, 18,389 sq km (7,100 sq miles) *Map J7*

Largest island: Great Britain, 229,850 sq km (88,745 sq miles) *Map D9*

THE MEDITERRANEAN

The region around the Mediterranean Sea has a distinctive climate of hot, dry summers and mild, rainy winters. These conditions are perfect for growing crops such as citrus fruits, grapes, and olives, shown here in southern Spain. Many trees, such as cork oaks, develop thick bark as a protection against the heat.

THE DANUBE

The Danube, western Europe's longest river, flows eastwards from its source in Germany to its mouth on the Black Sea. It serves as a trade route between the nine countries that lie along its course. The Danube delta, where the river divides into numerous channels, is an important wetland area. About 300 different bird species have been recorded in the delta as well as boars, deer, and wild cats.

PEOPLES OF EUROPE

EUROPE IS A CROWDED CONTINENT. It is the second smallest of the continents by area, yet it has the second highest population. As a result, population densities are very high, and most Europeans live in cities. Europe is also crowded with countries – more than 40 different nations jostle for position on the continent. Conflicts between these countries have often erupted into war. Two world wars have taken place on European soil this century alone. Yet, despite these problems, Europe is by and large a rich continent, and many European countries are among the wealthiest in the world. Some pockets of poverty exist, but in general the population enjoys a high standard of living compared to most other parts of the world. Much of this wealth has come as a result of industrial growth, and because of the large colonial empires established by many European countries in Africa, Asia, and the Americas.

EUROPEAN CITIES
A large proportion of Europeans live in cities. The most densely populated part of Europe lies in the west and forms a belt that stretches more or less continuously from southeast Britain, through northern France, Belgium, the Netherlands, and into Germany. In these densely populated areas, individual cities can merge into one another, forming what are known as conurbations. The largest of these is in the German industrial region known as the Ruhr. By contrast, in eastern Europe a greater proportion of the population live in country areas.

Population: approximately 578,240,000 people (This figure does not include the Russian Federation.)

Number of countries: 42

Largest country: Russian Federation – the European part covers 3,955,818 sq km (1,527,349 sq miles)

Most densely populated country: Netherlands, 410 people per sq km (1,062 per sq mile)

Least densely populated country: Iceland, 3 people per sq km (8 per sq mile)

KEY
1 NETHERLANDS
2 BELGIUM
3 LUXEMBOURG
4 SWITZERLAND
5 LIECHTENSTEIN
6 MOLDAVIA
7 ANDORRA
8 MONACO
9 SAN MARINO
10 VATICAN CITY
11 SLOVENIA
12 CROATIA
13 BOSNIA AND HERZEGOVINA
14 YUGOSLAVIA
15 ALBANIA
16 MACEDONIA

ICELAND
Faeroe Is. (Den)
NORWAY
SWEDEN
FINLAND
ESTONIA
LATVIA
LITHUANIA
RUSSIAN FED.
BELORUSSIA
DENMARK
UNITED KINGDOM
IRELAND
Channel Is. (UK)
GERMANY
POLAND
CZECH REP.
SLOVAKIA
UKRAINE
AUSTRIA
HUNGARY
FRANCE
ROMANIA
RUSSIAN FEDERATION
PORTUGAL
SPAIN
ITALY
BULGARIA
GREECE
GEORGIA
ARMENIA
AZERBAIJAN
AZERBAIJAN
Gibraltar (UK)
MALTA

Smallest country: Vatican City, 0.44 sq km (0.17 sq miles)

POPULATION DENSITY
Over 578 million Europeans are crammed into an area little more than the size of Australia. As a result, European countries have some of the highest population densities in the world. In the Netherlands, for example, there are nearly 410 people per sq km (1,062 per sq mile). Population densities in eastern Europe are lower, but even these are above the world average.

Population density chart

The figures on the chart show the number of people per sq km (per sq mile). Countries outside Europe are included as a comparison.

Netherlands: 410 (1,062)
Germany: 225 (583)
Poland: 123 (319)
World average: 41 (106)
USA: 27 (70)

THE TWO EUROPES

Economically, Europe can be divided into two main sets of countries. Western Europe contains some very rich countries, such as Germany, Switzerland, and France, which have strong economies. By contrast, eastern Europe contains former communist countries such as Poland, Hungary, and Romania, which are much poorer. They are still struggling to adjust their economies in order to compete in world markets.

During the period of communist rule, many people in eastern Europe had to queue for hours to buy food.

THE CHANGING POPULATION

Compared to Asia and Africa, the populations of most European countries are stable – they are not increasing or decreasing to any great extent. Birth rates are low, and average life expectancy is very high – about 75 years in most countries, compared to less than 60 years in India and most of Africa. As a result of these two factors, Europe's population is relatively elderly, with a large number of people aged over 65 years.

Age of population

	Ages 0–14	Ages 15–64	Ages 65+
Germany (Europe)	16.7%	68.7%	14.6%
Kenya (Africa)	49.1%	47.9%	3%
India (Asia)	36.5%	59%	4.5%

Ages 0–14

Ages 15–64

Ages 65+

CULTURAL MELTING POT

Europe's wealth and relative political stability have attracted large numbers of migrants to its shores, many from former colonies. As a result, most countries, particularly in western Europe, contain large numbers of people from ethnic minorities. In France, for example, north Africans from Algeria and other former colonies have settled in cities such as Marseilles and Paris.

The UK's population contains migrants from many countries, including the Caribbean, India, Pakistan, and Bangladesh.

New European countries

Former Czechoslovakia split apart peacefully in 1993, when the Czech Republic and Slovakia voted to separate.

Former Yugoslavia has been shattered by war since 1991, as various regions have declared themselves independent countries.

The European Parliament, elected by the people of the EU, meets in this building in Strasbourg, France.

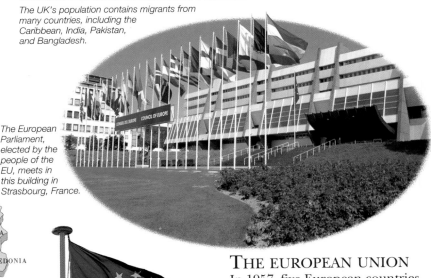

New European countries have also been formed from the former USSR – see page 136.

SPLITTING APART

Europe is a fragmented continent made up of more than 40 independent countries. Even within individual countries there are sometimes separate groups, such as the Basques in Spain, who claim some form of independence from the national government. New countries are still being formed. The former USSR, Yugoslavia, and Czechoslovakia are among the European countries that have split apart in recent years, sometimes violently.

The stars on the flag of the European Union represent the member countries.

THE EUROPEAN UNION

In 1957, five European countries agreed to form the European Economic Community (EEC). They believed that economic co-operation would reduce the likelihood of wars between the member countries, and would bring prosperity to the peoples of Europe. Since that time, more countries have joined, and the EEC has been renamed the European Union (EU). Today it consists of 15 member states and as well as closer economic co-operation, there are moves to encourage greater political union.

SCANDINAVIA AND FINLAND

THE NORTHERN EUROPEAN countries of Norway, Sweden, and Denmark are together known as Scandinavia. Along with neighbouring Finland, all four countries have small populations and enjoy a high standard of living with extensive social welfare systems that distribute wealth evenly among the people. Much of Norway, Sweden, and Finland is covered by forests of pine, spruce, and birch trees and contains many lakes gouged out by glaciers during the last Ice Age. Norway and Sweden are mountainous, while Finland and fertile Denmark are low-lying.

FINLAND

0 50 100 150 200 250 km
0 50 75 100 125 150 miles

Copenhagen, Denmark

Jan 0°C (32°F)
July 18°C (64°F)

Jan 49 mm (1.9 in)
July 71 mm (2.8 in)

NORWAY

Inari, Finland

Jan -13°C (8°F)
July 13°C (56°F)

Jan 22 mm (0.9 in)
July 53 mm (2.1 in)

SWEDEN

THINGS TO LOOK FOR ON THE MAP

Longest river: Kemijoki, Finland, 547 km (340 miles) *Map J5*

Highest point: Mt. Galdhopiggen, Norway, 2,469 m (8,101 ft) *Map E7*

Largest lake: L. Vänern, Sweden, 5,580 sq km (2,154 sq miles) *Map G9*

DENMARK

THE MIDNIGHT SUN

Much of northern Norway, Sweden, and Finland lies in the Arctic Circle. Here, the sun never sets at the height of summer – giving 24 hours of light – and never rises in the middle of winter – giving 24 hours of darkness. The periods of light or dark lengthen the further north you go. In the far north, the winter darkness lasts for almost two months.

Midnight sun in Senja, Norway.

COASTLINE CITIES

Most people in the region live in towns and cities around the coast or on lakesides. These stretches of water provide the best form of transport in an area where fast-flowing rivers are unsuitable for transport and where much of the interior is rugged. The capitals of all four countries are on the coast, including Stockholm, the Swedish capital, which lies on the edge of the Baltic Sea.

NORWAY

NORWAY LIES ALONG the western coast of Scandinavia. It is a long country, narrow in its northern half and only 80 km (50 miles) wide at one point. Despite its northerly location, Norway's lengthy coastline is kept free of ice by the warm Gulf Stream. Most of the country is mountainous, the spectacular landscape containing thousands of lakes and offshore islands. Many people work in industry, including offshore oil and gas production, shipbuilding, and mining. Fishing, forestry, and agriculture employ only about 6 per cent of the total workforce.

NORWAY	
Capital city: Oslo	
Area: 323,900 sq km (125,060 sq miles)	
Population: 4,233,116	
Official language: Norwegian	
Major religions: Christian 92%, other 8%	
Government: Multi-party democracy	
Currency: Norwegian krone	
Adult literacy rate: 99%	
Life expectancy: 77 years	
People per doctor: 500	
Televisions: 420 per 1,000 people	

OIL INDUSTRY

The discovery of oil and gas under the North Sea in 1969 transformed the Norwegian economy, turning the country into Europe's largest oil producer. Thousands of people work in the industry, constructing tankers and oil rigs and refining the crude oil. Today Norway is self-sufficient in energy, and exports most of its oil and natural gas to the rest of Europe.

Low-lying meadows are suitable for livestock.

Deep water allows cruise and other ships to sail far inland.

Rough upland grazing for herds of sheep and goats.

Once-thriving coastal fishing communities are declining as fish stocks diminish, but fish farming is increasing.

South facing slopes are warm enough to support crops of soft fruit in the summer months.

Traditional stave church in Sogne Fjord.

FJORDS

Only 3 per cent of Norway is suitable for farming, as most of the country consists of rugged mountain ranges and deep lakes. Most farmland is situated at the head of fjords, the long inlets of sea which cut into Norway's coast. Fjords were created by glaciers gouging out valleys as they descended to the sea. The fjords are natural harbours, sheltering small communities of fishermen and farmers. Tourists visit the spectacular scenery in cruise ships.

SHIPPING

Norway has one of the largest shipping fleets in the world. Many thousands of people are employed in shipyards and repair docks, and on board the many merchant ships and ferries that supply the ports and islands of the west coast. The most important port is the capital city, Oslo. Almost half a million people live in this bustling, lively city, which is the cultural, intellectual, and industrial centre of the country.

SKIING

Norway is the home of skiing. The earliest remains of skis were found in a glacier here, and the word "ski" is of Norwegian origin. During the snowy winter months, the most efficient way for many Norwegians to travel is on skis. The ski jump is a feature of most towns in Norway. Annual ski festivals are popular events, as is the sport of cross-country skiing.

WOODEN CHURCHES

Ancient stave churches are found throughout Norway. Unlike log cabins, which are made of horizontal logs, stave churches are built with vertical, curved strips of wood, called staves. Not a single nail is used in the construction, which is powerful enough to withstand heavy winter snowfalls.

Find out more
GAS: *163, 198, 211*
GLACIERS: *79*
GULF STREAM: *76*
OIL: *152, 281*

DENMARK

THE LONG, NARROW Jutland Peninsula that makes up mainland Denmark extends from Germany towards Norway and Sweden. To the east of the peninsula, more than a hundred islands make up the rest of the country. Denmark is the most southerly country in Scandinavia and is one of the flattest lands in the world. Like its neighbours, it enjoys political stability and a high standard of living. Industry has developed rapidly, and today a third of the people work in small factories.

DENMARK	
Capital city: Copenhagen	
Area: 43,070 sq km (16,629 sq miles)	
Population: 5,200,000	
Official language: Danish	
Major religions: Christian 93%, other 7%	
Government: Multi-party democracy	
Currency: Danish kroner	
Adult literacy rate: 99%	
Life expectancy: 75 years	
People per doctor: 390	
Televisions: 540 per 1,000 people	

COPENHAGEN

Denmark's capital is situated on the island of Sjaelland. It is the biggest city in Scandinavia and the largest trading centre in Denmark. Visitors wandering down old alleyways and pedestrianized streets will soon find historic churches, colourful market places, and a network of canals. This is also a city of bicycles, with bike paths leading out towards areas where many city-dwellers have summer homes.

ARCHITECTURE

Like the rest of the region, Denmark is famous for its architecture. Danish architects combine local materials such as cement, brick, and timber to create beautiful buildings that harmonize with the environment. Many housing developments have been built where each house runs on a designed system of solar panels and insulation designed to keep energy wastage to a minimum. Design is very important in Denmark, especially for furniture, glassware, kitchenware, and porcelain.

Solar panels use the Sun's rays to heat the water.

The ventilation system ensures that fresh air is taken in and stale air is drawn out.

Sun rooms made almost entirely from glass attract the warmth of the Sun's rays.

Air trapped between the inner and outer walls of the house acts as insulation and keeps out the cold.

PIG AND DAIRY FARMING
Denmark is well known for its co-operative organizations. To keep up with modern agricultural development, the farmers have had to work together closely. Part of their strategy has been to establish co-operatively owned dairies and bacon factories and to concentrate their energies on promoting these foods abroad.

LEGOLAND
"Lego" – the colourful interlocking building blocks designed for children – was first produced by a carpenter in Jutland in the 1930s. Now Jutland is home to a massive Legoland theme park, where all the buildings are made of Lego. The name "Lego" comes from the two Danish words, *leg* and *godt*, meaning "play well".

FAMILY LIFE

Throughout much of the Western world (Europe and North America), many people are taking a more open-minded attitude towards family life. This is particularly so in Denmark and the rest of Scandinavia. A high proportion of children in Denmark are brought up by unmarried parents, who have the same legal rights here as married couples, or by one parent. Men also play a large role in home life and childcare, and the number of working women has soared.

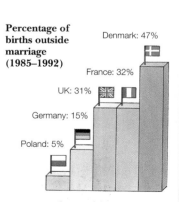

Percentage of births outside marriage (1985–1992)

Denmark: 47%
France: 32%
UK: 31%
Germany: 15%
Poland: 5%

Find out more

CYCLING: *92, 192*
EUROPEAN FAMILIES: *81*
INSULATED HOUSES: *143*
WORKING WOMEN: 137, *141*

SWEDEN

LYING BETWEEN NORWAY and Finland, Sweden stretches from the Arctic north to the fertile south, where most of its small population lives. Sweden's long industrial traditions and a highly skilled workforce have made it one of the world's most advanced manufacturing countries. Like its neighbours, Sweden is a prosperous place, where equal rights for all groups in society is a very important issue.

SWEDEN	
Capital city: Stockholm	
Area: 449,960 sq km (173,730 sq miles)	
Population: 8,585,907	
Official language: Swedish	
Major religions: Christian 97%, other 3%	
Government: Multi-party democracy	
Currency: Swedish krona	
Adult literacy rate: 99%	
Life expectancy: 78 years	
People per doctor: 370	
Televisions: 470 per 1,000 people	

Recycling system

Customers return their empty aluminium cans to shops with machines that flatten the cans, allowing many more to be collected.

The flattened cans are taken away, melted down, and rolled into new sheets of aluminium.

Soon, brand new cans made from the sheets are rolling off the production line, ready to start the cycle all over again.

CONSERVATION

Swedes are very concerned about conserving their environment. This includes their historic buildings as well as the countryside. There are many nature reserves in Sweden and some of Europe's largest national parks in the mountainous north. Many people are worried about water pollution and Sweden is a leading campaigner in the movement to clean up the Baltic Sea. It has also restricted industrial development in some coastal areas. Conserving resources is part of everyday life and Sweden runs a highly successful recycling system (right).

SUMMER HOMES

Holiday homes are common in this wealthy country. Pretty wooden houses, often painted red, are found along the coast, lakeshores, and river valleys. They provide the perfect escape for city-dwellers at the weekend or during holidays. When they are not there themselves, families often rent out these retreats to friends or to the growing number of tourists that visit Sweden.

SOCIAL WELFARE

Sweden has led the way in social welfare, and a small population means that it is easier for the government to take care of everyone. Childcare and facilities for the sick and the elderly are excellent. Unemployment figures have been among the lowest in Europe (see chart below). However, to pay for these benefits the government must impose high taxes. Also, the country's economic problems have put some of the benefits under threat.

UK: 10% France: 10%
Netherlands: 7%
Germany: 5%
Sweden: 5%

Percentages of unemployed people (1992 figures)

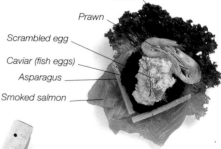

Lettuce
Prawn
Scrambled egg
Caviar (fish eggs)
Asparagus
Smoked salmon

SMÖRGASBORD

Smörgas means a slice of bread and *bord* is the Swedish word for table, but this Scandinavian speciality is much more than a table of sandwiches. It usually refers to a vast buffet of tempting cold foods, such as herrings in mustard sauce, various cheeses, meats, and salads.

DESIGN

Sweden, along with Scandinavia as a whole, is renowned for the clean, simple lines of its design style which is admired and copied all over the world. Swedish designers first began to make an impact in the 1960s. Good design has helped sell cars, such as Saab and Volvo, electrical equipment, textiles, glassware, and furniture, which is usually made from home-grown softwood.

This Swedish children's chair is designed to adjust to a child's height.

Find out more
HEALTH, EDUCATION: *276–277*
RECYCLING: *94*
RICH AND POOR: *278-279*
STOCKHOLM: *82*

FINLAND

KNOWN AS "SUOMI" to its people, Finland is the most northerly independent country in the world. An aerial view of this land would show a spectacular pattern of forests, swampy peatland, massive lakes, and islands – scattered in the lakes and along the coastline. Most of it is covered with pine, spruce, and birch trees, and for up to half of the year it is carpeted with snow. After centuries of Swedish rule, Finland became part of Russia before independence in 1917. Finland has a distinctive language and culture that marks it apart from the rest of Scandinavia.

FINLAND

Capital city: Helsinki

Area: 338,130 sq km (130,552 sq miles)

Population: 4,998,478

Official languages: Finnish, Swedish

Major religions: Christian 95%, other 5%

Government: Multi-party democracy

Currency: Markka

Adult literacy rate: 99%

Life expectancy: 75 years

People per doctor: 410

Televisions: 500 per 1,000 people

LAPLAND

The icy north of Norway, Sweden, and Finland is called Lapland. The people who live in the scattered villages of this region, the *Samer*, or Lapps, have their own language and customs and some herd reindeer for their meat and milk. However, their traditional way of life is slowly changing. Lapland is also known as the home of Father Christmas, and thousands of children send letters to him there each year.

HELSINKI

Surrounded on three sides by water, Finland's capital, Helsinki, has an open, spacious feel. Its magnificent harbour boasts a colourful street market selling fish, fruit, vegetables, and flowers. The city is filled with exciting modern buildings that are designed to blend with the old and create a distinctive national style.

LOGGING INDUSTRY

Timber is a major industry in this forested country – Finland and Sweden are Europe's top producers of the softwoods pine and spruce. The timber is transported by truck to processing plants where the wood is boiled down to a pulp. The liquid produced, wood alcohol, is used in various chemicals, while the pulp is made into plywood, board, and paper. Sawdust, bark, and waste are burned to produce electricity.

What the land is used for

Forest: 76%

Other: 15%

Crops: 8%

Grassland: 1%

LAND OF LAKES

Well over 50,000 lakes take up about 10 per cent of the country's area and are a major tourist attraction. Lake Saimaa is the largest lake and contains hundreds of islands. Ferries provide a vital link between the coastal islands. During the long, cold winters, lakes may freeze up and icebreakers keep coastal waters open for merchant shipping.

People beat themselves with birch twigs to stimulate their blood circulation and so refresh their bodies.

After a session in the sauna, it is time to cool off under a cold shower – or in the nearby lake!

Saunas are fuelled by wooden logs in the country, and by electricity in towns and cities.

SAUNAS

Finland is the home of the sauna. The Finns have used the steam bath for centuries, and today most houses in Finland have one. A sauna is a small, very warm room which people sit in to relax and cleanse their bodies. From time to time they throw water over hot stones and, as the water crackles and spits, the air fills with clouds of steam. Most families enjoy a shared sauna every week.

Find out more

ARCTIC PEOPLES: *25, 266*
LOGGING: *26, 69, 244*
NORTHERN FORESTS: *15, 132*

THE BRITISH ISLES

Tucked away in the northwest corner of Europe, the British Isles consists of the United Kingdom (UK) and Ireland. The UK includes Scotland, England, Wales, and Northern Ireland. The rest of Ireland is an independent country. Once, the whole of Ireland was dominated by England, a Protestant nation. This caused resentment among the Catholic Irish and in 1922 the south broke away. Despite differences between the two countries – Ireland is mainly rural, while the UK is heavily urbanized – both share a strong sense of identity that comes from being isolated from the rest of Europe by sea.

THINGS TO LOOK FOR ON THE MAP

Longest river: Shannon, Ireland, 386 km (240 miles) *Map F8*

Highest point: Ben Nevis, UK, 1,343 m (4,406 ft) *Map H5*

Largest lake: Lough Neagh, UK, 396 sq km (153 sq miles) *Map G7*

Deepest reservoir in Europe: Loch Morar, UK, 310 m (1,017 ft) *Map H4*

UNITED KINGDOM

Oban, UK
Jan 4°C (39°F)
July 14°C (57°F)
Jan 146 mm (5.8 in)
July 120 mm (4.7 in)

IRELAND

Cork, Ireland
Jan 6°C (42°F)
July 16°C (61°F)
Jan 119 mm (4.7 in)
July 70 mm (2.8 in)

London, UK
Jan 4°C (39°F)
July 18°C (64°F)
Jan 54 mm (2.1 in)
July 57 mm (2.2 in)

0   50   100   150 km
0   25   50   75   100 miles

THE EMERALD ISLE
Ireland gets its nickname, "The Emerald Isle", from the lush green grass that thrives in the island's mild and wet climate. This pasture makes excellent grazing land for cattle, and so dairy produce and beef are major products in a land where agriculture has always been the main industry. The beauty of the landscape, particularly its dramatic west coast, has also made Ireland a major tourist destination.

North Yorkshire coastline, England.

LANDSCAPE
The landscape of the British Isles varies greatly within a small area. High, craggy mountains in northern England, Scotland, Wales, and Ireland contrast with the flat Fens (marshlands) of East Anglia, and the rolling green fields of southern England. Three-quarters of the land is used for farming, and the crops grown vary from region to region, depending on the climate and soil.

UNITED KINGDOM

FOR A SMALL COUNTRY, the United Kingdom (UK) has had a huge influence on world affairs. At one time it controlled a vast empire, which is why English is now spoken across the globe. The Industrial Revolution of the late 1700s, which brought large-scale factory production, began here before spreading worldwide. Today many of the UK's traditional industries have declined. This highly urban society is now more reliant on service industries, such as banking and insurance, while huge reserves of oil in the North Sea meet much of its energy needs.

UNITED KINGDOM	
Capital city: London	
Area: 244,880 sq km (94,550 sq miles)	
Population: 55,701,000	
Official language: English	
Major religions: Christian 61%, Muslim 3%, other 36%	
Government: Multi-party democracy	
Currency: Pound sterling	
Adult literacy rate: 99%	
Life expectancy: 76 years	
People per doctor: 710	
Televisions: 430 per 1,000 people	

Red London buses rush past the Houses of Parliament, home of the United Kingdom's government.

Visitors to top 7 tourist sites charging admission (1994)

Alton Towers, Staffordshire: 3,011,000

Madame Tussaud's, London: 2,631,538

Tower of London: 2,407,115

St Paul's Cathedral, London: 1,900,000

Blackpool Tower: 1,305,000

Chessington World of Adventures: 1,614,000

Natural History Museum, London: 1,625,000

A MULTICULTURAL SOCIETY

Since the 1950s, the UK has become an increasingly multicultural society. Large numbers of people from the UK's former colonies in Africa, the West Indies, and the Indian Subcontinent have made their home here, establishing their own distinctive communities and enriching British life with their culture and traditions.

EDINBURGH

The beautiful city of Edinburgh lies on the chilly east coast of Scotland. Perched on a hill, Edinburgh Castle looks out over a city of winding medieval streets and splendid Georgian townhouses. The city is home to a major international arts festival held every summer.

Street performers at the Edinburgh Festival.

LONDON

Founded by the Romans in AD43, London is now a city of 7 million people, and is one of the largest cities in Europe. The capital is one of the world's leading centres of culture, finance, and tourism. Each year millions of people visit London to sample its theatres, museums, and historic buildings. Tourism is now a major industry throughout the whole of the UK. Places such as the west coast of Scotland and the ancient cities of Bath, York, and Stratford-upon-Avon attract thousands of tourists.

HOMES

Many people in the UK live in suburbs on the outskirts of towns and cities. Suburbs offer a cleaner environment, more space, and transport links, making commuting to jobs in city centres possible. British life is closely centred on the home, which most people aim to buy. Houses tend to be more popular than flats, and gardening or home improvements are popular leisure activities.

Typical styles of housing in the UK

1960s apartment block, or flats, with communal garden at the front.

Semi-detached house, 1930s.

Victorian terraced house, 1880s.

Detached house, 1980s.

Where people live

89% live in the city.   11% in the country.

WELSH MINING

Wales was until recently a major supplier of coal, and many towns and villages depended on the mines for their existence. But the coal industry has now been dismantled and large amounts of coal are imported, so that mines all over the UK have closed down. Wales especially has been badly hit, and there is high unemployment in many areas. Some towns, however, have succeeded in attracting new industries and the beautiful mountainous scenery brings increasing numbers of tourists.

SPORT

Sport is close to the hearts of many British people. Football (soccer) and rugby are generally played in the winter, and cricket and golf are popular in the summer months. Rugby, cricket, and golf – now played all over the world – originated in the UK, and the rules of football developed from games played in English boys' schools.

Hat made from Welsh wool.

Scottish tartan scarf

Waistcoat made from Irish linen.

NATIONAL IDENTITY

The UK's government is based in England, and there are strong independence movements in Scotland, Wales, and Northern Ireland. A sense of national identity in each of these regions is kept alive through traditional crafts and customs. For example, some Scotsmen still wear the tartan kilt of their family "clan" on special occasions.

Banking and financial services in particular have helped to boost the UK economy.

INDUSTRY

Heavy industry once supplied many jobs in the UK, but this pattern has changed. Now light engineering products, machinery, cars, and weapons are the major exports, and large numbers of people are employed in financial and service industries. These have helped an economy that was flagging, partly because the UK has to import so much of its food and raw materials. Many powerful multinational companies, with offices throughout the world, are also based here.

FINANCE

Each day more currency changes hands in London than in any other city in the world. The City of London, or the "square mile" as it is also known, contains more than 500 banks, attracted to the capital because of its leading role in world finance. This situation partly stems from the former importance of the British Empire, but today it is more to do with the city's convenient location – midway between Tokyo and New York, the other main world financial centres – and the expertise in banking and financial services built up over many years.

The Lloyd's Insurance Building in the heart of the City of London.

NORTHERN IRELAND

Since the 1960s Northern Ireland and its capital, Belfast (above), have suffered violent conflict. The large Protestant community, descended from British settlers, wants to stay within the UK, while Irish Catholics, who have been discriminated against in jobs and housing, wish to join southern Ireland. Both sides have kept up terrorist campaigns, and the Catholic Irish Republican Army have also bombed the British mainland. The Irish and British governments are now trying to organize talks between all parties, but a solution is proving difficult to find.

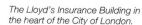

Find out more

COAL MINING: *96, 112, 162*
ETHNIC MIX: *81*
EUROPEAN CITIES: *80*
SERVICE INDUSTRIES: *281*

IRELAND

IRELAND

Capital city: Dublin

Area: 70,280 sq km (27,135 sq miles)

Population: 3,523,401

Official languages: Irish, English

Major religions: Christian 96%, other 4%

Government: Multi-party democracy

Currency: Irish pound

Adult literacy rate: 99%

Life expectancy: 75 years

People per doctor: 630

Televisions: 290 per 1,000 people

THE GREEN PASTURES of Ireland are kept fertile by the country's mild, wet climate. Ireland was once ruled by Britain. In 1922, southern Ireland – which makes up about two-thirds of the island – became an independent republic, while Northern Ireland remained part of the United Kingdom. The small population lives mainly by farming, though recently many young people have moved to the towns or left the country to look for work. Natural resources are few, and despite a growth in tourism and industry, Ireland remains one of the poorer countries in Europe.

RELIGIOUS LIFE

The Irish are a devout people and the Catholic Church plays an important role in daily life. Religious processions are held regularly, and shrines, many dedicated to the Virgin Mary (Jesus' mother), are dotted around the country. As well as running schools and hospitals, the Church has an influence on the social life of the country and opposes abortion and birth control. Divorce was illegal in Ireland until recently.

IRISH PUBS

Much social life in Ireland centres on the pub, or bar, where people meet to drink, chat, and exchange news. Stories from Irish history are told through songs, and bars are often alive with the sound of folk music. Irish stout – a strong, dark beer with a creamy, pale head – is the favourite drink. The largest brewery in Europe is found in Dublin and was opened by the Guinness family 200 years ago.

Bustling O'Connell Street is Dublin's major roadway.

DUBLIN

The capital of Ireland, Dublin, is steeped in the country's history. This compact city was the focus for the revolt against British rule and it was here, in 1922, that the Irish state was born. In recent years, Dublin has attracted manufacturing and service industries, as well as many people from other parts of the country that have come here in search of work.

RACEHORSES

The lush pastures of Ireland provide excellent grazing land for racehorses. These fine Irish thoroughbreds are world famous and frequently win major international races. The animals, bred on stud farms, are valuable sources of income for the Irish economy. Buying and selling horses is also popular, and country horse fairs are a familiar sight.

Many Irish peat bogs are a distinctive domed shape.

Over thousands of years, mud and plants compress to form peat.

The peat is cut out in blocks and then stacked and left to dry.

Peat is still gathered by hand in many parts of Ireland.

PEAT

Ireland has few natural resources, such as coal or oil, that produce energy. What it does have are huge peat bogs. Peat consists of dead, rotted plants that have been compressed and can be burned as fuel. Some villages have their own peat supplies, and there are also vast government-owned areas that are dug out by mechanical cutters. These provide fuel for large power stations that generate electricity.

Find out more

BEER-BREWING: *115*

COAL AND OIL: *96, 152, 162*

NORTHERN IRELAND: *89*

RELIGIONS: *274–275*

THE LOW COUNTRIES

THE THREE COUNTRIES IN THIS REGION – Belgium, the Netherlands, and Luxembourg – are known as the Low Countries because much of their land is flat and low-lying. The Low Countries are also called "Benelux" after the economic union they formed in 1948. The Benelux union allows the free flow of goods between the three countries, although each keeps its own currency and tax system. These are the most densely populated countries in Europe, yet their people generally enjoy a high standard of living. Although the region's traditional heavy industries, such as coal mining, are declining, they are being replaced by modern, manufacturing industries and service activities, such as banking and administration.

THINGS TO LOOK FOR ON THE MAP
Longest river: Meuse, France/Belgium/Netherlands, 901 km (560 miles) *Map J8*
Highest point: Botrange, Belgium, 694 m (2,277 ft) *Map J10*
Largest lake: Ijsselmeer, Netherlands, 1,210 sq km (467 sq miles) *Map I5*

De Bilt, Netherlands
Jan 2°C (36°F)
July 18°C (64°F)
Jan 68 mm (3 in)
July 77 mm (3 in)

Luxembourg, Luxembourg
Jan 1°C (33°F)
July 18°C (64°F)
Jan 61 mm (2 in)
July 60 mm (2 in)

Rotterdam is the world's busiest and largest port.

RIVERS
Some of Europe's most important rivers flow through these countries, linking the interior of the region with the coast. The most useful rivers for transport and trade are the Rhine, Mosel, and Meuse. At the mouth of the River Rhine stands the port of Rotterdam. Stretching for 20 km (12 miles) along the river, the port can handle 300 cargo ships at a time. Canals are also important for linking the ports with the rivers and inland areas.

FARMLAND
The region's flat plains are used for grazing dairy cattle and for growing flowers and vegetables. Much of the farmland has been reclaimed from the sea by enclosing an area with earth barriers, called dykes, and draining the water from it. The only areas of high land are the forested Ardennes Mountains which run across the south of Belgium and into Luxembourg.

NETHERLANDS

THIS SMALL, DENSELY POPULATED country is also referred to as Holland, the name of two of its provinces. In the 16th and 17th centuries, Dutch merchants and sailors travelled far and wide, trading in gold and spices. The empire they established stretched from southeast Asia to the Caribbean. Trade is still of great importance to the Netherlands today, since several large international companies are Dutch, and exports make up about half the country's income. The Dutch are known for their tolerance and for their liberal social attitudes.

NETHERLANDS

Capital cities: Amsterdam, The Hague

Area: 37,330 sq km (14,410 sq miles)

Population: 15,300,000

Official language: Dutch

Major religions: Christian 66%, Muslim 2%, other 32%

Government: Multi-party democracy

Currency: Netherlands guilder

Adult literacy rate: 99%

Life expectancy: 77 years

People per doctor: 410

Televisions: 500 per 1,000 people

Tulips were first brought to the Netherlands from Turkey in the 1630s, as much for their edible bulbs as for their flowers.

Asian lily bulb

Gladioli bulbs

More than half a million people in Amsterdam use a bicycle to travel to school or work.

AMSTERDAM

This historic city is the capital of the Netherlands and is much visited by tourists. In the 17th century, Amsterdam was a centre of world trade. Merchants built the network of canals which crisscross the city and the tall, narrow houses which line the canals. Today, Amsterdam is a world centre for diamond cutting and polishing.

CYCLING

The extreme flatness of the Dutch countryside makes cycling one of the easiest and most popular ways of getting about. Country areas have long-distance cycle routes, clearly signposted and shown on maps. Town centres are planned for bicycles rather than for motor cars. The lack of traffic means that more people can live in town centres, and so small, family-run shops are still thriving businesses.

AGRICULTURE

The Dutch have developed intensive farming methods to get the most from their limited but fertile land. Among the main crops grown are potatoes, barley, and salad vegetables, such as lettuce and tomatoes. Bulbs and flowers are probably the Netherlands' most famous export, particularly tulips. Other major exports are meat and dairy products, including cheeses, such as Gouda and Edam.

Making a polder

Earth dykes are built around a shallow area of water.

A mat of woven twigs is laid across the land surface.

A plane sows the seeds of reeds which grow up through the twigs.

The reeds are burned down. Their ashes are dug into the soil.

Years 1–2
The water is gradually drained off the land and pumped away.

Years 3–6

Year 7

Year 8

Only eight years since it was beneath the sea, the land is now ready to be used for farming and for building houses and roads.

LAND RECLAMATION

About a third of the Netherlands is land which has been reclaimed from the sea. These areas of land are called polders. Most of the reclaimed land is used for crop production and dairy farming, although about 25 per cent is set aside for housing, roads, and open spaces. Since so much of the land lies at or below sea-level, flooding is a serious problem. Huge barrier dams are built to keep the sea at bay, and water levels are monitored.

ETHNIC MIX

Many people from the former Dutch colonies in southeast Asia settled in the Netherlands in the 1940s and 1950s. They were followed in the 1960s by a flow of foreign workers from southern Europe, Turkey, and Morocco. Immigrants now make up about a fifth of the population of the Netherland's major cities. Most have full Dutch citizenship. The Dutch pride themselves on their policy of welcoming immigrants and refugees.

Find out more

CYCLING: *192*
ETHNIC MIX: *81*
POPULATION DENSITY: *80*
TRADE: *280–281*

BELGIUM

BELGIUM IS A FAIRLY NEW country that became independent from its Dutch rulers in 1830. Its current borders were only settled in 1919. The country is split in two by the valley of the River Meuse. To the north lie flat, fertile plains stretching to the coast. A thriving textile industry grew up here in the 16th century around cities such as Bruges, which is still known for its lace-making. To the south lie the Ardennes Mountains, a region of poor soil and scattered farms.

BELGIUM	
Capital city: Brussels	
Area: 33,100 sq km (12,780 sq miles)	
Population: 9,978,681	
Official languages: Dutch, French, and German	
Major religions: Christian 90%, Muslim 3%, other 7%	
Government: Multi-party democracy	
Currency: Belgian franc	
Adult literacy rate: 99%	
Life expectancy: 76 years	
People per doctor: 310	
Televisions: 450 per 1,000 people	

LUXEMBOURG	
Capital city: Luxembourg	
Area: 2,586 sq km (998 sq miles)	
Population: 384,400	
Official language: Letzeburgish	
Major religions: Christian 96%, other 4%	
Government: Multi-party democracy	
Currency: Luxembourg franc	
Adult literacy rate: 99%	
Life expectancy: 75 years	
People per doctor: 550	
Televisions: 260 per 1,000 people	

LANGUAGES

Three languages are spoken in Belgium. People in the southern part of the country, close to the border with France, speak French. North of Brussels, most people speak Flemish, a dialect of Dutch. In the far east, the official language is German. In Brussels, most people speak French, but Dutch is also widely spoken.

Main languages

BELGIUM

- ☐ Dutch
- ☐ French
- ■ German

The three languages Dutch, French, and German are spoken in Belgium.

A Brussels newsstand sells papers in three languages.

The medieval Grand Place is at the heart of Brussels.

BRUSSELS

Brussels is the capital of Belgium and the centre of government and trade. It is also an important international city. As a centre of the Benelux union, Brussels has a long history of administering international relations. The city is now home to the administrative centre of the European Union.

Chips

Mussels

FOOD AND DRINK

Belgian food is a mixture of French and Flemish influences. Soup is very popular and many regions have their own local recipes. A speciality is mussels and chips, which can be eaten in an expensive restaurant or bought from a street stall.

INDUSTRY

Belgium's traditonal heavy industries, such as coal mining and steel-making are now in decline. They are being replaced by newer industries such as the manufacture of chemicals and electrical equipment (shown here), and service industries, such as banking and administration. Two out of three Belgians now work in service industries.

LUXEMBOURG

SQUEEZED BETWEEN Germany, France, and Belgium, the Grand Duchy of Luxembourg is a tiny state. It has the highest standard of living in Europe and is famous as a centre of international finance and a tax haven. Most of its wealth comes from heavy industry and services. Despite its small size, Luxembourg plays a vital part in the European Union, as headquarters of the European Parliament and the European Court of Justice.

This tiny country has been at the crossroads of Europe for centuries. Walled towns and castles, built to offer protection from passing armies, are still dotted across the landscape.

TOURISM

As part of the Ardennes Mountain region, much of Luxembourg's countryside is hilly and forested. Tourism is a growing industry as visitors come to discover the unspoilt scenery with its picturesque castles and ancient walled towns.

Find out more
EUROPEAN PLAIN: 79
EUROPEAN UNION: 81, 273
RICH AND POOR: 278–279
SERVICE INDUSTRIES: 281

GERMANY

LYING AT THE HEART OF EUROPE, Germany is one of the world's wealthiest nations. In its present form, Germany is one of the newest countries in Europe. After World War II, it was divided into two separate countries – West Germany, a western-style democracy, and East Germany, a communist state. In 1990, the two parts of Germany were reunited as one country. The eastern part is now struggling to overcome the legacy of economic decay and pollution left by its communist past.

GERMANY
Capital city: Berlin
Area: 356,910 sq km (137,800 sq miles)
Population: 80,300,000
Official language: German
Major religions: Christian 82%, other 18%
Government: Multi-party democracy
Currency: Deutschmark
Adult literacy rate: 99%
Life expectancy: 76 years
People per doctor: 370
Televisions: 570 per 1,000 people

EDUCATION
Young German children go to nursery school, then to primary school. At the age of 10, they move to either a *Gymnasium* (grammar school), a *Hauptschule* (secondary school) or a *Realschule* (middle school). These last two types of schools specialize in training students in technical skills.

RECENT HISTORY
The reunification of Germany took place on October 3, 1990. Growing protests in East Germany, together with the collapse of communism in the USSR, finally led the government to make changes. The Berlin Wall, symbol of Germany's division, was demolished, and East Germans started to flood into West Berlin. The capital has since moved from Bonn back to its former home, in Berlin.

FEDERAL STATES
Germany has only been a single country since 1871. Before that, it was divided into many independent states. Today, Germany is still made up of 16 states, or *Länder* (shown left), with a federal system of government, similar to the USA. Each *Land* has its own state government and controls local issues such as education. Many Germans still have a strong sense of regional identity, thinking of themselves as Bavarians, for example, first, and Germans second.

Many provincial cities in Germany were formerly the capitals of independent states. Dresden, shown here, is now the capital of Saxony, a region that was once part of the former East Germany.

THE ENVIRONMENT
Thanks to the success of the Green Party, Germans are well aware of the need to protect the environment. There are very strict controls on pollution – Germany has led the way in fitting catalytic converters to cars and in using lead-free petrol. Most houses have three separate dustbins for different types of waste, so that household rubbish can be recycled.

Paper waste is collected separately from people's houses and taken to a refuse site like this one for recycling.

FOOD AND DRINK
The annual Munich *Oktoberfest* is the biggest of the many beer festivals held all over Germany. It lasts for two weeks and attracts millions of beer-drinkers. Beer is Germany's national drink, with wine a close second. Popular types of food include bread, pastries, pretzels, cold meats, and cheese. *Wurst* (sausage) is another German speciality. Many regions make their own local sausages.

Wine from the Rhine Valley

Pretzels

Smoked cheese

Blue-veined cheese

A B C D E F G H I J K L

1

ARCTIC CIRCLE

2

3

4

| 0 | 25 | 50 | 75 | 100 | 125 km |

| 0 | 25 | 50 | 75 miles |

Cologne
- Jan 3°C (35°F)
- July 19°C (66°F)
- Jan 60 mm (2.4 in)
- July 69 mm (2.7 in)

THINGS TO LOOK FOR ON THE MAP

Longest river: Rhine, Switzerland/Germany/France/Netherlands 1,320 km (820 miles) *Map D6*

Highest point: Zugspitze, 2,962 m (9,718 ft) *Map H12*

Largest lake: L. Müritz 117 sq km (45 sq miles) *Map J3*

World's busiest canal: Kiel, 98 km (61 miles) long *Map G2*

Berlin
- Jan -0.5°C (31°F)
- July 19°C (66°F)
- Jan 46 mm (1.8 in)
- July 73 mm (2.9 in)

Munich
- Jan -2°C (29°F)
- July 18°C (65°F)
- Jan 59 mm (2.3 in)
- July 139 mm (5.5 in)

N

DENMARK

BALTIC SEA

NORTH SEA

North Frisian Is.
Sylt
Föhr
Nordstrand
Helgoland Bay
East Frisian Is.

Schleswig
Husum
Kiel
Neumünster
Kiel Canal
Cuxhaven
Bremerhaven
Wilhelmshaven
Emden
Oldenburg
Bremen

Fehmarn
Mecklenburg Bay
Lübeck
Wismar
Schwerin
L. Schwerin
Hamburg
Lüneburg
Elbe

Rostock
Greifswald
Stralsund
Rügen
Neubrandenburg
L. Müritz

NETHERLANDS

BELGIUM
LUXEMBOURG
FRANCE

Rhine
Dortmund-Ems Canal
Ems
Weser
Münster
Osnabrück
Bielefeld
Gelsenkirchen
Duisburg
Krefeld
Essen
Dortmund
Hagen
Wuppertal
Düsseldorf
Remscheid
Leverkusen
Aachen
Cologne
Bonn
Siegen
Giessen
Koblenz

Hamm
Paderborn
Hanover
Celle
Wolfsburg
Braunschweig
Hildesheim
Salzgitter
Göttingen
Kassel
Mühlhausen
Gotha
Erfurt
Fulda
Ruhr
Eder
Fulda

GERMANY

Mittelland Canal
Stendal
Brandenburg
Magdeburg
Dessau
Nordhausen
Halle
Leipzig
Jena
Gera
Zwickau
Plauen
THURINGIAN FOREST
Suhl
Saale

BERLIN
Potsdam
Wittenberg
Riesa
Dresden
Chemnitz
ORE MTS.
Cottbus
Bautzen
Görlitz

POLAND
Oder
Frankfurt an der Oder

CZECH REPUBLIC

RHINELAND
Mosel
Trier
Wiesbaden
Mainz
Kaiserslautern
Saarbrücken
Frankfurt am Main
Offenbach
Darmstadt
Mannheim
Heidelberg
Heilbronn
Main
Würzburg
Schweinfurt
Bamberg
Erlangen
Nuremberg
Hof
Bayreuth
FRANCONIAN JURA

BLACK FOREST
Rhine
Neckar
Karlsruhe
Pforzheim
Stuttgart
Tübingen
Ulm
SWABIAN JURA
Danube
Augsburg
Regensburg
Ingolstadt
Landshut
Passau
Danube
Inn
BOHEMIAN FOREST

Freiburg im Breisgau
Konstanz
Friedrichshafen
L. Constance
SWITZERLAND
Ammersee
Starnberger See
Munich
Rosenheim
Chiemsee
Zugspitze
BAVARIAN ALPS
AUSTRIA

GERMANY

5

6

7

8

9

10

11

12

THE LANDSCAPE
From the flat, fertile plains of the north, to the snow-capped peaks of the Bavarian Alps, shown here, the German landscape is extremely varied. One of the country's most famous and most picturesque regions is the Black Forest in the southwest, which gets its name from its dark coniferous trees.

INLAND WATERWAYS
Germany's extensive network of canals and rivers is vitally important for transporting cargo. Barges are a common sight along rivers, such as the Rhine, carrying goods around Germany and into other parts of Europe. In eastern Germany, the River Oder is an important waterway for taking goods into Poland. On land, Germany has excellent motorways and a fast, efficient railway system.

RELIGION
In the 16th century, a German monk, Martin Luther, attacked the teachings of the Roman Catholic Church in Germany and preached his own brand of Christianity. The movement he started was called the Reformation, and his followers, Protestants. His movement gained most support in northern Germany which is still largely Protestant. Most people in southern Germany are Catholic.

This Gutenberg Bible was printed in Germany.

SPORT
Many of the world's top sports stars come from Germany, including Boris Becker, Steffi Graf (shown here), and Michael Stich in tennis, Michael Schumacher in motor racing, and Katja Seizinger in skiing. Football is Germany's most popular spectator sport. The national team has been outstandingly successful, winning the World Cup several times, most recently in 1990.

NEW GERMANS
As the German economy grew, so did the need for labour. In the 1960s, thousands of people came from Turkey and former Yugoslavia to work in Germany. Life has not been easy for them. They have suffered discrimination and been refused citizenship, despite their contribution to German life. Since 1990, more than a million German-speaking immigrants have arrived from eastern Europe.

Foreign workers often took unskilled jobs that Germans were unwilling to do.

Almost half of German workers are employed in industry.

THE ECONOMY
Germany's industries were completely rebuilt and modernized after World War II. Today, Germany is one of the world's leading industrial nations. This success is largely due to its very strong manufacturing industry. Germany is one of the world's top producers of trucks, ships, electrical goods, and cars, with such famous makes as Volkswagen, Mercedes, and BMW. These are exported for sale all over the world.

Cross-section through a deep coal mine

Coal deposits, or seams, are removed from the Earth by mining.

Surface works of coal mine

Upper layers of rock are younger and do not contain coal.

Vertical shaft leads down to the coal seams.

Seam of coal

Horizontal shafts lead to the seams where the coal is mined.

Coalfields in the Ruhr Valley

- Current coalfields
- Exhausted surface coalfields
- Coal reserves over 1,000 m (3,300 ft) deep
- Coal reserves under 1,000 m (3,300 ft) deep

Wesel •   • Recklinghausen   • Dortmund
Oberhausen •   Essen •   • Bochum   • Hagen

THE RUHR VALLEY
The Ruhr Valley is the most heavily industrialized region in Germany, and also the most densely populated area, with many large towns and cities. In the 19th century, huge deposits of coal were discovered there. This led to the region's development as the centre of iron and steel production, vital for Germany's car industry. At first, coal was mined in the south of the coalfield where it lay near the surface. These seams are now exhausted. Today, mining is concentrated in deeper mines in the north.

COAL MINING
The Ruhr coalfield is one of the largest in the world, producing both black coal and brown coal (lignite). Brown coal is found on the surface, but black coal has to be extracted from deep mines, like the one shown here. Today, the Ruhr region faces serious problems. Coal supplies are running out, and other sources of fuel are being found, leaving many people without jobs.

Find out more

BREAK-UP OF USSR: *136*
COAL MINING: *112, 162*
EUROPEAN IMMIGRANTS: *81*
PROTESTANTS: *274*

FRANCE

THE LARGEST COUNTRY IN western Europe, France includes the island of Corsica in the Mediterranean Sea. Two major mountain chains, the Pyrenees to the south and the Alps to the east, provide dramatic natural borders to neighbouring countries. Several rivers, including the Loire, the Rhône, and the Seine, are important for transport and irrigation of farmland. The tiny countries of Monaco and Andorra lie tucked in the south.

LANDSCAPE
The landscape and climate of France varies from north to south. Northern France has gently rolling farmland with cool, wet weather, while the middle of the country is dominated by the rugged hills of the Central Massif. The south, with its Mediterranean climate, is dry and warm with lavender fields a typical scene in the region of Provence.

FRANCE

Paris
Jan 6°C (43°F)
July 23°C (73°F)
Jan 43 mm (1.7 in)
July 11 mm (0.4 in)

Lyon
Jan 2°C (36°F)
July 21°C (70°F)
Jan 52 mm (2.1 in)
July 56 mm (2.2 in)

MONACO

ANDORRA

THINGS TO LOOK FOR ON THE MAP
Longest river: Loire, 1,020 km (634 miles) *Map D5*
Highest point: Mont Blanc, 4,807 m (15,772 ft) *Map J6*
Largest lake: L. Geneva, 580 sq km (224 sq miles) *Map I6*

Marseille
Jan 5°C (42°F)
July 23°C (73°F)
Jan 43 mm (1.7 in)
July 11 mm (0.4 in)

FRENCH HISTORY

For hundreds of years, France was ruled by kings and queens. They built magnificent palaces and castles, such as Chenonceau, along the River Loire. All this was swept away in the revolution of 1789. The monarchy was overthrown and King Louis XVI and his queen, Marie Antoinette, were publicly beheaded. In 1792, France became a republic. Despite some efforts to restore the monarchy, France remains a republic.

FRANCE

THE INFLUENCE OF French culture, fashion, and food can be seen all over the world. As a leading industrialized nation, and founder member of the European Union, France also plays a key role in world affairs. In the last 50 years, the country has become Europe's major agricultural producer and exporter with main crops of wheat, sugar beet, sunflower seeds, apples, and grapes used for wine. France boasts the world's fastest train, the TGV, which can travel at speeds up to 515 km/h (320 mph).

FRANCE	
Capital city: Paris	
Area: 551,500 sq km (212,930 sq miles)	
Population: 57,200,000	
Official language: French	
Major religions: Christian 92%, Jewish 1%, Muslim 1%, other 6%	
Government: Multi-party democracy	
Currency: Franc	
Adult literacy rate: 99%	
Life expectancy: 77 years	
People per doctor: 350	
Televisions: 400 per 1,000 people	

MONACO	
Capital city: Monaco	
Area: 1.95 sq km (0.75 sq miles)	
Population: 28,000	
Official language: French	
Major religions: Christian 95%, other 5%	
Government: Monarchy	
Currency: French franc	
Adult literacy rate: 99%	
Life expectancy: No figures available	
People per doctor: 373	
Televisions: 786 per 1,000 people	

ANDORRA	
Capital city: Andorra la Vella	
Area: 468 sq km (181 sq miles)	
Population: 58,000	
Official language: Catalan	
Major religions: Christian 86%, other 14%	
Government: Multi-party democracy	
Currency: French franc and Spanish peseta	
Adult literacy rate: 99%	
Life expectancy: No figures available	
People per doctor: 467	
Televisions: 149 per 1,000 people	

The Eiffel Tower is 300 m (984 ft) high and was built for the Paris World Exposition of 1889. The observation gallery can hold 800 people.

CITY OF CULTURE
Situated on the banks of the River Seine, Paris is the capital of France and its cultural and political centre. One of the world's most visited cities, its famous landmarks include the Eiffel Tower, the Louvre, and the cathedral of Notre Dame. There are also many museums, shops, and restaurants. Each spring, the world's leading fashion designers arrive in Paris to present their latest collections.

The second level is reached by lift or by climbing a further 700 steps.

Visitors reach the first level by lift or by climbing up 360 steps.

VILLAGE LIFE
Although many French people have moved from the countryside to live in the cities, village life is still important. Throughout France villages have kept a strong identity, with local festivals, fairs, and weekly food markets. Life centres around the village square where people often gather to play *boules*, the national game of France.

INDUSTRY
One of the world's leading industrial nations, France has large manufacturing, steel, and chemical industries, and stands at the front of engineering and technology. The country is a major producer of cars and aircraft, such as this Airbus in its Toulouse factory. France has a large nuclear industry which generates about 75 per cent of the country's electrical power. With millions of visitors a year, tourism is also important to the economy.

FOOD OF FRANCE
Famous for its excellent food and fine wines, France has such a range of climates and landscapes that it can produce many different types of food. Each region has its own speciality dish. Central France, for example, is famous for *boeuf bourguignon* (beef in red wine), while Marseille on the Mediterranean coast specializes in *bouillabaisse* (fish soup with garlic). France is also known for its breads and pastries, such as *croissants*, and different types of cheeses.

Crottins de Chavignol cheese

Croissant

Garlic

French people relax with friends in a café or restaurant.

A FINE FRAGRANCE
Some of the world's finest perfumes, or scents, come from France. Most perfume is made in Grasse in southern France where fields of lavender, roses, and jasmine are grown. Their essential oils are extracted and blended to make a variety of scents. As many as 300 oils may be used in one perfume.

Oil from the lavender flower is an important ingredient in many perfumes, as well as in soaps and bath oils.

WINE-MAKING

France produces about a quarter of the world's wine, and vineyards are a feature of the French landscape. Wine is made from the juice of black or white grapes (which are actually red or pale green in colour). Although juice was once extracted by people trampling on the picked grapes, today's methods are generally more modern. There are several processes in the production of wine, including fermentation, which mixes a natural yeast on the grape skin with the sugar in the grape. Pressing grapes using a modern press is shown here.

A French vineyard

The rows of vines are positioned so the Sun warms the earth and also helps the grapes to ripen.

wind

Black or white grapes can be used to make white wine. It is the skins that give red wine its colour.

Tall trees, such as poplars, protect young vines from wind damage.

Grape plants, called vines, are planted in rows in vineyards.

Pneumatic press

Black grapes go through a crusher which tears off the stalks and pumps the grapes into the press.

Pressed grapes

Air pumped in here to inflate rubber bag.

The press revolves to move the grapes around.

As the bag fills with air it gently pushes grapes against the cylinder to press out the juice.

Trough to collect grape juice before it is turned into wine.

White wine is usually drunk from a tall glass that holds the flavour.

IMMIGRATION
France has about 4 million immigrants, mainly Muslims from Morocco, Tunisia, and Algeria – France's former colonies in North Africa. People also arrive from Italy, Spain, and Poland in the hope of finding work. Immigrants often face problems such as discrimination, unemployment, and poor housing.

WORLD OF CINEMA
The film industry began in France in 1895 when the Lumiere brothers showed a film to an audience of 33. Today France is one of the leading makers of internationally acclaimed films. The crystal-shaped Kinemax in Poitiers has 10 different cinemas and boasts the biggest screen in Europe.

MONACO

A TINY COUNTRY ON THE Mediterranean coast, Monaco lies close to the Italian border. The heart of the country is the sophisticated city of Monte-Carlo, famous for its gambling casinos and motor racing Grand Prix. Monaco is an independent principality, ruled for much of its history by the Grimaldi family. Only a small part of the population is originally from Monaco; more than half the people are citizens of France.

TOURISM
Monaco's warm climate and glamorous image attracts thousands of tourists. Many rich people, with yachts moored in the old harbour, also choose to live there because it has a low rate of tax. Monaco is also a major international business centre.

ANDORRA

HIGH IN THE PYRENEES MOUNTAINS, on the border between France and Spain, nestles the country of Andorra. The people are governed jointly by the President of France and the Bishop of Urgel in northeastern Spain. Catalan is the official language, although many people also speak French and Spanish. The country's only large town is the capital city of Andorra la Vella.

THE PYRENEES
The main source of income in Andorra is tourism. Many people come to ski in the Pyrenees, although the only road between France and Spain is often blocked by heavy snow in winter.

Find out more

ETHNIC GROUPS: *81*
EUROPEAN CITIES: *80*
EUROPEAN UNION: *81, 273*
FORMER COLONIES: *208–212*

SPAIN AND PORTUGAL

SPAIN AND PORTUGAL OCCUPY a peninsula of land in southwest Europe called Iberia. For hundreds of years the area was ruled by the Moors, North African Muslims, who introduced orange trees to the region. Iberia is separated from the rest of Europe by the Pyrenees Mountains in the north, and from Africa by the Strait of Gibraltar to the south. Both countries share a warm Mediterranean climate and have economies based on tourism. Fishing off the Atlantic coast is also important.

LANDSCAPE

The landscape of Iberia is dominated by a vast, almost treeless, central plain called the *Meseta*. In summer, it is so hot here that nearly all the streams dry up. In winter, the temperature often falls below freezing and blizzards are common. Rain is in such short supply that farmers have to rely on irrigation to water their crops.

Barcelona, Spain
- Jan 9°C (49°F)
- July 24°C (75°F)
- Jan 31 mm (1.2 in)
- July 27 mm (1.1 in)

0   50   100   150 km
0   25   50   75   100 miles

Lisbon, Portugal
- Jan 11°C (52°F)
- July 22°C (72°F)
- Jan 111 mm (4.3 in)
- July 3 mm (0.1 in)

SPAIN

PORTUGAL

THINGS TO LOOK FOR ON THE MAP

Longest river: Tagus, Spain/Portugal, 1,007 km (626 miles) *Map E5*

Highest point: Mulhacén, Spain, 3,478 m (11,411 ft) *Map F8*

Most westerly point in mainland Europe: Cabo da Roca, Portugal *Map A6*

The Rock of Gibraltar lies at the entrance to the Mediterranean Sea.

GIBRALTAR

The tiny colony of Gibraltar stands on a rock just 5 km (3 miles) long. An important port for access to the Mediterranean, it was captured by Britain in 1704. Spain claims ownership of the colony but, in 1967, the people of Gibraltar voted to remain British. After years of closure, the frontier between Spain and Gibraltar was reopened in 1985.

*Map labels:*

ATLANTIC OCEAN

A Coruña, El Ferrol, Avilés, Gijón, Oviedo, Santander, Bilbao, San Sebastián, Bay of Biscay, BASQUE PROVINCES, Vitoria, Pamplona, FRANCE, ANDORRA, Roses, Girona, Costa Brava

Santiago, GALICIA, Lugo, CORDILLERA CANTABRICA, León, Burgos, Logroño, Huesca, PYRENEES, CATALONIA

Pontevedra, Vigo, Miño, Minho, Ourense, Douro, Esla Res., Zamora, Valladolid, Palencia, Duero, Soria, Zaragoza, Mequinenza Res., Lleida, Terrassa, Sabadell, Badalona, Barcelona

Viana do Castelo, Bragança, Braga, Porto, Espinho, Aveiro, Viseu, Salamanca, Segovia, SIERRA DE GUADARRAMA, Ávila, SIERRA DE GREDOS, Móstoles, MADRID, Getafe, Guadalajara, Teruel, Castellón de la Plana, Tarragona, Golf de Sant Jordi

Coimbra, Guarda, PORTUGAL, Castelo Branco, Atcántara Res., Tagus, Toledo, Cáceres, SPAIN, VALENCIA, Júcar, Valencia, Mahón, Minorca, Palma, Majorca, Balearic Islands

Leiria, Caldas da Rainha, Santarém, Portalegre, Maranhão Res., Mérida, Orellana Res., Guadiana, Ciudad Real, Albacete, Benidorm, Ibiza, Formentera

LISBON, Barreiro, Setúbal, Évora, Badajoz, Guadiana, Alicante, Elche, Costa Blanca

Cabo da Roca, Sines, Beja, PORTUGAL, SIERRA MORENA, Guadalquivir, Córdoba, Jaén, SIERRA DE SEGURA, Segura, Murcia, Cartagena, MEDITERRANEAN SEA

Portimão, Huelva, Seville, ANDALUSIA, C. St Vincent, Faro, Gulf of Cadiz, Jerez de la Frontera, Málaga, Granada, SIERRA NEVADA, Motril, Mulhacén, Almería

Cádiz, Marbella, Costa del Sol, San Fernando, Algeciras, Gibraltar (UK), Strait of Gibraltar

ARCTIC CIRCLE

SPAIN

FIESTAS AND FLAMENCO provide much of the flavour of Spain. Most Spaniards are Roman Catholic and fiestas, often to celebrate a local saint's day, include processions of people in traditional costume, music, and dancing. After a bitter civil war in 1936–39, Spain was ruled by a dictator, Francisco Franco, until 1975. His successor, King Juan Carlos I, has restored democracy. Today, Spain is a major industrial nation, with a large agricultural sector, and a booming tourist trade. These activities are mainly based near the coasts while central regions are less developed.

SPAIN	
Capital city: Madrid	
Area: 504,780 sq km (194,900 sq miles)	
Population: 39,100,000	
Official language: Spanish	
Major religions: Christian 99%, other 1%	
Government: Multi-party democracy	
Currency: Peseta	
Adult literacy rate: 98%	
Life expectancy: 77 years	
People per doctor: 280	
Televisions: 400 per 1,000 people	

CITIES OF SPAIN

Madrid, shown here, became Spain's capital in 1561 because King Philip II liked its climate and central location. Today, the city has a population of some 4 million people, and is Spain's centre of finance and government. Barcelona is Spain's second city and the capital of Catalonia. It lies at the heart of a large industrial area in the north and was the site of the 1992 Olympic Games.

Fan held by flamenco dancer.

Wooden castanets played by dancers.

FLAMENCO

Flamenco is the name given to the music and dance style developed by the gypsies of Andalusia in the 15th century. Dancers in traditional costumes, men in black and women in frilled dresses, stamp their heels and click castanets while flamenco music is played on a guitar.

The guitar originated in Spain in the 16th century. This model is a 19th century court guitar.

PEOPLE OF SPAIN

The Spanish are divided into regional groups, some with their own language and culture. Local languages, known as dialects, include Catalan, Gallego, and Euskera from the Basque region which stretches from northern Spain into France. The official dialect of Spain is Castilian which is taught in all schools, along with either English or French. Children in Spain tend to stay up late. They have a snack called *merienda* after school, then play outside before eating a late family dinner at around 9 p.m.

INDUSTRY

Farming and fishing used to be the basis of the Spanish economy. The country has now developed a large steel industry, centred around Barcelona, and is also an important centre for making cars. In the 1980s, many new electronics and high-tech industries were set up, often supported by money from foreign investment. Major agricultural products include cereals, olives, grapes for wine, and citrus fruits, especially oranges from around Seville.

Top six exports (1994)

Figures show percentage of country's total exports

Cars and other vehicles: 18.3%

Car parts: 4.1%

Oranges: 2.4%

Petrol and mineral oils: 1.8%

Shoes: 1.8%

SPANISH RESORTS

About 55 million tourists flock to Spain each year to enjoy the beaches and admire the architecture of cities such as Barcelona and Seville. Beaches on the Costa del Sol, as well as the Balearic Island of Majorca, shown here, are popular with tourists from Britain and Germany. Bullfighting, held in arenas in most cities, either attracts or repels tourists.

Find out more

OLIVE GROWING: *130*
POLITICAL SYSTEMS: *270–271*
ROMAN CATHOLICS: *274*
SPANISH EMPIRE: *42*

PORTUGAL

A NATION OF GREAT SEAFARERS, Portuguese explorers sailed the world in the 15th and 16th centuries. They claimed territories as far apart as Africa and Asia, and they also colonized Brazil. From 1932–1968 Portugal was ruled by the dictator, Oliveira Salazar, but after a military coup in 1974 the armed forces finally withdrew from politics. In 1986 Portugal joined the European Community, but it remains one of the poorest countries in western Europe. Tourism, particularly in the Algarve, is important to the economy.

PORTUGAL	
Capital city: Lisbon	
Area: 92,390 sq km (35,670 sq miles)	
Population: 9,900,000	
Official language: Portuguese	
Major religions: Christian 98%, other 2%	
Government: Multi-party democracy	
Currency: Escudo	
Adult literacy rate: 86%	
Life expectancy: 74 years	
People per doctor: 490	
Televisions: 180 per 1,000 people	

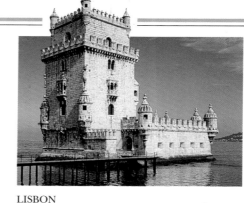

LISBON

The capital of Portugal, Lisbon lies at the mouth of the River Tagus. In the 15th century, Lisbon was a major port and world centre for the spice and gold trade. The Tower of Belem, shown here, sits on the site where the explorer Vasco da Gama set sail. Today, many old palaces and mansions have been converted into elegant restaurants and bars, shops, and art galleries.

RURAL LIFE

Traditional farming methods, unchanged for centuries, are still used in many parts of Portugal. In some villages, oxen wearing carved wooden yokes still pull the ploughs. One of the country's main crops is maize, which was brought back from the Americas by Christopher Columbus in the 15th century. Other crops include olives and figs. Wine, cork, and tomatoes are exported abroad and fishing remains important along the Atlantic coast.

CRAFTS

Traditional Portuguese handicrafts include ceramic tiles, called *azulejos* which are often used to decorate buildings. Street markets also display other local specialities, such as brightly coloured pottery, painted furniture, glassware, and porcelain. Delicate silver filigree jewellery and richly embroidered cloth from the island of Madeira are exported all over the world.

The cork process

The cork oak tree grows to about 20 m (65 ft).

Bark has been removed from tree but will grow back over the years.

Workers strip cork away from the tree.

THE CORK INDUSTRY

About one-third of Portugal is covered with cork oak trees, the bark of which is used to make cork products. The thick, spongy bark is expertly stripped off and left to dry. It is then steamed or boiled to soften it and pressed into sheets ready for use. Portugal is the world's leading exporter of cork for products such as stoppers, tiles, and the insides of shuttlecocks. By law, the bark is only removed every nine years so the trees can recover. Trees can provide cork for more than 100 years.

Cork bark

Cork tiles for home decoration

Cork used for shuttlecock

THE PORTUGUESE

Most Portuguese people are Roman Catholics. Family life is very important and girls often live at home until they marry, although more are now going to university and taking up careers. The *Queima das Fitas,* a festival held each May, celebrates the end of university life. In recent years, about 3 million Portuguese have gone abroad in search of work. Some leave families behind but send money home to support them.

Students celebrate the end of university.

Stoppers for bottles

Find out more

EUROPEAN UNION: *81, 273*
OLIVE GROWING: *130*
POLITICAL SYSTEMS: *270–271*
ROMAN CATHOLICS: *274*

ITALY

FOR MUCH OF ITS HISTORY, Italy has been a divided land. It was first united under the ancient Romans, whose great empire spread right across Europe. However, during the Middle Ages, Italy split into many separate states and did not reunite until 1870. This boot-shaped country stretches from the glaciers and lakes of the mountainous north to the rocky Mediterranean coastline of the hot south. The two nearby Mediterranean islands of Sicily and Sardinia both belong to Italy. Just south of Sicily lies a group of islands that make up the separate country of Malta. The mainland of Italy also includes the two tiny independent states of San Marino and Vatican City.

Milan, Italy
- Jan 2.5°C (36°F)
- July 25°C (76°F)
- Jan 44 mm (1.6 in)
- July 64 mm (2.5 in)

Brindisi, Italy
- Jan 9°C (48.5°F)
- July 25°C (77°F)
- Jan 77 mm (3 in)
- July 14 mm (0.6 in)

Valletta, Malta
- Jan 12°C (54°F)
- July 25°C (78°F)
- Jan 90 mm (3.5 in)
- July 0 mm (0 in)

SAN MARINO

VATICAN CITY

ITALY

MALTA

THINGS TO LOOK FOR ON THE MAP

Longest river: Po, 652 km (405 miles) *Map B4*

Highest active volcano in Europe: Mt. Etna, 3,263 m (10,705 ft) *Map H13*

Largest lake: L. Garda, 370 sq km (143 sq miles) *Map D3*

LANDSCAPE
The Alps sweep across the north of the region, and the Apennine Mountains form a central spine down the length of Italy, continuing beneath the sea to Sicily. Once covered in dense forest, much of the region's hills are now rocky scrubland, while the lowlands are used for growing crops.

AUSTRIA
SWITZERLAND
FRANCE
SLOVENIA
A L P S
Bolzano
Trento
DOLOMITES
Udine
Aosta
L. Como
L. Maggiore
Bergamo
L. d'Iseo
L. Garda
Vicenza
Treviso
Trieste
Piave
Novara
Monza
Milan
Brescia
Verona
Mestre
Padua
Venice
Gulf of Venice
Turin
Asti
Po
LOMBARDY
Mantova
Adige
Po
Piacenza
Cremona
Ferrara
Alessandria
Parma
Modena
Comacchio Lagoon
Cuneo
Reggio nell'Emilia
Reno
Bologna
Ravenna
Savona
Genoa
A P E N N I N E S
Forlì
San Remo
La Spezia
Rimini
LIGURIAN SEA
Gulf of Genoa
Viareggio
Pistoia
Prato
Pesaro
Pisa
Arno
Florence
SAN MARINO
Ancona
Livorno
TUSCANY
Arezzo
Siena
L. Trasimeno
Potenza
ADRIATIC SEA
Elba
Grosseto
Perugia
Tuscan Arch.
L. Bolsena
Tiber
Terni
San Benedetto del Tronto
Pescara
L'Aquila
Tremiti Is.
L. Bracciano
Civitavecchia
VATICAN CITY
ROME
Sangro
L. Varano
Manfredonia
Frosinone
Campobasso
Foggia
TYRRHENIAN SEA
Pontine Is.
Benevento
Ofanto
Bari
Altamura
Naples
Bradano
Ischia
Salerno
Bay of Naples
Capri
Potenza
Taranto
Brindisi
Lecce
Gulf of Salerno
Agri
Sassari
Olbia
Alghero
Nuoro
Tirso
Sardinia
Oristano
Mannu
Iglesias
Cagliari
San Pietro
Sant Antioco
Gulf of Cagliari
Cosenza
CALABRIA
Crotone
Catanzaro
Gulf of Squillace
Lipari Is.
Stromboli
IONIAN SEA
Filicudi
Salina
Alicudi
Lipari
Vulcano
Messina
Reggio di Calabria
Egadi Is.
Palermo
Cefalù
Strait of Messina
Trapani
Belice
Sicily
Mt. Etna
Salso
Catania
Agrigento
Caltanissetta
MEDITERRANEAN SEA
Gulf of Gela
Syracuse
Ragusa
Pantelleria
Gozo
VALLETTA
Pelagie Is.
Linosa
MALTA
Lampione
Lampedusa

ARCTIC CIRCLE

N

0   50   100   150 km
0   25   50   75   100 miles

ITALY

ANCIENT TRADITIONS and historic wealth
have left Italy a rich legacy of art and
architecture. Although Italy is today one of
the world's leading industrial powers, there is
a great divide between the wealthy, industrial
north and the poorer, agricultural south.
This economic division affects many aspects
of Italian life and is one of the reasons
behind the country's rapid turnover of
governments. Most people throughout Italy
follow the Roman Catholic religion.

ITALY

Capital city: Rome	
Area: 301,270 sq km (116,320 sq miles)	
Population: 56,411,290	
Official language: Italian	
Major religion: Christian 100%	
Government: Multi-party democracy	
Currency: Italian lira	
Adult literacy rate: 97%	
Life expectancy: 77 years	
People per doctor: 210	
Televisions: 420 per 1,000 people	

TOURISM
Some of the world's most stunning sights can
be found in Italy's cities. Tourists flock to the
ancient ruins of Rome, and to the palaces
and churches of Florence, where the great
revolution in art known as the Renaissance
was born in the 15th century. The
northern ski resorts and lakes
are also much visited. Tourism
is vital to Italy's economy.

Tall vines scramble up rows of posts and any available fruit trees.

An opera performance in Verona's Roman arena.

OPERA
The three great national
passions are fast cars,
football (soccer) – and
opera. Opera was
virtually invented in
Italy and performers
such as Luciano
Pavarotti are household
names worldwide. Italian
opera is unique in being a
part of everyday life, and
not a pastime for the wealthy
few, as it tends to be elsewhere.

A cereal crop such as maize is grown in a block between a row of vines and land left for grazing cattle.

AGRICULTURE
Small, family-run farms cover
the Italian countryside, and
many farmers are part-time.
In the fertile northern plain
surrounding the River Po, small-
scale farmers get the most from
their land by growing a variety
of different crops close together.
Cereals, fruit trees, vines, and
vegetables are widely grown, and
there are olive groves in the
south. Italy is a leading producer
of fruit, wine, and olive oil.

On many small farms, a variety of different crops are grown mixed up together in what is known as polyculture. Vines, fruit, vegetables, and cereals are main crops.

Crops such as potatoes are grown in the soil beneath vines.

Vine roots reach down to a deep layer of soil.

INDUSTRY
Once an agricultural
nation, Italy is now a leading
industrial country. Since it
does not have many natural
resources, Italy imports raw
materials and uses its highly
skilled workforce to turn
them into manufactured
goods, like the computers
shown here. Italy is a world
leader in industrial and
product design.

The hard, strong-tasting Parmesan cheese is made from cow's milk in the north of Italy.

A popular meal is pasta with tomatoes, and often Parmesan cheese.

Tomatoes grow well in the warm sun around Naples.

Pasta comes in many shapes.

FAMILY MEALTIMES
To Italians, life revolves around the family, which
means a large, extended network of different
generations, usually living nearby. Mealtimes
are important family gatherings, where the food
differs from region to region. In the north, the
popular pasta is often replaced by rice or polenta,
made from maize flour. Olive oil and fresh
vegetables are also important in Italian cooking.

A family enjoying a lunch together of pasta and fresh vegetables on the southern Italian island of Lipari.

Find out more
EUROPEAN CITIES: *80*
OLIVE GROWING: *131*
ROMAN CATHOLICS: *274*
WINE MAKING: *99*

MALTA

DUE TO ITS STRATEGIC POSITION on Mediterranean shipping routes, Malta has been ruled by many powers over the centuries. It finally became an independent country in the 1960s. Perhaps because of this history, the Maltese people cling to a strong sense of national identity, mostly following Roman Catholicism and speaking their own language. The country consists of two main islands, Malta and Gozo, and the smaller island of Comino.

MALTA

Capital city: Valletta

Area: 320 sq km (124 sq miles)

Population: 400,000

Official languages: Maltese and English

Major religion: Christian 100%

Government: Multi-party democracy

Currency: Maltese lira

Adult literacy rate: 87%

Life expectancy: 76 years

People per doctor: 890

Televisions: 740 per 1,000 people

SHIPPING
The busy Grand Harbour of Malta's capital, Valletta, is a sign of how vital shipping is to the Maltese economy. This has been true for centuries, due to Malta's position on the trade route between Europe and Africa. Many ships still come here to use the port and facilities for ship refitting.

TOURISM
A major source of Malta's income is provided by tourism. Visitors are drawn by its sheltered beaches and coves, and its good climate. Another attraction is the country's imposing architecture, a legacy of its history as part of the Roman and Byzantine empires, and later as an Italian and British colony. As for other industries, the poor soil means that farming produces little income and is now overshadowed by light industry, such as clothes manufacture.

VATICAN CITY

VATICAN CITY

Capital city: Vatican City

Area: 0.44 sq km (0.17 sq miles)

Population: 1000

Official languages: Italian and Latin

Major religion: Christian 100%

Government: Ruled by the Pope

Currency: Italian lira

No figures available for remaining statistics

THE WORLD'S SMALLEST independent state, Vatican City lies at the heart of Rome. This tiny state is the centre of the Roman Catholic Church and the home of the Pope. States ruled by the Pope once stretched right across Italy, and the Vatican is the last survivor. Many visitors are drawn by its religious significance and also its rich cultural legacy. The Vatican has its own flag, national anthem, stamps, and coins, as well as a newspaper and radio station.

A spectacular view from St Peter's basilica. The Pope delivers his messages and blessings to packed crowds in this grand piazza.

SAN MARINO

Capital city: San Marino

Area: 61 sq km (24 sq miles)

Population: 23,000

Official language: Italian

Major religions: Christian 96%, other 4%

Government: Multi-party democracy

Currency: Italian lira

No figures available for remaining statistics

SAN MARINO

SITUATED IN ITALY'S MOUNTAINOUS NORTH, San Marino is Europe's smallest republic. It is also one of the oldest, possibly founded around AD900. During the Middle Ages, Italy was divided into powerful "city-states", such as Venice and Florence. These states gradually became absorbed into other, larger territories, but San Marino held on to its independence. Despite being so tiny, the republic boasts a football (soccer) team good enough to be entered for the World Cup.

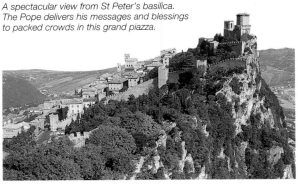

TOURISM
The fairytale fortress of Rocca Tower, perched high on a rocky outcrop, overlooks San Marino. With few resources, the republic relies heavily on a thriving tourist trade.

Find out more

POLITICAL SYSTEMS: *270–271*
ROMAN CATHOLICS: *274*
SMALL EUROPEAN STATES: *80–81*

SWITZERLAND AND AUSTRIA

HOME TO EUROPE'S TALLEST MOUNTAINS, the Alps, this region includes Switzerland, Austria, and the tiny state of Liechtenstein. The mountains have shaped the way Switzerland and Austria are organized politically, since communication has been difficult. Each is split up into individual districts which have great control over their own affairs. With no direct access to the sea and few natural resources, all three countries have had to maintain good relations with their neighbours and develop specialized industries.

MOUNTAINS AND LAKES
Idyllic scenes of towns and villages next to peaceful lakes are just one of the sights that inspire so many tourists to visit this part of the world. Europe's largest lakes and its highest mountains are found in these two countries.

Innsbruck, Austria
Jan -3°C (27°F)
July 19°C (66°F)
Jan 54 mm (2.1 in)
July 134 mm (5.3 in)

AUSTRIA

LIECHTENSTEIN

Zurich, Switzerland
Jan 1°C (31°F)
July 20°C (66°F)
Jan 74 mm (2.9 in)
July 136 mm (5.4 in)

SWITZERLAND

N

THINGS TO LOOK FOR ON THE MAP
Longest river: Rhône, Switzerland/France, 813 km (505 miles) *Map C9*

Highest point: Mt. Dufourspitze, Switzerland/Italy, 4,634 m (15,204 ft) *Map C9*

Largest lake: L. Constance, Switzerland/Austria/Germany, 540 sq km (208 sq miles) *Map E7*

0 25 50 75 100 125 km
0 25 50 75 miles

For centuries, narrow mountain passes have provided the main link with surrounding countries.

COMMUNICATIONS
The towering Alps cut through these two countries and form a massive wall that separates northern Europe from the Mediterranean countries further south. In the past, people had to cross the mountains via steep passes that were often blocked by snow. Today, tunnels and high bridges provide year-round access for road and rail transport, and Swiss engineering firms have become world experts in tunnel construction.

Ski resorts are built in the snowy peaks where few plants can grow.

On the higher slopes, patches of conifer trees are cleared for small farms.

The lower slopes are used as meadowland where cows can graze.

ALPINE VEGETATION
The different plants able to grow at different levels on the Alps show how vegetation is affected by climate. On the upper, colder slopes much hardier plants grow than those further down. Unlike the deciduous trees on the lower slopes, conifer trees have downward sloping branches so they can shed heavy snow. Above the tree line, there is scrubland where only small, flowering plants and shrubs can thrive.

Crops such as fruit and vines are grown in the fertile valley bottom.

106

SWITZERLAND	
Capital city: Bern	
Area: 41,290 sq km (15,940 sq miles)	
Population: 6,873,687	
Official languages: German, French, and Italian	
Major religions: Christian 92%, other 8%	
Government: Multi-party democracy	
Currency: Swiss franc	
Adult literacy rate: 99%	
Life expectancy: 78 years	
People per doctor: 630	
Televisions: 400 per 1,000 people	

LIECHTENSTEIN	
Capital city: Vaduz	
Area: 160 sq km (62 sq miles)	
Population: 29,868	
Official language: German	
Major religions: Christian 95%, other 5%	
Government: Multi-party democracy	
Currency: Swiss franc	

No figures available for remaining statistics

SWITZERLAND

SWITZERLAND HAS BEEN a neutral country since 1815, and has stayed out of all the wars that have affected Europe since that time. It is a country of isolated mountain communities, whose people speak several different languages. Despite this, Switzerland is remarkably unified in many ways, and has pooled its few resources to create a flourishing economy. Its neutrality and political stability have helped make it a major financial centre.

GENEVA
Many of Switzerland's banks and businesses are based in the beautiful lakeside city of Geneva. This city is also home to many international organizations, who have been attracted here by Switzerland's political stability and its neutral status. These include the Red Cross, the World Health Organization, and the European headquarters of the United Nations.

MANUFACTURING
Even though it has virtually no raw materials, Switzerland has made itself a major industrial power. The Swiss have a skilled workforce specializing in producing high-value, lightweight products. Since Switzerland is a small country, Swiss companies have had to export goods in order to find large markets and many businesses now have branches worldwide.

Making medicines and drugs is an important industry.

As many as 50 million watches are exported each year.

AGRICULTURE
Farming is not easy in such mountainous terrain, but the fertile valley bottoms are used extensively, and fruit and vines are grown on warmer, south-facing slopes. Dairy farming is a traditional way of life here. Cattle, sheep and goats graze the rich pasture of the upland slopes in the warmer months, and are brought down to the valleys for the winter. Their milk is used to produce a variety of cheeses, such as Emmental.

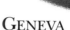

LIECHTENSTEIN

NESTLING IN THE RHINE VALLEY between Switzerland and Austria, this tiny, German-speaking principality is one of very few small European states to hold on to its independence. It is not totally independent, though, as Liechtenstein's Swiss neighbours provide its currency, as well as its postal and telephone services, and also direct the country's foreign policy.

French-speaking Swiss people at a street market in Lausanne.

SWISS LANGUAGES
Four different languages are spoken in Switzerland, Europe's most multi-lingual country. German, French, and Italian are the official languages, but a fourth, "Romansch", spoken in remote Alpine villages, has been given the status of a national language.

Liechtenstein produces highly decorative postage stamps that are much sought after by collectors. This one celebrates the anniversary of the king and queen.

Stamp sales make up about 10 per cent of the state's income each year.

THE ECONOMY
Financial services are vital to the economy, and investors are drawn here by liberal banking laws and political stability. Intensive agriculture, a thriving small-scale manufacturing industry, and tourism bring in large amounts of revenue. Its varied economy makes this is an extremely wealthy state.

Find out more
INTERNATIONAL ORGANIZATIONS: *272–273*
RICH AND POOR: *278–279*
SERVICE INDUSTRIES: *281*

AUSTRIA

THE SMALL, MOUNTAINOUS republic of Austria was once the centre of the vast Austro-Hungarian empire. It first became an independent country in 1955. The Alps cover much of western Austria and fertile lowlands stretch across the east. Dairy herds graze on the mountain slopes and crops such as cereals and fruit grow well in the north. Modern-day Austria is a highly industrialized nation, with major cities such as Linz producing iron, steel, heavy engineering, and chemicals. Austria joined the European Union in 1995.

AUSTRIA	
Capital city: Vienna	
Area: 83,850 sq km (32,375 sq miles)	
Population: 7,812,100	
Official language: German	
Major religions: Christian 91%, Muslim 2%, other 7%	
Government: Multi-party democracy	
Currency: Austrian schilling	
Adult literacy rate: 99%	
Life expectancy: 76 years	
People per doctor: 230	
Televisions: 470 per 1,000 people	

VIENNA

Austria's capital city was once the glittering centre of the Austro-Hungarian Empire. In the late 1700s and 1800s, Vienna was one of the most sophisticated cities in Europe and today the splendid architecture from that era attracts many visitors. Others come to soak up musical history – the imperial city was a magnet for composers, such as Beethoven, hoping to win commissions from the Austrian aristocracy or from the emperor himself.

HYDROELECTRIC POWER

Austria has little coal and no oil of its own, and so other ways of producing power have been developed. Plentiful rivers and steep Alpine valleys provide the opportunity of harnessing the power of moving water to generate electricity. This is known as hydroelectric power. In the mountains, as water is released from an upper to a lower reservoir, it powers generators that produce electricity.

Water is collected in a reservoir high up in the mountains.

The movement of the turbine drives an electricity generator.

The water falls down to a motor called a turbine.

The energy of the falling water drives the turbine.

Steep roofs are built to shed heavy winter snowfalls.

MOUNTAIN HOUSES

In the past, Austrians farming in the Alps built their steep-roofed houses from wood because trees were plentiful. Animals, hay, and humans were often housed in the same building. Hay was kept under the roof; cattle were kept in the basement; and the farmer's family lived in between. This kind of housing can still be seen in some farming villages, although tourism is changing the face of rural areas.

Tourism in the Austrian Alps

This chart shows the percentage of tourists visiting Austria in the winter or summer. Winter visitors go skiing; summer visitors go hill-walking.

TOURISM

Tourism accounts for nearly 15 per cent of the country's income. As well as exploring Austria's historic cities, visitors come to go skiing and hill-walking. Some of the world's best ski resorts are found here, and favourite summer haunts include the huge lakes nestling in the Alps. Conservation measures are being introduced to protect the land from damage by large numbers of visitors.

VARIED FOOD

Austrian food blends a range of influences – the result of all the different countries that once fell within the empire. For example, the famous *Wiener Schnitzel* (Viennese cutlet) is a breaded and fried piece of veal or pork that may have come originally from Italy. Viennese coffee houses are famous worldwide for their vast choice of cakes and pastries.

Austrians drink their coffee with milk, whipped cream, or strong and black.

Dobostorte is a rich, layered cake of sponge and chocolate cream, topped with caramel.

People enjoy a coffee break with lavish cakes mid-morning or afternoon.

Find out more

ALPINE LANDSCAPE: *106*
EUROPEAN UNION: *81, 273*
HYDROELECTRIC POWER: *262*
RIVER DANUBE: *78*

BELORUSSIA AND THE BALTIC STATES

Tucked away in the northwestern corner of the vast landmass that was once the USSR, these four states are now independent countries. Three of the states – Estonia, Latvia, and Lithuania – border the chilly Baltic Sea. The fourth, Belorussia, lies inland. The countries are low-lying, with hills, lakes, and marshes and a cool, moist climate. There are few natural resources in this thinly populated area. The peoples represent many different cultural groups and have suffered centuries of hardship from invasions and uprisings.

Tallinn, Estonia
Jan -7°C (20°F)
July 16°C (61°F)
Jan 39 mm (1.5 in)
July 68 mm (2.7 in)

THINGS TO LOOK FOR ON THE MAP
Longest river: Western Dvina, Russian Federation/Belorussia/Ukraine, 1,018 km (633 miles) *Map J8*
Highest point: Gaizin Kalns, Latvia, 312 m (1,024 ft) *Map H6*
Largest lake: L. Peipus, Estonia/Russian Federation, 3,626 sq km (1,400 sq miles) *Map I4*

Vilnius, Lithuania
Jan -8°C (18°F)
July 18°C (64°F)
Jan 30 mm (1.2 in)
July 51 mm (2 in)

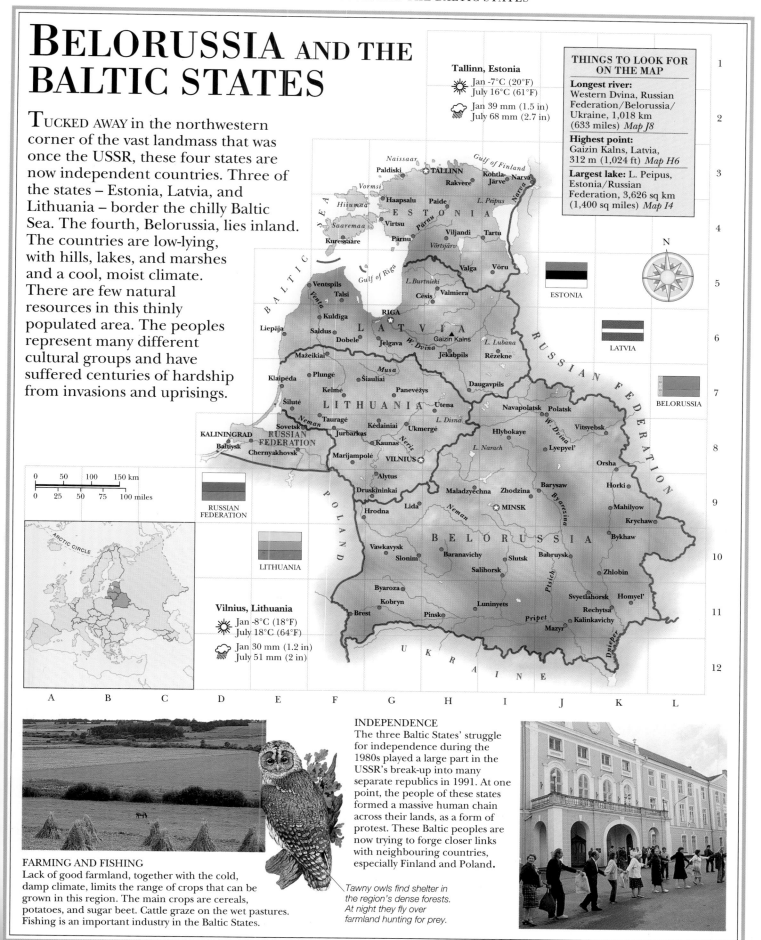

FARMING AND FISHING
Lack of good farmland, together with the cold, damp climate, limits the range of crops that can be grown in this region. The main crops are cereals, potatoes, and sugar beet. Cattle graze on the wet pastures. Fishing is an important industry in the Baltic States.

Tawny owls find shelter in the region's dense forests. At night they fly over farmland hunting for prey.

INDEPENDENCE
The three Baltic States' struggle for independence during the 1980s played a large part in the USSR's break-up into many separate republics in 1991. At one point, the people of these states formed a massive human chain across their lands, as a form of protest. These Baltic peoples are now trying to forge closer links with neighbouring countries, especially Finland and Poland.

BELORUSSIA

THIS POOR, RURAL republic is sparsely populated and has few natural resources. However, living conditions have improved greatly since the 1960s when a drive began to develop industry and to provide better housing. In 1986, an explosion at the Chernobyl nuclear power station in the Ukraine seriously affected people's health across the country. Two hundred years of Russian rule ended in 1991 with the break-up of the former USSR, and Belorussia became an independent republic.

BELORUSSIA

Capital city: Minsk

Area: 207,600 sq km (80,154 sq miles)

Population: 10,199,709

Official language: Belorussian

Major religions: Christian 68%, other 32%

Government: Multi-party democracy

Currency: Belorussian rouble

Adult literacy rate: 98%

Life expectancy: 71 years

People per doctor: 250

Televisions: 27 per 1,000 people

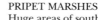

PRIPET MARSHES
Huge areas of southern Belorussia are covered in misty, marshy land. The Pripet Marshes form the largest expanse of marshland in Europe. Much of this area is forested with pine, alder, aspen, and oak trees which supply a growing timber industry. Animals such as elk, lynx, wild boar, and grouse have made the marshes and forests their home.

LOCAL FOODS
Mushrooms and potatoes are staple foods. Potatoes cooked in different ways are eaten for breakfast, lunch, and dinner. Mushrooms and sour cream are served with meat dishes, such as baked rabbit or pork. As well as being enjoyed fresh, mushrooms may be dried or salted and pickled.

Glass-making
Glass is actually cooled liquid sand. It is made from sand, limestone, soda, and waste glass. These four ingredients are fed into a furnace where they are heated to produce molten glass.

Dried chanterelle mushrooms

Mushrooms flourish in the country's thick, damp forests, and mushroom-picking is so popular it has been called the national sport.

Boletus or cèpe mushrooms

INDUSTRY
Heavy industries such as oil-refining and the manufacture of machinery are important to Belorussia. Under the former USSR, large factories were located here to process raw materials from Russia and the Ukraine. Reserves of useful minerals, such as oil, rock-salt, and types of sand have been discovered. The sands are used to make high-quality glassware.

The furnace is heated up to 1400°C (2550°F) to melt the raw ingredients.

As glass cools, it can be carefully shaped. To make sheets of glass, the liquid glass is floated on a river of molten tin. To make bottles, the glass is poured into bottle-shaped moulds.

A lump of molten glass called a gob is dropped into a mould.

The liquid glass sinks to the far end.

Air is blown in to make the glass fill the mould.

The glass bottle is left to cool and set before being taken out of the mould.

MINSK
The centrally placed capital city has a history of changing fortunes. Although it was devastated by bombing in World War II, in peaceful times Minsk has blossomed as a centre of government, education, culture, and communications. Recently, industrial growth has brought rapid expansion to the city. It is also the headquarters of the Confederation of Independent States (CIS), an organization that brings together former Soviet states.

EDUCATION
During the rule of the USSR, almost everyone in Belorussia was taught to read and write and education was free between the ages of 7 and 17. This firm educational foundation has led to the development of a strong literary and musical heritage within the republic.

Find out more

EDUCATION: *277*

EUROPEAN CITIES: *80*

FORMER USSR: *134*

OIL: *135, 152, 281*

ESTONIA	
Capital city: Tallinn	
Area: 45,125 sq km (17,423 sq miles)	
Population: 1,118,829	
Official language: Estonian	
Major religion: Christian 100%	
Government: Multi-party democracy	
Currency: Kroon	
Adult literacy rate: 99%	
Life expectancy: 71 years	
People per doctor: 210	
Televisions: No figures available	

LATVIA	
Capital city: Riga	
Area: 64,589 sq km (24,938 sq miles)	
Population: 2,666,567	
Official language: Latvian	
Major religion: Christian 100%	
Government: Multi-party democracy	
Currency: Lats	
Adult literacy rate: 99%	
Life expectancy: 71 years	
People per doctor: 210	
Televisions: No figures available	

LITHUANIA	
Capital city: Vilnius	
Area: 65,200 sq km (25,174 sq miles)	
Population: 3,689,779	
Official language: Lithuanian	
Major religion: Christian 100%	
Government: Multi-party democracy	
Currency: Litas	
Adult literacy rate: 98%	
Life expectancy: 73 years	
People per doctor: 220	
Televisions: No figures available	

ESTONIA

A LAND OF FORESTS, low hills, and lakes, Estonia is the smallest of the Baltic States. Once a farming nation, the Soviets transformed Estonia into an urban, industrialized region. Today its industries include timber, shipbuilding, and food processing. Since becoming independent from the former USSR in 1991, tensions have sprung up between the native Estonians and the third of the population that is Russian.

TALLINN
Roughly one-third of the people of Estonia live in or around the capital city of Tallinn. Many of the state's regular flow of tourists come to wander around the narrow, medieval streets of the city's old quarter.

LATVIA

SANDWICHED BETWEEN the other Baltic States, Latvia's central position, with easy access to the coast and three major ports, has done much to help trade. The cool, damp climate is well suited to dairy farming and meat production. Since becoming independent from the USSR in 1991, Latvia has concentrated on developing its farming, fishing, and timber industries, which had been overshadowed by large-scale factory production under the Soviets.

RIGA
The capital has been an important trading port since the Middle Ages. This is perhaps the most lively capital in the Baltic States and it is a vital cultural centre. Latvia has strong historic links with Germany, and this can be seen at every turn in Riga – in the buildings, the fashions, and the many German visitors.

LITHUANIA

IN MANY WAYS, LITHUANIA is the odd one out among the Baltic States. First, most of its people are native Lithuanians, whereas Estonia and Latvia have large Russian populations. Secondly, life here tends to be concentrated in the interior of the country, and away from the coast. The third major difference lies in the fertile soil, which makes farming vital to the economy.

FOLK TRADITIONS
The songs, dances, music, and crafts of their folk history have great value for the people of the Baltic States. Keeping their folk traditions alive became especially important as a way of maintaining a sense of identity under Russian rule. Now, each country has annual folk festivals and parades.

Amber can be cut or polished to make jewellery.

A fly is attracted to the tree's sticky resin and then caught as it hardens into amber.

AMBER
Up to 90 per cent of the world's amber comes from the shores of Lithuania, buried in sands dating back 50 million years. Amber is a fossilized tree resin, found in chunks of different shapes and sizes. Some is opaque and brown, but the most sought-after amber is yellow or gold. One small piece may contain the remains of insects or plants, trapped forever in the golden resin.

Find out more
EUROPEAN CITIES: *80*
FOLK TRADITIONS: *114, 116*
FORMER USSR: *134*
SHIPBUILDING: *183*

CENTRAL EUROPE

THE HEART OF EUROPE consists of a block of four countries: Poland, the Czech Republic, Slovakia, and Hungary. This region lies on the north European plain and is largely flat, broken only by low mountains in the south. The country borders within Central Europe have been redrawn many times over the centuries. This is because the flat landscape provides an easy target for invaders, and because the region was surrounded by four mighty empires: Russia, Austro-Hungary, Prussia, and the Ottoman Turks. After World War II, Central Europe came under the control of the former Soviet Union, and the countries have only been fully independent since the late 1980s.

ROMAN CATHOLICISM
The celebration of saints' days and religious festivals is a regular feature of life in Central Europe, where Roman Catholicism is the main religion. This region was first converted to Christianity about 1,000 years ago. Repeated invasions have led its people to cling to their sense of national identity, and Roman Catholicism is an important part of this.

Each year, thousands of people visit the Black Madonna at Czestochowa, Poland's holiest shrine.

A Hungarian musician in traditional costume.

FOLK MUSIC
Weddings, harvest festivals, Christmas, and other kinds of family and religious occasions are marked by music, song, and dance. Local styles vary widely, but traditions are particularly strong in rural areas. In Poland, for example, most musicians are amateurs, only picking up their instruments after a hard day's work. Slovakian folk music traditions survive mainly in the mountain villages, and are associated with brightly coloured folk dress.

THE RIVER DANUBE
This major waterway links Slovakia and Hungary to Germany and the River Rhine in the west, and to the Black Sea in the southeast. In the past, the Danube has been a vital trading route for Central Europe, although river traffic has declined recently as trade with the former Soviet Union has fallen off sharply. However, the waters have been dammed to produce an important source of hydroelectric power – a dam at Gabcikovo now provides 15 per cent of Slovakia's electricity.

How coal and lignite are formed

In swamps millions of years ago, plants died and were covered in mud.

The dead plant material was gradually compressed into peat.

Over centuries, layers of peat and rock sediment are laid down.

A chunk of lignite, also known as brown coal.

Underlying bedrock

The weight of all the layers pushes downwards.

The pressure turns the peat into lignite.

Over time, lignite may eventually become harder, black coal.

Cabbage is very popular and is often eaten stuffed, or pickled as sauerkraut.

Potatoes are served with most main courses.

Root vegetables such as beetroot are used to make thick soups.

HEARTY FOOD
The more northerly areas of Central Europe tend to have warm summers but very cold winters. Plummeting temperatures have made heavy, warming foods popular here. Influences are strongly German, Austrian, and Russian, and potatoes, dumplings, soups, and meat stews are favourite dishes. To the south, Hungary has a more exotic tradition, featuring highly spiced foods such as goulash – its famous beef stew.

Meat, such as this Polish salt pork called oczek, is a central part of most meals.

LIGNITE
Brown coal, or lignite, is the main fuel in Central Europe. It is burned in power stations to produce much of the region's electricity. However, lignite is very rich in sulphur and, when it is burned, its fumes join with moisture droplets in the air to produce a mild form of sulphuric acid, or "acid rain". This can eat into stone buildings and destroy plant life. Air pollution in this region is made even worse by vehicle exhaust fumes. Although car ownership is relatively low, the cars on the road are frequently old models running on inefficient engines.

A B C D E F G H I J K L
1 2 3 4 5 6 7 8 9 10 11 12

ARCTIC CIRCLE

POLAND

Warsaw, Poland
☀ Jan -3°C (27°F)
July 19.5°C (66.5°F)
🌧 Jan 27 mm (1.1 in)
July 96 mm (3.8 in)

0   50   100   150 km
0 25 50 75 100 miles

CZECH REPUBLIC

Brno, Czech Republic
☀ Jan -2°C (29°F)
July 19.5°C (67°F)
🌧 Jan 30 mm (1.2 in)
July 81 mm (3.2 in)

N

**THINGS TO LOOK FOR
ON THE MAP**
Longest river: Vistula, Poland,
1,091 km (678 miles) *Map H2*
Highest point: Gerlachovka,
Slovakia, 2,655 m (8,711 ft)
Map I8
Largest lake: L. Balaton,
Hungary, 598 sq km
(231 sq miles) *Map G11*

SLOVAKIA

HUNGARY

Debrecen, Hungary
☀ Jan -3°C (27°F)
July 21°C (70°F)
🌧 Jan 34 mm (1.3 in)
July 56 mm (2.2 in)

BALTIC SEA
Pomeranian Bay
Gulf of Danzig
RUSSIAN FEDERATION
LITHUANIA
BELORUSSIA
UKRAINE
ROMANIA
YUGOSLAVIA
CROATIA
SLOVENIA
AUSTRIA
GERMANY

POMERANIA
POLAND
KUJAWY
SILESIA
PODLASIE
GALICIA
WYZYNA MAŁOPOLSKA
CARPATHIANS
BOHEMIA
MORAVIA
CZECH REPUBLIC
SLOVAKIA
HUNGARY
HUNGARIAN PLAIN
ORE MOUNTAINS
SUDETEN MOUNTAINS

Słupsk, Gdynia, Koszalin, Gdańsk, Elbląg, L. Mamry, Suwałki, Słupia, Wda, Olsztyn, Ełk, L. Śniardwy, Chojnice, Szczecin, Grudziądz, L. Jeziorak, Narew, Białystok, Piła, Bydgoszcz, Toruń, Ostrołęka, Noteć, Włocławek, Płońsk, Gorzów Wielkopolski, Poznań, L. Włocławskie, Płock, WARSAW, Ursus, Bug, Krzna, Warta, Zielona Góra, Leszno, Prosna, Łódź, Vistula, Kalisz, Piotrków Trybunalski, Radom, Lublin, Legnica, Wrocław, Chełm, Odra, Wałbrzych, Częstochowa, Kielce, Opole, Warta, Bytom, Vistula, Ústí nad Labem, Liberec, Hradec Králové, Gliwice, Sosnowiec, Rzeszów, Karlovy Vary, Ohře, Labe, Jizera, Katowice, Tarnów, San, PRAGUE, Pardubice, Rybnik, Kraków, Plzeň, Ostrava, Bielsko-Biała, Dunajec, Wisłoka, Úhlava, L. Vitava, Tábor, Jihlava, Olomouc, L. Soliński, Blanice, České Budějovice, Lužnice, Jihlava, Brno, Žilina, Gerlachovka, Prešov, Ondava, Martin, Váh, Poprad, Torysa, Laborec, Trenčín, SLOVAKIA, Košice, Morava, Nitra, Banská Bystrica, Slaná, Trnava, Váh, Hron, Banská Štiavnica, Lučenec, Tisza, Nitra, Ipel', Miskolc, Nyíregyháza, BRATISLAVA, Gabčíkovo, Danube, Győr, Berettyó, Debrecen, Szombathely, Székesfehérvár, Szolnok, Veszprém, Kecskemét, Körös, Réba, Sárvíz, Danube, Zala, L. Balaton, Tisza, Zalaegerszeg, Nagykanizsa, Kapos, Szekszárd, Szeged, Pécs, Baja

113

WILD FOREST ANIMALS
The Bialowieza National Park
in Poland is northern Europe's
largest area of woodland. Wild
animals native to the forest
include elk, deer, wolves, and
bears, and conservation
campaigns have done
much to protect them.
Special animal
breeding programmes
have been set up here,
and it is now the only
natural breeding place
for wild bison in Europe.

*A bison cow feeding
her calf in Bialowieza
National Park, Poland.*

FOREST AREAS
Woodland covers a quarter of
Central Europe. In some places, the
forest dates back many thousands of
years – there are centuries-old oaks
near Poznan, in Poland. Acid rain
has harmed trees across the region,
but especially in Poland,
where almost half the
trees have been affected.

*Ancient forest in
Bialowieza National
Park, Poland.*

POLAND

POLAND IS A MIX OF SCATTERED farming villages and magnificent medieval towns. This mainly flat country is larger than the other three countries of Central Europe put together. Once a land of many different peoples, warfare, migration, and border changes in 1945 have meant that the majority of the people are now Polish-speaking Roman Catholics. During the 1980s, Poland broke free from Soviet communist control and began the difficult journey towards a more democratic political system.

POLAND	
Capital city: Warsaw	
Area: 312,680 sq km (120,720 sq miles)	
Population: 38,500,000	
Official language: Polish	
Major religions: Christian 95%, other 5%	
Government: Multi-party democracy	
Currency: Zloty	
Adult literacy rate: 99%	
Life expectancy: 72 years	
People per doctor: 490	
Televisions: 300 per 1,000 people	

RECENT POLITICS

It was a trade union leader, Lech Walesa, who led the country away from communism. He became president of a newly democratic Poland in 1990. Ten years earlier, workers at the Lenin Shipyard in Gdansk had been protesting against poor conditions under Soviet rule, and the Solidarity trade union, led by Walesa, formed a mouthpiece for their discontent. The change to democracy, however, brought a new era of political instability.

HEAVY INDUSTRY

Under the former Soviet Union, Poland was part of a vast centralized economy. For example, iron would be shipped into Poland, where it was then made into goods such as tractors for export to other parts of the Soviet Union. However, with the arrival of democracy, the country has tried to move swiftly to a free-market economy, and is struggling to transfer the huge, old-fashioned Soviet-style factories to private ownership.

The Katowice steelworks in Poland.

Machinery: 26%
Food: 18%
Metal goods: 15%
Textiles: 8%
Fuels: 10%
Chemicals: 10%
Other: 13%

Polish exports, 1993

Major exports include vehicles, machinery for industry and farming, and crops such as potatoes and other vegetables. Poland is also a major world exporter of coal and metals.

Painted wooden eggs are exchanged at Easter.

Wooden box carved with a traditional pattern.

A TRADITIONAL WAY OF LIFE

This nation of small-scale farmers clung fiercely to its local traditions throughout the years of Soviet control. As a result, unlike other countries under Soviet rule, the many small farms were not merged into larger state-run farms. Today, traditions such as horse-drawn ploughing are still common in parts of Poland. Local folk arts and crafts flourish too. Embroidery and woodcarving are often used to decorate household objects, and wooden furniture may be colourfully painted.

MEDIEVAL KRAKOW

The superb medieval buildings found along the city streets of Krakow are a reminder that Poland was a major power during the 15th and 16th centuries, before it was divided up among other countries. Poland has some of the finest old churches, palaces, and public buildings in Europe. Many were lost or damaged during World War II, but Krakow's buildings escaped relatively unscathed. Unfortunately, this is also one of the most air-polluted cities in Europe, due mainly to the nearby Nowa Huta steelworks.

The main market square in Krakow

AGRICULTURE

About a quarter of the nation's workforce is employed in agriculture. The most important products are potatoes, sugar beet, cereals, and livestock. Some farms specialize in commercial crops, but most grow some crops for selling and some for feeding the family. This is partly because most farms are still small and privately owned, often operated part-time, frequently by elderly or retired owners.

Find out more

AIR POLLUTION: *112*
POLITICAL SYSTEMS: *270–271*
ROMAN CATHOLICS: *274*
SOVIET UNION: *136*

CZECH REPUBLIC

As CENTRAL EUROPE's most industrialized country, the Czech Republic has a modern economy and a good standard of living. From 1918 until 1993, the Republic was part of the union forming Czechoslovakia. By the 1950s, Czechoslovakia was under Soviet control, but democratic elections in 1990 led to its peaceful split into two countries – the Czech Republic and Slovakia. Much of the Republic lies on a high, mountain-ringed plateau, and its people have a strong national identity.

Bridges over the Vltava River in Prague.

CZECH REPUBLIC	
Capital city: Prague	
Area: 78,370 sq km (30,260 sq miles)	
Population: 10,302,215	
Official language: Czech	
Major religions: Christian 72%, other 28%	
Government: Multi-party democracy	
Currency: Czech koruna	
Adult literacy rate: 99%	
Life expectancy: 71 years	
People per doctor: 310	
Televisions: 470 per 1,000 people	

PRAGUE
Not far from the historic core of this ancient city, one of the most beautiful capitals in Europe, a booming commercial centre has sprung up. The capital is now host to ever-increasing numbers of visitors, coming for both pleasure and business. However, as elsewhere in Central Europe, air pollution is a major problem. It is caused mainly by factories in the commercial quarter, and in the extensive industrial suburbs beyond.

The main grain crops are wheat, rye, barley, hops, and rapeseed.

AGRICULTURE
In contrast to Poland, most of the agricultural land in the Czech Republic is given over to large farms owned by the state or by co-operatives. But, as in Poland, the changeover from a communist to a capitalist economy has proved difficult for farmers as they fight to compete in an open "market economy". Czech farms are very productive, with the highest grain yields in Central Europe. But, as in neighbouring countries, a large proportion of this grain is fed to livestock, since the Republic concentrates on meat and milk production.

The brewing process in the Czech Republic

Malted barley grains and water are fed into the mash tun.

When heated, the starch in the barley is converted into sugar.

Dried hops are added for flavour.

Yeast is added. It converts the sugar into alcohol.

The mixture is boiled with hops for 1–2 hours.

The beer stays in the fermenting tank for about a week.

The beer is bottled or stored in casks.

THEATRE
It is extremely appropriate that the Czech Republic's first president, Vaclav Havel, was also a playwright, since this region has a powerful theatrical tradition that stretches back to the 13th century. It has also made contributions to other areas of the arts, particularly music, literature, and film.

The Smetana Concert Hall, in Prague, was named after a Czech composer.

Intricate, highly decorated glassware.

BOHEMIAN GLASS
For centuries, the fine sands found in this region, once known as Bohemia, have been used for glass-making. Medieval craftsmen were praised for their breathtaking stained-glass windows. Bohemian glass is renowned for its high quality and delicacy and is still made today.

INDUSTRY
Beer is one of the best-known products to come out of this highly industrialized country. Its centuries-old brewing traditions have created such famous brands as Pilsner, made in Plzen since 1925, and Budweiser Budvar. Industry in general has a long history here. As long ago as the 1200s, mountains were excavated for their rich mineral deposits, and mining is still a major employer. Other important industries produce vehicles, explosives, plastics, and textiles.

Budweiser beer is a well-known export.

Find out more
AIR POLLUTION: *112*
GLASS-MAKING: *110*
NEW EUROPEAN COUNTRIES: *81*
POLITICAL SYSTEMS: *270–271*

SLOVAKIA

ONCE THE EASTERN PART of Czechoslovakia, this small, beautiful country is much more rural than its highly industrialized neighbour, the Czech Republic. When Czechoslovakia broke free of Soviet control in 1990, the Slovaks felt they were being dominated by the wealthier Czechs and campaigned for independence, which came in 1993. The Slovakian economy was hit hard by the split, as it relied on Czech money and resources. In this mountainous land, the Slovak population is divided between different valleys, and the country lacks a geographical focus. Most people speak Slovak, but various dialects are still spoken in the more isolated areas.

SLOVAKIA
Capital city: Bratislava
Area: 49,500 sq km (19,100 sq miles)
Population: 5,274,335
Official language: Slovak
Major religions: Christian 72%, other 28%
Government: Multi-party democracy
Currency: Slovak koruna
Adult literacy rate: 99%
Life expectancy: 71 years
People per doctor: 310
Televisions: 300 per 1,000 people

SLOVAKIA

A map of main industries

Bratislava

7 Timber

⛏ Mining

Two women dress up in their national costume.

BRATISLAVA

This city is one of the youngest capitals in the world – it became the new capital of a new country in 1993. This former residence of an archbishop has been made into the parliament buildings. Bratislava is the only large city in Slovakia and historically has better links with Hungary than with the rest of Slovakia. However, the city's good communications and modern industry have helped attract interest from foreign investors.

FOLKLORE FESTIVALS

Slovaks love to celebrate with traditional music, dancing, and dress. Folk traditions are important, and are different from those of their Czech neighbours. While Czechs look north for their roots, Slovaks look south and east, towards Hungary and Russia. Unusually, the communist rulers encouraged folk customs, in order to foster a sense of regional pride.

INDUSTRY

Today, one-third of the workforce have jobs in industry, as Slovakia fights for a place in the industrialized world. This has not been easy, as the large state-owned companies set up by the former communist rulers have proved difficult to break up. Mining and metal production have a long history in Slovakia, and mines at Bánska Stiavnica claim to have been the first in Europe to use gunpowder, in 1657. Much of east Slovakia is still forested, so timber and paper-making are also important.

VILLAGE LIFE

This is a country of mountain villages and small towns. Slovakian farms are either tiny, family-run affairs, or they are large businesses run by the state or a group of people called a co-operative. As in the Czech Republic, the main crops are potatoes, sugar beet, and cereals, as well as livestock. Although Slovakia is traditionally rural, only a small proportion of the population are now employed in agriculture. There has been a great drive to develop industry, and many people are moving from the country to the towns.

The well-fortified walls of Orava Castle were built to guard the trade route with Poland.

Traditional wooden houses in Cicmany, Slovakia.

UNSPOILED LANDSCAPE

The natural beauty of Slovakia's countryside gives it huge potential as a tourist destination, as long as it remains unspoiled. Here are stunning mountain landscapes, castles perched on rocky outcrops, ancient walled towns, and mineral-rich spas. Great efforts are being made to develop the tourist trade, since there are as yet few facilities for visitors.

Find out more

CEREALS: *34, 120, 162*
NEW EUROPEAN COUNTRIES: *81*
POTATOES: *110*
SOVIET UNION: *136*

HUNGARY

A BROAD, FERTILE PLAIN sweeps across much of this country, while gentle hills and low mountains are found in northern and western parts. The most southern country in Central Europe, Hungary has been home to many different peoples, including Germans, Slovaks, Serbs, Croats, Romanians, and Gypsies. Most Hungarians, however, are descended from the Magyars, who were fierce nomadic horsemen. After World War II, the communists established a harsh rule here, putting down a rebellion in 1956. A democratic government is now in place.

HUNGARY	
Capital city: Budapest	
Area: 93,030 sq km (35,919 sq miles)	
Population: 10,374,823	
Official language: Hungarian (Magyar)	
Major religions: Christian 93%, other 7%	
Government: Multi-party democracy	
Currency: Forint	
Adult literacy rate: 99%	
Life expectancy: 70 years	
People per doctor: 340	
Televisions: 410 per 1,000 people	

Flowers being gathered at a vast flower farm run by a co-operative.

Paprika is used in many recipes, and Hungary grows over 40 per cent of the world's paprika.

Paprika

AGRICULTURE
Since this fertile land is warmed by hot summers and short, mild winters, a wide variety of crops are found here. Cereals flourish, as in other parts of Central Europe, but Hungary also produces sunflowers, fruit, and vegetables, as well as olives, figs, and grapes – there is a thriving wine trade. However, the changeover from a communist to a capitalist economy has caused problems.

Goulash was originally a basic dish eaten by shepherds.

A sauce of tomatoes, paprika, onions, and sour cream is served with fish, as well as with meat dishes such as goulash.

CUISINE
The varied crops produced in Hungary mean that it has developed some distinctive dishes. Hungary's national dish is a famous beef and vegetable mix called goulash, served as a stew or a thick soup. A hot red pepper called paprika is added to give goulash its spicy flavour. Other examples of the rich and heavy cuisine include carp in paprika sauce, pastry filled with liver pâté, and a mixed grill served with stuffed peppers.

THERMAL SPRINGS AND SPAS
The grand architecture of Budapest's old Turkish baths is a distant echo of the country's past as part of the Ottoman Empire. There are baths and spas right across Hungary, centred on the hundreds of warm springs that gush naturally from the ground. Since earliest times, people have flocked to bathe in these mineral-rich waters, often seeking to cure their ailments.

The parliament buildings on the River Danube in Budapest.

BUDAPEST
If you were to take a cruise ship through Budapest along the great River Danube, you would discover that the capital is actually two cities. Buda, on one bank of the river, is the old royal capital, filled with ancient buildings. Across the water lies Pest, the heart of modern business and political life, where the government buildings are found. Budapest has more foreign visitors than any other Central European capital, and almost two-thirds of foreign money invested in Hungary is centred on the city.

Foreign film companies are drawn to Hungary by the climate, scenery, and cheap, skilled labour.

INDUSTRY
Hungary's wide range of industries produces metals, chemicals, and vehicles as well as textiles and electrical goods. Since a democratic government gained control in 1990, the country has had to compete in a worldwide market. Many firms have been privatized, and some industry has declined. However, Hungary's population has highly developed skills, especially in science and engineering, and it attracts more foreign investment per person than any other country in Central Europe.

Find out more
CEREALS: *34, 120, 162*
EUROPEAN PLAINS: *79*
POLITICAL SYSTEMS: *270–271*
WINE MAKING: *99*

UKRAINE, MOLDAVIA, AND THE CAUCASIAN REPUBLICS

THE GRASSY STEPPE LOWLANDS of the Ukraine and Moldavia lie in the east of Europe. Further east, the three mountainous Caucasian Republics of Georgia, Armenia, and Azerbaijan lie between the Black Sea and the Caspian Sea, cradled by the Caucasus Mountains. From the 17th century, the Russian Empire dominated this region, and in this century it became part of the USSR, regaining independence only in the 1990s. Fertile farmland and a wealth of natural resources have made this area one of the richest parts of the former USSR. The region's mountains give it protection from the extreme cold of the Russian winters, and this has helped encourage a large tourist industry, particularly along the Black Sea coast.

These children at a wedding in Azerbaijan are from different ethnic groups.

PEOPLES

The people of the Ukraine and Moldavia are mostly European and Slavic, while over 50 different ethnic groups exist in the Caucasian Republics. The USSR tried to wipe out differences between the peoples of its empire by forcing them to use the Russian language and by suppressing local culture. However, many of the people of this region have a proud and ancient history and have struggled to hold on to their own languages and culture.

NATURAL RESOURCES

Large deposits of coal, gas, and oil have made this region among the world's leading producers of energy. In 1990, a quarter of all the energy used in the USSR came from this area. In addition to coal from the Donbass Basin in the Ukraine, and oil and natural gas from the Caspian Sea off Azerbaijan, nuclear reactors, hydroelectric schemes, and wind-power plants have been built in the region. Metal ores such as iron, manganese, lead, zinc, copper, and uranium are also mined here.

Kiev, Ukraine
Jan -7°C (19°F)
July 20°C (68°F)
Jan 58 mm (2.3 in)
July 91 mm (3.6 in)

BELORUSSIA

Styr
Sluch
Chernobyl
Luts'k
Korosten'
Kiev Res.
Rivne
Zhytomyr
KIEV
L'viv
Ternopil'
Bila Tserkva
SLOVAKIA
Khmel'nyts'kyy
Ivano-Frankivs'k
Dniester
Vinnytsya
CARPATHIAN MTS
Kam"yanets'-Podil's'kyy
UK
Chernivtsi
HUNGARY
Southern B
ROMANIA
Bălţi
MOLDAVIA
Dubăsari
CHISINAU
Tiraspol
Tighina
Odesa
MOLDAVIA
Bilhorod-Dnistrovs'kyy
ARCTIC CIRCLE
Reni

Simferopol, Ukraine
Jan -1°C (31°F)
July 22°C (71°F)
Jan 46 mm (1.8 in)
July 64 mm (2.5 in)

This coal mine is at Donetsk, in the Ukraine's Donbass region.

Key

🅐 Coal mine
🝙 Gas field
🏭 Power station
⚓ Oil field

H I J K L M

THINGS TO LOOK FOR ON THE MAP

Longest river: Dnieper, Russian Federation/
Belorussia/Ukraine, 2,285 km (1,420 miles)
Map G5

Highest point: Shkhara, Georgia, 5,203 m
(17,071 ft) *Map O12*

Largest lake: L. Sevan, Armenia, 1,414 sq km
(546 sq miles) *Map Q14*

N

RUSSIAN FEDERATION

Desna

Sula

Sumy

Kharkiv

Kremenchuk
Res.

Poltava

Donets'

Kremenchuk

U K R A I N E

Dniester

Kramators'k

Luhans'k

Dnipropetrovs'k

Horlivka

DONBASS

vyy Rih

Zaporizhzhya

Donets'k Makiyivka

Nikopol'

Kakhovka
Res.

Kherson

Mariupol'

Melitopol'

Berdyans'k

Pivnichno Krims'kyy Kanal

SEA OF AZOV

kinil'
Gulf

C R I M E A

Kerch Strait

evpatoriya

Kerch

Simferopol' Feodosiya

amit
Gulf

vastopol' Yalta

B L A C K   S E A

RUSSIAN FEDERATION

Gagra

C A U C A S U S

Sokhumi

Shkhara

Och'amch'ire

Enguri

K'ut'aisi

P'ot'i

G E O R G I A

TBILISI

Bat'umi

Kura

Rust'avi

T U R K E Y

Vanadzor

Gyumri

YEREVAN

A R M E N I A

Sevan
Hrazdan

L. Sevan

Xankändi

NAGORNO
KARABAKH

AZERBAIJAN

Naxçivan

I R A N

Alazani

M T S

Mingäçevir
Res.

Gäncä

A Z E R B A I J A N

Quba

Sumqayit

BAKU

Kura

Aras

Länkäran

C A S P I A N   S E A

O P Q R S T

UKRAINE

Tbilisi, Georgia

Jan 3°C (37°F)
July 25°C (77°F)

Jan 17 mm (0.7 in)
July 46 mm (1.8 in)

GEORGIA

0   50   100   150 km
0   25   50   75   100 miles

AZERBAIJAN

Yerevan, Armenia

Jan -6°C (22°F)
July 26°C (78°F)

Jan 23 mm (0.9 in)
July 15 mm (0.6 in)

ARMENIA

FARMING

The Caucasus Mountains protect
the three republics from cold
northerly winds and allow farmers
to cultivate many exotic crops that
cannot be grown elsewhere in the
region. Crops such as tea, vines,
nuts, tobacco, and cotton are sold
to countries of the former USSR.
Cattle and sheep are grazed on
the high mountain pastures.

*A variety of crops are grown
on the broad, plain beneath
Mount Ararat, in Armenia.*

Figs

Tea

Almonds and raisins

*Crops such as tea, figs,
almonds, and grapes
flourish in the region's
fertile soil and mild climate.*

CONFLICTS IN THE REGION

Since these countries gained their
independence from the USSR,
several conflicts have sprung up.
Different ethnic groups are
trying to stake their claim to
territory, particularly in the
Caucasian Republics.
Tension exists in the
Ukraine and Moldavia
between the local
ethnic groups and
the large numbers
of Russians who
were brought into
the area under
Soviet rule.

*A funeral in Azerbaijan for
people killed in fighting over
disputed territory.*

FERTILE PLAINS

Vast fields of cereal crops such as wheat, barley, oats,
and maize cover the gently rolling, treeless steppes of
the Ukraine and Moldavia. There is less rain here than
in the Caucasian Republics, but broad, slow-flowing
rivers, such as the Dnieper and the Dniester, provide
plentiful water to irrigate the fertile, dark soil.

UKRAINE

WITH ITS VAST, FERTILE PLAINS and huge coal resources, the Ukraine is one of the most powerful countries of the former USSR. Since independence in 1991, relations with the Russian Federation have been poor, as the two countries argue over ownership of weapons and ships belonging to the former USSR. Ethnic tension is a problem too, as one in five of the population is Russian. In 1986, the world's worst nuclear accident, at the Chernobyl nuclear power plant, contaminated a huge area, affecting people, animals, and even the soil.

Kiev is situated on the Dnieper River, the Ukraine's main waterway.

UKRAINE
Capital city: Kiev

Area: 603,700 sq km (223,090 sq miles)

Population: 51,706,742

Official language: Ukrainian

Major religions: Majority of population is Christian

Government: Multi-party democracy

Currency: Karbovanets

Adult literacy rate: 95%

Life expectancy: 70 years

People per doctor: 230

Televisions: 330 per 1,000 people

MOLDAVIA
Capital city: Chisinau

Area: 33,700 sq km (13,000 sq miles)

Population: 4,337,592

Official language: Romanian

Major religions: Majority of population is Christian

Government: Multi-party democracy

Currency: Moldavian leu

Adult literacy rate: No figures available

Life expectancy: 69 years

People per doctor: 250

Televisions: No figures available

KIEV
The Ukraine's capital city has been overrun repeatedly by powerful invaders. In the 9th century, it was the centre of a trading empire founded by the Vikings. It was invaded by the Mongols, and then by the Polish–Lithuanian Empire in the 14th century. In the 17th century, Kiev fell to the Russian Empire, later to become part of the USSR. Heavily bombed in World War II, Kiev was rebuilt in the 1950s–1960s and is now a centre for communications, culture, and education.

HEAVY INDUSTRY
The Donbass Basin in eastern Ukraine is Europe's largest coalfield. It is also a major industrial area, with local coal and hydroelectricity powering the world's fifth largest iron and steel industry. Factories process metals into finished products, including ships and machinery. However, many mines and factories are inefficient and new investment is needed.

CEREAL CROPS
Almost three-quarters of the Ukraine is covered by fertile plains known as the steppes. Much of this land is used to grow cereals. The huge quantities of wheat, maize, barley, oats, buckwheat, and rye that the Ukraine produces earned it the title "bread-basket of the Soviet Union". In 1990, the Ukraine grew more than 20 per cent of the Soviet Union's agricultural produce.

Oats

Rye

Wheat germ

Grains of cereal grow on the ears of each plant. This grain can be eaten whole or ground into flour.

Wholemeal bread

Caraway roll

Rye bread

Bread is the main food and is eaten with every meal. Ukrainians bake a great variety of bread in all shapes, sizes, and textures.

Granary loaf

MOLDAVIA

THIS SMALL, RURAL country was part of Romania, before being taken over by the USSR in 1940. Although it is the most densely populated republic of the former USSR, native Moldavians make up fewer than two-thirds of the population. Since independence, ethnic unrest has broken out. Ukrainians and Russians want to split off from Moldavia, while Moldavian nationalists want to reunite the country with Romania.

Most of the population live in country areas and make their living from small-scale farming.

AGRICULTURE
Moldavia's fertile soil and mild climate allow a variety of crops to be grown, such as maize, sunflower seeds, tobacco, and vines. Much of the produce is exported to countries of the former USSR to raise cash for vital imports such as oil, as Moldavia has few mineral resources of its own. Industries related to farming, such as food processing, are important too.

Find out more
BREAK-UP OF USSR: *136*
CEREALS: *34, 162*
COAL MINING: *96, 112, 162*
ROMANIA: *128*

GEORGIA

GEORGIA IS A LAND OF MOUNTAINS. The Caucasus range forms a barrier with Russia in the north, while snowy peaks overlook the Black Sea in the west. The country's sheltered fertile soil is suited to growing grapes, and Georgia is said to be the birthplace of wine. Its position between the Caspian and Black Seas, gives Georgia control over the movement of oil and other goods between countries in the region.

GEORGIA

Capital city: Tbilisi

Area: 69,700 sq km (26,911 sq miles)

Population: 5,443,359

Official language: Georgian

Major religions: Christian 97%, Muslim 2%, other 1%

Government: Multi-party democracy

Currency: Coupon

Adult literacy rate: 99%

Life expectancy: 73 years

People per doctor: 170

Televisions: No figures available

TBILISI
The buildings of Georgia's capital rise steeply from the banks of the Kura River. Tbilisi is a uniquely multicultural city, with a synagogue, mosque, Georgian basilica, Armenian church, and a Zoroastrian fire-worshipper's temple within a few minutes walk of each other.

A LONG LIFE
Georgia holds a remarkable world record. More people here live to be over 100 years old than anywhere else in the world. Many people continue to lead active lives even after the age of 120. Scientists cannot explain this, but they think the combination of good climate, a healthy, balanced diet, the rural environment, and outdoor work are all part of the secret.

AZERBAIJAN

THIS HOT, DRY COUNTRY lies along the coast of the Caspian Sea. In the 8th century, the Persians named the area Azerbaijan, "the land of flames", when they saw burning natural gas seeping from the ground. The Azerbaijani people are Muslims who conquered the region in the 11th century. Recently, there have been outbreaks of ethnic violence.

OIL PRODUCTION
Before oil was discovered in the Gulf states, Azerbaijan supplied half the world's oil output from oil fields near its capital, Baku. Today, villages on floating platforms house workers who drill for oil under the Caspian Sea. The transport network and electricity supplies set up for the oil industry have helped the development of other industries, such as the manufacture of textiles.

AZERBAIJAN

Capital city: Baku

Area: 86,600 sq km (33,436 sq miles)

Population: 7,037,867

Official language: Azerbaijani

Major religions: Muslim 70%, other 30%

Government: Multi-party democracy

Currency: Manat

Adult literacy rate: 96%

Life expectancy: 71 years

People per doctor: 250

Televisions: No figures available

ARMENIA

Capital city: Yerevan

Area: 29,000 sq km (11,505 sq miles)

Population: 3,304,776

Official language: Armenian

Major religions: Majority of population is Christian

Government: Multi-party democracy

Currency: Dram

Adult literacy rate: 99%

Life expectancy: 72 years

People per doctor: 250

Televisions: No figures available

ARMENIA

THIS TINY, MOUNTAINOUS state is the smallest of all the former republics of the USSR. Armenia was the first state in the world to adopt Christianity and is today surrounded by Islamic countries. Having no access to the sea, Armenia relies on its neighbours for road and rail links with the outside world, but conflict with both Azerbaijan and Georgia has affected much-needed supplies of raw materials and fuel.

FARMING
Farming is the main source of employment in Armenia. Sheep and cattle graze on the high mountain slopes, while fruit trees and cereals are grown lower down.

Find out more

BREAK-UP OF USSR: *136*
GAS: *163, 198, 211*
OIL: *135, 152, 281*
RELIGIONS: *274–275*

WESTERN BALKANS

MUCH OF THE WESTERN BALKANS consists of steep-sided, flat-topped mountain ranges, separated by deep river valleys. The word Balkan, meaning "mountains", was first used by the Turks, who ruled this area for 500 years until the early part of this century. From 1918 until its collapse in 1991, all the states except Albania were part of Yugoslavia, homeland of the South Slavs. After 1991, vicious fighting between the states led to the biggest conflict in Europe since World War II. Today, a fragile peace exists, allowing the region to try to rebuild its shattered economies.

LANDSCAPE
Forests of deciduous trees and conifers cloak the slopes of the mountains that dominate the region, as shown here in Montenegro. This part of Europe also boasts some fine examples of limestone scenery, known as *karst*, where scanty vegetation supports sheep and goats. Beneath the surface of this porous rock lies a vast network of passages with more than 7,000 underground caves.

Ethnic groups of former Yugoslavia (1991)

—————— Former Yugoslavia

Slovenia
Slovenes: 90.5%
Croats: 3%
Serbs: 2.2%
Others: 4.3%

Serbia and Montenegro
Serbs: 62.6%
Albanians: 14.5%
Muslims: 3.2%
Hungarians: 4.2%
Montenegrins: 5.5%
Others: 10%

Bosnia and Herzegovina
Muslims: 40%
Serbs: 32%
Croats: 18.5%
Others: 9.5

Croatia
Croats: 75%
Serbs: 12%
Others: 13%

Macedonia
Macedonians: 67%
Albanians: 20%
Turks: 4.5%
Serbs: 2%
Others: 6.5%

A LAND DIVIDED
The old country of Yugoslavia, shown on this map, contained many different peoples. Croats, Bosnians, Serbs, and others lived in the same country despite their different languages and religions. When Yugoslavia enjoyed a strong central government, under communist leader Tito, friction was kept to a minimum. His death, and the fall of communism in Europe, led to a weakening of the national government. This allowed the age-old rivalries between peoples to emerge, leading to the collapse of Yugoslavia in 1991 and the outbreak of war as nations struggled for independence.

GENERAL TITO
Communist leader Josip Broz, better known as Tito, kept the peace between the different people in the former Yugoslavia. Born in Croatia, he rose to power during World War II when he led an army against invading German and Italian forces. He died in 1980.

FOLK CULTURE
Traditional dance styles and folk music, as played by this group from Dubrovnik, flourish across the western Balkans. These are often a feature at social events such as weddings, or at religious festivals held on saints' days. In the countryside, communities celebrate the planting and harvesting of crops with communal round dances, known as *kolos*. Male combat dances imitate battles from the past, especially those fought against the Turks.

TRANSPORT
Getting from one place to another in the Balkans has never been easy. The mountainous terrain makes building roads and railway lines slow and expensive, and it is only in recent years that a system has been constructed that links the different parts of the region. Even today, roads are often blocked by snow or fallen rocks, a problem faced by UN troops during the conflict.

SLOVENIA

CROATIA

Sarajevo, Bosnia
- Jan -1°C (31°F)
- July 20°C (68°F)
- Jan 66 mm (2.6 in)
- July 71 mm (2.8 in)

THINGS TO LOOK FOR ON THE MAP

Longest river: Sava, Slovenia/Croatia/Bosnia and Herzegovina/Yugoslavia, 938 km (583 miles) *Map C3*

Highest point: Triglav, Slovenia, 2,864 m (9,395 ft) *Map A2*

Largest lake: L. Scutari, Yugoslavia/Albania, maximum size 531 sq km (205 sq miles) *Map H10*

YUGOSLAVIA

BOSNIA AND HERZEGOVINA

Dubrovnik, Croatia
- Jan 8°C (46°F)
- July 25°C (77°F)
- Jan 139 mm (5.5 in)
- July 26 mm (1 in)

AGRICULTURE

One of the most fertile regions in the Balkans lies in northern Serbia, where the land is watered by the Danube and other rivers. A range of vegetables, such as cabbages, peppers, and beans, are grown here, while cattle are grazed in pastures. Further south, in Croatia, hot summers are ideal for growing olives, figs, citrus fruits, rice, and grapes for making wine.

Cattle are kept for their meat and milk.

Pig-rearing is widespread in Croatia.

MACEDONIA

ALBANIA

BUTRINT

One of the most important historical sites in Europe lies in Albania. Butrint was founded by the Greeks, whose buildings still dominate the city. Under the Romans, it became a thriving port where rich merchants built their villas on the hills.

SLOVENIA	
Capital city: Ljubljana	
Area: 20,250 sq km (7,820 sq miles)	
Population: 1,900,000	
Official language: Slovene	
Major religions: Christian 98%, other 2%	
Government: Multi-party democracy	
Currency: Tolar	
No figures available for remaining statistics	

CROATIA	
Capital city: Zagreb	
Area: 56,540 sq km (21,830 sq miles)	
Population: 4,600,000	
Official language: Croatian	
Major religions: Christian 89%, Muslim 1%, other 10%	
Government: Political system in transition	
Currency: Kuna	
No figures available for remaining statistics	

SLOVENIA

THE MOUNTAINOUS COUNTRY of Slovenia lies to the north of the Balkans. Formerly ruled by Austria, and later part of Yugoslavia, Slovenia regained its independence in 1991. The natural beauty of the landscape, with its lakes and forests, encouraged tourists. However, the conflict in neighbouring regions has damaged the economy, particularly the tourist trade.

RIDING SCHOOLS
As long ago as 1580, a stud farm was set up in what is now Slovenia to supply horses to the Spanish Riding School in Vienna. The farm eventually bred the famous snow-white Lippizaner horse. Today they are considered the finest riding horses in the world.

SLOVENE PEOPLE
Despite being ruled for almost a thousand years by German-speaking Austrians, the Slovenes have kept their Slav language and folk culture. Colourful embroidery and distinctive headwear, as worn by women at this wedding, are part of that culture. Most people live in small towns or in one of the numerous villages scattered across the country. Only 300,000 people live in Ljubljana, making it the second smallest capital in Europe.

Slovene women attend a village wedding.

ECONOMY
Widespread forests provide wood for sawmills, furniture, and paper-making industries in Slovenia. In recent years, licence agreements with companies in western Europe have allowed local factories to produce a range of cars, trucks, motorcycles, and refrigerators.

Tourists once flocked to the islands along the Adriatic coast.

CROATIA

THE CRESCENT-SHAPED COUNTRY of Croatia was part of Hungary for hundreds of years until it was joined to Yugoslavia in 1918. In 1991 it became the first province to declare its independence. Almost immediately, Croatia had to defend its territory against Serbian forces, and across the region the age-old hatred between Croat and Serb led to war. The country is rich in resources of oil, coal, and bauxite, which may aid its recovery from war.

TOURISM
A long coastline, with hundreds of bays, coves, and secluded beaches often backed by dramatic mountains, has drawn generations of tourists to Croatia. In 1990 alone, the country had more than 12 million visitors. Since the outbreak of war, however, the tourist industry has all but collapsed as ancient walled towns, such as Dubrovnik, have been shelled by the Serbian army.

The flax plant is harvested when the lower stalk starts to turn yellow.

Linen fibre is obtained by crushing the stalks of the flax plant.

CROATIAN CROPS
The fertile river valleys in the north have a warm climate that is ideal for growing fruits such as plums, apricots, and grapes. Flax is also grown, both for its fibre, which is made into linen clothing and canvas, and for its seeds, which are used for linseed oil.

Find out more	
BREAK-UP OF YUGOSLAVIA: *81, 122*	
OIL AND COAL: *96, 152, 162*	
TIMBER INDUSTRY: *26*	

YUGOSLAVIA

WHEN THE FORMER YUGOSLAVIA broke up in 1991, the states of Serbia and Montenegro combined to form the new Federal Republic of Yugoslavia. Its capital city, Belgrade, lies on the River Danube, which winds its way across flat farmland. The new country claimed to be the successor state of the former Yugoslavia, and helped local Serbs to fight in Croatia and Bosnia. As a result, many countries have imposed sanctions, or penalties, and have refused to continue trading with Yugoslavia.

YUGOSLAVIA

Capital city: Belgrade

Area: 25,715 sq km (9,929 sq miles)

Population: 10,580,892

Official language: Serbian

Major religions: Christian 70%, Muslim 19%, other 11%

Government: Political system in transition

Currency: Dinar

No figures available for remaining statistics

BOSNIA AND HERZEGOVINA

Capital city: Sarajevo

Area: 51,130 sq km (19,741 sq miles)

Population: 4,200,000

Official language: Serbo-Croat

Major religions: Christian 50%, Muslim 40%, other 10%

Government: Political system in transition

Currency: Bosnian dinar

No figures available for remaining statistics

Industry in Yugoslavia

- Novi Sad
- Belgrade
- Pancevo
- Kragujevac
- Paracin
- Krusevac
- Nis

⚗ Chemical
△ Metallurgy
❀ Light engineering
✿ Heavy engineering
⚡ Electronics
✿ Textiles
🗋 Food processing
✐ Pharmaceuticals

INDUSTRY

Serbia was once the industrial heartland of the former Yugoslavia, with extensive engineering, food, and textile industries. Reserves of coal, as well as hydroelectricity from the Danube and Drina rivers, provided power, while oil deposits in the north supplied one-third of oil needs. However, the pressure of sanctions has now severely damaged Serbian industry.

PEOPLE

More than 60 per cent of the people are Serbs, with Hungarians in the northern region of Vojvodina, and Albanians in and around the southern region of Kosovo. Most people speak Serbian which can be written in two ways. Serbs write in the Cyrillic alphabet, as used for Russian. Croats write using the Roman alphabet, as used for English. Voting papers, being handed in here, are printed in both versions.

Green and red peppers

Raznjici is made with skewers of grilled lamb.

Skewer

DISHES OF SERBIA

A wide variety of tasty dishes are eaten in Serbia. *Raznjici*, grilled lamb with sweet peppers, shown here, is usually served with a bowl of yogurt. Meatballs served with onions and cream, called *cevapcici*, and vegetables such as cabbage stuffed with meat, onions, herbs, and garlic, are all popular dishes.

BOSNIA AND HERZEGOVINA

THE TWIN STATE OF Bosnia and Herzegovina was the last of the former republics of Yugoslavia to declare independence, in 1992. For centuries, the area contained a mixture of Muslim Bosnians, Catholic Croats, Orthodox Serbs, and Jews. After independence, outbreaks of violence eventually lead to a civil war as Serbs, Muslims, and Croats fought for control of the region. A peace treaty was signed in Dayton, USA, at the end of 1995.

ETHNIC CLEANSING

Serbs fighting in Bosnia undertook a policy of ethnic cleansing. This involved removing, or "cleansing", Muslims and Croats from areas they inhabited alongside Serbs. Thousands of non-Serbs were murdered. Others were frightened into leaving their homes and seeking safety in more welcoming countries. Many Muslims sought refuge in Germany and Turkey.

Muslim girls and women traditionally wear a headscarf to cover their hair.

CITY OF SARAJEVO

By 1990, the ancient town of Sarajevo had grown into a large, modern city. But war exposed the city to Serb gunfire from the surrounding hills, and many citizens were killed. Those that remained led a primitive existence, often with no food, heat, or proper housing.

Bosnian refugees in Europe 1995

Germany: 330,000
Sweden: 86,445
Turkey: 36,800
Italy: 36,000

Find out more

BREAK-UP OF YUGOSLAVIA: *81, 122*

RELIGIONS: *274–275*

RIVER DANUBE: *79*

MACEDONIA	
Capital city: Skopje	
Area: 25,715 sq km (9,929 sq miles)	
Population: 1,900,000	
Official language: Macedonian	
Major religions: Christian 86%, Muslim 14%	
Government: Multi-party democracy	
Currency: Denar	
No figures available for remaining statistics	

ALBANIA	
Capital city: Tirana	
Area: 28,750 sq km (11,100 sq miles)	
Population: 3,300,000	
Official language: Albanian	
Major religions: Muslim 70%, Christian 30%	
Government: Multi-party democracy	
Currency: New lek	
No figures available for remaining statistics	

MACEDONIA

THE NEWLY INDEPENDENT state of Macedonia faces many threats to its survival. Serbia refuses to recognize the independence of its neighbour, while Greece rejects the state, claiming that its name is their property. As a result, both Serbia and Greece have sealed their borders with Macedonia. Despite these problems, the country has the potential to survive. Its Mediterranean climate allows the cultivation of early fruit crops, and industrial crops such as cotton, tobacco, and rice for export. Hydroelectric power supplies a range of textile, chemical, and steel industries.

Freshwater carp

EARTHQUAKES

The capital city of Skopje is located where several geological fault lines meet, making it a likely place for earthquakes. In fact, earth tremors in Skopje are frequent, and the city has been destroyed four times in its history. In 1963 an earthquake registering 6.8 on the Richter scale destroyed much of the city. Fortunately, the Turkish area, parts of which date from 1392, survived the destruction.

LAKELAND AREAS

The mountainous area of southwest Macedonia contains two of Europe's most beautiful freshwater lakes. When the country had more tourists, visitors flocked to Lake Ohrid, and to the smaller Lake Prespa, to enjoy the scenery, and visit the ancient towns along the shores. Both lakes are teeming with fish, particularly carp, trout, and eels, that are used for local fish dishes. Colonies of pelicans and cormorants also feed on fish from Lake Prespa.

ALBANIA

ONE OF THE POOREST countries in Europe, most of Albania is rugged mountains, suitable only as pasture for sheep and goats. For most of its history, Albania was ruled by the Ottoman Turks, who withdrew in 1913 leaving no roads, railways, or industries. During this century, Albania has been ruled by a fascist king, and then governed by a communist dictator. Democratic elections were held in 1991, and the country is now struggling to modernize its economy.

Employment in 1994

Jobs are scarce in Albania, and rates of pay are low. About two-thirds of those with jobs work in agriculture, while the rest work in industry or services, such as education. Recently, thousands of people have moved to Greece or Italy to look for work.

Services: 18%   Industry: 26%   Agriculture: 56%

COMMUNISM

From 1944–1985, Albania was led by the communist leader Enver Hoxha. Under his rule, Albania was cut off from the rest of Europe. The borders with Yugoslavia and Greece were sealed, and no contact with Italy was permitted. All trade after 1960, through ports in Durres and Vlore, was with China. The Communists developed heavy industry at the expense of agriculture, leaving the country poor and undeveloped. This mural at Tirana Museum represents the people's struggle.

FAMILY LIFE

The family is an important part of Albanian life and, until recently, men were encouraged by the state to father large families. From an early age, Albanians are taught the importance of the promised word, known as *besa*. To break one's word, in a business deal for example, is considered a disgrace.

Find out more
EARTHQUAKES: *13*
HYDROELECTRIC POWER: *108*
MEDITERRANEAN CLIMATE: *15*
POLITICAL SYSTEMS: *270–271*

ROMANIA AND BULGARIA

DIVIDED BY THE MIGHTY River Danube, which flows eastwards along most of the shared border to the Black Sea, Romania and Bulgaria have much in common. The most fertile land in the region is found in the valley of the Danube, while forests of oak, pine, and fir grow on the sides of the Carpathian and the Balkan Mountains. For hundreds of years, Black Sea ports, around areas such as Constanta and Burgas, provided access to trade routes and remain important for international shipping.

TOURIST ATTRACTIONS
Picturesque landscapes and colourful folk traditions make Romania popular with tourists. The legend of Count Dracula, from the forested region of Transylvania, shown here, attracts tourists who come to visit his castle. Black Sea beaches as well as mountain ski resorts cater for both summer and winter visitors.

ROMANIA

Bucharest, Romania
Jan -3°C (27°F)
July 23°C (73°F)
Jan 46 mm (1.8 in)
July 53 mm (2.1 in)

THINGS TO LOOK FOR ON THE MAP
Longest river: Danube, Germany/Austria/Hungary Yugoslavia/Romania/ Bulgaria, 2,850 km (1,771 miles) Map F10

Highest point: Musala, Bulgaria, 2,925 m (9,597 ft) Map F12

Largest lake: L. Razim, Romania, 390 sq km (151 sq miles) Map L8

ARCTIC CIRCLE

Sofia, Bulgaria
Jan -1°C (30°F)
July 22°C (71°F)
Jan 36 mm (1.4 in)
July 68 mm (2.7 in)

Women hand-sort the tobacco leaves, ready for making cigarettes and pipe tobacco.

AGRICULTURE
Much of Bulgaria is used for farming. In the south, around the Maritsa River valley, tobacco plants are grown and then dried into tobacco for export. In Romania, maize is the major crop, and is used for food as well as fuel. The climate in parts of both countries is suitable for growing grapes to export as wine.

UKRAINE
HUNGARY
MOLDAVIA
Satu Mare
Baia Mare
Botoşani
Suceava
Siret
Oradea
Someş
Sângeorz-Băi
Bistriţa
Iaşi
Piatra-Neamţ
Cluj-Napoca
Bistriţa
Târgu Mureş
Vaslui
Bacău
Arad
TRANSYLVANIA
ROMANIA
Alba Iulia
Copşa Mică
Bârlad
Prut
Mureş
Timişoara
Deva
Sibiu
Sfântu Gheorghe
Focşani
Braşov
Galaţi
UKRAINE
Reşiţa
CARPATHIAN MTS.
Timiş
Buzău
Brăila
Tulcea
Danube Delta
YUGOSLAVIA
Târgu Jiu
Râmnicu Vâlcea
Târgovişte
Buzău
L. Razim
Băile Herculane
Piteşti
Ploieşti
Ialomiţa
L. Sinoe
Drobeta-Turnu-Severin
Slobozia
Craiova
Slatina
BUCHAREST
Alexandria
Argeş
Călăraşi
Danube-Black Sea Canal
Constanţa
Jiu
Olt
Giurgiu
Eforie-Nord
Vidin
Danube
Corabia
Ruse
Mangalia
Dobrich
Mikhaylovgrad
Pleven
Razgrad
BLACK SEA
Vratsa
Lovech
Golden Sands
Shumen
Varna
BULGARIA
Kamchiya
Iskŭr
Pravets
Gabrovo
Nesebŭr
SOFIA
BALKAN MTS.
Kazanlŭk
Sliven
Burgas
Pernik
Yambol
Sozopol
L. Iskŭr
Tundzha
Rila
Pazardzhik
Stara Zagora
Musala
Velingrad
Plovdiv
MACEDONIA
Struma
RHODOPE MTS.
Khaskovo
Maritsa
TURKEY
Sandanski
Arda
GREECE

N

BULGARIA

0 25 50 75 100 125 km
0 25 50 75 miles

ROMANIA

ONCE PART OF THE ROMAN EMPIRE – hence its name – Romania is one of the largest countries in Europe. The Carpathian Mountains form an arc across the country, curving around the region of Transylvania. Elsewhere the land is rich and fertile. Romania became independent from Turkey in 1878, but its borders have been redrawn several times as a result of war. A revolution in 1989 overthrew the harsh communist government and today Romania is struggling to improve the life of its people. Although Romanians can now travel and worship in freedom, there is also high unemployment and food has become more expensive.

ROMANIA	
Capital city: Bucharest	
Area: 237,500 sq km (91,700 sq miles)	
Population: 22,760,449	
Official language: Romanian	
Major religions: Christian 85%, other 15%	
Government: Multi-party democracy	
Currency: Leu	
Adult literacy rate: 97%	
Life expectancy: 70 years	
People per doctor: 560	
Televisions: 200 per 1,000 people	

POLITICS
From 1965 until his overthrow and execution in 1989, communist leader Nicolae Ceaucescu ruled Romania. During his brutal dictatorship, he tried to boost the population by encouraging women to have large families. Many people could not afford to keep their babies, however, and had to leave them in orphanages. Some were adopted, but many children remain in care.

WOODEN BUILDINGS

The vast forests of Romania provide an ideal material for building, and wooden houses and churches are found throughout the country. Many are surrounded by wooden fences and elaborately carved gateways. The walls are constructed using horizontal planks of wood, unlike the rest of Europe where they are placed vertically. House styles vary from one region to another. The steep-roofed home shown here is from a snowy area in the Carpathian Mountains; homes in wine-growing areas would have large cellars to store wine and fruit from the orchards.

FOREIGN ORDERS
In order to modernize old industries and create new jobs, foreign companies are being encouraged to set up business in Romania. France, Spain, Italy, the USA, and South Korea all now have manufacturing plants in or near Bucharest.

Homes in the mountains have steep roofs so that snow will slide off.

Wood from pine, beech, or spruce trees is used to build houses.

Columns may be hand-carved in a local design.

Houses are built on foundations of local stone to prevent the wood from rotting.

Rooms are decorated with carved wooden furniture and brightly painted plates.

Bedspreads are embroidered with traditional designs.

PEOPLE OF ROMANIA

Romania is home to many peoples, with Hungarians and Germans sharing the land with native Romanians. Ukrainians and Turks settled areas near the Black Sea coast, now popular as a holiday resort. In the past, people lived and worked on the land, but with the growth of industry the majority now live in Bucharest, the capital, and other towns and cities.

GYPSY POPULATIONS
Today, about 250,000 gypsies (or Romanies) live in Romania. Gypsies once travelled widely, but today they mostly live on the outskirts of towns, and work as horse traders or scrap metal dealers. They have a colourful folk tradition that includes music and dancing.

Find out more

CITIES: *80*
COUNTRIES OF EASTERN EUROPE: *81*
POLITICAL SYSTEMS: *270–271*

BULGARIA

FOR MUCH OF ITS HISTORY, the area that is now Bulgaria has lived in the shadow of stronger neighbours. The Greeks, Romans, and Turks have all ruled here, and from 1944–1989 Bulgaria was part of the Russian communist bloc. Most of today's population are Bulgars, with sizeable minorities of Macedonians and Turks. In Bulgaria's move towards democracy, state-run farms are being reorganized, and western tourists are encouraged to visit the old towns and villages as well as lakes and resorts on the Black Sea.

BULGARIA	
Capital city: Sofia	
Area: 110,910 sq km (42,822 sq miles)	
Population: 8,472,724	
Official language: Bulgarian	
Major religions: Christian 85%, Muslim 13%, Jewish 1%, other 1%	
Government: Multi-party democracy	
Currency: Lev	
Adult literacy rate: 94%	
Life expectancy: 72 years	
People per doctor: 320	
Televisions: 250 per 1,000 people	

Women wear traditional costumes during the Festival of the Roses.

Roses are picked before fully open to avoid exposure to the sun.

Damask rose

CITY OF SOFIA
The capital city of Sofia is home to more than a million people. Set in an area of mountains and lowland dairy farming, the city is a thriving industrial centre. It is also a showcase for many fine Roman buildings, as well as the Alexander Nevsky cathedral, shown here, that was built to honour Russian soldiers who liberated Sofia from Turkish rule in 1878. Bulgaria has a good transport system. Many people in Sofia travel by trolleybuses that get their power from overhead electric cables.

ROSE GROWING
Situated in the foothills of the Balkan Mountains, near the town of Kazanluk, lies the Valley of the Roses. Fields of roses are grown here for their essential oil, called attar, which is used to make perfume. At dawn each day in May and June, before the sun has time to dry out their oil, blossoms of the damask rose are picked, and the petals packed into sacks. These are taken by donkey cart to a distillery where they are made into attar. Every June there is a festival to celebrate the rose harvest.

FESTIVAL MASKS
Folk customs play an important part in keeping Bulgarian traditions alive. Many towns have their own festival, featuring music and parades. People often make and paint their own masks, and decorate them with beads and ribbons.

ECONOMY
Bulgaria lacks the high-grade coal and iron necessary to support heavy industry. In the past, its factories relied on cheap supplies of coal and oil from the former USSR, but now have to buy these on the open market. Bulgaria has recently arranged large loans from the West to finance development of new industries, such as computer technology. Textile mills and food processing are important.

Bulgarian industries
Ruse
Shumen
Pleven
Varna
Pernik
Burgas
Sofia
Plovdiv

NUCLEAR POWER
Bulgaria does not have enough coal or power from its hydroelectric plants to provide itself with energy. Forty per cent of its electricity now comes from the Kozloduy nuclear power station. Because the station was built by the Soviet Union, and lies in an earthquake zone, there has been great concern about its safety. Since 1990, the European Union has helped to make the plant safer.

🚗	Vehicle assembly	◻	Steel
✿	Engineering	✹	Textiles
🌿	Tobacco	⚓	Shipbuilding
▯	Oil refining	▤	Food processing
🍇	Wine	💻	Computers

Find out more
BREAK-UP OF USSR: *136*
COUNTRIES OF
EASTERN EUROPE: *80*
POLITICAL SYSTEMS: *270–271*

GREECE

THE SOUTHERN BALKAN state of Greece is one of the oldest nations in Europe, with a rich history stretching back thousands of years. Yet Greece only won its independence from the Turks in 1832, and it took control of some islands as recently as 1947. With its mountainous terrain, more than 2,000 scattered islands, and lack of natural resources, Greece is the poorest member of the European Union. However, its large shipping fleet and earnings from tourism contribute to an economy that is struggling to overcome years of low investment.

GREECE

Capital city: Athens

Area: 131,990 sq km (50,961 sq miles)

Population: 10,269,074

Official language: Greek

Major religions: Christian 98%, Muslim 1%, other 1%

Government: Multi-party democracy

Currency: Drachma

Adult literacy rate: 94%

Life expectancy: 77 years

People per doctor: 580

Televisions: 200 per 1,000 people

Main tourist nationalities

The majority of tourists visiting Greece are European, although large numbers of people also travel to Greece from North America and Australasia.

Germany	UK	Italy	France	Other
22%	19%	7%	6%	46%

SHIPPING

The cheapest and easiest way to travel round Greece is still by boat. Fleets of merchant ships connect the many islands with the mainland, moving supplies and industrial products, while ferries carry vehicles, local people, and tourists. Ship-owners have built up huge fleets of ships, with the result that Greece now has the largest merchant fleet in the world.

Icons being blessed at an Easter ceremony.

GREEK ORTHODOX CHURCH

The state religion of Greece is Greek Orthodox, making it the only officially Orthodox Christian country in the world. Almost every Greek is a member of the church. Priests play an important part in national events, and are recognized as leaders of their local communities. The churches are not allowed statues, but many contain holy pictures of saints known as icons.

TOURISM

More than 8 million tourists a year come to Greece to enjoy the beautiful island scenery, the historic monuments, and the summer sun. Hotels, shops, and restaurants employ thousands of people to cater for the visitors, whose spending boosts the national economy enormously. The Greek government encourages tourism by giving grants for hotel building. However, some islands are being developed too rapidly, and suffer from problems such as water shortages. Recently, the number of visitors has declined as tourists choose cheaper holidays elsewhere.

Holidaymakers enjoying the beach on the island of Samos.

Olives are treated, pickled, and fermented before being eaten whole.

To make olive oil, the olives are ground to a thick paste before being pressed.

Olives can be eaten when green or black, but must ripen to black when used for oil.

Olive trees are usually quite small but they can live for hundreds of years.

ATHENS

The ancient capital of Greece is dominated by the Acropolis and the dramatic ruins of the Parthenon temple. Much of the city, however, consists of modern buildings, for many people have left the countryside to seek employment in the city. As a result, Athens is one of the world's most polluted cities; cars are banned from entering the city on certain days of the week in order to reduce the level of smog.

Olives are harvested in autumn. The trees are shaken by hand or by machine, and the olives are gathered up in large nets and sorted.

FARMING

Only a third of the mountainous terrain of Greece can be farmed, and much of the soil is poor. Many people are needed to work this land – nearly one-third of the Greek workforce is employed in agriculture, which is more than anywhere else in Europe.

The most important crop is olives, grown on hillsides across the country. Greece is the third biggest producer of olive oil after Italy and Spain, as well as a major producer of grapes and wine, citrus and other fruits, figs, cotton, tomatoes, and tobacco.

Thessaloniki, Greece
☀ Jan 5.5°C (42°F)
☀ July 26.5°C (80°F)
🌧 Jan 44 mm (1.7 in)
🌧 July 22 mm (0.9 in)

THINGS TO LOOK FOR ON THE MAP

Longest river: Aliákmonas, 314 km (195 miles) *Map D3*

Highest point: Mt. Olympus, 2,917 m (9,570 ft) *Map D4*

Largest lake: L. Prespa, Greece/Albania/ Macedonia, 290 sq km (112 sq miles) *Map C2*

World's narrowest navigable strait: between Évvoia and the mainland, 40 m (131 ft) wide *Map F7*

Naxos, Greece
☀ Jan 12.5°C (54°F)
☀ July 24.5°C (76.5°F)
🌧 Jan 91 mm (3.6 in)
🌧 July 2 mm (0.1 in)

GREECE

Athens, Greece
☀ Jan 9.5°C (49.5°F)
☀ July 28°C (82.5°F)
🌧 Jan 62 mm (2.4 in)
🌧 July 6 mm (0.2 in)

BULGARIA
MACEDONIA
ALBANIA
GREECE
THRACE
TURKEY

Corfu
Igoumenitsa
Ioannina
Preveza
Lefkada
Arta
Astakos
Mesolongi
Lixouri
Argostóli
Patrai
Andravida
Zakynthos
Kyllini
Pyrgos
Katakolo
Olympia
Kalamata
Pilos
Gytheio
Neapoli
Kythira

Florina
L. Prespa
Kastoria
Kozani
Grevena
Veroia
Edessa
Kilkis
Vardar
Katerini
Mt. Olympus
Trikala
Karditsa
Larisa
Lamia
Stylis
Amfissa
Itea
Delphi
Corinth
Mycenae
Tripoli
Nafplio
Sparti
Leonidi

Thessaloniki
Polygyros
Serres
Drama
Kavala
Xanthi
Komotini
Alexandroupoli
Thasos
Samothraki

Volos
Loutra Aidipsou
Chalkida
Marathon
Corinth Canal
Piraeus
ATHENS
Lavrio
Epidaurus
Karystos

Sporades
Skiathos
Skiros
Évvoia
Kymi
Limnos
Ayios Evstratios
Lesvos
Mytilini
Chios
Chios

AEGEAN SEA

Andros
Tinos
Ikaria
Samos
Samos
Mykonos
Siros
Kéa
Kithnos
Sérifos
Sifnos
Milos
Paros
Naxos
Ios
Amorgos
Astipálaia
Thira
Kos
Kos
Rhodes
Monólithos
Rhodes
Karpathos

CYCLADES
DODECANESE

SEA OF CRETE
Chania
Rethymno
Knossos
Irakleio
Crete
Agios Nikolaos

MEDITERRANEAN SEA

IONIAN SEA
Ionian Is.
Corfu
Lefkada
Kefallonia
Zakynthos
PINDUS MOUNTAINS
Acheloos
L. Trichonida
Gulf of Patras
PELOPONNESE
Gulf of Corinth
Gulf of Messini
Gulf of Laconia

ARCTIC CIRCLE

N

0 25 50 75 km
0 25 50 miles

ANCIENT GREEK HISTORY
The remains of temples and other buildings from Greece's long and complex history can still be seen today. From about 2000BC, advanced civilizations existed on Crete and on the mainland at Mycenae. By the 5th century BC, powerful city states emerged, including Athens and Sparta. Philosophers, mathematicians, architects, and dramatists contributed to a rich culture that spread around the Mediterranean.

Signs of Greece's rich classical past are revealed in its many ancient ruins, such as this temple of Apollo at Delphi.

Find out more
EUROPEAN UNION: *81, 273*
MEDITERRANEAN LANDSCAPE: *79*
ORTHODOX CHURCH: *274*
WINE MAKING: *99*

ASIA

STRETCHING FROM THE frozen Arctic to the hot Equator, Asia is by far the world's largest and most mountainous continent. Much of the land is barren, with vast, empty deserts in southwest and central Asia, and the remote, windswept plateau of Tibet to the north of the Himalayan Mountains. Asia also has some of the world's most fertile plains and valleys beside rivers that include the Mekong, Indus, and Euphrates. In southeast Asia, the land is mainly mountainous or covered in tropical rainforests that are teeming with wildlife.

Away from the mainland, scattered either side of the Equator, lie thousands of islands, many of them volcanic.

SIBERIA

Most of Siberia, the Asian part of Russia, is bitterly cold in winter. In the north lies the tundra, where part of the soil has been frozen since the end of the last Ice Age. Beneath its surface there are vast supplies of minerals. To the south lies the world's largest coniferous forest. This cold forest makes way for a dry grassland area, known as steppe, which forms Russia's main farming region.

THE YANGTZE RIVER
From its source in the Tanggula Mountains on the plateau of Tibet, the Yangtze River flows through mountainous land for most of its course. On its final stages, it follows the southern edge of the Great Plain of China until it reaches the East China Sea. In the flatter areas, the Yangtze supplies water for irrigation. In the past, flooding has caused thousands of deaths.

CENTRAL DESERTS
Unlike most deserts, the Takla Makan and Gobi in central Asia have hot summers but extremely cold winters. Much of their landscape is made up of bare rock with huge expanses of shifting sand. Vegetation is sparse, except in river valleys, as shown here in the Takla Makan. Some animals, including wild camels, can survive cold winters in the Gobi.

A Bactrian camels has two humps.

Highest temperature: Tirat Zevi, Israel, 54°C (129°F)

THE HIMALAYAS
The Himalayas, right, form a massive land barrier between the Indian Subcontinent and Tibet. The range is permanently snow-capped, and contains the world's highest peak, Mount Everest. The mountains began to form about 50 million years ago when a moving plate, carrying the subcontinent, began to push against the Eurasian plate. When the plates collided, the edge of the Indian plate was forced under the Eurasian plate, and the sea-bed in between was folded up to form the Himalayas.

0 250 500 750 1000 1250 km
0 250 500 750 miles

Lowest temperature:
Verkhoyansk, Russian
Federation, -68°C (-90°F)

N

KARA SEA

Pioneer I. *Severnaya*
Zemlya
October
Revolution I.
Bolshevik I.
Vil'kilskiy Strait

A R C T I C   O C E A N

LAPTEV SEA

New Siberian Is.

EAST SIBERIAN SEA

GYDA
NINSULA

TAYMYR PENINSULA

L. Taymyr

CENTRAL
SIBERIAN
PLATEAU

Wrangel I.

CHUKCHI
SEA

Taz

Khatanga

Olenëk

Yana

Indigirka

Kolyma

Omolon

OLOY
RANGE

C. Navarin

Yenisey

Lower Tunguska

Lena

Verkhoyansk

VERKHOYANSK RANGE

KOLYMA RANGE

KORYAK RANGE

ERIAN
AIN

S I B E R I A

Vilyuy

Aldan

C. Olyutorskiy

Stony Tunguska

Vitim

Lena

DZHUGDZHUR
RANGE

Karaginskiy Is.

BERING SEA

Ob'

Angara

STANOVOY RANGE

Olekma

Shantar Is.

SEA OF
OKHOTSK

C. Sivuchiy

AZAKH
LANDS

L. Baikal

Amur

Sakhalin

KAMCHATKA

Kurile Is.

**THINGS TO LOOK FOR
ON THE MAP**

Area: 44,680,718 sq km
(17,251,315 sq miles)

Highest point: Mt. Everest,
China/Nepal, 8,848 m
(29,029 ft) *Map H11*

ALTAI MOUNTAINS

Hulun
Nur

Songhua

Tatar Strait

balkhash

L. Uvs

GOBI DESERT

MANCHURIAN
PLAIN

Hokkaido

yk-Kul

TIEN SHAN

Tarim

TAKLA MAKAN
DESERT

ALTUN MTS.

Yellow River (Huang He)

YELLOW
SEA

SEA OF
JAPAN

Oki Is.

Honshū

Longest river: Yangtze,
China, 5,520 km
(3,430 miles) *Map K10*

Largest lake: Caspian Sea,
Azerbaijan/Iran/
Turkmenistan/Kazakhstan/
Russian Federation,
378,400 sq km
(146,101 sq miles) *Map D8*

Largest island: Borneo,
743,250 sq km (286,969
sq miles) *Map K14*

KUNLUN SHAN

IRS

PLATEAU
OF TIBET

TANGGULA MTS.

GREAT
PLAIN OF
CHINA

Kyushū

EAST
CHINA
SEA

O   P   Q   R   S

RAKORAM

Brahmaputra

RED
BASIN

Yangtze

▲ Mt. Everest

ERT

HIMALAYAS

Hongshui He

Ganges

Irrawaddy

Mehong

Taiwan

Bay of
Bengal

Hainan

Andaman
Is.

SOUTH
CHINA
SEA

Luzon

Yap

Nicobar
Is.

SULU
SEA

Mindanao

Palau

Sri
Lanka

I N D I A N   O C E A N

CELEBES
SEA

Sumatra

Borneo

Sulawesi

BANDA
SEA

New Guinea

15

JAVA SEA

Java

Timor

ARAFURA
SEA

16

H   I   J   K   L   M   N

P A C I F I C   O C E A N

THE RING OF FIRE

Volcanoes erupt so often on the rim of land
and islands around the Pacific that the
region is called the "Ring of Fire". The most
famous eruption took place in 1883, when
the volcanic island of Krakatoa, west of Java,
erupted. The explosion was so loud it was
heard in Australia. In 1928, a new volcano
burst into life on the island. It was named
Anak Krakatoa, meaning "son of Krakatoa".

PEOPLES OF ASIA I

OF ALL THE CONTINENTS, Asia has the largest population with the greatest variety of cultures. The history of civilization here stretches back for many thousands of years. Cities and writing, the development of which are closely connected, first appeared in Asia. More than 5,000 years ago the earliest cities, such as Babylon, emerged in the valley of the Tigris and Euphrates rivers, an area that is now known as Mesopotamia. Today, Asia contains two-thirds of the world's population, much of which is concentrated in the southern and eastern regions of the continent. Although most of the population are farmers, city populations are growing very rapidly.

Stone reliefs in Persepolis, capital of the ancient Persian Empire.

EARLY CIVILIZATIONS
The world's earliest civilizations grew up around river valleys in Asia, in an area known as the fertile crescent which stretches in an arc from the Persian Gulf to the Mediterranean Sea. Many cities here can trace their history back for several thousand years.

Population: approximately 3,497,760,000 people (This figure includes the whole of the Russian Federation.)
Number of countries: 48

Largest country: Russian Federation – the Asian part covers 13,444,468 sq km (5,190,909 sq miles)

RUSSIAN FEDERATION

KAZAKHSTAN

MONGOLIA

UZBEKISTAN
KYRGYZSTAN
TURKMENISTAN
TAJIKISTAN

NORTH KOREA
SOUTH KOREA
JAPAN

TURKEY

CYPRUS
LEBANON SYRIA
ISRAEL
JORDAN
IRAQ
IRAN

AFGHANISTAN

CHINA

KUWAIT
BAHRAIN QATAR
U.A.E.

PAKISTAN

NEPAL BHUTAN

BANGLADESH

TAIWAN

Least densely populated country: Mongolia, 1 person per sq km (4 per sq mile)

SAUDI ARABIA

OMAN

YEMEN

INDIA

BURMA

Hong Kong (UK)
Macao (Port)

Most densely populated country: Hong Kong, 5,798 people per sq km (15,017 per sq mile)

Smallest country: Maldives 300 sq km (116 sq miles)

LAOS
THAILAND
CAMBODIA
VIETNAM

PHILIPPINES

Andaman Is. (Ind)

Nicobar Is. (Ind)

SRI LANKA

MALDIVES

MALAYSIA
BRUNEI
SINGAPORE

INDONESIA

EMPTY PLAINS
Although Asia has a huge population, many areas are hardly peopled at all. At just 1 person per sq km (4 per sq mile), Mongolia has the world's lowest population density.

GROWING CITIES

A large proportion of Asia's population still live in the countryside as farmers, but the number living in cities is rising steeply. The largest cities in Asia now have populations of over 10 million people. These super-cities, along with many other cities in the continent, are destined to grow even faster as people move from the countryside to towns.

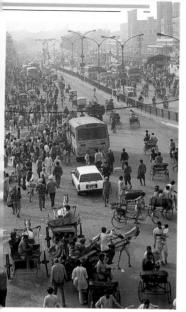

This crowded street scene is in India's capital, New Delhi. India is one of the world's most densely populated countries.

LARGEST CITIES IN ASIA	
Tokyo, Japan	18.1 million
Shanghai, China	13.4 million
Calcutta, India	11.8 million
Bombay, India	11.2 million
Seoul, South Korea	11 million

Population density

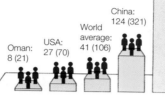

The figures on the chart show the number of people per sq km (per sq mile). Countries outside Asia are included as a comparison.

Bangladesh: 830 (2,150)

China: 124 (321)

World average: 41 (106)

Oman: 8 (21)

USA: 27 (70)

POPULATION DENSITY

Large areas of the Middle East and central Asia are empty wilderness, unsettled by people because of their extreme dryness or cold temperatures. Most of the continent's population is concentrated in the fertile river valleys and coastal lowlands of south and east Asia. Apart from the two island city-states of Hong Kong and Singapore, Bangladesh is the most densely populated country in Asia with 830 people per sq km (2,150 per sq mile).

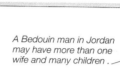

A Bedouin man in Jordan may have more than one wife and many children.

POPULATION GROWTH

Two out of every three people in the world live in Asia. Seven of the world's ten most populated countries are located here, with China and India heading the list. Between them these two countries account for about 40 per cent of the world's population. In mainland China a strictly enforced government policy to restrict family size to just one child has slowed the rate of population growth, but elsewhere in the continent it is still very high. By the year 2000, India's population will have risen to over 1,000 million and Indonesia's will be over 220 million.

In China, a family with just one child receives free education and a housing allowance.

RIVER VALLEYS

The first peoples settled in fertile river valleys where they could grow crops. They built irrigation systems to channel water from the river to the crops. Today, rivers are still of great importance to the people of southern and eastern Asia. As well as irrigation, rivers are used for fishing and for drinking. They are dammed to produce hydroelectric power. Rivers often provide a country's main means of transport, and some are the focus around which countries have grown up.

World's top rice-growing countries (1991)

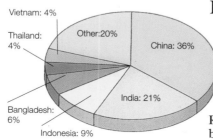

Vietnam: 4%
Thailand: 4%
Other: 20%
China: 36%
India: 21%
Bangladesh: 6%
Indonesia: 9%

RICE

Half the world's population depend on rice as their principal source of food, so a rice shortage can cause terrible famine. This plant, which is native to southeast Asia, has been cultivated in the region for at least 7,000 years. In recent decades, new varieties of rice have been developed to help feed Asia's growing population. These new strains of rice are part of the "Green Revolution", which applies scientific knowledge to plant breeding and uses technology to increase productivity.

PEOPLES OF ASIA II

ALTHOUGH SOME ASIAN COUNTRIES, such as Japan and China, have been independent for a long time, others have only recently emerged from being colonies. At the start of this century, much of the Middle East, the whole Indian Subcontinent, and large areas of southeast Asia were controlled by European powers. Nationalist movements grew up across Asia and the countries regained their independence. Many countries here have had very fast economic growth which, together with the recent pressures for change, means that societies across the region are now changing very rapidly.

INDEPENDENCE
Each year, many countries in the region celebrate their freedom from colonial rule in independence day celebrations, like those in Pakistan shown above. Some countries, such as India, gained their independence through peaceful protest, while fierce fighting occurred in others, such as Burma. These countries are now struggling to forge a sense of national unity.

The former USSR
This map shows the former USSR and the 15 republics that it divided up into.

USSR
(Much of this area is now the Russian Federation.)

BREAK-UP
The Soviet Union, or USSR, was the world's largest nation. However, in 1991, the USSR split up into 15 republics which set up their own governments. Nine of the republics are in Europe and the other six are in Asia. Now they are no longer part of a large, centralized economy, the republics are struggling to compete in a world market. The USSR's collapse also freed some eastern European countries from Soviet control.

Chechnya's capital Grozny was heavily bombed by the Russian Federation in 1994.

WORLD RELIGIONS
Asia was the birthplace of all the main world religions, including Hinduism, Buddhism, Judaism, Christianity, and Islam. Religious beliefs still have a strong influence on the people of the region today. Religions often emphasise modesty in wealth and the importance of donating to charity for spiritual reward rather than any personal gain.

This temple is in Thailand, where Buddhism is the main religion.

Most young men in Thailand live in a monastery as monks for a few months.

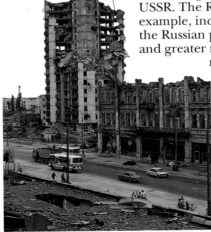

ETHNIC GROUPS
Fighting between ethnic groups is still continuing in several parts of the former USSR. The Russian Federation, for example, includes some regions where the Russian population is in the minority and greater numbers of people belong to native ethnic groups, such as Chechnya where only about a third of the population is Russian. Since the break-up of the USSR, the Chechens have been fighting for independence. However, the Russian Federation is not prepared to grant independence to any of these territories since this could lead to the break-up of Russia itself.

PRESSURES FOR CHANGE

In Asian societies today, the traditional rural ways of life and religious beliefs conflict with an increasingly money-oriented way of life, influenced by the west. As Asian societies become more open to western influences, so the pressures on traditional ways of life will intensify. Societies react to pressures for change in different ways. In Iran, for example, religious leaders violently opposed the growing influence of western ideas, leading to the setting up of a republic based on traditional Islamic values under Ayatollah Khomeini.

The influence of the USA and capitalism can be seen on the streets of Tokyo, in Japan.

These Islamic fundamentalists in Iran were supporting the government and Ayatollah Khomeini.

OIL AND THE MIDDLE EAST
Before oil was discovered, many desert countries in the Middle East were very poor. Oil has transformed their fortunes. More than half the world's known reserves of crude oil and a third of all natural gas occur here and the countries have become wealthy through the export of oil and natural gas throughout the world. New cities have sprung up such as Dubai (shown above) and foreign workers have arrived in great numbers.

WESTERN INFLUENCE
In some societies, change happens gradually and without violent demonstrations. In Japan, for example, economic development was seen by its rulers as a way of avoiding becoming dependent on European nations. Japan has therefore accepted western capitalism while still managing to preserve traditional Japanese values. Even China, so long closed to western ideas, is now beginning to embrace capitalism.

Shaded areas on the map show southeast Asia's newly industrializing countries.

Asia's tiger economies

SOUTH KOREA

HONG KONG

TAIWAN

PHILIPPINES

THAILAND

MALAYSIA

SINGAPORE

LITTLE TIGERS
In the last 20 years, following in the footsteps of Japan, the economies of many southeast Asian countries have developed at a rapid pace. Because of the speed and dynamism of economic growth, these newly industrialising countries have been nicknamed the "Little Tigers". Cheap and plentiful labour, along with very strict governments that stifle any unrest, have encouraged foreign investment and the development of manufacturing industry.

Kazakh people in northern China outside a tent, known as a yurt.

NOMADIC EXISTENCE
The collapse of the USSR has led to a revival of traditional ways of life among the nomads of central Asia. Goods that were made in factories, such as felt which is used to line the inside of nomads' tents, ceased to be available and now have to be made by hand using traditional methods. The same is true when it comes to moving home. In recent years, many nomads have moved their belongings around in motor vehicles, but petrol is now in very short supply and nomads have returned to using camels and horses.

ROLE OF WOMEN
Women's lives differ hugely over such a large continent, influenced by each nation's culture, religion, and politics. In some areas, such as India and the Islamic countries of the Middle East, the vast majority of the workforce is male. Yet Islamic women in southeast Asian countries such as Indonesia often work outside the home. In other areas, such as communist China and North Korea, and the former communist republics of the USSR, women make up a large proportion of the workforce and carry out most household chores.

Women in the workforce

This chart shows the percentage of men and women in the workforce in five countries.

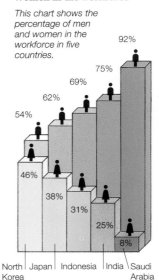

	North Korea	Japan	Indonesia	India	Saudi Arabia
Men	54%	62%	69%	75%	92%
Women	46%	38%	31%	25%	8%

RUSSIAN FEDERATION

STRETCHING ACROSS two continents – Europe and Asia – and extending halfway around the globe, the Russian Federation is by far the largest country in the world. Because of the bitterly cold climate and harsh living conditions, this vast land is sparsely populated. However, Russia has areas of fertile land, rich mineral deposits, and abundant natural resources. The country was once the head of a powerful communist state, the Union of Soviet Socialist Republics (USSR). After the collapse of communism in 1991, many parts of the old Soviet Union declared independence. The government of the newly formed Russian Federation are now struggling to establish a Western-style democracy and economy.

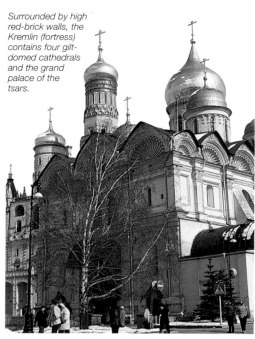

Surrounded by high red-brick walls, the Kremlin (fortress) contains four gilt-domed cathedrals and the grand palace of the tsars.

St Petersburg
Jan -10°C (14°F)
July 17°C (63°F)
Jan 35 mm (1.4 in)
July 72 mm (2.8 in)

RUSSIAN FEDERATION

Perm
Jan -17°C (2°F)
July 19°C (65°F)
Jan 40 mm (1.6 in)
July 89 mm (3.5 in)

THINGS TO LOOK FOR ON THE MAP

Longest river: Lena, 4,261 km (2,648 miles) *Map N6*

Highest point: Klyuchevsk, 4,750 m (15,585 ft) *Map T5*

Largest lake: Baikal, 31,468 sq km (12,150 sq miles) *Map M10*

World's largest straits: Tatar Strait, 800 km (497 miles) long *Map S9*

POLITICAL CHANGE

The Moscow Kremlin reflects the changing political face of Russia. Once the home of the tsars (emperors), who ruled Russia for many centuries, it later became the headquarters of the world's first communist government in 1917. The government created the USSR, which became an industrial and military superpower, but at great cost to its people. The communist state collapsed in 1991, and the Kremlin is now the symbolic home of the new rulers of the Russian Federation.

VOLGA RIVER
The mighty Volga River rises northwest of Moscow and flows 3,530 km (2,193 miles) southwards to the Caspian Sea. The Volga is the most important inland waterway in Russia. Hundreds of ships use it every day to transport goods to vast industrial sites that lie alongside the river. Six huge dams have created a string of reservoirs providing water and electricity for the people who live on or near its banks.

138

J K L M N O P Q R S T U

1 2 3 4 5 6 7 8 9 10 11 12

Verkhoyansk
Jan -51°C (-59°F)
July 14°C (57°F)
Jan 5 mm (0.2 in)
July 28 mm (1.1 in)

Franz Josef Land

Wrangel I.

CHUKCHI SEA

EAST SIBERIAN SEA

Pevek

C. Navarin

Pioner I.

October Revolution I.

Severnaya Zemlya

Ayon I.

Bolshevik I.

Bear Is.

C. Chelyuskin

Ambarchik

New Siberian Islands

LAPTEV SEA

C. Olyutorskiy

TAYMYR PENINSULA

L. Taymyr

Tiksi

Indigirka

Kalyma

OLOY RANGE

KORYAK RANGE

BERING SEA

Bay
Belyy I.

CENTRAL SIBERIAN PLATEAU

Olenk

Korkodon

Ossora

Karaginskiy Is.

GYDA PENINSULA

Pyasina

Khatanga

Anabar

Verkhoyansk

Adycha

KOLYMA RANGE

C. Sivuchiy

Noril'sk

PUTORANA MTS.

Olenëk

Bytantay

Sartang

Magadan

Ust'-Kamchatsk

Klyuchevsk

Nakhodka

Lena

VERKHOYANSK RANGE

Yana

KAMCHATKA

R U S S I A N

Taz

S I B E R I A

Vilyuy

Yakutsk

Okhotsk

Petropavlovsk-Kamchatskiy

Oktyabr'skiy

Lower Tunguska

Amga

Aldan

DZHUGDZHUR RANGE

Moya

SEA OF OKHOTSK

C. Lopatka

F E D E R A T I O N

Yenisey

Stony Tunguska

Lena

Olëkma

Paramushir Is.

Ket'

Angara

Vitim

C. Yelizavety

Okha

The Kurile Islands are administered by the Russian Federation, but claimed by Japan.

Tomsk

Ust'-Ilimsk

STANOVOY RANGE

Zeya Res.

Sakhalin

Kurile Islands

osibirsk

Achinsk

Krasnoyarsk

Kansk

Bratsk

Skovorodino

Komsomol'sk-na-Amure

Sovetskaya Gavan'

Poronaysk

Kemerovo

Svobodnyy

Talar Strait

ovokuznetsk

Abakan

Oka

L. Baikal

Romanovka

Chita

Shilka

Svobodnyy

Blagoveshchensk

Khabarovsk

Yuzhno-Sakhalinsk

naul

Biysk

Irkutsk

C H I N A

Amur

SEA OF JAPAN

Kyzyl

Ulan-Ude

Olovyannaya

Ussuri

M O N G O L I A

Vladivostok

PACIFIC OCEAN

0   200   400   600 km

0   100   200   300   400 miles

NORTH KOREA

SIBERIA

To the east of the Ural Mountains lies Siberia, a vast tract of largely uninhabited land that stretches across to the Pacific Ocean. Most of Siberia is covered with coniferous forest known as the taiga, which contains about a quarter of the world's wood reserves. In the north, the forest thins out as the climate gets colder and the land becomes a barren waste, called tundra. Here, the ground remains frozen throughout the year.

SIBERIAN WILDLIFE

The forests of Siberia provide a vital source of food for animals, such as reindeer, bears, and squirrels, especially during the long winter months. The region is also home to the largest tiger in the world, the Siberian tiger, which has thick fur to withstand the bitter winters.

Arctic ground squirrel

RUSSIAN FEDERATION

THE URAL MOUNTAINS form the boundary between European and Asian Russia. European Russia lies to the west of the mountains. This vast stretch of land is home to more than 100 million people, two-thirds of the entire Russian population. Most people live in the big cities of Moscow – the capital of the country – and St Petersburg, or along the Volga river valley. The land is rich in minerals. It is also intensively farmed, with wheat and other grains in the north giving way to tobacco, citrus fruit, and a variety of crops in the warmer south.

RUSSIAN FEDERATION

Capital city: Moscow	
Area: 173,750,400 sq km (6,592,800 sq miles)	
Population: 147,021,869	
Official language: Russian	
Major religions: Russian Orthodox 75%, other 25%	
Government: Multi-party democracy	
Currency: Rouble	
Adult literacy rate: 99%	
Life expectancy: 70 years	
People per doctor: 210	
Televisions: No figures available	

ST PETERSBURG

With its network of canals and rivers, the elegant city of St Petersburg is known as the "Venice of the North". It is a centre for arts and culture, and has many fine 18th century buildings. It was the capital of Russia between 1713 and 1917. Under communist rule the city was renamed Leningrad to honour Lenin, the leader of the 1917 Russian revolution. With the collapse of communism in 1991, it reverted to its old name.

Potatoes are grown on a huge scale in Russia. The large, open fields are ploughed into furrows and then the potatoes are planted in neat rows by machine.

At harvest time, the potatoes are dug out of the ground.

The potatoes are sorted and graded according to size and condition.

AGRICULTURE

Because of the harsh climate, only 10 per cent of Russian land is used for growing crops, mostly in an area known as the "fertile triangle" (see map right). The country is the world's leading producer of barley, oats, rye, and potatoes, and the world's third biggest producer of wheat. During the 1950s a vast area of barren land in south-central Russia was cultivated, the largest expansion of agriculture this century. The new wheat fields freed up more fertile areas in the west to grow fodder for animals.

The fertile triangle

Most of Russia's crops are grown in "the fertile triangle" which stetches from St Petersburg and the Ukraine in the west to southern Siberia in the east.

RUSSIAN BALLET
Ballet arrived in Russia from France in the 19th century, thanks to close cultural and diplomatic ties between Paris and St Petersburg, the old Russian capital. By the early 20th century, Russia had transformed traditional ballet, making it more creative and exciting. Today, the Bolshoi Ballet of Moscow and the Kirov Ballet of St Petersburg are known throughout the world.

RELIGIOUS REVIVAL

The Russian Orthodox Church was suppressed for many years by the former Soviet government, but became legal once more with the ending of communism. Today churches and monasteries are reopening across the country, and many people regularly attend religious services. As Russian society continues to change rapidly, the unchanging traditions of the Orthodox Church are a great comfort to many people.

The head of the Russian Orthodox Church is known as the "Patriarch of Moscow and All Russia".

FOOD AND DRINK

The basic Russian diet, consisting of grain, potatoes, oil, and sugar, tends to be fattening. Fresh fruit, vegetables, and meat are regarded as a luxury. In the last few years, however, increased food production and a better system of supply has led to a wider range of foods on sale in the big cities.

Sour cream

Borscht, a soup made from beetroot.

Vodka, a strong alcohol made from grain or potatoes, is the national drink. Alcoholism is a problem throughout Russia.

Black bread made from hard wheat.

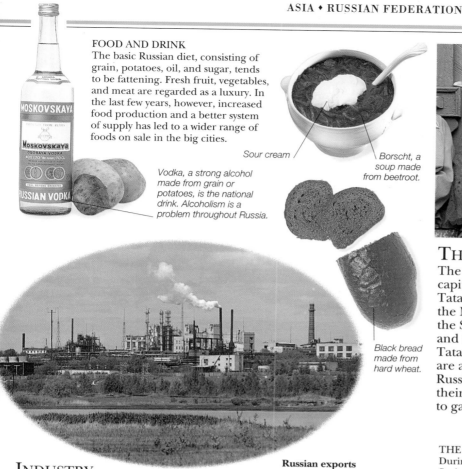

THE TATARS

The ancient town of Kazan, on the Volga, is the capital of Tatarstan, home to more than 4 million Tatars. These Islamic peoples are descendants of the Mongols, who overran Russia in 1240. Under the Soviet Union, the Tatars were suppressed and their Islamic mosques closed. Today the Tatars – along with other non-Russian peoples – are asserting their independence within the Russian Federation. The Tatars are reviving their traditional customs, and are taking steps to gain control of the local economy.

INDUSTRY

The former Soviet Union invested heavily in its industry. Vast industrial complexes were built in the iron-rich Ural Mountains and in the Kuzbass coalfield of southern Siberia. The production of coal, iron, and other minerals soared, and heavy industries, such as engineering, steel, iron, and chemical production, dominated the economy. However, Russia is now paying a price for this big advance. Many factories are old and inefficient, polluting the environment with harmful emissions.

Russian exports

Machinery and industrial equipment: 43%
Petroleum and gas: 15%
Iron and steel: 12%
Food and cereals: 4%
Wood and paper: 6%
Other: 9%
Chemicals: 11%

THE MOSCOW METRO

During the 1930s, the Soviet government built a huge underground railway system beneath the streets of Moscow. The system is fast and efficient and is used daily by more than 7 million people. The stations were built deep down in the ground so that they could be used as air-raid shelters during wartime. Many are beautifully decorated with paintings, sculptures, and mosaics.

The range of goods on offer in Russian cities is slowly expanding and new shops are opening daily.

MARKET ECONOMY

The old state-run, planned economy collapsed with the break-up of the Soviet Union. It is being replaced with a market economy based on profit, as in western Europe and the USA. Old state-run enterprises are being turned into private businesses. Many international companies are now investing in the new Russia.

WOMEN WORKERS

Many more Russian men than women died during World War II and in the labour camps set up by the Soviet leader Stalin. As a result, there are far more women than men in Russia, and women make up more than 50 per cent of the workforce. Good child care and medical services enable women with children to go out to work. Many work on the railways or drive buses and trams. Most factories have large female workforces and many professions, such as medicine, dentistry, and teaching, are dominated by women.

This woman worker is helping to clear heavy snow in Moscow.

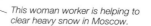

RUSSIAN FEDERATION

TO THE EAST of the Ural Mountains lies Asian Russia. This vast expanse of land, known as Siberia, is bigger than the combined size of the USA and western Europe. Yet, because of the harsh climate, only 40 million people live here. Parts of Siberia are colder in winter than the North Pole. To the north are frozen plains, or tundra, while further south it is just warm enough to grow some hardy crops. For centuries, Siberia remained undeveloped, home only to peoples who trapped animals for their meat and fur and caught fish in the local rivers. But the discovery of minerals, such as gold and diamonds, has opened the region up to economic and industrial development.

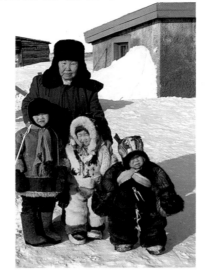

KAMCHATKA

Hanging off the eastern end of Siberia, the Kamchatka Peninsula is one of the most isolated parts of Russia. Under the Soviet Union, Kamchatka bristled with military bases because of its closeness to both Japan and the USA. Today the military presence is reduced and people are returning to more traditional ways of making a living. Once more, people are fishing in the many rivers, herding reindeer, or hunting seals, sea otters, and bears for their skins.

Major mineral deposits

Moscow

URAL MTS

Omsk

Trans-Siberian railway

Vladivostock

RAW MATERIALS

Siberia is rich in natural resources, with huge reserves of oil, gas, coal, metals, diamonds, and gold. The Trans-Siberian railway transports vast amounts of minerals from Siberia to European Russia. Western Siberia contains one-third of the world's natural gas reserves, as well as a huge oilfield producing 8.4 million barrels of oil a day, more than two-thirds of the entire Russian output. Development of these resources, however, is difficult, for the climate is harsh and laying pipelines to carry fuel over such long distances is expensive.

- Coal
- Gas
- Oil
- Copper
- Diamonds
- Gold
- Iron

The elegant dining car of the Trans-Siberian Express.

THE TRANS-SIBERIAN RAILWAY

The Trans-Siberian railway is the world's longest continuous rail line. It begins at Moscow's Yaroslavl station in the west and stretches 9,440 km (5,866 miles) across to Vladivostok in the east. Trains cross eight time zones and take eight days to complete the journey. In recent years the line has become increasingly congested. New lines, including the Baikal-Amur Mainline, have been built alongside to relieve this problem.

The boxes are often decorated with scenes from fairy tales.

CLOSED AND SECRET CITIES

Under Soviet Union rule, two types of city were out of bounds for security reasons to all but an authorized few. Closed cities, including Vladivostok (shown left), were sites of military or industrial importance. Secret cities were places of research in chemical and nuclear warfare. They did not appear on a map and were located in remote areas surrounded by no-go zones and patrolled by armed guards. Today, most of the closed cities are open to visitors, but the secret cities remain out of bounds.

ARTS AND CRAFTS

The rise in Russian nationalism has been accompanied by a return to traditional crafts, folk tales, and music and dance. Skilled craftworkers make boxes and other items from wood or *papier mâché*. The lacquered boxes are decorated with miniature paintings.

Hand-painted Russian chess set.

CHESS

The ancient game of chess became popular in Russia as a way of spending long, dark winter evenings by the fireside. Today, chess is still widely played here. Russian Grand Masters such as Karpov and Spassky have dominated world chess tournaments. During a big match, giant chessboards are displayed in big city squares for the public to follow the competitors' moves.

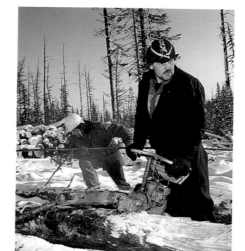

FORESTRY

The taïga forest of northern Russia and Siberia provides work in logging, paper production, chemicals, and furniture making. In the past, most forestry jobs were in the more accessible parts of northern Russia. But many of these forests have been cleared, and new seedlings take up to 80 years to produce mature wood. As a result, the centre of the forestry industry has moved south and east into Siberia. Today, most timber production is located in southern Siberia near Lake Baikal or on the Amur River near the Pacific coast.

LIVING IN A COLD CLIMATE

The Yakut people of eastern Siberia are used to living in a cold climate, as winter temperatures drop to –43°C (–45°F). Engines are kept running 24 hours a day to prevent them freezing up. Drinking water is delivered as chunks of ice sawn out of the local river. Even during the brief summer, most ground remains frozen hard. Houses are often built on raised concrete platforms or wooden stilts to protect them from frost damage.

Window frames are often attractively decorated.

Food is stored in bags outside the windows and defrosted when needed.

The Yakut survive the winter by wearing many layers of warm clothing made from animal skins and fur. People wear felt or reindeer-fur boots, as leather freezes and cracks quickly.

Milk is sold in frozen brick form with wooden handles inserted so that it can be carried home easily.

A sled pulled by dogs or reindeer is a traditional way of travelling through the snow.

The Yakut people make their living by herding reindeer in the north of the region and rearing cattle in the centre.

Windows are triple-glazed to keep out the cold. The air between the three layers of glass acts as insulation.

Fur hats with ear-flaps protect their wearers from Russian winters.

FUR FARMS

For centuries, hunters and trappers have worked the Siberian forests to catch ermine, mink, sable, lynx, and fox. In order to protect some species from over-hunting, the Soviet government introduced fur farms, where breeders raise rare animals for their furs. Furs from Siberian animals are turned into hats, coats, and linings for boots and gloves.

LAKE BAIKAL

Known as the "blue eye of Siberia", Lake Baikal in southeastern Siberia covers 31,468 sq km (12,150 sq miles) and is up to 1,940 m (6,367 ft) deep. It is the deepest lake in the world and the largest freshwater lake, containing more than 20 per cent of the world's entire supply of fresh water. In recent years, logging and chemical industries have polluted the water, prompting a major campaign to protect this unique environment.

Lake Baikal is home to the world's only freshwater seal, the Baikal seal. A wide variety of flora and fauna, unique to the area, are found in and around the lake.

Find out more
BREAK-UP OF USSR: *136*
FORESTRY: *69, 86, 244*
ORTHODOX CHURCH: *274*
POLITICAL SYSTEMS: *270–271*

TURKEY

TURKEY LIES PARTLY IN EUROPE and partly in Asia, and is divided by a narrow waterway. For more than 600 years, Turkey was part of the powerful Ottoman Empire. Today, Turkey is a republic and the country is a mix of Islamic and Western traditions. Most people are Turkish-speaking Muslims, although there is no official state religion. Turkey has a varied landscape and climate, and is a popular tourist destination. Many types of crop are grown, and the country is self-sufficient in food.

TURKEY	
Capital city: Ankara	
Area: 779,450 sq km (300,950 sq miles)	
Population: 59,600,000	
Official language: Turkish	
Major religions: Muslim 99%, other 1%	
Government: Multi-party democracy	
Currency: Turkish lira	
Adult literacy rate: 82%	
Life expectancy: 67 years	
People per doctor: 1,260	
Televisions: 174 per 1,000 people	

CYPRUS	
Capital city: Nicosia	
Area: 9,251 sq km (3,572 sq miles)	
Population: 700,000	
Official languages: Greek and Turkish	
Major religions: Christian 77%, Muslim 23%	
Government: Multi-party democracy	
Currency: Cyprus pound and Turkish lira	
Adult literacy rate: 94%	
Life expectancy: 77 years	
People per doctor: 750	
Televisions: 207 per 1,000 people	

KEMAL ATATURK
Kemal Ataturk was the founder and first president of the modern state of Turkey after the collapse of the Ottoman Empire in the early 20th century. He brought about many reforms in Turkish society, including greater freedom for women and better education for all.

This depiction of Kemal Ataturk towers over Antalya, in southern Turkey.

THE KURDS
The Kurds, numbering about 25 million, are one of the largest groups of people in the world who have no homeland. They live in a mountainous area split between four countries: Turkey, Iran, Iraq, and Syria. The Kurds have sought to form their own state – Kurdistan.

Kurdish children living in Harran in Turkey.

AGRICULTURE
About half of the Turkish workforce is employed in agriculture – growing crops such as wheat, cotton, tobacco, sugar beet, and fruit. Tea is grown along the Black Sea coast and is a popular drink. Much of the work in the fields is done by women. With plenty of fertile farmland, Turkey can produce enough food not only for its own needs, but for export too.

EPHESUS
Each year, millions of tourists visit Turkey for its sunny weather, sandy beaches, and ancient sites. These include the ruined city of Ephesus on the Aegean coast, famous for its huge, open-air theatre, carved out of the hillside in the first century AD, with seating for 24,000 people. Tourism is one of Turkey's major industries.

MARKETS
Bustling street markets, or bazaars, are a common sight in many Turkish towns and cities. Turkey is famous for its arts and crafts, particularly for its fine carpets, pottery, beaten copperware, and leatherwork. Carpets are woven from silk, wool, and cotton and decorated with beautiful geometric and floral designs, often symbolizing the maker's family or area of origin.

This carpet stall is in the Grand Bazaar in Kusadasi in western Turkey.

STREET CAFÉS
Street cafés are popular meeting places, especially with men. They visit them to drink tea or Turkish coffee, smoke pipes, and chat. Games, such as cards or backgammon, are often played.

Men smoke pipes called hubble-bubbles. Smoke is drawn into the mouth through a long tube.

Rich, dark Turkish coffee is a popular drink.

Men often play cards in street cafés.

Istanbul, Turkey
☀ Jan 5.5°C (41.5°F)
July 23°C (73.5°F)
🌧 Jan 109 mm (4 in)
July 34 mm (1.3 in)

Kars, Turkey
☀ Jan -12°C (10°F)
July 17°C (63°F)
🌧 Jan 28 mm (1.1 in)
July 53 mm (2.1 in)

THINGS TO LOOK FOR ON THE MAP
Longest river: Kizil Irmak, 1,151 km
(715 miles) *Map F5*

Highest point: Mt. Ararat, 5,123 m (16,800 ft)
Map K6

Largest lake: L. Van, 3,763 sq km
(1,453 sq miles) *Map K6*

World's only city on two continents: Istanbul
Map C5

TURKEY

Nicosia, Cyprus
☀ Jan 10°C (50.5°F)
July 29°C (84°F)
🌧 Jan 76 mm (3.0 in)
July 1 mm (0 in)

CYPRUS

ISTANBUL

Istanbul is the only city in the world to lie in two
continents. It is split between Europe and Asia by
a narrow channel of water called the Bosphorus.
Bridges link the two parts of the city. Istanbul is a
mixture of old and new, eastern and western, with
elegant mosques side-by-side with sprawling slums.
It is Turkey's largest city and main port. Until the
move to Ankara in 1923, it was also Turkey's capital.

CYPRUS

CYPRUS IS A LARGE,
picturesque island in the
eastern Mediterranean,
popular as a tourist
destination. It was under
Turkish, then British control
until its independence in
1959. The majority of the
islanders are Greeks; about
a fifth are Turkish. Conflict
between the two groups led
to the division of the island
in 1974, into the Greek south
and Turkish north.

*This house stands on Hermes Street in
Nicosia, the capital of Cyprus. The street
marks the division between the Greek
south and Turkish north. Turkey is the
only country to recognize Turkish
Northern Cyprus officially.*

Find out more
CARPET MAKING: *155,
165, 210*
ISLAM: *275*
TEA: *172, 238*

THE NEAR EAST

BETWEEN EUROPE AND THE MIDDLE EAST, at the eastern edge of the Mediterranean Sea, lies the region known as the Near East. The area includes the countries of Israel, Lebanon, Jordan, and Syria. It is the birthplace of some of the world's oldest civilizations and has close ties with three major religions – Judaism, Christianity, and Islam. The land is mostly dry and barren, particularly to the east, but is lusher and more fertile along the Mediterranean coast. After centuries of invasion by Arabs, Christian Crusaders, and Turks, the present-day countries took shape in the last 100 years. Since then, they have been plagued by civil wars and conflicts.

A LAND OF CONTRASTS
A range of mountains stretches from Lebanon in the north to Israel in the south, which contrasts with the deserts to the east and the coast to the west. In Lebanon, the mountains drop away to rich, fertile plains where cereal crops are grown. The mountain tops are covered in snow for most of the year and are popular with skiers.

Noisy or smelly market stalls, such as those belonging to metalsmiths (above) or leatherworkers, are placed at a distance from the main mosque.

A CITY IN THE NEAR EAST

Many traditional Muslim cities follow a distinctive pattern. At the heart of the city is the main mosque, which is usually the largest building. This is surrounded by other important buildings and market stalls. The narrow, irregular streets which radiate out towards the city walls provide shade and keep down wind and dust. Privacy is important – doors opening on to narrow streets must not face each other.

The main mosque stands at the centre of the city.

Streets are narrow and irregular.

The market stalls selling religious goods, such as candles, incense, and books (above), are placed closest to the main mosque in the centre of the city.

Many houses face on to courtyards.

PALESTINE

In 1948, the Jewish state of Israel was created from the country of Palestine, the ancient land of the Jews and the home of the Palestinian Arabs. Thousands of Palestinians were driven from their homes and land. Many went to live in the neighbouring Arab territories of the West Bank and the Gaza Strip. In 1967, Israel captured and occupied these areas. Recently, peace agreements have been reached between Arab and Israeli leaders, giving Palestinians some control of the Gaza Strip and the West Bank city of Jericho.

Yasser Arafat is the leader of the Palestine Liberation Organization (PLO), which represents the interests of Palestinian Arabs.

Gaza Strip   **West Bank**

Dead Sea

▲ Israeli settlements
● Major cities

THE DEAD SEA
On the border between Israel and Jordan lies a large lake known as the Dead Sea. It is the lowest place on Earth – some 400 m (1,312 ft) below sea level. Salt deposits rise up like pillars out of the water. No fish can live there, which is how the lake got its name. Mud from the shores of the Dead Sea is said to have healing properties.

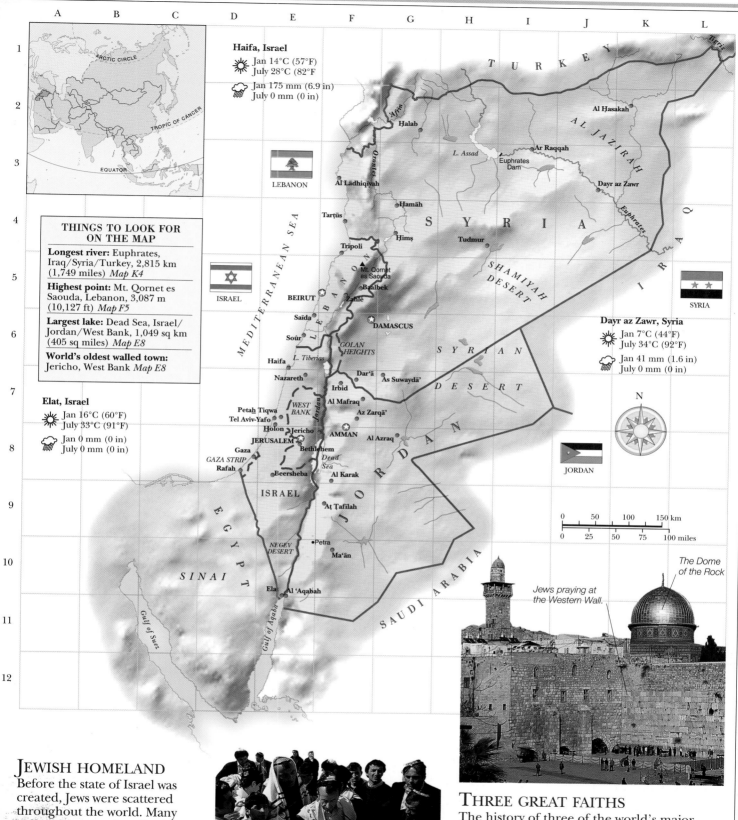

Haifa, Israel
☀ Jan 14°C (57°F)
   July 28°C (82°F)
🌧 Jan 175 mm (6.9 in)
   July 0 mm (0 in)

LEBANON

ISRAEL

SYRIA

Dayr az Zawr, Syria
☀ Jan 7°C (44°F)
   July 34°C (92°F)
🌧 Jan 41 mm (1.6 in)
   July 0 mm (0 in)

JORDAN

THINGS TO LOOK FOR ON THE MAP

Longest river: Euphrates, Iraq/Syria/Turkey, 2,815 km (1,749 miles) *Map K4*

Highest point: Mt. Qornet es Saouda, Lebanon, 3,087 m (10,127 ft) *Map F5*

Largest lake: Dead Sea, Israel/Jordan/West Bank, 1,049 sq km (405 sq miles) *Map E8*

World's oldest walled town: Jericho, West Bank *Map E8*

Elat, Israel
☀ Jan 16°C (60°F)
   July 33°C (91°F)
🌧 Jan 0 mm (0 in)
   July 0 mm (0 in)

TURKEY

Al Ḥasakah
Ḥalab
AL JAZIRAH
L. Assad
Euphrates Dam
Ar Raqqah
Dayr az Zawr
Al Lādhiqīyah
Euphrates
Ḥamāh
Tartūs
SYRIA
Ḥimṣ
Tudmur
Tripoli
Mt. Qornet es Saouda
Baålbek
SHAMIYAH DESERT
Zahlé
BEIRUT
Saïda
DAMASCUS
IRAQ
Soûr
GOLAN HEIGHTS
SYRIAN
Haifa
L. Tiberias
Nazareth
Dar'ā
As Suwaydā'
DESERT
Irbid
WEST BANK
Al Mafraq
Petaḥ Tiqwa
Tel Aviv-Yafo
Az Zarqā'
Holon
Jericho
JERUSALEM
AMMAN
Al Azraq
Bethlehem
Gaza
Dead Sea
GAZA STRIP
Rafah
Beersheba
Al Karak
ISRAEL
JORDAN
EGYPT
Aṭ Ṭafīlah
SINAI
NEGEV DESERT
Petra
Ma'ān
Elat
Al 'Aqabah
Gulf of Aqaba
Gulf of Suez
SAUDI ARABIA

MEDITERRANEAN SEA

LEBANON

N

The Dome of the Rock

Jews praying at the Western Wall.

0   50   100   150 km
0   25   50   75   100 miles

JEWISH HOMELAND

Before the state of Israel was created, Jews were scattered throughout the world. Many suffered persecution. During World War II, 6 million Jews were killed by the Nazis in Germany. After the war, thousands of Jews from all over the world emigrated to Israel, the home of their ancestors.

THREE GREAT FAITHS

The history of three of the world's major religions is closely linked to the Near East. Judaism and Christianity began here, whilst Islam spread to the region from nearby Saudi Arabia. Jerusalem in Israel is a holy city for all three faiths. The Dome of the Rock, sacred to Muslims, and the Western Wall, sacred to Jews, stand on the same site.

SYRIA

SYRIA IS AN ANCIENT LAND. Its capital, Damascus, is one of the world's oldest cities. Because of its important position on major trade routes, Syria has been invaded and occupied many times – by the Romans, Arabs, Greeks, and Turks. After World War I, it came under French control, becoming independent in 1946. Since then Syria has been involved in several wars with Israel. Most Syrians are Muslim and speak Arabic. More than half of Syria is desert, but the river floodplains provide fertile land.

SYRIA	
Capital city: Damascus	
Area: 185,180 sq km (71,498 sq miles)	
Population: 13,800,000	
Official language: Arabic	
Major religions: Muslim 90%, Christian 10%	
Government: One party dictatorship	
Currency: Syrian pound	
Adult literacy rate: 67%	
Life expectancy: 66 years	
People per doctor: 1,160	
Televisions: 60 per 1,000 people	

PALMYRA

The rich and varied history of Syria is reflected in the many ancient ruins from past civilizations found scattered throughout the country. In the 3rd century AD, Palmyra, with its palaces, temples, and theatres, was a flourishing city, but it was destroyed by the Romans for refusing to give up its independence. It lies in an oasis on the edge of the desert, and is one of the best preserved ancient cities in the world.

MARKET LIFE

Markets, or *souks*, are held in villages and towns throughout Syria. The *souks* are lively, bustling places, with market stalls set out on winding alleyways, selling anything from spices and vegetables, to carpets, jewellery, basketwork, and coffee pots. People come here to buy and sell, meet their friends, and haggle (bargain) over prices. *Souks* are more than just trading centres, they are a central feature of the Arab way of life.

Craftsmen and women are often seen working at their stalls in the souk: beating and engraving copper, carving wood, and weaving baskets.

The stalls selling fresh bread, fruit, and vegetables jostle for space with the craft stalls.

THE GOLAN HEIGHTS

The mountainous area known as the Golan Heights was seized from Syria by Israel in 1967. It is important to the Israelis because it overlooks the Hula Valley in Israel, offering a good strategic position. It is a major issue in recent peace talks between the two countries, and it has been suggested that the Golan Heights should become a non-military zone and be returned to Syria.

MUSLIM GROUPS

The majority of Syrians belong to the traditionally powerful Sunni Muslim group. But there are other Muslim sects, such as the Shi'as, Ismailis, and Alawis. The Alawis believe not only in Islam, but in some aspects of Christianity. For example, they celebrate Christmas and Easter. The Alawis were persecuted in the past, but many have now become rich and powerful. President Assad of Syria is himself an Alawi Muslim.

A minaret (tower) on a Muslim mosque, from which the faithful are called to prayer five times a day.

THE EUPHRATES DAM

The Euphrates River flows through the northeast of Syria, on its journey from Turkey to Iraq. A gigantic dam has been built across the river to harness the power of the water and produce hydro-electricity. The dam's hydro-electric plants now provide three-quarters of Syria's electricity. A huge lake, Lake Assad, was also created by the dam. Water from the lake is used to grow crops.

LEBANON

LEBANON IS A SMALL COUNTRY at the eastern end of the Mediterranean, bordered by Syria and Israel. The people of Lebanon are mostly Arabs, belonging to a great variety of religious groups. Lebanon was once the cultural and business centre of the Near East. But in 1975, tensions between Muslim and Christian groups led to the outbreak of a violent civil war which almost destroyed the country. Peace terms were agreed in 1989 and some stability was restored.

LEBANON	
Capital city: Beirut	
Area: 10,400 sq km (4,015 sq miles)	
Population: 2,900,000	
Official language: Arabic	
Major religions: Muslim 75%, Christian 25%	
Government: Multi-party democracy	
Currency: Lebanese pound	
Adult literacy rate: 81%	
Life expectancy: 68 years	
People per doctor: 670	
Televisions: 325 per 1,000 people	

DRUZES
The Druze faith is an offshoot of Islam that is now considered a religion in its own right. There are about 200,000 Druzes in Lebanon, mainly living in the southern mountains. They have many customs designed to protect their community. It is impossible to become a Druze unless you are born one, and you cannot give up your faith. Marriage is only allowed within the community to ensure that the Druze faith continues.

RELIGIOUS GROUPS
The Lebanese population is a jigsaw of religious groups, including different Christian and Muslim sects. The largest Christian group is the Maronites, who practise a form of Catholicism. Other Christian groups include the Greek Orthodox and Greek Catholics. The Muslims are divided into the Sunnis and the Shi'as.

Although Beirut is no longer formally divided into Muslim West and Christian East, both groups have remained in their own area.

Beirut

☐ Greek Orthodox
☐ Maronites
■ Sunni Muslim
☐ Shi'a Muslim
■ Druze

REBUILDING BEIRUT
Before its destruction in the civil war, Beirut was a cultured and lively city. It was known as the "Paris of the East" and was one of the region's most important ports and business centres. Today, much of Lebanon's capital lies in ruins. The goverment has now launched an ambitious programme to rebuild the financial heart of the city and attract visitors back to Beirut.

Where people live

84% live in cities   16% live in the country

CEDAR TREES
The cedars of Lebanon are the country's symbol and appear on the national flag. In biblical times, great forests of cedar trees covered the slopes of the Lebanese mountains. Today, they survive only in a few protected groves. Some of these trees are more than 1,500 years old.

LEBANESE FOOD
The national dish of Lebanon is *kibbe*, made of lamb, burghul (cracked wheat), and onions, pounded together. The mixture is shaped into balls or patties and baked or fried. Sweet pastries, stuffed with nuts and dates and covered in honey, are also popular.

Sweet pastries

Kibbe is the Lebanese national dish.

TYRE AND SIDON
The civil war ruined Lebanon's thriving tourist industry. Attempts are now being made to attract visitors back to the country's fine beaches and historical sites, such as the two cities of Tyre and Sidon. These were built by the Phoenicians some 3,000 years ago and were famous in Roman times for their glassware and purple dyes.

Vegetables, such as swede, and spicy foods, such as chillies, are often eaten with the main meal.

Swede

Chillies

Find out more
LEBANESE FLAG: *147*
LEBANESE LANDSCAPE: *146*
RELIGION: *274–275*
WARS IN THE REGION: *146*

ISRAEL

ISRAEL IS A LONG, THIN STRIP of land running along the eastern coast of the Mediterranean Sea. Its landscape is varied, with fertile valleys, dry deserts, mountains, lakes, and rivers. It has a wide range of industries and a modern agricultural system. The state of Israel was created in 1948 as a homeland for Jews from all over the world. The country was previously called Palestine. Much of the Palestinian Arab population was forced to leave Israel and live as refugees in Jordan and Lebanon. This has created conflict between Israel, the Palestinians, and neighbouring Arab states ever since.

ISRAEL*	
Capital city: Jerusalem	
Area: 20,700 sq km (7,992 sq miles)	
Population: 5,400,000	
Official languages: Hebrew and Arabic	
Major religions: Judaism 82%, Muslim 14%, Christian 2%, other 2%	
Government: Multi-party democracy	
Currency: New shekel	
Adult literacy rate: 95%	
Life expectancy: 76 years	
People per doctor: 350	
Televisions: 260 per 1,000 people	

* Figures include the West Bank and Gaza Strip.

JERUSALEM
The city of Jerusalem is a holy place for Jews, Muslims, and Christians. Within the walls of the Old City is the Jewish Western Wall, the only remaining part of Herod's Temple, and the Temple Mount from where the Muslim prophet Mohammed rose up to heaven. The major Christian shrine is the Church of the Holy Sepulchre, the traditional site of Christ's burial and resurrection.

KIBBUTZ
Almost half of Israel's food is grown on large communal farms, called *kibbutzim*, on which many families live and work together. People share everyday tasks such as cleaning and cooking, as well as work on the farm. Use of computerized irrigation to water the land has made large areas of barren desert fertile.

Families live and work together on a kibbutz.

Some crops, such as tomatoes, are grown inside plastic greenhouses.

People from other countries, attracted by the way of life, come to stay and work on kibbutzim during busy periods.

Citrus fruits, such as oranges, lemons, and grapefruit, are grown.

Water is pumped through pipes to irrigate the land.

Efficient irrigation is essential for farming in a hot, dry climate.

AT PRAYER
Judaism is one of the world's oldest religions. Jews believe in one God and follow the teachings of the *Torah*, the first five books of the Bible. At prayer, many Jewish men wear blue-edged prayer shawls and small boxes called phylacteries, or *tephillin*, which contain verses from the *Torah*. Saturday is the Jewish holy day, or Sabbath.

Tephillin are worn on the head and left arm, near the heart, to show that God's teachings control a person's thoughts and feelings.

Knotted tassels serve to remind Jews of God's commandments.

Prayer shawl

ISRAELI SOLDIERS
Because of the conflict between Israel and the Palestinians, and repeated wars with neighbouring countries, the army plays a crucial part in Israeli life. From the age of 18, Israeli men and women must serve in the army for a number of years. Women receive the same training as men, but do not take part in direct combat.

DIAMOND CUTTING
About 25 per cent of Israel's export earnings come from its diamond industry. The rough diamonds are imported, and then skilfully cut and polished for use in jewellery settings.

Find out more
DIAMONDS: *226, 248*
IRRIGATION: *155, 156, 217*
JUDAISM: *275*
PALESTINE: *146*

JORDAN

JORDAN LIES TO THE NORTHWEST of the Arabian Peninsula. Apart from a short coastline along the Gulf of Aqaba, it is completely landlocked, or cut off from the sea. Much of eastern Jordan is desert, with mountains in the north and south. Most of its people are Muslim and speak Arabic. Jordan is a relatively new country (it became fully independent in 1946), but some of the world's oldest sites are found here. In recent years, the government has played a part in peace talks between the Israelis and their Arab neighbours.

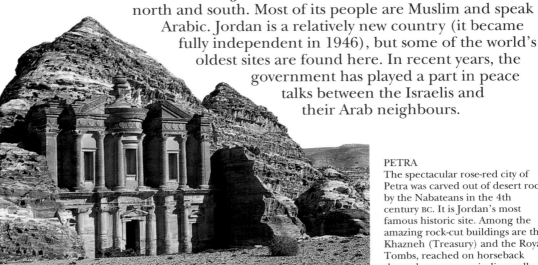

JORDAN

Capital city: Amman

Area: 89,210 sq km (34,444 sq miles)

Population: 4,453,000

Official language: Arabic

Major religions: Muslim 93%, other 7%

Government: Monarchy with democratic system

Currency: Jordanian dinar

Adult literacy rate: 82%

Life expectancy: 67 years

People per doctor: 770

Televisions: 81 per 1,000 people

PETRA
The spectacular rose-red city of Petra was carved out of desert rock by the Nabateans in the 4th century BC. It is Jordan's most famous historic site. Among the amazing rock-cut buildings are the Khazneh (Treasury) and the Royal Tombs, reached on horseback through a narrow, winding gully.

Ed-Deir (The Monastery) is the largest monument in Petra.

REFUGEE CAMPS
When Israel was formed in 1948, tens of thousands of Palestinians were forced to flee their homes and become refugees in Jordan and other Arab countries. More than 40 years later, they are still there. In Jordan alone, there are 1.8 million Palestinian refugees. Many have been born and brought up in refugee camps. This Palestinian refugee camp is near Amman.

Houses being built in Amman.

POPULATION GROWTH
The population of Jordan, roughly equally divided between Jordanians and Palestinian refugees, is growing rapidly. Providing housing, jobs, schools, and healthcare for the growing number of people is one of the Jordanian government's most urgent problems.

In millions

Population growth in Jordan

1978 1984 1988 1993

GULF OF AQABA
The Gulf of Aqaba is the narrow, northeastern arm of the Red Sea between Saudi Arabia and the Sinai Peninsula. It is 160 km (99 miles) long and up to 27 km (17 miles) wide. At its head lies Jordan's one seaport, Aqaba. This short stretch of coastline is Jordan's only outlet to the sea. It is also popular with holidaymakers.

RIVER JORDAN
Water is in short supply throughout the Near East. Control of the River Jordan, which forms the border between Jordan and Israel, has become an important issue in peace talks between the two countries. Jordan, a relatively poor country, has a particular need for a greater share of the water to irrigate its land and produce more crops.

Find out more

ANCIENT SITES: *134*
ISLAM: *275*
NEAR EAST HISTORY: *146–147*
POPULATION GROWTH: *16–17*

THE MIDDLE EAST

THE MIDDLE EAST IS IN SOUTHWEST ASIA. Much of the area is covered by dry, barren desert or rugged mountains. Earlier this century, large deposits of oil were discovered around the Persian Gulf. Today, oil is the main source of income for many Middle Eastern countries. Historically, the Middle East was the site of the world's first cities and the birthplace of one of the world's great religions – Islam. The majority of the population today is Muslim and the most widely spoken language is Arabic. In recent years, the region has suffered a series of wars and conflicts between neighbouring countries.

ROCKY DESERT
Part of the Middle East is rocky desert, where the bare rock floor has been stripped clean by intense heat, drying winds, and occasional but heavy rainstorms.

Sand dunes are created by a build-up of sand carried along by strong winds.

Sand storms arise when strong winds blow sand and dust across the desert, causing the sky to darken.

Settlements may grow up around oases – these are often created by water coming to the surface through a fault (split) in the rock.

When the wind blows in one direction, it causes a ripple effect in the sand.

Some hardy plants can survive all year in the desert because their long roots collect water over a wide area.

Bedouin nomads face a constant fight for survival as they move from place to place with their animals in search of food and water.

DESERT
Apart from fertile patches of land along the Tigris and Euphrates rivers, by the coast, and near isolated oases, much of the Middle East is covered by hot, dry deserts, both rocky and sandy. These include the Rub'Al Khali, the Empty Quarter, a vast sandy desert in Saudi Arabia. Large areas of desert are uninhabited because of the lack of water for drinking and farming.

OIL PRODUCTION
More than 65 per cent of the world's oil is found in the Middle East, and the region supplies almost a third of the world's daily oil production. The discovery of oil has brought great wealth to the Middle East, leading to rapid industrial and social change in a formerly underdeveloped region. It has also greatly increased the region's international importance and influence on world affairs.

Drilling for oil

Drilling rig

Distribution of oil production in the Middle East

Yemen and Bahrain: 1.3%
Iraq: 2.5%
Qatar: 2.6%
Oman: 4%
Kuwait: 10.5%
United Arab Emirates: 13%
Iran: 19.5%
Saudi Arabia: 46.6%

Oil wells are drilled deep down into the ground to extract the oil trapped between layers of rock.

WARFARE
In recent years, the Middle East has been constantly troubled by wars, in which thousands of people have lost their lives. In 1980, the long-standing rivalry and border disputes between Iran and Iraq erupted into a war which lasted until 1988. At the start of the Gulf War in 1990, Iraq invaded Kuwait and an international force, led by the USA, intervened.

Rusting tanks in Iraq serve as a reminder of recent warfare.

A sign marks part of the border between Iran and Iraq.

DISPUTED BORDERS
Many Middle Eastern countries are relatively new, created earlier this century when the region was divided up by its Western rulers. These artificial divisions, sometimes poorly defined, have led to many border disputes, especially between Iraq and its six neighbouring countries.

ARCTIC CIRCLE
TROPIC OF CANCER
EQUATOR

0 100 200 300 400 500 km
0 100 200 300 miles

AZERBAIJAN

THINGS TO LOOK FOR ON THE MAP

Longest river: Euphrates, Iraq/Syria, 2,815 km
(1,749 miles) *Map E5*

Highest point: Qolleh-ye-Damāvand, Iran,
5,671 m (18,605 ft) *Map H4*

World's largest oilfield: Ghawar, Saudi Arabia,
8,400 sq km (3,243 sq miles) *Map F8*

IRAN

Tehran, Iran
Jan 2°C (36°F)
July 30°C (86°F)
Jan 46 mm (1.8 in)
July 3 mm (0.1 in)

TURKEY
ARMENIA
AZERBAIJAN
TURKMENISTAN

L. Urmia
Tabrīz
Orūmīyeh
Ardabīl
CASPIAN SEA
Mosul
Irbīl
Rasht
SYRIA
Kirkuk
Zanjān
As Sulaymānīyah
IRAQ
Qazvīn
Sārī
ELBURZ MTS.
Mashhad
Wādī Hawrān
Diyālā
Sanandaj
Karaj
TEHRAN
Qolleh-ye-Damāvand
KUWAIT
Ar-Ramādī
Bakhtarān
Qom
Semnān
Babylon
BAGHDAD
DASHT-E KAVIR
Karbala
Arāk
Al-Hillah
An-Najaf
Wādī 'Ar'ar
Kāshān
BAHRAIN
Al 'Amārah
Dezfūl
Eşfahān
Ur
An Nāsirīyah
Eşfahān
I R A N
Gulf of Aqaba
L. al Hammar
Ahvāz
EGYPT
Al-Basrah
Ābādān
Yazd
QATAR
Tabūk
Yāsūj
KUWAIT
AN NAFUD
ZAGROS MTS.
L. Sīstān
AFGHANISTAN
Kermān
DASHT-E LUT
Hā'il
KUWAIT CITY
Shīrāz
UNITED ARAB
EMIRATES
RED SEA
Buraydah
Persian Gulf
Bandar-e-Būshehr
Zāhedān
Medina
NEJD
Jaz Mūriān Salt Lake
Ad Dammām
Bandar-e 'Abbās
PAKISTAN
OMAN
Ghawar Oilfield
BAHRAIN
Khasab (to Oman)
SAUDI
MANAMA
Strait of Hormuz
SAN'A
Al Hufūf
DOHA
Sharjah
Dubai
RIYADH
Harad
Gulf of Oman
Al Khābūrah
ARABIA
ABU DHABI
UNITED ARAB
EMIRATES
MUSCAT
Jedda
Mecca
Nazwā
Samā'il
Ta'if
ASIR
OMAN
Riyadh, Saudi Arabia
Jan 15°C (58°F)
July 34°C (93°F)
Abhā
RUB 'AL KHALI (EMPTY QUARTER)
Jan 3 mm (0.1 in)
July 0 mm (0 in)
Masirah I.
Gulf of Masirah
N
Jīzān
RAMLAT AS SAB'ATAYN
Kuria Muria Is.
YEMEN
Hodeida
SAN'A
Y E M E N
Salālah
Dhamār
HADHRAMAUT
Wādī Hajr
Al Mukhā
Ta'izz
Al Mukallā
ARABIAN SEA
Aden
Bab el Mandeb

*Dubai, United
Arab Emirates*

ISLAM

Islam originated in the Middle East
in the 6th century AD and is still the
dominant religion of the region.
Muslims, the followers of Islam, believe
in one God, Allah, and in Mohammed,
his prophet. Mohammed was born in
Mecca, in modern-day Saudi Arabia.
The Muslims' holy book is the Koran,
which contains Allah's teachings as
revealed to Mohammed.

A devout Muslim reading the Koran.

CITIES
The Middle East has some of the most
rapidly growing cities in the world. This is
because of the enormous wealth brought to the
region by the discovery of oil and by the growth
in population. These large cities are built along
the lines of many modern cities in Western
countries, with high-rise apartment and office
blocks of glass, steel, and concrete.

IRAQ

IRAQ IS ONE OF THE LARGEST and most powerful countries in the Middle East. Most of its people are Muslim and Arabic speaking. There are also some 4 million Kurds living in the north. Apart from the fertile plains of the Tigris and Euphrates rivers, most of Iraq is mountainous or covered in desert. Only about a sixth of the country is suitable for farming and much of Iraq's food is imported. Since Iraq became a republic in 1958, it has experienced great political unrest. During the 1980s a bitter war was fought against Iran, and Iraq's invasion of Kuwait led to the Gulf War (1990–91) and to intervention by an international force.

IRAQ	
Capital city: Baghdad	
Area: 438,320 sq km (169,235 sq miles)	
Population: 19,335,199	
Official language: Arabic	
Major religions: Muslim 97%, other 3%	
Government: One-party dictatorship	
Currency: Iraqi dinar	
Adult literacy rate: 62%	
Life expectancy: 66 years	
People per doctor: 1,810	
Televisions: 72 per 1,000 people	

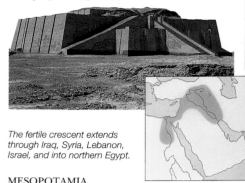

This ziggurat is in Ur, once a thriving city in Mesopotamia.

The fertile crescent extends through Iraq, Syria, Lebanon, Israel, and into northern Egypt.

MESOPOTAMIA

Many ancient peoples settled in Mesopotamia (part of which is now Iraq) because it lay in the fertile crescent of land formed by the Tigris and Euphrates rivers. The area has many ancient ruins, including stepped, pyramid-like structures, called ziggurats, found at Babylon and Ur. The steps led to a temple at the top.

SADDAM HUSSAIN

Since 1979, Iraq has been ruled by Saddam Hussain. Under his dictatorship, many ordinary Iraqis, especially the Kurds, have suffered badly. The government is backed up by the army and secret service who help to prevent any political opposition. Saddam's invasion of Kuwait was condemned by the West and by some Arab countries, and led to Iraq's isolation in world affairs.

PIPING OIL

Iraq's most important natural resources are oil and natural gas. Oil production began on a large scale in 1945 and now dominates the economy. Because Iraq has only a short stretch of coastline along the Persian Gulf, it relies on pipelines through Turkey, Syria, and Saudi Arabia to export its oil.

BAGHDAD

Baghdad, the capital of Iraq, lies on the banks of the River Tigris. It is the largest city in Iraq and the country's centre of business and government. A city of contrasts, it is a mixture of ancient mosques, modern high-rise buildings, and packed bazaars. Baghdad has been a centre of Islamic culture for more than a thousand years.

The huts, or mudhifs, are made of reeds bound tightly together.

The Marsh Arabs wend their way through the narrow reed-lined waterways in small wooden canoes, or mashhufs.

MARSH ARABS

The Marsh Arabs have hunted and fished in the marshes of southern Iraq for more than 5,000 years. Today, their lifestyle is threatened by the government's decision to drain the marshes and use the water for growing crops. The unique environment and wildlife of the marshes will also vanish if the drainage scheme continues.

The white pelican is one species of bird that makes its home in the marsh lands in winter.

The reed huts are built on platforms made of mud.

Find out more
ANCIENT SITES: *134*
DICTATORSHIP: *271*
KURDS: *144*
OIL: *137, 152, 281*

IRAN

IRAN IS THE LARGEST NON-ARAB country in the Middle East; its people are Persian in origin. In ancient times, Iran was called Persia, and it was at the centre of a great empire. The Persian language has survived from that time and is spoken by most Iranians. The country consists of a huge, central plateau, ringed by the Zagros and Elburz mountains. In 1979, the last Shah, or king, of Iran was overthrown by an Islamic revolution and the country was declared a republic. Today, oil is Iran's biggest export.

IRAN	
Capital city: Tehran	
Area: 1,648,000 sq km (636,293 sq miles)	
Population: 61,600,000	
Official language: Farsi	
Major religions: Muslim 99%, other 1%	
Government: Islamic republic	
Currency: Iranian rial	
Adult literacy rate: 56%	
Life expectancy: 67 years	
People per doctor: 3,140	
Televisions: 65 per 1,000 people	

Minaret

MOSQUE

Mosques are Muslim places of worship. All mosques have at least one tall tower, or minaret, from which the faithful are called to prayer. Many mosques are beautifully decorated with abstract patterns and verses from the Koran, the holy book of Islam. Artists avoid representing living things, as Muslims believe nothing should be worshipped apart from God, and that God is the only creator of life.

QANAT IRRIGATION

Less than half of the Iranian countryside is suitable for farming, and then only if it is well irrigated, or watered. Traditional irrigation methods include dams, wells, and qanats. A qanat is an underground channel that transports water from a source to an area that can be farmed. Some qanats are more than 40 km (25 miles) long.

Shepherds leading their flock of sheep through the Elburz Mountains.

AGRICULTURE

In recent years, Iran has tried to become less dependent on food imports, and has returned to growing more crops, such as cereals, tea, and cotton. Herds of cattle, sheep, and goats continue to be kept by many farming families.

The wells are used as ventilation and repair shafts, as well as to draw water.

Rainwater runs down and seeps into the ground.

The water flows along an underground channel that slopes gently downwards.

A series of wells are used to dig the channel and then to draw water from it.

A settlement often grows up near the mouth of the qanat.

Islamic fundamentalists carrying posters of Ayatollah Khomeini.

THE AYATOLLAH

Ayatollah Khomeini was a key figure in the Iranian revolution and remained Iran's political and religious leader until his death in 1989. The Shah had tried to introduce Western ideas to Iran, but Khomeini wanted the country to be governed by traditional Islamic laws and values. His ideas still dominate Iran.

PERSIAN CARPETS

Iran is famous for its hand-woven Persian carpets. Each consists of thousands of pieces of wool knotted into elaborate patterns. The weavers always make a deliberate mistake in their work because, as Muslims, they believe that nothing is perfect except God. Carpets are Iran's second largest export, after oil.

This woman is weaving a carpet on a vertical loom.

Graceful patterns of flowers and leaves combined with abstract shapes are a feature of Persian carpets.

SAUDI ARABIA

SAUDI ARABIA IS BY FAR the largest country in the Arabian Peninsula. Some 90 per cent of this Muslim nation is covered by the hot, dry, sandy Arabian Desert, including the vast Rub'Al Khali, or Empty Quarter, in the south. There are no permanent rivers, and years may pass without any rainfall. The discovery of huge oil reserves has made Saudi Arabia extremely rich and powerful, and enabled it to develop and improve its industry, agriculture, and standard of living.

OPEC
Saudi Arabia has the largest oil reserves in the world. Oil accounts for almost 90 per cent of the country's exports. Saudi Arabia is a key member of OPEC (Organization of Petroleum Exporting Countries). OPEC sets guidelines for the production and export of oil, and protects the interests of its member countries.

SAUDI ARABIA	
Capital city: Riyadh	
Area: 2,149,690 sq km (829,995 sq miles)	
Population: 15,431,000	
Official language: Arabic	
Major religion: Muslim 100%	
Government: Absolute monarchy	
Currency: Saudi riyal	
Adult literacy rate: 64%	
Life expectancy: 69 years	
People per doctor: 660	
Televisions: 269 per 1,000 people	

MECCA

Mecca, the birthplace of the prophet Mohammed and the holiest city of Islam, is in the west of Saudi Arabia. Each year, more than a million pilgrims from all over the world flock to Mecca to visit the sacred Ka'ba shrine in the Great Mosque. Muslims are expected to undertake the *hajj*, or pilgrimage to Mecca, at least once in their lives.

The Ka'ba stands on the remains of an ancient shrine, which, according to the Koran (the Muslim holy book), was built by Abraham.

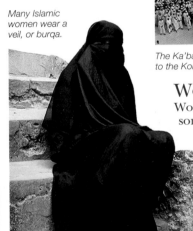

Many Islamic women wear a veil, or burqa.

WOMEN'S ROLE

Women in Saudi Arabia and some other Muslim countries live restricted lives by Western standards. Many women wear traditional Muslim dress, with long robes and veils covering their heads and faces. In Saudi Arabia, women are not allowed to work with men nor to drive cars, although every girl has the right to a good education.

WATERING THE LAND
Much of Saudi Arabia's land is scrubby, barren, and unsuitable for growing food. Farmers rely on irrigation to water their fields. Recent projects have been so successful that farmers can now grow melons, tomatoes, wheat, and barley in the desert.

Disc-shaped fields are created by sprinklers that rotate to water the land.

THE BEDOUIN

For centuries, Bedouin nomads have roamed the deserts of Saudi Arabia in search of food and water for their animals. Some Bedouin are camel herders; others keep sheep and goats. The Bedouin traditionally live in tents that are light and easy to transport. Today, their way of life is under threat as the government encourages people to settle in towns and cities.

Camels are ideally suited to desert life and are highly valued by the Bedouin.

A Bedouin tent is made from long strips of tightly woven goat's hair.

The tent is divided into male and female quarters.

Modern Bedouin use cars and trucks for transport as well as camels and horses.

Bedouin women weave tent cloth, drapes, and cushion covers, and saddle bags for their camels and horses.

Long, loose-fitting robes protect the skin from the sun, and keep the body cool during the day.

Find out more
DESERT NOMADS: 181, 209
DESERTS: 15, 132, 152
ISLAM: 275
OIL: 137, 152, 281

KUWAIT	
Capital city: Kuwait	
Area: 17,820 sq km (6,880 sq miles)	
Population: 2,212,000	
Official language: Arabic	
Major religions: Muslim 85%, other 15%	
Government: Absolute monarchy with parliament	
Currency: Kuwaiti dinar	
Adult literacy rate: 74%	
Life expectancy: 75 years	
People per doctor: 690	
Televisions: 271 per 1,000 people	

BAHRAIN	
Capital city: Manama	
Area: 680 sq km (263 sq miles)	
Population: 518,000	
Official language: Arabic	
Major religions: Muslim 85%, Christian 7%, other 8%	
Government: Absolute monarchy	
Currency: Bahrain dinar	
Adult literacy rate: 79%	
Life expectancy: 71 years	
People per doctor: 930	
Televisions: 414 per 1,000 people	

QATAR	
Capital city: Doha	
Area: 11,000 sq km (4,247 sq miles)	
Population: 500,000	
Official language: Arabic	
Major religions: Muslim 95%, other 5%	
Government: Absolute monarchy	
Currency: Qatar riyal	
Adult literacy rate: 76%	
Life expectancy: 70 years	
People per doctor: 530	
Televisions: 445 per 1,000 people	

KUWAIT

KUWAIT LIES AT THE NORTHERN end of the Persian Gulf. It is a small country, largely covered by sandy desert. Huge oil reserves have made Kuwait rich, and oil-refining has become its chief industry. In 1990, at the start of the Gulf War, Kuwait was occupied by Iraq. It was liberated in 1991 by an international force.

KUWAIT'S WEALTH

Until the discovery of oil in the 1940s, Kuwait was a poor, underdeveloped country. The wealth gained by selling oil has transformed it into one of the most prosperous nations in the world. Its people enjoy a high standard of living, with free education, free health care and social services, and no income tax.

POLLUTION
Kuwait suffered badly during its invasion by Iraq. Many of its oil wells were set on fire, causing enormous damage to the economy and the environment. A huge slick of oil spilled into the Gulf, poisoning the water and killing wildlife. Abandoned ammunition and unexploded mines littered the desert. The clearing up process continues today.

Kuwait's wealth is reflected in its impressive buildings, such as these water towers which dominate Kuwait City's skyline.

BAHRAIN

BAHRAIN IS MADE UP OF A SMALL GROUP of islands in the Persian Gulf. Little rain falls, so farming is only possible on irrigated, or watered, land. Bahrain was one of the first Arab states to discover oil in the 1930s. Its oil reserves are now running out.

PEARLING
As Bahrain's oil runs low, traditional industries such as pearling are once again growing in importance. The pearl season lasts from June to September. Divers descend on weighted ropes, equipped only with nose-clips, knives, and collecting bags. The most valuable pearls are bright white, tinged with pink.

A pearl taken from an oyster shell.

LINKED ISLANDS

The main island of Bahrain is linked by a series of road causeways to the neighbouring islands of Al Muharraq and Sitrah, and to the Saudi Arabian mainland, with which Bahrain has close relations. Bahrain island is only 48 km (30 miles) long, and the other islands are even smaller.

QATAR

QATAR IS A LONG PENINSULA of land jutting out into the Persian Gulf. It is mainly desert with a hot, dry climate. Oil production and refining form the basis of its economy. The government is trying to encourage the growth of fishing and agriculture to reduce the country's dependence on oil.

An Indian construction worker.

WORKERS FROM ABROAD
In the 1940s, the smaller oil states such as Qatar and Kuwait encouraged workers from other parts of the Middle East, India, and Pakistan to work in their rapidly growing oil industries. Their own labour forces were simply too small to cope. Today, these migrant workers outnumber the local Qatari people.

Find out more
DESERTS: *15, 132, 152*
GULF WAR: *152, 154*
IRRIGATION: *155, 156, 217*
OIL: *137, 152, 281*

UNITED ARAB EMIRATES

THE UNITED ARAB EMIRATES (UAE) lies on the southern coast of the Persian Gulf. Three-quarters of this Islamic country is sandy desert, with a hot, dry climate all year round. Only a tiny proportion of the land is suitable for farming and most food has to be imported. Oil was discovered in 1958 and has turned the UAE into one of the world's most prosperous countries, with a high standard of living for most people. There are many huge oil refineries along the coast.

Abu Dhabi

TOURISM
The UAE has a growing tourist industry. Some 50,000 people arrive each year, mainly from Europe and Japan. Most visit in winter when it is warm but not too hot. Attractions include luxury hotels and duty-free shops, traditional markets, fine beaches, and trips into the desert.

Al Mamza Beach Park, Dubai.

SEVEN STATES
The United Arab Emirates is a federation of seven small states, or emirates, each ruled by an emir, or sheik. The emirs have absolute power over their own states, but they also meet regularly to make decisions affecting the whole federation. Abu Dhabi is the largest of the emirates and its capital is also that of the UAE.

ISLAMIC FESTIVALS
The two most important festivals of the Islamic year are *Id al-Fitr* and *Id al-Adha*. *Id al-Fitr* literally means "the breaking of the fast". It celebrates the end of the holy month of Ramadan, during which Muslims must fast from dawn to dusk. *Id al-Adha* is the festival of sacrifice. Prayers are followed by the sacrifice of a sheep, cow, or camel.

A Muslim family celebrating Id al-Fitr (left). The feast consists of typical Middle Eastern foods, such as those shown on the right.

Dates

Dried apricots

Apricots and dates are often eaten as appetizers.

Lentils are used to make soups.

Courgettes (zucchinis) often accompany a meat dish.

OMAN

THE SULTANATE (KINGDOM) OF OMAN lies on the southeast coast of the Arabian Peninsula. Much of the land is desert, dotted with oases, but parts of the coastline are more fertile. Here farmers grow dates, pomegranates, limes, tobacco, and wheat. People also raise goats, sheep, and cattle. Oil is Oman's main export.

Omani fishermen

FISHING
The Oman coastline is 1,700 km (1,056 miles) long, and fishing is a valuable source of income and food. Omani fishermen catch large amounts of sardines, tuna, anchovies, cod, and cuttlefish. They use traditional dug-out canoes, fitted with outboard motors for greater speed.

LOST CITY OF THE SANDS
According to Arabian legend, a magnificent city called Ubar lies buried under the desolate sands of southern Oman. Archaeologists have excavated a watering hole and the remains of a city dating from about 3000BC near the Yemen border. Some experts believe that this is the lost city of Ubar.

___ *Find out more* ___

DESERTS: *15, 132, 152*
ISLAM: *275*
OIL: *137, 152, 281*
OIL WEALTH: *137, 278*

YEMEN

THE COUNTRY OF YEMEN was formed in 1990 when North and South Yemen were reunited. Yemen lies at the southern tip of the Arabian Peninsula. It is more fertile than other Middle Eastern countries, with good farmland in the western highlands where there is regular rainfall. The coast and mountains of the east are hot, dry, and barren. Yemen is a poorer, less developed country than its neighbours, although the discovery of oil in the 1980s may help increase its prosperity in the future.

THE PORT OF ADEN
Aden is one of the biggest cities in Yemen and the country's main port. Because of its location on the Gulf of Aden, it has been the region's chief trading city since ancient times. Today, it is an important industrial centre, with a huge oil refinery, factories, and an international airport.

YEMEN	
Capital city: San'a	
Area: 527,970 sq km (203,850 sq miles)	
Population: 12,533,000	
Official language: Arabic	
Major religions: Muslim 97%, other 3%	
Government: Multi-party democracy	
Currency: Yemen riyal	
Adult literacy rate: 41%	
Life expectancy: 52 years	
People per doctor: no figures available	
Televisions: 29 per 1,000 people	

YEMENI TERRACES

In many places, the mountain slopes of Yemen are terraced to provide extra space for crops. Some terraces are more than 1,300 years old. More than half the people of Yemen are farmers. They grow cereal crops, such as wheat and sorghum, along with citrus fruits and dates, and raise sheep, goats, and cattle. Coffee and cotton are grown mainly for export.

Traditional Yemeni tower houses are scattered throughout the terraced hills.

The remaining floors are used as living quarters.

The terraces are built up into the mountains.

The first floor is often used for storage.

Animals, such as goats and sheep, are kept on the ground floor of the house.

A variety of crops, such as coffee and cotton, are grown on the Yemeni terraces.

Coffee is often served in traditional Bedouin pots.

COFFEE AND QAT
Coffee is thought to have originated as a drink in Yemen and the country produces some of the world's finest quality beans. Yemen is also famous for a plant called qat. Its leaves contain a mild drug and are often chewed. Qat parties are an important part of Yemeni social life.

Tribal men often wear a ceremonial dagger, or jambiya, strapped to the waist.

TRIBAL SOCIETY

Most Yemeni people are Muslim Arabs belonging to various tribal groups. Each tribe elects a sheik as its leader and has its own customs, costumes, and folklore. Within each tribe, people live in large, closely knit, extended families. Several generations of the same family usually share the same house. The tribal tradition is particularly strong in north Yemen.

SAN'A

San'a, the capital of Yemen, is an ancient city, famous for its traditional Yemeni-style architecture. In the old city you can still see clusters of 400-year-old multi-storeyed, mud and brick tower houses, their outer walls often decorated with friezes. An international conservation effort has been launched to protect this unique city and preserve it for the future.

Find out more
ANCIENT SITES: *134*
COFFEE: *50, 62, 66*
OIL: *137, 152, 281*
TERRACE FARMING: *173, 201*

CENTRAL ASIA

CENTRAL ASIA LIES FAR FROM the world's oceans. The winds are dry and there is little rainfall, so the area is generally arid. With cold, dry winters, and hot, dry summers, lack of water is a problem for farmers. The north consists of a flat, grass-covered plain, or steppe. In the centre of the region are two vast deserts, the Kyzyl Kum ("Red Sands") and the Kara Kum ("Black Sands"). In the south are long chains of snow-capped mountain ranges that join the neighbouring Himalayas. The entire region, apart from Afghanistan, used to be part of the Soviet Union. Industrialization and collective farms brought huge changes to a region once occupied mainly by nomads.

A hoarding displaying a communist poster in Uzbekistan.

INDEPENDENCE

In 1991, the communist state of the Soviet Union fell apart and the central Asian countries became independent. While the countries were under Soviet rule, many Russian people settled there and Russian replaced the local languages. Today, the peoples of central Asia are re-establishing their own languages and national identities.

Nomadic herders in the hills of Afghanistan.

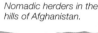

This girl's hat from Uzbekistan is embroidered with gold thread.

Child's hat from Afghanistan.

A LAND OF MANY PEOPLES

There is a great variety of peoples living in central Asia. The original inhabitants include the Kazakhs, Turkmens, and Uzbeks, related to the Turks, and the Tajiks and Afghans, related to the Iranians. Each group has its own distinctive style of hat, often woven in silk with brightly coloured geometric patterns.

Silver ornaments adorn this Turkmen girl's hat.

NOMADIC LIFESTYLE

Many people living in central Asia are nomads, moving from place to place with their animals in search of new pastures. Nomads live in tents and have few belongings, making travelling easier and quicker. They live by herding animals such as camels, goats, and sheep, which give them milk, meat, and wool, some of which they sell, but most of which they use themselves. Nomads mostly stay in the open country, but they visit the towns and cities occasionally to sell their products.

The Aral Sea in 1960

Fishing village on the coast.

Fishing village stranded inland.

DRILLING FOR OIL

The northern states of central Asia are sitting on huge reserves of oil and gas. Kazakhstan is slowly exploiting one of the world's biggest oil fields under the Caspian Sea, while Turkmenistan is beginning to make use of a vast reservoir of natural gas trapped beneath its land. Exploitation of these riches is hampered by lack of investment and a poorly skilled workforce.

Miners drilling for oil in the Tengiz oil field in Kazakhstan.

The Aral Sea in 1995

The lake is about half its original size. By 2010, it may have almost disappeared.

SHRINKING SEA

The Aral Sea, once the fourth largest freshwater lake in the world, is shrinking. Fishing villages that once stood on the sea coast are now stranded inland, depriving villagers of their livelihood. This environmental disaster has been caused by water from the Amu Darya River, which flows into the Aral Sea, being drained for irrigation projects. Huge areas of useless land have been laid bare. Wind storms are common, sweeping up polluted dust and dumping it on the surrounding countryside.

A B C D E F G H I J K L

1 2 3 4 5 6 7 8 9 10 11 12

RUSSIAN FEDERATION

KAZAKHSTAN

Almaty, Kazakhstan
☀ Jan -9°C (15°F)
July 22°C (71°F)
🌧 Jan 33 mm (1.3 in)
July 36 mm (1.4 in)

RUSSIAN FEDERATION

Petropavlovsk

Ural'sk
Aksay

Kustanay

Kokchetav

Pavlodar

Akmola

Semipalatinsk
Ust' Kamenogorsk

Aktyubinsk
Alga

Arkalyk

KAZAKH UPLANDS

Temirtau
Karaganda

Zyryanovsk

L. Tengiz

KIRGHIZ STEPPE

Atyrau

Emba

L. Zaysan

KAZAKHSTAN

Ural

Nikol'skiy
Zhezkazgan

Aral'sk

Balkhash

CHINA

Fort Shevchenko
Beyneu

Baykonur

L. Balkhash

KARA KUM

Aktau

USTYURT PLATEAU

ARAL SEA

Syr Darya

Taldykorgan

Ili

Novyy Uzen'

Muynak

Kzyl-Orda

Chu

Kapchagay

UZBEKISTAN

L. Sarykamysh

Nukus

TURAN LOWLAND

KYZYL KUM

Uchkuduk

Zhambyl

ALMATY

CASPIAN SEA

Zaliv Kara-Bogaz-Gol

Dashkhovuz
Urgench

Shymkent

BISHKEK
Tokmak

Karakol

Krasnovodsk

L. Aydarkul'

TASHKENT

KYRGYZSTAN

Issyk-kul'

Nebitdag

Navoi
Samarkand

Andizhan
Fergana

Naryn

Osh

TURKMENISTAN

Zeravshan

Bukhara

Khujand

TIEN SHAN

Kizyl-Arbat

Chardzhev

Karshi

TAJIKISTAN

Communism Peak

Kizyl-Atrek

ASHGABAT

Amu Darya

DUSHANBE

Bartang

UZBEKISTAN

Mary

Karakum Canal

Kurgan-Tyube
Kulyab

PAMIRS

Panj

IRAN

Tedzhen

Mazar-e Sharif

Kunduz

Pamir

TURKMENISTAN

Morghab

TORKESTAN MTS.

Qonduz

Krasnovodsk, Turkmenistan
☀ Jan 2°C (35°F)
July 56°C (83°F)
🌧 Jan 13 mm (0.5 in)
July 5 mm (0.2 in)

Herat

Harirud

HINDU KUSH

KYRGYZSTAN

Kowl-e-Namaksar

AFGHANISTAN

KABUL
Jalalabad

Khyber Pass

PAKISTAN

Hamun-e-Saberi

Helmand

Arghandab

Kandahar

Gowd-e Zereh

TAJIKISTAN

ARCTIC CIRCLE

TROPIC OF CANCER

EQUATOR

N

AFGHANISTAN

Kabul, Afghanistan
☀ Jan -3°C (27°F)
July 22°C (72°F)
🌧 Jan 31 mm (1.2 in)
July 3 mm (0.1 in)

0 100 200 300 400 km
0 50 100 150 200 250 miles

THINGS TO LOOK FOR ON THE MAP

Longest river: Amu Darya, Afghanistan/Tajikistan/Turkmenistan/Uzbekistan, 1,403 km (872 miles) *Map F8*

Highest point: Communism Peak, Tajikistan, 7,495 m (24,590 ft) *Map H7*

World's largest lake: Caspian Sea, Russian Federation/Kazakhstan/Turkmenistan/Iran/Azerbaijan, 378,400 sq km (146,111 sq miles) *Map B6*

World's longest irrigation canal: Karakum Canal, Turkmenistan, 1,100 km (683 miles) *Map E8*

CAVIAR

The largest inland lake in the world, the Caspian Sea covers 378,400 sq km (146,111 sq miles) and borders five countries. The lake is home to a variety of fish, such as sturgeon, from which caviar (fish eggs) is made. However, pollution of the waters by industrial waste has led to a drop in the numbers of fish.

Caviar served on toast.

ISLAM

Throughout central Asia, Islam is the main religion. It arrived in the region in the early 8th century. While central Asia was part of the Soviet Union, Islam was suppressed. Traditional Muslim wedding ceremonies were forbidden. Throughout this time, however, people continued to worship in secret. With the end of communism, Islam has gained strength in every country.

KAZAKHSTAN

STRETCHING FROM THE Caspian Sea to China, Kazakhstan is a vast country, almost the size of western Europe. It is also one of the most underpopulated countries in the world. With vast mineral reserves, fertile soil, and a stable government, Kazakhstan has the potential to be a wealthy country. However, industrial and agricultural pollution, and the presence of many ageing nuclear weapons left behind by the former Soviet Union, have caused considerable environmental problems.

KAZAKHSTAN

Capital city: Almaty

Area: 2,717,300 sq km (1,049,150 sq miles)

Population: 16,536,511

Official language: Kazakh

Major religions: Muslim 47%, other 53%

Government: Democracy

Currency: Tenge

Adult literacy rate: 98%

Life expectancy: 69 years

People per doctor: 250

Televisions: No figures available

THE VIRGIN LANDS
In the 1950s the Russian government increased grain production by cultivating the vast grassland steppes, or plains, of Kazakhstan. Huge farms were set up to grow corn and wheat on land that had been barren. Millions of Russians migrated or were forced to move to this empty region, known as the "Virgin Lands". The programme met with mixed success. It left Kazakhstan self-sufficient in grain and other crops, but it led to enormous environmental damage.

RICH IN MINERALS
Mining is the most important industry in Kazakhstan. The country has huge coal and iron-ore reserves, the world's largest chrome mine, and one of its biggest gold fields, as well as plentiful supplies of copper, zinc, lead, uranium, and other minerals. Most coal in Kazakhstan comes from open-cast mines, where coal is extracted near the surface of the ground, rather than from deep mine shafts.

At the processing plant, the coal is cleaned and dried and sorted into different sizes.

In the filter bed, any remaining pieces of rock and clay are removed.

Trucks transport the extracted coal along a haul road.

Steps are cut into the sides of the pit so that the coal can be reached safely.

Surface rock is loosened by explosives so that the digging machines can remove the rock and reach the coal.

Machines dig the coal out of the pit.

The government building in Almaty, the capital of Kazakhstan.

THE CITY OF APPLES
Almaty means "father of apple trees", and the capital is known for its apple orchards. The city nestles at the foot of the Tien Shan mountains in the far south of the country. It has many parks and fountains, and narrow canals called *aryks* run along the sides of streets to cool the city during the hot summers. However, there are plans to move the capital to Akmola in the north.

SPACE RACE
History was made in Kazakhstan in 1957 when the world's first artificial satellite, *Sputnik I*, was launched from the Baykonur Cosmodrome, or space station, in the centre of the country. The first person in space, Yuri Gagarin, was sent into orbit around the Earth from Baykonur in 1961. The site is still used today by the Russian government for its space programme.

THE KAZAKHS
Native Kazakhs make up only about 40 per cent of the total population of their country and live mainly in the west and south. Many are farmers and have worked hard to preserve the natural beauty of the land, setting up reserves to protect wildlife and the environment. The rest of the population consists mainly of Russians, Germans, and Ukranians.

Find out more

CEREALS: *34, 120*
COAL MINING: *96, 112*
POPULATION DENSITY: *135*
STEPPE (GRASSLANDS): *15*

UZBEKISTAN

UZBEKISTAN IS ONE OF the wealthiest and one of the more populated countries in central Asia. It also has a varied landscape. While two-thirds of the land is made up of desert and arid steppe land, there are also fertile areas, fast-flowing rivers, and snowy mountain tops. The ancient cities of the Silk Road are beginning to attract large numbers of tourists, and foreign investors are helping to develop the country's huge mineral and energy resources. Uzbekistan is also the world's fourth largest producer of cotton, known locally as "white gold".

UZBEKISTAN

Capital city: Tashkent	
Area: 1,138,910 sq km (439,733 sq miles)	
Population: 19,905,158	
Official language: Uzbek	
Major religions: Muslim 78%, other 22%	
Government: Democracy	
Currency: Som	
Adult literacy rate: 97%	
Life expectancy: 69 years	
People per doctor: 280	
Televisions: No figures available	

TAJIKISTAN

Capital city: Dushanbe	
Area: 143,100 sq km (55,251 sq miles)	
Population: 5,108,576	
Official language: Tajik	
Major religions: Muslim 85%, other 15%	
Government: Democracy	
Currency: Rouble	
Adult literacy rate: 97%	
Life expectancy: 70 years	
People per doctor: 350	
Televisions: No figures available	

ISLAMIC CITIES

The Silk Road is an old trading route that linked China with central Asia, the Middle East, and Europe. Ancient Islamic cities, once major trading centres, are found along its route. These include Samarkand, which contains many fine examples of Islamic architecture, Bukhara, an important place of pilgrimage for Muslims, and Tashkent, the capital of Uzbekistan and known as the "city of fountains".

NATURAL GAS
Uzbekistan is rich in natural resources. It has plentiful supplies of oil, natural gas, coal, gold, and uranium. A huge pipeline used for exporting natural gas stretches from Bukhara to the Urals in Russia. Much of the local industry, producing machinery, chemicals, and aircraft, is based on energy from gas.

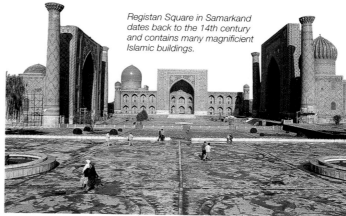

Registan Square in Samarkand dates back to the 14th century and contains many magnificient Islamic buildings.

TAJIKISTAN

THE POOREST OF THE FORMER Soviet Union states, Tajikistan is a mountainous country with only about six per cent of its land available for farming. Most people work on the land, growing fruit, cotton, and tobacco and herding animals, or work in small factories producing textiles, silk, and carpets. Since independence in 1991, Tajikistan has been split by armed conflict between the government and rebel groups.

In the Pamir mountain region, a different tribal group is found in almost every valley.

Peaches

Melon

Pistachios

FERTILE VALLEYS
In spring, melted snow from the Tien Shan and Pamir mountains flows down into the Fergana and other river valleys of Tajikistan, bringing with it rich, fertile mud. Irrigation channels direct this water into the surrounding fields, enabling farmers to grow a variety of crops, such as those above.

PAMIR VALLEY PEOPLES

Less than 100,000 people live in the Pamir mountain region, growing grain and fruit in the deep valleys, or herding sheep and yaks on the bleak high plains in the east. Because of the remoteness of the area and the isolation of the valleys from each other, there is a bewildering variety of peoples, languages, and dialects.

Find out more
COTTON: *36, 215, 216*
GAS: *198, 211*
ISLAM: *275*
ISLAMIC ARCHITECTURE: *155*

TURKMENISTAN

TURKMENISTAN

KYRGYZSTAN

ALMOST 90 PER CENT of Turkmenistan consists of the vast Kara Kum ("Black Sands") Desert, where temperatures reach more than 50°C (122°F). A fertile strip of land stretches around the southern borders of the desert; here people grow cotton and other crops for export. Since Turkmenistan became independent in 1991, Turkmen has replaced Russian as the state language and Islam is once again the major religion. The country is poor and isolated from the rest of the world, but possesses huge reserves of natural gas.

ASHGABAT
In 1948, the bustling market town of Ashgabat was totally destroyed by a huge earthquake. The town was completely replanned and rebuilt and is now the capital city of Turkmenistan. Ashgabat is the centre for food processing and silk, lace, and carpet manufacturing.

TURKMENISTAN	
Capital city: Ashgabat	
Area: 488,100 sq km (188,455 sq miles)	
Population: 3,533,925	
Official language: Turkmen	
Major religions: Muslim 85%, Christian 10%, other 5%	
Government: Democracy	
Currency: Manat	
Adult literacy rate: 98%	
Life expectancy: 66 years	
People per doctor: 290	
Televisions: No figures available	

KYRGYZSTAN	
Capital city: Bishkek	
Area: 198,500 sq km (76,640 sq miles)	
Population: 4,290,442	
Official language: Kyrgyz	
Major religions: No figures available	
Government: Democracy	
Currency: Som	
Adult literacy rate: 97%	
Life expectancy: 68 years	
People per doctor: 280	
Televisions: No figures available	

THE TURKMENS
The Turkmen people live in various parts of central Asia and many follow a nomadic lifestyle. In Turkmenistan, however, many Turkmens have settled as farmers and expert horse breeders. They visit local horse fairs and buy and sell horses for export to neighbouring countries. The Turkmens are known for producing highly prized racehorses, such as the Akhal-Teke, a breed able to move quickly in desert conditions.

Ashgabat Karakum Canal

Amu Darya

• Main towns
⚓ Cotton

KARAKUM CANAL
The world's longest irrigation canal stretches from the Amu Darya River in the east to beyond Ashgabat in the west, a distance of 1,100 km (683 miles). Known as the "River of Life", the Karakum Canal provides water for a large area of arid land, so that cotton and other crops can be grown.

KYRGYZSTAN

The Kyrgyz people follow Islam. They speak a Turkic language and live a nomadic life in the countryside.

KNOWN AS THE SWITZERLAND of central Asia because of its mountainous landscape, over half of Kyrgyzstan is 2,500 m (8,200 ft) or more above sea level. The snow-capped Tien Shan mountains dominate the countryside, but the river valleys are fertile and green. Most people are farmers. Animal breeding is particularly important because there is so little land to farm.

THE KYRGYZ PEOPLE
More than half the population is native Kyrgyz. These nomadic people are known for their skilled horsemanship. The largest minority group are Russians, who live in the towns and, until independence in 1991, ran the economy. As a result of rising nationalist feeling among the Kyrgyz, many Russian people have now returned to Russia.

Gold nugget

MOUNTAIN RICHES
The mountains of Kyrgyzstan are rich in minerals. Gold and mercury are mined for export, while coal, oil, and gas are exploited for domestic use. The fast-flowing rivers are ideal for generating electricity and new hydro-electric power stations have been built.

Find out more
DESERTS: *15, 132, 152*
GAS: *163, 198, 211*
NOMADS: *160*
USSR BREAK-UP: *136, 160*

AFGHANISTAN

AFGHANISTAN OCCUPIES AN IMPORTANT position between central Asia to the north and the Indian Subcontinent to the south. As a result, the country has been fought over for centuries, especially by Russian and British armies. Afghanistan is a land of contrasts, made up of high, grassy plains, low, flat, stony desert, and high mountain peaks. The country has few roads and no railways, and almost three-quarters of this bleak land is inaccessible. In the last 20 years, the country has been in the grip of civil war and is currently ruled by a fragile government. Afghanistan is one of the poorest countries in the world.

AFGHANISTAN	
Capital city: Kabul	
Area: 652,090 sq km (251,770 sq miles)	
Population: 20,500,000	
Official languages: Dari (Persian), Pashtu	
Major religions: Muslim 99%, other 1%	
Government: Islamic republic	
Currency: Afghani	
Adult literacy rate: 32%	
Life expectancy: 43 years	
People per doctor: 6,430	
Televisions: 8 per 1,000 people	

ISLAMIC SCHOOLS
Most Afghan people are Muslim. Children are taught about Islam in their local mosque and school. As teenagers, they attend a *madrasah*, or religious college. Here they memorize huge extracts of the Koran (Islamic holy book) and study theology, religious law, and logic.

THE MUJAHIDEEN

In 1979, the Soviet Union invaded Afghanistan to prop up the new communist government. Islamic rebels, known as the *mujahideen*, retaliated by launching a full-scale war. By 1989 they had forced the Soviet army to withdraw, and by 1992 had taken over the entire country. Once in power, they introduced strict Islamic laws. However, fighting between the main *mujahideen* groups has led to a state of civil war.

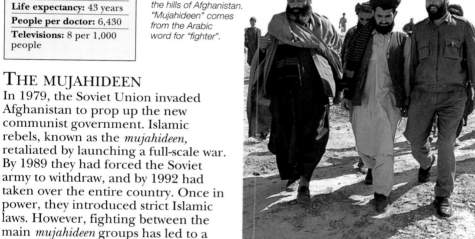

Some mujahideen groups are based in the hills of Afghanistan. "Mujahideen" comes from the Arabic word for "fighter".

The Turkmen nomads in the north of the country live in reddish-brown, dome-shaped tents.

The Pushtoon nomads of the south live in black tents spread low over the ground.

TENTS
Some Afghans are nomads, or *kochis* as they are known locally. The different groups can be distinguished by the unique designs of the felt or animal-skin tents they live in, each design having been passed down through countless generations.

CARPET WEAVING
The Turkmens of northern Afghanistan are skilled carpet makers, hand-knotting and weaving fine wool from the karakul sheep into geometric red, brown, and maroon patterns. The carpets are usually made by women and are used as saddle-cloths, tent hangings, and prayer mats.

MANY PEOPLES

More than 20 different groups of people live in Afghanistan. In the south, the Pushtoons, or Afghans, are the largest group; the country is named after them because they have controlled its government for the last 200 years. In the big cities and the rural areas of the northeast live the Dari- (Persian-) speaking Tajiks, many of whom are merchants and traders. The Hazara people (above) live in the centre of the country.

Major peoples in Afghanistan
1. Uzbek
2. Tajik
3. Aimaq
4. Hazara
5. Nuristani
6. Pushtoon

Find out more
CARPET MAKING: *144, 155, 210*
ISLAM: *275*
NOMADS: *160*
TENTS: *156, 181*

THE INDIAN SUBCONTINENT

FRINGED BY THE INDIAN OCEAN, the Arabian Sea, and the Bay of Bengal, and bordered to the north by the mighty Himalayas, the Indian Subcontinent covers a vast area. At least a fifth of the world's people live here. Dominated by India, the area also includes Pakistan, Bangladesh, Nepal, the island of Sri Lanka, and the tiny state of Bhutan. The Subcontinent has a long and turbulent history and has been invaded many times. In the 19th and early 20th centuries, most of the area, apart from Nepal and Bhutan, was ruled by Britain. The landscape and climate of the Subcontinent vary greatly, with snow-capped mountains in the north, dry, sandy desert in the northwest, and hot, tropical rainforest in the south.

INDEPENDENCE
India became independent in 1947. The country was divided into Hindu India and the new Muslim country of Pakistan, split into West and East. In 1971, East Pakistan became the independent country of Bangladesh.

Mahatma Gandhi, a central figure in India's struggle for independence, believed in using peaceful methods to achieve his country's aims.

Most villagers are farmers, but others follow a trade such as weaving or pottery-making.

Most village people live in small houses with two or three rooms.

VILLAGE LIFE

Most people in the Subcontinent live in closely knit villages and make their living from farming. In India alone, more than 70 per cent of the population live in some 500,000 villages scattered across the country. Some consist of small clusters of houses, others have thousands of inhabitants. Most families have lived in the same village for many years, passing on their knowledge and skills from one generation to the next.

The houses of many villages are clustered round a village square. Here the village council (Panchayat) will meet to make decisions.

The well is one of the focal points of village life. Women collect water every day and meet to exchange news.

Because Bangladesh is flat and low-lying, it is particularly prone to flooding.

→ Southwest winds (June to October)

→ Northeast winds (November to February)

MONSOON

The climate of much of the Subcontinent is dominated by the monsoon winds which bring rain to the area each summer. Farmers rely on this rainfall to water their crops. If the rains fail, they face ruin. Sometimes the rainfall is very heavy and causes terrible floods. Whole villages and fields of crops may be swept away.

SEASONAL WINDS

These winds blow from the southwest in summer and from the northeast in winter. As the summer winds sweep across the Indian Ocean, they pick up moisture which turns into rain on reaching the hot, dry land.

TREKKING IN THE HIMALAYAS
Each year, thousands of tourists travel to Nepal to trek in the mountains. The Nepalese Himalayas include eight peaks more than 8,000 m (26,247 ft) high. The world's tallest mountain, Everest, stands on the border between Nepal and Tibet. Many expeditions are accompanied by Sherpas. These Nepalese people are skilled climbers.

A B C D E F G H I J K L

Kashmir: a "line of control"
was established in 1972 by
the Simla Agreement between
Pakistan and India

Aksai Chin is
controlled by
China but
claimed by
India

Demchok is
claimed by both
India and China

Islamabad, Pakistan
Jan 9°C (49°F)
July 31°C (87°F)
Jan 64 mm (2.5 in)
July 233 mm (9.2 in)

THINGS TO LOOK FOR ON THE MAP
Longest river: Ganges, India, 2,510 km
(1,560 miles) *Map G5*
Highest point: Mt. Everest, China/Nepal, 8,848 m
(29,029 ft) *Map J5*
Largest lake: L. Chilka, India, 910 sq km
(351 sq miles) *Map H8*
World's largest delta: Ganges, India/Bangladesh,
75,000 sq km (28,957 sq miles) *Map J7*

NEPAL
BHUTAN

AFGHANISTAN
IRAN
TOBA KAKAR RANGE
CHAGAI HILLS
PAKISTAN
MAKRAN
Quetta
Tarbela Res.
Peshawar
ISLAMABAD
Rawalpindi
Jhelum
Srinagar
KASHMIR
HIMALAYAS
CHINA
Gujrat
Gujranwala
Sargodha
Lahore
Faisalabad
Amritsar
Jalandhar
Chandigarh
Okara
Ludhiana
Dera
Ghazi Khan
Multan
PUNJAB
Meerut
Bahawalpur
Rahimyar
Khan
NEW DELHI
Bareilly
Shikarpur
Larkana
Sukkur
SINDH
THAR DESERT
Nawabshah
Jodhpur
Jaipur
Agra
Aligarh
Shahjahanpur
Nepalganj
KATHMANDU
Mt. Everest
THIMPHU
BHUTAN
Itanagar
Karachi
Hyderabad
Indus
Chambal
Gwalior
Yamuna
Ganges
Lucknow
Kanpur
Gorakhpur
Biratnagar
Rangpur
Brahmaputra
Guwahati
Shillong
RANN OF
KUTCH
Kota
Varanasi
Allahabad
Patna
Ganges
Gaya
Son
BANGLADESH
Jamalpur
Sylhet
Imphal
Gulf of
Kutch
Jammagar
Rajkot
Ahmadabad
Vadodara
Indore
Bhopal
Govind Ballash
Pant Res.
Dhanbad
Rajshahi
DACCA
Aizawl
Bhavnagar
Narmada
Jabalpur
Ranchi
Asansol
Calcutta
Gulf of
Khambhat
Surat
Daman
Dhule
Tapti
Nagpur
Raipur
Jamshedpur
Khulna
Chittagong
BURMA
Nasik
Thane
Bombay
Pune
Nanded
Godavari
Hirakud
Res.
Ganges Delta
ARABIAN
SEA
DECCAN
Sholapur
PLATEAU
Hyderabad
Krishna
Nagarjuna
Res.
Vishakhapatnam
Rajahmundry
Vijayawada
Mahanadi
Cuttack
Bhubaneswar
L. Chilka
Bay of Bengal
BANGLADESH
INDIA
Panaji
Dharwad
Davangere
WESTERN GHATS
EASTERN GHATS
Nellore
MALABAR COAST
Mangalore
Mysore
Bangalore
Salem
Coimbatore
Tiruchchirappalli
Madras
COROMANDEL COAST
Cochin
Madurai
Jaffna
Mannar
Trivandrum
Trincomalee
Nagercoil
SRI
LANKA
Kandy
COLOMBO
Galle
SRI LANKA

N

0 100 200 300 400 km
0 50 100 150 200 250 miles

Hyderabad, India
Jan 23°C (72°F)
July 27°C (80°F)
Jan 8 mm (0.3 in)
July 152 mm (6 in)

Chittagong, Bangladesh
Jan 20°C (67°F)
July 28°C (82°F)
Jan 5 mm (0.2 in)
July 597 mm (23.5 in)

ARCTIC CIRCLE
TROPIC OF CANCER
EQUATOR

SACRED RIVER
Followers of five of the world's major religions
live in the Indian Subcontinent – Hindus,
Muslims, Buddhists, Sikhs, and Christians. The
majority of people are Hindu and their holiest
city is Varanasi, in northern India. The city
stands on the banks of the Ganges, the sacred
river of the Hindus. Millions of pilgrims come to
Varanasi each year to bathe in the river. This is
believed to wash away their sins.

ENDANGERED WILDLIFE
The Subcontinent is rich in wildlife,
from elephants and rhinoceros to
monkeys and mongooses. Loss of
habitat and poaching are serious
threats to India's most famous
animals, including tigers. Despite the
establishment of protected reserves,
illegal tiger-hunting continues. Fewer
than 3,000 tigers are left in the wild.

PAKISTAN

PAKISTAN WAS CREATED IN 1947 as a home for Muslims in India. The country was originally divided into East and West, but in 1971 East Pakistan broke away to become Bangladesh and West Pakistan became Pakistan. Today most people make their living from farming, but industry – especially cotton and textiles – is growing steadily. Handicrafts, such as carpet-making and metal work, are also important. Since Pakistan became independent, it has been in dispute with India over the largely Muslim state of Kashmir, which forms part of India but is claimed by Pakistan.

PAKISTAN	
Capital city: Islamabad	
Area: 796,100 sq km (307,374 sq miles)	
Population: 128,100,000	
Official language: Urdu	
Major religions: Muslim 97%, other 3%	
Government: Multi-party democracy	
Currency: Pakistani rupee	
Adult literacy rate: 36%	
Life expectancy: 58 years	
People per doctor: 2,940	
Televisions: 18 per 1,000 people	

● major cities
▣ irrigated land

WHERE PEOPLE LIVE
The population of Pakistan is unevenly distributed across the country. More than 80 per cent live in the provinces of Punjab and Sind, on the fertile floodplains of the rivers.

ISLAMABAD
About a third of Pakistani people live in cities. The capital is Islamabad (right), a brand new city built in the early 1960s. The name Islamabad means the "place of Islam". The city is well planned, with lots of open spaces and wide, tree-lined avenues. Karachi is the major port and largest city, with more than 10 million people living there.

PEOPLES OF PAKISTAN
There are many different groups of people living in Pakistan, all of whom have their own distinctive language and culture. The Pathan tribes of the Northwest Frontier are known for their fierce loyalty to family and tribe. The Sindhis (above) are a farming community living in the south of the country with a rich tradition in literature and music. The Punjabis live in the fertile plains of the Punjab.

BRIGHT BUSES
Many people in Pakistan travel on the brightly coloured buses that run between the towns and cities. The buses often have flowers and patterns painted on them and are decorated with tinsel and fairy lights. Trucks used to transport all sorts of goods are also often highly decorated.

WATERING THE LAND
The flat, fertile plains of the Punjab form the farming heartland of Pakistan. The rich soil is watered by the River Indus, which also provides water for drinking and for electricity. The river has five tributaries, the Jhelum, Chenab, Ravi, Sutlej, and Beas, which give the region its name, as Punjab means "five waters". In other parts of the country, huge irrigation (watering) schemes have converted scrubland and semi-desert into fertile farmland.

WOMEN'S LIFE
Islamic law is very important in Pakistan. It sets out how people should worship and behave. It is Islamic custom for women to live in *purdah* (behind the veil). This means that when women appear in public, they cover themselves with a *burqa* (hooded gown) or a *chaddar* (veil), to ensure that men cannot see their faces. Traditional households are often divided into a men's section at the front and a women's section at the back.

Chaddar, or veil

Kamiz, or tunic

Find out more
COTTON: *36, 215, 216*
IRRIGATION: *155, 156, 217*
ISLAM: *275*
RIVER VALLEYS: *135*

BANGLADESH

IN 1971, EAST PAKISTAN broke away from West Pakistan to become the independent country of Bangladesh. Like Pakistan, it remains a largely Muslim country. The official language is Bengali. Bangladesh is one of the poorest and most crowded countries in the world, suffering from frequent cyclones and floods which cause devastation, especially along the coast. Efforts are being made to control the floods, to slow down the rate of population growth, and to modernize industry and farming.

BANGLADESH

Capital city: Dhaka

Area: 143,998 sq km (55,598 sq miles)

Population: 109,876,977

Official language: Bengali

Major religions: Muslim 83%, Hindu 16%, other 1%

Government: Multi-party democracy

Currency: Taka

Adult literacy rate: 37%

Life expectancy: 52 years

People per doctor: 6,670

Televisions: 5 per 1,000 people

GROWING JUTE

Known to Bangladeshis as "the golden fibre", jute is a tough, fibrous plant which has proved a valuable source of income for farmers. Jute is used to make sacking, rope, and carpet backing. It has traditionally been Bangladesh's most important export, but now faces competition from artificial fibres. Rice is a major food crop in Bangladesh, with tea and sugarcane grown for export.

The flooded delta
The map shows the varying depths of water during the annual flood.

Most Bangladeshi people make their living from fishing and farming. The annual floods provide plenty of fish and keep the land very fertile.

FLOODED LAND

Much of Bangladesh is made up of the delta (mouth) of three major rivers – the Ganges, Brahmaputra, and Meghna. During the monsoon season (June to October) the rivers flood and huge amounts of rich silt are left behind, making the soil extremely fertile for farming. But the flooding can also cause devastation, killing many people and animals, and sweeping away homes and crops. Despite the risks, most Bangladeshis live in tiny villages scattered across the floodplains.

Depth of water
- up to 1 m (3 ft)
- 1-2 m (3-6 ft)
- more than 2 m (6 ft)

Houses are often raised up on stilts or embankments to protect them from the floods.

Boats are a vital means of transport. People travel in all types of craft, which are often very crowded. Huge rafts are used to carry jute, bamboo, and other goods.

HEALTH CARE
Despite government health-care programmes, the death rate in Bangladesh is very high, especially among children in remote, rural areas. This is largely due to poor diet and to unclean water, which helps spread diseases such as cholera. Medical teams travel around the country immunizing people from disease and teaching them about diet and birth control.

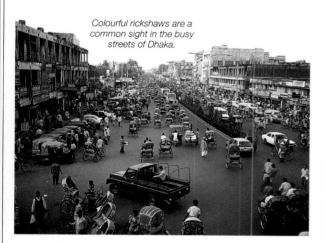

Colourful rickshaws are a common sight in the busy streets of Dhaka.

LIFE IN THE CITY

Only about a third of Bangladeshis live in cities, mainly in Dhaka, the capital, or the two ports of Chittagong and Khulna. City dwellers can enjoy a higher standard of living than people in the villages, with better homes and facilities such as piped water and electricity supplies. As the cities become more crowded with people looking for work, however, many new arrivals are being forced to live in slums and shanty towns.

Find out more

HEALTH: *276*
ISLAM: *275*
MONSOON: *166*
RIVER VALLEYS: *135*

INDIA

THE WORLD'S SEVENTH LARGEST and second most populated country, India is a vast, colourful land, full of variety in religion, language, and culture. Three of the world's major faiths, Hinduism, Buddhism, and Sikhism, originated here. More than 200 languages are spoken, though 40 per cent of the population speak Hindi. Despite much poverty, India is one of the world's top industrialized nations. Both agriculture and industry have expanded during the past 15 years and have attracted investment from international companies. India is also the world's largest democracy. Some 450 million people are eligible to vote.

BOLLYWOOD
More films are produced in India than anywhere else in the world, including the USA. About 800 full-length feature films are shot each year, mainly in Bombay, nicknamed "Bollywood". Indian films are often packed with songs, dancing, romance, glamorous stars, and non-stop action. Going to the cinema is a favourite pastime in India, and many films last for four or five hours.

INDIA

Capital city: New Delhi

Area: 3,287,590 sq km (1,269,338 sq miles)

Population: 844,324,222

Official languages: Hindi, English

Major religions: Hindu 83%, Muslim 11%, Christian 2%, Sikh 2%, other 2%

Government: Multi-party democracy

Currency: Rupee

Adult literacy rate: 50%

Life expectancy: 60 years

People per doctor: 2,440

Televisions: 32 per 1,000 people

These farm workers are winnowing, or sifting, grain after the harvest. Huge amounts of grain are kept in reserve in case the harvest fails.

GREEN REVOLUTION

One of India's most pressing problems has been to produce enough food for its ever-growing population. Today, it is self-sufficient in food, production of rice and wheat having risen more than 200 per cent since independence. This improvement is partly due to the "Green Revolution" of the 1960s, when farming methods were modernized and higher yielding varieties of rice and wheat were planted.

FOOD PRODUCTION
India is the world's biggest producer of the crops shown below. Percentages indicate India's share in world production.

sugar 11% — bananas 13% — tea 28% — sesame seeds 33% — jute 44% — mangoes 60%

Cinnamon is used in both sweet and savoury dishes.

Garlic is added to many spice mixtures.

Coriander is an essential ingredient in many Indian dishes.

Turmeric is used as a spice and a dye.

INDIAN FOOD

Many Indian people are vegetarians. They do not believe in killing animals to eat. Most Hindus never eat beef because they consider cows to be sacred, and Muslims do not eat pork. Food varies from place to place, but a typical meal might consist of several spicy vegetable dishes, *dhal* (lentils), *dahi* (yoghurt), rice or *chappatis* (flat bread), and *poppadums*. The food is flavoured with many spices, including turmeric, chilli, coriander, cumin, and cardamom.

Rice

Vegetables in a spicy sauce.

INDUSTRY

Since independence, industry has expanded in India. Factories produce and process goods such as cars, chemicals, food and drink, and computers. Jet aeroplanes and space rockets are now being made. Textiles and leather goods are major exports. About half of India's industrial output comes from small, family-run "cottage" industries producing traditional handicrafts such as brasswork, mirror work, and tie-dye.

BUSY CITIES

India's cities are bustling, chaotic places where modern, high-rise office blocks stand next to ancient temples, mosques, and monuments. New Delhi is the capital, but the two largest cities are Calcutta (left) and Bombay. Both are major industrial centres. Overcrowding is a serious and growing problem in India's cities, as more and more people arrive from the countryside in search of work. Many people live in slums and shanty towns, or on the streets.

MEMORY IN MARBLE

The Taj Mahal in Agra was built in the 17th century by Shah Jahan, one of the Mughal emperors who ruled India from the 16th to 18th centuries. Built in white marble as a tomb for his beloved wife, it is a fine example of Islamic architecture and attracts many visitors. Tourism is an increasingly important industry in India, bringing millions of people every year.

HINDU WEDDING

Hindu weddings are elaborate affairs, with ceremonies and feasting lasting for several days. Most marriages take place among members of the same *caste*, or social group, and are arranged by the couple's parents. After the wedding, the bride lives with her husband's family. Family life is very important to Hindus. They often live as part of an extended family, with several generations sharing the same house.

The bride and groom wear garlands round their necks.

After the sheet has been lifted, the bride and groom take seven steps around the sacred fire. Each step represents an aspect of their future life together, such as happiness, children, and lifelong friendship.

At the beginning of the wedding ceremony, the bride and groom sit facing each other, holding hands through a silk sheet held as a screen between them.

Traditionally, a Hindu bride wears a red silk sari, embroidered with gold thread, together with special jewellery and make-up. Her hands and feet are decorated with mehndi (henna).

The henna lasts for weeks, reflecting the woman's new status as a wife.

A silk sari

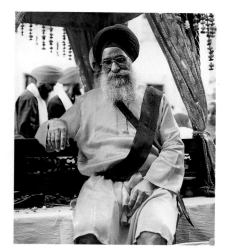

OTHER FAITHS

Most people in India are Hindu, but many other faiths are followed, such as Sikhism and Jainism. Sikhs believe in one god. Their holiest shrine is the Golden Temple, in Amritsar. Many male Sikhs wear turbans (left), a symbol of purity. Jainism is similar to Hinduism. Jains have respect for all life, and monks wear masks to prevent insects from entering their mouths.

SARI

The traditional dress for Indian women is the sari, a length of brightly coloured silk or cotton, some 20 m (66 ft) long, which is wrapped around the body and draped over one shoulder. One end of the sari is left hanging or used to cover the head. Traditional dress for men is a *dhoti*, a length of cotton cloth usually wrapped around the waist and between the legs.

Find out more

DEMOCRACY: *270*
GROWING CITIES: *17, 135*
RELIGION: *274–275*
SPICES: *57, 198, 264*

SRI LANKA

SRI LANKA IS A TEARDROP-SHAPED island that lies off the southeast coast of India. It is known for its tropical, palm-fringed beaches, rugged mountains, and varied wildlife which attracts thousands of tourists. In recent years, Sri Lanka and its tourist trade have been badly hit by fighting between the Sinhalese people and the minority Tamil group, who want an independent state. Agriculture is important to Sri Lanka. Tea, rubber, and coconuts are grown on large plantations and are the island's main export crops. Rice is the main food crop.

SRI LANKA	
Capital city: Colombo	
Area: 65,610 sq km (25,332 sq miles)	
Population: 17,900,000	
Official language: Sinhalese	
Major religions: Buddhist 69%, Hindu 15%, Christian 8%, Muslim 8%	
Government: Multi-party democracy	
Currency: Sri Lanka rupee	
Adult literacy rate: 89%	
Life expectancy: 71 years	
People per doctor: 7,140	
Televisions: 35 per 1,000 people	

THE SACRED TOOTH
The most important Buddhist festival in Sri Lanka takes place in Kandy in August. A beautifully decorated elephant parades through the streets, carrying a gold casket containing the sacred tooth of the Buddha. For the rest of the year, the tooth is kept in the Temple of the Tooth. It is said that the tooth was snatched from the Buddha's funeral pyre (fire) in 543BC.

Sapphire stone

Sapphire earrings

SAPPHIRE BLUE
Sri Lanka is known for its gemstones, particularly those from Ratnapura, the "City of Gems". Sapphires, rubies, topazes, amethysts, and garnets are all found in the rocks nearby. Many are made into superb jewellery or exported abroad.

Many Tamil women are employed as tea pickers.

THE TAMILS

Tensions between the Sinhalese government and the Tamils erupted into civil war in 1983 and have continued ever since. The Tamils object to the domination of the island by the Sinhalese and are demanding their own independent state in the north. Tamils, who are mostly Hindu, make up about 20 per cent of the population. The mainly Buddhist Sinhalese form the majority, accounting for about 75 per cent.

BEAUTIFUL BEACHES
Tourism is among Sri Lanka's most important industries. Badly hit by political troubles in the 1980s and early 1990s, it is now starting to recover and tourists are returning to the island in huge numbers. Sri Lanka is well known for its beautiful sandy beaches, especially on the south and southwest coasts, and for its Buddhist temples and monuments further inland.

Tea seeds are first sown in a nursery bed and then the young plants are transplanted to a field.

The women hang the baskets from their heads, so that both hands are free for picking.

TEA GROWING

Tea is grown mainly on large plantations in the central highlands. The cooler climate allows the tea to grow slowly, adding to its flavour. Only the youngest, tenderest leaves are harvested, and then processed quickly to retain quality. Tea makes up about a third of the island's exports. Recently, the tea industry has suffered fierce competition from countries producing cheaper, lower quality tea.

The tea plants are plucked once a week. Picking is still done by hand as machines would bruise the leaves and spoil their flavour.

When the tea picker's basket is full, it is taken for weighing. The picker is paid by the basket.

The leaves are then fermented and dried to produce the final product.

Find out more

BUDDHISM: *275*
GEMSTONES: *62, 191*
RUBBER: *194, 226*
TEA GROWING: *238*

NEPAL

THE SMALL, ISOLATED country of Nepal lies in the Himalayan mountains and is cut off from the sea (landlocked). It is a Hindu state, although many people practise a mixture of Hinduism and Buddhism. Until 1991, the king was the absolute ruler. In that year, democratic elections were held for the first time. Nepal is now ruled by an elected government. Trekkers and tourists flock to Nepal every year, bringing valuable income to this very poor country.

KATHMANDU
Kathmandu is the capital and largest city in Nepal. In the old part of the city there are many narrow streets and squares lined with ancient temples and monuments. In one temple lives the Kumari Devi, or living goddess. She is a young girl chosen to represent the Hindu goddess, Parvati, until she reaches puberty.

NEPAL	
Capital city: Kathmandu	
Area: 140,800 sq km (54,363 sq miles)	
Population: 21,100,000	
Official language: Nepali	
Major religions: Hindu 90%, Buddhist 5%, Muslim 3%, other 2%	
Government: Multi-party democracy	
Currency: Nepalese rupee	
Adult literacy rate: 27%	
Life expectancy: 53 years	
People per doctor: 16,670	
Televisions: 2 per 1,000 people	

BHUTAN	
Capital city: Thimpu	
Area: 47,000 sq km (18,147 sq miles)	
Population: 1,700,000	
Official language: Dzongkha	
Major religions: Buddhist 70%, Hindu 24%, other 6%	
Government: Absolute monarchy	
Currency: Ngultrum	
Adult literacy rate: 41%	
Life expectancy: 48 years	
People per doctor: 13,110	
Televisions: Bhutan does not have a TV service	

MOUNTAIN TERRACES
About 90 per cent of Nepalese people work on the land. Crops such as rice are grown on immaculately kept terraces cut into the mountainside. This allows farmers to grow crops on land that would otherwise be inaccessible. Farmers depend on the monsoon rains for a good harvest.

These Sherpa women are carrying heavy loads as they trek through the mountains.

NEPALESE PEOPLES
There are many different groups of people living in Nepal. The Sherpas of the eastern mountains are known for their climbing skill. The Gurkha people are famous for their courage and military skills. Their reputation has spread all over the world. The Newars of Kathmandu Valley are known for their magnificent wood carvings which decorate many Nepali temples and houses. More than half of the people are Nepalese, of Indian descent.

BHUTAN

THE HIMALAYAN KINGDOM of Bhutan is a mysterious, isolated place because of its location in the mountains and its restrictions on tourism. With limited natural resources, Bhutan has been trying to exploit the fast-flowing mountain rivers to produce hydroelectricity. Bhutan is a Buddhist country, ruled by an absolute monarch, the Dragon King.

Drupkas speak Dzonghkha, the national language of Bhutan, which is closely related to Tibetan.

Bhutanese people eat yak meat, use their milk to make butter and cheese, and use their dung as fuel.

Yak hair is used for tents and clothes and yak tails are used as fans or dusters.

USEFUL YAKS
For many people living in the mountains of Bhutan, life revolves around their herds of yaks. These tough, hardy animals can carry heavy loads and survive freezing temperatures.

DRUPKAS
About 70 per cent of the Bhutanese are Drupkas of Tibetan origin. Clashes between the Drupkas and the Nepali-speaking Lhotsampa people of the south led to violent demonstrations against the government in 1990. Further immigration into Bhutan is banned.

Find out more	
HIMALAYAS: *132, 166*	
HINDUISM & BUDDHISM: *275*	
POLITICAL SYSTEMS: *270–271*	
TERRACE FARMING: *159, 201*	

EAST ASIA

EAST ASIA IS DOMINATED by the vast country of China, but it also includes the windswept plains of Mongolia, North and South Korea, the fertile island of Taiwan, and the tiny colonies of Hong Kong and Macao. China itself is full of contrasts. In the west, high ranges of mountains tower over rocky valleys and semi-desert plains. Tibet, a previously independent country occupied by China since 1950, is known as the "roof of the world" because it is so high above sea level. In the north of the country is the harsh and empty Gobi Desert. In eastern China and North and South Korea, river valleys and flood plains are farmed intensively, providing food for the millions of people who live in the cities on or near the coast.

Urumqi, China
☀ Jan -17°C (3°F)
July 21°C (70°F)
🌧 Jan 15 mm (0.6 in)
July 18 mm (0.7 in)

THE YELLOW RIVER
The Yellow River, or Huang He, is one of the world's most destructive rivers. It has flooded the surrounding land many times, causing enormous loss of life. For this reason, the river is known as "China's Sorrow". As it slowly glides eastwards through central China, it erodes huge amounts of fertile loess (fine soil) from the land which stains the river yellow, hence its name.

THE GREAT WALL
Snaking across northern China, from the Yellow Sea in the east to the deserts of central Asia in the west, is one of the technological wonders of the ancient world. Much of the Great Wall was built in the 1400s to protect Chinese farmers from invasion by nomads from Mongolia. At almost 6,400 km (4,000 miles) long, it is the world's longest structure, and can be seen by astronauts in outer space.

ANCESTOR WORSHIP
One of the main ideas of Confucianism, the ancient religion of China, is the importance of family loyalties and the honouring of ancestors. Because of this, traditional funerals in East Asia follow a set ritual to ensure that the soul of the dead person is well provided for. At the graveside, mourners make food offerings and burn paper money and paper models of cars, bikes, and other goods to accompany the soul to heaven.

People throw paper money to pacify spirits that are thought to haunt the road.

Mourners often wear over-garments made of sackcloth, and white headdresses.

Buddhist priests often lead the funeral procession. They chant prayers and play musical instruments.

Effigies (models) of Confucius, the founder of Confucianism, are carried along the way.

The richer the family, the more ornate the coffin.

| | G | H | I | J | K | L | M | N | O | P | Q | R |

THINGS TO LOOK FOR ON THE MAP

Longest river: Yangtze, China 5,520 km (3,430 miles) *Map L11*

Highest point: Mt. Everest, on border of China/Nepal/Tibet, 8,848 m (29,029 ft) *Map D12*

Largest lake: Qinghai Hu, China 4,460 sq km (1,722 sq miles) *Map H9*

World's largest square: Tiananmen Square, Beijing, China 396,606 sq m (4,269,027 sq ft) *Map M8*

0 100 200 300 400 km
0 50 100 150 200 250 miles

MONGOLIA

N

RUSSIAN FEDERATION

L. Hövsgöl
L. Uvs
Ulaangom
L. Hyargas
Mörön
Sühbaatar
Erdenet
Darhan
Har Us L.
Uliastay
Tsetserleg
ULAN BATOR
Öndörhaan
Choybalsan
Uldz
Kerulen
Orhon
Etsyn
Agun

Altay
Arvayheer
Saynshand
Erenhot

MONGOLIA

GOBI DESERT

Hami

INNER MONGOLIA

Xilinhot

Manzhouli
Hailar
Hulun Nur
Yakeshi
Zalantun
Qiqihar

LESSER KHINGAN MTS.
Amur
Yichun
Bei'an
Jiamusi
L. Khanka

Harbin
Ulanhot
Jixi

GREATER KHINGAN RANGE
MANCHURIA

Tongliao
Changchun
Jilin

Liaoyuan

Ch'öngjin

SEA OF JAPAN

NORTH KOREA

Chifeng
Shenyang
Fushun
Anshan

NORTH KOREA
Hamhüng
Wönsan

Hohhot
Baotou
Jining
Great Wall
Datong
BEIJING
Tianjin
Tangshan

Sinüiju
PYONGYANG
Namp'o
Haeju
Kangnüng

SOUTH KOREA

BAIDAN JARAN DESERT
Linhe
Wuhai
Dongsheng
ORDOS DESERT

Dalian
Yantai
Bo Hai
Korea Bay
SEOUL
Inch'ön
Taejön
Taegu

Yumen
Great Wall
Great Wall
Yinchuan
Great Wall

Shijiazhuang
Taiyuan
Yellow R.

YELLOW SEA
SHANDONG PENINSULA

SOUTH KOREA
Pusan
Korea Strait
Kwangju

Lenghu
Da Qaidam
Delingha
Wuwei
Wuwei
Great Wall
Xining
Qinghai Hu

Handan
Jinan
Zibo
Tai'an
Qingdao

Cheju

Golmud
Lanzhou

Changzhi
Zaozhuang
Lianyungang

QINGHAI
BAYAN HAR MTS.

Baoji
Xi'an
Luoyang
Zhengzhou
Xuzhou
Hongze Hu
Grand Canal

Beijing, China

Yushu
GULA MTS.
Qamdo

Mianyang

QIN LING
Ankang

Huainan
Nanjing
Hefei
Wuxi
Suzhou
Shanghai

Jan -4°C (24°F)
July 26°C (79°F)
Jan 4 mm (0.2 in)
July 243 mm (9.6 in)

Nyingchi
Litang
Chengdu
Wanxian
Yichang

Xiangfan
Xinyang
Jingmen
Wuhan
Yangtze
Hangzhou
Shaoxing
Ningbo

INDIA

Leshan
Zigong
Chongqing

Dongting Hu
Poyang Hu
Yueyang
Nanchang
Jingdezhen
Wenzhou

Mekong
Salween
Jinsha

Xichang
Panzhihua
Zunyi
Changsha
Shaoyang
Pingxiang
Nanping
Fuzhou

EAST CHINA SEA

Dongchuan
Dali
Guiyang
Guilin
Shaoguan
Ganzhou
Xiamen

Chi-lung
TAIPEI
TAIWAN

TAIWAN

Kunming
Gejiu

GUANGXI ZHUANG AUTONOMOUS REGION
Liuzhou
Wuzhou
Canton
Dongguang
Shantou
Kao-hsiung

Taiwan Strait

BURMA
Salween
Mekong

Nanning
Pingxiang
Zhanjiang
Xuwen
Macao
Kowloon
HONG KONG
MACAO
(Portugal)
Hong Kong (UK)

VIETNAM
LAOS

LEIZHOU PENINSULA
Gulf of Tongking
Haikou

Shantou

SOUTH CHINA SEA

Hainan
Sanya

Lhasa, China
Jan -1°C (29°F)
July 16°C (62°F)
Jan 0 mm (0 in)
July 122 mm (4.8 in)

CHINA

Taipei, Taiwan
Jan 16°C (60°F)
July 29°C (84°F)
Jan 86 mm (3.4 in)
July 231 mm (9.1 in)

CHINA

CHINA

Capital city: Beijing	
Area: 9,396,960 sq km (3,628,166 sq miles)	
Population: 1,133,682,501	
Official language: Mandarin	
Major religions: Traditional religions 20%, Buddhist 6%, Muslim 2%, other 72%	
Government: One-party state	
Currency: Yuan	
Adult literacy rate: 80%	
Life expectancy: 71 years	
People per doctor: 730	
Televisions: 30 per 1,000 people	

ONE IN FIVE PEOPLE in the world today lives in just one country – China. This vast nation is almost the same size as the whole of Europe, and is the third largest country in the world after Russia and Canada. It has also one of the world's oldest civilizations, with a history stretching back more than 7,000 years. Ruled by a succession of emperors, China became a republic in 1911 and a communist state in 1949. Under the communists, every aspect of life was controlled by the state and China became a major industrial and military power. In recent years it has begun to move towards a more competitive economy which encourages investment from other countries.

THE FORBIDDEN CITY
When the emperor Zhu Di rebuilt China's capital, Beijing, in the 15th century, he created a vast imperial palace in the centre of the new city. The palace became known as the Forbidden City as only the emperor's family and closest advisers could enter it. Encircled by walls, it contains nearly 1,000 buildings, including temples, stables, and a library.

CHINESE WRITING

Unlike English or French, which use an alphabet of 26 letters, Chinese writing uses more than 50,000 characters or symbols. Each character depicts a different word or idea. Simple words, such as "sky", or "rain", use one character. Complex words use two or more – "telephone" uses the characters for "electric" and for "talk".

The art of handwriting, or calligraphy, is highly prized in China because great care is required to draw each character correctly.

CHINESE COMMUNISM

The Communist Party took control of China in 1949. Led by Mao Zedong, the party believed in a society in which everyone was equal and property was owned by the whole community. Land was taken from wealthy landowners and given to groups of peasant farmers who worked together on large, collective farms. Industry was put under state control. These attempts to transform China met with mixed success. Since Mao's death in 1976, private ownership has again been allowed to develop.

Portraits of Mao Zedong still hang in Tiananmen Square in Beijing, the largest public square in the world.

RICE GROWING

Two-thirds of China's large population live and work on the land. The most fertile areas are found in the south. The main crop is rice, though tea, cotton, fruit, and vegetables are also grown. The rice is planted in flooded paddy fields (shown below). Two crops of rice and one of vegetables or cereals are harvested in a good year. In the north and west of the country, which is drier and hillier, farmers grow a single crop of cereals and tend sheep and cattle.

Ploughing
Water buffaloes are used to plough, rake, and flatten the muddy paddy fields ready for planting.

Low earth barriers known as bunds separate the paddy fields.

Planting
Women do the back-breaking work of planting out the rice shoots.

Sowing

While the paddy fields are being prepared, rice seeds are sown in a separate flooded field, or seed-bed.

After a month, the tightly packed rice shoots are ready for transplanting into the paddy fields.

Some farms in China have tractors, but most use water buffaloes or oxen.

Water in the paddy fields keeps down the weeds.

CHINESE FOOD

Chinese people take great pleasure in their food, which varies from region to region. Western cuisine from Sichuan province uses spices, while northern cuisine from Beijing is famous for its tasty roast duck. Cantonese food from the south is renowned across the world for its fish dishes and delicate flavours. Meals are cooked by steaming or stir-frying in a large pan called a wok. Rice is served in the south of the country, wheat buns or noodles in the north. The food is held in small bowls and chopsticks are used for eating.

Bean sprouts

Green mung beans are eaten as a savoury or sweet.

Native to China, star anise is a spice that has a similar flavour to aniseed.

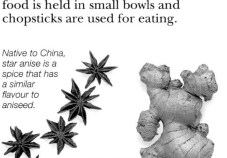

Root ginger adds a fresh, spicy taste to many dishes in western China.

Chilli peppers are added to make hot, spicy dishes.

Rice, whether boiled, steamed, or fried, forms the basis of many Chinese dishes.

China bowl

Tea is served in handleless china cups.

Tea, made without milk and sugar, is the most popular drink in China.

Chopsticks are used for eating.

Knives are not needed because food is sliced before cooking.

Jasmine tea is a light refreshing drink made from green leaves. Black and Oolong are other types of Chinese tea.

Harvesting

Farmers cut the stalks with sickles and tie them into bundles.

The rice stalks are beaten to shake off the grain.

Piles of rice grains are left in the sun to dry.

When the rice is dry, the outer shells, or husks, are removed, and the rice is sifted.

CITY LIFE

More than 250 million Chinese people live in towns and cities, many of which are overcrowded. Accommodation is scarce and families usually live in one or two rooms rented from the company they work for. The city streets are full of bicycles, and public transport, while cheap and frequent, is always packed. The main industrial and commercial city is Shanghai, home to 12 million people and one of the biggest cities in the world.

ONE-CHILD FAMILIES

The Chinese population is growing by about 15 million people a year, which is almost the total population of Australia. In order to reduce this rapid growth, the government introduced a policy in 1979 to limit each family to one child only. The single children are known as "Little Emperors" because they are often spoiled. The one-child policy has succeeded in the towns, but not in the country, where large families are needed to provide labour in the fields.

FOOD PRODUCTION

Every patch of fertile soil in China is used for agriculture. Crops are planted alongside roads and railway lines, and one type of crop is often planted between rows of another. China is the world's biggest producer of the crops shown below. Percentages indicate China's share in world production.

85%
36%
31%
29%
23%
20%

carrots
water-melons
pears
cucumbers
rice
sweet potatoes

NEW YEAR CELEBRATIONS

Every year, in late January or early February, Chinese people prepare to celebrate the New Year. They spring-clean their houses, put up red decorations to bring them luck, and give new clothes and toys to their children. The festival itself lasts for several days. Every shop and office is closed, and people take to the streets, letting off firecrackers and joining in the displays of lion and dragon dances.

THE BUDDHISTS OF TIBET

Tibet, once an independent country, has been part of China since 1950. Tibetans are devout Buddhists and their religion has been suppressed by the Communist Party, which discourages any religious practice. However, the Buddhist faith remains strong in Tibet. Buddhists devote their lives to prayer. They hang up flags with prayers printed on them to bring fortune and good luck.

Tibetan Buddhists hang prayer flags from their houses, across bridges, or on mountainsides.

THE GRAND CANAL

The world's longest waterway, the Grand Canal, stretches for 1,790 km (1,110 miles) across China. It was begun in the 5th century BC to connect the cities of the north with the rice growing valleys of the south. Near its southern end, the canal passes through Suzhou, a picturesque city known as the "Venice of the East" because it is crisscrossed by rivers and canals.

LIFE IN THE PARK

Because most city people live in flats with no gardens, parks play an important part in everyone's life. Exercise is encouraged in China, and people go regularly to the park to keep fit. Early in the morning, many people practise *tai chi* or the more vigorous *kung-fu*. Children fly kites on windy days, and adults play table tennis, cards, or chess, or just sit and chat with their friends.

Table tennis is very popular in China; tables are set up in parks for people to enjoy a game out in the open air.

Kites are made by pasting brightly coloured paper on to simple bamboo frames, often in the shape of animals or birds.

People often play Chinese chess and cards.

Cycling is popular, as a means of transport and as a way of keeping fit.

Tai chi is a form of gentle exercise with slow movements, which resembles shadow boxing.

Chinese parks are beautifully kept and contain rockeries and trees that blossom in the spring.

INDUSTRY

China has huge coal reserves and deposits of most minerals. After the Communists took power in 1949, the government concentrated on heavy industry, building huge iron and steel works and chemical plants. In recent years, light engineering and the production of consumer goods have been encouraged, and China is now a leading producer of fertilizers, textiles, clothing, and electronics.

CHINESE MEDICINE

The Chinese believe that a person falls ill because the opposing forces of *yin* and *yang* in the body become unbalanced. Doctors rebalance the body with herbal remedies and acupuncture, which involves sticking thin needles into various parts of the body to relieve pain. Many people are treated by "barefoot doctors", or locally trained healers.

Bugbane rhizome (sheng ma) is used to treat headaches, colds, and measles.

Wolfberry (guo qi zi) is used for diabetes and is said to improve eyesight.

Senn leaf (fan xie ye) is a herb used to cleanse the system.

Chain fern bark (gou ji) helps ease back pain.

Find out more
BUDDHISM: 275
POLITICAL SYSTEMS: 270–271
POPULATION GROWTH: 16–17
RICE GROWING: 135, 185, 197

HONG KONG

HONG KONG*	
Capital city: None	
Area: 1,045 sq km (403 sq miles)	
Population: 5,674,114	
Official languages: English, Cantonese	
Major religions: Buddhist and Daoist 74%, Christian 9%, other 17%	
Government: Under British Administration	
Currency: Hong Kong dollar	

* Hong Kong is not an independent country. It is a territory ruled by Britain.

MACAO*	
Capital city: Macao	
Area: 16 sq km (6 sq miles)	
Population: 355,693	
Official languages: Chinese, Portuguese	
Major religions: Buddhist 45%, Christian 16%, other 39%	
Government: Under Portuguese administration	
Currency: Pataca	

* Macao is not an independent country. It is a territory ruled by Portugal.

HONG KONG

Tucked into a corner of southeast China, Hong Kong occupies only a small area, yet almost 6 million people live squashed on its rocky islands and mountainous mainland. It is one of the world's most important finance centres and has one of its most prosperous economies. In 1898, the New Territories of Hong Kong were leased by China to Britain for 99 years. In 1997, Hong Kong will be returned to China.

FLOATING HOMES

Many people in Hong Kong live not on the land but on boats. Families are squashed on to wooden junks and sampans, mostly making their living by fishing. Floating schools, shops, and restaurants serve their needs, while doctors, dentists, and hairdressers do their rounds by boat. Thousands of people still live in these floating villages, but, increasingly, deep sea trawlers are replacing the traditional boats and forcing the fisherfolk to look for work on land.

MACAO

Overshadowed by its richer and bigger neighbour, Macao consists of a mainland and two islands linked by a bridge and causeway. Macao will be returned to China in 1999. When its Portuguese rulers give up power – after almost 450 years – it will be the end of the longest surviving European settlement in Asia.

TOURISM

Macao's skyline is dominated by casinos and hotels. The casinos are a big tourist attraction because gambling is very popular with the Chinese and casinos are outlawed in Hong Kong. Gambling is a major industry in Macao, providing about one-third of the country's income.

HONG KONG SHANGHAI BANK
In the central business district of Hong Kong stands the impressive Hong Kong Shanghai Bank. This masterpiece of technological engineering was completed in 1985. At every stage of its construction, experts in *feng shui*, the ancient Chinese belief in the natural forces of wind and water, were consulted to ensure that the building would bring health, prosperity, and good fortune to its many occupants.

TEXTILES
Across Hong Kong, many thousands of people are employed in small workshops making jeans, T-shirts, suits, and shirts for export around the world. The textile industry is a major employer in Hong Kong, but recently electronics factories have grown in number, producing calculators, radios, watches, and computers.

INDUSTRY
Macao produces a variety of goods for export, ranging from textiles and electronic goods to fireworks (shown above), toys, and artificial flowers. Every day, low-paid workers from China come to work in the many factories of Macao.

Find out more
COLONIAL RULE IN ASIA: *136*
DEPENDENT TERRITORIES: *271*
POPULATION: *16–17, 135*
TIGER ECONOMIES: *137*

TAIWAN

WHEN PORTUGUESE SAILORS first visited this island in 1590, they named it *Ilha Formosa* – "Beautiful Island" – because of its lush, mountainous scenery. For many years part of China, Taiwan has been isolated from the mainland since 1949, when the nationalist government of China fled to the island after it was overthrown by the communists. Both nationalists and communists consider Taiwan to be a province of China, but cannot agree who has the right to rule the whole country. Few nations recognize Taiwan as a separate country, but despite this the island has a thriving economy that exports a wide range of goods around the world.

TAIWAN	
Capital city: Taipei	
Area: 36,179 sq km (13,969 sq miles)	
Population: 20,800,000	
Official language: Mandarin	
Major religions: Buddhist, Confucian, and Taoist 93%, Christian 5%, other 2%	
Government: Multi-party democracy	
Currency: New Taiwan dollar	
Adult literacy rate: 86%	
Life expectancy: 75 years	
People per doctor: No figures available	
Televisions: 300 per 1,000 people	

TAIPEI

For most of its 120-year history, Taipei has been a city of unimpressive low-rise buildings. But during the last 20 years the city has been transformed into the modern hi-tech capital of the island, with many new tower blocks, public buildings, and landscaped gardens. Almost 3 million people live in Taipei, and the city is still growing rapidly. The capital has problems with congestion and pollution. Most people travel to work on motorcycles, contributing to the smog that covers the city for most of the year.

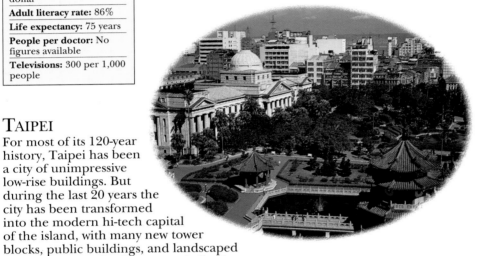

INDUSTRY

Once a poor agricultural island, Taiwan has succeeded in developing one of the world's most successful industrial economies. It is a world exporter of electronic and electrical goods, machinery, textiles, shoes, sports equipment, TV sets, and watches. This huge export trade pays for the oil and other raw materials the economy needs, for Taiwan has few natural resources of its own.

OPERA
Traditional Chinese opera is popular in Taiwan. The basic stories are simple – concerning good against evil, or boy meets girl – and there are few props on stage. Instead, the actor's movements, elaborate costumes, and facial make-up all convey character and plot.

TRIBAL GROUPS
Long before the Chinese first came to Taiwan, the island was home to a variety of peoples. Each tribe had its own distinct language, but all had many customs and skills in common. In the 1600s, the Chinese came to the island and fought the tribes for control. Today the surviving tribes make up only 2 per cent of the total population.

The largest surviving tribe are the Ami, who are expert potters and farmers. The Ami live in large villages, with women holding power in the family home.

TAOISM

The major religions practised in Taiwan are Buddhism, Taoism, and Confucianism. These faiths are closely linked and many people follow aspects of all three. Taoism, which began in China around 300BC, teaches how people can follow the *tao* (path) to a life of simplicity and freedom from desire. Taoists aim to live in harmony with nature, balancing the calm, feminine side of the body (*yin*) with the active, male side (*yang*).

Temples are used as social centres and playgrounds as well as places of worship.

Major tribes in Taiwan

- ☐ Tsou
- ☐ Paiwan
- ☐ Ami
- ☐ Atayal
- ☐ Bunun

Find out more
GROWTH OF CITIES: *17*
PACIFIC RIM ECONOMIES: *137*
RELIGION: *274–275*
TRADE: *280–281*

MONGOLIA

THE REMOTE, SPARSELY POPULATED country of Mongolia was once the centre of a vast empire. For most of this century, however, Mongolia was a communist nation linked to Soviet Russia, until democratic rule was introduced in 1990. Many people live on the grassy plains in the centre of the country, tending their flocks as they move in search of new pasture. The climate is harsh: summers are short, winters are long and cold. Mountain ranges ring the country to the north and west, while the south is bordered by the Gobi Desert. The country is rich in natural resources, with huge deposits of coal and oil, but it is only recently that these have been developed.

MONGOLIA	
Capital city: Ulan Bator	
Area: 1,565,000 sq km (604,247 sq miles)	
Population: 2,043,400	
Official language: Khalkh Mongol	
Major religions: No figures available	
Government: Multi-party democracy	
Currency: Tughrik	
Adult literacy rate: No figures available	
Life expectancy: 63 years	
People per doctor: No figures available	
Televisions: 41 per 1,000 people	

GENGHIS KHAN
During the 13th century, the Mongol leader Genghis Khan carved out a huge empire that stretched across much of central Asia and China. By the time of his death, it was said that it took almost a year to ride from one side of his empire to the other. He was succeeded by his grandson, Kublai Khan, but in the 1300s the empire was conquered by China.

The framework of a yurt consists of a circular latticework frame with a central ring to support the roof. The frame is covered with felt lashed together with rope.

Smoke from the iron stove escapes through a chimney in the roof of the yurt.

NOMADIC LIFE
The nomadic farmers of Mongolia move with their yaks, sheep, goats, camels, and cattle from the summertime pastures high in the mountains down to the grassy lowland steppes during the winter months. Yaks are ideally suited to the harsh Mongolian climate, and provide milk, butter, meat, and wool. As the nomads move with their flocks, they take their portable dome-shaped yurts with them.

A yurt may have as many as eight layers of felt to keep out the winter cold.

Flaps may be drawn over the single wooden or felt door.

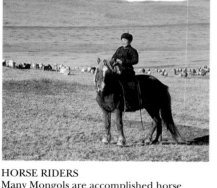

HORSE RIDERS
Many Mongols are accomplished horse riders. From a very early age, Mongolian children learn to ride horses, becoming jockeys as early as three years old. Every July 11 they get the chance to show off their skills at the Nadam Festival, a nationwide sporting event which includes horse-racing, archery, and wrestling competitions.

ULAN BATOR
The capital city of Mongolia lies at the centre of road and rail networks in the country. Until this century, Ulan Bator was a small country town, but development by its communist rulers in the last 50 years has turned it into a major city. The influence of Soviet Russia is reflected in the style of many of the city's major buildings.

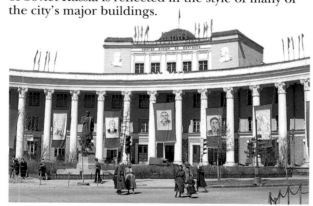

The scroll is carved in the shape of a horse's head.

Traditional wooden Mongolian fiddle

Bow

MAKING MUSIC
Mongol nomads like to entertain themselves in the evening with music. Stringed instruments, such as the Mongolian fiddle, are popular.

Find out more

NOMADS: *156, 160, 209*
POLITICAL SYSTEMS: *270–271*
STEPPE (GRASSLANDS): *15*
YAKS: *173*

NORTH KOREA

WITH ITS RUGGED, HILLY INTERIOR and limited fertile land, North Korea is a harsh country. Winds from central Asia produce extreme winter temperatures, and snow covers the ground for many months. Politically, North Korea is equally harsh. The communist government maintains a tight grip on its people. It limits contact with the outside world and forbids all foreign newspapers, but also provides excellent health and education services. The country is rich in mineral resources, and has built up its industrial and military strength to ensure that it is self-sufficient in every way.

NORTH KOREA

Capital city: Pyongyang

Area: 120,540 sq km (46,540 sq miles)

Population: 23,100,000

Official language: Korean

Major religion: No figures available

Government: One-party state

Currency: Won

Adult literacy rate: No figures available

Life expectancy: 71 years

People per doctor: 370

Televisions: 15 per 1,000 people

A DIVIDED LAND

At the end of World War II, Korea was occupied by Russian and American armies. In 1948, the country became divided in two. A communist government ruled the North and an American-backed, democratic government ruled the South. Today, the two hostile sides face each other along one of the most heavily armed borders in the world.

Most farm houses are built of brick with tile or slate roofs.

Both men and women work on the land, growing rice, vegetables, grain, and fruit.

COLLECTIVE FARMING

Under the communist government, thousands of small, family-owned farms were abolished and replaced by 3,800 enormous state-controlled farms. These collective farms are run by people who work together to produce enough food to supply the country's needs. Because North Korea is so mountainous, every piece of available land is farmed intensively, with irrigation (watering) systems, advanced machinery, and fertilizers used to improve the annual harvest.

Health services are free for everyone, with doctors and nurses employed on each collective farm.

Every farm has its own day-care centre and nursery school where babies and young children stay while their parents work on the land.

KOREAN FOOD

In North and South Korea, the whole meal is served at the same time, rather than in separate courses. Rice is always the main dish, often combined with barley and red beans and eaten with a range of spicy vegetables, herbs, and meats. Steamed rice-cakes are prepared for important celebrations.

Ginseng is exported around the world.

Kimchi, made from pickled cabbage and radishes mixed with garlic, salt, red pepper, and other spices, is a popular dish.

In jeolme, a type of rice-cake powdered with soya flour, is served as a sweet.

GINSENG

The root of the ginseng plant is grown in both North and South Korea. It is believed to promote good health and energy. After being washed, steamed, and dried it can be ground into pills or made into lotions.

KIM IL SUNG

The world's longest-serving ruler, Kim Il Sung, dominated North Korea from 1948 until his death in 1994. He established an image as the father of working people. His portrait was hung in every office and huge statues were erected to him in public places. Under his rule, North Korea became increasingly isolated politically and economically from the rest of the world. He was succeeded by his son, Kim Jong Il.

Find out more

FARM "SHARING": 115, 140, 150
HEALTH, EDUCATION: 276, 277
IRRIGATION: 155, 156, 217
POLITICAL SYSTEMS: 270–271

SOUTH KOREA

LIKE NORTH KOREA, much of South Korea is mountainous and forested. Unlike its northern neighbour, however, it has a thriving economy that trades with many other countries, such as Japan and the USA. After becoming independent in 1948, South Korea was invaded by North Korea. By the end of the Korean War (1950–53), the cities and factories of South Korea were devastated and thousands of refugees had arrived in the country from the North. Within 20 years, a remarkable turnaround had taken place. New factories began to produce world-class products, and new cities sprang up. Today South Korea has a well-educated workforce producing high-technology goods for export.

SOUTH KOREA	
Capital city: Seoul	
Area: 99,020 sq km (38,232 sq miles)	
Population: 43,410,899	
Official language: Korean	
Major religions: Christian 49%, Buddhist 47%, Confucianist 3%, other 1%	
Government: Multi-party democracy	
Currency: Won	
Adult literacy rate: 97%	
Life expectancy: 70 years	
People per doctor: 1,370	
Televisions: 207 per 1,000 people	

SEOUL

More than 7 million people live in the capital, Seoul. Most of this modern city has been built in the 40 years since the end of the Korean War. As more people have moved here from the countryside, the city has become increasingly crowded. To cope with this, Seoul has an excellent public transport system, linking buses, trains, boats, and planes into one timetable.

Shipbuilding has expanded rapidly in South Korea, which is now the second biggest shipbuilder, after Japan, in the world.

A Korean shaman is usually a woman, called a mundang.

People bring offerings of money and food to the mundang.

SHAMANISM

People in South Korea belong to a number of religions. About half are Buddhists, the rest are Christian or Confucianist. Many people in rural areas still believe in shamanism – that an invisible spirit world lives alongside the visible human world. When the spirits interfere in the lives of humans, a shaman (priest) acts as a link between the two worlds.

Burnt offerings are made to pacify the spirits.

Apart from obtaining blessings from spirits, a mundang will try to cure people's diseases and help with personal problems.

INDUSTRY

After the devastation of the Korean War, South Korea had to rebuild its industry from scratch. It concentrated on producing and exporting manufactured goods, setting up huge industrial companies, known as *chaebol*, to make shoes, clothes, ships, cars, and more recently computers and video sets. Large iron and steel works were built to supply the factories with raw materials. South Korea now has one of the most successful economies in the world.

Figures show South Korea's share in world production.

Ship production in South Korea

1980	1990	1991
4%	12%	15%

FARMING

Unlike North Korea, most farms in South Korea are small and family-owned. Rice is the main crop, but barley, wheat, fruit, vegetables, and spices are also grown. As much of the land is mountainous, farms can be found clustered along the river valleys and lowlands near the coast.

The traditional Korean fan dance is performed by women only. As the women dance, they move faster and faster around each other while making patterns with their fans.

Women wear long, brilliantly coloured, high-waisted dresses.

KOREAN DANCE

Korean dancing is popular in both the South and North. Dancers dress up in traditional clothes called *hanbok*. The aim of Korean dancing is to create a mood rather than to tell a story.

Find out more
PACIFIC RIM ECONOMIES: *137*
POLITICAL SYSTEMS: *270–271*
RELIGION: *274–275*
TRADE: *280–281*

JAPAN

JAPAN IS A CHAIN OF SOME 4,000 ISLANDS stretching for more than 2,500 km (1,553 miles) off the east coast of mainland Asia. Most people live on the four largest islands – Honshu, Hokkaido, Shikoku, and Kyushu. Flat land is in short supply. More than three-quarters of the country is hilly, leaving less than a quarter suitable for building and farming. To create more level ground, hillsides are being cut back and land is being reclaimed from the sea. Japan's climate is a varied one. The islands in the south are warm all year round, while in the north it is cooler, with snowfall on the mountains in winter. The Japanese call their country *Nippon*, "the land of the rising Sun", as the Sun can be seen rising above the Pacific Ocean.

ISLAND LINKS
Travel between the islands is made easier by a network of bridges and tunnels linking them together. The Seto Ohashi bridge (above) connects several of the smaller islands. The Akashi Kaikyo Road Bridge, linking Honshu and Shikoku, is due to open in 1998. It will be the world's longest suspension bridge, with an overall span of 1,990 m (6,529 ft).

THE EMPEROR
Japan has the oldest hereditary monarchy in the world, dating back to before the 6th century. In the past, the emperor was very powerful and many Japanese people believed he was a god. But the emperor's status changed after Japan's defeat in World War II, and his role was reduced to a symbolic one.

The present emperor, Akihito, is the 125th in the imperial line. He is highly respected by Japanese people, but he has no political power.

Mount Fuji is a huge, cone-shaped volcano. It last erupted in 1707.

SACRED MOUNTAIN

At 3,776 m (12,388 ft), Mount Fuji on Honshu is Japan's highest mountain. For the followers of Shinto, one of Japan's major religions, Mount Fuji is a sacred mountain. Each year, thousands of pilgrims make the long climb to visit the Shinto shrine on the summit. Many Japanese consider Mount Fuji to be a symbol of their country and keep a photograph or painting of the mountain on display in their homes.

UNSTABLE LAND

Japan suffers from hundreds of earthquakes a year. Slight shakes are recorded almost every day, while larger tremors causing minor damage can be felt several times a year. Strong earthquakes occur more rarely, causing damage, injury, and death. Buildings and bridges topple, roads, and railways are destroyed, and devastating fires break out. In 1995, a massive earthquake struck the port of Kobe and killed more than 5,000 people. Regular earthquake drills are held in schools, homes, and workplaces.

Children are taught to duck under desks to protect themselves from falling objects.

Modern skyscraper

Pagoda

Strong central column

BUILT TO LAST
Both new and old buildings in Japan have been designed with earthquakes in mind. A pagoda has a strong central column sunk into the ground to give it added stability. A modern skyscraper has a regular shape and thick walls reinforced by steel columns, which help make the building more secure.

Skyscrapers are often built on pads made of steel and rubber that absorb earthquake tremors.

PEACEFUL PLACES

Japanese gardens are carefully designed places of peace and beauty. They contain sand, rocks and pebbles, trees, ponds, and streams. The elements are arranged in a particular way to create a balanced, harmonious setting in which people can relax and meditate. Many gardens are influenced by Zen Buddhism, a branch of Buddhism that emphasizes the need for meditation.

A Japanese garden represents the world in a miniature form.

Trees represent forests.

Rocks symbolize mountains.

Ponds represent oceans, rivers, and streams.

JAPAN

Hakodate
☀ Jan -4°C (26°F)
☀ July 20°C (67°F)
🌧 Jan 66 mm (2.6 in)
🌧 July 137 mm (5.4 in)

THINGS TO LOOK FOR ON THE MAP

Longest river: Shinano, 370 km (230 miles) *Map G8*

Highest point: Mt. Fuji, 3,776 m (12,388 ft) *Map H9*

Largest lake: L. Biwa, 673 sq km (260 sq miles) *Map F9*

World's longest undersea rail tunnel: Seikan Tunnel between Hokkaido and Honshu, 53.85 km (33.46 miles) *Map H4*

Tokyo
☀ Jan 3°C (38°F)
☀ July 25°C (77°F)
🌧 Jan 48 mm (1.9 in)
🌧 July 142 mm (5.6 in)

0 50 100 150 km
0 50 100 miles

Nagasaki, Japan
☀ Jan 6°C (43°F)
☀ July 26°C (79°F)
🌧 Jan 71 mm (2.8 in)
🌧 July 257 mm (10.1 in)

RICE GROWING
Although only about a tenth of the land is suitable for farming, Japan has traditionally produced all the rice it needs. Rice is Japan's main food crop, and is eaten almost every day. It is intensively cultivated on small farms, using sophisticated farm machinery such as rice planters and harvesters. The work is done very quickly, so fewer workers are needed, and farmers often have a second job.

JAPAN

FOR MANY CENTURIES, Japan was closed to foreigners and wary of the outside world. Today, it is a leading industrial and technological power and one of the world's richest countries. This transformation is even more remarkable given Japan's mountainous landscape and lack of natural resources. Most raw materials have to be imported from abroad. Japanese people are hard-working and enjoy a high standard of living, with good health and education systems. Average life expectancy is the highest in the world. Western influence is strong, although people remain proud of their culture and traditions.

JAPAN

Capital city: Tokyo

Area: 377,800 sq km (145,869 sq miles)

Population: 123,611,167

Official language: Japanese

Major religions: Shinto and Buddhist 92%, other 8%

Government: Multi-party democracy

Currency: Yen

Adult literacy rate: 99%

Life expectancy: 79 years

People per doctor: 610

Televisions: 620 per 1,000 people

MAKING MONEY

Japan has huge economic power. It invests in land and property around the world. Of the ten largest commercial banks, seven are Japanese. Japan's economic and industrial heartland is in the capital, Tokyo. The world's largest stock exchange and the headquarters of many major banks and corporations are found in Tokyo's Central Business District. It is said that if an earthquake hit this area, the world would suffer economic chaos.

Electronic goods produced in Japan

Electronic components: 34%

Computers: 24%

Other 5%

Consumer goods: 18%

Industrial equipment: 19%

The Japanese excel at making electronic goods, such as televisions, cameras, digital watches, and computers, which are sold worldwide. Many Japanese companies are world leaders in research and development of new technology.

Workers often begin the day by exercising.

WORKING LIFE

One of the main reasons why the country's industries have grown so quickly is that the Japanese are very hard-working. People take great pride in their work and are loyal to their companies. Many of the larger companies are like families, providing housing and health care for their employees. Japanese businesses export huge amounts of goods ranging from cars to electronic and scientific equipment. Japan has the largest motor industry in the world.

Traditional folding fans made of bamboo covered with paper are carried by both men and women.

Black silk kimono

TRADITIONAL DRESS

People in Japan wear kimonos for religious festivals and other special occasions. A kimono (which means "clothing") is a long-sleeved, wrap-around robe, tied with a broad sash. It may be made of silk, cotton, or wool. Many formal silk kimonos are richly coloured and beautifully embroidered.

CHERRY BLOSSOM

Japanese people share a love of nature and pay close attention to the changing seasons. The blossoming of the cherry trees is a reminder that spring has arrived. The first blossoms appear in southern Kyushu, and their progress is plotted on maps shown on the television news. The blossoms last for a few days, and people celebrate by picnicking under the cherry trees.

Wooden clogs, or geta

OVERCROWDING

With a large population and a lack of flat land for settlement, Japan is a crowded country. Land is expensive, especially in the cities, and many people commute long distances to work. During rush hour, subway trains are so crowded that guards have to push commuters on board. The uncomfortable journeys that people endure inspired Japanese technicians to invent personal stereos so people could listen to music while travelling.

CHILDREN'S LIVES

Children are well looked after in Japan. There is even a national holiday, Children's Day, dedicated to them. In another festival, "seven-five-three day", children are dressed in traditional clothing and taken to religious shrines. Japanese children are expected to study hard at school. In addition to the long school day, many pupils attend extra classes on Saturdays and in the evenings.

TEA-MAKING CEREMONY

The Japanese tea-making ceremony is an elaborate ritual. Mastering the art of making, serving, and drinking tea takes several years. The ceremony takes place in a quiet, peaceful place. The host boils water over a fire and makes a thick brew with powdered green tea. Bowls of thinner tea are served later.

Flowers are arranged in a vase hung on the wall.

Water is boiled over a charcoal fire.

Sweets are served with the tea.

Tea ladle

A tea whisk is used to whip the thin tea into a fine froth.

Japanese tea cup

Green tea, the most popular drink in Japan, is ground into a powder for the tea ceremony.

SPORTING LIFE

Whether watching or taking part, Japanese people love sport. The national team sport is baseball, which came to Japan from the USA. An ancient sport unique to Japan is sumo wrestling. Success in the ring depends on weight and strength, so wrestlers follow high-protein diets.

Golf is very popular in Japan. Practice-ranges are often built on several levels to save space.

FISHING FOR FOOD

As a nation of islands, Japan depends heavily on the surrounding seas for food. The Japanese catch and eat more fish than any other country, and have the largest fishing fleet in the world. There are hundreds of villages dotted along the coast from which small fishing boats venture out, while deep-sea fish are caught by larger trawlers. Some trawlers are floating fish factories that process the catch on board. Millions of fish are also bred each year on fish farms.

Deep-sea trawlers may stay at sea for months at a time.

Fish are cleaned and filleted on board.

Many types of fish and seafood are eaten raw, as sushi, and artistically presented on lacquered dishes or trays.

After filleting, the fish are frozen or canned.

Fish are stored in the hold.

Find out more

EARTHQUAKES: *13*
GROWING CITIES: *17, 136*
LIFE EXPECTANCY: *276*
PACIFIC RIM ECONOMIES: *137*

MAINLAND SOUTHEAST ASIA

STRETCHING FROM THE FOOTHILLS of the Himalayas in the north almost to the Equator in the south, the seven countries of mainland southeast Asia are largely mountainous. About half the region is covered with forest. Most people live in the river valleys that cut through the fertile countryside. Burma is isolated, poor, and underdeveloped. In comparison, Thailand, Malaysia, and above all the island of Singapore are rich countries with modern industrial economies. Vietnam, Cambodia, and Laos are recovering from years of war. The region has a monsoon climate, with a dry season from November to March and a wet season from May to October.

THE COMING OF THE RAIN
As the wet season starts in May, the people of Laos and northeast Thailand celebrate *bun bang fai*, the skyrocket festival. They build huge rockets up to 4 m (13 ft) long from steel or plastic pipes and pack them with up to 500 kg (1,100 lb) of gunpowder. The rockets are launched into the sky to prompt the rain god, Vassakarn, to send the annual rains.

In the uplands, the river picks up silt which it carries down to the valleys.

During the monsoon season, the river bursts its banks and floods the surrounding fields.

THE MEKONG DELTA
The delta of the Mekong River in Vietnam is one of the world's great rice-growing areas, producing much of the surplus that has made Vietnam the world's sixth largest rice exporter. Farmers in the delta also grow fruit and catch the many breeds of fish that thrive in the muddy river waters.

RIVER VALLEYS
From ancient times, people have settled in the valleys of the great rivers, such as the Irrawaddy, Mekong, and Salween, because the land there is suitable for growing rice. All the major cities in the region are situated on a river. In the valleys, farmers cultivate every corner of the land, often constructing terraces on the hillsides to grow rice and other crops. They use the river waters to irrigate (water) their crops.

Silt from the uplands helps to fertilize the paddy fields.

This Akha village on the border of Thailand and Burma is surrounded by land that is cleared for slash-and-burn farming.

Rice is grown near the river, where the paddy fields can be easily watered.

1 and 2: in January an area of forest is cut down and left to dry. During the dry season in April, the area is burnt.

SLASH-AND-BURN FARMING
In the uplands, where there is lots of land but few people to work it, farmers use a technique called slash-and-burn. An area of forest is cleared and cultivated for a few years, then the farmer moves on to another patch, leaving the original land to recover. In this way, the land is never exhausted, and the forest is not destroyed to create permanent fields.

THE UPLANDS
In contrast to the crowded river valleys, the uplands are sparsely populated and largely covered by forests. Here the hill peoples live in villages, farming small plots of land and gathering fruit and other food from the forests. This traditional way of life is now threatened by the region's growing population, which has brought more people to the uplands, and by logging companies cutting down the forests.

3 and 4: crops are planted during the monsoon rains in May, and harvested in October.

Stages 3 and 4 are repeated for 2–4 years, until the soil becomes less fertile.

5 and 6: the area is left fallow for 15–25 years, and the forest grows back.

① ② ③ ④ ⑤ ⑥

N

1

INDIA

2

Chindwin

KUMON RANGE

Hkakabo Razi

Myitkyina

3

BANGLADESH

CHIN HILLS

C

Irrawaddy

Lashio

H

I

N

A

4

Monywa

Mandalay

Sagaing Amarapura

Pakokku

BURMA

Pagan

5

Sittwe

Minbu

Taunggyi

L. Inle

Mekong

Nam Ou

Red R.

L. Thac Ba

Viet Tri

Thai Nguyen

Hong Gai

HANOI

Hai Phong

Nam Dinh

Ha Long Bay

Black R.

6

Ramree I.

Pyinmana

Prome

Sandoway

Salween

Sittang

Chiang Mai

Mekong

Louang Phrabang

L A O S

Thanh Hoa

Gulf of Tongking

VIETNAM

7

BURMA

Bay of Bengal

Henzada

Pegu

Insein

Bhumiphol Res.

Thaton

Pa-an

Moulmein

Sirikit Res.

Tak

Muang Phitsannlok

VIENTIANE

Udon Thani

Nam Theun

Savannakhét

Vinh

VIETNAM

8

C. Negrais

Gulf of Martaban

Amherst

T H A I L A N D

Nakhon Sawan

Mae Nam Ping

Khon Kaen

Mae Nam Mun

Ubon Ratchathani

Mekong

Hue

Da Nang

Quang Ngai

9

ANDAMAN SEA

Srinagarind Res.

Tavoy

Mae Klong

Ayutthaya

BANGKOK

Nakhon Ratchasima

Pakxé

Sên

San

Qui Nhon

10

Mergui

Rat Buri

Chon Buri

Angkor Wat

Bátdâmbâng

Tônlé Sap

C A M B O D I A

Mekong

Lumphát

Buon Me Thuot

Nha Trang

Da Lat

11

Mergui Archipelago

ISTHMUS OF KRA

Gulf of Thailand

Kâmpóng Chhnăng

Kâmpóng Cham

PHNOM PENH

Takêv

Bien Hoa

Ho Chi Minh City

Long Xuyen

Rach Gia

Can Tho

SOUTH CHINA SEA

12

Phangan I.

Samui I.

Nakhon Si Thammarat

13

Phuket

Phuket I.

Luang Lagoon

Hat Yai

Songkhla

Yala

Langkawi

Kota Baharu

14

George Town

Taiping

Ipoh

CAMERON HIGHLANDS

Kuala Terengganu

Kuantan

15

KUALA LUMPUR

Kelang

M A L A Y S I A

Pahang

Seremban

16

Melaka

Johor Baharu

SINGAPORE

Mandalay, Burma
☀ Jan 20.5°C (68.5°F)
July 30°C (85.5°F)
🌧 Jan 3 mm (0.1 in)
July 69 mm (2.7 in)

Hanoi, Vietnam
☀ Jan 16.5°C (62°F)
July 29.5°C (84.5°F)
🌧 Jan 18 mm (0.7 in)
July 323 mm (127 in)

LAOS

Bangkok, Thailand
☀ Jan 26°C (78.5°F)
July 28°C (83°F)
🌧 Jan 8 mm (0.3 in)
July 160 mm (6.3 in)

0 100 200 300 km
0 50 100 150 200 miles

Kuala Lumpur, Malaysia
☀ Jan 27°C (81°F)
July 27.5°C (81.5°F)
🌧 Jan 158 mm (6.2 in)
July 99 mm (3.9 in)

ARCTIC CIRCLE

TROPIC OF CANCER

EQUATOR

MALAYSIA

SINGAPORE

CAMBODIA

THAILAND

HA LONG BAY
A Vietnamese legend tells of a gigantic dragon that thrashed its way into the sea, smashing the limestone coastline into thousands of islands and rocky outcrops. Today, Ha Long Bay, which means "where the dragon descends into the sea", has some of the most dramatic scenery in this region, and has inspired many poets and painters.

PINEAPPLES
Thailand is the world's leading producer of pineapples, but this fruit is grown in many parts of southeast Asia. Much of the crop is canned and exported.

BIRDS' NEST SOUP
The brown-rumped swift builds its nest high in the roofs of caves throughout southeast Asia. Local men risk death climbing flimsy ladders to collect these nests, which form the main ingredient of birds' nest soup. The nests are made from the birds' saliva, but when they are plunged in boiling water they look like noodles.

**THINGS TO LOOK FOR
ON THE MAP**

Longest river: Mekong, Thailand/Laos/Cambodia/Vietnam, 4,184 km (2,600 miles) *Map F6, H8*

Highest point: Hkakabo Razi, Burma, 5,881 m (19,294 ft) *Map D1*

Largest lake: Tônlé Sap, Cambodia, maximum size in wet season 6,475 sq km (2,500 sq miles) *Map G10*

Ha Long Bay: Vietnam *Map I5*

A B C D E F G H I J

THAILAND

THAILAND	
Capital city: Bangkok	
Area: 513,120 sq km (198,116 sq miles)	
Population: 56,900,000	
Official language: Thai	
Major religions: Buddhist 95%, Muslim 4%, other 1%	
Government: Multi-party democracy	
Currency: Baht	
Adult literacy rate: 94%	
Life expectancy: 69 years	
People per doctor: 5,000	
Televisions: 114 per 1,000 people	

These young men wear orange robes and have shaved their heads to show that they are monks.

THE KINGDOM OF THAILAND was established in the 13th century, and the country has remained independent for most of its history. It was the only country in mainland southeast Asia not to be colonized by Britain or France. Modern Thailand is an economically successful nation, with rapid economic growth and a huge tourist industry. The north, west, and south are mountainous and fairly empty. About a third of the people live in the fertile and densely populated centre of the country. Thailand was once covered in forest, but so much of it has been cut down for timber that logging is now banned.

THE KING OF THAILAND
King Bhumibol Adulyadej has ruled Thailand since 1946, making him one of the longest-serving heads of state in the world. The king is a powerful unifying force in the country and has often intervened in politics to restore order. He is highly respected by Thais and any criticism of him or his family is frowned upon.

BANGKOK
Officially 6 million people live in Bangkok, but the true figure is probably closer to 10 million. Originally built on a network of canals, the city still has relatively few major roads and a limited public transport system. As a result, Bangkok has some of the worst traffic jams in the world. In July 1992, after a monsoon storm, it took 11 hours for one jam to clear. Some commuters have converted their cars into mobile offices, even installing chemical toilets, so they can work while they are driven in.

A MODERN ECONOMY
Thailand is the world's biggest producer of pineapples, and also exports large quantities of rubber and rice. However, in recent years manufacturing has overtaken agriculture in economic importance. American and Japanese companies have set up factories in Thailand, which is now a leading producer of electronic goods, such as integrated circuits for computers. Many of the workers in these new factories are women.

Women are often employed in the electronics industry because they earn lower wages than men and their smaller hands can cope with the fiddly assembly work.

BUDDHISM
Monks from Sri Lanka introduced Theravada Buddhism to this region in the 12th century and it soon became Thailand's main religion. Theravada Buddhism – the "Way of the Elders" – encourages its followers to obey the Law of Karma and do all they can to reduce suffering in the world. Traditionally young men were expected to became monks for a period of their lives, and many still follow this custom today.

The Emerald Temple in Bangkok is named after the green jade statue of the Buddha that it contains.

TOURISM
The thousands of ornate Buddhist temples and monasteries in Thailand have always drawn tourists from around the world to admire their beautiful architecture. Today, visitors also come to lie on the long, unspoilt beaches, trek in the wild hills of the north, or play on one of the new golf courses that are being constructed to attract businessmen from Japan.

Find out more
BUDDHISM: *275*
GROWING CITIES: *17, 135*
LOGGING: *69, 227, 244*
PACIFIC RIM ECONOMIES: *137*

BURMA

OVERSHADOWED BY THE POWERFUL neighbouring countries of India, China, and Thailand, Burma (also known as Myanmar) is little known to the outside world. When the country became independent in 1948, it adopted a policy of political and economic isolation that reduced this once-rich nation to one of the poorest on Earth. Revolts by the hill peoples and, in recent years, political repression by a military government have kept nearly all foreign influences away. Yet Burma is rich in natural resources, is well watered by the great Irrawaddy River, and is fertile enough to support intensive farming.

BURMA	
Capital city: Rangoon	
Area: 676,550 sq km (261,200 sq miles)	
Population: 44,600,000	
Official language: Burmese	
Major religions: Buddhist 89%, Muslim 4%, Christian 4%, Animist 1%, other 2%	
Government: Military government	
Currency: Kyat	
Adult literacy rate: 82%	
Life expectancy: 57 years	
People per doctor: 12,500	
Televisions: 2 per 1,000 people	

The Akha people value silver highly. This chief and his family wear silver neck-rings, bracelets, and ornaments on their clothes to show their wealth and status.

THE HILL PEOPLES

In the upland areas of the east, north, and west of Burma live the hill peoples. They include the Shan, Akha, Karen, and Kachin tribes, and make up more than a quarter of the total Burmese population. Most hill peoples live in small villages and make their living from slash-and-burn farming on the land around their villages. They are fiercely independent and resent interference from outside. As a result, more than 200,000 Karen and others have lost their lives fighting the Burmese government for independence.

TEAK

Hard, easily carved, and containing an oil that resists water and stops iron rusting, teak is a highly desirable wood for furniture, flooring, and other building uses. About 70 per cent of the world's teak trees grow on the hills of Burma, but intensive felling means that few trees will be left standing by the end of the century unless action is taken to replant the forests.

The map legend:
◆ Rubies
▩ Poppy-growing area

The opium poppy has white, pink, or purple flowers and can grow to a height of 1.2 m (4 ft).

Seed head

NATURAL WEALTH

Rubies and sapphires are among the many gemstones produced in northern Burma. Many people consider Burmese rubies to be the finest in the world because of their deep red colour. Burma is also rich in silver, copper, jade, lead, zinc, and tin, and has extensive reserves of oil and natural gas.

Ruby crystals are often found in calcite rock.

Burmese ruby crystal

THE GOLDEN TRIANGLE

The area where Burma, Thailand, and Laos meet is known as the Golden Triangle. Here the hill peoples grow opium poppies as one of their few sources of income. Opium is a useful painkiller, but it can also be used to make dangerous drugs. Two-thirds of the world's heroin comes from this region. In order to combat this lethal trade, the government is encouraging the local people to plant other crops for export, such as tobacco or flowers.

Opium is made from the sap that oozes out of cuts scored in the seed head.

RANGOON

Situated in the delta of the great Irrawaddy River, the capital city of Burma was established in 1852 by the British, who laid out the streets in a grid pattern. Since then, Rangoon has grown to be the country's major port and industrial centre. Dominating the city is a Buddhist temple called the Shwe Dagon Pagoda. Situated on a hill just north of the city centre, the gold-covered pagoda towers 99 m (325 ft) above the city streets.

Find out more

BUDDHISM: *275*
DRUG TRADE: *58*
GEMSTONES: *62, 172*
LOGGING: *69, 227, 244*

VIETNAM

EVERY DAY FOR 13 YEARS, Vietnam appeared on television sets and in newspapers around the world as the communist-led north of the country fought the American-backed south in a vicious war. When the war ended in 1975, with victory for the north, Vietnam had been devastated by the years of fighting and many of its people wanted to leave. Today, the country is back in the news. Some economists have called Vietnam "the tiger on a bicycle", because its economy is strong, but its people are poor and can only afford bicycles. Foreign firms are investing in new industry, and tourists have begun to visit this beautiful country.

VIETNAM	
Capital city: Hanoi	
Area: 329,560 sq km (127,243 sq miles)	
Population: 64,375,762	
Official language: Vietnamese	
Major religions: Buddhist 55%, Christian 7%, other 38%	
Government: One-party state	
Currency: New dong	
Adult literacy rate: 89%	
Life expectancy: 63 years	
People per doctor: 2,860	
Televisions: 29 per 1,000 people	

RUSH HOUR ON A BICYCLE
Cars dominate most large cities in the world, but in Vietnam the bicycle rules the road. Everyone has a bicycle which they use to get to work, or for shopping, because few people are rich enough to afford a car. In the morning and evening rush hours, streets like this one in Ho Chi Minh City are packed with cyclists, ringing their bells and shouting out loud to warn pedestrians and other cyclists to get out of the way.

Many of the boat people died at sea from disease or because their boats were not strong enough for the hazardous voyage.

THE BIRTH OF A CHILD
In the past, many Vietnamese babies did not live for long, so families didn't celebrate the birth of a child, but its survival for a month. This ritual continues today. Later, when the child is a year old, the family celebrates *Thoi Noi*. The child is shown a tray with objects on it. Whichever one the child chooses shows which career he or she will follow – for example a pen for a teacher, scissors for a tailor.

THE BOAT PEOPLE
After the end of the war, many Vietnamese people tried to leave in search of jobs abroad or out of fear of persecution. They took to the sea in boats, hoping to reach the West via Hong Kong, Malaysia, or Singapore. By 1980 about half a million people had set sail. The flood of refugees stopped when neighbouring countries began to send them home.

RICE GROWING
Two-thirds of the farmland in Vietnam is under water for part of the year, but deliberately so, because the fields are flooded to grow rice. During the rainy season, the fields slowly fill with rainwater, which is kept in place by low earth dykes. Soon a series of shallow, muddy paddy fields appear. Women plant the rice by hand. It takes two to three months to grow to full strength and is then harvested.

Most villages have an electricity supply, and some families own a television set.

House made of concrete.

Outdoor shower

Plot for growing vegetables and maize.

VILLAGE LIFE
Three out of every four people in Vietnam live in the countryside. Because cars are rare, and there is only one railway line, few of them will ever visit the great cities of Hanoi or Ho Chi Minh. The vast majority live in small villages and earn their living as farmers or labourers. Here they live in simple houses made of concrete, brick or, more traditionally, wood, straw, and palm leaves. A typical house has two rooms – one for eating and living, the other for sleeping – but no running water, which comes from a well outside.

Families live on the fruits and vegetables they grow on their farm. They eat meat only on special occasions.

Find out more
CYCLING: 92
PACIFIC RIM ECONOMIES: 137
POLITICAL SYSTEMS: 270–271
RICE GROWING: 135, 176, 197

CAMBODIA

Angkor Wat consists of a central temple building, surrounded by smaller temples and palaces, and huge moats and reservoirs.

FEW COUNTRIES HAVE SUFFERED as much as Cambodia. In 1970 it was drawn into the fighting in neighbouring Vietnam. Then, from 1975–79, the country was ruled by Pol Pot and the Khmer Rouge, a revolutionary group who killed more than a million Cambodians. In 1979 the Vietnamese invaded to overthrow Pol Pot, and the country fell into civil war, which lasted until 1991. Today Cambodia is slowly rebuilding its shattered society.

CAMBODIA

Capital city: Phnom Penh

Area: 181,040 sq km (69,000 sq miles)

Population: 9,000,000

Official language: Khmer

Major religions: Buddhist 95%, other 5%

Government: Multi-party democracy

Currency: Riel

Adult literacy rate: 38%

Life expectancy: 50 years

People per doctor: 25,000

Televisions: 8 per 1,000 people

LAOS

Capital city: Vientiane

Area: 236,800 sq km (91,428 sq miles)

Population: 4,600,000

Official language: Lao

Major religions: Buddhist 85%, other 15%

Government: One-party state

Currency: Kip

Adult literacy rate: no figures available

Life expectancy: 50 years

People per doctor: 4,350

Televisions: 7 per 1,000 people

ANGKOR WAT

For 600 years, the vast temple complex of Angkor Wat lay hidden in the jungles of north Cambodia. It was built in the 12th century by the Khmer King, Suryavarman II, in honour of the Hindu god Vishnu, and was once the centre of a huge empire. When the Khmers fell from power, Angkor Wat was abandoned and the jungle gradually grew over the buildings. The site has been uncovered only this century.

CLASSICAL DANCE
In the temple of Angkor Wat, royal dancers performed religious dances based on the Indian epic tales of the Ramayana and the Mahabharata. This type of classical dance is highly stylized, with graceful movements requiring years of training to perfect. The dancers wear richly embroidered costumes so tight that they have to be sewn into them before each performance.

THE WORLD'S BIGGEST MINEFIELD

The lengthy wars in Cambodia have left the country in a desperate state. The road and rail systems have collapsed, and industry barely exists. Up to 3 million mines are thought to lie buried in the ground. Despite the efforts of mine clearers, like the man in this picture, many mines are discovered only when someone steps on one. As a result, some 20,000 people have been disabled.

LAOS

Hmong men often have more than one wife. Each wife is responsible for bringing up her children, and looks after her own poultry and vegetable garden.

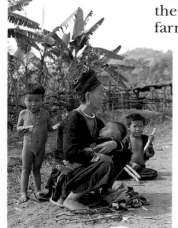

LAOS IS A COMMUNIST STATE, and one of the poorest and most isolated countries in the world. Three-quarters of its people are farmers; many of them grow only enough food to feed their families. Apart from the fertile Mekong Valley, the land is rugged and unsuitable for farming. Yet Laos is rich in gold and other minerals, and also produces timber and coffee.

THE FRIENDSHIP BRIDGE
Spanning the Mekong River near the capital city of Vientiane is the graceful Friendship Bridge, which opened in 1994. Laos is landlocked (it has no coastline), and the bridge provides the only direct route to Thailand and its sea ports.

THE HILL PEOPLES

Peoples such as these Hmong have lived in the isolated hill areas of Laos for many years. They grow maize and rice to eat, and opium poppies to sell. But this traditional way of life has been badly affected by the wars in this region and many Hmong have left the country and settled in Thailand or the USA.

Find out more

HILL PEOPLES: *188, 191*

HINDUISM: *275*

OPIUM: *191*

POLITICAL SYSTEMS: *270–271*

MALAYSIA

Spread across the South China Sea is the divided land of Malaysia. Part of the country lies on the Malay Peninsula, which hangs off the corner of mainland southeast Asia, but the states of Sarawak and Sabah are on the island of Borneo to the east. More than 17 million people live in the country, most of them in the rapidly growing cities on the mainland. Every five years Malaysia gets a new head of state: nine sultans, who each rule one of the states that make up the country, take it in turns to be king.

THE PEOPLE OF MALAYSIA
Almost half the population of Malaysia are Malays, like this family. About one-third are Chinese; the rest are either descendants of settlers from the Indian Subcontinent, or local tribespeople. This mix of peoples has led to racial conflict in the past.

MALAYSIA

Capital city: Kuala Lumpur

Area: 329,750 sq km (127,317 sq miles)

Population: 17,566,982

Official language: Malay

Major religions: Muslim 53%, Buddhist 18%, Chinese faiths 11%, Hindu 7%, Christian 7%, other 4%

Government: Multi-party democracy

Currency: Ringgit

Adult literacy rate: 80%

Life expectancy: 70 years

People per doctor: 2,700

Televisions: 148 per 1,000 people

SINGAPORE

Capital city: Singapore City

Area: 620 sq km (239 sq miles)

Population: 2,705,100

Official languages: Malay, Chinese, Tamil, and English

Major religions: Buddhist/Taoist 53%, Muslim 16%, Hindu 4%, Christian 1%, other 26%

Government: Multi-party democracy

Currency: Singapore dollar

Adult literacy rate: 90%

Life expectancy: 74 years

People per doctor: 920

Televisions: 378 per 1,000 people

NATURAL RESOURCES

Malaysia is rich in natural resources, with large oil and gas reserves off the coast of Sarawak. The country is the world's top producer of palm oil, used to make soap and for cooking, and the second biggest producer of natural rubber. The rainforests of Sarawak are rich in hardwood trees, but experts are worried that the timber industry is cutting down trees faster than the forest can renew itself.

Peas, beans, and other vegetables are often grown between the rows of trees.

Strips of bark are cut away to let the latex run down the trunk and into a collecting cup.

RUBBER
Hidden inside the bark of the rubber tree is a white liquid, called latex, that is used to make natural rubber. Rubber trees grow in hot, wet climates and flourish on the lower slopes of the mountains that run down the length of the Malay Peninsula. Collected latex is sent to a local factory. There it is mixed with water and acid in a large pan to make a sheet of rubber that is then smoked or hung on a line to dry.

Rubber tappers go out before dawn to collect the latex before the high daytime temperatures stop its flow.

Two out of every three cars sold in Malaysia are Protons.

MODERN INDUSTRY

The first car to be manufactured in Malaysia – the Proton – rolled off the production line outside Kuala Lumpur in 1985. Today more than 110,000 Protons are produced every year, many for export to Indonesia, Singapore, and the UK. The Proton has been so successful that Malaysia is now starting a second car project. Malaysia is also an international centre for the electronics industry and is the world's biggest producer of disk drives for computers.

THE CHANGING ECONOMY
1970s: in 1970 Malaysia had few factories, and most of its raw materials, such as rubber and tin, were exported to be manufactured into finished goods abroad.

1990s: today, Malaysia's economy is one of the most successful in the world. Malaysia continues to produce large amounts of raw materials, and its manufacturing sector has grown dramatically. Two-thirds of all exports are now finished goods, such as cars, electronics, textiles, and foods.

Exports in 1970

42.5%
15%
25%
12.5%
5%

Manufactured goods: 64%

Exports in 1993

Oil and gas: 8%
Other: 26%
Rubber: 1.5%
Tin: 0.5%

ISLAM

In 1414, the people of Malacca (modern-day Melaka) converted to Islam when their ruler married a Muslim princess from Sumatra. The new faith spread rapidly throughout the country. Today, more than half the population of Malaysia is Muslim. Islamic law is widely obeyed and many women wear a head-dress in the street.

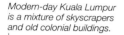

Modern-day Kuala Lumpur is a mixture of skyscrapers and old colonial buildings.

LIFE ON STILTS

Faced with the problem of building on the banks of rivers or next to the sea, villagers developed an ingenious solution – they built their houses on stilts. Villages of these houses, called *kampungs*, are found throughout southeast Asia. The wooden houses stand high enough above the water to protect them from flooding, while the raised floors and many windows help to keep the houses well ventilated.

A high, steep roof protects the inhabitants from the heavy monsoon rains.

Animals are often kept under the raised floor.

Many kampung villagers make their living from fishing.

Fish are laid out to dry in the sun so that they can be stored for future use.

KUALA LUMPUR

In 1857, a group of miners in search of tin set up a camp where the Kelang and Gombak rivers join. They called their settlement Kuala Lumpur, which is Malay for "muddy meeting place". The camp soon grew in size and importance as a centre of the tin mining and rubber industries. Today it is Malaysia's capital city and home to more than 1.3 million people.

SINGAPORE

OFF THE TIP OF MALAYSIA lies the tiny island state of Singapore, one of the most densely populated countries on Earth. Singapore was originally a trading settlement on the shipping route between India and China. It was founded in 1819 by Sir Stamford Raffles, an official of the British East India Company. Today rapid economic growth has turned the island into one of the world's most successful economies.

SINGAPORE SOCIETY

Three-quarters of the people of Singapore are Chinese; the rest are Malays and descendants of people from the Indian Subcontinent. Because Singapore is so wealthy, most people lead comfortable lives. The government keeps tight control over the country: it regulates the press, owns the television and radio services, and limits car ownership to prevent congestion on the roads. It is illegal to drop litter in the street, eat in the underground, or chew gum in public.

Singapore's banks and stock exchange, based in this part of the city, generate about a quarter of the country's income.

THE PORT OF SINGAPORE

Every three minutes a ship enters or leaves the bustling harbour of Singapore, making it the busiest port in the world. Tankers from the Persian Gulf bring crude oil to be refined into petrol and other products, which are then shipped out to ports throughout eastern Asia. Cargo ships on the way to and from China and Japan stop to use the harbour's facilities, and most of Malaysia's large export trade goes out through this port.

Singapore's skyline is dominated by modern high-rise buildings, built because land is in such short supply.

Find out more

ISLAM: *275*
OIL: *137, 152, 281*
PACIFIC RIM ECONOMIES: *137*
RUBBER: *226*

MARITIME SOUTHEAST ASIA

MARITIME MEANS "CONNECTED WITH THE SEA" and maritime southeast Asia is a belt of thousands of islands strung out across a vast expanse of ocean. Here, sandwiched between mainland southeast Asia and Australia, are four countries: the eastern part of Malaysia, Brunei, Indonesia, and the Philippines. This is one of the world's most volcanic regions, and the monsoon climate makes some areas among the wettest places on Earth. A huge variety of animals and plants live here, because the environment is slightly different on each island. There are many different peoples, too. More than 250 languages are spoken on the islands of Indonesia alone.

WATER TRANSPORT
In this island region, boats have traditionally provided the main method of getting from place to place. Small boats, such as this outrigger canoe, are ideal for navigating the waterways between clusters of islands.

TYPHOON CLIMATE

Each year, about 20 tropical storms called typhoons batter the islands of the Philippines. They bring flooding and winds travelling at over 100 km/h (62 mph). Many people are killed in storms, and thousands of homes are destroyed. Low-lying coastal areas are most at risk, but people are forced to live there because land is in short supply, and these areas are cheap.

PHILIPPINES

Manila, Philippines
☀ Jan 25.5°C (77.5°F)
July 27.5°C (81.5°F)
🌧 Jan 23 mm (0.9 in)
July 432 mm (17 in)

BRUNEI

MALAYSIA

Medan, Sumatra
☀ Jan 25.5°C (78°F)
July 27°C (80.5°F)
🌧 Jan 137 mm (5.4 in)
July 135 mm (5.3 in)

N

INDONESIA

Jakarta, Java
☀ Jan 26°C (79°F)
July 27°C (80°F)
🌧 Jan 300 mm (11.8 in)
July 64 mm (2.5 in)

VOLCANOES

Volcanic eruptions and earthquakes are a frequent part of life in this region. They are caused by the movement of huge pieces of the Earth's crust, called tectonic plates. Much of maritime southeast Asia lies over a massive arc-shaped join between two of these plates. Despite the terrible destruction that eruptions cause, the islanders risk growing crops on the slopes of active volcanoes because their ash makes the soil fertile.

Scientists studying the rainforests in this region have discovered that they contain one-sixth of all the world's bird species.

NATURAL VARIETY

This Australasian Komodo dragon lives on an island to the east of Wallace's Line.

During the 1850s the British naturalist, Alfred Russel Wallace, journeyed through these islands. He noticed that most of the animals on the island of Bali were Asian in origin, but those on neighbouring Lombok were mainly Australasian. "Wallace's Line" is an imaginary line drawn across the region to divide the islands with Asian animals from those with Australasian animals.

Islands to the west of Wallace's Line are filled with Asian animals, such as this orang utan.

THE TROPICAL RAINFORESTS

Individual islands provide different natural habitats, so the animals and plants that have evolved on one island may be very different to those on the next. This means that the region's dense rainforests contain the greatest variety of species in the world. This is why it is so vital that these forests should be protected and not cut down or cleared.

THE RAFFLESIA FLOWER

This rare plant, found deep in the rainforests, is named after Sir Stamford Raffles, a British governor in this region during the 19th century. It has the world's largest flowers, measuring up to 91 cm (3 ft) across. *Rafflesia* is famous for its foul smell, which attracts insects.

THINGS TO LOOK FOR ON THE MAP

Longest river: Kapuas, Indonesia, 1,142 km (710 miles) *Map G9*

Highest point: Puncak Jaya, Indonesia, 5,030 m (16,502 ft) *Map R10*

World's largest volcano crater: Toba, Indonesia, 1,775 sq km (685 sq miles) *Map B8*

World's largest cave: Sarawak Chamber, Malaysia, 700 m (2,296 ft) long *Map I7*

USING THE PADDY FIELDS

Rice is the main, or staple, food for most people in this region, and much of it is grown in specially flooded paddy fields. All kinds of plants and animals are raised in and around these fields, including vegetables, fruit trees, fish, shellfish, crabs, and frogs. They provide food and income for the people, give nutrients to the waters, and the animals eat pests that could otherwise do great damage to this finely balanced underwater world.

PACIFIC OCEAN

Morotai
Halmahera
Waigeo
Supiori Biak
Gulf of Weda
Sorong
Yapen
Mamberamo
Jayapura
Moluccas
Misool
Gulf of Berau
SERAM SEA
Seram
IRIAN JAYA
Ambon
Banda Is.
MAOKE MTS
Puncak Jaya
ARAFURA SEA
PAPUA NEW GUINEA
Kai Is.
Digul
Aru Is.
Dolak
Komoran
Leti Is.
Babar
Yamdena
TIMOR SEA

Ambon, Moluccas
☀ Jan 27.5°C (82°F)
  July 25°C (77.5°F)
☁ Jan 127 mm (5 in)
  July 602 mm (23.7 in)

| 0 | 100 | 200 | 300 | 400 | 500 km |
| 0 | 100 | 200 | 300 miles |

O   P   Q   R   S   T

Trees grown by the paddy fields supply fruit and firewood.

Local people eat and sell fish that are raised in the paddy fields.

The paddy field waters are slightly acid. This encourages the growth of tiny plants and animals that help to keep the waters full of nutrients.

Fish and frogs eat insects that live on the rice plants.

INDONESIA

EVERYTHING ABOUT INDONESIA IS BIG. It is the world's largest archipelago, made up of 13,677 islands, of which only about 1,500 are inhabited. It stretches for 5,100 km (3,169 miles), and is spread across 8 million sq km (3 million sq miles) of sea and three time zones. The population contains 362 different peoples, speaking over 250 languages and dialects. More than 160 million Indonesians are Muslims, making it the world's biggest Muslim country. It is also a land of contrasts: along with its modern cities and industries, Indonesia contains peoples whose lifestyles have not altered for centuries.

INDONESIA	
Capital city: Jakarta	
Area: 1,904,570 sq km (735,355 sq miles)	
Population: 179,247,783	
Official language: Bahasa Indonesia	
Major religions: Muslim 87%, Christian 9%, other 4%	
Government: Military government	
Currency: Rupiah	
Adult literacy rate: 84%	
Life expectancy: 62 years	
People per doctor: 7,140	
Televisions: 60 per 1,000 people	

BRUNEI	
Capital city: Bandar Seri Begawan	
Area: 5,770 sq km (2,228 sq miles)	
Population: 260,482	
Official language: Malay	
Major religions: Muslim 66%, Buddhist 14%, Christian 10%, other 10%	
Government: Absolute monarchy	
Currency: Brunei dollar	
Adult literacy rate: 85%	
Life expectancy: 74 years	
People per doctor: 1,460	
Televisions: 241 per 1,000 people	

THE SPICE ISLANDS

For centuries, the Moluccas islands in eastern Indonesia were Europe's main source of cloves, nutmeg, cinnamon, and other spices. While Indonesia was a Dutch colony, the merchants of the Dutch East India Company had total control of this trade and grew fabulously rich. Indonesia became an independent country in 1949.

Pepper · Nutmeg · Cloves · Cinnamon

JAKARTA

Indonesia's capital is home to more than 7 million people, making it the largest city in southeast Asia. It was originally a small trading port at the mouth of the Ciliwung River, shipping spices throughout eastern Asia. In 1618 the Dutch made Jayakarta, as it was then called, the capital of their East Indies empire. They renamed the town Batavia and rebuilt it around canals to look like Amsterdam.

The temple of Borobudur is the world's largest Buddhist monument.

BOROBUDUR

Situated in the heart of Java is one of the architectural wonders of the world. The vast Buddhist temple of Borobudur – which means "monastery on the hill" in Javanese – was built between AD778–856. The temple consists of a series of platforms, each one representing a different stage in the Buddhist's spiritual journey from ignorance, through enlightenment, to *nirvana*, or heavenly bliss.

OIL AND GAS

The first oil well was drilled in Sumatra in 1871, and oil has dominated the Indonesian economy ever since. By 1981 oil and gas products made up more than 80 per cent of exports, but this figure is now dropping as the oil reserves begin to run out. To reduce its dependence on oil, Indonesia is exploiting its huge reserves of natural gas. The gas is usually exported in a liquid form, called liquefied natural gas.

THE INDONESIAN ECONOMY

Indonesia's factories produce a wide range of manufactured and simple electronic goods. Yet more than half the people still work on the land, growing enough food to feed the expanding population of the cities. Indonesia used to be the world's largest importer of rice, but in the last 10 years has increased rice production to grow enough for its own needs.

Indonesian exports 1994

Oil and gas: 24%
Other manufactured goods: 19%
Other: 17%
Textiles: 6%
Food and drink: 9%
Wood: 12%
Clothes and shoes: 13%

BALI

With lush plants and trees covering the island in a carpet of green, and sandy beaches stretching along the coast, Bali is one of the most beautiful places in the world. It is a favourite destination for tourists, who come to enjoy the scenery and to watch local groups of actors and musicians perform ancient dances. Most Balinese are Hindu, and processions, like these women taking offerings to the temple, are part of everyday life.

PEOPLES OF INDONESIA

More than 179 million people live in Indonesia, 60 per cent of them packed on to the island of Java. Yet this island occupies just 7 per cent of the country's total land area. Many of the other islands are barely occupied, despite their vast size. In 1950 the government began to resettle people from Java on other islands. More than 6 million people have been resettled in this way, despite opposition from local people who are sometimes moved to make way for the new settlers.

THE BUGIS

The Bugis people of south Sulawesi are famous for their seafaring skills and, in previous centuries, for their ferocity in battle. They built elegant wooden ships in which they terrorized the inhabitants of neighbouring islands. It is thought that our English words "bogeyman" and "bugbear" come from Bugis.

The Bugis still build their wooden ships, although they now have diesel engines.

BORNEO	SULAWESI
16 people per sq km	66 people per sq km
(42 people per sq mile)	(171 people per sq mile)

IRIAN JAYA
27 people per sq km
(71 people per sq mile)

A longhouse is usually constructed of timber and bamboo.

Covered gallery

Loft storage area, where rice is kept in large baskets.

JAVA
813 people per sq km
(2,107 people per sq mile)

Women separating rice grains from the chaff.

Field of crops

THE DAYAKS

The native inhabitants of Borneo, the Dayaks, are expert builders who construct elaborate longhouses on stilts. Several families live in a longhouse, each with their own cooking and sleeping quarters. Meetings are held in the covered gallery which runs along the length of the building, and rice, fish, and other foods are dried on the open verandah in front.

Dani houses are made of wood and thatch.

The Dani barter for goods, such as pigs.

Entrance *Hearth*

BATIK

The people of Java have perfected a complex printing process, called *batik*. A layer of wax is applied to the areas of fabric which are to stay uncoloured. The cloth is then dyed with the first colour, and when dry, rewaxed in different places before it is dyed again with a second colour. After many waxings and dyeings, the fabric is ready for use.

Batik printing block

Batik is often used to decorate the wrap-around cotton garment called a sarong, which is worn by both men and women.

THE DANI

The people who live in Indonesia's easternmost province of Irian Jaya are related to the dark-skinned peoples of the Pacific Ocean rather than the lighter-skinned inhabitants of the rest of southeast Asia. Among the many tribes who live in this isolated area are the Dani, whose agricultural way of life has changed little in thousands of years.

BRUNEI

SQUASHED BETWEEN THE MALAYSIAN STATE of Sarawak and the South China Sea lies the tiny country of Brunei. It consists of a humid tropical rainforest with a swampy plain along the coast. Once a forgotten outpost of the British Empire and a haven for pirates, this small country was transformed by the discovery of oil in 1929. Today Brunei is one of the world's wealthiest nations, with huge resources of oil and natural gas. It is so rich that the people pay no income tax, and receive free education, health care, and pensions.

THE SULTAN OF BRUNEI

Brunei is ruled by one of the wealthiest people on Earth. Thanks to the country's vast oil and gas reserves, Sultan Hassanal Bolkiah is worth about US$25 billion, although he denies this figure. In recent years the Sultan has spent more than US$450 million building one of the world's largest mosques in Brunei's capital city, Bandar Seri Begawan.

Find out more

ISLAM & BUDDHISM: *275*
OIL & GAS: *137, 152, 163, 211*
POPULATION DENSITY: *16, 135*
SPICES: *57, 264*

THE PHILIPPINES

THE PHILIPPINES

THE PHILIPPINES	
Capital city: Manila	
Area: 300,000 sq km (115,839 sq miles)	
Population: 60,703,206	
Official languages: Filipino and English	
Major religions: Christian 92%, Muslim 5%, other 3%	
Government: Multi-party democracy	
Currency: Philippine peso	
Adult literacy rate: 90%	
Life expectancy: 65 years	
People per doctor: 8,330	
Televisions: 48 per 1,000 people	

LOCATED ON THE "RING OF FIRE" – the arc of volcanoes running through maritime southeast Asia – and in the path of violent tropical storms, the Philippines suffers from earthquakes and volcanic eruptions. The country consists of 7,107 islands, of which only about 1,000 are inhabited. Most of the people live on the northern island of Luzon, which contains the capital, Manila. For almost 400 years the Philippines was governed by Spain; in fact the country is named after the Spanish king, Philip II. In 1898 control passed to the USA, then in 1946 the Philippines became an independent nation. Most Filipinos are of Malay origin, but there are some Chinese immigrants and mixed-blood *mestizos.*

MANILA
Much of the Philippines' capital city lies below sea level, and it suffers from floods during the rainy summer season. The Spanish captured Manila in 1571, fortifying its walls and making it the centre of their Asian empire. Over the centuries Manila has been an important trading port, with merchants arriving from as far afield as Arabia, India, and Japan. Today, it is a bustling modern city with more than 7 million inhabitants.

2 April 1991: the growth of a lava dome shows that Mt Pinatubo is about to erupt.

14 June 1991: the mountain begins to spew deadly clouds of gas and ash.

15 June 1991: a huge blast blows out the mountainside, and molten lava floods down the slopes.

MOUNT PINATUBO
In June 1991, Mount Pinatubo, a volcano north of Manila on the island of Luzon, burst into life. For 10 days, it spewed out volcanic ash and rocks in one of the biggest volcanic eruptions ever recorded. The landscape was soon covered with a layer of debris some 7 m (23 ft) deep. Heavy rainfall turned much of this to sludge, blocking rivers and filling up valleys. The local Aeta tribespeople lost their land and houses overnight.

SMOKY MOUNTAIN
On the edge of Manila lies a vast mountain. Unlike other mountains, this one is not made of rock, but of rubbish. Every day the dust carts of Manila arrive there to dump their loads of household waste. Many people, some of them children as young as four, live on the mountain, searching the refuse daily for bottles, cans, plastics, and cardboard that they can sell for recycling.

Filipinos working abroad in 1995

Europe: 2.4%

Asia: 40.3%

The Americas: 3.3%

Middle East: 53.1%

Africa: 0.6%

Australasia: 0.3%

About 2% of the workforce are working abroad at any one time, sending money home to support their families. Each year, more than US$1 billion flows into the country's economy in this way.

THE ECONOMY
Once one of the richer nations in Asia, in the last 40 years the Philippines has fallen behind its economically powerful neighbours. Half the population live in poverty, and many Filipinos can only support their families by working abroad. The Philippines is rich in natural resources, with reserves of gold, copper, and chrome. The main export crops are tobacco, sugar, and a wide range of tropical fruits.

AMAZING JEEPS
At the end of World War II, the US Army left thousands of unwanted jeeps in the Philippines. Local people soon converted these for their own use, decorating them in amazing colours and patterns. The jeep can cope with the rugged conditions and poor roads of the countryside, and is now one of the main forms of transport in the Philippines.

POLITICS

In 1965 Ferdinand Marcos became president of the Philippines. He governed the country ruthlessly, fixing election results to stay in power, and illegally making a huge personal fortune. In 1983, the leader of the opposition, Benigno Aquino, was assassinated. Unrest against Marcos' government reached a peak in 1985. Supported by the Catholic Church, millions of people took to the streets in protest, forcing Marcos to leave the country. Corazon Aquino, Benigno's widow, became president, and a democratic system of government was restored.

RELIGION

Roman Catholicism was introduced to the Philippines by the explorer, Magellan, who visited the island of Cebu in 1521 during his voyage round the world. Under Spanish rule, many Filipinos converted to Catholicism. It became the major religion in all but the southern, Muslim, island of Mindanao. Today, the Philippines is the only Christian country in Asia, and the Catholic Church continues to exert a powerful influence on everyday life.

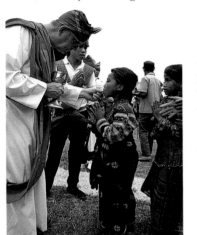

ANCIENT TERRACES, MODERN METHODS

The Ifugao people have farmed the mountainous landscape in the north of Luzon island for thousands of years, laboriously constructing terraces on the steep hillsides to grow rice. These ancient terraces are now a major tourist attraction. But not all rice-growers in the Philippines use such traditional methods. The country is also home to the International Rice Research Institute, where scientists have bred new species of rice that yield more grains per plant, and are also developing rice-planting and harvesting machines.

Farmers here sow rice in the ground like any other cereal crop, rather than in a flooded paddy field.

The terraces are held in place by stone walls, built entirely by hand.

COCONUTS

Reaching a height of up to 30 m (100 ft), the coconut is one of the most beautiful palm trees in the world. Long leaves form on top of the slender trunk, and cream flowers grow on long spikes.

The coconut palm flourishes in the warm, damp climate of the Philippines, producing nuts for up to 70 years. The nuts ripen in bunches of 15–20, and are harvested by farmers who knock them out of the trees with long bamboo poles. After Indonesia, the Philippines is the world's second largest producer of coconuts, and the world's biggest producer of copra, the fleshy meat inside the nut, exporting its many products around the world.

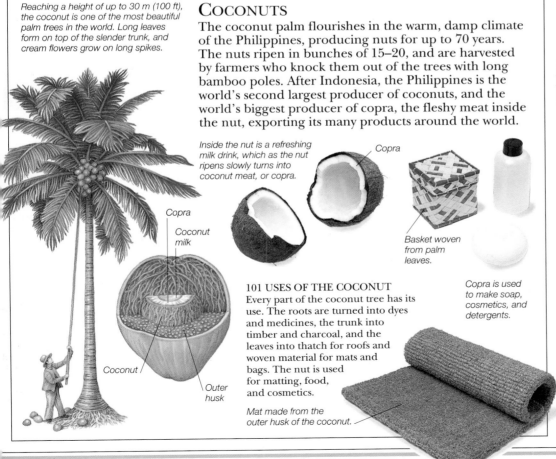

Copra
Coconut milk
Coconut
Outer husk

Inside the nut is a refreshing milk drink, which as the nut ripens slowly turns into coconut meat, or copra.

Copra

Basket woven from palm leaves.

101 USES OF THE COCONUT

Every part of the coconut tree has its use. The roots are turned into dyes and medicines, the trunk into timber and charcoal, and the leaves into thatch for roofs and woven material for mats and bags. The nut is used for matting, food, and cosmetics.

Copra is used to make soap, cosmetics, and detergents.

Mat made from the outer husk of the coconut.

HUNTER-GATHERERS

On some of the more remote islands of the Philippines live groups of hunter-gatherers, who roam the countryside fishing, hunting animals, and gathering vegetables, fruit, and berries. These people are among the last in the world to continue this ancient way of life, but their lifestyle is under attack as the forests in which they live are felled for timber.

Find out more

RICE GROWING: *135, 176, 197*
ROMAN CATHOLICS: *274*
TERRACE FARMING: *159, 173*
VOLCANOES: *13, 197*

THE INDIAN OCEAN

THE THIRD LARGEST of the world's oceans, the Indian Ocean, covers 73 million sq km (28 million sq miles) and contains some 5,000 islands, many of them surrounded by coral reefs. This ocean is unique because, unlike the Atlantic and Pacific, it has no outlet to the north. It has the saltiest sea (the Red Sea), and the warmest sea (the Persian Gulf) on Earth. The Indian Ocean is also at risk from pollution, especially from oil tankers leaving the Persian Gulf. Heavy monsoon rain and tropical storms can bring disastrous flooding to the northern coasts.

ISLAND PARADISE
The islands of the Indian Ocean include coral atolls, like the Maldives and Seychelles, which attract thousands of tourists every year. Although this brings money to the islands, it also threatens to damage the environment. Gradual erosion of the coral reefs also leaves the islands exposed to ocean tides and flooding. This Maldive island has a barrier to protect it from sea damage.

CORAL ISLANDS
Coral is formed in warm waters by tiny creatures known as polyps. These marine creatures build limestone skeletons around themselves. Over many thousands of years, these skeletons gradually grow up towards the surface of the ocean to form a coral island. An atoll, shown right, is a form of circular coral reef that grows around an underwater volcano. As the volcano sinks, the coral forms an atoll. The water in the centre is called a lagoon.

1. Corals grow in shallow waters around volcanic island.

2. Coral reef builds up as movements in the Earth's surface make the island sink.

3. Island finally disappears, leaving a coral atoll.

This port in Fremantle, Australia handles freight from across the world.

SHIPPING ROUTES
More than 200 large ships a day sail round the Cape of Good Hope at the southern tip of Africa as they enter or leave the Indian Ocean. Many are vast tankers laden with oil from the Persian Gulf. Smaller ships are able to pass through the Suez Canal. On the other side of the Indian Ocean, ships pass through the Strait of Malacca carrying cargo to ports in eastern Asia.

MADAGASCAR
Madagascar lies off the east coast of Africa and, because of its isolation, is home to many unique plants and animals. Most people in Madagascar scratch a living by farming, clearing a new patch of land each year to plant their crops. The main export on the island is vanilla, grown for use in ice cream and cola drinks. Women traditionally have elaborate hairstyles that indicate which village they are from.

THE SALTY SEA
Oceans are salty because minerals dissolved from rocks by rivers are washed into the seas. Around the shores of the Indian Ocean, people extract the salt by channelling water into shallow pans. The sun's heat evaporates the water, leaving the salt behind, as shown here in Mauritius.

The dried salt is stored in baskets. Workers then carry the heavy baskets on their heads to a waiting truck.

MALDIVES	
Capital city: Male	
Area: 300 sq km (116 sq miles)	
Population: 200,000	
Official language: Dhivehi	
Major religion: Muslim 100%	
Government: One-party state	
Currency: Rufiyaa	

COMOROS	
Capital city: Moroni	
Area: 2,230 sq km (861 sq miles)	
Population: 600,000	
Official languages: Arabic and French	
Major religions: Muslim 86%, Christian 14%	
Government: Multi-party democracy	
Currency: Comoros franc	

MAURITIUS	
Capital city: Port Louis	
Area: 1,860 sq km (718 sq miles)	
Population: 1,000,000	
Official language: English	
Major religions: Hindu 52%, Christian 28%, Muslim 17%, other 3%	
Government: Multi-party democracy	
Currency: Mauritian rupee	

MADAGASCAR	
Capital city: Antananarivo	
Area: 587,040 sq km (226,660 sq miles)	
Population: 12,800,000	
Official languages: Malagasy and French	
Major religions: Christian 41%, other 59%	
Government: Multi-party democracy	
Currency: Malagasy franc	

SEYCHELLES	
Capital city: Victoria	
Area: 280 sq km (108 sq miles)	
Population: 68,000	
Official language: Creole	
Major religions: Christian 98%, other 2%	
Government: Multi-party democracy	
Currency: Seychelles rupee	

A B C D E F G H I J K L

MALDIVES

THINGS TO LOOK FOR ON THE MAP

World's longest archipelago: Indonesian Islands, 5,600 km (3,480 miles) *Map J5*

Deepest trench: Java Trench, 7,125 m (23,376 ft) *Map J6*

World's highest rainfall: Réunion, 1,870 mm (73.62 in) in 24 hours *Map E7*

Maldives
- Jan 26°C (79°F)
- July 27°C (80°F)
- Jan 46 mm (1.8 in)
- July 226 mm (8.9 in)

SEYCHELLES

COMOROS

Antananarivo, Madagascar
- Jan 21°C (70°F)
- July 14°C (58°F)
- Jan 300 mm (11.8 in)
- July 9 mm (0.3 in)

MADAGASCAR

MAURITIUS

Parson's chameleon

Mauritius
- Jan 26°C (79°F)
- July 20°C (68°F)
- Jan 216 mm (8.5 in)
- July 58 mm (2.3 in)

Map labels:
Port Said, Suez, Suez Canal, Nile, Euphrates, Tigris, KUWAIT CITY, Persian Gulf, Gulf of Oman, Indus, Karachi, ASIA, HIMALAYAS, Ganges, Calcutta, Irrawaddy, RED SEA, ARABIA, ARABIAN SEA, Bombay, RANGOON, Bay of Bengal, Madras, Andaman Is. (India), DJIBOUTI, Aden, Gulf of Aden, Socotra (Yemen), Laccadive Is. (India), Cochin, Sri Lanka, Colombo, Nicobar Is. (India), ANDAMAN Sea of MALACCA, Strait of Malacca, Mekong, Gulf of Thailand, George Town, SOUTH CHINA SEA, SINGAPORE, MALDIVES, MALE, British Indian Ocean Territory (UK), Sumatra, INDONESIA, Borneo, JAVA SEA, Java, Java Trench, AFRICA, Mombasa, Amirante Is. (Seychelles), Mahé, VICTORIA, Aldabra Is. (Seychelles), Dar es Salaam, Grande Comore, MORONI, COMOROS, Bobaomby, Antsiranana, Mayotte (France), Mahajanga, SEYCHELLES, Maldive Ridge, Mascarene Plateau, Cargados Ridge, Cocos Is. (Australia), Christmas I. (Australia), Ashmore & Cartier Is. (Australia), Zambezi, ANTANANARIVO, Toamasina, MAURITIUS, PORT LOUIS, INDIAN, Beira, MADAGASCAR, Fianarantsoa, Le Port, Réunion (France), Mascarene Is., AUSTRALIA, Toliara, Farafangana, West Australian Basin, North West C., Limpopo, Madagascar Basin, OCEAN, Mid-Indian Ridge, Broken Ridge, Durban, Madagascar Ridge, Fremantle, CAPE TOWN, Cape of Good Hope, C. Leeuwin, Amsterdam I. (France), St Paul I. (France), Crozet Basin, Southeast Indian Ridge, Southwest Indian Ridge, Crozet Is. (France), Kerguelen (France), Kerguelen Plateau, Prince Edward Is. (South Africa), Heard I., Macdonald Is. (Australia), South Indian Basin, Atlantic-Indian Basin, ANTARCTICA

WILDLIFE
Half of all the chameleons – a type of lizard – in the world are found on Madagascar. Although harmless, they are feared by local people who believe the animals represent human spirits not yet at rest. The chameleon is best known for its ability to change colour when angry or frightened.

FISHING
Large-scale fishing is less developed in the Indian Ocean than in the Atlantic or Pacific because there are not as many areas of shallow sea. Most of the fish are caught by shore-based fishermen for family use or to sell in a local market.

Fishermen bring in the catch in the Maldives.

These men are following a traditional method of fishing with a square net raised and lowered by wooden poles.

Find out more
CORAL REEFS: *47, 255, 258*
FISHING: *29, 76*
MONSOON: *166*
SUEZ CANAL: *216*

AFRICA

THE SECOND LARGEST CONTINENT, Africa is a land of contrasts. To the north lies the great Sahara, the largest desert in the world. The central parts, which the Equator runs through, are covered in dense tropical rainforests, while further south a series of grassy plateaux (areas of flat highland) give way to narrow coastal plains. Major mountain ranges include the Atlas in the north and the Ruwenzori range on the Uganda-Zaire border. Africa's highest mountain is Kilimanjaro, a dormant volcano in Tanzania. To the east is the Great Rift Valley, which contains several huge lakes. Some of the world's longest rivers drain the continent, including the Nile, Niger, Zaire, and the Zambezi.

DESERTS

Africa has three huge deserts. The vast Sahara is the world's largest desert, and dominates the northern third of the continent. Thousands of years ago, the Sahara had a moist climate. Today, the path of wet winds blowing in from the sea is blocked by other winds blowing outwards from the desert. The Namib and Kalahari deserts cover large areas of southwest Africa. Although it lies along the coast, the Namib Desert (shown here), is particularly barren and dry.

GREAT RIFT VALLEY

The Great Rift Valley stretches from Mozambique in the south, through east Africa and the Red Sea, into Syria. In most places the valley is 30–100 km (19–62 miles) wide, with steep sides rising up to 2,000 m (6,562 ft). The valley was formed as blocks of land sank between faults in the Earth's crust. In east Africa, the valley has two main branches. The Rift Valley is marked by volcanoes, hot springs, and a long chain of lakes.

Formation of a rift valley

Movements deep within the Earth's crust cause stretching, and cracks appear on the surface.

Surface cracks

Block mountains

Lake

Volcano

The cracking creates long faults. Some blocks of land slip down between parallel faults to create a rift valley.

RAINFORESTS

The world's second largest rainforest, after the Amazon, lies in central Africa. It teems with plant and animal life, including rare creatures such as okapis. It was also the home of several groups of pygmies, but many now live in settled villages, as vast areas of forest have been destroyed for logging and farming. One group, the Mbuti, still live in the forests of northeast Zaire.

Millions of flamingos flock to Lake Turkana and other Rift Valley lakes to nest and feed on tiny water plants.

LAKE VICTORIA

Lake Victoria is Africa's largest lake and the second largest freshwater lake in the world. Lying on the Equator, between Kenya, Tanzania, and Uganda, it covers about 69,484 sq km (26,828 sq miles) and reaches 82 m (269 ft) at its deepest point. The River Nile flows out of the northern end of the lake. Lake Victoria is rich in fish, which provide an important source of income for the large numbers of people living along the lake shores.

DRAKENSBERG MOUNTAINS

The highest mountains in southern Africa are the Drakensberg. They form part of the rim of a saucer-shaped plateau of high land, called the Great Escarpment. In the local Zulu language, the mountains are known as *Quathlamba*, which means the "barrier of pointed spears". The highest peak, Thabana Ntlenyana, rises 3,482 m (11,424 ft) above sea level, and is capped with snow in winter.

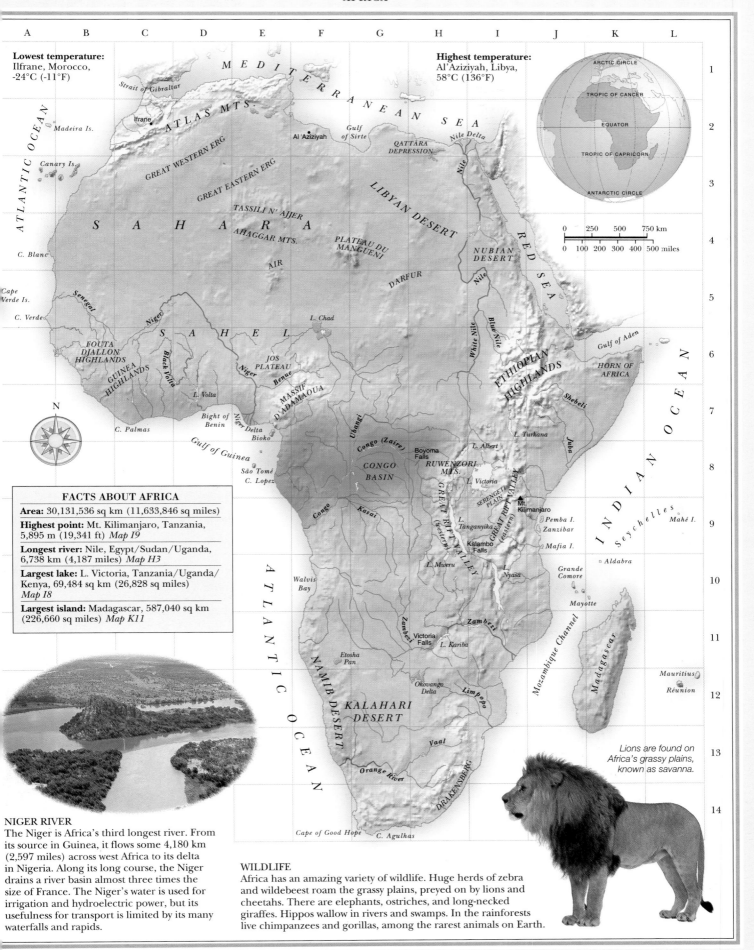

A B C D E F G H I J K L

AFRICA

Lowest temperature:
Ilfrane, Morocco,
-24°C (-11°F)

Highest temperature:
Al'Aziziyah, Libya,
58°C (136°F)

ARCTIC CIRCLE
TROPIC OF CANCER
EQUATOR
TROPIC OF CAPRICORN
ANTARCTIC CIRCLE

M E D I T E R R A N E A N   S E A

Strait of Gibraltar

Ifrane
A T L A S   M T S.
Madeira Is.
Al 'Aziziyah
Gulf
of Sirte
QATTARA
DEPRESSION
Nile Delta

Canary Is.

C. Blanc

S A H A R A
GREAT WESTERN ERG
GREAT EASTERN ERG
TASSILI N' AJJER
AHAGGAR MTS.
AIR
PLATEAU DU
MANGUENI
DARFUR

LIBYAN   DESERT
Nile

NUBIAN
DESERT

Nile

R E D   S E A

Cape
Verde Is.
C. Verde

Senegal
Niger
L. Chad
S A H E L
FOUTA
DJALLON
HIGHLANDS
GUINEA
HIGHLANDS
Black Volta
Niger
JOS
PLATEAU
Benue
L. Volta
MASSIF
D'ADAMAOUA

White Nile
Blue Nile
Gulf of Aden
ETHIOPIAN
HIGHLANDS
HORN OF
AFRICA
Shebeli

C. Palmas
Bight of
Benin
Niger Delta
Bioko
Gulf of Guinea
São Tomé
C. Lopez

Ubangi
Congo (Zaire)
Boyoma
Falls
CONGO
BASIN
RUWENZORI
MTS.
L. Albert
L. Victoria
SERENGETI
PLAIN
Mt.
Kilimanjaro
Juba
L. Turkana

I N D I A N   O C E A N
Seychelles
Mahé I.

Congo
Kasai
GREAT RIFT VALLEY (western)
GREAT RIFT VALLEY (eastern)
L. Tanganyika
Kalambo
Falls
L. Mweru
L. Nyasa
Pemba I.
Zanzibar
Mafia I.
Aldabra
Grande
Comore

Walvis
Bay
Zambezi
Zambezi
Victoria
Falls
L. Kariba
Mayotte
Mozambique Channel
Madagascar
Mauritius
Réunion

A T L A N T I C   O C E A N
NAMIB   DESERT
Etosha
Pan
Okovango
Delta
Limpopo
KALAHARI
DESERT
Vaal
Orange River
DRAKENSBERG
Cape of Good Hope
C. Agulhas

N

FACTS ABOUT AFRICA

Area: 30,131,536 sq km (11,633,846 sq miles)

Highest point: Mt. Kilimanjaro, Tanzania, 5,895 m (19,341 ft) *Map I9*

Longest river: Nile, Egypt/Sudan/Uganda, 6,738 km (4,187 miles) *Map H3*

Largest lake: L. Victoria, Tanzania/Uganda/Kenya, 69,484 sq km (26,828 sq miles) *Map I8*

Largest island: Madagascar, 587,040 sq km (226,660 sq miles) *Map K11*

0   250   500   750 km
0   100 200 300 400   500 miles

Lions are found on Africa's grassy plains, known as savanna.

NIGER RIVER

The Niger is Africa's third longest river. From its source in Guinea, it flows some 4,180 km (2,597 miles) across west Africa to its delta in Nigeria. Along its long course, the Niger drains a river basin almost three times the size of France. The Niger's water is used for irrigation and hydroelectric power, but its usefulness for transport is limited by its many waterfalls and rapids.

WILDLIFE

Africa has an amazing variety of wildlife. Huge herds of zebra and wildebeest roam the grassy plains, preyed on by lions and cheetahs. There are elephants, ostriches, and long-necked giraffes. Hippos wallow in rivers and swamps. In the rainforests live chimpanzees and gorillas, among the rarest animals on Earth.

PEOPLES OF AFRICA

Population: approximately 689,000,000 people

Number of countries: 53

AFRICA IS HOME TO about 689 million people – one in eight of the world's population. The most densely populated areas are along the northern and western coasts, especially in the fertile valleys of the Nile, Niger, Congo, and Senegal rivers. The population of Africa is growing rapidly, as birth rates in many African countries are extremely high. Families are often large, and about half the population is young, aged below 15 years. Although most Africans live in the countryside, a growing number are now found in towns and cities. Many people have moved there because of poverty and lack of work in country areas; others have gone to escape civil wars, droughts, and famines.

Largest country:
Sudan,
2,505,810 sq km
(967,493 sq miles)

Smallest country:
Seychelles
280 sq km
(108 sq miles)

Least densely populated country:
Namibia, 2 people per sq km (6 per sq mile)

Most densely populated country:
Mauritius, 549 people per sq km (1,421 per sq mile)

THE FIRST PEOPLE

The history of human beings appears to begin in Africa. The skeletons of people who walked upright and lived up to 2 million years ago have been found in the Rift Valley that runs through Tanzania and Ethiopia. Archaeologists now believe that this region was the birthplace of our human ancestors. From here, these early human beings, known as *Homo Erectus*, soon moved into other parts of the continent and rapidly spread even further afield.

Richard Leakey discovered some of the earliest known human remains in Africa's Rift Valley.

Percentage of population under 15 years of age

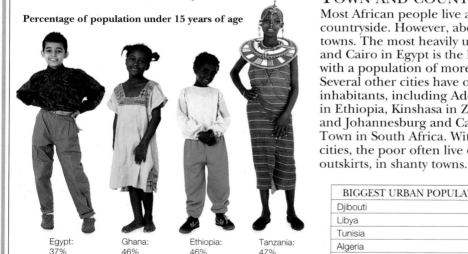

Egypt:
37%

Ghana:
46%

Ethiopia:
46%

Tanzania:
47%

YOUNG POPULATION

The population of Africa is growing rapidly. Death rates are falling as a result of improved medical care, and birth rates are extremely high. In countries such as Burundi and Kenya, the average birth rate is more than six children per woman, compared with only one or two in Europe and North America. Children are viewed as an economic necessity, especially in country areas, where they are used to help farm the land.

TOWN AND COUNTRY

Most African people live as farmers or herders in the countryside. However, about one in five people now live in towns. The most heavily urbanized region is north Africa, and Cairo in Egypt is the largest city on the continent, with a population of more than 6 million. Several other cities have over a million inhabitants, including Addis Ababa in Ethiopia, Kinshasa in Zaire, and Johannesburg and Cape Town in South Africa. Within the cities, the poor often live on the outskirts, in shanty towns.

BIGGEST URBAN POPULATION	
Djibouti	86%
Libya	84%
Tunisia	57%
Algeria	53%
South Africa	50%

SMALLEST URBAN POPULATION	
Lesotho	21%
Guinea Bissau	20%
Niger	19%
Burkina	17%
Ethiopia	13%

Many people go to the cities on a temporary basis in search of work. In Johannesburg, shown here, migrants seek work in the gold and diamond mines.

THE PEOPLE

The vast Sahara Desert separates the peoples of northern Africa, who are mostly Berbers and Arabs, like these Tunisian men, from those to the south, who are mostly Negroid. Northern Africa is predominantly Islamic, but south of the Sahara people follow a variety of religions, including Christianity and traditional animist beliefs. Two other groups are also important: there are about 5 million people of European descent, who live mainly in southern Africa, as well as a large number of Indians who live along the eastern coast and in South Africa.

PEOPLES AND COUNTRIES

There are more than 600 ethnic or tribal groups in Africa, and only 53 countries. Many of today's national boundaries were created in the late 19th century by the colonial rulers. Borders sometimes follow natural features, such as rivers, but often they just follow straight lines on the map. As a result, tribes are often split between different countries. The Ewe people, for example, are divided between Ghana and Togo. After independence, it has often proved difficult to create unity among the different peoples in one country.

Groups of nomadic Fulani people are found throughout the area shaded brown on this map of west Africa. They roam across many countries.

WEST AFRICA

INDEPENDENCE

During the 19th and early 20th centuries, most African countries were ruled by European powers, such as Britain, France, Germany, and Belgium. This is known as the colonial period. Since the 1960s, most countries have regained their independence, although many retain links with their former colonial rulers.

Celebrating 25 years of independence in Nairobi, Kenya.

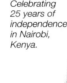

These refugees at a camp in Rwanda are Hutu people from neighbouring Burundi. War between the Hutu and Tutsi peoples has forced thousands of people in this region to leave their homes.

Groundnuts (peanuts) are one of the main export crops in west Africa.

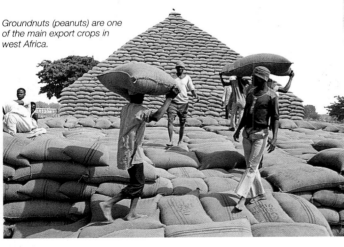

ECONOMIC PROBLEMS

Most African countries rely on exporting raw materials, such as coffee, cocoa, or oil. In recent years, the prices of these products have been falling. In contrast, the cost of importing machinery and other manufactured goods has risen. So the amount that African countries can earn from their exports is often less than what they have to spend on imports. These factors, along with the growing population and the effects of drought and war, mean that the economies of many African countries are in difficulty.

REFUGEES

More than 40 per cent of all the world's refugees come from Africa. Wars, drought, famine, and poverty are among the many factors that have caused millions of Africans to leave their homes. Estimates of the numbers of refugees vary, but today there may be as many as 6 million Africans who have been forced to move to another country. Up to 2 million refugees have fled the wars in Angola and Mozambique, while fighting in Ethiopia, Sudan, and Somalia has also displaced vast numbers of people.

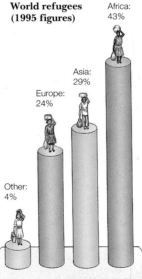

World refugees (1995 figures)

Africa: 43%
Asia: 29%
Europe: 24%
Other: 4%

NORTHWEST AFRICA

THE FOUR COUNTRIES of Morocco, Algeria, Tunisia, and Libya make up the northwest corner of Africa. This region has a long and varied history, due to its situation between the rest of Africa, Western Europe, and the Middle East. Most of its people are Arabic-speaking Muslims whose ancestors came to northwest Africa from the Middle East. From the 1530s to the 1830s, the region was part of the Turkish Ottoman Empire. It was then ruled by the colonial powers of France, Italy, and Spain, until the various countries gained independence in the mid-1900s. The countries of northwest Africa are relatively wealthy, thanks largely to their rich supplies of oil and gas.

ALONG THE COAST
The vast majority of northwest Africa's 63 million people live along the narrow coastal plain that borders the Mediterranean Sea and the Atlantic Ocean. Here, the climate is warm and wet in winter, and hot and dry in summer, making it more suitable for farming than the arid desert further inland. Citrus fruits, dates, olives, tomatoes, and flowers are grown. The major towns and cities are located here too.

A GROWING POPULATION
One of the most serious problems facing northwest Africa is the rapid growth of its population. In Algeria alone, the population increased from 12 million to 25 million between 1966–1990. Millions of people have moved from the countryside to the cities in search of work. This has led to severe housing shortages in the city centres and to the rise of overcrowded shanty towns on the outskirts.

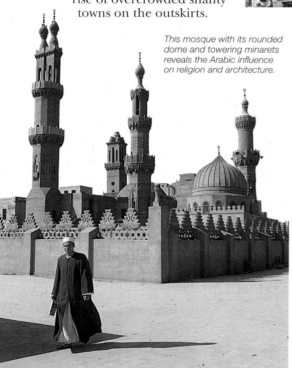

This mosque with its rounded dome and towering minarets reveals the Arabic influence on religion and architecture.

ARAB INFLUENCE
The Arab invasions of the 7th and 11th centuries have had a long-lasting effect on northwest Africa. The Arabs soon outnumbered the local Berber people who rebelled against their rule. They quickly established their own language, Arabic, and their own religion, Islam, throughout the region. Despite the later arrival of European colonists, northwest Africa today, in its language, culture, religion, and architecture, remains firmly part of the Arab world.

Marrakesh, Morocco
- Jan 11°C (53°F)
- July 29°C (84°F)
- Jan 25 mm (1 in)
- July 3 mm (0.1 in)

MOROCCO

WESTERN SAHARA

Tangier
Této
Kénitra
RABAT
Casablanca
Meknès
Safi
MOROC
Khouribga
Essaouira
Beni Mellal
Marrakesh
Er R
Djebel Toubkal ▲ Boumalne-
Agadir
Dadès
Tiznit
AT

Tan-Tan

EL AAIUN ⊙

A T L A N T I C   O C E A N

Semara
Tindouf

W E S T E R N   S A H A R A

Ad Dakhla

M A U R I T A N I A

Morocco occupied the whole of Western Sahara in 1979.

Lagouira

| 0 | 100 | 200 | 300 | 400 km |
| 0 | 50 | 100 | 150 | 200 | 250 miles |

TROPIC OF CANCER

EQUATOR

TROPIC OF CAPRICORN

N

In Salah, Algeria
- Jan 14°C (56°F)
- July 37°C (98°F)
- Jan 3 mm (0.1 in)
- July 0 mm (0 in)

A   B   C   D   E   F   G

The Tuareg ride on camel back, although motorbikes and four-wheeled drive trucks are increasingly used.

SAHARA DESERT

Much of northwest Africa is covered by the scorching sand and rocks of the Sahara Desert. The world's largest desert, the Sahara is expanding at an alarming rate as the land at its edges is overgrazed and gradually turned to dust. Despite daytime temperatures of up to 50°C (122°F), freezing nights, and years on end without rain, the desert is home to some amazing animals which have adapted to survive the conditions.

The fennec fox's huge ears let heat escape from its body, cooling it down.

DESERT PEOPLES

Few people can survive in the harsh environment of the Sahara Desert. The hardy Tuareg are desert nomads who may travel vast distances a day, carrying salt to trade in markets. Traditionally, the Tuareg use camels for transport, and also to provide milk, meat, and hides. However, many Tuareg are now abandoning their centuries-old nomadic lifestyle and settling in the cities.

THINGS TO LOOK FOR ON THE MAP

Longest river: Oued Chelif, Algeria, 700 km (435 miles) *Map K2*

Highest point: Djebel Toubkal, Morocco, 4,165 m (13,665 ft) *Map G4*

World's highest sand dune: is in the Erg Tifernine, Algeria, 430 m (1,411 ft) *Map M7*

World's highest recorded temperature: Al' Aziziyah, Libya, 58°C (136.4°F) *Map O4*

TUNISIA

Tunis, Tunisia
Jan 10°C (51°F)
July 26°C (79°F)
Jan 64 mm (2.5 in)
July 3 mm (0.1 in)

Benghazi, Libya
Jan 14°C (57°F)
July 26°C (78°F)
Jan 66 mm (2.6 in)
July 0 mm (0 in)

ALGERIA

LIBYA

MEDITERRANEAN SEA

ALGIERS
Bejaïa
Skikda
Bizerte
Mostaganem
Blida
Sétif
Annaba
TUNIS
Oran
Oued Chelif
Constantine
Jendouba
Sidi Bel Abbès
Tiaret
Batna
Tébessa
Kairouan
Sousse
Monastir
Tlemcen
Biskra
Sfax
Laghouat
Chott Melrhir
Gafsa
Gabès
El Oued
Tozeur
Jerba I.
Chott El Jerid
Medenine
Ghardaïa
Touggourt
TRIPOLI
Al Khums
Al Bayḍā
Dernah
Gharyān
Al' Aziziyah
Mişrātah
Al Marj
Tobruk
Ouargla
Yafran
Benghazi
Gulf of Sirte
Marsá al Burayqah
Al Jaghbūb
Surt
Ajdābiyā
Ghadāmis
Great Man-made River Project
GREAT WESTERN ERG
GREAT EASTERN ERG
Great Man-made River Project
Hūn
A L G E R I A
L I B Y A
Adrar
In Salah
Birāk
Adīrī
Sabhā
LIBYAN DESERT
Erg Tifernine
Illizi
Awbārī
Great Man-made River Project
Murzuq
Al Kufrah
TASSILI N'AJJER
Ghāt
S A H A R A
E G Y P T
AHAGGAR MTS.
Tamanrasset
N I G E R
C H A D
S U D A N
L I B

J K L M N O P Q R S T U

1 2 3 4 5 6 7 8 9 10 11

MOROCCO

Berber wedding ceremony

MOROCCO'S WARM CLIMATE, sandy beaches, and stunning mountain scenery make it a popular winter destination for holiday makers. Tourism, along with agriculture and phosphate production, is vital to the country's economy. In 1956, Morocco gained its independence from the French who had governed it since 1912. It is one of the few Arab countries to be ruled by a king, Hassan II. Since coming to the throne in 1961, King Hassan has won international recognition for his strong leadership. The main issues facing Morocco today are Islamic fundamentalism and the undecided fate of the Western Sahara region in the south.

MOROCCO*

Capital city: Rabat

Area: 698,670 sq km (269,757 sq miles)

Population: 27,000,000

Official language: Arabic

Major religions: Muslim 99%, other 1%

Government: Monarchy with democratic system

Currency: Moroccan dirham

Adult literacy rate: 52%

Life expectancy: 63 years

People per doctor: 4,840

Televisions: 74 per 1,000 people

* Figures include Western Sahara

BERBERS

Since the Arab invasions of the 11th century, the local Berber people have lived in villages high up in the Atlas Mountains. Most Berbers converted to Islam but kept their own culture and way of life. They call themselves *Imazighen*, or "people of the land". Today, about a third of Moroccans are Berber-speaking, although most also speak Arabic and French.

Carpets with symbolic patterns and ornate metalwork lanterns are made by local people.

AN ISLAMIC CITY

The ancient Moroccan city of Fez is a good example of a traditional Islamic town. Each part has been designed with a purpose, as set out in the Koran, the Muslim holy book. The streets are narrow to provide shade, but wide enough to let a pair of fully laden camels pass through. Houses have small, high-up windows on to the street, to guard their owners' privacy. In the city centre stands the largest mosque, surrounded by the *souks*, or markets.

The numerous, carefully planned streets in the old city of Fez look chaotic from a distance.

ARTS AND CRAFTS

Millions of tourists visit Morocco each year to relax on the beaches along the Atlantic coast or to explore the historical cities of Fez and Marrakesh. The cities' colourful *souks*, or markets, are a treasure chest of traditional goods and handicrafts, such as Moroccan leather, silver jewellery, and hand-woven carpets.

A supporter of the Polisario in the Western Sahara.

WESTERN SAHARA

This is a desert region south of Morocco with a population of some 200,000 people. It was formerly ruled by Spain. Since 1976, Morocco has been fighting a war for control of the region and its valuable mineral resources. Opposing the Moroccans are the Polisario, a guerilla force of desert tribesmen who are aiming for complete independence for the Western Sahara.

A phosphate-processing factory in the south of Morocco.

ECONOMY

Morocco's economy depends on three major industries – tourism, agriculture, and phosphates. Farm products make up about a third of exports. The main crops are cereals, vegetables, citrus fruits, and dates. Irrigation systems pipe water to many dry areas for farming. Morocco is the world's third largest producer of phosphates, which are used to make chemicals and fertilizers. Large factories process the phosphates for export.

Find out more

CARPET MAKING: *144, 155, 165*
IRRIGATION: *155, 156, 217*
ISLAM: *275*
MONARCHY: *270–271*

ALGERIA

STRETCHING FROM THE MEDITERRANEAN coast deep into the Sahara Desert, Algeria is the second largest country in Africa. It won independence from France in 1962, after a bitter, eight-year struggle that claimed one million lives. During French rule, tens of thousands of Europeans arrived, many of them later leaving after independence. Since then, Algeria has played an important part in world affairs as a member of the United Nations and the Arab League. The main challenge facing the military government today comes from the rapidly growing number of Islamic fundamentalists who support the setting up of an Islamic government.

ALGERIA	
Capital city: Algiers	
Area: 2,381,740 sq km (919,590 sq miles)	
Population: 27,100,000	
Official language: Arabic	
Major religions: Muslim 99%, other 1%	
Government: Military government	
Currency: Algerian dinar	
Adult literacy rate: 61%	
Life expectancy: 66 years	
People per doctor: 2,330	
Televisions: 74 per 1,000 people	

The leaves of date palms are used for thatching.

Arabs selling local produce at a market in Ghardaia, Algeria.

Dates can be eaten in many ways.

Wood is used for timber

Date palms are grown at desert oases, where water comes up to the surface.

ALGIERS
Algiers, the capital of Algeria, is the country's largest city and most important port. The city was founded in the 10th century by Muslims from Arabia. It was seized by the Turks in 1518 and by the French in 1830. The French influence can still be seen in these buildings in the modern part of the city along the Bay of Algiers. The old city, with its narrow streets, mosques, and markets, stands on the slopes of the Sahel Hills.

ETHNIC MIX
About 27 million people live in Algeria. Although the vast majority of Algerians are Arabs, about a fifth of the population are descendants of the earlier Berber settlers. Arabic is the official language and Islam the main religion. Of the million or so Europeans who settled in Algeria before independence, only a few thousand still live here. These include people of French, Spanish, and Italian descent.

Algerian exports 1991

Gas and gas products: 60%

Oil and oil products: 36%

Other: 4%

ECONOMY
Algeria's economy is dependent on its oil and gas reserves. These come from large deposits in the Sahara Desert. Oil production began in 1958 and, by 1979, had reached 1.2 million barrels a day. Although falling world oil prices in the 1980s and 1990s caused a drop in oil production, the exploitation of natural gas has since increased. Algeria supplies both France and Spain with gas.

FARMING
Algeria cannot grow enough crops to feed its rapidly increasing population and has to import about three-quarters of the food it needs. However, about half the population earns its living by farming. Major crops include cereals, citrus fruits, grapes, olives, and tobacco. Figs and dates are important too. Algeria is one of the world's leading producers of dates and of cork, which is made from cork oak bark. Dates are eaten fresh, dried or ground into flour. Roasted and ground date stones are made into date coffee.

TERRORIST ATTACKS
Islamic fundamentalists, like these members of the Islamic Salvation Front (FIS), are in open revolt against Algeria's military government. Thousands of Algerians have died in recent years as a result of terrorist violence. Westerners have also been attacked and bombs have been planted in Paris and other French cities.

Find out more	
COLONIAL PERIOD:	207
ISLAM:	275
OIL & GAS:	137, 152, 163, 211
SAHARA:	204, 209

TUNISIA

NORTHWEST AFRICA'S SMALLEST country, Tunisia lies between Libya to the south and Algeria to the west. Throughout its history, Tunisia has had close links with Europe. It was at the heart of the ancient empire of Carthage in the 4th century BC, and later became part of the mighty Roman empire. In the 7th century AD, Tunisia was colonized by Muslim Arabs, and, in the early 1880s, by French forces. It became independent in 1956. The government has since been restructured and a multi-party system introduced.

TUNISIA

Capital city:	Tunis
Area: 163,610 sq km (63,170 sq miles)	
Population: 8,600,000	
Official language: Arabic	
Major religions: Muslim 98%, Christian 1%, other 1%	
Government: Multi-party democracy	
Currency: Tunisian dinar	
Adult literacy rate: 68%	
Life expectancy: 67 years	
People per doctor: 1,870	
Televisions: 81 per 1,000 people	

TUNISIAN FOOD

Traditional food is influenced by Arabic, Turkish, and French cooking. The national dish is *couscous*, a mix of semolina, meat, and vegetables. Spicy stews cooked in clay pots, called *tajines*, are also popular. For dessert, people eat fruit, dates stuffed with almond paste, or *baklava*, a sweet nut and honey pastry. To drink, there is strong black coffee or mint tea. Many Tunisian men go to cafés in the evening to meet friends and drink coffee.

A heap of steamed couscous served with roast chicken and sausages.

Brightly dyed wool will soon be woven into carpets.

A glass of strong, sweet mint tea.

INDUSTRY

Until the collapse of world oil prices in the 1980s, Tunisia's major exports were oil and gas. Today, textiles and agricultural products have become much more important. Tunisia is also one of the world's leading producers of calcium phosphates, used to make chemicals and fertilizers. Most of the country's industries are located in and around the capital city, Tunis.

TOURISM

Libya: 25%

Germany: 15%

France: 14%

Algeria: 14%

Other: 32%

Most tourists come from neighbouring Algeria and Libya, and from Europe. Cheaper air travel and the search for an exotic holiday location have made Tunisia a favourite destination for Europeans.

Tunisia's warm winter climate and historic sites attract numerous tourists each year. Until 1976, tourism was Tunisia's highest earner of foreign currency. Numbers fell in the early 1980s but have now risen again to almost 4 million per year. The government has encouraged the building of new hotels and the development of resorts to meet the growing demand. Thousands of Tunisians are employed in the tourist industry.

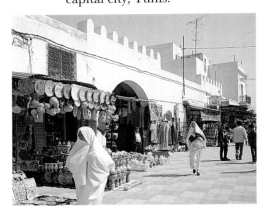

ARTS AND CRAFTS

One of the liveliest parts of a Tunisian city is the *souk*, or market. The souk is a maze of narrow, winding streets, each crowded with traders and craftsmen selling their wares. Here, you can buy a wide range of traditional arts and crafts, including copper pots and pans, carpets, leather goods, jewellery, and embroidered cloth. Other stalls sell fish, meat, fruit, and vegetables.

Grapes grow well in Tunisia's light soil and strong sunshine.

Oranges and limes come from groves along the fertile coast.

Dates are grown in the desert oases in the dry south.

AGRICULTURE

About two-thirds of Tunisia is suitable for farming. Many areas suffer from a lack of rainfall and rely on irrigation to water crops. The main crops include cereals, such as wheat and barley, citrus fruits, grapes, figs, dates, and olives. Tunisia is the world's fourth largest producer of olive oil. Despite efforts to improve output, however, Tunisia still has to import many basic foods.

Find out more

OIL & GAS: *137, 152, 163, 211*

OLIVES: *130*

POLITICAL SYSTEMS: *270–271*

LIBYA

SITUATED ON THE MEDITERRANEAN COAST between Egypt and Algeria, Libya is the fourth largest country in Africa. It has been part of the Roman, Byzantine, Arab, and Ottoman empires, and from 1911 to 1943 was an Italian colony. The Sahara Desert covers about 90 per cent of the country, so farming is only possible along the coastal strip, where many people work as sheep or goat herders. The discovery of oil in 1959 very quickly transformed Libya from a poor to a wealthy country. Many foreigners have since arrived to work in the oil industry.

LIBYA

Capital city: Tripoli	
Area: 1,759,540 sq km (679,358 sq miles)	
Population: 5,500,000	
Official language: Arabic	
Major religions: Muslim 97%, other 3%	
Government: Dictatorship	
Currency: Libyan dinar	
Adult literacy rate: 66%	
Life expectancy: 62 years	
People per doctor: 690	
Televisions: 99 per 1,000 people	

OIL AND GAS

The production of oil and gas dominates the Libyan economy, with oil making up 99 per cent of the country's exports. Before oil was discovered, Libya's major exports were rushes and scrap metal. Most of the oil is produced in western Libya but there are also some offshore oil reserves. As the oil industry has grown so have Libya's cities, providing more houses, jobs, and services. Some 84 per cent of the population are now city dwellers. Before this, many people lived in the countryside as farmers or nomads.

Where people live

84% live in cities 16% live in the country

FAMILY GROUPS

Most Libyans are Arabs, with some Berbers and Tuaregs in the south. Almost all are Muslim. They belong to large, extended family groups, called tribes or clans. The clan is an important part of society and also has an influence on politics. Many of Colonel Gaddafi's government ministers are members of his clan. People's names often reveal which clan they belong to.

COLONEL GADDAFI

Since 1969, Libya has been ruled by Colonel Muammar Gaddafi, who overthrew the king to become president. Gaddafi rules through military committees. His politics are a very personal mix of socialism, Islam, and Arab nationalism. Since all political parties were banned in 1971, any opposition to Gaddafi's rule has to come from outside Libya. Colonel Gaddafi's support for terrorist organizations has sometimes brought him into conflict with Western governments.

OASIS TOWN

In the vast, arid desert, small towns and villages have grown up around oases. Here, underground water rises to create rare patches of fertile land where crops are grown. The communities that live around oases rely on farming, receiving money from relations working in the cities, and dealing with passing traders. In the past, oasis towns were important stopping places for camel caravans transporting goods across the desert. Today, many of these journeys are made by truck instead.

People grow crops such as date palms, grapes, figs, and peaches.

Rain falls in the mountains and sinks into the porous rock.

A small village grows up at the edge of the oasis.

Impermeable rock stops the water sinking further.

Rainfall is stored in porous rock called an aquifer.

Water seeps up through a split in the rock layers.

ROMAN RUINS

Signs of Libya's rich classical past can still be seen in its many historical ruins. It has some of the finest Roman ruins in North Africa, such as the impressive site of Leptis Magna which has a forum, aqueduct, and amphitheatre (shown left). This port was founded by the Phoenicians in about 800BC and became a major centre for trade with Africa. It was then part of the Roman empire, before the Arab invasions of the 7th century AD led to the city's downfall.

Find out more

ISLAM: *275*
OIL: *137, 152, 281*
OIL WEALTH: *137, 278*
SAHARA: *204, 209*

NORTHEAST AFRICA

NORTHEAST AFRICA CONTAINS EGYPT and Sudan, two desert lands watered by the River Nile, and the region known as the Horn of Africa, so-called because it is shaped like an animal horn. The region consists of Somalia, Djibouti, Ethiopia, and Eritrea, four of the poorest countries in the world. The boundaries that divide them date from this century and follow the borders drawn up by the old colonial rulers of the area. Many people that live here are nomadic herders and take little notice of the borders as they travel over vast areas in search of pasture for their animals.

BASIC TOOLS
Farming methods in the area are often inefficient and simple tools, such as hoes, digging sticks, and sickles, are widely used. The ox-drawn scratch plough (above) is light and can be carried to scattered fields. But it only turns over the surface layer of the soil and does not allow nutrients to spread deeper, so after a few years the soil is no longer fertile.

TROUBLED LANDS
In recent years, the countries of Somalia, Sudan, Ethiopia, and Eritrea have been devastated by war. In 1993, Eritrea gained independence from Ethiopia, after a civil war that lasted 20 years. Somalia has been torn apart by civil war between its rival groups, or clans. Conflict continues in Sudan between the Arabic-speaking Muslims in the north and the African, non-Muslim peoples in the south.

Thousands of Eritrean women fought alongside men in the war against Ethiopia, and many held positions of command.

INTERNATIONAL AID
Many parts of northeast Africa have suffered from drought and famine in recent years. In 1984–85, a terrible famine swept through Ethiopia. It was caused by a combination of drought, warfare, and population growth. The famine drew the world's attention to the region and a huge international aid effort was launched, helped by the pop charity, Band Aid.

The White Nile meanders slowly through the Sudd, a vast region of dense reed swamps in Sudan.

The White Nile and the Blue Nile meet at Khartoum in Sudan to form the Nile River.

As the Nile reaches the border of Sudan and Egypt, it flows into Lake Nasser, one of the world's largest artificial lakes. The lake was created by the building of the Aswan High Dam.

Many birds, including storks, herons, and pelicans, make their home in the Sudd.

The Blue Nile begins at Lake Tana. It flows through the mountains of Ethiopia, collecting rainfall along the way.

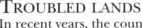
Fertile farmland

THE RIVER NILE
The world's longest river, the River Nile, flows northwards from Lake Victoria in Kenya through the Sahara Desert to the Mediterranean Sea. It passes through Ethiopia, Sudan, and Egypt, providing precious water for drinking, farming, and fishing. The river is also a major tourist attraction. People travel along the Nile on cruise liners and traditional sailing boats, called *feluccas*, to see the ancient sites of Egypt.

North of the Aswan Dam, the Nile is surrounded by desert, but rich, fertile land lies along the banks of the river.

Feluccas are now mainly used by tourists.

A B C D E F G H I J K L

1 2 3 4 5 6 7 8 9 10 11 12

MEDITERRANEAN SEA
Marsa Matrûh
El Mansûra
Port Said
Alexandria
Suez Canal
Tanta
Ismâ'iliya
CAIRO
Suez
QATTÂRA DEPRESSION
Giza
Helwân
SINAI
EGYPT
El Faiyûm
Gulf of Suez
El Minya
Gulf of Aqaba
Asyût
Bûr Safâga
Sohâg
Qena
LIBYA
Nile
Luxor
LIBYAN DESERT
ISRAEL

Cairo, Egypt
☀ Jan 13°C (56°F)
☀ July 29°C (83°F)
🌧 Jan 5 mm (0.2 in)
🌧 July 0 mm (0 in)

EGYPT

Aswân High Dam
Aswân
RED SEA
L. Nasser
Administration Border
Wadi Halfa
NUBIAN DESERT
ERITREA

CHAD
SUDAN
Nile
Port Sudan
Atbara
Atbara
Khartoum North
Omdurman
Kassala
KHARTOUM
ASMARA
Wad Medani
ERITREA
Adwa
Dahlak Archipelago

El Fasher
El Obeid
White Nile
Blue Nile
Ras Dashen Terara
Mekele
Assab
DJIBOUTI
Nyala
En Nahud
Gonder
DJIBOUTI
DJIBOUTI
Kaduqli
Ed Damazin
L. Tana
Bahir Dar
Dese
Awash
Gulf of Aden
Berbera
Boosaaso
HORN OF AFRICA

THINGS TO LOOK FOR ON THE MAP
World's longest river: Nile, Egypt/Sudan/Uganda, 6,738 km (4,187 miles) *Map E5*
Highest point: Ras Dashen Terara, Ethiopia, 4,620 m (15,157 ft) *Map G7*
Largest lake: L. Tana, Ethiopia, 2,849 sq km (1,100 sq miles) *Map G8*
World's longest shipping canal: Suez Canal, Egypt, 163 km (101 miles) *Map E1*

Addis Ababa, Ethiopia
☀ Jan 15°C (59°F)
☀ July 16°C (60°F)
🌧 Jan 13 mm (0.5 in)
🌧 July 279 mm (11 in)

Debre Markos
ETHIOPIAN
ADDIS ABABA
Dire Dawa
Harer
Hargeysa
Garoowe
Nekemte
HIGHLANDS
ETHIOPIA
Gore
Jima
SUDD
Malakal
Awasa
Gaalkacyo
SUDAN
Wau
Jonglei Canal
Omo
L. Abaya
Genale
Shebeli
SOMALIA
CENTRAL AFRICAN REPUBLIC
Rumbek
Southeast Sudan is administered by Kenya
Beledweyne
SOMALIA

ZAIRE
Juba
L. Rudolf
UGANDA
KENYA
Juba
Baydhabo
MOGADISHU
Marka

0 100 200 300 400 500 km
0 100 200 300 miles

SUDAN

Mogadishu, Somalia
☀ Jan 27°C (80°F)
☀ July 26°C (78°F)
🌧 Jan 0 mm (0 in)
🌧 July 64 mm (2.5 in)

ETHIOPIA

Jilib
Kismaayo

INDIAN OCEAN

Pyramids

Cairo

Many people live on the banks and delta of the Nile.

New land has been formed in the delta by mud and rock deposited by the river.

As the river nears the Mediterranean Sea, it separates into many tributaries and forms a fertile triangle of land called a delta.

COTTON FIELDS
Largely as a result of European colonization in the last century, cotton growing and processing are important industries in Egypt and Sudan. Production was begun in these areas by the British to provide cotton for their textile mills. The cotton is grown on large, highly mechanized farms that lie along the fertile banks of the River Nile.

EGYPT

IT IS SAID THAT EGYPT is the gift of the River Nile. The site of one of the world's first great civilizations, Egypt grew up under the rule of the pharaohs along the banks of the Nile more than 5,000 years ago. Most of the country is dry, sandy desert with a narrow, fertile strip which follows the river valley and widens into the delta. This is where the vast majority of Egypt's population lives. Most of the people are Arab and follow the Muslim faith. The economy is dominated by farming, oil, tourism, income from ships passing through the Suez Canal, and money earned by Egyptians working abroad.

EGYPT	
Capital city: Cairo	
Area: 1,001,450 sq km (386,660 sq miles)	
Population: 56,100,000	
Official language: Arabic	
Major religions: Muslim 94%, other 6%	
Government: Multi-party democracy	
Currency: Egyptian pound	
Adult literacy rate: 50%	
Life expectancy: 61 years	
People per doctor: 1,320	
Televisions: 109 per 1,000 people	

CAIRO
With a population of some 9.5 million, Cairo is the largest city in Africa and one of the fastest growing. The city faces terrible housing problems. New arrivals often have to live in dirty, overcrowded slums. Some live among the graves of the City of the Dead, a huge cemetery on the outskirts of the city. People also live on the roofs of the many high-rise buildings in Cairo.

The Suez Canal is used by more than 20,000 ships every year.

SUEZ CANAL
The Suez Canal runs from the Red Sea to the Mediterranean Sea. It is the one of the world's largest and most important artificial waterways, providing a short cut from Europe to India and East Asia. The canal was built with French and British help and was completed in 1869. It has since been made deeper and wider to allow for the increasing size of ships and tankers. In 1956 the canal came under Egyptian control. Today, the tolls taken from the ships that use the canal are an important source of income for the Egyptian government.

→ Route before Suez Canal
→ Route after Suez was built

The Suez Canal offered a short cut from Europe to India and East Asia. Earlier, ships from Europe had sailed around Africa.

FUL MEDAMES
This Egyptian dish is made by boiling brown beans with onions, vegetables, and spices. This may be eaten with an egg for breakfast. A similar mixture is used to stuff *aysh* (flat bread), to make sandwiches.

THE RIVER NILE
Some 99 per cent of Egyptians live in the valley or delta of the River Nile. The river is Egypt's lifeline, providing water for farming, industry, and home use. When the Aswan High Dam was built on the Nile, it created the world's largest reservoir, Lake Nasser.

The Sphinx, built of soft sandstone, has the body of a lion and the head of a man.

FARMING IN EGYPT
Many Egyptian farmers, or *felahin*, use traditional farming methods to grow cotton, wheat, rice, sugar, fruit, and vegetables. Egypt is the world's largest producer of dates. Another important crop is *berseem*, a type of clover that is grown for animal feed. Egypt is also one of the world's biggest cotton growers. Many people are employed in the textile industry, spinning, weaving, and dyeing the fine quality cotton to make clothes and other goods.

ANCIENT SITES
Egypt is littered with ancient monuments. Every year, millions of tourists flock to Egypt to see the pyramids and other sites, or to take a boat trip on the River Nile. The pyramids, built more than 4,000 years ago as tombs for the pharaohs, are one of the seven wonders of the ancient world, and the only one to survive.

Cool and comfortable cotton tunics, called jelabas, are often worn by Egyptian men.

SUDAN

SUDAN, THE LARGEST COUNTRY in Africa, is one of the poorest and least developed countries in the world. The River Nile flows from south to north, and most people live along its fertile banks. The landscape ranges from rocky desert in the north, to swampland in the south. Sudan is also divided culturally. The people of the north are mainly Arabic-speaking Muslims, while in the centre and south, African languages and religions, together with Christianity, dominate. Clashes between the two sides have led to decades of civil war.

SUDAN	
Capital city: Khartoum	
Area: 2,505,5810 sq km (967,493 sq miles)	
Population: 25,000,000	
Official language: Arabic	
Major religions: Muslim 70%, traditional beliefs 20%, Christian 5%, other 5%	
Government: Military government	
Currency: Sudanese dinar	
Adult literacy rate: 28%	
Life expectancy: 51 years	
People per doctor: 11,110	
Televisions: 71 per 1,000 people	

NOMADIC LIFE

Many of Sudan's tribal people live by herding cattle, moving from place to place in search of fresh pasture. The more cattle a person owns, the greater his importance in the tribe. The civil war has disrupted the lives of many herders, destroying their pastures and their herding routes.

The Dinka tribe are nomadic cattle herders who live on the plains east of the Nile.

WATERING THE LAND

Much of Sudan is too dry to live or farm in, and large areas of suitable farmland have been destroyed by war. The majority of people live by the River Nile and use its water to irrigate their fields. Two-thirds of the people make their living from the land, growing crops such as cotton, peanuts, gum arabic, millet, and dates. A large-scale irrigation scheme set up by the government has helped farmers to grow more crops for export.

TRIBES

The people of Sudan are divided into more than 500 different tribes and groups speaking more than 100 languages and dialects. Each tribe shares a common ancestor. Many, such as the Dinka and Juhaynah tribes, are nomadic. Others have settled in particular areas, such as the Shilluk tribe, who are farmers living on the west bank of the Nile. The people shown left are from the Beni Amer tribe, a Muslim group.

KHARTOUM

Since Sudan became independent in 1956, the Muslim government in the capital, Khartoum, has tried to impose Islam on the rest of the population, leading to civil war and famine. Millions of refugees have poured into Khartoum from the south and west to escape the fighting and to find food and work. Many now live in shanty towns on the outskirts of the city.

HOUSING

Life in the Arab north of Sudan is very different from that of the African south. There are differences in language, religion, customs, and style of housing. The Nubian people of the north (an African people who adopted Islam as their religion) build rectangular, flat-roofed houses of sun-dried bricks. The Nubans of central Sudan (a tribe of hill farmers) build round huts with conical roofs made of grass, wooden poles, and millet stalks.

Flat-roofed houses built of mud brick are common in northern Sudan.

Conical-roofed huts are common in central and southern Sudan. Each hut has its own purpose.

Storeroom

Living quarters

A small "keyhole" doorway helps keep the hut warm and dry inside.

Wrestling is a popular sport among the Nuban people.

Find out more

IRRIGATION: *155, 156*
PEOPLES OF AFRICA: *206–207*
REFUGEES: *207*
RELIGION: *274–275*

ETHIOPIA

A LAND RICH in its own unique traditions, Ethiopia has in recent years suffered from drought, famine, and warfare. In 1984–85, a terrible famine, caused by a combination of civil war, drought, overpopulation, and overfarming, struck the northern highlands. During this time, Ethiopia was involved in a long, bitter war with the Eritreans, which ended in 1991. Four out of five Ethiopians live off the land, growing crops such as *teff* (a type of grass) or herding cattle. Coffee is Ethiopia's major export crop. It is mostly grown in the mountains of Kaffa province, from which it gets its name.

ETHIOPIA

Capital city: Addis Ababa

Area: 1,221,900 sq km (471,775 sq miles)

Population: 51,300,000

Official language: Amharic

Major religions: Muslim 43%, Christian 37%, indigenous beliefs 17%, other 3%

Government: Provisional government

Currency: Ethiopian birr

Adult literacy rate: No figures available

Life expectancy: 46 years

People per doctor: 33,330

Televisions: 2 per 1,000 people

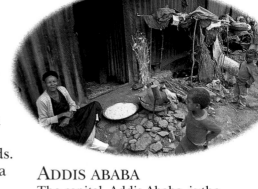

ADDIS ABABA

The capital, Addis Ababa, is the biggest city in Ethiopia with some 3 million inhabitants. It is a rapidly growing city, home to many refugees from the north and Eritrea. Housing is in short supply and there are about 20,000 children living on the streets. Many people live in crowded slums without toilets or running water. It is not unknown for a family of eight to ten people to share one room.

MUSIC AND DANCE

There are many groups of Ethiopians, each with their own language and traditions in storytelling, music, and dance. Traditional dances tell stories from everyday life. The music and songs that accompany them are an important means of passing on information about local cultures and customs.

Traditional instruments include the kra (a type of lyre).

Traditional Ethiopian dancers shake their shoulders as they dance.

Traditional dress consists of an embroidered white dress and shawl for women, and white shirts and trousers for men.

Coffee-making ceremonies are elaborate. The coffee is brewed with added spices, incense is burned, and grass spread over the floor.

Ethiopian Orthodox priests at a religious festival in Addis Ababa.

ETHIOPIAN CHURCH

The Ethiopian Orthodox Church can be traced back to the 4th century AD. Its most impressive monuments are the 12th century churches in the village of Lalibela, which are carved out of solid rock. The Ethiopian Church has similarities with other Eastern churches and some Jewish customs have been retained, but its colourful ceremonies and festivals have their own distinctive flavour.

FIREWOOD

Women are responsible for cutting, carrying, and selling firewood, a major source of fuel and income. Much of Ethiopia's forests have now been destroyed, however. This has led to the soil, no longer protected by trees, being blown or washed away and to the loss of valuable farmland.

A typical vegetable dish made from cabbage, carrots, garlic, and red lentils.

Wot, made from red onions, chillies, garlic, ginger, and other herbs and spices, is added to meat and vegetable dishes.

Hard-boiled eggs are often eaten with the meal.

Chicken stew, made from chicken, egg, and red peppers.

Enjera

Beef stew, made from beef, cinnamon, peppers, red chilli, and tomatoes.

FOOD

The national dish of Ethiopia is *enjera*, a type of soft, flat bread made from *teff*, eaten with a mixture of meat and vegetables. These are cooked in a hot, spicy sauce, called *wot*. Traditionally, the sauce is served on top of the *enjera*. Raw beef, served with hot spices and melted butter, is eaten at festival times.

Find out more

CHRISTIANITY: *274*
CITIES: *17, 206*
COFFEE: *50, 62, 66*
SOIL EROSION: *55, 244*

SOMALIA

SOMALIA GAINED INDEPENDENCE from Italy in 1960. However, this diverse country with a rich history did not achieve peace. Since 1991, Somalia has been torn apart by civil war, resulting in widespread famine. Many Somalians are nomadic herders, wandering through the dry, barren countryside with their camels, sheep, and goats in search of food and water.

MOGADISHU
Mogadishu is the capital of Somalia and its major port and commercial centre. The various styles of the buildings reflect the history of the country. Arabs settled there in the 9th century, and it became a European colony in the 20th century.

RELIEF CAMPS
Since war broke out, many thousands of Somalis have moved into relief camps for food, safety, and shelter. The troubles, however, have made it difficult for international aid to be distributed. Up to 1 million refugees are in neighbouring countries and are likely to remain for some time until a solution to the war can be found.

WOMEN'S DRESS
Many Somali women wear a cotton, sari-like garment called a *guntimo*, and a shawl, called a *garbasaar*. Unlike many Muslims in other countries, Somali women do not wear veils that cover the face.

SOMALIA

Capital city: Mogadishu

Area: 637,660 sq km (246,200 sq miles)

Population: 9,500,000

Official languages: Somali, Arabic.

Major religion: Muslim 100%

Government: None at present

Currency: Somali shilling

Adult literacy rate: 27%

Life expectancy: 46 years

People per doctor: 14,290

Televisions: 12 per 1,000 people

DJIBOUTI

Capital city: Djibouti

Area: 23,200 sq km (8958 sq miles)

Population: 500,000

Official languages: Arabic, French

Major religions: Muslim 94%, other 6%

Government: Multi-party democracy

Currency: Djibouti franc

Adult literacy rate: No figures available

Life expectancy: 48 years

People per doctor: 4,180

Televisions: 5 per 1,000 people

ERITREA

Capital city: Asmara

Area: 93,680 sq km (36,170 sq miles)

Population: 3,500,000

Official languages: Tigrinya, Arabic

Major religions: Christian 45%, Muslim 45%, other 10%

Government: Provisional government

Currency: Ethiopian birr

Adult literacy rate: No figures available

Life expectancy: No figures available

People per doctor: No figures available

Televisions: No figures available

DJIBOUTI

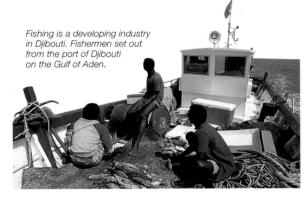

Fishing is a developing industry in Djibouti. Fishermen set out from the port of Djibouti on the Gulf of Aden.

THE SMALL, MAINLY DESERT country of Djibouti became independent in 1977. Many of its people are nomads. Djibouti is of great importance to this part of Africa because of its port and capital city, also called Djibouti. The country's economy relies almost entirely on income from the port.

ERITREA

AFTER 20 YEARS OF WAR, the mountainous land of Eritrea achieved independence from Ethiopia in 1991. The Eritrean People's Liberation Front (EPLF) drove the last Ethiopian troops out, and went on to form the government. The Eritrean people are now trying to rebuild the shattered economy.

This theatre in Asmara, the capital of Eritrea, is an example of the fine Italian-style architecture found in parts of the city. Eritrea was once an Italian colony.

Find out more

COLONIAL PERIOD: *207*
DESERTS: *15, 204, 209*
ISLAM: *275*
REFUGEES: *207*

WEST AFRICA

MANY CENTURIES AGO, great civilizations such as the Asanti and Mali were thriving in the region now known as West Africa. Word of rich gold deposits brought Europeans flocking here, and by the 1880s they had colonized nearly all of this vast region. West Africa did not win back its independence until the 1960s. Although this region is rich in oil, gold, timber, and other natural resources, most of the 15 countries in West Africa are very poor. There are large numbers of ethnic groups here – over 200 different peoples live in Nigeria alone. The combination of poverty and clashes between different peoples has made political turmoil another all-too-familiar feature of the region.

RELIGION
West Africa divides roughly into northern and southern regions where the landscape and climate are concerned, and this also applies to its religions. Islam is dominant in the north, while there are more Christians in the south. Throughout the region, many people follow ancient traditional religions such as voodoo, which is especially strong in Benin.

Desert
The burning Sahara Desert forms the northern "lid" of West Africa. Very little grows here. The border of the desert advances or retreats, depending on how dry it becomes in neighbouring areas.

Sahel
The arid northern grasslands that border the desert are called sahel – the word means "shore" of the desert in Arabic. Few trees can survive in this region.

Savanna
Moving south, a little more rain falls in the vast expanses of savanna – grassland scattered with acacias, baobabs, and other trees. Much of West Africa consists of savanna.

Tropical forest
Moist forests flourish under the heavy rains of the far south. Many animals and plants live here, although there are not as many different species as in the rainforests of central Africa.

Climate zones in West Africa

Desert
Sahel
Savanna
Tropical forest

THE CLIMATE
If you set out on a journey from north to south across this huge region, you would pass through a fascinating variety of hot, tropical landscapes. The vegetation of each zone has developed because of the amount of rain that falls there. Plenty of rain falls in the far south, whereas the arid northerly region is prone to serious drought. In some parts, there is a distinct wet season that lasts about 4–6 months and no rain at all falls for much of the rest of the year.

WESTERN SAHARA
Zou
Fdérik

Ras Nouâdhibou
Nouâdhibou
Atar

Ras Timirist

M A U R I

SENEGAL
⊙NOUAKCHOTT
Tidjikd

L. Rkiz
Rosso
Aleg
Saint-Louis
Louga
Senegal
Kaédi
Matam

C. Verde ⊙DAKAR
S E N E G A L
Kaolack
Tambacounda

BANJUL
GAMBIA

Ziguinchor
Kolda
Bafatá

GUINEA-BISSAU ⊙ BISSAU
Labé

GAMBIA
Bijagos Archipelago
Boké
G U I N
Fria
Kindia
CONAKRY ✪
SIERR

GUINEA-BISSAU   **GUINEA**
Makeni
LEO
✪FREETOWN
Bo

MONR

Freetown, Sierra Leone
☀ Jan 26.5°C (80°F)
July 25.5°C (78.5°F)
🌧 Jan 13 mm (0.5 in)
July 894 mm (35.2 in)

SIERRA LEONE

LIBERIA

There are many nomadic cattle herders in Burkina, which lies in the dry sahel region.

WEST AFRICAN FARMERS
This region is home to two very different types of farmer – settled and nomadic. Settled farmers live near small plots of land where they grow enough to feed their families and perhaps some cash crops such as cocoa or oil palms. Nomadic cattle herders, such as the Fulani, roam constantly across the region in search of good grazing land. They are more common towards the drier north, where the land is not as good for growing crops.

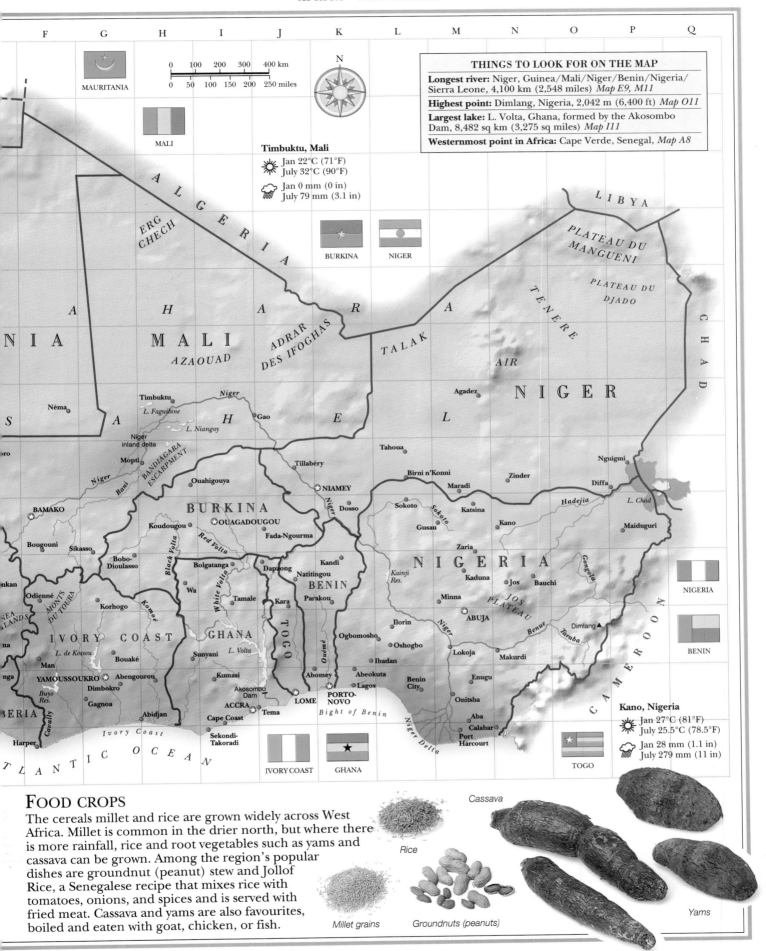

F G H I J K L M N O P Q

MAURITANIA

0   100   200   300   400 km
0   50   100   150   200   250 miles

N

MALI

Timbuktu, Mali
Jan 22°C (71°F)
July 32°C (90°F)
Jan 0 mm (0 in)
July 79 mm (3.1 in)

THINGS TO LOOK FOR ON THE MAP
Longest river: Niger, Guinea/Mali/Niger/Benin/Nigeria/
Sierra Leone, 4,100 km (2,548 miles) *Map E9, M11*
Highest point: Dimlang, Nigeria, 2,042 m (6,400 ft) *Map O11*
Largest lake: L. Volta, Ghana, formed by the Akosombo
Dam, 8,482 sq km (3,275 sq miles) *Map I11*
Westernmost point in Africa: Cape Verde, Senegal, *Map A8*

BURKINA   NIGER

A L G E R I A

L I B Y A

PLATEAU DU
MANGUENI

PLATEAU DU
DJADO

ERG
CHECH

S A H A R A

A

H

A

MALI

AZAOUAD

ADRAR
DES IFOGHAS

H

TALAK

TENERE

AIR

CHAD

R

A

E

L

NIGER

Néma

Timbuktu
L. Faguibine
Niger
L. Niangay
Gao

Agadez

Niger
inland delta
Mopti

Tahoua

Nguigmi

BANDIAGARA
ESCARPMENT

Tillabéry

NIAMEY

Birni n'Konni
Maradi

Zinder

Diffa

L. Chad

Maiduguri

Niger
Bani

Ouahigouya

Dosso

Sokoto
Sokoto

Katsina

Kano

Hadejia

BAMAKO

BURKINA

Gusau

Bougouni
Sikasso

Koudougou

OUAGADOUGOU

Fada-Ngourma

Zaria

Kaduna

Jos   Bauchi

NIGERIA

NIGERIA

Bobo-
Dioulasso

Black Volta

Red Volta

Kandi

Kainji
Res.

Minna

JOS
PLATEAU

Odienné

MONTS
DU TOURA

Korhogo

White Volta

Wa

Bolgatanga

Dapaong

Natitingou

BENIN

Parakou

Kaina
Res.

Ilorin

ABUJA

Dimlang ▲

BENIN

Komoé

Tamale

Kara

Benue

Taraba

IVORY   COAST

GHANA

TOGO

Ouémé

Ogbomosho

Niger

Lokoja

Makurdi

L. de Kossou

Sunyani

L. Volta

Oshogbo

Enugu

CAMEROON

Man

Bouaké

Kumasi

Ibadan

Benin
City

YAMOUSSOUKRO   Abengourou

Dimbokro

Abomey

Abeokuta
Lagos

Onitsha

Buyo
Res.

Gagnoa

Akosombo
Dam

LOME

PORTO-
NOVO

Aba

Abidjan

ACCRA   Tema

Bight of Benin

Port
Harcourt

Calabar

Gongola

Harper

Cape Coast

Sekondi-
Takoradi

Niger Delta

Kano, Nigeria
Jan 27°C (81°F)
July 25.5°C (78.5°F)
Jan 28 mm (1.1 in)
July 279 mm (11 in)

A T L A N T I C   O C E A N

Ivory Coast

IVORY COAST   GHANA

TOGO

FOOD CROPS

The cereals millet and rice are grown widely across West
Africa. Millet is common in the drier north, but where there
is more rainfall, rice and root vegetables such as yams and
cassava can be grown. Among the region's popular
dishes are groundnut (peanut) stew and Jollof
Rice, a Senegalese recipe that mixes rice with
tomatoes, onions, and spices and is served with
fried meat. Cassava and yams are also favourites,
boiled and eaten with goat, chicken, or fish.

Rice

Cassava

Millet grains

Groundnuts (peanuts)

Yams

MAURITANIA

COVERING AN AREA TWICE THE SIZE of Spain, but with a population smaller than Madrid's, Mauritania is one of the emptiest countries in the world. In recent years, many of the people have left the countryside to live and work in the towns, and Nouakchott, the capital, has grown from 20,000 people in 1960 to 500,000 today. The country is dominated by the Arab Maures (Moors) from the north, but their political control is resented by the black peoples from the south. Mining is an important industry, as Mauritania is rich in phosphates, copper, gold, and other minerals. Drought is a major problem in this region.

MAURITANIA
Capital city: Nouakchott
Area: 1,025,520 sq km (395,953 sq miles)
Population: 2,200,000
Official language: French
Major religion: Muslim 100%
Government: Multi-party democracy
Currency: Ouguiya
Adult literacy rate: 35%
Life expectancy: 47 years
People per doctor: 11,900
Televisions: 23 per 1,000 people

NIGER
Capital city: Niamey
Area: 1,267,000 sq km (489,188 sq miles)
Population: 8,500,000
Official language: French
Major religions: Muslim 85%, traditional beliefs 14%, other 1%
Government: Multi-party democracy
Currency: CFA franc
Adult literacy rate: 31%
Life expectancy: 46 years
People per doctor: 33,330
Televisions: 5 per 1,000 people

Projects like this one for planting trees and grass to hold the soil in place are helping to stop erosion.

THE SAHEL

Two-thirds of Mauritania is covered by the Sahara, and only the land along the Senegal River is suitable for farming. The semi-desert land in between, known as the sahel, is the grazing land for nomadic farmers. This area suffers from frequent droughts and from soil erosion, made worse by people cutting down the few trees for firewood and overgrazing cattle. For these reasons – both natural and human – the sahel is gradually becoming more desert-like.

FISHING
Fleets from all over the world come to fish off the coast of Mauritania, where some of the richest fish stocks in West Africa are found. By law, all fish caught here must be landed and processed in Mauritania before they are exported to overseas markets. However, overfishing of the seas by fleets of trawlers has led to concern about the future of the industry.

Areas at risk of desertification

This map shows the areas of West Africa that are at risk of turning into desert.

- Very high risk
- High risk
- Medium risk

NIGER

THE VAST STATE OF NIGER is completely surrounded by other countries. Its main link to the sea is the River Niger, the only major river in the country. Most of Niger's 8 million people live in the semi-desert sahel region, which stretches in a narrow ribbon across the south of the country. North of the sahel lies the vast and inhospitable Sahara, home to the nomadic Tuareg peoples. Niger has few natural resources apart from uranium, which brought in considerable wealth during the 1980s. Most of the people, however, remain poor, earning their living herding flocks or growing crops in the few fertile parts of the country.

THE TUAREG
As a result of frequent droughts in northern Niger, many Tuareg lost all their animals and were forced to give up their nomadic lifestyle. Many moved south to the towns in search of food and work. In reaction to this enforced move, some Tuareg are campaigning for a country of their own.

FARMING
Every year, the River Niger floods. As the floodwaters retreat, local farmers quickly plant their crops of cereals, rice, vegetables, groundnuts, and cotton in the fertile soils left behind. The banks of the Niger also provide pasture for cattle and other livestock reared for meat and milk.

> ### *Find out more*
> RIVER NIGER: *205*
> SAHEL: *220*
> SOIL EROSION: *55, 244*
> TUAREG: *209*

MALI

THE LANDSCAPE OF MALI ranges from the vast desert plains of the Sahara in the north, through the semi-desert sahel region in the centre, to wetter savanna in the south. A thin belt of fertile land stretches either side of the Niger and Senegal rivers. The country gets its name from the great Muslim empire of the Malinke people, which flourished in this region in the 13th and 14th centuries. Today, Mali is a poor country where most people make their living from farming or herding cattle.

MALI	
Capital city: Bamako	
Area: 1,240,190 sq km (478,837 sq miles)	
Population: 10,100,000	
Official language: French	
Major religions: Muslim 90%, traditional beliefs 9%, Christian 1%	
Government: Multi-party democracy	
Currency: CFA franc	
Adult literacy rate: 36%	
Life expectancy: 45 years	
People per doctor: 20,000	
Televisions: 1 per 1,000 people	

MOSQUES

Islam arrived in Mali with merchants travelling across the Sahara from the Arab north. By the 13th century, Mali was entirely Muslim, with mosques built in most towns. Mosques like this one at Mopti are constructed of clay around a wooden framework that sticks out in turrets above the roof. The wooden beams jutting out through the walls allow villagers to climb all over the building to carry out its annual repairs.

TIMBUKTU
Founded by Tuareg nomads in 1100, Timbuktu became one of the most famous cities in Africa. Because of its position on the trade route across the Sahara, it soon developed into a major town. Arab traders from the north brought salt, cloth, and horses to exchange for gold and slaves from the south. By 1400, Timbuktu had become a major centre of Islamic learning.

The River Niger at Bamako, in southern Mali.

THE NIGER

The River Niger is the lifeline of Mali, flowing through the country from west to east before turning south to pour into the Atlantic Ocean. Most people in the country live along its banks, using the river as a source of water and food and the main means of transport. The capital of Mali, Bamako, on the upper reaches of the river, is a major port, shipping cement and petrol down river and receiving rice and groundnuts (peanuts) for export in exchange.

Granaries are built of thick clay to keep the grain cool and free of rats.

Dogon houses are made of clay, often with terraces above the main living area.

The flat rooftops are used to dry onions and to store pots and baskets.

Compound

Outer wall

Entrance

The Dogon live in walled compounds built on steep hillsides for protection against attack from their enemies.

RICE GROWING

In the centre of Mali, the River Niger splits into several branches. This area is called the river's inland delta, and is one of the most fertile regions of the country. Here, as the river begins to flood, farmers plant a special "floating" rice that grows up to 30 cm (12 in) a day to keep pace with the rising waters. When the crop is ready, the farmers harvest it from boats.

THE DOGON

South of Timbuktu, the flat river plain gives way to sandstone cliffs surrounding the Bandiagara plateau. Living in the cliffs are the Dogon people, who first settled in the area in the 1500s. The Dogon worship their own gods, and have many legends about the creation of the world. Because of the harsh conditions in which they live, the Dogon are expert farmers, using every available strip of land to grow crops of rice, millet, and maize.

Find out more
ISLAM: *275*
MALINKE PEOPLE: *225*
RICE GROWING: *135, 176, 197*
RIVER NIGER: *205*

SENEGAL	
Capital city: Dakar	
Area: 196,720 sq km (75,950 sq miles)	
Population: 7,900,000	
Official language: French	
Major religions: Muslim 92%, traditional beliefs 6%, Christian 2%	
Government: Multi-party democracy	
Currency: CFA franc	
Adult literacy rate: 40%	
Life expectancy: 49 years	
People per doctor: 20,000	
Televisions: 36 per 1,000 people	

GAMBIA	
Capital city: Banjul	
Area: 11,300 sq km (4,363 sq miles)	
Population: 900,000	
Official language: English	
Major religions: Muslim 90%, Christian 9%, traditional beliefs 1%	
Government: Multi-party democracy	
Currency: Dalasi	
Adult literacy rate: 30%	
Life expectancy: 44 years	
People per doctor: 11,690	
Televisions: No figures available	

SENEGAL

THE MIGHTY SENEGAL RIVER dominates large areas of this country. Every year the river floods, and seasonal crops are grown on the fertile land that the flood waters leave behind. Senegal is relatively wealthy compared to other countries in this region, as it was once the capital of French West Africa and still has close links with France. Among the mix of ethnic groups, such as the Wolof and Mandinke, there are still many French inhabitants. There is a similar mix of religions – Islam exists side-by-side with traditional beliefs. Senegal's beautiful, palm-fringed coastline makes tourism an important feature of life here.

MUSICAL STORYTELLING

History is a living thing in West Africa. For centuries, history and other information has been passed on by word of mouth, and from one generation to the next, through stories, poems, and songs. In Senegal, the people who take these from village to village are called *griots*. They play a variety of traditional instruments, such as the *kora*.

The kora has 21 strings.

Front view of kora

The soundbox is made from a hollowed-out gourd.

DAKAR
The lively city of Dakar, Senegal's capital, perches on a rocky peninsula that forms the westernmost point of Africa. This major port was once the capital of French West Africa, as can be seen from its grand colonial buildings. Today great poverty is found on the streets of Dakar, alongside the expensive restaurants and modern hotels.

FARMING AND FISHING

Nearly three-quarters of Senegal's people work in farming. In the north, cereals such as millet and sorghum are the main food crops and groundnuts (peanuts) are a vital cash crop. Rice is common in the wetter southern areas. Groundnuts were once grown on nearly half the farmland, but fish is now taking over as the country's main export. A common sight is local fishermen setting out in dug-out canoes called *pirogues*, made from local trees.

GAMBIA

THE TINY COASTAL COUNTRY of Gambia is a long, thin sliver of land carved out of Senegal, which surrounds it on three sides. At its widest point, Gambia measures no more than 80 km (50 miles) from north to south. Like Senegal, Gambia has a wide ethnic mix and Islam is very important. Most of the people work in farming, relying heavily on the groundnut crop. Women play a major role in agricultural life. Rice growing is their main occupation, but near the coast large areas of swampy rice land have been ruined by the build-up of salt in the soil. Many women now grow vegetables to sell in local markets.

Most tourists stay along the coast, but many take trips inland to see the crocodiles, monkeys, and many species of bird that live along the Gambia River.

TOURISM
The tourist trade is the fastest growing part of the Gambian economy. More and more North Europeans are coming here to escape their cold winters, attracted by the magnificent beaches. Gambia is particularly popular with visitors from the UK, because English is widely spoken in this former British colony. But fears are already mounting that the easy-going local lifestyle will soon be ruined by advancing tourism.

Find out more

AFRICAN CITIES: *206*
COLONIAL PERIOD: *207*
RELIGION: *274–275*
RICE GROWING: *135, 176, 197*

GUINEA

ONCE A FRENCH COLONY, this fertile, hilly country is rich in minerals, and has perfect weather conditions for growing many crops, including bananas, citrus fruits, and rice. These factors should have made Guinea a rich country. Instead, it is one of the poorest in the world, with a life expectancy of just 44 years and very basic medical and education facilities. This is largely the result of the French leaving Guinea without financial support, poor management of the economy, and years of harsh political rule under Sekou Touré, who was president from 1958–84.

GUINEA	
Capital city: Conakry	
Area: 245,860 sq km (94,926 sq miles)	
Population: 5,600,000	
Official language: French	
Major religions: Muslim 95%, traditional beliefs 4%, Christian 1%	
Government: Provisional government	
Currency: Guinea franc	
Adult literacy rate: 27%	
Life expectancy: 44 years	
People per doctor: 50,000	
Televisions: 7 per 1,000 people	

GUINEA BISSAU	
Capital city: Bissau	
Area: 36,120 sq km (13,940 sq miles)	
Population: 1,000,000	
Official language: Portuguese	
Major religions: Traditional beliefs 54%, Muslim 38%, Christian 8%	
Government: One-party state	
Currency: Guinea peso	
Adult literacy rate: 39%	
Life expectancy: 43 years	
People per doctor: 7,260	
Televisions: No figures available	

THE GUINEA HIGHLANDS
Thick forest covers the mountainous Guinea Highlands in the south of the country. As well as providing timber products, conditions in this highly fertile area are ideal for growing various crops, including coffee. Three of the region's major rivers – the Niger, the Gambia, and the Senegal – have their sources here. Rich iron deposits are also to be found, and the whole area is nourished by abundant rainfall.

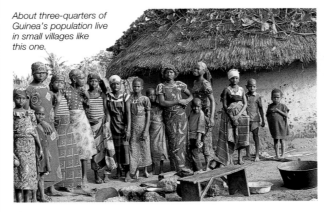

About three-quarters of Guinea's population live in small villages like this one.

PEOPLE OF GUINEA
A varied mix of peoples, including the Malinke, Fulani, and Soussou, live in Guinea. Most of them are Muslim. The Malinke make up about a third of the population, and are named after a mountainous area on the Mali border. This was once part of the great Mali empire, which dominated West Africa in medieval times. Today, the Malinke are famous for their centuries-old storytelling and musical skills.

MINING
The mountainous areas of Guinea are rich in a mineral ore called bauxite. Ores are substances from which metals can be obtained, and bauxite is used to make aluminium. Guinea is the world's second largest producer of bauxite, after Australia, and it accounts for more than 80 per cent of the country's earnings from exports. Guinea's mountain regions yield other valuable minerals, including iron, gold, and diamonds.

GUINEA BISSAU

Groundnuts (peanuts)

SANDWICHED BETWEEN SENEGAL and Guinea, this low-lying, swampy country is a particularly unspoilt place. Once ruled by Portugal, Guinea Bissau was the first Portuguese colony to gain independence, in 1974. Today it is very poor, and heavily dependent on financial aid from other countries. The people are a mix of ethnic groups, the largest of which are the Balante, from the south. Most people scrape a living by growing coconuts, cotton, groundnuts (peanuts), or cashew nuts. Timber and fishing are also important.

Cashew nuts

ALONG THE COAST
Like its neighbours, Guinea Bissau has spectacular beaches. Its coastline is edged with mangrove swamps, mud flats, and estuaries leading to a maze of inland waterways. A huge variety of fish are found off the coast, and many people in this coastal region make their living from fishing.

GROUNDNUTS
As the name suggests, the actual nuts of the groundnut, or peanut, plant grow underground. The nut pods are pulled out of the ground and left to dry before being shelled and skinned. Some of the nuts are sold in local markets, but most are used to extract groundnut oil, used in food production, or crushed to make peanut butter.

Find out more

COLONIAL PERIOD: 207
ISLAM: 275
LIFE EXPECTANCY: 276
POOR COUNTRIES: 298–299

SIERRA LEONE

IN 1787, THE BRITISH colonized this region and created a settlement for freed African slaves. This is how Sierra Leone's capital, Freetown, got its name. Today, there are still a few descendants of the freed slaves, known as Creoles, living here. The main peoples, however, are the Mende in the south and the Temne in the north. In recent years, conflicts between the various ethnic groups have led to civil war. Sierra Leone is one of the poorest countries in the world, and three-quarters of the people make their living from small-scale farming.

SIERRA LEONE

Capital city: Freetown

Area: 71,740 sq km (27,699 sq miles)

Population: 4,500,000

Official language: English

Major religions: Traditional beliefs 60%, Muslim 30%, Christian 10%

Government: Military government

Currency: Leone

Adult literacy rate: 24%

Life expectancy: 42 years

People per doctor: 14,290

Televisions: 10 per 1,000 people

LIBERIA

Capital city: Monrovia

Area: 111,370 sq km (43,000 sq miles)

Population: 2,800,000

Official language: English

Major religions: Christian 68%, traditional beliefs 18%, Muslim 14%

Government: Military government

Currency: Liberian dollar

Adult literacy rate: 42%

Life expectancy: 55 years

People per doctor: 9,340

Televisions: 18 per 1,000 people

Diamonds

Diamonds found among the gravel in rivers are called alluvial diamonds.

Cut diamond

Rice grains

MINING
Sierra Leone's rich mineral deposits have made mining a vital industry, with diamonds among the main products. Diamond mining methods vary from using fully mechanized diggers, to chipping gemstones out of the rock by hand, or panning for them in rivers. Other mineral exports include gold, iron ore, bauxite (from which aluminium is made), and rutile (from which titanium is made).

FARMING
Sierra Leone's main cash crops are cocoa, coffee, nuts, and palm kernels (seeds from which oil is extracted). The main food crop is rice, which is grown in the river valleys. "Dry" rice is grown in the soil on the valley sides, and "wet" rice is grown in flooded fields on the valley floor. Attempts have been made to raise production – for example, clearing mangrove swamps to make way for extra rice-fields.

LIBERIA

LIBERIA BECAME AN INDEPENDENT country in 1847 and has never been colonized, making it the oldest independent republic in Africa. In the 19th century, the American Colonization Society helped thousands of freed African slaves to return from the USA and settle here. They gave Liberia its name, which means "freed land". Links between the USA and Liberia remain strong today. Since 1990, Liberia has suffered from civil war, and the economy has virtually collapsed.

THE RUBBER TRADE
One of Liberia's strongest links with the USA are the extensive, American-owned rubber plantations. Over the years, these have employed huge numbers of people and have accounted for a very large slice of the country's income from exports. The American Firestone company, which makes world-famous tyres, has been at the forefront of this rubber production. Rubber is made from a sticky substance called latex, which can be "tapped" from rubber trees by cutting slits in the bark.

This camp at Pern is home to refugees from the war.

CIVIL WAR
In recent years there have been clashes between Liberia's different ethnic groups, which include the Kpelle, Bassa, and Kru peoples. These problems erupted into civil war in the early 1990s, which did a great deal of damage to an already weakened economy. The war has forced about half the population to leave their homes, and many people have starved because of food shortages.

Find out more

DIAMONDS: *150, 248*
REFUGEES: *207*
RICE GROWING: *135, 176, 197*
RUBBER: *194*

IVORY COAST

IVORY COAST HAS a reputation for being one of the most politically and economically stable countries in Africa. Some of this may be explained by the fact that it had the same president, Félix Houphouët-Boigny, for 33 years, until his death in 1993. He encouraged the export of a wide range of products, which can often help to keep an economy healthy. Coffee and cocoa are the main cash crops. Other products include cotton, fruit, tobacco, and timber. Ivory Coast was once a French colony, which gained independence in 1960, and still has strong ties with France.

IVORY COAST

Capital city: Yamoussoukro

Area: 322,463 sq km (124,503 sq miles)

Population: 13,400,000

Official language: French

Major religions: Traditional beliefs 63%, Muslim 25%, Christian 12%

Government: Multi-party democracy

Currency: CFA franc

Adult literacy rate: 56%

Life expectancy: 52 years

People per doctor: 16,670

Televisions: 61 per 1,000 people

These hardwoods all come from Ivory Coast.

Mahogany

Iroko

Idigbo

TIMBER INDUSTRY
Ivory Coast once had vast areas of forest, containing ebony, mahogany, and other hardwood trees. Today hardly any is left. For years the country's economy was heavily dependent on the timber industry. Timber exports were seen as vital for paying off foreign debts, and large areas of forest were cleared to make way for coffee and cocoa plantations. A programme was recently started to help save the forests and plant new ones.

ETHNIC GROUPS
More than 60 ethnic groups live side-by-side in Ivory Coast, with relatively few clashes. The Dan people, for example, live deep in the heart of the western forests and are famous for their carving skills. They make wooden masks that are worn by the members of special secret societies to keep their identities hidden. Only members of these societies are allowed to take part in the Dan stilt dances.

YAMOUSSOUKRO
The dome of the world's largest Christian church rises up above the rooftops of Yamoussoukro, a small town in the centre of the country which recently became Ivory Coast's capital city. Personally overseen by former president Boigny, the cathedral was completed in 1989 at huge cost. It seats 7,000 people and has an open-air area for another 350,000 – three times the city's population. There has been much controversy about undertaking such an extravagant project in a country where there is still widespread poverty.

Pineapple

Bananas

Coffee beans

THE ECONOMY
Compared to much of West Africa, Ivory Coast is a fairly prosperous country. This is partly the result of the policy of growing a variety of crops. Ivory Coast is the world's leading cocoa grower – in some years, it has produced about a third of the world's cocoa exports – but competition from southeast Asia may change this. It is also Africa's biggest coffee producer and grows vast numbers of pineapples and bananas.

World's top five cocoa producers (1992/3)

Figures show the share of total world cocoa production.

- Malaysia: 9%
- Indonesia: 10%
- Brazil: 12.5%
- Ghana: 13%
- Ivory Coast: 29%

Many of Abidjan's banks and businesses are based in the skyscrapers of the Plateau district.

ABIDJAN
This modern port, with its glittering glass skyscrapers, is the country's largest city. Abidjan is filled with smart shops and restaurants that show a powerful French influence, reminding visitors of Ivory Coast's historical ties with France. It was also the country's capital until the 1990s, when Yamoussoukro took over that role.

Find out more

CHRISTIANITY: *274*
COCOA: *228, 234*
COFFEE: *50, 62, 66*
LOGGING: *69, 244*

GHANA

GHANA SHOULD BE A RELATIVELY wealthy country. Its many riches include fertile farmland, reserves of gold, bauxite, and oil, and a young population that is among the best educated in Africa. However, years of unstable government, low earnings from exports, and bad management of the economy have hindered Ghana's development. More than 50 different ethnic groups live in Ghana, each with its own language and traditions. Among the largest groups are the Akan peoples, who include the Asante in the south of the country, the Dagomba in the north, and the Ewe in the southeast.

INDEPENDENCE
In 1957, Ghana became the first black African country to gain independence from its colonial rulers. Ghana's first prime minister was Kwame Nkrumah, who had led the resistance to British rule. At first Nkrumah was very popular, but he lost favour in the economy declined, and was eventually overthrown in 1966.

GHANA

GHANA	
Capital city: Accra	
Area: 238,540 sq km (92,100 sq miles)	
Population: 16,400,000	
Official language: English	
Major religions: Traditional beliefs 38%, Muslim 30%, Christian 24%, other 8%	
Government: Multi-party democracy	
Currency: Cedi	
Adult literacy rate: 63%	
Life expectancy: 55 years	
People per doctor: 25,000	
Televisions: 15 per 1,000 people	

THE AKOSOMBO DAM
One of the world's largest artificial lakes, Lake Volta, is formed by the Akosombo Dam on the Volta River. When the dam was built in the 1960s, about 85,000 people had to be moved from areas flooded by the lake. The dam's power station generates electricity for factories in the city of Tema and for domestic use. Some power is exported to Togo and Benin.

Asante gold head showing a defeated enemy general.

MARKETS
Every Ghanaian town has a bustling market, drawing people in from the surrounding area. Here they can buy and sell a wide range of goods, from food and animals to household supplies and even false teeth. Many of the market traders are women. Some of them make a lot of money from it. Others are involved in marketing because it is part-time and leaves the rest of the day free for other work.

Women traders at the market in Accra.

THE ASANTE
When Europeans first visited Ghana in the 15th century, they named it the Gold Coast because of the gold offered to them in trade by local people. The main gold workers were the Asante, whose kings and priests wore gold ornaments to show their high status. The symbol of Asante unity was a golden stool, which they believed had come down from the sky. Gold from the Asante mines is still an important export for Ghana.

A mature cocoa tree produces 20–30 fruit pods a year.

Cocoa pods grow directly from the trunk. They are harvested once they have ripened to a yellow colour.

COCOA
Cocoa trees need plenty of shade when they are young and water when they are mature. This is why they grow so well in the humid forests of southern Ghana. Here young cocoa plants are grown between rows of other food crops, which provide the necessary shade. The trees only begin to produce fruit after about seven years. Cocoa production is a major industry, accounting for up to 80 per cent of the country's exports, but Ghana now faces stiff competition from neighbouring Ivory Coast and from southeast Asia.

Each pod contains up to 40 pale pink beans covered in a pink pulp.

Roasted cocoa beans

Cocoa pod

Cocoa beans are fermented, roasted, and ground to produce a chocolate liquid. This is used to make cocoa butter for cosmetics, or is reheated and moulded to make blocks of chocolate.

Find out more
COCOA: *227, 234*
COLONIAL PERIOD: *207*
GOLD MINING: *253*
TRADE DEPENDENCY: *281*

BURKINA

Landlocked Burkina (formerly known as Upper Volta) is one of the world's poorest countries. Like the other countries in the sahel region, Burkina is at constant risk from drought, and in recent years large amounts of grazing land have turned to desert as the Sahara has expanded southwards. Burkina has few cities, and most of the people live in villages, making their living from farming and herding. Burkina's economy has suffered badly from political unrest. Because the country is so poor, almost one-third of the workforce have to go abroad to find jobs.

BURKINA

Capital city: Ouagadougou

Area: 274,200 sq km (105,870 sq miles)

Population: 9,800,000

Official language: French

Major religions: Traditional beliefs 65%, Muslim 25%, Christian 10%

Government: Multi-party democracy

Currency: CFA franc

Adult literacy rate: 20%

Life expectancy: 48 years

People per doctor: 33,330

Televisions: 5 per 1,000 people

TOGO

Capital city: Lomé

Area: 56,790 sq km (21,927 sq miles)

Population: 3,900,000

Official languages: French, Kabye, and Ewe

Major religions: Traditional beliefs 70%, Christian 20%, Muslim 10%

Government: Multi-party democracy

Currency: CFA franc

Adult literacy rate: 45%

Life expectancy: 54 years

People per doctor: 12,500

Televisions: 6 per 1,000 people

FOREIGN AID

Burkina is very dependent on foreign aid. Each year more than $US400 million of aid comes into the country, much of it from Burkina's former colonial ruler, France, and from the European Union. The money is used for both large-scale projects, such as dams to generate hydroelectric power, and smaller schemes, like this well that provides clean water for a village.

Many farmers have a vegetable garden where they grow food for their families.

AGRICULTURE

Lack of water and poor soil cause huge problems for Burkina's farmers. Before any crops can be planted, a farmer has to clear the land, burning the scrub and ploughing the ash into the ground to act as a fertilizer. The new field can only be used for four to five years before it is exhausted. Then it has to be left for at least another five years to recover.

The Fulani carry many of their possessions in large bowls called calabashes, which are made from the dried fruit shells of the gourd.

The calabash rests on a roll of cloth.

THE FULANI

The Fulani are nomads who live by cattle herding. They travel wherever there is grazing land, pitching their huts or tents when they want to sleep. The Fulani live off the produce of their animals, eating mainly milk, butter, and cheese. Their wealth is measured by how many animals they own, so they rarely kill and eat them. Many Fulani have now abandoned this nomadic way of life and settled in one place.

The Fulani's animals are mainly cattle, like these zebu, but they also keep goats, sheep, and, in the north of the region, camels.

TOGO

Sandwiched between Ghana and Benin, Togo is a former French colony that gained its independence in 1960. The population is a mix of about 30 different ethnic groups; the two largest are the Ewe in the south of the country and the Dagomba in the north. Phosphates – minerals used to make fertilizers – account for half of Togo's exports, but the economy has been badly affected by rises and falls in world phosphate prices. Togo's capital city, Lomé, is one of the major ports in West Africa.

FARMING AND FISHING

Although Togo is a very poor country, it produces nearly all its own food. About three-quarters of the population live in the countryside and are employed in farming. They grow maize, yams, rice, and cassava to eat, and cocoa, coffee, and cotton to sell and export. Along the coast, many people make their living from fishing.

Find out more
FULANI: *207*
PHOSPHATES: *210*
RICH AND POOR : *278–279*
SAHEL: *220, 222*

NIGERIA

NIGERIA IS HOME TO AN AMAZING mix of more than 250 different peoples. The largest groups are the Hausa-Fulani, who live in the north, the Yoruba in the west, and the Ibo in the east. Nigeria could be one of Africa's most successful economies. It has large reserves of oil, gas, and minerals, and abundant farmland. The population of 88 million is the largest of any African country, and one of the best educated. Yet a series of military coups has weakened the government, and conflicts between the ethnic groups led to civil war in 1967. Today, Nigeria is struggling to pay off huge debts and to modernize its industry and agriculture.

NIGERIA

Capital city: Abuja

Area: 923,770 sq km (356,668 sq miles)

Population: 88,514,501

Official language: English

Major religions: Muslim 50%, Christian 40%, traditional beliefs 10%

Government: Military government

Currency: Naira

Adult literacy rate: 52%

Life expectancy: 52 years

People per doctor: 66,670

Televisions: 32 per 1,000 people

BENIN

Capital city: Porto-Novo

Area: 112,620 sq km (43,480 sq miles)

Population: 5,100,000

Official language: French

Major religions: Traditional beliefs 70%, Christian 15%, Muslim 15%

Government: Multi-party democracy

Currency: CFA franc

Adult literacy rate: 25%

Life expectancy: 46 years

People per doctor: 14,290

Televisions: 5 per 1,000 people

LAGOS
The city of Lagos is situated on a coastal island in the southwest corner of Nigeria. The island was first settled in the 15th century by local Yoruba people. The town grew rapidly as a trading port used by European merchants, and became the capital of independent Nigeria in 1960. In 1992 the capital was moved to Abuja, in central Nigeria, but Lagos is still the biggest city.

OIL

Oil was first produced in Nigeria in 1956 and within 20 years the new industry dominated the economy. Today it makes up about 98 per cent of the country's exports. Nigerian oil is high quality with a low sulphur content, making it ideal as aircraft fuel. However, it is dangerous for a country to rely on just one product. When world oil prices fell in the 1980s, Nigeria suffered badly. Efforts are now being made to develop other products so that the country is not so dependent on oil.

The Niger Delta in the south of the country contains huge oil reserves, enough to last for at least another 25 years. Four huge refineries prepare the crude oil for export.

Main exports in 1992

Oil: 98%

Others: 2%

PLANTATIONS

In recent years huge plantations have been set up throughout Nigeria to produce crops in large quantities, mainly for export. Plantations make use of modern machinery to plant, grow, and process the crops, which include cotton, coffee, sugar, cocoa, and oil palms. Today Nigeria is one of the world's largest producers of palm oil. Oil from the fleshy fibre of the palm nut is used in cooking oil, margarine, soap, candles, and paint.

Farmers clear and plough the land ready to plant crops.

SMALL FARMS
Most Nigerian farmers work on their own small farms. They use hoes, ploughs, and other simple tools to grow food crops such as cassava, rice, yams, and maize to feed their families. They also grow crops such as cocoa, oil palms, rubber, and groundnuts (peanuts) to sell. These are known as cash crops. Despite the recent investment in plantations, most of Nigeria's cash crops are still grown on these small farms.

Oil palm tree

Palm nuts grow in large bunches. When they are ripe, they are cut down and taken to factories where the oil is extracted.

Fleshy fibre

Kernel

Cross-section of a palm nut

VILLAGE LIFE

Most Nigerians are born and die in the same village, and think of it as home even if they move to a big city for a while. Most of the villagers work as farmers, although each village usually has a traditional doctor, blacksmith, and carpenter. Villagers are almost self-sufficient, growing much of their own food, building their own houses, weaving cloth for clothes, and making pots for cooking. Anything they cannot make, they buy with money earned by selling goods in the local market.

MOVING TO THE CITY

Many young Nigerians leave their villages for a few years and move to a city. They go to study, or to earn money that they can send back to their families when profits from farming are low. This money may be used to buy food, or sometimes it is spent on books for a child going to school. Once the migrants have finished their studies or saved up enough money, they return home to their villages.

Corrugated iron has replaced traditional building materials in many villages

Firewood for cooking

Migrants add to the overcrowding in Nigeria's cities, and are often forced to live in shanty towns without proper drains or water supplies.

Villagers return from the market in the local town with chickens, cloth, and other goods.

Millet, an important part of the diet, is pounded in a clay pot to make flour.

In the south of Nigeria most meals include yams or other vegetables. Yams have to be peeled, boiled, and mashed before they can be eaten.

Women carry babies in slings made of cloth.

One of the main dyes is indigo, a blue colour produced by pulping the leaves of the indigo vine.

DYEING

The Yoruba people of southwest Nigeria are skilled cloth dyers, making intricate patterns from a range of natural dyes. The cloth is usually dyed in earthenware pots, although the Hausa people in the northern city of Kano use large pits in the ground, lined with a local cement.

RELIGION

Nigeria is divided in its religious beliefs. In the north, people follow Islam, which was introduced by Arab traders from across the Sahara Desert during the 11th century. Religious festivals, such as this Sallah procession to mark the end of Ramadan (the Islamic month of fasting), are important local events. Five hundred years later, European merchants brought Christianity into the south. Many Nigerians, however, still follow traditional African religions.

BENIN

SQUASHED UP AGAINST THE WESTERN border of Nigeria, Benin is a long, thin country that stretches north from its narrow Atlantic Ocean coastline to the Niger River. Originally called Dahomey (it was renamed Benin in 1975), the country gained its independence from France in 1960. Since then Benin has had a series of military governments, and been a one-party state. In 1991 it became the first African nation to move from one-party rule to a multi-party democracy. Although it is a poor country, Benin has a growing economy based on agricultural products, such as cotton, cocoa, and coffee.

COASTAL REGIONS

For centuries, the inhabitants of these stilt houses along the shores of Lake Ganvie have made their living from fishing in the lake. But many former lakes and lagoons have become partly silted up, and many of the fishermen have had to take up sea fishing or move to the towns to try to find work.

Find out more

AFRICAN CITIES: *206*
COCOA: *227, 228, 234*
OIL: *137, 152, 281*
RELIGION: *274–275*

CENTRAL AFRICA

In fertile central Africa, steaming rainforests cluster around the Equator, and the mighty Congo River snakes its way through Congo and Zaire. In the 1400s, Europeans began a cruel slave trade here; by the late 19th century, the region was colonized. Independence came in the 1960s, but democracy has been slow to arrive. The area has met with mixed fortunes. Countries range from stable, prosperous Cameroon to the Central African Republic, which has been crushed by poverty and harsh dictatorships.

Faya, Chad
- Jan 21°C (69°F)
- July 34°C (93°F)
- Jan 0 mm (0 in)
- July 0 mm (0 in)

CHAD

THINGS TO LOOK FOR ON THE MAP

Longest river: Congo (Zaire), Zaire/Congo, 4,666 km (2,900 miles) *Map G10*

Highest point: Mt. Stanley (Margherita Peak), Zaire, 5,110 m (16,765 ft) *Map K11*

Largest lake: L. Tanganyika, Zaire, 32,893 sq km (12,700 sq miles) *Map K12*

N

0 100 200 300 400 500 km
0 100 200 300 miles

CAMEROON

EQUATORIAL GUINEA

SÃO TOMÉ & PRÍNCIPE

GABON

CENTRAL AFRICAN REPUBLIC

CONGO

ZAIRE

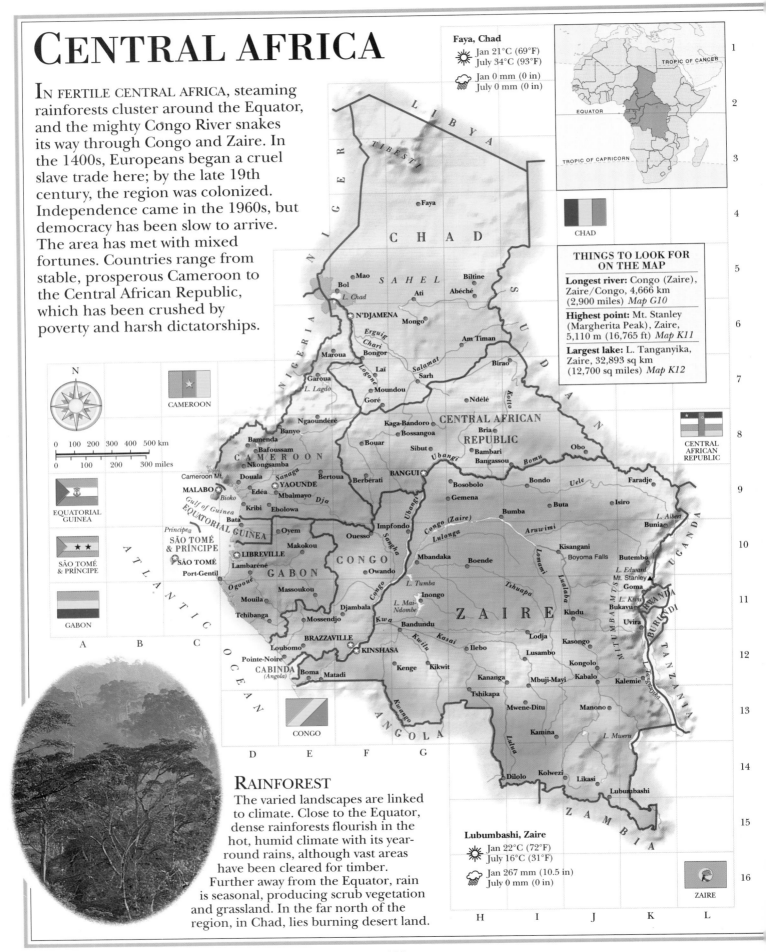

RAINFOREST

The varied landscapes are linked to climate. Close to the Equator, dense rainforests flourish in the hot, humid climate with its year-round rains, although vast areas have been cleared for timber. Further away from the Equator, rain is seasonal, producing scrub vegetation and grassland. In the far north of the region, in Chad, lies burning desert land.

Lubumbashi, Zaire
- Jan 22°C (72°F)
- July 16°C (31°F)
- Jan 267 mm (10.5 in)
- July 0 mm (0 in)

CAMEROON

IN AN AREA THAT HAS SEEN many troubles since independence, Cameroon is a relatively prosperous and stable success story, thanks to sensible government policies. Along with its southern neighbours, Gabon and Congo, the country has earned money from oil, and has used this to develop its economy. Many different peoples live in Cameroon, and its geography is just as varied. The humid coastal plain in the south gives way to a drier central plateau, while a finger of land points up to the marshes around Lake Chad.

CAMEROON	
Capital city: Yaoundé	
Area: 475,440 sq km (183,570 sq miles)	
Population: 12,500,000	
Official languages: French, English	
Major religions: traditional beliefs 51%, Christian 33%, Muslim 16%	
Government: Multi-party democracy	
Currency: CFA franc	
Adult literacy rate: 57%	
Life expectancy: 55 years	
People per doctor: 12,500	
Televisions: 23 per 1,000 people	

Pearl millet grows to a height of 1.5–3 m (5–10 ft).

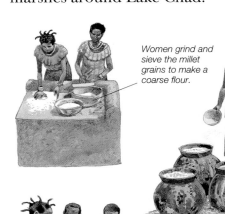

Women grind and sieve the millet grains to make a coarse flour.

Millet can also be used to make beer. It is dried, pounded, and then brewed in large pots.

A stiff white porridge made from millet flour is a popular breakfast dish.

PEOPLES

With more than 130 ethnic groups, Cameroon has one of the richest mixes of peoples and cultures in Africa. These range from the Fulani cattle herders, who live in the north and follow Islamic beliefs, to forest dwellers further south who practise traditional religions. Most people are settled farmers producing enough for their own needs, like this Hausa farmer tending his cattle.

GROWING MILLET

Most farmers in Cameroon grow crops, such as millet, for their own use (subsistence farming) and also produce crops to sell. Millet is cultivated widely in northern Cameroon, where there is less rainfall, because it grows well in poorer, drier soils. There has also been great investment in the production of commercial "cash" crops such as cocoa and coffee, oil palms, and bananas.

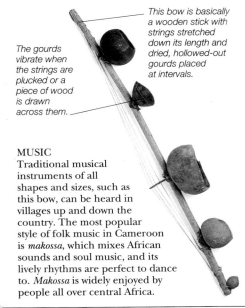

This bow is basically a wooden stick with strings stretched down its length and dried, hollowed-out gourds placed at intervals.

The gourds vibrate when the strings are plucked or a piece of wood is drawn across them.

MUSIC
Traditional musical instruments of all shapes and sizes, such as this bow, can be heard in villages up and down the country. The most popular style of folk music in Cameroon is *makossa*, which mixes African sounds and soul music, and its lively rhythms are perfect to dance to. *Makossa* is widely enjoyed by people all over central Africa.

INDUSTRY

Cameroon has an expanding timber industry. The country has extensive forests, and mahogany, ebony, and teak are all exported abroad. However, the industry is hampered by roads that are impassable during the rainy season. Much of the country's wealth is based on its reserves of oil, and other natural resources include bauxite, iron, and gold.

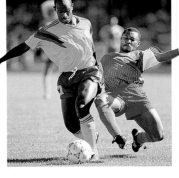

FOOTBALL
Cameroon has won a place as Africa's most celebrated football (soccer) team after some spectacular displays of skill on home territory and in the World Cup. The people of Cameroon love football, and at lunchtime and in the evenings informal matches spring up on any spare piece of open ground that they can find.

Find out more
COCOA: *227, 228, 234*
LOGGING: *69, 227, 244*
OIL: *152, 230, 281*
OIL PALMS: *230*

CENTRAL AFRICAN REPUBLIC	
Capital city: Bangui	
Area: 622,980 sq km (240,530 sq miles)	
Population: 3,300,000	
Official language: French	
Major religions: traditional beliefs 60%, Christian 35%, Muslim 5%	
Government: Multi-party democracy	
Currency: CFA franc	
Adult literacy rate: 40%	
Life expectancy: 47 years	
People per doctor: 25,000	
Televisions: 4 per 1,000 people	

EQUATORIAL GUINEA	
Capital city: Malabo	
Area: 28,050 sq km (10,830 sq miles)	
Population: 400,000	
Official language: Spanish	
Major religions: Christian 90%, other 10%	
Government: Multi-party democracy	
Currency: CFA franc	
Adult literacy rate: 52%	
Life expectancy: 47 years	
People per doctor: No figures available	
Televisions: 9 per 1,000 people	

CENTRAL AFRICAN REPUBLIC

SITUATED AT THE CORE OF AFRICA, the north of the Central African Republic (CAR) is arid, while lush rainforest covers the south. Drought and political unrest have caused great problems. In 1965, Emperor Bokassa began a 14-year reign of terror, which was followed by military dictatorship. The first multi-party elections were held in 1993, but the economy is still unstable, and this is one of the poorest places in the world.

This woman is sifting diamonds from a river bed.

INDUSTRY
A large part of the country's income comes from diamonds. There is potential for developing other industries, too, as gold, iron ore, copper, and uranium are also found here. Flooding caused by heavy seasonal rains, however, is a constant threat to any kind of mining.

RIVER ROUTES
The CAR is totally surrounded by land, has no railway system and few well surfaced roads, so its rivers are vital for transport and trade. Nearly three-quarters of trading goods are shipped down the 7,000 km (4,350 miles) of inland waterways. Many goods travel to Brazzaville in Congo. Here they are loaded on to trains and taken to the Atlantic coast.

PYGMIES
Small huts made from banana leaves are found deep in the country's rainforests. These are the homes of a people known as pygmies, called this because they rarely grow taller than about 1.5 m (5 ft). Pygmies are "hunter-gatherers", living on food collected from the rainforest. They are a shining example of people living in harmony with the natural world, without damaging the environment.

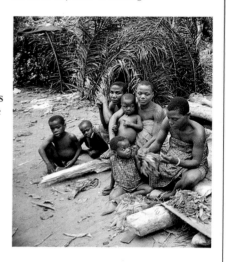

EQUATORIAL GUINEA

THE ECONOMY AND PEOPLE of Equatorial Guinea have suffered badly because of brutal leadership. Macias Nguema ruled as a cruel dictator during the 1970s, but a more moderate government came to power in the 1990s. This tiny, beautiful country, which includes five islands, is now working hard to rebuild its economy.

Hippopotamus tooth

Animal bone

Cowrie shell

TRADITIONAL MEDICINE
Traditional medicine is still widely practised in Africa. Animal bones, shells, and wooden sticks are used in public healing ceremonies. The healer will often sing and dance around the patient, using chants to cry out to the spirits for help.

FARMING
Although the hot climate and fertile volcanic soil of the largest island, Bioko, are perfect for growing crops, there are few good roads and the workforce is unskilled. Concentrating on growing cocoa for export has left little land for people to grow food for themselves.

Tree root

Find out more
COCOA: *227, 228*
DIAMONDS: *150, 226, 248*
HUNTER-GATHERERS: *201*
POLITICAL SYSTEMS: *270–271*

CHAD

MUCH OF CHAD falls inside a wide belt of hot, dry grassland called the sahel, which extends across the African continent. Drought is a frequent occurence in the sahel. This has proved a disaster for the country because its economy is heavily dependent on agriculture. Politically, Chad is an unstable place, and recent decades have seen a series of military coups and civil wars.

CHAD

Capital city: N'Djamena

Area: 1,284,000 sq km (495,752 sq miles)

Population: 6,000,000

Official language: French

Major religions: Muslim 44%, Christian 33%, traditional beliefs 23%

Government: Multi-party democracy

Currency: CFA franc

Adult literacy rate: 33%

Life expectancy: 47 years

People per doctor: 33,330

Televisions: 1 per 1,000 people

SÃO TOMÉ AND PRÍNCIPE

Capital city: São Tomé

Area: 964 sq km (372 sq miles)

Population: 117,504

Official language: Portuguese

Major religions: Christian 99%, other 1%

Government: Multi-party democracy

Currency: Dobra

Adult literacy rate: No figures available

Life expectancy: 67 years

People per doctor: 1,940

Televisions: No figures available

Camels being brought to drink at the waters of Lake Chad.

THE KANIMBO
Chad's northern deserts stretch up into the Arab lands of North Africa, so the country is a mixture of Arabic and black African influences. More than 100 languages are spoken. One of Chad's many peoples is the Arabic and Muslim group, the Kanimbo, who live as nomads in the arid north.

Original size of the lake, more than one million years ago.

Areas of damp fertile land are left behind as the waters of the lake retreat.

Lake Chad today.

DISAPPEARING WATERS
Lake Chad was once a huge expanse of water that formed the meeting point of Chad, Cameroon, Niger, and Nigeria. In the past, water poured into Lake Chad from surrounding rivers, but as the climate has become drier (over the past 10,000 years), so the lake has dried up. The shrinking lake poses a serious problem for the local people, who rely on its fish for food.

Gourds are one of the crops grown on the fertile land surrounding Lake Chad. When cut and dried, gourds can be carved and decorated.

SÃO TOMÉ AND PRÍNCIPE

THE VOLCANIC ISLANDS of São Tomé and Príncipe lie off the coast of Equatorial Guinea and Gabon. Dense tropical forest cloaks the upper slopes whilst lower down farms and large plantations growing cocoa and sugar can be found. The islands were ruled by Portugal until 1975. Today, the people make a living from farming and fishing, and cocoa remains a vital crop.

The creole people of São Tomé and Príncipe are called filhos de terra, which is Portuguese for "sons of the earth".

VOLCANIC LANDSCAPE
This part of Africa lies on a fault line – a crack in the Earth's crust. Molten rock can seep through this crack and cool to form volcanoes. These islands are the peaks of such volcanoes. Their soil is enriched by volcanic ash, which makes it extremely fertile.

CREOLE CULTURE
No one was living on these islands when the Portuguese first landed in the 1400s. Soon most of the population was made up of slaves imported from the mainland. Today, one of the main groups of people are of both African and Portuguese ancestry, creating a "creole" culture with a distinctive language and style of building.

Find out more
COCOA: *227, 228, 234*
PEOPLES OF AFRICA: *206–207*
SAHEL: *220, 222*
VOLCANOES: *13*

GABON

SITTING ASTRIDE THE EQUATOR, and with plentiful rain all year round, three-quarters of Gabon is covered with tropical rainforest. Timber is an increasingly valuable resource, though Gabon's biggest earner is oil. This should have made Gabon a wealthy country, but most people are very poor. This is partly because after independence in 1960, a one-party state was created that wasted much of the wealth. In 1990, Gabon became a multi-party democracy.

GABON	
Capital city: Libreville	
Area: 267,670 sq km (103,347 sq miles)	
Population: 1,300,000	
Official language: French	
Major religions: Christian 60%, traditional beliefs 40%	
Government: Multi-party democracy	
Currency: CFA franc	
Adult literacy rate: 62%	
Life expectancy: 53 years	
People per doctor: 2,790	
Televisions: 37 per 1,000 people	

CONGO	
Capital city: Brazzaville	
Area: 342,000 sq km (132,040 sq miles)	
Population: 2,400,000	
Official language: French	
Major religions: Traditional beliefs 50%, Christian 48%, Muslim 2%	
Government: Multi-party democracy	
Currency: CFA franc	
Adult literacy rate: 59%	
Life expectancy: 52 years	
People per doctor: 8,320	
Televisions: 6 per 1,000 people	

LIBREVILLE
The capital city, Libreville, means "free town" in French, and was founded in 1849 as a haven for freed slaves. French influence is strong because Gabon was colonized by France during the 1800s. Libreville is a bustling modern city, where some people enjoy great wealth, in contrast to the poverty suffered by most people on the city streets.

PEOPLE
Although just 1 million people live in Gabon, there are around 40 different ethnic groups here, each speaking their own dialect. The largest group is the Fang, once famed as warriors and skilled wood carvers. Many people in Gabon moved here from other African countries in search of work.

MINERAL RICH
Oil and manganese became important exports in the 1960s. This manganese mine is in southeast Gabon. The country is one of the world's biggest producers of the mineral, which is used to make paints, batteries, and steel. There are also large reserves of uranium and iron ore, but these have yet to be properly developed.

CONGO

CONGO'S EASTERN BORDER follows the course of the Congo River and the Ubangi, its main tributary, or offshoot. Oil reserves have made Congo one of the richest countries in Africa. Although ordinary people have benefited from this more than those in Gabon, many scratch out a living from farming, producing just enough to feed themselves. Cassava, a starchy root vegetable, is the major food crop.

Oil is of vital importance to Congo, bringing in 90 per cent of the country's export income.

Animal skin stretched across the top and fixed with pegs.

DRUM BEAT
As in other parts of Africa, music is a vital part of life, and drum beats form the backbone of this music. Many drums are wooden, and the one shown here is almost as tall as its players. One popular style in the region is called Congo Music, which is similar to soul music.

OIL WEALTH
The government has wisely invested the money that comes from oil in the economy, in projects such as dams, paper mills, transport systems, and forest-planting. Though industry is limited, there is a skilled workforce. Most industries are found around the towns and cities, especially Congo's capital, Brazzaville.

Find out more
CASSAVA: *221, 240*
OIL: *152, 230, 281*
POLITICAL SYSTEMS: *270–271*
RAINFORESTS: *15, 69, 204*

ZAIRE

APART FROM A TINY FINGER of land that stretches to the coast, the vast country of Zaire is landlocked. Nine other countries cluster around its edges. The Congo, or Zaire, River snakes its way through the country, providing a watery lifeline for its people. The climate is warm and wet and most people are farmers. Since independence from Belgium in 1960, Zaire has suffered from civil war and a harsh dictator. These problems, plus falling prices for its products, have made Zaire one of the poorest countries in the world.

ZAIRE	
Capital city: Kinshasa	
Area: 2,345,410 sq km (905,563 sq miles)	
Population: 41,200,000	
Official language: French	
Major religions: Christian 70%, Muslim 10%, traditional beliefs 10%, other 10%	
Government: Multi-party democracy	
Currency: New zaire	
Adult literacy rate: 74%	
Life expectancy: 52 years	
People per doctor: No figures available	
Televisions: 1 per 1,000 people	

Shells sewn onto material made from vegetable fibres.

AFRICAN ART
Zaire is famous for its distinctive art. The Kuba people of central Zaire, whose ancestors date back many centuries, use shells, beads, and raffia (fibres from palm leaves) to create geometric patterns. A Kuba chief would have worn the haunting mask shown above in order to take on some of the power of a great spirit.

A hydro-electric dam has been built on the Congo at Inga. The dam harnesses the power of the water to create electricity.

Boats stop at river ports for repair work and to refuel.

Tug-boat pushing logs along the river.

CONGO (ZAIRE) RIVER

The people here call the Congo River the Zaire. One of the largest rivers in the world, this wide ribbon of water forms the nation's transport system as it cuts a great upside-down "U" through miles of forest. People travelling from place to place crowd into motorized boats and dug-out canoes. Some large boats are even floating health clinics or bars. The river's fish provide vital food, while crops are grown on the fertile river banks.

The course of the Congo River

Kisangani
Mbandaka
EQUATOR
Kinshasa

Traders taking their produce to a river market.

The curving Congo River crosses the Equator twice.

People travel downstream in dug-out canoes produced by local craftsmen or in passenger boats with outboard motors.

MINING WEALTH

Zaire's mining industry seems to hold the key to greater wealth in the future. There are vast seams of copper, cobalt, gold, uranium, silver, and diamonds here, and reserves of oil lie just off the coast. Copper mining, shown below, is very important, but when the price of copper fell in the 1970s the economy virtually collapsed.

Diamond production in Zaire

x 1,000 carats
25,000
20,000
15,000
10,000
5,000

1948 1970 1980 1990 1991

Zaire is one of the biggest producers of diamonds in the world. Together with copper and cobalt, they provide nearly 80% of Zaire's export earnings.

MARKETS
Colourful, bustling river ports are meeting points for trade and travel along the Congo River. Shops selling travel provisions or farming tools nestle alongside markets where people from riverside villages come to sell their goods. Markets are not only based on land. Traders often sell their fresh vegetables and fish direct from their dug-out canoes.

Find out more

COPPER MINING: *73, 245*
DIAMONDS: *150, 226, 248*
HYDRO-ELECTRICITY: *108, 262*
POLITICAL SYSTEMS: *270–271*

CENTRAL EAST AFRICA

A LINE OF DRAMATIC HIGHLANDS, volcanic mountains, gorges, and vast lakes runs through this region from Uganda in the north to Malawi in the south. This is part of a huge split in the Earth's crust, known as the Great Rift Valley. Much of the rest of the landscape is flat grassland, called savanna – the perfect environment for the big game animals which draw thousands of tourists to countries such as Kenya and Tanzania. Growing tea and coffee provides another important source of income for the seven countries of the region. Mining and small-scale farming have always been important, and other industries are now increasing.

SAVANNA LANDSCAPE

Golden grasses that can grow up to 4 m (13 ft) tall cover the flat savanna. The rains come only once a year, so the grasses make the most of whatever water is available by spreading long roots deep into the soil. Needle-like leaves on acacia trees minimize water loss, while baobab trees can store water in their swollen trunks. To protect this landscape and its wildlife, vast areas have been turned into nature reserves, such as the Serengeti in Tanzania and the Masai Mara in Kenya.

ANIMALS OF THE SAVANNA
Herds of giraffes, elephants, antelopes, and zebra wander across the savanna in search of pasture and water. They are closely watched by cheetahs, lions, and leopards, waiting to kill any weak animals. Finally, jackals and vultures will move in to finish off the carcasses.

Masai warriors and women wear jewellery – usually bead necklaces, large earrings, and copper bracelets.

Most Masai men have more than one wife. Each wife lives in a separate hut with her children.

FARMING IN THE HIGHLANDS

Most farmers in this region produce only enough food to feed their own families, either from small plots of land or from cattle herding. In the highland areas, which have a cool, moist climate, the volcanic soils are particularly fertile and companies own large farms where tea and coffee are grown for export. However, as the population has grown, many farms have been divided up into impossibly small units. The soil has begun to erode as farmers cultivate even the steepest slopes.

Tea is made from the leaves of the tea bush. Pickers have to push their way into the bushes to reach the freshest shoots, so they wear rubber aprons to protect themselves.

THE RIFT VALLEY

The Great Rift Valley stretches 7,000 km (4,350 miles) from Syria in Asia to Mozambique. Over millions of years, movement between two of the plates that form the Earth's crust have created this dramatic landscape. In some places, this movement has formed steep-sided valleys such as Kenya's Mau Escarpment. Elsewhere, volcanic peaks have erupted and wide plateaux, such as the Athi Plains in Kenya, have formed where lava has seeped through the Earth's surface.

Africa's tallest mountain is Mount Kilimanjaro, a dormant volcano in the Tanzanian part of the Rift Valley.

NOMADIC CATTLE FARMERS
In the lowland areas of central east Africa, where lack of rainfall makes growing crops difficult, nomadic people travel with herds of cattle, sheep, goats, and sometimes donkeys and camels in search of water and grazing. In Kenya, the Masai people herd humpbacked zebu cattle in the area south of Nairobi straddling the Tanzanian border. The Masai keep their cattle for milk and for blood, which they draw off from a vein through a thin reed to drink.

Kampala, Uganda
Jan 23°C (74°F)
July 21°C (70°F)
Jan 46 mm (1.8 in)
July 46 mm (1.8 in)

UGANDA

KENYA

Nairobi, Kenya
Jan 19°C (66°F)
July 16°C (60°F)
Jan 38 mm (1.5 in)
July 15 mm (0.6 in)

RIFT VALLEY FISHING

A chain of large fresh and saltwater lakes runs along the Rift Valley. Many of the lakes are home to vast numbers of fish, and along the shores of Lake Albert (Mobutu Sese Seko), Lake Nyasa (Lake Malawi), and Lake Tanganyika many people make their living by fishing with small nets or spears.

TROPIC OF CANCER

EQUATOR

RWANDA

BURUNDI

TROPIC OF CAPRICORN

0   100   200   300   400 km
0   50   100   150   200   250 miles

N

TANZANIA

Dar es Salaam, Tanzania
Jan 28°C (82°F)
July 24°C (75°F)
Jan 66 mm (2.6 in)
July 31 mm (1.2 in)

Lusaka, Zambia
Jan 22°C (71°F)
July 16°C (61°F)
Jan 231 mm (9.1 in)
July 0 mm (0 in)

ZAMBIA

MALAWI

THINGS TO LOOK FOR ON THE MAP

Longest river: Luangwa, Zambia/Mozambique, 804 km (500 miles) *Map G11*

Highest point: Mt. Kilimanjaro, Tanzania, 5,895 m (19,341 ft) *Map J6*

Largest lake: L. Victoria, Tanzania/Uganda/Kenya, 69,484 sq km (26,828 sq miles) *Map G6*

Southeast Sudan is administered by Kenya

SUDAN

ETHIOPIA

SOMALIA

Lokichokio

Mandera

Moyale

CHALBI DESERT

L. Turkana

Arua

Gulu

Pakwach

Moroto

Mbale

Kitale

Wajir

Albert Nile

Victoria Nile

L. Albert

L. Kyoga

RWENZORI MTS.

UGANDA

KENYA

Fort Portal

Kasese

KAMPALA

Jinja

Eldoret

Kakamega

Meru

Mt. Kenya

Nakuru

Nyeri

Thika

ABERDARE RANGE

GREAT RIFT VALLEY

Tana

Garissa

Entebbe

Masaka

Mbarara

L. Edward

Lake

Victoria

NAIROBI

Machakos

Bukoba

Musoma

Galana

Malindi

Mombasa

ZAIRE

L. Kivu

KIGALI

Butare

RWANDA

BUJUMBURA

BURUNDI

Kigoma

Mwanza

Shinyanga

Olduvai Gorge

Mt. Kilimanjaro

Arusha

Moshi

L. Eyasi

L. Manyara

Pangani

Wembere

Singida

Tabora

MASAI STEPPE

Tanga

Pangani

Pemba I.

INDIAN OCEAN

TANZANIA

DODOMA

Zanzibar

Zanzibar

GREAT RIFT VALLEY

L. Tanganyika

L. Rukwa

Sumbawanga

Great Ruaha

Iringa

Rufiji

Morogoro

Dar es Salaam

Mafia I.

Mbala

Mbeya

Njombe

Kilwa Masoko

L. Mweru

Kasama

Lindi

ZAIRE

Mansa

L. Bangweulu

Mpika

Luangwa

Mzuzu

Songea

Mtwara

Ruvuma

Solwezi

Chingola

Mufulira

Kitwe

Ndola

Luanshya

MUCHINGA MTS.

Lundazi

Nkhotakota

Bua

L. Nyasa

MOZAMBIQUE

Zambezi

ZAMBIA

Chipata

LILONGWE

Salima

MALAWI

ANGOLA

Mongu

Kafue

KAFUE FLATS

Kabwe

LUSAKA

Kafue

MOZAMBIQUE

Zomba

Blantyre

Zambezi

L. Kariba

Choma

Kariba Dam

Victoria Falls

Livingstone

Nsanje

NAMIBIA

BOTSWANA

ZIMBABWE

UGANDA

BEFORE INDEPENDENCE, Uganda was a prosperous country, which Winston Churchill called the "Pearl of Africa". But by 1986, the country lay shattered and bankrupt. From 1971–79, President Idi Amin ruled Uganda as a dictator. During this period, thousands of people were persecuted or murdered, Europeans and Asians were expelled, and their property was seized. International aid was cut off when other countries realized how corrupt Amin's government was. In 1979, Amin was deposed, but the disruption continued until 1986, when President Yoweri Museveni came to power. His government restored peace and has begun to rebuild the economy and re-establish democracy.

UGANDA	
Capital city: Kampala	
Area: 235,880 sq km (91,073 sq miles)	
Population: 16,582,700	
Official language: English	
Major religions: Christian 66%, traditional beliefs 18%, Muslim 16%	
Government: One-party state	
Currency: New Uganda shilling	
Adult literacy rate: 51%	
Life expectancy: 43 years	
People per doctor: 25,000	
Televisions: 10 per 1,000 people	

FISHING IN LAKE VICTORIA
The vast, shallow Lake Victoria is shared by Uganda, Tanzania, and Kenya. Huge Nile perch fish were introduced to the lake 30 years ago to increase fish production and provide sport fishing for tourists. Since then the perch have spread to every corner of Lake Victoria and have devoured most of its original species.

The cassava plant grows up to 90 cm (3 ft) tall. It is grown for its roots, which can be eaten as a vegetable or ground to make flour.

Kampala is said to be built on seven hills. The city centre lies on just one of them – Nakasero Hill.

FARMING
Fertile, volcanic soil and high levels of rainfall make more than four-fifths of Uganda's land suitable for farming. Large plantations produce the coffee, cotton, and tea which make up 90 per cent of the country's exports. Although 90 per cent of Ugandans work on farms, most are involved in small-scale farming, growing crops such as maize, millet, cassava, and sweet potatoes for their own use or to sell in local markets.

Sweet potato (left) and cassava (right) are common vegetables in this region.

KAMPALA
People in Uganda's capital, Kampala, rarely go out without an umbrella, as most days see a heavy downpour in the afternoon. Kampala has an average of 242 days a year with violent thunderstorms. By evening, the rain has stopped and the air is cool. Kampala suffered much destruction during and immediately after Amin's period in power, but is now being restored with the help of foreign investment.

What Have You Heard About AIDS?

What Does It Mean?
How Does It Harm Us?
Who Can Get It?
What Causes It?
How Can We Stop It?
What Can We Do For People Who Have It?
How Can It Be Cured?
What Does It Look Like?
Which Of Us Has It?

Don't GUESS the Answers! LEARN THE TRUTH ABOUT AIDS!

AIDS AWARENESS
Uganda has one of the highest number of AIDS sufferers in the world. In some parts of the country about 20 per cent of the population is infected. AIDS is a sexually transmitted disease, and as yet there is no cure for it, so doctors are trying to teach people how to avoid catching it. Special campaigns, like this poster produced by UNICEF, are aimed at educating children to be aware of the risk of AIDS.

WILDLIFE
In Ruwenzori National Park, tourists can take a boat trip down the Kazinga Channel to see thousands of hippos and pelicans. Much of Uganda's wildlife was wiped out during the years of conflict, and today there are not many places in Africa where you are likely to see so many hippos.

Find out more
COFFEE: *50, 62, 66*
LAKE VICTORIA: *204*
POLITICAL SYSTEMS: *270–271*
TEA: *172, 238*

RWANDA

SINCE 1993, RWANDA HAS rarely been out of the news. War between the two main ethnic groups – the Tutsi and Hutu – has torn Rwanda apart and wrecked its economy, leaving it one of the poorest countries in the world. Before the war, Rwanda's main export was coffee. Today, although 95 per cent of the people still work on the land, few crops are grown for export. The country's instability has also hindered attempts to develop manufacturing and mining industries.

RWANDA
Capital city: Kigali
Area: 26,340 sq km (10,170 sq miles)
Population: 7,164,994
Official languages: French and Kinyarwanda
Major religions: Traditional beliefs 50%, Christian 45%, other 5%
Government: One-party state
Currency: Rwanda franc
Adult literacy rate: 52%
Life expectancy: 47 years
People per doctor: 50,000
Televisions: No figures available

BURUNDI
Capital city: Bujumbura
Area: 27,830 sq km (10,750 sq miles)
Population: 6,000,000
Official languages: French and Kirundi
Major religions: Christian 60%, traditional beliefs 39%, Muslim 1%
Government: Multi-party democracy
Currency: Burundi franc
Adult literacy rate: 52%
Life expectancy: 48 years
People per doctor: 16,670
Televisions: 1 per 1,000 people

HEALTH

Rwanda is one of Africa's most densely populated countries, and the population continues to grow. Most Rwandan women have at least six children, compared to an average of only one or two in developed countries. However, few Rwandans live to be over 50. Diseases such as malaria and AIDS are common, and medical facilities are in short supply and are rarely free, so few people can afford them.

There are only about 650 gorillas left in the world. The mountain gorilla is found only in this region of Africa.

ETHNIC WARFARE

The worst ethnic violence in Africa's recent history has dominated Rwanda and Burundi since 1993, resulting in the loss of at least 200,000 lives. This is not a new conflict, but one which has continued over many centuries, as the minority but powerful Tutsi tribe struggles to maintain control over the majority but less powerful Hutu. The recent struggles have ruined Rwanda's economy, and sent 1.5 million people fleeing from the country.

MOUNTAIN GORILLAS

One of the last known refuges for the mountain gorilla is the Volcanoes National Park in Rwanda. Even though the gorilla is protected, it is still in danger of extinction by poachers, and its habitat is threatened by farming.

BURUNDI

UNTIL INDEPENDENCE IN 1962, Burundi and neighbouring Rwanda formed one country. Like Rwanda, Burundi is home to both Tutsi and Hutu people, and the wars between these tribes have been part of Burundi's history too. In 1972, about 10,000 Hutu were killed by Tutsis. Almost as densely populated and poor as its neighbour, Burundi is struggling to cope with the huge numbers of refugees who have fled from war-torn Rwanda.

POPULATION PRESSURE

Most people in Burundi make their living from farming. So many people live in the most fertile areas that land is very scarce. Plots of land are usually just large enough to support a family in good years, but bad weather or disease can lead to widespread famine. In some areas, the land is so over-used that the soil has begun to erode.

DRUMMING GROUPS

In Burundi, stories, songs, and music are passed down from generation to generation rather than written down in a formal way. Tutsi folk dancing is one of the highlights of traditional culture, as are the groups of 12 to 15 drummers who play together with no other instruments.

Find out more
HEALTH: *276*
POPULATION: *16–17, 206*
REFUGEES: *207*
SOIL EROSION: *55, 244*

KENYA

UNLIKE MANY AFRICAN countries, Kenya has been stable and relatively democratic since it gained its independence from Britain in 1963. Under British rule, large farms were created in many areas to produce cash crops, and a network of roads and railways were built to link ports and towns. Today, Kenya is one of Africa's richest countries, producing crops such as coffee and tea for export, and welcoming tourists to its vast game reserves. Side-by-side with this, many people still make their living from small farms or cattle herding. Kenya has one of the world's fastest growing populations, which has led to increasing poverty, rivalry over land, and some ethnic violence.

KENYA

Capital city: Nairobi

Area: 580,370 sq km (224,081 sq miles)

Population: 26,100,000

Official language: Swahili

Major religions: Christian 66%, traditional beliefs 26%, Muslim 6%, other 2%

Government: Multi-party democracy

Currency: Kenya shilling

Adult literacy rate: 71%

Life expectancy: 59 years

People per doctor: 71,430

Televisions: 10 per 1,000 people

Kenya's main crops

The main farming area, shown enlarged on the map below, is in the southwest of the country.

KENYA

- Coffee
- Tea
- Sisal
- Sugarcane
- Rice
- Forest
- Other

On game reserves such as Kenya's Masai Mara and Amboseli National Park, tourists can photograph wild animals close up.

Tea

Coffee beans

Green beans

NAIROBI

Lions, giraffes, and cheetahs roam the plains which surround Kenya's capital, Nairobi, with the tower blocks of the modern city as a backdrop. This is the largest city in east Africa, with a population of about a million people. It developed after European colonization as a convenient stopping place on the railway from Uganda to Kenya's main port of Mombassa.

TOURISM

Tropical beaches and some of Africa's best game reserves attract thousands of tourists to Kenya. Tourism is vital to the country's economy, and the government has invested in roads, airports, and hotels to make Kenya one of the easiest and most comfortable African countries for tourists to visit. Because most people come to see the animals on game reserves, the government has placed a high priority on protecting wildlife and stamping out poaching.

FARMING
AND THE ECONOMY

Farming is Kenya's chief export earner, but much of the country is far too dry to grow crops. In the highlands – where there is more rain – tea, coffee, wheat, maize, sisal, and sugarcane are grown. Where less water is available, dairy and meat cattle are farmed on large ranches. Dams and lakes provide water to irrigate land for growing market garden crops, such as green beans, which are exported by air to foreign supermarkets.

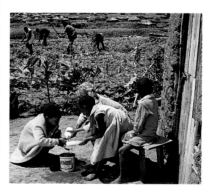

KENYAN PEOPLES

These villagers belong to Kenya's largest tribe, the Kikuyu, who live around Mount Kenya. The Kikuyu god, Ngai, is believed to live on the mountain, so the Kikuyu traditionally built their houses with the door facing the mountain. Like two-thirds of the country's 70 tribal groups, the Kikuyu speak Bantu. Small numbers of Asians, Arabs, and Europeans also live in Kenya.

KENYAN ATHLETES

Athletes from Kenya's Rift Valley area excel at running long-distance races. They have won five out of the last seven Olympic 3,000 m steeplechase events, and Kenyan Moses Kiptanui, shown here, holds the world records for the 3,000 m and the 3,000 m steeplechase. The runners' skill may stem from the high altitude they live and train in, or perhaps from years of running long distances to school.

Find out more

AFRICAN CITIES: *206*
HIGHLAND FARMING: *238*
POPULATION: *16–17, 206*
RIFT VALLEY: *204*

TANZANIA

TANZANIA, Tanzania

TANZANIA WAS CREATED in 1964, when the mainland country of Tanganyika and the island of Zanzibar united. Until recently, Tanzania had a socialist government, which tried to encourage people to work together on schemes such as state-run plantations. Although some of these schemes have been successful, Tanzania is much poorer than neighbouring Kenya, and is one of the least urbanized countries in Africa. About 120 different peoples live here, most of whom speak Swahili, a language which developed as a means of communication between Africans and foreign traders.

TANZANIA	
Capital city: Dodoma	
Area: 945,090 sq km (364,900 sq miles)	
Population: 25,635,000	
Official languages: English and Swahili	
Major religions: Traditional beliefs 42%, Muslim 31%, Christian 26%, other 1%	
Government: One-party state	
Currency: Tanzanian shilling	
Adult literacy rate: 55%	
Life expectancy: 51 years	
People per doctor: 33,330	
Televisions: 2 per 1,000 people	

OLDUVAI GORGE

The steep sides of Olduvai Gorge in northern Tanzania were carved out of the flat Serengeti Plain by the flow of water over millions of years. Here, archaeologists have unearthed fossils of the earliest humans, dating back 2 million years. Yet more ancient footprints of human-like creatures have been discovered too, left by two adults and a child walking across the still-soft lava that formed the plain, 3.5 million years ago.

Making sisal fibre

The outer leaves of the sisal plant are cut off close to the stalk when they reach their full length.

The sisal fibre is usually obtained by crushing the leaves between rollers. The pulp is removed, leaving strands of white fibre over 1 m (3 ft) long.

The strands of fibre are washed and then hung out to dry.

DAR ES SALAAM

Although Tanzania's capital is now the purpose-built inland city of Dodoma, the old capital Dar es Salaam remains the country's biggest city and port. It is also the end of the TanZam railway which carries goods from land-locked Zambia to the sea.

The name Dar es Salaam means "Haven of Peace". The city is still fairly small, with few high-rise buildings and many low, red-tiled roofs.

SISAL

One of Tanzania's main crops is sisal, a plant with leaves that are used to make rope and twine, and also mats, brushes, hats, and baskets. Sisal ropes are particularly useful on board ships since they do not rot in sea-water. However, Tanzania's sisal trade is now under threat because many products made with sisal in the past can now be made with synthetic substitutes.

String made from sisal.

TANZANIAN VILLAGES

The country's population used to be scattered in small villages. Then, in 1970, the government started a programme to resettle the population in larger villages of about 250 households. By grouping people together in this way, it is easier and more economic to provide schools, water, and other services, and to distribute fertilizers and seeds. Today, 75 per cent of Tanzanians live in villages in the countryside, more than in any other African country.

The buildings and style of clothes reflect Zanzibar's continuing Arabic flavour.

ZANZIBAR

Off Tanzania's coast lies the island of Zanzibar. In the 18th and 19th centuries, the port of Zanzibar, on the island's western side, was used as an Arab trading post. African slaves passed though here, en route to the Arab world. The island's main crop, cloves, was also shipped out of the port. The clove tree was only introduced to the island in 1818, but today Zanzibar is the world's largest producer.

Find out more

EARLY PEOPLE: *206*
POLITICAL SYSTEMS: *270–271*
POPULATION DISTRIBUTION: *206*
TANZAM RAILWAY: *245*

MALAWI

LYING ON A PLATEAU at the southern end of the Great Rift Valley, Malawi is one of the most stable countries in this region of Africa. Its six major tribal groups live together peacefully. Malawi's economy is based on agriculture, but the government is trying to encourage the growth of agricultural processing industries, such as food canning and cooking oil manufacture, as well as mining and other heavy industries. Although relations with its neighbours have been tense, Malawi still accepted more than a million refugees during Mozambique's recent civil war.

MALAWI	
Capital city: Lilongwe	
Area: 118,480 sq km (45,745 sq miles)	
Population: 10,700,000	
Official languages: Chewa and English	
Major religions: Christian 75%, Muslim 20%, traditional beliefs 5%	
Government: Multi-party democracy	
Currency: Malawian kwacha	
Adult literacy rate: 54%	
Life expectancy: 45 years	
People per doctor: 50,000	
Televisions: No figures available	

Fishermen collect these brightly coloured fish, called cichlids, for export to aquariums around the world.

LAKE NYASA

Over one-fifth of Malawi's total area is taken up by Lake Nyasa, one of the largest and deepest lakes in the world. A huge fishing industry has developed around the lake, which is home to more than 500 species of fish. A sardine-like fish called the usipa is one of the main catches. The fish are dried on the shore and sold throughout Malawi, providing the main source of protein for a nation of nearly 11 million people.

Many people grow just enough food to feed themselves and their family. If there is any extra produce, they sell it in local markets like this one.

FARMING

Farming is the most important business in Malawi. Tobacco, tea, and sugar make up 85 per cent of exports, and more than 80 per cent of Malawi's population make their living by farming. To increase the land available to farm, swamps have been drained, and woodland has been cleared. Rivers have been dammed and wells dug to water dry grasslands. Poor harvests can lead to extreme hardship among Malawi's people.

Soil erosion

Wind blows away soil on exposed areas.

Water runs down the hillside, washing the soil away to form gulleys.

Tree roots help to bind the soil together.

If the trees are cut down, wind and rain wear away the soil.

PEOPLE OF MALAWI

Malawi is one of the least urbanized countries in Africa, with 88 per cent of its population living in villages in the countryside, mostly near the seasonal wetlands, called *dambos*. Villages are small and are usually made up of people who are closely related. Unlike many other African countries, Malawi's main ethnic groups, the Chewas, Nyanja, Tumbuka, Tonga, Ngonis, and Yao, live together peacefully.

HASTINGS BANDA

For 30 years after independence, Dr Hastings Banda was president of Malawi, and ruled the country virtually alone. His government helped the country to become strong and self-reliant, but other political opinions were not tolerated and many people were tortured or imprisoned. In 1993, calls for democracy led to Banda's downfall.

FORESTS

Forests and woodlands cover nearly half the country, but huge areas have been cut down for fuel and to clear land for farming. Malawi has no oil and little coal, so the most popular fuel is charcoal, made by partially burning wood so that it becomes smokeless and slow-burning. Where more land is needed for farming, trees are cut down and burned, and then crops are grown in the ashes. Such land is fertile for only a short time, as the forest soil is quickly eroded.

Find out more

DEFORESTATION: *69, 227, 233*
PEOPLES OF AFRICA: *206–207*
POLITICAL SYSTEMS: *270–271*
REFUGEES: *207*

ZAMBIA

ZAMBIA OCCUPIES A BROAD plateau scattered with mountains and deep valleys. After independence from Britain in 1963, political violence based on tribal differences rocked the country until 1972, when President Kenneth Kaunda declared a one-party state. In 1991, Kaunda was defeated in the first democratic elections for 19 years. Today, the country is less affected by ethnic conflict than many African states, even though there are 14 main tribal groups. Zambia is the world's fourth largest producer of copper, and the country's economy depends almost entirely on the fortunes of this industry.

ZAMBIA	
Capital city: Lusaka	
Area: 752,610 sq km (290,563 sq miles)	
Population: 8,900,000	
Official languages: English, Bemba, and Nyanja	
Major religions: Christian 63%, Hindu 36%, traditional beliefs 1%	
Government: Multi-party democracy	
Currency: Zambian kwacha	
Adult literacy rate: 75%	
Life expectancy: 46 years	
People per doctor: 11,110	
Televisions: 31 per 1,000 people	

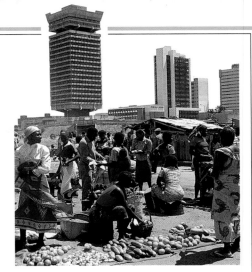

CITIES

A chain of shanty towns lies along the railway linking Zambia's copperbelt with the capital Lusaka. The makeshift shacks have no water, power, or drains, and disease is widespread. Most people here have jobs in the copper industry. In fact, 42 per cent of Zambians live in the towns, making it one of the most urbanized countries in Africa. Many Zambian families have been city-dwellers for three or four generations, which is rare for Africa.

Mineral deposits in Zambia

⚒ Copper

⚒ Cobalt

The copperbelt

ZAMBIA

TanZam railway

Kasama

Lusaka

Livingstone

Zambia's exports (1990)

Copper: 85%

Other: 7%

Cobalt: 6%

Zinc: 2%

Copper ore

TANZAM RAILWAY
Landlocked Zambia has to rely on roads and railways through other countries to export copper and other products to ports, so good relations with its neighbours are important. Until the 1960s, most goods went through Rhodesia (now Zimbabwe), but relations between the two countries broke down. Today, the main trade route is the TanZam railway, through Tanzania.

The TanZam railway links Zambia to the port of Dar es Salaam, in neighbouring Tanzania.

COPPER MINING
Seams of copper run through an area over 320 km (200 miles) long and 50 km (30 miles) wide in central Zambia, called the copperbelt. First developed commercially in the 1930s, copper mining has funded much of Zambia's development. Copper accounts for 85 per cent of the country's exports, and if the world price of copper were to fall, Zambia's economy could be wrecked. To add to this problem, the copper reserves are beginning to run out.

ZAMBEZI RIVER
Forming Zambia's southern border, the Zambezi River is one of the country's main tourist attractions. Visitors can go white-water rafting on the river, take a wildlife safari in one of the area's game parks, and visit the magnificent Victoria Falls. A huge dam at Kariba provides power in the form of hydroelectricity for Zambia's copperbelt and for neighbouring Zimbabwe. Lake Kariba, the artificial lake formed by the dam, is a popular fishing destination for tourists.

FISH EAGLE
National parks, set up to protect wildlife, take up more than one-third of the country's area. The fish eagle is Zambia's national symbol, and appears on the country's flag. It is common around open stretches of water, where it swoops down to snatch fish from the surface and rises up with a fish in its talons.

___*Find out more*___
EXPORT DEPENDENCY: *281*
HYDROELECTRICITY: *108, 262*
POLITICAL SYSTEMS: *270–271*
VICTORIA FALLS: *250*

SOUTHERN AFRICA

THE EIGHT COUNTRIES THAT MAKE UP southern Africa have much in common. Once governed by European settlers, almost all of them had to struggle to achieve independence. Many endured years of vicious warfare. Today, all eight countries are independent, multi-racial democracies. Their climate ranges from warm and mild in the south to tropical in the north, while the landscape includes both deserts and rainforests, vast plains, and towering mountain ranges. The population varies in wealth from extremely rich industrialists and landowners in South Africa to hunter-gatherer Bushmen in the Kalahari Desert.

Before 1994, demonstrations against apartheid were held throughout South Africa.

The magnificent Table Mountain towers above Cape Town in the Cape Peninsula, South Africa. The Cape is home to many unique species of plants and flowers.

POLITICS

Southern Africa is dominated by the politics of South Africa. After 1948, South Africa pursued a policy of separate development for white and black people known as apartheid. South Africa tried to weaken the neighbouring countries that opposed it. It supported rebels fighting the Angolan and Mozambique governments, and helped those resisting black rule in Zimbabwe and Namibia. The ending of white rule in 1994 led to better relations between South Africa and its neighbours.

A LAND OF CONTRASTS

The landscape of Southern Africa varies from the Namib and Kalahari deserts in the west and centre to lush vegetation and tropical forests in the north. Inland, vast grassy savannas and woodlands are home to much of the region's wildlife, from the minute *dik-dik* (the world's smallest antelope) to the African elephant. Game reserves and national parks have been set up to protect endangered species. Tourists come from all over the world to visit the reserves and enjoy the dramatic scenery.

OKAVANGO DELTA

Unlike most rivers, which run out to the sea, the Okavango River runs inland into a desert. The river begins in Angola, then flows southeast through Namibia into a delta in the Kalahari Desert in Botswana. The vast swamps and waterways of the river and its delta cover an area of more than 22,000 sq km (8,500 sq miles). This provides a haven for a wide variety of plants and animals. People travel into the swamps in dug-out canoes, called *mokoros*.

KALAHARI BUSHMEN

The Bushmen, or San, of the Kalahari Desert are one of the few groups of hunter-gatherers left in Africa. These people live and work together in small, tightly knit communities. Traditionally they moved from place to place, searching for insects and edible plants and hunting small animals with poisonous arrows. Today, however, many of the San live a more settled existence.

MINERAL RICHES

Southern Africa is rich in mineral resources. Much of the world's gold, diamonds, uranium, and copper come from the region, and have transformed the local economies. Botswana is the most dependent upon its mineral resources. Almost 80 per cent of the country's export earnings come from diamonds. South Africa is the world's leading producer of gold, and Namibia has the world's largest uranium mine. Coal is southern Africa's major source of energy. South Africa, Zimbabwe, Botswana, and Mozambique all have large coal reserves.

Major mineral deposits

- Uranium
- Coal
- Iron
- Diamonds
- Copper
- Oil
- Gold

THINGS TO LOOK FOR ON THE MAP

Longest river: Zambezi, Mozambique/Zimbabwe/Zambia/Namibia/Angola, 2,700 km (1,678 miles) *Map J5*

Highest point: Mt. Thabana-Ntlenyana, Lesotho, 3,482 m (11,424 ft) *Map H10*

Largest lake: L. Nyasa, Mozambique/Malawi/Tanzania 28,490 sq km (11,000 sq miles) *Map J4*

ZIMBABWE

MOZAMBIQUE

ANGOLA

NAMIBIA

Francistown, Botswana
Jan 25°C (77°F)
July 15°C (58°F)
Jan 107 mm (4.2 in)
July 0 mm (0 in)

BOTSWANA

SWAZILAND

LESOTHO

SOUTH AFRICA

Port Elizabeth, South Africa
Jan 21°C (70°F)
July 13°C (56°F)
Jan 31 mm (1.2 in)
July 48 mm (1.9 in)

TROPIC OF CANCER

EQUATOR

TROPIC OF CAPRICORN

CITY GROWTH

Across southern Africa, people are leaving the countryside and moving to the cities in search of work. The urban area surrounding Johannesburg in South Africa now houses a population of more than 9 million, making it the second biggest African city, after Cairo. Maputo, the capital of Mozambique (right), doubled in size between 1975 and 1983, and now contains more than 1.5 million people.

WOMEN'S ROLE

In traditional African society, women generally acted as wives and mothers and were responsible for routine household tasks and growing crops. Today, many African men work away from home in the mines and cities for one or two years at a time, leaving women to form the majority in their villages. This means that women are now taking on more responsibility in the households.

ANGOLA

ANGOLA SHOULD BE ONE of the most successful countries in Africa. The land is largely fertile, with dense tropical forests in the north giving way to drier grasslands in the south. Farmers produce enough food to support the small population, while huge oil and mineral reserves bring wealth to the economy. However, Angola has been torn apart by a civil war that began in 1975. Few parts of the country have been left unaffected by the fighting, which has killed or injured thousands of people and reduced this potentially rich country to poverty.

ANGOLA	
Capital city: Luanda	
Area: 1,246,700 sq km (481,351 sq miles)	
Population: 10,300,000	
Official language: Portuguese	
Major religions: Christian 90%, traditional beliefs 10%	
Government: Multi-party democracy	
Currency: New kwanza	
Adult literacy rate: 43%	
Life expectancy: 46 years	
People per doctor: 14,290	
Televisions: 6 per 1,000 people	

- Major towns
- ······ Benguela railway

The Benguela railway runs from the coastal ports of Benguela and Lobito in Angola, and heads eastwards across country until reaching Zaire.

CIVIL WAR
In 1975, Portuguese rule in Angola ended and civil war broke out. The conflict was between the Angolan People's Liberation Movement (MPLA), supported by the Soviet Union and Cuba, and the National Union for Total Angolan Independence (UNITA), supported by South Africa and the USA. After a ceasefire in 1991, the MPLA were elected into power, but fighting broke out again. A peace agreement was reached in 1994–5.

BENGUELA RAILWAY
Opened in 1931, the Benguela railway was built to transport copper and other minerals from the mines of landlocked Zambia and Zaire to the coastal ports of Lobito and Benguela for export round the world. The railway and ports provided work for many Angolans, who lost their jobs when the railway was destroyed in the civil war. After the ceasefire of 1991, engineers began to rebuild sections of the track, and plans have been made to reopen the railway.

LUANDA
The port of Luanda is Angola's capital and biggest city. Founded by the Portuguese in 1576, for centuries it was a centre for shipping slaves to the Portuguese colony of Brazil. The Portuguese built a fort and many other fine buildings which stand alongside modern skyscrapers. On the hills surrounding the city vast shanty towns house thousands of people.

INDUSTRY
The tiny Angolan territory of Cabinda, to the north of the main part of the country, is one of the richest oil-producing regions in Africa. Offshore oil fields contain reserves of 1,500 million barrels of oil and vast quantities of natural gas. Some of the richest diamond deposits in the world are found in the northeast of the country, while iron and other minerals are mined further south. However, constant fighting has destroyed some mines and factories.

A brace divides the bow string into two unequal lengths.

MUSICAL BOW
The Humbi people of southwestern Angola use an ordinary hunting bow as a musical instrument. The musician supports the bow with one hand and holds it in his mouth. As he hits the string with a stick held in his other hand, he produces different notes by altering the shape of his lips.

Find out more

AFRICAN CITIES: *206*
DIAMONDS: *150, 226, 248*
OIL: *152, 230, 281*
RAILWAYS: *245*

BOTSWANA

BOTSWANA IS ONE OF Africa's few real success stories. When it became independent in 1966, this poor country depended on small-scale farming for its livelihood. The discovery of diamonds in 1967, and the development of vast cattle ranches in the last 20 years, have transformed the economy into one of the fastest growing in the world. The country is well managed by a stable, democratic government.

BOTSWANA	
Capital city: Gaborone	
Area: 581,730 sq km (224,600 sq miles)	
Population: 1,325,291	
Official language: English	
Major religions: traditional beliefs 50%, Christian 30%, other 20%	
Government: Multi-party democracy	
Currency: Pula	
Adult literacy rate: 75%	
Life expectancy: 60 years	
People per doctor: 5,150	
Televisions: 16 per 1,000 people	

NAMIBIA	
Capital city: Windhoek	
Area: 824,290 sq km (318,260 sq miles)	
Population: 1,401,711	
Official language: English	
Major religions: Christian 90%, traditional beliefs 10%	
Government: Multi-party democracy	
Currency: South African rand	
Adult literacy rate: 40%	
Life expectancy: 58 years	
People per doctor: 4,620	
Televisions: 21 per 1,000 people	

GABORONE
When Botswana became independent, the country had no capital city, as it had previously been governed from Mafikeng in South Africa. The new country therefore built a new capital, called Gaborone. Today more than 150,000 people live in the city, which houses the national government and is the centre of communications and industry.

Parents and young children live in the main sleeping hut.

People cook, eat, and receive guests in the lolwapa.

Trees are valued for their shade.

Women are responsible for building and maintaining the huts.

TSWANA HOMES

The Tswana people, who make up most of the Botswana population, traditionally organize themselves into chiefdoms. Each chiefdom consists of a capital town, around which are a number of satellite villages. Families live in dwellings made up of three or four huts, each hut serving a particular purpose. The huts are arranged around a central courtyard, or *lolwapa*.

The lolwapa is surrounded by a low wall.

The thatched roof is supported on poles which encircle the wall of the hut. The space between the wall and the roof gives ventilation.

The huts are decorated with finger markings in earth shades of brown, red, and orange.

NAMIBIA

ORIGINALLY A GERMAN COLONY, Namibia was governed by its neighbour, South Africa, from 1915 until independence in 1990. Rich in minerals and other natural resources, the country is dominated by the Namib Desert, which runs in a thin strip down the west of the country near the Atlantic Ocean, and the vast Kalahari Desert, which lies in the south.

Copper

MINING
Namibia is one of the four biggest mineral producers in Africa, with large deposits of copper, diamonds, tin, and other minerals. The world's largest uranium mine is located at Rössing, in the Namib Desert in the centre of the country. Namibia is also the world's second largest producer of lead.

To show that she is married, a Himba woman will lengthen her hair by adding hair cut from her brother's head.

RURAL LIFE

Most Namibian people live on the high plains in the north of the country. Here the Ovambo people build fenced-in enclosures known as *kraals*. The Himba people live further west in the rugged land bordering Angola. These semi-nomadic people make their living from tending cattle, which provide them with meat, milk, and clothing. The number of cattle owned is a reflection of wealth and status.

Find out more
COPPER MINING: *73, 237, 245*
DEMOCRACY: *270*
DESERTS: *15, 204*
DIAMONDS: *150, 226, 248*

ZIMBABWE

ZIMBABWE WAS ONCE PART OF a great trading empire. Many centuries ago, central African merchants exported gold and copper to India and China. The centre of this empire was Great Zimbabwe ("house of the chief"), a huge stone palace, from which Zimbabwe took its name when it became independent in 1980. Modern-day Zimbabwe has one of the most diverse and successful economies in Africa, although ethnic tensions between the majority Shona and minority Ndebele peoples, and the constant threat of drought, have hindered its recent development.

ZIMBABWE

Capital city: Harare	
Area: 390,580 sq km (150,800 sq miles)	
Population: 10,401,767	
Official language: English	
Major religions: Syncretic (part Christian, part traditional beliefs) 50%, Christian 25%, traditional beliefs 24%, other 1%	
Government: Multi-party democracy	
Currency: Zimbabwe dollar	
Adult literacy rate: 69%	
Life expectancy: 56 years	
People per doctor: 62,500	
Televisions: 30 per 1,000 people	

HARARE
The capital of Zimbabwe is known as the "City of Flowering Trees" because of the many flowering shrubs and trees that line its wide streets. Formerly called Salisbury, at independence it was renamed in honour of Neharare, a local chieftain who ruled the area before the British took control. Today this attractive, modern city is the bustling heart of the country.

VICTORIA FALLS
As the Zambezi River flows eastwards along the border between Zambia and Zimbabwe, it drops 128 m (420 ft) down into a narrow chasm. The thick mist and loud noise produced by the waterfall can be seen and heard up to 40 km (25 miles) away. Local people call the falls *Mosi-oa-tunya* ("the smoke that thunders"), but internationally they are known as the Victoria Falls.

MANUFACTURING

After South Africa, Zimbabwe has the widest range of industries in Africa. The southern city of Bulawayo lies at the heart of the national road and railway network and is Zimbabwe's main industrial centre. Steel and cement, and a wide range of manufactured goods, including vehicles, light machinery, textiles, and footwear, are made in Bulawayo. The city is also a major centre for food processing and for the tobacco industry.

THE SHONA PEOPLES
The majority of Zimbabweans are Shona (or Mashona) peoples, who live in the centre and east of the country. Many make a living from farming or, increasingly, work in industry. Many Shona people are Christians, but they also believe in animism, that is that natural objects such as lakes and trees have spirits. The Shona are known for their pottery and sculpture.

FARMING THE LAND

The centre of Zimbabwe is rich in fertile farm land, producing tobacco and other crops for selling (commercial farming.) But, while a fairer division of land has now been made, the best land is still in the hands of a few thousand landowners who are mainly white, leaving the poorer areas to be farmed by about 5 million black people, who grow just enough to live on (subsistence farming.)

How the land is farmed

- Commercial farming
- Subsistence farming
- Land unsuitable for farming
- Tobacco
- Cattle

Tobacco plant

Find out more
AFRICAN CITIES: *206*
PEOPLES OF AFRICA: *206–207*
RELIGION: *274–275*
TOBACCO: *52*

MOZAMBIQUE

WHEN MOZAMBIQUE BECAME independent from Portugal in 1975, its former rulers fled the country, destroying transport and machinery as they left. Years of civil war, drought, and flooding have since reduced the country to one of the poorest in the world. Mines left over from the war still litter the countryside, and few bridges remain standing. But Mozambique has the potential to overcome its disastrous recent history. The land is rich and fertile, and its mineral resources are largely untouched.

MOZAMBIQUE	
Capital city: Maputo	
Area: 801,590 sq km (309,493 sq miles)	
Population: 15,300,000	
Official language: Portuguese	
Major religions: traditional beliefs 60%, Christian 30%, Muslim 10%	
Government: Provisional government	
Currency: Metical	
Adult literacy rate: 24%	
Life expectancy: 47 years	
People per doctor: 50,000	
Televisions: 3 per 1,000 people	

BEIRA
The Indian Ocean port of Beira is the second city of Mozambique, and its major port. Most of neighbouring Zimbabwe's imports and exports pass through the port, using the rail, road, and pipeline links that run between Beira and the Zimbabwean capital of Harare. During the civil war, up to 10,000 Zimbabwean soldiers guarded this vital lifeline.

Workers taking a health-care class in Mozambique.

HEALTH CARE

After independence, the Mozambique government brought all health services under national ownership and provided free health care for all. However, years of civil war have destroyed most rural hospitals and clinics, and diseases such as tuberculosis, malaria, and pneumonia continue to kill many people. Today, almost the entire population live in poverty, and more than half rely on food aid supplied from abroad. Each year Mozambique receives millions of pounds worth of aid, mainly from European nations and the USA.

Where the aid comes from (1993)

Other: 42%
Germany: 19%
Italy: 13%
Sweden: 10%
Norway: 8%
USA: 8%

During the civil war, millions of refugees fled the country or left villages to find safety in the towns.

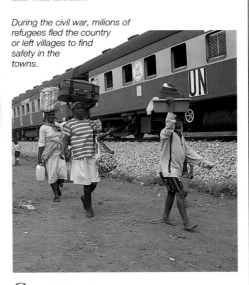

CIVIL WAR

After independence in 1975, civil war broke out between the communist Frelimo government and the Mozambique National Resistance (Renamo) rebels, supported by South Africa. The war led to the deaths of 900,000 people and to widespread starvation. Withdrawal of international support from Renamo and the decision of the Frelimo government to hold multi-party elections resulted in a peace treaty being signed between the two sides in 1992.

FARMING
More than 85 per cent of Mozambique's people work on the land. Farmers grow crops such as sugar, cotton, tea, cashew nuts, and citrus fruits on the fertile coastal plains, and grow tobacco and herd cattle on the inland pastures. The seas are rich in fish, the export of shrimps, lobsters, and other seafoods providing much needed income for the national economy.

Workers carrying bundles of sugarcane after the harvest.

LOCAL MUSIC
The coastal Chopi people produce music based on the sound of the *timbila*, a type of xylophone. *Timbila* orchestras provide the music for poetic songs and elaborate *migodo* (dance suites) reflecting village life. *Timbila* music is the national music of Mozambique.

Find out more	
HEALTH CARE:	*276*
REFUGEES:	*207*
RICH & POOR:	*278–279*
SUGAR:	*52*

SOUTH AFRICA

In 1994 SOUTH AFRICA moved from minority rule by its white population to majority government under the multi-racial control of the African National Congress (ANC). Since 1948, the South African government had practised apartheid, keeping the different races apart and restricting power to white people. South Africa became isolated from the rest of the world and violence between the races grew. Since the election of the ANC leader, Nelson Mandela, as South Africa's president, the apartheid system is being dismantled and South Africa has resumed full international relations.

NELSON MANDELA
Jailed in 1964 as a senior member of the ANC, Nelson Mandela (shown above with F. W. de Klerk) spent 26 years in prison until he was released in 1990. This was a result of President de Klerk's decision to legalize black freedom groups, with a view to ending apartheid. Under Nelson Mandela's leadership, the ANC won political power in 1994, and Mandela became the first black president of South Africa.

SOUTH AFRICA

Capital cities: Pretoria, Cape Town, Bloemfontein

Area: 1,221,040 sq km (471,443 sq miles)

Population: 40,800,000

Official languages: 9 African languages, English, Afrikaans

Major religions: Christian 47%, other 53%

Government: Multi-party democracy

Currency: Rand

Adult literacy rate: 80%

Life expectancy: 62 years

People per doctor: 1,640

Televisions: 97 per 1,000 people

SWAZILAND

Capital city: Mbabane

Area: 17,360 sq km (6,703 sq miles)

Population: 800,000

Official languages: Siswati, English

Major religions: Christian 60%, traditional beliefs 40%

Government: Absolute monarchy

Currency: Lilangeni

Adult literacy rate: 71%

Life expectancy: 57 years

People per doctor: 18,820

Televisions: 21 per 1,000 people

LESOTHO

Capital city: Maseru

Area: 30,350 sq km (11,718 sq miles)

Population: 1,900,000

Official languages: English, Sesotho

Major religions: Christian 90%, traditional beliefs 10%

Government: Military government

Currency: Loti

Adult literacy rate: 78%

Life expectancy: 60 years

People per doctor: 18,610

Televisions: 6 per 1,000 people

THE TOWNSHIPS

As part of South Africa's apartheid policies, black workers and their families were excluded from the main towns and forced to live in specially built townships a great distance from their work. The biggest and most famous of these townships is Soweto, home to more than 1 million people. Everyday, black workers leave Soweto and commute for many hours on over-crowded buses and trains to work in the mines and factories of neighbouring Johannesburg.

THE NDEBELE
South Africa is a multi-racial country, with many different ethnic groups and 11 official languages. One group, the Ndebele, are known for their distinctive houses, which are brightly decorated in strong, geometric shapes. Women are responsible for the upkeep of the huts, and repaint the outer walls each spring.

Grapefruit

Lime   *Lemon*

FRUIT GROWING
South Africa is a major exporter of food, thanks to its warm, dry climate and fertile soil. Citrus fruits, apples, and grapes are grown and then exported around the world. South Africa is also known for its fine wines.

THE GOLDEN CITY

South Africa has three capital cities, with the administration in Pretoria, the law courts in Bloemfontein, and the parliament in Cape Town. However, the financial and industrial heart of South Africa is Johannesburg (shown right), known as "the golden city". Gold mines deep beneath the surface have created enormous wealth, encouraging the development of a sprawling industrial area manufacturing cars, textiles, and hi-tech and heavy engineering products.

DIGGING FOR GOLD

Over the last century, the Witwatersrand gold field around Johannesburg has produced almost half the world's gold, and still accounts for more than 30 per cent of the world's total output each year. Diamonds and other minerals are also mined in huge quantities, and the country has a large manufacturing industry and financial sector. As a result, South Africa has the strongest and most advanced economy in Africa. However, population growth and rising unemployment are putting the economy under pressure.

Huge underground rooms known as stoped-out areas are created by drilling and blasting the surrounding rock.

What the gold is used for

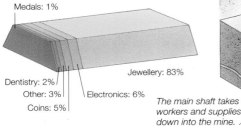

Medals: 1%
Dentistry: 2%
Other: 3%
Coins: 5%
Electronics: 6%
Jewellery: 83%

In the reduction plant, gold ore is removed from its surrounding rock.

A ventilation shaft lets air into the mine.

Tunnels lead from the main shaft to the reef – the thin, slanting layer of rock which contains the gold.

Reef

Diesel trains take the gold ore to large containers called ore skips which carry the gold up to the surface.

Ore skip

Shafts may be more than 3 km (2 miles) deep.

The main shaft takes workers and supplies down into the mine.

SPORT

Under apartheid, sporting facilities were segregated and black and white players belonged to different teams. As a result, South Africa was banned from international sporting competition. With the ending of apartheid, sport became multi-racial and South African teams were allowed once more to compete in world sporting events. In 1995 the national rugby team, the Springboks (shown above), won the Rugby World Cup.

SWAZILAND

THE KINGDOM OF SWAZILAND is dominated by its powerful neighbour, South Africa, relying on it for much of its wealth and energy supplies. Swaziland's main export is sugarcane, although it also exports wood pulp, coal, and asbestos. The king of Swaziland holds great power, running its affairs as head of government and appointing many members of its parliament. His power is reflected in his title, *Ngwenyama*, meaning "lion".

The coronation of King Mswati III in 1986.

LESOTHO

ENTIRELY SURROUNDED BY South Africa, the mountainous kingdom of Lesotho is the only country in Africa where all the land is above 1,000 m (3,300 ft). Its main natural resource is water; a huge hydro-electric scheme currently being built will eventually supply all of Lesotho's energy needs and vast quantities of water for South Africa. Until then, Lesotho is economically dependent on its wealthy neighbour.

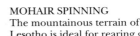

MOHAIR SPINNING

The mountainous terrain of Lesotho is ideal for rearing goats, whose mohair wool is much prized. Using foot-powered treadle wheels, women spin the mohair into yarn to make finely woven material for clothes and other products.

Find out more
AFRICAN CITIES: *206*
HYDRO-ELECTRICITY: *108, 262*
POLITICAL SYSTEMS: *270–271*
SUGARCANE: *52*

AUSTRALASIA AND OCEANIA

THIS VAST ISLAND REGION is spread over a huge area of the Pacific Ocean, to the south of southeast Asia. Australasia is made up of Australia, New Zealand, Papua New Guinea and several nearby islands. Australia is the only country which is also a continent in its own right, the smallest of the seven. Australasia is often linked with three groups of Pacific islands – Melanesia, Micronesia, and Polynesia – which form an even wider region, called Oceania. The climate and geography of Australasia and Oceania are as diverse as the region itself, ranging from the rainforests of northern Australia, and the glaciers of southern New Zealand, to the coral atolls and volcanoes which form many of the Pacific islands.

PAPUA NEW GUINEA

Papua New Guinea is the eastern end of the island of New Guinea. The western end is Irian Jaya, part of Indonesia. Papua is a country of high mountains and thick forests. The highest peak, Mount Wilhelm, reaches 4,300 m (14,107 ft) and is often snow-capped, despite lying close to the Equator. Lower down, the climate is hot and humid, ideal for the growth of the rich, tropical rainforests which cover two-thirds of the island.

The frilled lizard lives in the deserts of the outback.

THE AUSTRALIAN OUTBACK

Australia has four major deserts – the Simpson, Gibson, Great Sandy, and Great Victoria. Together, they cover most of the heart of the continent in a vast, barren area, known as the outback. Very few people live in the outback, though the dry conditions are good for raising sheep and cattle.

Highest temperature:
Bourke, Australia,
53°C (128°F)

Lowest temperature:
Canberra, Australia,
-22°C (-8°F)

THINGS TO LOOK FOR ON THE MAP

Area: 8,508,238 sq km (3,285,048 sq miles)

Highest point: Mt. Wilhelm, Papua New Guinea, 4,300 m (14,107 ft) *Map F7*

Longest river: Murray-Darling, Australia, 3,824 km (2,376 miles) *Map F12*

Largest lake: L. Eyre, Australia, maximum size 9,690 sq km (3,742 sq miles) *Map E11*

Largest island: New Guinea, 787,878 sq km (304,200 sq miles) *Map E7*

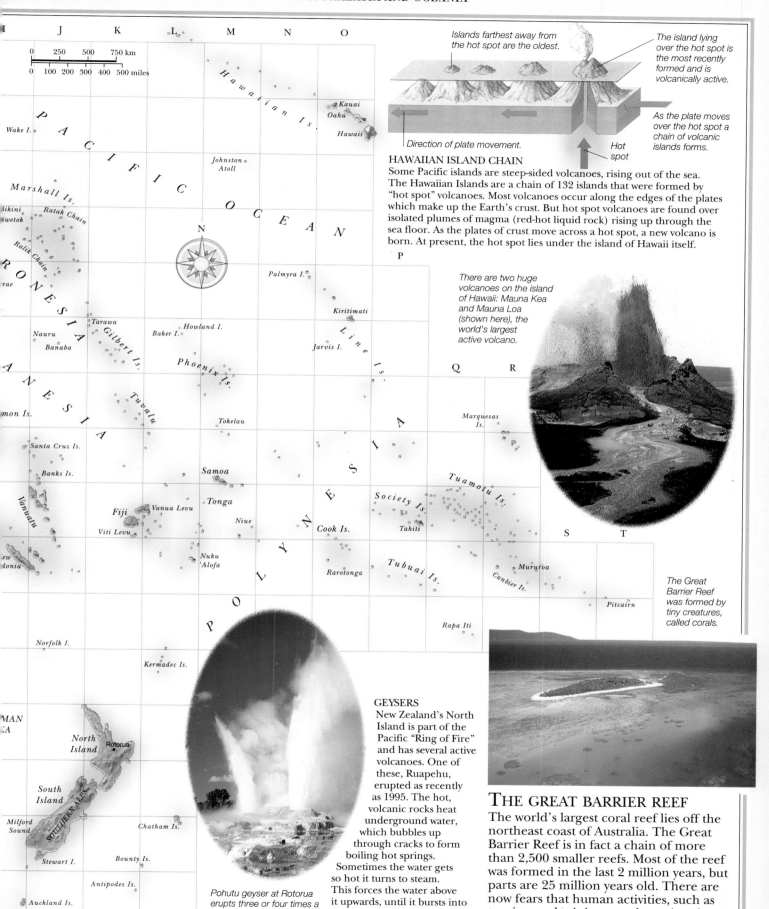

0 250 500 750 km
0 100 200 300 400 500 miles

Hawaiian Is.

Wake I.

Kauai
Oahu
Hawaii

Johnston Atoll

PACIFIC OCEAN

Islands farthest away from the hot spot are the oldest.

The island lying over the hot spot is the most recently formed and is volcanically active.

Direction of plate movement.

As the plate moves over the hot spot a chain of volcanic islands forms.

Hot spot

HAWAIIAN ISLAND CHAIN

Some Pacific islands are steep-sided volcanoes, rising out of the sea. The Hawaiian Islands are a chain of 132 islands that were formed by "hot spot" volcanoes. Most volcanoes occur along the edges of the plates which make up the Earth's crust. But hot spot volcanoes are found over isolated plumes of magma (red-hot liquid rock) rising up through the sea floor. As the plates of crust move across a hot spot, a new volcano is born. At present, the hot spot lies under the island of Hawaii itself.

There are two huge volcanoes on the island of Hawaii: Mauna Kea and Mauna Loa (shown here), the world's largest active volcano.

Marshall Is.
Bikini
Eniwetok
Ratak Chain
Ralik Chain

MICRONESIA

N

Palmyra I.

Kiritimati

Tarawa
Nauru
Banaba
Baker I.
Howland I.
Jarvis I.

Gilbert Is.

Tuvalu

Phoenix Is.

Tokelau

Line Is.

Marquesas Is.

MELANESIA

Solomon Is.

Santa Cruz Is.
Banks Is.

Samoa

Vanuatu

Fiji
Vanua Levu
Viti Levu

Tonga
Niue

Cook Is.

Society Is.
Tahiti

Tuamotu Is.

POLYNESIA

New Caledonia

Nuku 'Alofa

Rarotonga

Tubuai Is.

Mururoa
Ganbier Is.

Pitcairn

Rapa Iti

The Great Barrier Reef was formed by tiny creatures, called corals.

Norfolk I.

Kermadec Is.

TASMAN SEA

North Island
Rotorua

South Island

SOUTHERN ALPS

Milford Sound

Chatham Is.

Stewart I.
Bounty Is.

Antipodes Is.

Auckland Is.

GEYSERS

New Zealand's North Island is part of the Pacific "Ring of Fire" and has several active volcanoes. One of these, Ruapehu, erupted as recently as 1995. The hot, volcanic rocks heat underground water, which bubbles up through cracks to form boiling hot springs. Sometimes the water gets so hot it turns to steam. This forces the water above it upwards, until it bursts into the air in a tall, spectacular spout, called a geyser.

Pohutu geyser at Rotorua erupts three or four times a day, occasionally reaching a height of 30 m (98 ft).

THE GREAT BARRIER REEF

The world's largest coral reef lies off the northeast coast of Australia. The Great Barrier Reef is in fact a chain of more than 2,500 smaller reefs. Most of the reef was formed in the last 2 million years, but parts are 25 million years old. There are now fears that human activities, such as tourism and mining, are damaging the fragile balance of the reef and its wildlife.

PEOPLES OF AUSTRALASIA AND OCEANIA

ISOLATED FROM THE REST of the world, parts of this region were among the last places on Earth to be settled. The first inhabitants came from Asia, and include the Aboriginals of Australia, the Maoris of New Zealand, and the peoples of the Pacific Islands. In the 18th century, settlers started to arrive from Europe, and both Australia and New Zealand became British colonies. Many Pacific Islands were European colonies. Today, links with the European colonizers are no longer so strong. In recent decades, people have migrated to Australia and New Zealand from the Middle East and southeast Asia, and they have both become multicultural societies with successful modern economies.

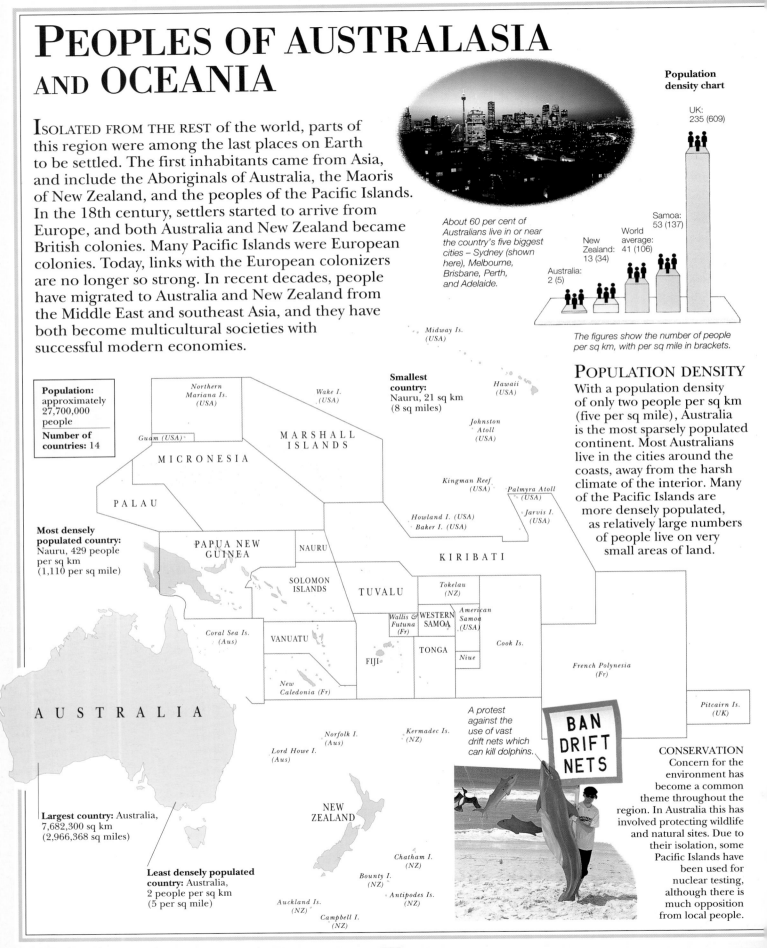

About 60 per cent of Australians live in or near the country's five biggest cities – Sydney (shown here), Melbourne, Brisbane, Perth, and Adelaide.

Population density chart

UK: 235 (609)

Samoa: 53 (137)

World average: 41 (106)

New Zealand: 13 (34)

Australia: 2 (5)

The figures show the number of people per sq km, with per sq mile in brackets.

POPULATION DENSITY

With a population density of only two people per sq km (five per sq mile), Australia is the most sparsely populated continent. Most Australians live in the cities around the coasts, away from the harsh climate of the interior. Many of the Pacific Islands are more densely populated, as relatively large numbers of people live on very small areas of land.

Population: approximately 27,700,000 people

Number of countries: 14

Smallest country: Nauru, 21 sq km (8 sq miles)

Midway Is. (USA)

Northern Mariana Is. (USA)

Wake I. (USA)

Hawaii (USA)

Johnston Atoll (USA)

Guam (USA)

MARSHALL ISLANDS

MICRONESIA

Kingman Reef (USA)

Palmyra Atoll (USA)

PALAU

Howland I. (USA)
Baker I. (USA)

Jarvis I. (USA)

Most densely populated country: Nauru, 429 people per sq km (1,110 per sq mile)

PAPUA NEW GUINEA

NAURU

KIRIBATI

SOLOMON ISLANDS

TUVALU

Tokelau (NZ)

Wallis & Futuna (Fr)

WESTERN SAMOA

American Samoa (USA)

Cook Is.

Coral Sea Is. (Aus)

VANUATU

FIJI

TONGA

Niue

French Polynesia (Fr)

New Caledonia (Fr)

AUSTRALIA

Norfolk I. (Aus)

Kermadec Is. (NZ)

Pitcairn Is. (UK)

Lord Howe I. (Aus)

A protest against the use of vast drift nets which can kill dolphins.

BAN DRIFT NETS

Largest country: Australia, 7,682,300 sq km (2,966,368 sq miles)

NEW ZEALAND

Chatham I. (NZ)

CONSERVATION
Concern for the environment has become a common theme throughout the region. In Australia this has involved protecting wildlife and natural sites. Due to their isolation, some Pacific Islands have been used for nuclear testing, although there is much opposition from local people.

Least densely populated country: Australia, 2 people per sq km (5 per sq mile)

Bounty I. (NZ)

Antipodes Is. (NZ)

Auckland Is. (NZ)

Campbell I. (NZ)

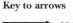

Key to arrows

→ 50,000–70,000 years ago

→ 5,000–1,000 BC

→ AD100–200

→ AD700–950

Early peoples sailed from New Guinea to the nearest islands, known as Melanesia. Over the next few thousand years they settled other islands. To the north they arrived in the region known today as Micronesia.

The early settlers sailed in outrigger canoes. Today, similar canoes are still used by islanders for fishing.

NEW GUINEA

Towards Hawaii

Towards Easter Island

EARLY SETTLERS

The first settlers were the Aboriginals, who arrived in Australia between 50,000 and 70,000 years ago, when the continent was still connected by a land bridge to New Guinea. The inhabitants of the Pacific Islands arrived next, when, about 7,000 years ago, people from southeast Asia began to settle the islands. Parts of this region have been settled for little more than 1,000 years – the Maoris, for example, arrived in New Zealand in about AD950.

AUSTRALIA

The Maoris sailed to New Zealand around AD950.

NEW ZEALAND

Australia's history as a British colony is reflected in its flag, which features the British flag, the Commonwealth Star, and the Southern Cross constellation.

POPULATION TODAY

As a legacy of their colonial past, most people in New Zealand and Australia today are of British descent. In the last few decades, however, new settlers have arrived in the region from throughout the world. For more than two million Australians, English is not their first language. The various groups of migrants have brought their own customs, traditions, festivals, and food, making Australia and New Zealand multicultural societies.

AUSTRALIA'S EXPORT MARKETS	
1 Japan	26% of exports
2 South Korea	8% of exports
3 New Zealand	7% of exports
3 USA	7% of exports
5 Singapore	5% of exports

TRADING PARTNERS

Traditionally, the UK was the main trading partner for both Australia and New Zealand. However, since the UK joined the European Union in 1973, Australia and New Zealand have had to look for new export markets. Both countries are now concentrating on the growing Asian market. In 1960, Asia accounted for only 25 per cent of Australia's exports. Today 60 per cent of Australia's trade is with Asia, and Japan is its most important market.

Today, Aboriginals make up between one and two per cent of Australia's population.

ABORIGINAL RIGHTS

For many years, Aboriginal children in Australia and Maoris in New Zealand were taught only in English and were discouraged from learning their own languages. Today the situation is very different. The Maori language is officially recognized in New Zealand, and in Australia schoolchildren learn about Aboriginal culture and traditions. But many people feel that the future also depends on reclaiming the land and resources taken from the original peoples when European settlers first arrived.

The England-Australia Test Matches are played every four years.

SPORT

In both Australia and New Zealand, sport has played an important role in creating a sense of national identity. Rugby is the national sport of New Zealand, while Australia's two main sports are football (soccer) and cricket. Success in these sports is a great source of national pride.

AUSTRALIA AND PAPUA NEW GUINEA

Raggiana's bird of paradise – two-thirds of all birds of paradise live in the forests of Papua New Guinea.

BOUNDED BY THE INDIAN and Pacific Oceans, Australia is the world's largest island, but the smallest continent. It is vast, nearly the size of the USA, and very dry. There is little rain, and arid desert stretches across about two-thirds of the land. Most of the people live in the big cities along the coasts. To the north, only 150 km (93 miles) across the Torres Strait, lies Papua New Guinea. An Australian colony until 1975, it consists of the eastern end of the island of New Guinea and more than 600 surrounding islands.

ISLAND OF MOUNTAINS AND FORESTS

Papua New Guinea lies entirely in the tropics and has a hot, wet climate. Running from west to east along the island is a range of high rugged mountains, covered with dense rainforest. These remote forests are home to a vast range of plants and animals, many of which are found nowhere else in the world. Mangrove swamps grow along many of the island's coasts.

When rains do come, there are flash floods, and plants like this Sturt's Desert Pea flower from seeds that have lain dormant for years.

THE OUTBACK

Most of Australia is a flat plain without mountains, forests, or rivers. The huge central region, known as the outback, is one of the hottest and driest places on Earth. It has sandy or stony deserts, which can be baked by intense heat during the day, and frozen by extreme cold at night. In places where there is some vegetation, or the land has been irrigated, farmers raise cattle and sheep.

ULURU (AYERS ROCK)

This massive block of sandstone stands almost in the middle of Australia. It measures 9.4 km (5.8 miles) around the base, and rises to 348 m (1,142 ft). To the Aboriginals, the first people of Australia, the rock is known as Uluru. It is a sacred site and features in their beliefs about the creation of the world. Once called Ayers Rock after a former premier of South Australia, the rock regained its Aboriginal name in 1985.

GREAT BARRIER REEF

The Great Barrier Reef, the largest living thing on Earth, stretches for 2,000 km (1,243 miles) along the northeast coast of Australia. It is the world's largest coral reef and home to more than 2,000 species of fish. Its coral is made of layer upon layer of tiny anemone-like creatures called polyps. The Great Barrier Reef is a major tourist attraction, but swimmers and divers can easily pollute and damage it. To protect it, the reef has been made a World Heritage Area.

Perth, Australia

☀ Jan 23°C (74°F)
☼ July 13°C (55.5°F)

🌧 Jan 8 mm (0.3 in)
July 170 mm (6.7 in)

THINGS TO LOOK FOR ON THE MAP

Longest river: Murray-Darling, Australia 3,824 km (2,376 miles) *Map I10, K9*

Highest point: Mt. Wilhelm, Papua New Guinea, 4,300 m (14,107 ft) *Map K11*

Largest lake: L. Eyre, Australia, maximum size 9,690 sq km (3,742 sq miles) *Map I9*

PAPUA NEW GUINEA

FEWER THAN FOUR MILLION PEOPLE live in Papua New Guinea, most of them in small, isolated villages. By western standards, many people are poor. Papua is rich in natural resources, especially minerals such as copper and gold. The copper mine at Panguna on the island of Bougainville is one of the world's main producers. Timber from the rainforests is another major export. The challenge is to develop these resources without damaging the environment.

PAPUA NEW GUINEA

PAPUA NEW GUINEA	
Capital city: Port Moresby	
Area: 462,840 sq km (178,700 sq miles)	
Population: 3,529,538	
Official language: English	
Major religions: Christian 66%, traditional beliefs 34%	
Government: Multi-party democracy	
Currency: Kina	
Adult literacy rate: 65%	
Life expectancy: 55 years	
People per doctor: 12,500	
Televisions: No figures available	

Port Moresby, Papua New Guinea
☀ Jan 28°C (82.5°F)
July 25.5°C (78°F)
☂ Jan 178 mm (7 in)
July 28 mm (1.1 in)

PAPUA NEW GUINEA (flag)

Alice Springs, Australia
☀ Jan 28.5°C (83.5°F)
July 11.5°C (53°F)
☂ Jan 43 mm (1.7 in)
July 8 mm (0.3 in)

Sydney, Australia
☀ Jan 22°C (71.5°F)
July 12°C (53°F)
☂ Jan 89 mm (3.5 in)
July 117 mm (4.6 in)

0   100 200 300 400 500 km
0   100   200   300 miles

BIG BUTTERFLY
Queen Alexandra's Birdwing butterfly, with a wingspan of 25 cm (10 in), is the world's largest butterfly.

Tribespeople from Mendi, wearing head-dresses made from bird of paradise feathers.

TRIBAL PEOPLE
The mountains and forests of Papua New Guinea have always restricted contact between the various groups of people who live there. As a result, the country is now home to about 1,000 tribes, speaking more than 700 different languages. Most of these people live off the land they farm.

PORT MORESBY
The capital, Port Moresby, is a sprawling city built around a natural harbour on the island's southern coast. Unlike the rest of the country, it is dry for much of the year. Port Moresby has grown rapidly in recent years, as people from remote regions have moved there to find work.

Find out more	
AUSTRALIAN OUTBACK:	*254*
COPPER MINING:	*73, 237, 245*
GREAT BARRIER REEF:	*255*
SETTLING THE ISLANDS:	*257*

AUSTRALIA

UNTIL ABOUT 200 YEARS AGO, the land that is now Australia was occupied only by Aboriginals. Then, in 1770, the British explorer James Cook arrived in Botany Bay and claimed it for Britain. In 1901, Australia became an independent commonwealth. Over the years settlers from overseas, firstly from Britain and Europe, but more recently from Asia, have shaped the culture of this huge country. Wool and wheat, as well as mineral resources of iron ore, coal, and copper have made Australia wealthy, and most people benefit from a high standard of living.

AUSTRALIA
Capital city: Canberra
Area: 7,682,300 sq km (2,966,368 sq miles)
Population: 17,900,000
Official language: English
Major religion: Christian 76%, other 24%
Government: Multi-party democracy
Currency: Australian dollar
Adult literacy rate: 99%
Life expectancy: 77 years
People per doctor: 440
Televisions: 490 per 1,000 people

SETTLERS
In the 18th century, British prisons were overcrowded and criminals were often sent overseas. In 1778 the first ships arrived from Britain with 757 adult convicts, forming a settlement in what is now Sydney. By 1860 more than 160,000 convicts had been transported to Australia.

LIVING ON THE COAST
About 85 per cent of Australians live in or around cities along the coast. Most of the schools, hospitals, offices, and factories are located here, and life is easier than in the remote towns and farms of the outback. Homes in the city are built of wood or brick, often with verandas, as well as a patio or backyard for the barbecue. The five largest cities contain 60 per cent of the population. One of these is Sydney, shown left, with its Opera House overlooking the harbour.

ABORIGINAL BELIEFS
The word Aboriginal means "from the beginning", and Aboriginals believe they have occupied Australia since the beginning of time. They have a detailed knowledge of the land; women gathered fruits, nuts, and grubs, and men hunted animals such as kangaroos and possums. The Dreaming, long ago when the land and all living things were made, is the basis of Aboriginal culture.

MAIN CITIES BY POPULATION	
Sydney	3,699,800
Melbourne	3,153,500
Brisbane	1,385,000
Perth	1,193,100
Adelaide	1,065,300

Aboriginals act out their beliefs in their songs, ceremonies, and art. This group is from Queensland.

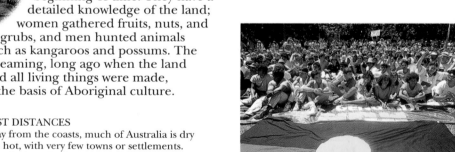

People in Sydney demonstrate for land rights. On the Aboriginal flag, black represents the people, yellow the Sun, and red the land.

VAST DISTANCES
Away from the coasts, much of Australia is dry and hot, with very few towns or settlements. Alice Springs, in the centre of the country, began as a station linking the telegraph line between Darwin and Adelaide. Separated by such large distances, many children cannot get to school and take lessons through the School of the Air learning scheme.

The journey from Darwin to Sydney, via Adelaide, is 4,822 km (2,996 miles). This would take about 2.5 days and nights of non-stop driving.

LAND RIGHTS
The arrival of the British changed life for the Aboriginals. Many lost their lands and thousands died of European diseases. Today, they no longer live off the land in the traditional way, but work in factories or farms. Many suffer poor health and bad housing. In 1967, they were granted the right to vote. Since then a series of laws have given Aboriginals control over some of the land.

- Major roads
- Route shown below

Darwin to Alice Springs	Alice Springs to Adelaide	Adelaide to Sydney
1,508 km (937 miles)	1,529 km (950 miles)	1,785 km (1,109 miles)

SHEEP FARMING

Australia is the world's chief wool-producing country, with
New South Wales the leading area. Most of Australia's sheep are
Merinos which were brought from South Africa and England in
the 1790s. Today, there are about 150 million sheep in Australia,
most of them kept on farms, called stations. Some stations are
huge, and can cover 15,000 sq km (5,792 sq miles), which is half
the size of Belgium. Motorbikes and four-wheel-drive vehicles
are now used to control livestock over such wide areas.

Sheep usually graze on grass, but eat hay or grain in the summer when pastures are dry.

Drovers ride horses to follow the flock.

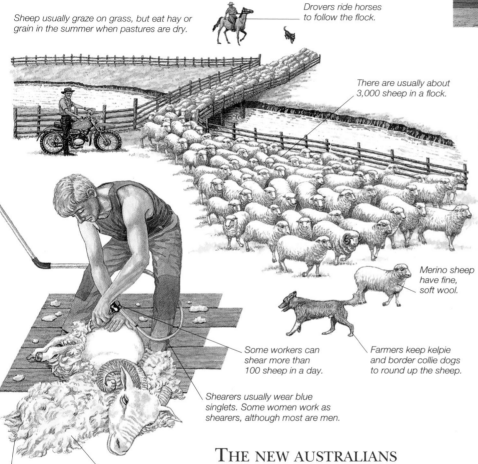

There are usually about 3,000 sheep in a flock.

Merino sheep have fine, soft wool.

Some workers can shear more than 100 sheep in a day.

Farmers keep kelpie and border collie dogs to round up the sheep.

Shearers usually wear blue singlets. Some women work as shearers, although most are men.

Merino sheep can survive the heat and still produce a heavy fleece of good wool.

Wool is graded and stored in bins.

RICHES FROM THE EARTH

In the 1850s, the discovery of gold in Victoria
and New South Wales attracted people to Australia
and helped boost the economy. Today, mining for
coal, copper, and iron ore, shown above, is still big
business. Australia is the world's largest coal
exporter, and also has the world's most productive
diamond mine, near Lake Argyle. However,
modern mining relies more on machinery than
on labour, and does not employ many people.

LOOKING EAST

For many years, Australia traded mainly with
Britain. However, since Britain joined the
European Union in 1973, Australia has
strengthened its trading links with the United
States as well as with countries that are closer,
such as Japan. Today, many foreign companies,
such as car manufacturers and computer
businesses, have set up factories in Australia.

THE NEW AUSTRALIANS

For many years, Australia allowed
only white people to settle there:
mostly people from Britain, Italy,
and Greece. In 1972, this policy was
changed and since then immigrants
have arrived from all over the world.
The "New Australians" include
Vietnamese, Japanese, and
Chinese. These groups
have brought their own
languages, festivals,
and types of food.

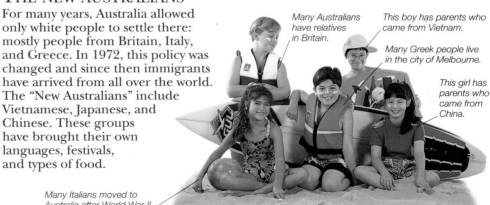

Many Australians have relatives in Britain.

This boy has parents who came from Vietnam.

Many Greek people live in the city of Melbourne.

This girl has parents who came from China.

Many Italians moved to Australia after World War II.

In Australian Rules football, players can kick or punch the ball, but they must not throw it.

SPORTING LIFE

Australians love the outdoors, and sport is a major part of
their lifestyle. Sandy beaches, warm water, and good surf
make swimming, sailing, water-skiing, and surfing extremely
popular. Australians also excel in international events at
cricket, tennis, athletics, and rugby. In the year 2000 Sydney
will host the Olympic Games for the first time.

Find out more

DIAMONDS: *150, 226, 248*
POPULATION DENSITY: *256*
SETTLING AUSTRALIA: *256–257*
TRADE (PACIFIC RIM): *257*

NEW ZEALAND

SITUATED ABOUT 1,500 KM (932 MILES) from Australia, its nearest neighbour, New Zealand consists of two large islands – North and South Island – and several smaller ones. The North Island has a warm, mild climate and is volcanically active. The South Island is colder, with glaciers, high mountain peaks, and forests. From 1840 to 1907 New Zealand was a British colony, but gained full independence in 1947. The original inhabitants – the Maoris – still make up about 9 per cent of the population. New Zealand is a wealthy and progressive country, and was the first in the world to give women the vote.

PEOPLE AND CITIES
There are only about 3.4 million people in New Zealand – fewer than half the population of London or Paris. Nearly three-quarters of New Zealanders live on the North Island, and most of them live in the cities. Wellington (shown here) is New Zealand's capital city.

NEW ZEALAND

Capital city: Wellington

Area: 270,534 sq km (104,454 sq miles)

Population: 3,434,950

Official language: English

Major religions: Christian 62%, other 22%, non-religious 16%

Government: Multi-party democracy

Currency: New Zealand dollar

Adult literacy rate: 99%

Life expectancy: 75 years

People per doctor: 580

Televisions: 440 per 1,000 people

FARMING
Large areas of grass and a warm, damp climate make New Zealand ideal for farming, especially raising sheep and cattle. There are about 60 million sheep (about 20 for every one person) and 8 million cattle. Three-quarters of New Zealand's exports are agricultural products. The country is one of the world's leading exporters of wool, frozen meat, and dairy products such as butter and cheese.

ENERGY
More than 80 per cent of New Zealand's electricity comes from hydro-electric plants, like the Clyde Dam on the South Island, which harness the power of its rushing rivers. New Zealand does not use nuclear power. This, together with its small population and the lack of heavy industry, make it one of the world's least polluted countries. New Zealand is very proud of its "clean, green" image.

Auckland, North Island
- Jan 19.5°C (66.5°F)
- July 10.5°C (51°F)
- Jan 79 mm (3.1 in)
- July 145 mm (5.7 in)

Dunedin, South Island
- Jan 14.5°C (58°F)
- July 6°C (3.1°F)
- Jan 86 mm (3.4 in)
- July 79 mm (3.1 in)

NEW ZEALAND

TASMAN SEA

PACIFIC OCEAN

Great Exhibition Bay
Waipapakauri
Waitangi
Whangarei
Kaipara Harbour
Great Barrier I.
Auckland
Coromandel
Thames
Bay of Plenty
Tauranga
Hamilton
Rotorua
Waikato
L. Taupo
Taupo
Gisborne
New Plymouth
NORTH ISLAND
Napier
Hawke Bay
Wanganui
Hastings
Palmerston North
Cook Strait
Levin
Masterton
Tasman Bay
WELLINGTON
Nelson
Picton
Westport
Blenheim
Wairau
Greymouth
Kaikoura
Hurunui
SOUTHERN ALPS
Pegasus Bay
Milford Sound
Mt. Cook
Rakaia
Christchurch
Timaru
Waitaki
Canterbury Bight
Queenstown
Taieri
L. Te Anau
L. Wakatipu
SOUTH ISLAND
Dunedin
Invercargill
Foveaux Strait
Stewart I.

EQUATOR
TROPIC OF CAPRICORN

N

| 0 | 50 | 100 | 150 km |
| 0 | 50 | 100 miles |

THINGS TO LOOK FOR ON THE MAP

Longest river: Waikato, North Island 425 km (264 miles) *Map F4*

Highest point: Mt. Cook, South Island, 3,754 m (12,316 ft) *Map C9*

Largest lake: L. Taupo, North Island, 606 sq km (234 sq miles) *Map G5*

THE FIRST NEW ZEALANDERS

New Zealand was one of the last places on Earth to be inhabited by people. The first settlers, the Maori, arrived from Polynesia in about AD950. Today, although most Maoris have adopted western lifestyles, their culture lives on in their language, art, and extended family groups. Maoris are represented in the government, and there are moves to ensure that they receive equal opportunities in health, education, and employment, which have been lacking in the past.

MAORI ART
This neck pendant represents Tiki, one of the Maori gods, and is worn to bring good luck. It is carved from greenstone, a kind of hard jade found on the South Island.

OUTDOOR LIFE
New Zealand's pleasant climate and beautiful countryside make it ideal for outdoor activities. New Zealanders enjoy sports of all kinds, from hiking and mountain climbing to canoeing, yachting, and rugby. The country's rugby team, the All Blacks, are shown in action above. Many tourists visit New Zealand for its outdoor lifestyle, and tourism is now a major source of income.

KIWI FRUIT

The Chinese gooseberry was introduced into New Zealand in about 1900, and was later renamed the kiwi fruit after the country's famous bird. New Zealand is now the world's principal producer, and exports kiwi fruit worldwide. The fruit, known as a subtropical, needs a warm, sunny climate. It is grown in special orchards, divided into sections by fences or hedges.

The orchards are divided into sections about 150 m by 40 m (492 ft x 131 ft).

Home of the orchard manager.

Strong supports hold the vines steady while the kiwi fruit grows.

Tall trees, or hedges, protect the vines from gusts of wind.

Pickers, wearing gloves to protect the fruit, pluck the kiwi fruit from the branch.

The fruit is placed in a special apron while the picker moves along the rows.

The kiwi fruit has a fuzzy, greenish-brown skin a little like the feathers of the bird after which it is named.

Pickers sort the fruit by size, then pack it in cardboard boxes.

ORCHARD FRUITS

Because New Zealand lies in the southern hemisphere, it can grow crops when its customers in the north are in the middle of their winter. The main types of fruit, with examples from each group shown below, are – pip fruit (apple), berry fruit (strawberry), stone fruit (peach), citrus fruit (orange), and subtropicals (tamarillo).

Orange

Apple

Strawberry

Peach

Tamarillo

FLIGHTLESS BIRDS
New Zealand's isolated position has allowed many unique plants and animals to develop there. The most famous are the flightless birds, such as the kakapo and kiwi. These birds lost the ability to fly because they had no enemies and did not need to be able to fly away.

The long-beaked kiwi is New Zealand's national emblem.

The rare kakapo, or owl parrot, nests under tree roots.

Find out more

HYDRO-ELECTRICITY: *108*
SETTLING PACIFIC ISLANDS: *257*
SHEEP FARMING: *261*
VOLCANIC ACTIVITY: *13, 255*

THE PACIFIC OCEAN

MICRONESIA
Capital city: Kolonia
Area: 2,900 sq km (1,120 sq miles)
Population: 101,000

NAURU
Capital city: None
Area: 21.2 sq km (8.2 sq miles)
Population: 9,000

PALAU
Capital city: Koro
Area: 508 sq km (196 sq miles)
Population: 300,000

SOLOMON ISLANDS
Capital city: Honiara
Area: 289,000 sq km (11,158 sq miles)
Population: 300,000

VANUATU
Capital city: Port-Vila
Area: 12,190 sq km (4,707 sq miles)
Population: 163,000

FIJI
Capital city: Suva
Area: 18,270 sq km (7,054 sq miles)
Population: 700,000

TUVALU
Capital city: Fingafale
Area: 26 sq km (10 sq miles)
Population: 9,000

TONGA
Capital city: Nuku'alofa
Area: 750 sq km (290 sq miles)
Population: 94,000

WESTERN SAMOA
Capital city: Apia
Area: 2,840 sq km (1,097 sq miles)
Population: 169,000

KIRIBATI
Capital city: Bairiki
Area: 710 sq km (274 sq miles)
Population: 66,000

MARSHALL ISLANDS
Capital city: Majuro
Area: 181 sq km (70 sq miles)
Population: 48,000

THE WORLD'S LARGEST, DEEPEST OCEAN, the Pacific covers one-third of the Earth's surface, stretching from the shores of Asia and Australia to America and Antarctica. About 20,000 volcanic and coral islands lie scattered over its vast expanse, many covered with lush vegetation. Over much of the Pacific the climate is hot and moist. The native island peoples, who originally came from southeast Asia, fall into three main groups, Polynesians, Melanesians, and Micronesians. Europeans began to arrive in the 1500s, and by the 1800s many islands were colonies of powerful countries overseas. Today, some of the islands are self-governing; in others foreign control is still strong.

Coconut palms provide the islanders with food, milk, and fibre to make rope.

Large families of 10 or more live together under one roof.

PACIFIC PEOPLES
Some islanders live in towns, but many people continue the traditional farming way of life, growing crops such as yams and sweet potatoes, or fishing from the sea. The shape of homes varies from island to island but most, like this Fijian *bure*, are simply built using a large wooden frame topped with a thatch of plant fronds. Today, corrugated iron is often used as roofing because it lasts longer than thatch. Community life on the islands is important, with large extended families ruled by tribal chiefs. Property and personal objects belong to everybody.

People often keep chickens and pigs.

Men wear a cloth skirt called a sulu.

A special meal might include fish, chicken, yams, vegetables, coconut, and bananas.

Boys learn to weave using green coconut leaves.

This area of the house is used for guests.

EXPORTS
Rich, volcanic soil and regular rainfall make these hot, sunny islands especially fertile. Some farmers produce surplus crops that they export. Sugar, ginger, black pepper, and copra (dried coconut) are among the main export crops. Fish, timber, livestock, and minerals are also important sources of income on certain islands.

The green fruit of the black pepper plant is dried to make black peppercorns.

Ground pepper

THE EFFECT OF TOURISM
Many of the "island paradises" are fast becoming major tourist destinations – especially around Fiji, Tonga, and Western Samoa. Tourism brings in valuable income, but it can also damage the environment and affect the life of local people. For example, already limited water supplies may be diverted away from villages to hotel pools and showers.

PACIFIC PROTESTS
Since the first atomic explosion more than 50 years ago, the Pacific has been used by Britain, France, and the USA for testing nuclear weapons. Some tests continue today, although groups such as Greenpeace have demonstrated against this. There are also local protests, but these are hindered by the fact that they involve relatively few people scattered across a huge area.

Marshall Islands
☀ Jan 27°C (81°F)
☀ July 28°C (83°F)
🌧 Jan 53 mm (2.1 in)
🌧 July 213 mm (8.4 in)

NAURU

THINGS TO LOOK FOR ON THE MAP

World's deepest trench: Mariana Trench 10,924 m (35,840 ft) *Map C4*

World's largest atoll: Kwajalein, Marshall Islands, coral reef that encloses a 2,174 sq km (839 sq mile) lagoon. *Map D5*

MARSHALL ISLANDS

KIRIBATI

PALAU

SOLOMON ISLANDS

VANUATU

FIJI

Fiji
☀ Jan 26°C (80°F)
☀ July 23°C (74°F)
🌧 Jan 290 mm (11.4 in)
🌧 July 125 mm (4.9 in)

| 0 | 500 | 1000 | 1500 | 2000 km |

| 0 | 250 | 500 | 750 | 1000 | 1250 miles |

TUVALU

TONGA

WESTERN SAMOA

Giant tortoise found only on the Galápagos Islands

GALÁPAGOS ISLANDS

When British naturalist Charles Darwin (1809-1882) went to the Galápagos Islands, off the west coast of South America, he found many unusual creatures, including giant tortoises. He also noticed differences between animals of the same kind living on different islands. This led him to believe that, over many generations, animals change, or evolve, to suit their habitat.

As a person travels west, they move into different time zones, and lose one hour for every 15° they travel round the Earth.

At the International Date Line, where the date changes, you lose or gain a day, depending on which way you are travelling.

Since 1884, time has been measured from Greenwich in Britain. Originally known as Greenwich Mean Time (GMT), it is now referred to as Universal Time.

As a person travels east, they move into different time zones, and gain one hour for every 15° they travel round the Earth.

INTERNATIONAL DATE LINE

The world is divided into 24 imaginary time zones, shown left, and the time of day changes by one hour from one zone to the next. At a half-way point – the International Date Line – the date changes. The line runs across the Pacific Ocean, although in some places it winds its way between the islands – life would be difficult if it was two different days on one island.

Find out more
CORAL ISLANDS: *202*
GREENPEACE: *273*
SETTLING PACIFIC ISLANDS: *257*
VOLCANOES: *13*

THE ARCTIC

THE MOST NORTHERLY CONSTELLATION of stars, Arktos, or the Great Bear, gives its name to the icy ocean beneath it that surrounds the North Pole. One of the coldest places on Earth, the Arctic Ocean is bordered by the northernmost parts of Europe, Asia, North America, and Greenland, the world's largest island. Most of the Arctic Ocean is covered by ice, although warmer currents from the Atlantic and Pacific flow northwards into it, warming the sea and air and clearing ice from the coasts in summer. Few people live in the Arctic, although the region is rich in minerals and wildlife.

CLIMATE

During the long winter months, the Sun never rises over the horizon, and temperatures drop as low as -70°C (-94°F). In the summer, the Sun never sets, bathing the region in constant daylight and raising temperatures considerably. This is because the Earth rotates at an angle to the Sun, plunging the Arctic from total light to total darkness as the North Pole moves towards and away from the Sun. The dark polar skies are lit by the Aurora, wispy curtains of red and green light caused by electricity in the upper atmosphere.

The polar bear is well adapted to Arctic life. It has acute senses, runs fast, swims well, and is camouflaged against the snow and ice by its white fur. Polar bears feed on seals and other animals, ranging far across the ice in search of prey.

Arctic terns breed in large colonies during the Arctic summer. When winter comes, they fly halfway around the world to take advantage of the daylight and rich food supply of the Antarctic summer.

NATURAL RESOURCES

The lands that surround the Arctic Ocean are rich in minerals. Vast oil and gas reserves lie under Alaska, while Norwegian and Russian companies are mining coal on the island of Svalbard (shown here). Smaller quantities of gold, iron, silver, tin, and other minerals are found throughout the region. Extracting these resources is expensive, but as supplies elsewhere begin to run out, oil and mining companies are turning their attention to the untapped wealth of the Arctic region.

ARCTIC WILDLIFE

The Arctic Ocean teems with wildlife. Seals, walrus, and many species of whale thrive in the icy waters, protected from the cold by layers of thick blubber beneath their skins. On land, reindeer, musk ox, hares, Arctic foxes, and wolves scavenge for food, migrating south to avoid the worst of the winter. In the brief summer hardy plants bloom, providing food for millions of insects. Birds such as the Arctic tern and Brent goose take advantage of this abundant food supply to breed and raise their young.

PEOPLE OF THE ARCTIC

The cold, inhospitable Arctic region is home to few people. The Sami of northern Scandinavia, the Yugyts and Nenets of Siberia, and the Inuit of Canada traditionally survived by hunting and trapping wild animals. Large herds of reindeer provided them with all their basic needs, such as food, clothing, tents, tools, and items to trade. Some native peoples still follow this nomadic lifestyle, but most now live in settled communities, like this one at Iqaluit in Canada.

Traditional Inuit clothing is often lined with fur to keep out the cold.

TRAVEL IN THE ARCTIC

Transport on land has always been difficult in the Arctic. In the winter, thick snow covers the ground, while the summer thaw turns much of the land into a boggy marsh. Snowshoes and skis stop people sinking into the soft snow, while boots with rough or spiky soles grip well on icy ground. In the past, teams of huskies pulled sledges with supplies over great distances, but in the last 20 years, the dogs have been replaced by snowmobiles. These small, motorized sledges on skis are easy to manoeuvre and can pull very heavy loads.

A B C D E F G H I J K L
1 2 3 4 5 6 7 8 9 10

Cape Deshnev

KEY
Research stations

CHUKCHI SEA

RUSSIAN FEDERATION

ALASKA (USA)

Wrangel
Pevek
Ambarchik

Wrangel I. (Russian Fed.)

Barrow

Prudhoe Bay

BEAUFORT SEA

EAST SIBERIAN SEA

Approximate Limit of Permanent Pack Ice

New Siberian Is. (Russian Fed.)

Tiksi

Kotelniy

LAPTEV SEA

THINGS TO LOOK FOR ON THE MAP

Highest point: Mt. Gunnbjørn, Greenland 3,700 m (12,139 ft) *Map D9*

Most northerly land on Earth: Oodaaq Island, *Map F7*

Lowest temperature in the Arctic: -70°C (-94°F) recorded at Nord station, Greenland *Map F7*

North Pole: *Map F5*

C. Kellett

Banks I. (Canada)

Prince Patrick I. (Canada)

Mould Bay

Melville I. (Canada)

ARCTIC OCEAN

Nordvik

TAYMYR PENINSULA

Cape Chelyuskin

Barrow, USA
☀ Jan -26.5°C (-15.5°F)
July 4.5°C (39.5°F)
❄ Jan 5 mm (0.2 in)
July 23 mm (0.9 in)

Resolute

Axel Heiberg I. (Canada)

Queen Elizabeth Is. (Canada)

North Pole

Severnaya Zemlya (Russian Fed.)

Mys Arktiskogo

Dikson

0 250 500 750 km
0 100 200 300 400 500 miles

Godthåb, Greenland
☀ Jan -9.5°C (14.5°F)
July 7°C (45°F)
❄ Jan 36 mm (1.4 in)
July 56 mm (2.2 in)

Devon I. (Canada)

Ellesmere Island (Canada)

Alert

Approximate Limit of Permanent Pack Ice

KARA SEA

North Pole
☀ Jan -45°C (-49°F)
July 0°C (32°F)

Thule
Dundas

Baffin Island (Canada)

Baffin Bay

KNUD RASMUSSEN LAND

PEARY LAND

Oodaaq Island

Nord

Franz Josef Land (Russian Fed.)

Krenkel

Novaya Zemlya (Russian Fed.)

BARENTS SEA

Pangnirtung

GREENLAND (Denmark)

SVALBARD (Norway)

Ny Ålesund
LONGYEARBYEN

B

Davis Strait

Upernavik

Godhavn

Søndre Strømfjord

Spitsbergen

GREENLAND SEA

GODTHÅB (NUUK)

Frederikshåb

Mt. Gunnbjørn
Ammassalik

Scoresbysund

Denmark Strait

Jan Mayen (Norway)

Julianehåb
Narsarsuaq

C. Farvel

ATLANTIC OCEAN

Nils Nordenskjöld discovered the northeast passage in the Vega in 1879.

REYKJAVIK ICELAND

ARCTIC CIRCLE
TROPIC OF CANCER
EQUATOR
A

ICE-BREAKERS
The Arctic sea ice is usually only about 2 m (6 ft) thick. Ships called ice-breakers are specially constructed with reinforced hulls and bows shaped for ploughing through this icy obstacle. Their powerful engines push the bow on top of the ice until the weight of the ship breaks it and clears a passage for other ships.

ARCTIC EXPLORATION
In the 16th century, European sailors first explored the Arctic seas in search of a new trade route to Asia. English sailors began to map the northwest passage around the top of Canada, while the Dutch explored the northeast passage around Siberia. By 1906, both routes had been successfully navigated. Three years later, the American, Robert Peary, claimed to have reached the North Pole itself. However the speed of his journey has led some explorers to doubt his achievement.

Roald Amundsen sailed through the northwest passage in the Gjöa in 1906.

CROSS-SECTION THROUGH THE ARCTIC
For centuries, some Arctic explorers believed that the polar ice lay on top of a vast continent. In 1958, an American atomic-powered submarine, the USS *Nautilus*, demonstrated that this was untrue by sailing from Alaska to Svalbard underneath the ice. Subsequent exploration beneath the ice has revealed the ridges and basins of the seabed below.

This cross-section follows the line A–B on the map above.

A Canada
Polar ice
Lomonsov Ridge
North Pole
Franz Josef Land
Russian Federation
B
Canada Basin
Fram Basin

THE ANTARCTIC

Unlike the arctic, which is an ocean surrounded by continents, the Antarctic is a continent surrounded by oceans. Antarctica is the remotest, most inhospitable place on Earth, and consists of a large land mass and numerous off-shore islands. Most of the mainland is covered by a vast ice-cap, which breaks up at the coastline, forming huge icebergs up to 200 km (125 miles) long. Antarctica is the only continent that has no permanent human population – the only inhabitants are visiting scientists studying the local environment. It is also unique in being governed by an international treaty that forbids countries from owning or exploiting the land.

CLIMATE

In the winter of 1983, the temperature at the Russian research station, Vostok, reached –89.2°C (–128.6°F), the lowest temperature ever recorded on Earth. Even at the height of summer, temperatures rarely rise above freezing point. Cold winds blow down from the central plateau towards the coasts, causing intense blizzards. The high winds and low temperatures make it dangerous for an unprotected person to be caught outside.

The American-owned Amundsen-Scott base is situated at the South Pole.

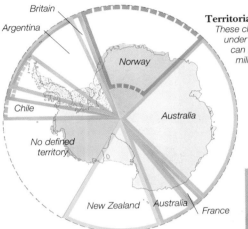

Territorial claims in the Antarctic
These claims have been suspended under the Antarctic Treaty. Stations can be set up for research, but military activities are forbidden.

Britain
Argentina
Norway
Chile
Australia
No defined territory
New Zealand
Australia
France

By taking samples of ice from deep inside the ice-cap, scientists are able to study changes in the climate.

STUDYING ANTARCTICA

Scientists from all over the world come to Antarctica to study its unique climate, weather, geology, and wildlife. The age-old rocks tell them much about the development of the Earth, while analysis of the many meteorites that hit the ice-cap provides valuable information about the universe.

RESEARCH STATIONS

Barely 1,200 people live in Antarctica in the winter, with another 2,500 joining them during the summer months. All are involved in scientific research and live on one of the 46 or so bases dotted around the continent. Each base is specially insulated against the intense cold and some have been constructed below the surface in order to conserve heat. Diesel fuel is used for heating and generating electricity, and enough fuel, food, and other supplies are kept to last an extra year in case the weather prevents new supplies being brought in.

THE ANTARCTIC TREATY

Earlier this century, many countries claimed territory in Antarctica. In order to prevent future conflict, 12 countries signed the Antarctic Treaty in 1959, which suspended all national claims to the land. The treaty designated Antarctica as "a continent for science", and stated that it should be used for peaceful purposes only. Today, more than 42 countries have signed the treaty, which is one of the most successful examples of international co-operation.

TOURISM

Each year, a few intrepid tourists visit Antarctica, exploring the dramatic coastline in cruise ships or flying inland over the ice to land at the South Pole. So far, the small number of tourists has had little effect on the environment which was, however, under threat from the rubbish that was slowly accumulating around the older scientific bases.

Captain Roald Amundsen taking sights at the South Pole in 1911.

ANTARCTIC EXPLORATION

It wasn't until 1820 that the shores of Antarctica were first sighted. From the 1840s onwards, explorers began to map the continent, but the South Pole remained unknown. In the summer of 1911–12, two expeditions – one from Norway led by Roald Amundsen, the other from Britain led by Robert Scott – set out to reach the Pole. Amundsen arrived on 14 December, followed by Scott a month later.

Cruise liners have been bringing tourists to Antarctica since the 1950s, and now bring about 5–6,000 people each year.

A B C D E F G H I J K L

1 2 3 4 5 6 7 8 9 10

Drake Passage

Orcadas *(Argentina)*

South Shetland Is. *(UK)*

South Orkney Is. *(UK)*

SCOTIA SEA

King George I. *(UK)*

Esperanza *(Argentina)*

Anvers I. *(USA)*
7
8

Larsen Ice Shelf

Stonington I. *(UK)*
9

Adelaide I. *(UK)*

ANTARCTIC PENINSULA

BELLINGSHAUSEN SEA

Peter the First I. *(Norway)*

AMUNDSEN SEA

WEDDELL SEA

SANAE *(S. Africa)*

Neumayer *(Germany)*

Riiser-Larsen Ice Shelf

Halley *(UK)*

Belgrano II *(Argentina)*

Filchner Ice Shelf

Ronne Ice Shelf

Vinson Massif ▲

ELLSWORTH MTS.

MARIE BYRD LAND

Getz Ice Shelf

C. Colbeck

ROSS SEA

C. Adare

Balleny Is.

SOUTHERN OCEAN

Fimbul Ice Shelf

QUEEN MAUD LAND

ENDERBY LAND

Syowa *(Japan)*

Lutzow-Holm Bay

Molodezhnaya *(Russian Fed)*

Mawson *(Australia)*

C. Darnley

ANTARCTICA

SOUTH POLAR PLATEAU

Amery Ice Shelf

Lambert Glacier

Prydz Bay

Heard I. *(Australia)*

DAVIS SEA

West Ice Shelf

Amundsen-Scott *(USA)*
South Pole

Vostok *(Russian Fed.)*

Mirnyy *(Russian Fed.)*

Shackleton Ice Shelf

TRANSANTARCTIC MTS.

Ross Ice Shelf

WILKES LAND

Casey *(Australia)*

B
C. Poinsett

McMurdo *(USA)*
Scott Base *(New Zealand)*

VICTORIA LAND

Deepest point of ice ★

Porpoise Bay

Dumont d'Urville *(France)*

SOUTHERN OCEAN

0 200 400 600 800 1000 km
0 200 400 600 miles

KEY
● Numbered Research stations
1 Signy *(UK)*
2 Comandante Ferraz *(Brazil)*
3 Teniente Rodolfo Marsh Martín *(Chile)*
4 Chang Cheng *(China)*
5 King Sejong *(Korea)*
6 Henryk Arctowsky *(Poland)*
7 Palmer *(USA)*
8 Faraday *(UK)*
9 Rothera *(UK)*

South Pole
☀ Jan -23°C (-9.5°F)
July -76°C (-105°F)

Stonington Island
☀ Jan 0°C (32°F)
July -12°C (10.5°F)
❄ Jan 10 mm (0.4 in)
July 33 mm (1.3 in)

EQUATOR
TROPIC OF CAPRICORN
ANTARCTIC CIRCLE

THINGS TO LOOK FOR ON THE MAP

Highest point: Vinson Massif, 4,896 m (16,063 ft) *Map D5*

Lowest temperature on Earth: -89.2°C (-128.6°F) recorded at Vostok Station, *Map H6*

Deepest point of ice: 4,776 m (15,669 ft) *Map H8*

South Pole: *Map F5*

CROSS-SECTION THROUGH THE ANTARCTIC

Antarctica is buried beneath an enormous ice-cap which covers 99.6 per cent of the land area. It has formed from the build up of snow compacted over 100,000 years. The ice-cap contains most of the fresh water on Earth, and 90 per cent of all the ice. If the ice were to melt, the oceans would rise by up to 64 m (210 ft). The ice weighs so much that it pushes much of Antarctica below sea level.

This cross-section follows the line A–B on the map above.

Sea level

Ross Ice Shelf

Transantarctic Mountains

Deepest point of ice

A

B

ANTARCTIC WILDLIFE

Antarctica's severe climate and isolated position have greatly reduced the variety of its wildlife. The largest animal that lives on land all year round is a tiny insect. During the brief summer, however, seals, penguins, and many birds visit the continent to take advantage of the safe breeding sites and plentiful food supply to raise their young. At sea, a dozen species of whale feed off the many seals, fish, and krill that live in the icy waters.

KRILL

Krill are shrimp-like crustaceans up to 5 cm (2 in) in length. They feed on plankton and other crustaceans and occur in such large numbers that they sometimes turn the oceans around Antarctica pink.

EMPEROR PENGUINS

The majestic emperor penguin stands up to 1.15 m (4 ft) tall and can weigh 30 kg (66 lb). After spending most of the year at sea, the emperors come ashore in April to breed. The male alone then incubates the single egg during the icy winter, holding it on his feet to keep it warm. The female returns in July to feed the new-born chick.

POLITICAL SYSTEMS

NO TWO COUNTRIES have identical systems of government, as over the years each country has made up a system that best suits its history, culture, and people. But it is possible to group the political systems of the world into five main categories. Within each category there are many variations. Some countries have a government that is in transition from one category to another, such as Eritrea in Africa, which is moving from colonial rule to full multi-party democracy.

Examples of presidential republics:
USA, Russia, France, Israel, India, Ireland, South Africa

The president of the USA, Bill Clinton (right), with former presidents, George Bush (left) and Gerald Ford (centre).

MULTI-PARTY DEMOCRACY

In a multi-party democracy, people are given a choice between several parties to elect into office. Because this allows different points of view to be expressed in public, and opposition to form against the elected government, not every country can make a multi-party democracy work. Some countries, such as the central Asian states that were once part of the USSR, claim to be multi-party democracies, but real power is actually held by the president.

In a multi-party election, voters choose between more than one candidate.

Voters

Candidates

Candidates from several parties are elected into office.

CONSTITUTIONAL MONARCHY

In a constitutional monarchy, the head of the ruling royal family is head of state and is succeeded by his or her closest relative in hereditary succession. Japan, for example, is a constitutional monarchy whose head of state is the emperor. The monarch has no real power. This is in the hands of the democratically elected government, led by the prime minister, the ruler of the largest party in parliament. Over the years, many countries have evolved from absolute to constitutional monarchies.

Examples of constitutional monarchies:
United Kingdom, Sweden, Spain, Netherlands, Thailand, Japan

Queen Elizabeth II is the UK's head of state.

PRESIDENTIAL REPUBLIC

A presidential republic is a true democracy where voters choose both the head of state – the president – and elect representatives to parliament. It is the most common form of government in the world. In countries such as the USA and South Africa, the president is both the head of state and of government. In France and Russia, the president is elected head of state and chooses the prime minister to run the government, but retains considerable power in the running of the nation. In many countries, such as Ireland, India, and Israel, the president is a symbolic figurehead and real power is held by the prime minister and government.

FEDERAL REPUBLIC

A number of nations, including Germany, are federal republics, with each local state in the republic having considerable power and electing its own prime minister. In Germany, the federal *Bundestag* (assembly) acts as an umbrella over the *Länder* (states), and elects a chancellor (prime minister) to rule the republic as a whole. The president is chosen by the *Länder* and *Bundestag* together.

Examples of a federal republic:
Germany, Austria

ONE-PARTY STATE

In a one-party state, only one political party is allowed to exist. All other parties are forbidden. All power in the state is held by the one party. The former communist states of eastern Europe and many of the African nations are now moving from being one-party states to establishing a multi-party democracy.

In an election, the party decides who its candidate will be and voters are only required to endorse that choice.

Examples of one-party states:
China, Vietnam, North Korea, Guinea Bissau

Voters

One party in office.

One candidate

THEOCRACY

In a theocracy, power is held by religious leaders who rule according to their scriptures. In Iran, the *mullahs* – Muslim scholars and priests – hold the real power, though the government is in non-religious hands. The Vatican City, the world's smallest state, is a mixture between a theocracy and an elected monarchy. The head of state is the Pope, leader of the world's Roman Catholics.

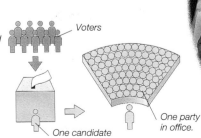

An Iranian mullah

Examples of theocracies:
Iran, Vatican City

ONE-PARTY DOMINATED STATES

Some countries, such as Egypt and Tunisia, claim to be multi-party democracies, but are run by a single party that keeps a firm hold on power, often with the support of the army, as in Syria.

Examples of one-party dominated states:
Egypt, Syria, Tunisia, Kenya, Zaire, Zimbabwe

MILITARY GOVERNMENT

General al-Bashir, head of the military regime in Sudan.

Military governments are usually set up after the army has seized leadership from a weak or unpopular government. All power is held by senior military officers, usually drawn from the army. Elections and parliament are abolished and political parties are declared illegal. Military governments have often held power in South and Central America, Africa, and Asia.

Examples of military governments: Burma, Sudan

DICTATORSHIP

A number of countries around the world are ruled by single rulers, called dictators, who have absolute authority. Most dictators gain power either through military coups (an army takeover), or by seizing leadership from an existing ruler, as in Iraq. Once in office, dictators rule in a personal, often brutal, fashion, eliminating all opposition to themselves.

Saddam Hussain has been the dictatorial ruler of Iraq since 1979.

Example of a dictatorship: Iraq

ABSOLUTE MONARCHY

King Hussein of Jordan

In an absolute monarchy, power is held by the ruling monarch of the country and is handed down through the royal family to his or her successor. In the past, absolute monarchs kept all power to themselves, but today most appoint a small advisory council to help them rule.

MONARCHY WITH A PARTIAL DEMOCRATIC SYSTEM

In some countries, the ruling monarch retains a strong grip on the government but allows some limited democracy. In Jordan, King Hussein has allowed direct elections to the lower House of Representatives, but keeps strong control by appointing all 30 members of the upper house, or Senate.

Examples of absolute monarchies: Saudi Arabia, Brunei, Bahrain, Qatar, Oman

Examples of monarchies with partial democratic systems: Jordan, Tonga, Morroco

POLITICAL TERMS

Alliance A formal agreement between nations for economic, political, or military reasons.

Apartheid A policy of separating people by race.

Capitalism A system in which wealth and profit in the hands of a few people drives the country's economy.

Communism A system in which property and land are owned by the whole community and each person is paid according to their needs and abilities.

Democracy A system in which people vote for the government of their choice.

Economy The organization of a country's finances, exports, imports, industries, and services.

Multi-party elections More than one party standing for election.

Nationalized Industries or services owned by the state.

Privatization State-owned organizations taken over by private companies.

Republic A state where people elect the head of state and the government.

Socialism A system in which the economy is controlled by the whole community.

Trade union An organized group of workers united to protect their rights and interests.

West, the Countries in Europe and North America with capitalist economies and democratic governments that share similar cultural values.

DEPENDENT TERRITORIES

Not every country rules itself. About 10 million people around the world live under the protection of either the UK, Denmark, Norway, France, Portugal, the USA, New Zealand, or Australia. Most dependent territories are relics of the colonial era that have remained attached to their former colonial rulers. Some territories are now changing status. Hong Kong, for example, reverts from British to Chinese rule in 1997. Some territories are retained because of their strategic or economic importance, while others remain colonies because they are too small, remote, or weak to survive on their own.

Examples of dependent territories

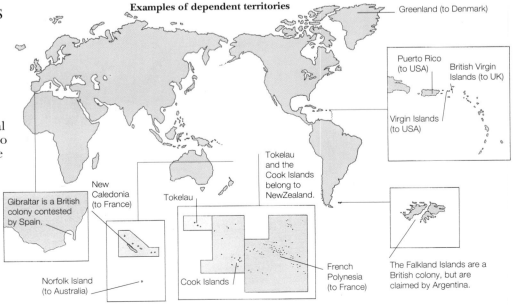

Greenland (to Denmark)

Puerto Rico (to USA)

British Virgin Islands (to UK)

Virgin Islands (to USA)

Tokelau and the Cook Islands belong to New Zealand.

Gibraltar is a British colony contested by Spain.

New Caledonia (to France)

Tokelau

Norfolk Island (to Australia)

Cook Islands

French Polynesia (to France)

The Falkland Islands are a British colony, but are claimed by Argentina.

INTERNATIONAL ORGANIZATIONS

As MORE AND MORE NATIONS have gained their independence, the need for international organizations to bring the different nations together has never been greater. Some, such as the United Nations (UN), are truly international, and seek to promote world peace and understanding. Others are continental or regional in character, and either link their members into a loose association with common aims, such as the Organization of African Unity, or else are more structured and bind their members closely together in trade and economic agreements, such as the European Union.

THE UNITED NATIONS

The United Nations (UN) was established in 1945 after World War II. The UN has four aims: to preserve world peace and security, to encourage nations to be just in their actions, to help nations co-operate, and to serve as an agency through which nations can work towards these goals. All member states agree to the principle of settling their disputes peacefully, and not using force against other nations, except in self-defence. Today almost every country in the world is a member of the UN.

THE ECONOMIC AND SOCIAL COUNCIL

The Economic and Social Council (ESC) looks after economic, social, cultural, educational, and health matters in UN member states. It also works to guarantee human rights. The Council has 54 members, elected by a two-thirds majority vote of the General Assembly, the main institution of the UN. A large number of specialized agencies report to the ESC (see below), some of which were in existence long before the UN itself was created.

UN aid in action at a camp for Rwandan refugees in Tanzania.

MAJOR AGENCIES UNDER THE ESC	
FAO Food and Agriculture Organization	**IMO** International Maritime Organization
IBRD International Bank for Reconstruction and Development (World Bank)	**ITU** International Telecommunications Union
ICAO International Civil Aviation Organization	**UNESCO** UN Educational, Scientific, and Cultural Organization
ILO International Labour Organization	**UPU** Universal Postal Union
IMF International Monetary Fund	**WHO** World Health Organization
	WMO World Meteorological Organization

Cambodians leaving refugee camps in Thailand under the protection of the UN.

THE SECURITY COUNCIL

The Security Council is the decision-making body of the UN, summoned in times of crisis to help secure peace. The Council can pass resolutions demanding that countries stop fighting each other, or agree to send troops to keep the peace. The troops are drawn from national armies but they serve under the UN. The Council has five permanent members – USA, Russia, China, Britain, and France.

MAJOR UN PEACE-KEEPING FORCES
UNFICYP UN Peacekeeping Force in Cyprus
UNIFIL UN Interim Force in Lebanon
UNOMIG UN Observer Mission in Georgia
UNOMIL UN Observer Mission in Liberia
UNOMOZ UN Operation in Mozambique
UNOMUR UN Observer Mission in Uganda-Rwanda

THE EUROPEAN UNION

The European Union (EU) grew out of the wish of European nations after World War II to prevent another war in Europe. The organization, originally called the European Economic Community (EEC), has set up a single market with all barriers to the free movement of goods, people, and services between the member countries abolished. The EU is now working towards full economic union, with one currency for all nations. The EU is also moving towards full political union, developing into a federal state of Europe.

Members of the EU

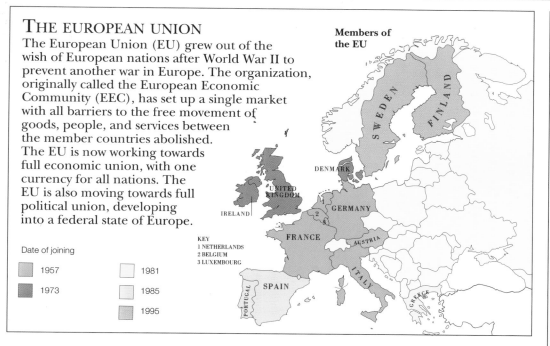

Date of joining

1957		1981	
1973		1985	
		1995	

KEY
1 NETHERLANDS
2 BELGIUM
3 LUXEMBOURG

Major international organizations

This map shows the member states of some of the major organizations around the world. A description of these groups is given on the right.

- NATO
- ASEAN
- OAU
- NAFTA
- Arab League
- OPEC

Greenpeace organizes many protests against environmental pollution.

SINGLE-ISSUE ORGANIZATIONS

There are various international groups (see below) that devote themselves to a particular political, social, or environmental issue. Some of these groups put pressure on governments to bring about change.

EXAMPLES OF SINGLE-ISSUE GROUPS

Amnesty International Group that campaigns for human rights around the world.

Greenpeace An international direct-action group that campaigns against abuse of the natural world.

IAEA The International Atomic Energy Agency promotes the peaceful use of atomic energy.

IOC The International Olympic Committee organizes the summer and winter Olympics.

IWC The International Whaling Commission promotes the conservation of whales and conducts whale research.

Non-Proliferation Treaty Signed by more than 140 nations, this 1968 treaty pledges its members not to export nuclear weapons to non-nuclear states, and to work towards arms control.

Red Cross An international organization concerned with the alleviation of human suffering and the promotion of public health. The Red Crescent serves Arab nations.

OTHER INTERNATIONAL ORGANIZATIONS

APEC Asia-Pacific Economic Co-operation promotes links across the Pacific between 15 Pacific Rim nations.

Arab League A forum for 21 Arab nations to discuss social, political, and military issues.

ASEAN The Association of South East Asian Nations promotes economic, cultural, and defence co-operation between six non-communist states in the region.

CBSS The Council of the Baltic States formed in 1992 to promote co-operation among 10 states around the Baltic Sea.

CEI The Central European Initiative evolved in 1991 to link together 10 central European and Adriatic states.

CIS The Commonwealth of Independent States grew out of the former USSR in 1991. It links Russia and 11 former Soviet republics in a variety of economic and political ways.

Commonwealth, The This grouping links the UK and 50 of its former colonies together. Although many member states are republics, the organization is headed by the British monarch, Queen Elizabeth II.

Council of Europe A Europe-wide organization, independent of the EU, that seeks to promote human rights and safeguard basic freedoms.

G7 Group of seven major industrial powers – Canada, France, Germany, Italy, Japan, the UK, and the USA, with the EU as an observer – which meets regularly to discuss the world economy.

GCC Six oil-rich Gulf states set up the Gulf Co-operation Council to promote regional economic and defence co-operation.

NAFTA The North American Free Trade Agreement links Canada, the USA, and Mexico in a free-trade zone.

NATO The North Atlantic Treaty Organization promotes defence co-operation between the USA and Western Europe.

OAU The Organization of African Unity promotes unity and co-operation between its 52 African member states.

OPEC The Organization of Petroleum Exporting Countries has 12 oil-rich members from around the world. It exists to co-ordinate the petroleum pricing and export policies of its members, so as best to protect their interests.

WORLD RELIGIONS

THROUGHOUT HISTORY, people have asked questions about the meaning of life and death and have sought answers through religion. There are many faiths throughout the world, each with its own practice and belief. Some religions, such as Christianity, have spread over the world; others, such as traditional African beliefs, have stayed in one place. The world's major faiths roughly divide into two groups – the Western tradition and the Eastern tradition. The Western tradition originated in the Near and Middle East and includes Judaism, Christianity, and Islam. The Eastern tradition began in India and includes Hinduism and Buddhism.

RELIGIOUS FOLLOWERS
This chart shows the percentage of people belonging to each of the major world religions. More than 1,800 million people are Christians, the greatest number of followers of any faith in the world. The fastest-growing religion is Islam, with 971 million followers. The figure for "others" includes those who do not follow any faith.

Christianity: 33.4% Others: 29.5% Islam: 17.7% Hinduism: 13.4% Buddhism: 5.7% Judaism: 0.3%

THE RELIGIOUS WORLD
The most widely distributed religion in the world is Christianity, which was spread to every continent by European colonists and traders. Both Hinduism and Islam are spreading away from their places of origin as their followers settle in cities in Europe and North America.

This map shows only the dominant religion in each country. The symbols indicate where there is a large minority of another faith.

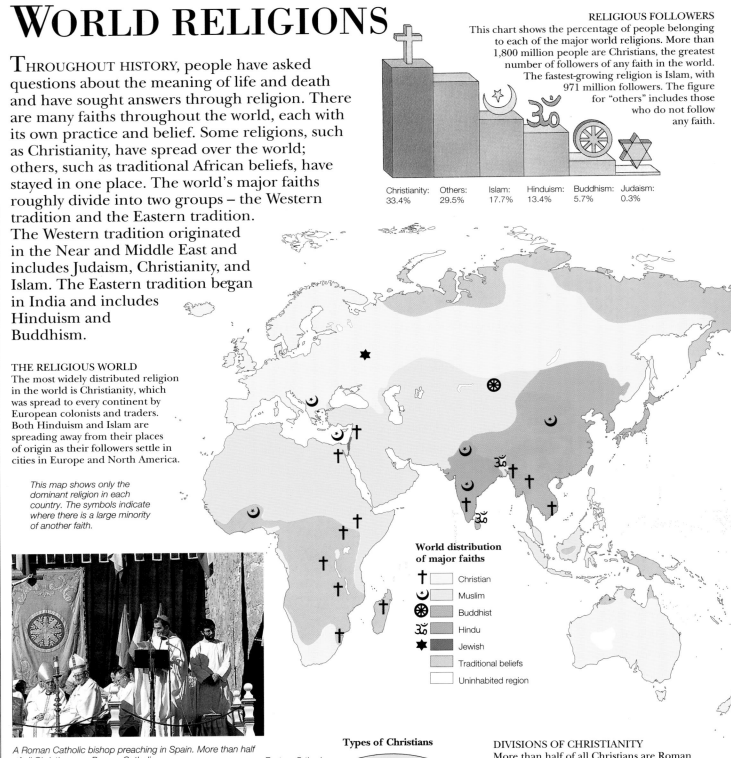

World distribution of major faiths
- ✝ Christian
- ☪ Muslim
- ✺ Buddhist
- ॐ Hindu
- ✡ Jewish
- Traditional beliefs
- Uninhabited region

A Roman Catholic bishop preaching in Spain. More than half of all Christians are Roman Catholic.

CHRISTIANITY
Christianity was founded almost 2,000 years ago by Jesus Christ, who was born in Bethlehem, in Israel. Jesus was born into the Jewish faith, but began to interpret the Jewish Bible in a new way. After his death, his teachings were written down and collected together in the New Testament of the Bible. Christians believe in one God. They claim that Jesus is the Son of God, that he rose from the dead, and that those who follow him will have eternal life. The Christian symbol is the cross on which Jesus was killed.

Types of Christians
- Eastern Orthodox: 9.3%
- Others: 10.2%
- Protestants: 24.5%
- Roman Catholics: 56%

DIVISIONS OF CHRISTIANITY
More than half of all Christians are Roman Catholics, who follow the leadership of the Pope in Rome. There are large numbers of Catholics in southern Europe, Central and South America, and the Philippines. One quarter of Christians are Protestants, who split from the Catholic Church 500 years ago, and belong to a number of self-governing churches. The main areas of Protestantism are in northern Europe and North America. About one in ten Christians belong to one of the Eastern Orthodox Churches of eastern Europe and Russia; each national church has its own Patriarch, or leader.

OTHER FAITHS

SIKHISM This faith began in the Punjab region of India in the 1400s. Its founder was Guru Nanak. He was succeeded by nine other Gurus who all helped to develop Sikhism. The *Guru Granth Sahib* is the Sikh holy book. The religion is based on the worship of one God and on the cycle of human rebirth. Sikhs believe that God is found in all things, and that all people are equal in the eyes of God. Sikhism is mainly practised in India, but followers are also found throughout the world.

CONFUCIANISM More like a philosophy than a religion, Confucianism was founded by Confucius, or K'ung Fu Tze, in around 500BC. It is not based on the worship of a god but on following a moral code. Confucianism is practised in China and other parts of east Asia.

TAOISM This faith was founded in China by Lao Tzu around 300BC. Taoists believe in many gods and aim to live in harmony with nature. Their symbol, *Yin Yang*, stands for balance and harmony. Taoism is followed in China and other parts of east Asia.

SHINTOISM The ancient religion of Japan is based on the worship of gods of nature and ancestor worship. Most Shinto shrines are in parks, gardens, and on mountains.

JAINISM Jains do not believe in a god; their faith is based on non-violence to all living things and a belief in rebirth. Most of its followers live in India.

ZEN BUDDHISM Very important in Japan, this branch of Buddhism originated in China. It aims at harmony in living and stresses the need for meditation.

TRADITIONAL BELIEFS Around the world, there are numerous local religions handed down by word of mouth from generation to generation. Many share a belief that there are spirits living in the world – in the sky, stars, trees, lakes, and rivers. Many traditional faiths are found in Africa, where beliefs vary widely depending on the individual tribe. The ancient faith of Shamanism, found in parts of Asia, centres on a priest, or *shaman*, who produces trances to enable people to leave their bodies and visit the spiritual world.

When they pray, Muslims face in the direction of Mecca.

ISLAM

Muslims follow the Islamic faith, which is based on a belief in one God, Allah. Islam shares the same roots as Judaism and Christianity, all three recognizing certain prophets, such as Abraham. The last and greatest of the Islamic prophets was Mohammed, who was born in Mecca, Saudi Arabia, in AD570. The words revealed to Mohammed by Allah were later written down in the Koran. After Mohammed's death, Islam split into two branches: the traditional Sunnis, who follow Mohammed's original successors (the Caliphs), and the radical Shi'ites, who followed Mohammed's cousin and son-in-law, Ali. Shi'ites are the majority in Iran and Iraq, Sunnis the majority elsewhere.

JUDAISM

Judaism, the religion of the Jews, began in about 2000BC when the ancient Hebrew people settled in what is now mainly Israel. Judaism is the parent of the other two major monotheist (one-god) religions, Christianity and Islam. There is no single founder, but Abraham was the first leader. The scripture is the Jewish Bible, of which the Torah (the first five books) is the most important part. After persecution in Europe, the Jewish people established a homeland in Israel in 1948, although Jews are found in most countries of the world. The Jewish symbol is the six-pointed Star of David.

The Jewish menorah, or seven-branched candleholder.

Shiva is the Hindu God of good and evil. Statues and pictures of gods are often found in Hindu homes.

HINDUISM

Hinduism originated in India in about 1750BC – the word "Hindu" comes from the Persian for "India". The faith has no single founder or scripture, though the earliest beliefs were written down in the *Vedas*, a collection of hymns and chants. Most Hindus believe in many gods but in one underlying reality (*Brahman*). They believe that when a person dies their soul is reborn again in another body. People who live good lives are born again in a higher life; bad lives lead to a lower life. Devout Hindus aim to be free from the cycle of rebirth and become one with *Brahman*. The Hindu symbol is a sacred sound, "Om".

A Tibetan Buddhist monk holding a prayer wheel.

BUDDHISM

Buddhism is based on the teachings of Buddha, the "Enlightened One", a prince who was born in India in about 563BC. Buddha taught that suffering is always present in daily life and is caused by desiring things. Freedom from desire leads to the end of suffering and the attainment of perfect peace, or *nirvana*. Although Buddhism began in India, most Buddhists today are found elsewhere, in China, Sri Lanka, Tibet, and southeast Asia.

HEALTH

IN THE LAST 100 YEARS, the world has become a healthier place to live. Advances in medical science, improved diet, higher standards of living, and better health education have all helped people to live longer and healthier lives. However, many problems remain, especially in the poorer countries of Africa and Asia. While immunization has protected millions of children against disease, many illnesses remain common. Tuberculosis and malaria are widespread, and thousands of babies die each year of tetanus. In the richer areas of the world, which include North America, Oceania, and Europe, cancer and heart disease affect many people.

HIGHEST LIFE EXPECTANCY	
Japan	79
Iceland	78
Sweden	78
Switzerland	78

LOWEST LIFE EXPECTANCY	
Sierra Leone	42
Afghanistan	43
Guinea Bissau	43
Uganda	43
Gambia	44
Guinea	44

LIFE EXPECTANCY
Life expectancy is a measure of how long a person is likely to live. In 1950, the average person expected to live for 40 years. Better health care and nutrition mean that most people now live to be at least 63. However, this figure hides the huge differences between rich and poor countries, and the social groups within them. Wealthier people are generally healthier than poor, and rich countries, such as Japan, which has the highest life expectancy in the world, are generally healthier places to live.

PEOPLE PER DOCTOR
One way of measuring the provision of health care in a country is to count the number of people cared for by each doctor (map and chart, right). Countries that are rich or have good welfare systems provide easy access to health services, and on average have one doctor for every 390 people. In contrast, there is only one doctor to every 50,000 people in the world's poorer African countries, and over half the population live more than 10 km (6 miles) from a doctor or medical centre.

Number of people per doctor
- Above 10,000
- 5,000–10,000
- 1,000–5,000
- Below 1,000
- Figures not available

Russsian Federation: 210

Australia: 440

Pakistan: 2,940

Kenya: 71,430

HIGHEST CHILD MORTALITY	
Country	*per 1,000 births*
Afghanistan	270
Sierra Leone	250
Guinea Bissau	240
Mozambique	240
Gambia	230
Malawi	230

CHILD MORTALITY
The child mortality rate is the number of deaths of children under five years of age per 1,000 births. In some areas of the world, such as Afghanistan and parts of Africa, poor medical care and lack of nourishment lead to a high number of child deaths. The story is much better in Europe and North America where less than 10 out of every 1,000 under-fives die.

PREVENTIVE MEDICINE
There are many ways of safeguarding against illness. Immunization protects people from catching diseases such as measles and tetanus. In rich countries most children are immunized, but in some poor countries only 30 per cent of children receive this care. Across the world, adults are warned of the dangers of smoking, alcohol, and drugs. Attention to water quality, food hygiene, sanitation, and good housing all play their part in keeping people healthy. Campaigns by the media and in schools and clinics help to educate people in health care.

This boy is having his weight checked. A balanced diet is essential to good health.

EDUCATION

EDUCATION IS ONE OF the most important ways of creating a better world, for it enables people to improve their own lives. Most children receive a primary education up to the age of 11, which gives them the basic skills of reading, writing, and mathematics. About half the world's children also receive a secondary education up to the age of 16 or 18, and some go on to higher education. But education provision varies greatly. Children in rich countries generally receive a better education than those in poorer areas. One of the biggest problems for poor countries is that having fewer educated people, they are less capable of coping with the demands of the modern world.

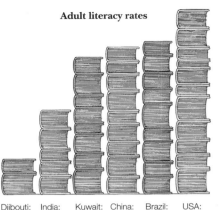

Adult literacy rates

Djibouti: 19% India: 50% Kuwait: 74% China: 80% Brazil: 82% USA: 99%

ADULT LITERACY
The adult literacy rate of a country shows how many adults over the age of 15 can read and write. The test involves asking a person to read and write a short, simple statement about their everyday life. In the USA, for example, the literacy rate is 99 per cent, which means that only one adult in 100 cannot read or write. In the poor country of Djibouti in east Africa the rate is only 19 per cent, which shows a low level of national education.

EDUCATION LEVELS
This map shows adult literacy rates across the world. A country's education level is related to its wealth, as mostly richer countries have the money to provide adequate schools, teachers, and books. In turn, education adds to the national wealth as it provides well-educated young people to work in the factories, offices, and farms. Better education helps farmers produce more crops, and office workers become better managers.

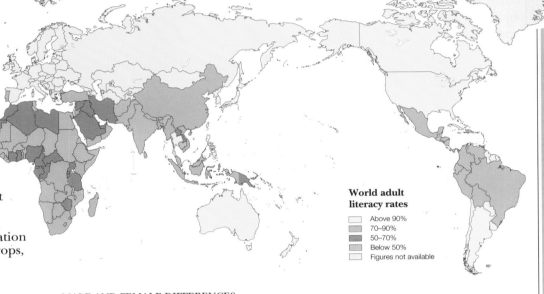

World adult literacy rates
- Above 90%
- 70–90%
- 50–70%
- Below 50%
- Figures not available

Children in Japan work hard to pass their exams. Many attend special classes on Saturdays or in the evenings.

EFFICIENT EDUCATION
Japan has one of the most efficient education systems in the world. Nearly all children attend a nursery before they are old enough to go to primary school, and one-third of children stay on for higher education. Japanese children do well in science and maths, which are subjects much in demand by industries to help them achieve success. South Korea and Taiwan, both strongly influenced by Japan, have similar education systems.

MALE AND FEMALE DIFFERENCES
In many poorer countries, girls are not educated as well as boys. Girls often have to help in the home and have little time left for education. But the situation is improving, as educating women has great benefits – it improves health care and hygiene, and helps reduce infant deaths.

Male and female differences in literacy rates

Male average: 100

Brazil: 96% Iraq: 70% Nigeria: 65% India: 55% Burkina Faso: 32%

In each case the female figure is a percentage of the male average, which is given as 100. The closer the figure to 100, the smaller the gap in literacy rates.

Children being taught in a rural school in Bangladesh.

RURAL AND URBAN SCHOOLING
In the poorer countries of Africa and Asia, children who live in towns usually receive a better education than those who live in the countryside. This is because many country children are needed to stay at home to work the land and help in the family, and would have to travel long distances to get to school. However, educating rural children can bring great advantages, because they can develop skills to increase productivity in agriculture and local industry.

RICH AND POOR

THE DIFFERENCE IN WEALTH between the richest and poorest countries is vast. The average person in Mozambique earns one six-hundredth of the average person in Switzerland. How wealthy a country is depends on its natural resources, industrial strength, population size, and political stability. Libya is much richer than its southern neighbour, Chad. Both are desert countries with small populations, but Libya has oil while Chad has few natural resources. Many poor countries borrow money from richer countries to finance new industries. Repayment of the debt is expensive, with the result that poor countries remain poor, while rich countries continue to grow richer.

RICHEST COUNTRIES (1991) (Based on real GDP per person)	
Country	US$
USA	22,130
Switzerland	21,780
Luxembourg	20,800
Germany	19,770
Japan	19,390

POOREST COUNTRIES (1991) (Based on real GDP per person)	
Country	US$
Ethiopia	370
Chad	447
Zaire	469
Mali	480
Guinea	500

NATIONAL WEALTH

There are two measures of national wealth. The Gross Domestic Product (GDP) measures the total value of finished goods and services produced by a national economy. The Gross National Product (GNP) measures GDP and the income from abroad that flows into the country. Both figures are usually expressed in US dollars. When the figures are divided by the total population of the country, they give an indication of how rich or poor that country is. The tables on the left show that whereas the five richest countries span three continents, the five poorest countries are all in Africa.

World distribution of wealth

The wealthiest areas of the world are North America, Japan, Australia, United Arab Emirates, and parts of Europe. The poorest areas are parts of Africa and southern Asia. Figures are based on real GDP per person.

Pounding millet in Burkina Faso. Millet is a basic food in many African countries.

ABSOLUTE AND RELATIVE POVERTY

About a quarter of the world's population live in "absolute poverty". This means that their basic needs for a healthy life are not met: they have little or no food to eat, are often homeless and are poorly clothed. The vast majority of these people live in southern and eastern Asia and the area south of the Sahara Desert in Africa. Many more people live in "relative poverty", that is, they are much poorer than the majority of people living in the same country.

THE NEWLY RICH

Historically, the wealthy countries of the world have been in Europe and North America. With the discovery of oil reserves in the Middle East in the past 60 years, the desert states of the Arabian Peninsula are now among the richest nations in the world. Also, the spectacular growth of the southeast Asian economies, such as Hong Kong, Taiwan, South Korea, and Singapore – which have all followed in the footsteps of Japan – means that these countries will soon join the world's wealthiest nations.

Oil has brought wealth to many people in Saudi Arabia, the largest country in the Arabian Peninsula.

SOCIAL POVERTY

In most countries, there are groups of people who are poorer than others. Women are usually poorer than men – they are often paid less (see chart right) or are housewives with no income. Also, women often have a lower standard of education, which means they do not have the qualifications to obtain higher-paid jobs. Single mothers and elderly single women are particularly at risk from poverty. Older people on low pensions and the sick are also poorer than average. In some places, such as São Paulo in Brazil (shown left), children are forced to live on the streets because they have no families to support them or homes to live in. They often beg or turn to crime to survive.

Male and female wages

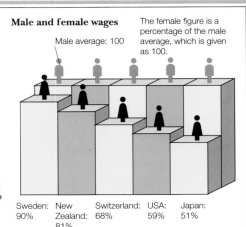

Male average: 100

The female figure is a percentage of the male average, which is given as 100.

| Sweden: 90% | New Zealand: 81% | Switzerland: 68% | USA: 59% | Japan: 51% |

Map key

Figures are in US$ and based on real GDP per person.

- Above 15,000
- 10,000–15,000
- 5,000–10,000
- 1,000–5,000
- Below 1,000
- Figures not available

Auckland, New Zealand. Most New Zealanders enjoy a high standard of living.

Wealthy city-dwellers walk past a beggar in San Francisco, USA.

DIFFERENCES IN WEALTH

Within many countries there are great differences in income between rich and poor. In Europe and North America there are many homeless people on the streets or seeking shelter in cardboard boxes. In some poor countries, such as India, rich landowners and industrial managers flourish. In Brazil, the poorest 20 per cent of the people earn only 2.1 per cent of the total income, while the richest 20 per cent earn 67.5 per cent, a difference of 32 times. In comparison, the poorest 20 per cent in Hungary earn 10.9 per cent, and the richest 20 per cent earn 34.3 per cent, a difference of only 3.2 times.

Some countries that give aid

Figures are a percentage of the government's budget.

- USA: 0.8%
- UK: 1.2%
- Japan: 1.3%
- Canada: 2%
- France: 3.2%
- Denmark: 3.2%

Some countries that receive aid

Figures shown are per person.

- Mozambique: $US 92
- Somalia: $US 62
- Ethiopia: $US 24
- Bangladesh: $US 14
- Afghanistan: $US 9
- India: $US 3

AID

In order to help the world's poorest countries, the richer nations give them aid in the form of grants, loans, or, when a natural disaster such as an earthquake occurs, food, tents, and clothing. Some African countries, such as Mozambique, depend on aid for much of their income. The largest source of aid is the USA, which provides more than $11 billion a year, though this is only 0.8 per cent of its total government spending.

EQUAL WEALTH DISTRIBUTION

Some countries strive for a more equal distribution of wealth among their citizens, so that there are few, if any, very rich or very poor people. Some governments spend a large proportion of national wealth on education, health care, social welfare, and job creation to help all people in society. New Zealand was the first country in the world to introduce a full welfare state, while Scandinavian countries such as Sweden concentrated on providing jobs for everyone. Today they are among the most equal societies in the world.

WORLD TRADE

TRADE BETWEEN THE COUNTRIES of the world allows each nation to specialize in the goods it produces best. A country sells its products abroad to buy goods that are produced more cheaply elsewhere. Trade creates wealth and jobs by encouraging countries to produce goods that can be sold abroad, or exported. However, the benefits of trade are not evenly spread across all countries – some produce a range of goods much more cheaply than others, and these gain the most from trading. Today, much of world trade is controlled by about 200 multinational companies, which have offices and factories across the globe.

USA: 13.2%
Germany: 11.5%
Japan: 8%
UK: 5.8%
France: 6.5%

THE BIG FIVE
Between them, five countries account for almost half the entire amount of world trade. The USA is the world's biggest trading nation, with 13.2 per cent of the total, Germany is second with 11.5 per cent, and Japan, France, and the UK are not far behind. The other 186 nations of the world share 55 per cent of world trade.

SHARE OF WORLD TRADE
The 23 richest countries in the world control 74 per cent of all world trade. The 40 poorest countries, such as Ethiopia and Laos, control only 5 per cent. The remaining 128 countries, such as the nations of eastern Europe and much of South America, control 21 per cent.

Rich: 74%
Low income: 5%
Middle income: 21%

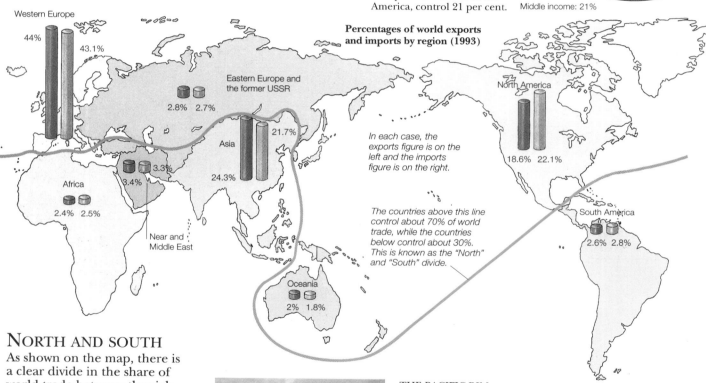

Percentages of world exports and imports by region (1993)

Western Europe
44% 43.1%

Eastern Europe and the former USSR
2.8% 2.7%

Asia
21.7%
24.3%

Near and Middle East
3.4% 3.3%

Africa
2.4% 2.5%

North America
18.6% 22.1%

South America
2.6% 2.8%

Oceania
2% 1.8%

In each case, the exports figure is on the left and the imports figure is on the right.

The countries above this line control about 70% of world trade, while the countries below control about 30%. This is known as the "North" and "South" divide.

NORTH AND SOUTH
As shown on the map, there is a clear divide in the share of world trade between the rich economies of the "North" and the poor economies of the "South". In order to prosper, a country needs to have a positive balance of trade, that is, earn more from exports than it spends on imports. Many nations have a negative balance of trade – importing more than they export. In order to improve their trade balance, many have grouped together to form regional trading blocs, such as the European Union (EU).

THE PACIFIC RIM
The centre of world trade is shifting from the USA and Europe to the USA and Asia, in particular those countries found around the edge of the Pacific Ocean, an area known as the Pacific Rim. Here, some of the fastest-growing economies in the world are found. Countries such as South Korea and Thailand, as well as the island states of Singapore (left), Hong Kong, and Taiwan, have developed hi-tech electronic industries, exporting their low-cost products around the world. Secure government and encouragement of foreign investment have helped generate trade.

Pacific Rim economies
Figures show the average percentage rate of economic growth (1980–93). The USA is included for comparison.

Thailand: 6.4%
South Korea: 8.2%
Singapore: 6.1%
USA: 1.7%
Hong Kong: 5.4%

Major oil exporters and importers

Arrows show the main oil trade routes.

THE OIL TRADE

Without oil, the world would grind to a halt. Industry and transport would stop, and many homes would be cold. This is why oil is the single most important product traded in the world today. Oil is produced and exported by a few countries, mostly in the Middle East, north and west Africa, and Central and South America, and is transported through pipelines or by tanker. The three main regions that import oil are eastern Asia (including Japan), Europe, and the USA.

Bananas are St Lucia's main export product.

SERVICE INDUSTRIES
During the past 30 years, the fastest-growing area in world trade has been the service industries. These include banking, insurance, finance, tourism, airlines, and shipping. Money earned from service industries, which do not make things but provide a service for others, is called "invisible earnings".

TRADE DEPENDENCY

Some countries rely almost entirely on one product to sell abroad. For example, many of the Caribbean islands, such as St Lucia, depend on bananas for a large percentage of their income. This dependency on one product can leave a country at the mercy of events beyond its control. If the price of a commodity rises around the world, the country will benefit, but if the price drops, or a natural disaster such as a hurricane destroys the harvest, the country can be plunged into economic hardship.

Other: 2.1%
Mining: 9.3%
Agriculture: 9.4%
Services: 21.9%
Manufacturing: 57.3%

WHAT IS TRADED

World trade is dominated by manufactured goods, such as cars and computers. Most of these are made by rich countries. Poorer countries generally produce food and raw materials (primary products). This means that rich countries are growing richer, because at present bigger profits are to be made by exporting expensive manufactured goods rather than cheaper primary products.

One-product economies

Figures show percentage of export earnings provided by one product.

Nigeria: Oil 98%
Ghana: Cocoa 80%
Laos: Timber 76%
Bangladesh: Jute 51%
St Lucia: Bananas 60%
Niger: Uranium 67%
Cuba: Sugar 75%

GLOSSARY

Aboriginals: the earliest known, original, inhabitants of a country; most often used to refer to the native peoples of Australia.

Acid rain: rain that has been polluted by gases from factories and traffic; when the rain falls it can damage crops, forests, and lakes.

Apartheid: the policy, developed in South Africa, of separating people according to their race.

Archipelago: a large group of islands

Arid: dry; with little rainfall.

Barren: lacking in vegetation; not able to produce fruit or crops.

Bauxite: the mineral ore from which aluminium is obtained.

By-product: a substance produced as a result of making something else.

Capitalism: an economic system based on private ownership of property, and on free and competitive conditions for business.

Cash crops: crops that are grown specifically to be sold for a profit.

Cattle ranch: a large farm where cattle are reared.

Civil war: a war between rival groups who live in the same country or region.

Collective farm: a farm owned and run by a group of people working together.

Colonize: to send a group of people to settle in another land and establish a colony.

Colony: a region or country that is controlled by another country; a group of people settled in a land outside their homeland but still ruled by its laws.

Commercial farming: raising crops or animals for sale and profit.

Communism: an economic and political system in which farms and factories and the goods they produce are owned by the state.

Consumer goods: goods such as cars, computers, and televisions, purchased by people for personal use.

Co-operative farm: see Collective farm

Crude oil: petroleum in its natural state, before it has been treated in any way.

Culture: the values, beliefs, and way of life of the people of a country or region.

Deforestation: the large-scale clearing of healthy trees, often to make room for cash crops or for cattle ranching.

Delta: the flat area (often triangular in shape) formed by material deposited at the mouth of some rivers where they enter the sea or a large lake; deltas usually have highly fertile soil.

Democracy: a form of government based on the rule of the people, usually through representatives who have been voted into office by the people.

Dependency: a land run by another, usually more powerful, country.

Deposit: a natural grouping of minerals, such as oil or coal, within the Earth.

Dictatorship: a system of government where the ruler, or dictator, has absolute power.

Economy: the system by which a society manages its resources, makes and distributes goods and services.

Emigrant: a person who leaves their native country to settle in another.

Empire: a country and the conquered lands which it rules.

Environment: the natural world around us.

Ethnic group: a group of people sharing a common racial, religious, or cultural background.

Ethnic mix: the mix of ethnic groups in a country or region.

Export earnings: the money a country earns from selling goods or services to other countries.

Exports: goods or services sold to another country.

Extended family: a family which may include grandparents and other relatives as well as their children.

Favela: name used in Brazil for a shanty town.

Fertility rate: the average number of children born to a woman of childbearing age.

Fundamentalism: the belief that all the teachings of a particular religion must be strictly obeyed.

Guerilla: a member of a small, military group fighting a stronger, official army, usually through surprise attacks.

Gulf: a large area of sea partly enclosed by land, such as the Persian Gulf or the Gulf of Mexico.

Hardwood: wood from broad-leaved trees, such as beech, oak, and mahogany.

Health care: medical services that diagnose and treat illness, and provide care for pregnant women, the elderly, and disabled.

High-tech industries: industries that use or make the most recently invented and technologically advanced products, such as computers.

Hunter-gatherers: people who feed themselves by hunting wild animals and gathering fruits, nuts, and berries.

Hydroelectric power: electricity created by capturing the power of running water.

Immigrant: a person who has come from another country to settle.

Imports: goods or services bought from another country.

Indigenous people: the first or native people of an area or country.

Industry: economic activity that is concerned with manufacturing goods or processing raw materials.

Investment: the provision of resources, usually money, for a business venture, with the aim of later making a profit from it.

Irrigation: supplying dry land with water through a system of canals or pipes so that crops will grow.

Landlocked: surrounded by land; with no access to the sea.

Latin America: those parts of the American continent where the official language is Spanish or Portuguese; often used to mean Mexico, Central and South America.

Life expectancy: the average number of years a person can expect to live.

Literacy rate: the percentage of people over the age of 15 who can read and write a simple sentence.

Manufactured goods: products made from raw materials using machines, or made by hand.

Mestizo: a person of mixed race with one parent European and the other native Indian.

Migrant: a person moving from one place or country to settle in another.

Mineral: a natural substance found in rocks of the Earth, such as a metal; removed by mining.

Missionary: a person who goes abroad trying to convert others to their particular religion.

Monarchy: a country ruled by a king or queen, who has usually inherited the position rather than been elected by the people.

Monsoon: a wind that changes direction with the change of seasons; it causes a rainy season from April to October in southern Asia.

Multicultural: a group of people or society made up of various different ethnic groups.

Native peoples: the people who belong by birth or origin to a place.

Natural resources: materials which occur naturally in an area, such as wood, coal, oil, or gas.

Nomads: people who move from place to place in search of food, water, and land to graze their animals.

Northern hemisphere: the half of the Earth which lies north of the Equator.

Oasis: a fertile place in the desert, where water lies near or on the surface.

Ore: a mineral or rock from which a valuable metal, such as iron, gold or copper, can be mined or extracted.

Overfarming: exhausting the soil by growing too many crops.

Overgrazing: exhausting the land by not moving animals around to graze in different places.

Overpopulation: when population growth exceeds economic growth and results in food shortages and lack of housing.

Paddy field: a flooded field where rice is grown.

Peninsula: a strip of land surrounded on three sides by water.

Petrochemicals: chemicals obtained from natural gas or petroleum.

Phosphate: a chemical compound used in fertilizers and detergents.

Pilgrim: a person who goes on a journey, or pilgrimage, to a sacred place.

Plantation: a large farm using hired workers to grow and harvest one main crop, such as coffee, sugarcane, rubber, or cotton.

Plateau: a high, flat area of land.

Population density: the number of people living in a given area of land.

Racism: the belief that one's own racial group is superior to others.

Raw materials: the basic materials used to make a product, such as minerals, or wood.

Refined oil: oil that has been treated to remove water, and other impurities, to separate out fuels such as petrol, diesel, and paraffin.

Refugee: a person who has fled to another country in search of safety because of war, or political or religious oppression.

Regime: a particular government, or system of government.

Republic: a country ruled by elected representatives of its people, with an elected president rather than a king or queen.

Reserves: the amount of a resource, such as copper, known to exist, but which has not yet been extracted.

Revolution: the overthrow of a government.

Ring of fire: the zone around the Pacific Ocean where there are many volcanoes and frequent earthquakes.

Rural: relating to the countryside.

Sahel, the: zone of semi-desert and dry grassland to the south of the Sahara Desert in Africa.

Sanctions: penalties imposed by one or more countries to persuade another country to follow a certain course of action.

Savanna: open grassland in a tropical or sub-tropical region.

Shanty town: an area in or around a city where people live in temporary shacks, often without basic services such as running water.

Silt: tiny particles of earth deposited by a river or lake.

Slash-and-burn agriculture: a method of clearing land to create fields, by cutting down trees or bushes and then burning away any remaining roots.

Social services: welfare services provided by a state or local authority.

Socialism: a system of society in which goods are owned collectively and the whole community exercises political power.

Softwood: wood from cone-bearing trees, such as pine or cedar.

Soil erosion: the natural wearing away of the soil by wind or rain.

Southern hemisphere: the half of the Earth which lies south of the Equator.

Standard of living: the quality of life in a country, usually measured by income, possessions, and levels of health care and education.

Staple crop or food: a crop that provides the main food, such as rice, potatoes, or wheat.

Steppe: a vast grass-covered plain, that stretches from eastern Europe across central Asia.

Stock exchange: an international market for buying and selling the stocks or shares of a public company.

Subsistence farming: raising just enough crops or animals to feed the farmer's family.

Technology: the development of methods, materials, and tools used in doing work.

Terrorist: a person who uses violence, often against ordinary people or buildings, to win demands or influence the policies of a government.

Third world: the poorer, less developed parts of the world in Asia, Africa, Central and South America.

Urban: relating to a town or city.

Vegetation: the plant life of a region.

Welfare system: the way a government organizes assistance to its people, particularly the young, the elderly, the sick, and the unemployed.

West, the: the western, industrially advanced countries of the world, specifically North America and western Europe.

Workforce: all the people available to work in a country; all the workers employed by a particular factory or place of work.

GAZETTEER

HOW TO USE THE GAZETTEER

This gazetteer helps you to find places on the maps. For example, to find the city of Paris in France, look up its name in the gazetteer. The entry reads:

Paris *Town* France 97 F3

The first number, 97, tells you that Paris appears on the map on page 97. The second number, F3, shows that it is in square F3 of the grid printed over the map. Turn to page 97. Trace down from the letter F along the top of the grid and then across from the number 3 along the side of the grid. You will find Paris in the square where the letter and the number meet.

A

Aachen *Town* Germany 95 D7
Abadan *Town* Iran 153 F6
Abeokuta *Town* Nigeria 221 K12
Aberdeen *Town* UK 87 J5
Abha *Town* Saudi Arabia 153 C10
Abidjan *Town* Ivory Coast 21 H12
Abilene *Town* Texas, USA 35 H10
Abu Dhabi *Town* United Arab Emirates 153 H9
Abuja *Town* Nigeria 221 M11
Acapulco *Town* Mexico 39 G9
Accra *Town* Ghana 221 I12
Aconcagua, Mt. Argentina 41 F11, 71 F7
Ad Dammam *Town* Saudi Arabia 153 F8
Adamaoua, Massif d' *Region* Cameroon 205 E7
Adana *Town* Turkey 145 F8
Adapazari *Town* Turkey 145 C5
Addis Ababa *Town* Ethiopia 215 G9
Adelaide *Town* South Australia, Australia 259 I11
Aden *Town* Yemen 153 C12, 203 D3
Aden, Gulf of 10 F8, 132 C13, 203 D3, 215 J8
Adriatic Sea S. Europe 78 G11, 103 G6
Aegean Sea 78 H12, 131 H6
Afghanistan *Country* Central Asia 18 G6, 161 F9
Africa *Continent* 10 C7, 205
Agadir *Town* Morocco 208 F4
Agalega Islands Indian Ocean 10 F10, 18 F10
Agra *Town* India 167 F5
Aguascalientes *Town* Mexico 39 F7
Ahaggar Mts *Mountain range* Algeria 205 E4, 209 L8
Ahmadabad *Town* India 167 D6

Ahvaz *Town* Iran 153 F5
Ajaccio *Town* Corsica 97 L10
Akosombo Dam Ghana 221 J12
Akron *Town* Ohio, USA 37 F5
Al 'Amarah *Town* Iraq 153 F5
Al Hufuf *Town* Saudi Arabia 153 F8
Al Ladhiqiyah *Town* Syria 147 F3
Al Mukha *Town* Yemen 153 C12
Al' Aziziyah *Town* Libya 205 F2, 209 O4
Al-Basrah *Town* Iraq 153 F6
Al-Hillah *Town* Iraq 153 E5
Alabama *State* USA 37 D10
Åland *Island group* Finland 82 I8
Alaska *State* USA 19 Q3, 33 C2, 267 E2
Alaska, Gulf of USA 11 Q4, 20 E6, 265 G2
Alaska Range *Mountain range* Alaska, USA 20 D4, 33 C2
Albania *Country* S.E. Europe 123 H12, 18 D5
Albany *Town* New York, USA 37 I5
Albany *Town* Western Australia, Australia 258 D11
Albert Canal Belgium 91 H9
Albert, Lake Uganda/Zaire 205 I8, 239 F4
Alberta *Province* Canada 27 E12
Ålborg *Town* Denmark 82 E10
Albuquerque *Town* New Mexico, USA 35 E9
Aldabra Islands Indian Ocean 203 D6, 205 K10
Ålesund *Town* Norway 82 E7
Aleutian Islands Alaska, USA 11 O4, 20 B7, 33 B3, 265 E2
Alexandria *Town* Egypt 215 D1
Algeciras *Town* Spain 100 D9
Algeria *Country* N.W. Africa 18 B6, 209 J6
Algiers *Town* Algeria 209 K2
Aliákmonas *River* Greece 131 D3
Alicante *Town* Spain 100 I6
Alice Springs *Town* Northern Territory, Australia 259 H7
Allahabad *Town* India 167 G6
Allentown *Town* Pennsylvania, USA 37 H5
Almaty *Town* Kazakhstan 161 I6
Alps *Mountain range* C. Europe 10 C5, 78 E11, 97 I7, 103 B3, 106 D8
Altai Mts. N. Asia 10 I5, 133 H7, 175 F5
Altiplano *Region* Bolivia 41 G9
Altun Mts. China 133 H9, 174 D9
Amarapura *Town* Burma 189 C4
Amarillo *Town* Texas, USA 35 G9
Amazon *River* Brazil/Peru 11 W9, 41 G6, 59 E5, 67 C4, G3
Amazonia *Region* S. America 11 W9, 41 G6, 59 E5, 67 E4
Ambato *Town* Ecuador 59 C5
Ambon *Town* Moluccas, Indonesia 197 O10
American Samoa *Dependent territory* Polynesia, Pacific Ocean 11 O10, 19 P10, 265 F6
Amherst *Town* Burma 189 D8
Amicante Islands Indian Ocean 203 E5
Amiens *Town* France 97 F2
Amman *Town* Jordan 147 F6
Amritsar *Town* India 167 E3
Amsterdam *Town* Netherlands 91 H6
Amsterdam Island Indian Ocean 18 H12, 203 G9
Amu Darya *River* Central Asia 132 E9,

161 F8
Amundsen Sea Pacific Ocean 269 B7
Amundsen-Scott *Research station* Antarctica 269 F5
Amur *River* China/Russian Federation 10 L4, 133 M7, 139 R10, 175 N2, Q3
An Nasiriyah *Town* Iraq 153 E5
An-Najaf *Town* Iraq 153 E5
Anchorage *Town* Alaska, USA 33 D2
Andalusia *Region* Spain 100 F8
Andaman Islands Indian Ocean 10 H8, 18 I8, 133 I13, 203 H3
Andaman Sea 189 C9, 203 I3
Andes *Mountain range* S. America 11 V9, W11, 41 E7, 59 D3, D9, 71 F6, G13
Andizhan *Town* Uzbekistan 161 H7
Andorra *Country* Europe 18 B5, 97 F10, 100 J2
Andorra la Vella *Town* Andorra 97 F10
Angel Falls *Waterfall* Venezuela 41 G4, 59 H3
Angkor Wat *Ancient site* Cambodia 189 G9
Anglesey *Island* UK 87 H9
Angola *Country* Southern Africa 18 D10, 247 D3
Angola Basin Atlantic Ocean 77 I9
Ankara *Town* Turkey 145 E6
Annaba *Town* Algeria 209 M2
Annapolis *Town* Maryland, USA 37 H6
Anne Arbor *Town* Michigan, USA 37 E5
Anshan *Town* China 175 O7
Antakya *Town* Turkey 145 G9
Antalya *Town* Turkey 145 D8
Antananarivo *Town* Madagascar 203 D7
Antarctic Peninsula Antarctic 269 B4
Antarctica *Continent* 265 I11, 269
Antigua and Barbuda *Country* West Indies 19 W7, 45 V11
Antipodes Islands New Zealand, Pacific Ocean 11 O13, 19 O13, 255 K16, 265 E9
Antofagasta *Town* Chile 41 E4
Antwerp *Town* Belgium 91 G9
Anvers Island Pacific Ocean 269 A3
Apeldoorn *Town* Netherlands 91 J6
Apennines *Mountain range* Italy 78 F11, 103 F6
Appalachian Mts. USA 11 V6, 21 M10, 37 G7
Apure *River* Venezuela 59 F2
Aqaba, Gulf of S.W. Asia 147 E11, 215 F2
Ar-Ramadi *Town* Iraq 153 E4
Arabian Peninsula S.W. Asia 10 E7
Arabian Sea 10 G7, 132 E12, 153 G12, 203 F3
Arad *Town* Romania 127 D6
Arafura Sea S.E. Asia 10 L9, 133 M16, 197 Q10, 265 B6
Arak *Town* Iran 153 G5
Aral Sea *Lake* Kazakhstan/Uzbekistan 10 G5, 132 E8, 161 D5, 258 E8
Ararat, Mt. Turkey 145 K6
Arauca *River* Colombia/Venezuela 59 E2
Arctic Bay *Town* Northwest Territories, Canada 27 H5
Arctic Circle 11 Z2
Arctic Ocean 10 K1, 267 F4
Ardabil *Town* Iran 153 G3
Ardennes *Region* Belgium 91 I11
Arequipa *Town* Peru 59 E10

Argentina *Country* S. America 19 W12, 71 G8
Argentine Basin Atlantic Ocean 77 F11
Århus *Town* Denmark 82 E11
Arica *Town* Chile 71 E2
Arizona *State* USA 33 K11
Arkansas *State* USA 35 K9
Arkhangel'sk *Town* Russian Federation 138 F4
Arlon *Town* Belgium 91 J12
Armenia *Country* S.W. Asia 18 E5, 119 P14
Armenia *Town* Colombia 59 D3
Arnhem *Town* Netherlands 91 J7
Arnhem Land *Region* Northern Territory, Australia 254 D8, 259 G4
Arno *River* Italy 103 D6
As Sulaymaniyah *Town* Iraq 153 E4
Ascension Island *Dependent territory* Atlantic Ocean 10 A9, 18 A9, 77 H8
Ashgabat *Town* Turkmenistan 161 D7
Ashmore and Cartier Islands Indian Ocean 18 K10, 203 K6
Asia *Continent* 10 I4, 132
Asmara *Town* Eritrea 215 G7
Assad, Lake Syria 147 H3
Assen *Town* Netherlands 91 K4
Astrakhan' *Town* Russian Federation 138 B8
Asunción *Town* Paraguay 71 J4
Aswân *Town* Egypt 215 E4
Aswân High Dam Egypt 215 E4
Asyût *Town* Egypt 215 D2
Atacama Desert Chile 11 V11, 41 F10, 71 F4
Athabasca, Lake Alberta/Saskatchewan, Canada 21 J6, 27 F11
Athens *Town* Greece 131 F7
Atlanta *Town* Georgia, USA 37 E9
Atlantic Ocean 10 B10, 11 X5, 77
Atlantic-Indian Ridge 77 J12
Atlas Mts *Mountain range* Morocco 10 B6, 205 D2, 208 F4
Auckland Islands New Zealand, Pacific Ocean 11 N13, 19 N13, 255 I16, 265 D9
Auckland *Town* New Zealand 262 F3
Augsburg *Town* Germany 95 H10
Augusta *Town* Maine 37 K4
Austin *Town* Texas, USA 35 I12
Australasia and Oceania 254-255
Australia *Country and continent* 10 K10, 18 K11, 259 G8
Australian Capital Territory *Territory* Australia 259 L11
Austria *Country* Europe 18 C5, 106 J6
Ayacucho *Town* Peru 59 D9
Ayers Rock *see* Uluru
Ayutthaya *Town* Thailand 189 E9
Az Zarqa' *Town* Jordan 147 F7
Azerbaijan *Country* S.W. Asia 18 F5, 119 P15
Azores *Island Group* Atlantic Ocean 11 Z5, 19 Y5, 77 G4
Azov, Sea of Russian Federation/ Ukraine 78 J10, 119 J9, 138 A7

B

Babruyck *Town* Belorussia 109 J10
Babylon *Ancient site* Iraq 153 E4
Bacau *Town* Romania 127 I6

Bacolod *Town* Philippines 196 L4
Badagastein *Town* Austria 106 H7
Baden *Town* Austria 106 K5
Badlands *Region* North/South Dakota, USA 35 F3
Baffin Bay Canada/Greenland 11 W2, 21 O3, 27 I4, 267 C7
Baffin Island Northwest Territories, Canada 11 V2, 21 N4, 27 J6, 267 B7
Bafoussam *Town* Cameroon 232 D8
Baghdad *Town* Iraq 153 E4
Baguio *Town* Philippines 196 K2
Bahamas *Country* West Indies 11 V7, 19 V7, 45 M5
Bahía Blanca *Town* Argentina 71 I9
Bahrain *Country* S.W. Asia 18 F7, 153 F8
Baia Mare *Town* Romania 127 F4
Baikal, Lake Russian Federation 10 J4, 133 J6, 139 M10
Baja California *Peninsula* Mexico 39 B3
Baker Island *Dependent territory* Pacific Ocean 19 P9, 255 L6, 265 E5
Bakersfield *Town* California, USA 33 H11
Bakhtaran *Town* Iran 153 F4
Baku *Town* Azerbaijan 119 T13
Balaton, Lake Hungary 113 G11
Balearic Islands Spain 78 E12, 100 J5
Bali *Island* Indonesia 196 I12
Balikesir *Town* Turkey 145 B6
Balikpapan *Town* Borneo, Indonesia 196 J9
Balkan Mts S.E. Europe 78 H11, 123 K9, 127 F11
Balkhash, Lake Kazakhstan 10 HS, 133 G8, 161 I5
Ballarat *Town* Victoria, Australia 259 J12
Baltic Sea N. Europe 10 D4, 78 G8, 82 I10, 109 E5
Baltimore *Town* Maryland, USA 37 H6
Bamako *Town* Mali 221 F9
Banda Sea S.E. Asia 133 M15, 196 M10
Bandar Seri Begawan *Town* Brunei 196 I7
Bandar-e 'Abbas *Town* Iran 153 H8
Bandar-e-Bushehr *Town* Iran 153 G7
Bandundu *Town* Zaire 232 E14
Bandung *Town* Java, Indonesia 196 F12
Bangalore *Town* India 187 E11
Bangkok *Town* Thailand 189 E9
Bangladesh *Country* S. Asia 18 H7, 167 J6
Bangui *Town* Central African Republic 232 G9
Banja Luka *Town* Bosnia and Herzegovina 123 E5
Banjarmasin *Town* Borneo, Indonesia 196 I10
Banjul *Town* Gambia 220 B8
Banks Island Northwest Territories, Canada 11 S2, 21 H3, 29 E5, 267 C4
Baotou *Town* China 178 K8
Baranavichy *Town* Belorussia 109 H10
Barbados *Country* Caribbean Sea 19 W8, 45 W14
Barbuda *Island* Antigua and Barbuda 45 V11
Barcelona *Town* Spain 100 K3
Barcelona *Town* Venezuela 59 G1
Bareilly *Town* India 167 G4
Barents Sea Arctic Ocean 10 E2, 78 K4, 138 G3, 267 H7
Bari *Town* Italy 103 J9
Barinas *Town* Venezuela 59 F2
Barisian Mts. Sumatra, Indonesia 196 C10
Barnaul *Town* Russian Federation 139 I10
Barquisimeto *Town* Venezuela 59 F1
Barranquilla *Town* Colombia 59 D1

Barysaw *Town* Belorussia 109 J9
Basque Provinces Spain 100 F2
Bassein *Town* Burma 189 B7
Basseterre *Town* St Kitts and Nevis 45 U11
Batangas *Town* Philippines 196 K3
Batdâmbâng *Town* Cambodia 189 G10
Baton Rouge *Town* Louisiana, USA 35 K11
Bavarian Alps *Mountain range* Austria/Germany 95 I11
Bayamo *Town* Cuba 45 L7
Baykonur *Space centre* Kazakhstan 161 F5
Beagle Channel Argentina 71 I16
Bear Island *Island group* Russian Federation 139 Q3
Beaufort Sea Arctic Ocean 11 Q2, 20 F4, 27 C6, 33 C1, 267 D3
Beaumont *Town* Texas, USA 35 J12
Beersheba *Town* Israel 147 E8
Beijing *Town* China 175 M8
Beira *Town* Mozambique 247 J6
Beirut *Town* Lebanon 147 F5
Bejaia *Town* Algeria 209 L2
Belém *Town* Brazil 67 H3
Belfast *Town* UK 87 G7
Belgium *Country* Europe 18 C4, 91 G10
Belgrade *Town* Serbia, Yugoslavia 123 I5
Belize *Country* Central America 19 U7, 44 D8
Belle Île *Island* France 97 B5
Bellevue *Town* Washington, USA 33 G4
Bellinghausen Sea Pacific Ocean 269 B5
Bello *Town* Colombia 59 D2
Belmopan *Town* Belize 44 D8
Belo Horizonte *Town* Brazil 67 I9
Belorussia *Country* E. Europe 18 D4, 109 I10
Ben Nevis *Mountain* UK 87 H5
Bengal, Bay of India 10 H7, 133 H12, 167 H9, 203 H3
Benghazi *Town* Libya 209 R4
Benidorm *Town* Spain 100 I6
Benin *Country* W. Africa 18 C8, 221 K10
Berbera *Town* Somalia 215 I8
Berbérati *Town* Central African Republic 232 F9
Bergen *Town* Norway 82 D8
Bergen op Zoom *Town* Netherlands 91 G8
Bering Sea Pacific Ocean 11 O3, 20 B6, 33 A3, 139 T3, 265 E2
Bering Strait Arctic Ocean/Pacific Ocean 11 P3, 20 C5, 33 B2, 265 F1
Berlin *Town* Germany 95 J5
Bermuda *Dependent territory* Atlantic Ocean 11 W6, 19 W6
Bern *Town* Switzerland 106 C8
Bethlehem *Town* West Bank 147 E8
Bhopal *Town* India 167 F6
Bhutan *Country* S. Asia 18 I6, 167 J5
Bialystok *Town* Poland 113 K3
Bielefeld *Town* Germany 95 F5
Bien Hoa *Town* Vietnam 189 I11
Bihac *Town* Bosnia and Herzegovina 123 D5
Bikini Island Marshall Islands, Pacific Ocean 265 D5
Bila Tserkva *Town* Ukraine 118 F5
Bilbao *Town* Spain 100 G1
Birmingham *Town* Alabama, USA 37 D9
Birmingham *Town* UK 87 J10
Biscay, Bay of 10 B5, 78 D11, 100 G1
Bishkek *Town* Kyrgyzstan 161 I6
Bismarck *Town* North Dakota, USA 35 H3
Bismarck Archipelago *Island group* Papua New Guinea 10 L9, 254 G6, 259 L1

Bissau *Town* Guinea-Bissau 220 B9
Bitola *Town* Macedonia 123 J12
Biwa, Lake Japan 185 F9
Black Forest *Region* Germany 78 F10, 95 E10
Black Hills South Dakota, USA 35 G4
Black Rock Desert Nevada, USA 33 H8
Black Sea Asia/Europe 10 E5, 78 J11, 127 L10, 132 B8, 138 A7
Black Volta *River* W. Africa 205 C6, 221 H10
Blackpool *Town* UK 87 I8
Blantyre *Town* Malawi 239 H14
Blenheim *Town* New Zealand 262 E7
Blida *Town* Algeria 209 K2
Bloemfontein *Town* South Africa 247 G10
Blue Mts. Oregon/Washington, USA 33 H6
Blue Nile *River* E. Africa 205 I5, 215 E7
Bobo Dioulasso *Town* Burkina 221 G10
Bogor *Town* Java, Indonesia 196 F12
Bogota *Town* Colombia 59 D3
Bohemia *Region* Czech Republic 113 C8
Bohemian Forest *Region* Germany 95 J9
Boise *Town* Idaho, USA 33 H6
Bolivia *Country* S. America 19 W10, 59 G10
Bologna *Town* Italy 103 E5
Bombay *Town* India 167 D8, 203 G3
Bonin Islands Pacific Ocean 10 L6
Bonn *Town* Germany 95 E7
Borås *Town* Sweden 82 F10
Bordeaux *Town* France 97 D8
Borneo *Island* S.E. Asia 10 J9, 133 K14, 196 I8
Bornholm *Island* Denmark 78 G8, 82 G12
Borobudur *Ancient site* Java, Indonesia 196 G12
Bosnia and Herzegovina *Country* S.E. Europe 18 D5, 123 F6
Bosporus Channel Turkey 145 C5
Boston *Town* Massachusetts, USA 37 J5
Bothnia, Gulf of Finland/Sweden 78 H6, 82 I6
Botosani *Town* Romania 127 I4
Botrange *Mountain* Belgium 91 J10
Botswana *Country* Southern Africa 18 D11, 247 F7
Bounty Islands New Zealand, Pacific Ocean 11 O13, 19 N13, 255 L15, 265 E9
Bourke *Town* New South Wales, Australia 254 G12
Bournemouth *Town* UK 87 J12
Bouvet Island *Dependent territory* Atlantic Ocean 77 I12
Boyoma Falls *Waterfall* Zaire 205 H8, 232 J10
Bradford *Town* UK 87 J8
Brahmaputra (Yarlung Zangbo) *River* India/China 133 H10, 167 K5, 174 C11
Braila *Town* Romania 127 K7
Brasília *Town* Brazil 67 H8
Brasov *Town* Romania 127 H7
Bratislava *Town* Slovakia 113 F10
Braunschweig *Town* Germany 95 H5
Bravo del Norte *River* Mexico 39 E2
Brazil *Country* S. America 19 W9, 67 F5
Brazil Basin Atlantic Ocean 77 G8
Brazilian Highlands *Mountain range* Brazil 41 J9, 67 I8
Brazzaville *Town* Congo 232 F12
Breda *Town* Netherlands 91 H8
Bremen *Town* Germany 95 F4
Brest *Town* Belorussia 109 F11
Bridgeport *Town* Connecticut, USA 37 I5
Bridgetown *Town* Barbados 45 W14

Brighton *Town* UK 87 K12
Brindisi *Town* Italy 103 K9
Brisbane *Town* Queensland, Australia 259 M8, 265 C7
Bristol *Town* UK 87 I11
British Columbia *Province* Canada 27 B12
British Indian Ocean Territory *Dependent territory* Indian Ocean 18 H9, 203 G5
British Isles *Country* Europe 10 B4, 78 C8, 87
British Virgin Islands *Dependent Territory* Caribbean Sea 45 T10
Brittany *Region* France 97 B4
Brno *Town* Czech Republic 113 F8
Broken Hill *Town* New South Wales, Australia 259 J10
Broken Ridge Indian Ocean 203 I9
Brooks Range *Mountain range* Alaska, USA 20 D4, 33 C1
Broome *Town* Western Australia, Australia 258 D6
Bruges *Town* Belgium 91 F9
Brunei *Country* Borneo, S.E. Asia 18 J8, 196 H7
Brussels *Town* Belgium 91 G9
Bucaramanga *Town* Colombia 59 D2
Bucharest *Town* Romania 127 I9
Budapest *Town* Hungary 113 H10
Buenaventura *Town* Colombia 59 C3
Buenos Aires *Town* Argentina 71 J8, 77 E10
Buenos Aires, Lake (Lake General Carrera) Argentina/Chile 41 F15, 71 G13
Buffalo *Town* New York, USA 37 G4
Bujumbura *Town* Burundi 239 E7
Bukavu *Town* Zaire 232 K11
Bukhara *Town* Uzbekistan 161 F7
Bulawayo *Town* Zimbabwe 247 H7
Bulgaria *Country* E. Europe 18 D5, 127 H11
Buon Me Thuot *Town* Vietnam 189 I10
Buraydah *Town* Saudi Arabia 153 D7
Burgas *Town* Bulgaria 127 J11
Burgundy *Region* France 97 H5
Burkina *Country* W. Africa 18 B8, 221 I9
Burma *Country* S.E. Asia 18 I7, 189 C5
Bursa *Town* Turkey 145 C6
Burundi *Country* Africa 18 E9, 239 E7
Butuan *Town* Philippines 196 M5
Buzau *Town* Romania 127 I8
Bydgoszcz *Town* Poland 113 G3

C

Cabanatuan *Town* Philippines 196 K2
Cabimas *Town* Venezuela 59 E1
Cabinda *Region* Angola 18 C9, 232 E12, 247 B1
Cabo da Roca *Cape* Portugal 78 C11, 100 A6
Cabot Strait Canada 29 J5
Cacak *Town* Serbia, Yugoslavia 123 I7
Cadiz *Town* Philippines 196 L4
Cádiz *Town* Spain 100 D8
Caen *Town* France 97 D3
Caernarfon *Town* UK 87 H9
Cagayan de Oro *Town* Philippines 196 M5
Cagliari *Town* Sardinia 103 C11
Cairns *Town* Queensland, Australia 259 K5
Cairo *Town* Egypt 215 D1
Calabria *Region* Italy 103 I12
Calais *Town* France 97 F1
Calama *Town* Chile 71 F4

Calbayog *Town* Philippines 196 M4
Calcutta *Town* India 167 J7
Calgary *Town* Alberta, Canada 27 E13
Cali *Town* Colombia 59 C3
California *State* USA 33 H10
Callao *Town* Peru 59 C8
Camaguey *Town* Cuba 45 L6
Cambodia *Country* S.E. Asia 18 I8, 189 H10
Cambrian Mts UK 87 H10
Cambridge *Town* UK 87 K10
Cameron Highlands *Mountain range* Malaysia 189 E14
Cameroon *Country* Central Africa 18 C8, 232 D8
Cameroon, Mt. *Volcano* Cameroon 232 D9
Campbell Island New Zealand, Pacific Ocean 19 N13, 265 E9
Campeche *Town* Mexico 39 K8
Campinas *Town* Brazil 67 H10
Can Tho *Town* Vietnam 189 H11
Canada *Country* N. America 19 S3, 26–27, 28–29
Canary Basin Atlantic Ocean 77 G6
Canary Islands Atlantic Ocean 10 A6, 18 A6, 77 H5, 205 A3
Canberra *Town* Australian Capital Territory, Australia 254 G13, 259 L11, 265 C8
Cancún *Town* Mexico 39 L7
Cannes *Town* France 97 J9
Canterbury *Town* UK 87 L11
Canton *Town* China 175 N14
Cape Basin Atlantic Ocean 77 I10
Cape Canaveral *Peninsula* Florida, USA 37 G12
Cape Cod *Peninsula* Massachusetts, USA 21 N9, 37 K5
Cape Horn *Peninsula* Chile 11 off W13, 41 off G16, 71 I16, 77 D12
Cape of Good Hope *Peninsula* South Africa 10 D12, 77 J10, 203 B9, 205 G14, 247 E12
Cape Town *Town* South Africa 203 B9, 247 E11
Cape Verde *Peninsula* Senegal 205 A5, 220 A8
Cape Verde Islands Atlantic Ocean 10 A7, 18 A7, 77 G6, 205 A5
Cape York *Peninsula* Queensland, Australia 254 F9, 259 J4
Cappadocia *Region* Turkey 145 G7
Capri *Island* Italy 103 G9
Caracas *Town* Venezuela 59 G1
Cardiff *Town* UK 87 I11
Caribbean Sea 11 V8, 41 F2, 44 J10, 77 C6
Caroline Islands Federated States of Micronesia, Pacific Ocean 10 L8, 254 G5
Carpathians *Mountain range* Central Europe 10 C4, 78 H10, 113 I8, 118 B6, 127 F10, H8
Carpentaria, Gulf of Northern Territory/Queensland, Australia 254 E8, 259 I5
Carson City *Town* Nevada, USA 33 H9
Cartagena *Town* Colombia 59 D1
Cartagena *Town* Spain 100 H7
Casablanca *Town* Morocco 208 G3
Cascade Range *Mountain range* USA 21 H7, 33 G6
Caspian Sea *Lake* Central Asia 10 F5, 78 M11, 132 D8, 138 B9, 161 B6
Castries *Town* St Lucia 45 V14
Catalonia *Region* Spain 100 J3
Catania *Town* Sicily 103 H13
Caucasus Mts Europe/Asia 10 E5, 78 L11, 119 O12, 132 C8

Cayenne *Town* French Guiana 59 L3
Cayman Islands *Dependent territory* Caribbean Sea 44 I7
Cebu *Town* Philippines 196 M4
Cedar Rapids *Town* Iowa, USA 35 K5
Celebes Sea S.E. Asia 133 L14, 196 K8
Central African Republic *Country* Central Africa 18 D8, 232 H8
Central America *Region* 11 U7, 41, 44
Central Siberian Plateau Russian Federation 133 K3, 139 M5
Ceuta *Spanish enclave* Morocco 208 H2
Cevennes *Mountain range* France 97 G8
Chad *Country* Central Africa 18 D7, 232 G4
Chad, Lake Central Africa 205 F5, 221 P9, 232 F5
Chagos Archipelago *Island group* Indian Ocean 10 H9
Chalbi Desert Kenya 239 J3
Chandigarh *Town* India 167 F3
Changchun *Town* China 175 O5
Changsha *Town* China 175 M12
Channel Islands UK 18 B4, 78 D10, 87 I13, 97 C3
Channel Tunnel UK/France 87 L11, 97 F1
Chapala, Lake Mexico 39 E7
Chardzhev *Town* Turkmenistan 161 E7
Charleroi *Town* Belgium 91 G11
Charleston *Town* South Carolina, USA 37 G10
Charleston *Town* West Virginia, USA 37 F7
Charlotte *Town* North Carolina, USA 37 F8
Charlottetown *Town* Prince Edward Island, Canada 29 J6
Chatham Islands New Zealand, Pacific Ocean 11 O13, 19 O13, 255 L15, 265 E8
Chattanooga *Town* Tennessee, USA 37 E8
Cheju *Town* South Korea 175 Q9
Chelyabinsk *Town* Russian Federation 138 F8
Chemnitz *Town* Germany 95 J7
Chengdu *Town* China 175 J11
Chenonceaux *Town* France 97 E5
Cherbourg *Town* France 97 C2
Cherkasy *Town* Ukraine 118 G6
Chernihiv *Town* Ukraine 118 G4
Chernivtski *Town* Ukraine 118 C6
Chernobyl *Town* Ukraine 118 F4
Cheyenne *Town* Wyoming, USA 35 F6
Chiang Mai *Town* Thailand 189 E6
Chicago *Town* Illinois, USA 37 C5
Chichén Itzá *Ancient site* Mexico 39 L7
Chiclayo *Town* Peru 59 B7
Chihuahua *Town* Mexico 39 E3
Chile *Country* S. America 19 V12, 71 F6, F14
Chilka, Lake India 167 H8
Chillán *Town* Chile 71 F9
Chimbote *Town* Peru 59 C7
China *Country* E. Asia 18 I6, 175 G8
Chingola *Town* Zambia 239 D12
Chios *Island* Greece 131 I7
Chisinau *Town* Moldavia 118 E8
Chittagong *Town* India 167 K7
Chitungwiza *Town* Zimbabwe 247 I6
Chon Buri *Town* Thailand 189 E9
Ch'ongjin *Town* North Korea 175 Q6
Chongqing *Town* China 175 K12
Christchurch *Town* New Zealand 262 E9
Christmas Island Indian Ocean 18 J10, 203 J6
Chugoku Mts. Japan 185 D10
Chukchi Sea Arctic Ocean 11 O2, 20 B4, 139 R1, 267 F1

Churchill *Town* Manitoba, Canada 27 I10
Cincinnati *Town* Ohio, USA 37 E6
Citlaltépetl (Orizaba) *Volcano* Mexico 39 H8
Ciudad Bolívar *Town* Venezuela 59 H2
Ciudad Guayana *Town* Venezuela 59 H2
Ciudad Juárez *Town* Mexico 39 E2
Clermont-Ferrand *Town* France 97 G6
Cleveland *Town* Ohio, USA 37 F5
Clipperton Island *Dependent territory* Pacific Ocean 19 T8, 265 I5
Cluj-Napoca *Town* Romania 127 F5
Coast Mts. Canada 11 R3, 20 G6
Coast Ranges *Mountain range* N. America 11 S5, 21 H9, 33 F8
Cobán *Town* Guatemala 44 C8
Cochabamba *Town* Bolivia 59 G10
Cochin *Town* India 167 E12
Coco *River* Honduras/Nicaragua 44 F10
Cocos Islands Indian Ocean 10 I10, 18 I10, 203 J6
Coihaique *Town* Chile 71 G13
Coimbatore *Town* India 167 E11
Coimbra *Town* Portugal 100 B4
Cologne *Town* Germany 95 E7
Colombia *Country* S. America 19 V8, 59 E3
Colombo *Town* Sri Lanka 167 F13, 203 H4
Colón *Town* Panama 44 H14
Colorado *River* Argentina 41 G13, 71 I10
Colorado *River* Mexico/USA 21 J9, 33 I12, 35 E6
Colorado *State* USA 35 E6
Colorado Springs *Town* Colorado, USA 35 F7
Columbia *River* Canada/USA 27 D13, 33 G5
Columbia *Town* South Carolina, USA 37 F9
Columbus *Town* Georgia, USA 37 E10
Columbus *Town* Ohio, USA 37 F6
Communism Peak *Mountain* Tajikistan 161 H7
Como, Lake Italy 103 C3
Comodoro Rivadavia *see* Rivadavia
Comoros *Country* Indian Ocean 10 E10, 18 E10, 203 D6
Conakry *Town* Guinea 220 C10
Concepción *Town* Chile 71 F9
Concord *Town* California, USA 33 G10
Concord *Town* New Hampshire, USA 37 J4
Congo (Zaire) *River* Central Africa 10 C9, 205 F9, G8, 232 F11, G10
Congo Basin *Region* Congo/Zaire 205 G8
Congo *Country* Central Africa 18 C9, 232 F10
Connecticut *State* USA 37 J6
Constance, Lake Switzerland/Austria/Germany 95 G12, 106 E7
Constanta *Town* Romania 127 K9
Constantine *Town* Algeria 209 M2
Cook Islands *Dependent territory* Polynesia, Pacific Ocean 11 P10, 19 P10, 255 O9, 265 F6
Cook Strait New Zealand 262 F7
Cook, Mt. New Zealand 262 C9
Copenhagen *Town* Denmark 82 F11
Copiapó *Town* Chile 71 F5
Coral Sea Islands *Dependent territory* Pacific Ocean 18 M10, 265 C7
Coral Sea Pacific Ocean 10 M10, 254 G8, 259 L4, 265 C6
Córdoba *Town* Argentina 71 H7
Córdoba *Town* Spain 100 E7
Corfu *Island* Greece 131 A5

Corinth *Town* Greece 131 E8
Cork *Town* Ireland 87 E10
Coromandel *Town* New Zealand 262 G3
Coromandel Coast India 167 G11
Corpus Christi *Town* Texas, USA 35 I13
Corrib, Lough *Lake* Ireland 87 E8
Corrientes *Town* Argentina 71 J5
Corsica *Island* France 78 E11, 97 L10
Costa Blanca *Coast* Spain 100 I7
Costa Brava *Coast* Spain 100 K3
Costa del Sol *Coast* Spain 100 F8
Costa Rica *Country* Central America 19 U8, 44 E13
Côte d'Azur *Coast* France 97 J9
Coventry *Town* UK 87 J10
Craiova *Town* Romania 127 F9
Crete *Island* Greece 78 H13, 131 H12
Crimea *Peninsula* Ukraine 119 H9
Croatia *Country* S.E. Europe 18 C5, 123 E4
Crozet Islands Indian Ocean 10 F13, 18 F13, 203 E10
Cuba *Country* Caribbean Sea 19 V7, 45 K6
Cúcuta *Town* Colombia 59 E2
Cuenca *Town* Ecuador 59 C5
Culiacán *Town* Mexico 39 D5
Cumaná *Town* Venezuela 59 H1
Curitiba *Town* Brazil 67 H10
Cusco *Town* Peru 59 E9
Cyclades *Island group* Greece 131 H9
Cyprus *Country* Europe 18 E6, 132 B10, 145 F10
Czech Republic *Country* Central Europe 18 C4, 113 E7

D

Da Lat *Town* Vietnam 189 J10
Da Nang *Town* Vietnam 189 I8
Dacca *Town* Bangladesh 167 J7
Dagupan *Town* Philippines 196 K2
Dakar *Town* Senegal 220 A8
Dalian *Town* China 178 O8
Dallas *Town* Texas, USA 35 I10
Dalmatia *Region* Croatia 123 D7
Damascus *Town* Syria 147 F6
Dampier *Town* Western Australia, Australia 258 C7
Danube *River* Central Europe 10 D5, 78 G10, H11, 95 G11, J10, 106 K5, 113 G10, H11, 123 H5, J5, 127 F10, K8
Danube Delta Romania 127 L7
Danzig, Gulf of Poland/Russian Federation 113 H1
Dar es Salaam *Town* 239 K9
Dardanelles *Channel* Turkey 145 A5
Darling *River* New South Wales, Australia 10 L11, 254 F12, 259 K9
Dartmoor *Region* UK 87 H12
Darwin *Town* Northern Territory, Australia 259 G4
Dashkhovuz *Town* Turkmenistan 161 D6
Datong *Town* China 175 L8
Daugavpils *Town* Latvia 109 H7
Davao *Town* Philippines 196 M6
David *Town* Panama 44 G15
Davis Sea Antarctica 269 K5
Davis Strait Canada/Greenland 11 W2, 21 O4, 27 L5, 267 B8
Dayr az Zawr *Town* Syria 147 J3
Dayton *Town* Ohio, USA 37 E6
De Bilt *Town* Netherlands 91 I6
Dead Sea *Lake* Israel/Jordan/West Bank 132 B10, 147 E8
Death Valley California, USA 21 I10
Debrecen *Town* Hungary 113 J10

Deccan Plateau *Region* India 10 H7, 167 E8
Delaware *State* USA 37 I7
Delphi *Ancient site* Greece 131 D7
Denali (Mt. McKinley) *Mountain* Alaska, USA 20 E5, 33 C2
Denizli *Town* Turkey 145 C7
Denmark *Country* Europe 18 C4, 82 E10
Denmark Strait Greenland/Iceland 10 A2, 267 E9
Denver *Town* Colorado, USA 35 F7
Derby *Town* UK 87 J9
Des Moines *Town* Iowa, USA 35 J6
Detroit *Town* Michigan, USA 37 E5
Devon Island Northwest Territories, Canada 11 U1, 27 H4, 267 C6
Dezful *Town* Iran 153 F5
Dhanbad *Town* India 167 I6
Dharwad *Town* India 167 D10
Dieppe *Town* France 97 E2
Dijon *Town* France 97 H5
Dimlang *Mountain* Nigeria 221 O11
Dinaric Alps *Mountain range* Bosnia and Herzegovina/Croatia 123 D7
Dire Dawa *Town* Ethiopia 215 H9
Diyarbakir *Town* Turkey 145 I7
Djebel Toubkal *Mountain* Morocco 208 G4
Djibouti *Country* E. Africa 18 F8 215 H8
Djibouti *Town* Djibouti 203 D3, 215 I8
Dnieper *River* E. Europe 10 E4, 78 I9, J10, 109 K12, 118 G5, I7
Dniester *River* Ukraine 78 I10, 118 C6
Dnipropetrovs'k *Town* Ukraine 119 I7
Dobrich *Town* Bulgaria 127 K10
Dodecanese *Island group* Greece 131 J9
Dodoma *Town* Tanzania 239 I8
Doha *Town* Qatar 153 G8
Dolomites *Mountain range* Alps, Italy 103 E3
Dominica *Country* Caribbean Sea 19 W7, 45 U13
Dominican Republic *Country* Caribbean Sea 19 W7, 45 P9
Don *River* Russian Federation 10 E4, 78 K9, K10
Donbass *Region* Ukraine 119 K7
Donegal Bay Ireland 87 E7
Donets'k *Town* Ukraine 119 K7
Dongguan *Town* China 175 N14
Dordogne *River* France 97 E7
Dordrecht *Town* Netherlands 91 H7
Dortmund *Town* Germany 95 E6
Douglas *Town* Isle of Man, UK 87 H8
Douro (Duero) *River* Portugal/Spain 78 C12, 100 D3, F3
Dovala *Town* Cameroon 232 D9
Dover *Town* Delaware, USA 37 H6
Dover *Town* UK 87 L11
Drake Passage *Channel* Atlantic Ocean/Pacific Ocean 269 A1
Drakensberg *Mountain range* South Africa 205 H14, 247 G11
Drava *River* S.E. Europe 78 G10, 123 C2, G4
Dresden *Town* Germany 95 K7
Drobeta-Turnu-Severin *Town* Romania 127 E8
Dubai *Town* United Arab Emirates 153 H8
Dublin *Town* Ireland 87 G8
Dubrovnik *Town* Yugoslavia 123 F9
Dufourspitze, Mt. Switzerland 106 C9
Duisburg *Town* Germany 95 D6
Duluth *Town* Minnesota, USA 35 K3
Dumont d'Urville *Research station* Antarctica 269 H9
Dundee *Town* UK 87 J5
Dunedin *Town* New Zealand 262 C11
Dunkirk *Town* France 97 F1

Durango *Town* Mexico 39 E5
Durban *Town* South Africa 247 I10
Dushanbe *Town* Tajikistan 161 G8
Düsseldorf *Town* Germany 95 D6
Dvina (Northern, Western) *River* Russian Federation 78 I8, L6, 109 G6, J8, 138 E5
Dzhugdzhur Range *Mountain range* Russian Federation 133 O6, 139 Q8

E

East China Sea China 10 K6, 133 L10, 265 A3
East Frisian Islands Germany 95 E3
East London *Town* South Africa 247 H11
East Siberian Sea, Arctic Ocean 11 N2, 133 P3, 139 P3, 267 H2
Easter Island *Dependent territory* Polynesia, Pacific Ocean 265 I7
Eastern Ghats *Mountain range* 167 G9
Ebro *River* Spain 78 D11, 100 H3
Ecuador *Country* S. America 19 V9, 59 C5
Edinburgh *Town* UK 87 I6
Edmonton *Town* Alberta, Canada 27 E13
Egypt *Country* N.E. Africa 18 D7, 147 D10, 215 D2
Eindhoven *Town* Netherlands 91 I8
El Aaiun *Town* Western Sahara 208 D5
El Faiyûm *Town* Egypt 215 D2
El Mansûra *Town* Egypt 215 D1
El Minya *Town* Egypt 215 D2
El Obeid *Town* Sudan 215 D7
El Paso *Town* Texas, USA 35 E11
El Salvador *Country* Central America 19 U8, 44 C10
El'brus, Mt Russian Federation 78 K11
Elat *Town* Israel 147 E10
Elâzig *Town* Turkey 145 I7
Elba *Island* Italy 103 D7
Elbe *River* Germany 78 F9, 95 H3, J6
Elbert, Mt. Colorado, USA 35 E7
Elburz Mts. Iran 132 D9, 153 G4
Ellesmere Island Northwest Territories, Canada 21 N1, 27 H2
Ellsworth Mts. Antarctica 269 D5
Emperor Seamounts Pacific Ocean 265 D3
Enderby Land *Region* Antarctica 269 H3
England *Region* UK 87 K10
English Channel France/UK 78 D9, 87 J12
Enschede *Town* Netherlands 91 J6
Entebbe *Town* Uganda 239 G5
Ephesus *Ancient site* Turkey 145 A7
Epidaurus *Ancient site* Greece 131 E8
Equator 11 Z9
Equatorial Guinea *Country* Africa 18 C9, 232 C9
Erfurt *Town* Germany 95 H7
Erg Tifernine *Desert region* Algeria 209 M7
Erie *Town* Pennsylvania, USA 37 G4
Erie, Lake Canada/USA 21 M9, 29 F9, 37 F5
Eritrea *Country* E. Africa 215 G6
Erzurum *Town* Turkey 145 J6
Esequibo *River* Guyana 59 I3
Esfahan *Town* Iran 153 G5
Eskisehir *Town* Turkey 145 C6
Esmeraldas *Town* Ecuador 59 B4
Essen *Town* Germany 95 E6
Estonia *Country* E. Europe 18 D3, 109 H4

Ethiopia *Country* E. Africa 18 E8, 215 H9
Ethiopian Highlands *Mountain range* Ethiopia 10 E8, 205 I6, 215 G9
Etna, Mt. *Volcano* Sicily 78 G12, 103 H13
Eugene *Town* Washington, USA 33 F6
Euphrates *River* S.W. Asia 132 C9, 145 H8, 147 K4, 153 E5
Europe *Continent* 10 C4, 78–79
Evansville *Town* Indiana, USA 37 D7
Everest, Mt. China/Nepal 10 H6, 133 H11, 167 J5, 174 D12
Everett *Town* Washington, USA 33 G4
Everglades Swamp *Region* Florida, USA 21 M11, 37 F13
Evvoia *Island* Greece 131 F6
Exeter *Town* UK 87 H11
Eyre, Lake South Australia, Australia 10 L11, 254 E11, 259 I9

F

Faeroe Islands *Dependent territory* Atlantic Ocean 10 B3, 18 B3, 77 H3, 78 C6
Fairbanks *Town* Alaska, USA 33 D2
Faisalabad *Town* Pakistan 167 D3
Falkland Islands *Dependent Territory* Atlantic Ocean 11 W13, 19 W13, 41 H16, 71 K15, 77 E11
Famagusta *Town* Cyprus 145 F9
Faro *Town* Portugal 100 B8
Fens, The *Region* UK 87 K10
Fergana *Town* Uzbekistan 161 H7
Fernando de Noronho *Island* Atlantic Ocean 19 J9, 77 G8
Fez *Town* Morocco 208 H3
Fianarantsoa *Town* Madagascar 203 D7
Fiji *Country* Melanesia, Pacific Ocean 11 O10, 19 O10, 255 K9, 265 E7
Finland *Country* Europe 18 D3, 82 K6
Finland, Gulf of 78 H7, 82 K9, 109 I3
Fitzroy *River* Western Australia, Australia 258 E6
Flinders Ranges *Mountain range* South Australia, Australia 259 I10
Flinders *River* Queensland, Australia 259 J6
Flint *Town* Michigan, USA 37 E4
Florence *Town* Italy 103 E6
Flores *Island* Indonesia 196 L12
Florida *State* USA 37 F11
Focsani *Town* Romania 127 J7
Formentera *Island* Balearic Islands, Spain 100 J6
Formosa *Town* Argentina 71 J4
Fort Lauderdale *Town* Florida, USA 37 G13
Fort Wayne *Town* Indiana, USA 37 E5
Fort Worth *Town* Texas, USA 35 I10
Fortaleza *Town* Brazil 67 K4
Forth *River* UK 87 I5
Foxe Basin Northwest Territories, Canada 21 M5, 27 J7
France *Country* Europe 18 B4, 97
Francistown *Town* Botswana 247 H7
Franconian Jura *Mountain range* Germany 95 I9
Frankfort *Town* Kentucky, USA 37 E7
Frankfurt am Main *Town* Germany 95 F8
Franz Josef Land *Island group* Russian Federation 10 F1, 139 J1, 267 H6
Fray Bentos *Town* Uruguay 71 J7
Fredericton *Town* New Brunswick, Canada 29 I6
Frederikshavn *Town* Denmark 82 E10

Freeport *Town* Bahamas 45 L3
Freetown *Town* Sierra Leone 220 C11
Fremantle *Town* Western Australia, Australia 203 K9, 258 C10
French Guiana *Country* S. America 19 X8, 59 K3
French Polynesia *Dependent territory* Pacific Ocean 19 Q10, 265 G6
Fresno *Town* California, USA 33 G10
Fribourg *Town* Switzerland 106 B8
Frobisher Bay Baffin Island, Northwest Territories, Canada 27 L7
Fuji, Mt. *Volcano* Japan 185 H9
Fundy, Bay of Canada 29 I7, 77 D4
Fushun *Town* China 175 O6
Fuzhou *Town* China 175 O12

G

Gabon *Country* Central Africa 18 C9, 232 F10
Gaborone *Town* Botswana 247 H8
Gaizin Kalns *Mountain* Latvia 109 H6
Galápagos Islands Pacific Ocean 11 V9, 19 V9, 265 I5
Galati *Town* Romania 127 K7
Galdhøppigen, Mt. Norway 82 E7
Galicia *Region* Poland 113 I8
Galicia *Region* Spain 100 C2
Galway Bay Ireland 78 B9
Gambia *Country* W. Africa 18 A8, 220 B8
Gäncä *Town* Azerbaijan 119 Q13
Gander *Town* Newfoundland, Canada 29 K4
Ganges *River* India 10 H7, 133 H11, 167 G5, I6, J7
Ganges Delta *River mouth* Bangladesh 167 J7
Garda, Lake Italy 103 D3
Garova *Town* Cameroon 232 E7
Gary *Town* Indiana, USA 37 D5
Gaza Strip *Region* 147 D8
Gaziantep *Town* Turkey 145 H8
Gdansk *Town* Poland 113 G2
Geelong *Town* Victoria, Australia 259 J12
Gelsenkirchen *Town* Germany 95 E6
General Santos *Town* Philippines 196 M6
Geneva *Town* Switzerland 106 A9
Geneva, Lake France/Switzerland 97 I6, 106 B9
Genoa *Town* Italy 103 C5
George Town *Town* Malaysia 189 E14
Georgetown *Town* Guyana 59 J1
Georgia *Country* S.W. Asia 18 E5, 119 O12
Georgia *State* USA 37 E9
Gerlachovka *Mountain* Slovakia 113 I8
Germany *Country* Europe 18 C4, 95
Ghana *Country* W. Africa 18 B8, 221 I11
Gharyan *Town* Libya 209 O4
Ghawar Oilfield Saudi Arabia 153 F8
Ghent *Town* Belgium 91 F9
Gibraltar *Dependent territory* Mediterranean Sea 18 B6 100 E9
Gibraltar, Strait of 78 C13, 100 D9
Gibson Desert Western Australia, Australia 10 K11, 254 C11, 258 D8
Gilbert Islands Kiribati, Pacific Ocean 11 N9, 255 K6, 265 D6
Gisborne *Town* New Zealand 262 H5
Giza *Town* Egypt 215 D1
Glana *River* Norway 82 F7
Glasgow *Town* UK 87 I6
Gobi Desert Central Asia 10 I5, 133 I8, 175 I7

Godavari *River* India 167 F8
Godoy Cruz *Town* Argentina 71 G8
Godthab (Nuuk) *Town* Greenland 267 B9
Goiânia *Town* Brazil 67 H8
Golan Heights *Region occupied by Israel* Syria 147 F6
Gold Coast *Town* Queensland, Australia 259 M9
Gonder *Town* Ethiopia 215 G8
Goose Lake California/Oregon, USA 33 G7
Gostivar *Town* Macedonia 123 J10
Göteborg *Town* Sweden 82 F10
Gotland *Island* Sweden 82 H11
Gough Island Atlantic Ocean 10 B12, 18 B12, 77 H10
Gozo *Island* Malta 103 G15
Grampian Mts UK 87 I5
Gran Chaco *Region* Argentina 41 G11, 71 H4
Granada *Town* Spain 100 F8
Grand Banks *Sea shelf* Atlantic Ocean 29 L4, 77 E4
Grand Canal China 178 O10
Grand Canyon Arizona, USA 21 I10, 33 J10
Grand Cayman *Island* Cayman Islands 44 F7
Grand Forks *Town* North Dakota, USA 35 I2
Grand Junction *Town* Colorado, USA 35 D7
Grand Rapids *Town* Michigan, USA 37 D4
Grasse *Town* France 97 J8
Graz *Town* Austria 106 K7
Great Australian Bight Australia 10 K12, 254 D13, 259 G10
Great Barrier Reef Australia 254 G9, 259 L6
Great Basin *Region* USA 21 I9
Great Bear Lake *Northwest Territories,* Canada 11 S2, 21 H5, 27 D8
Great Dividing Range *Mountain range* Queensland, Australia 10 M11, 254 G11, 259 L8
Great Eastern Erg *Desert region* Algeria 205 D3, 209 L5
Great Lakes Canada/USA 11 V4, 21 M8, 37 E2
Great Plain of China 10 J6, 133 K10
Great Plains USA 11 T5, 21 J8, 35 G6
Great Rift Valley E. Africa 10 D9, 205 H9, I9, 239 F9, I6
Great Salt Lake Utah, USA 21 I9, 33 J8
Great Salt Lake Desert Utah, USA 33 J8
Great Sandy Desert Western Australia, Australia 10 K11, 254 C10, 258 E7
Great Slave Lake *Northwest Territories,* Canada 11 S3, 21 I6, 27 E10
Great Victoria Desert Western/South Australia, Australia 10 K11, 254 C11, 258 F9
Great Wall *Ancient site* China 175 H8, I8, J9, K9, M7
Great Western Erg *Desert region* Algeria 205 C3, 209 J5
Greater Antilles *Island group* Caribbean Sea 11 V7, 41 E1, 45 M10
Greater Khingan Range *Mountain range* China 175 N5
Greece *Country* Europe 18 D5, 131
Green River W. USA 33 K9
Greenland *Dependent territory* Arctic Ocean 11 X1, 19 X1, 21 R3, 77 F2, 267 D7
Greenland Sea Arctic Ocean 11 Z2, 77 H2, 267 F8
Greensboro *Town* North Carolina, USA

37 G8
Grenada *Country* Caribbean Sea 19 W8, 45 U15
Greymouth *Town* New Zealand 262 D8
Groningen *Town* Netherlands 91 K4
Groznyy *Town* Russian Federation 138 B9
Guadalajara *Town* Mexico 39 E7
Guadalquivir *River* Spain 100 D7
Guadeloupe *Dependent territory* Caribbean Sea 45 V12
Guadiana *River* Portugal/Spain 100 C6, E6
Guam *Dependent territory* Micronesia, Pacific Ocean 18 L8, 254 F3, 265 B5
Guantánamo *Town* Cuba 45 M8
Guatemala *Country* Central America 19 U8, 44 B8
Guatemala City *Town* Guatemala 44 B9
Guayaquil *Town* Ecuador 59 B5
Guernsey *Island/Dependent territory* UK 87 I13
Guiana Highlands *Mountain range* S. America 41 G4
Guinea *Country* W. Africa 18 B8, 220 C10
Guinea Highlands *Region* W. Africa 205 C6, 221 E11
Guinea, Gulf of Atlantic Ocean 10 B8, 77 I7
Guinea-Bissau *Country* W. Africa 18 A8, 220 B9
Guiyang *Town* China 175 K13
Gujranwala *Town* Pakistan 167 E3
Gulf, The S.W. Asia 10 F6
Gunnbjørn, Mt. Greenland 267 D9
Guri *Reservoir* Venezuela 59 H2
Guwahati *Town* India 167 K5
Guyana Basin Atlantic Ocean 77 F7
Guyana *Country* S. America 19 W8, 59 I4
Gwalior *Town* India 167 F5
Gyda Peninsula Russian Federation 133 G3, 139 J5
Gyumri *Town* Armenia 119 P14

H

Ha Long Bay Vietnam 189 I5
Haarlem *Town* Netherlands 91 H6
Hagen *Town* Germany 95 E6
Hai Phong *Town* Vietnam 189 I5
Haifa *Town* Israel 147 E6
Haikou *Town* China 175 M15
Hainan *Island* China 175 L16
Haiti *Country* Caribbean Sea 19 V7, 45 O9
Hakodate *Town* Japan 185 H4
Halab *Town* Syria 147 G2
Halifax *Town* Nova Scotia, Canada 29 J6
Halle *Town* Germany 95 F6
Hälsingborg *Town* Sweden 82 F11
Hamada *Town* Japan 185 D10
Hamadan *Town* Iran 153 F4
Hamah *Town* Syria 147 G4
Hamburg *Town* Germany 95 G3
Hamersley Range *Mountain range* Australia 254 B10, 258 C7
Hamilton *Town* New Zealand 262 F4
Hamilton *Town* Ontario, Canada 29 F6
Hammar, Lake al Iraq 153 E4
Handan *Town* China 175 M9
Hangzhou *Town* China 175 O11
Hanoi *Town* Vietnam 189 H9
Hanover *Town* Germany 95 G5
Harad *Town* Saudi Arabia 153 F8
Harare *Town* Zimbabwe 247 I6
Harbin *Town* China 175 P5

Hardranger Fjord Norway 82 D8
Hargeysa *Town* Somalia 215 I9
Harrisburg *Town* Pennsylvania, USA 37 H6
Hartford *Town* Connecticut 37 J5
Hasselt *Town* Belgium 91 I9
Hastings *Town* New Zealand 262 G6
Hat Yai *Town* Thailand 189 E13
Havana *Town* Cuba 44 I5
Hawaii *Island* USA 33 H15, 255 O2
Hawaii *State* USA 19 P7, 33 G14
Hawaiian Islands Polynesia, Pacific Ocean 11 P7, 255 M1, 265 F4
Heard Island Indian Ocean 203 G11
Hefei *Town* China 175 N10
Helena *Town* Montana, USA 35 C3
Helsinki *Town* Finland 82 J9
Helwân *Town* Egypt 215 D2
Henzada *Town* Burma 189 C7
Herat *Town* Afghanistan 161 E9
Hilo *Town* Hawaii, USA 33 H14
Himalayas *Mountain range* S. Asia 10 H6, 133 G10, 167 H4, 174 D12
Hims *Town* Syria 147 G4
Hindu Kush *Mountain range* Central Asia 10 G6, 132 F9, 161 G9
Hiroshima *Town* Japan 185 D10
Hispaniola *Island* Caribbean Sea 41 F1
Hitachi *Town* Japan 185 I8
Hkakabo Razi *Mountain* Burma 189 D1
Ho Chi Minh City *Town* Vietnam 189 I11
Hobart *Town* Tasmania, Australia 259 K13
Hodeida *Town* Yemen 153 C11
Hohhot *Town* China 175 L7
Hokkaido *Island* Japan 10 L5, 133 N8, 185 I2
Holguín *Town* Cuba 45 M7
Holon *Town* Israel 147 E7
Holyhead *Town* UK 87 H9
Homyel' *Town* Belorussia 109 K11
Honduras *Country* Central America 19 U7, 44 E9
Hong Gai *Town* Vietnam 189 I5
Hong Kong *Dependent territory* E. Asia 18 J7, 175 N14, 285 A4
Honolulu *Town* Hawaii, USA 33 G14, 265 F4
Honshu *Island* Japan 10 L6, 133 N9, 185 H8
Horlivka *Town* Ukraine 119 K7
Hormus, Strait of Iran/Oman 153 I8
Horn of Africa *Region* Somalia 205 K6, 215 K8
Houston *Town* Texas, USA 35 J12
Howland Island *Dependent territory* Polynesia, Pacific Ocean 19P9, 255 L6, 265 E5
Hrodna *Town* Belorussia 109 F9
Huainan *Town* China 175 N10
Huancayo *Town* Peru 59 D8
Huang He, *see* Yellow River
Huascarán *Volcano* Peru 59 C7
Hudson Bay Canada 11 U3, 21 L6, 27 I10, 29 D4
Hudson *River* New York, USA 37 I5
Hudson Strait Northwest Territories, Canada 27 K8
Hue *Town* Vietnam 189 I8
Hungary *Country* Central Europe 18 D5, 113 G11
Huntsville *Town* Alabama, USA 37 D9
Huron, Lake Canada/USA 21 M8, 29 F8, 37 E3
Hyderabad *Town* India 167 F9
Hyderabad *Town* Pakistan 167 C5

I

Iasi *Town* Romania 127 J5
Ibadan *Town* Nigeria 221 K11
Ibiza *Island* Balearic Islands, Spain 100 J6
Ica *Town* Peru 59 D9
Iceland *Country* Atlantic Ocean 10 A3, 18 B44, 77 H2, 78 A5, 267 E10
Idaho *State* USA 33 H6
Iguaçu Falls *Waterfall* Brazil 41 I10, 67 F10
Ijsselmeer *Lake* Netherlands 91 C5
Île d'Ouessant *Island* France 97 A4
Ilebo *Town* Zaire 232 H12
Îles d'Hyères *Islands* France 97 J9
Iligan *Town* Philippines 196 M5
Illinois *State* USA 37 C6
Iloilo *Town* Philippines 196 L4
Ilorin *Town* Nigeria 221 L11
In Salah *Town* Algeria 209 K6
Inari *Lake* Finland 78 I4, 82 K3
Inch'on *Town* South Korea 175 Q8
Independence *Town* Missouri, USA 35 J7
India *Country* S. Asia 18 H7, 167 F6
Indian Ocean 10 H10, 203
Indiana *State* USA 37 D6
Indianapolis *Town* Indiana, USA 37 D6
Indonesia *Country* S.E. Asia 18 J9, 196 K11, 203 J5
Indore *Town* India 167 E7
Indus *River* Pakistan 132 F11, 167 B6, C4
Inner Hebrides *Island group* UK 78 C7, 87 G5
Innsbruck *Town* Austria 106 G7
Insein *Town* Burma 189 C7
International Date Line 265 E3
Invercargill *Town* New Zealand 262 B11
Ionian Islands Greece 131 A6
Ionian Sea Greece/Italy 103 J12, 131 A6
Ios *Island* Greece 131 H10
Iowa *State* USA 35 J5
Ipoh *Town* Malaysia 189 E14
Ipswich *Town* UK 87 L10
Iquique *Town* Chile 71 E3
Iquitos *Town* Peru 59 D5
Irakleio *Town* Crete 131 H12
Iran *Country* S.W. Asia 18 F6, 153 H5
Iranian Plateau S.W. Asia 10 G6, 132 D10
Iraq *Country* S.W. Asia 18 E6, 153 E4
Irbid *Town* Jordan 147 F7
Irbil *Town* Iraq 153 E3
Ireland *Country* Europe 18 34, 87 F8
Irian Jaya *Region* Indonesia 197 R10
Irish Sea Ireland/UK 87 H8
Irkutsk *Town* Russian Federation 139 M10
Irrawaddy *River* Burma 133 I12, 189 C4
Irtysh *River* N./Central Asia 10 H4, 133 G7, 138 H7, H8, 161 I2, 174 E5
Ischia *Island* Italy 103 G9
Ishim *River* Kazakhstan/Russian Federation 161 F2
Iskenderun *Town* Turkey 145 G8
Islamabad *Town* Pakistan 167 D2
Ismâ'iliya *Town* Egypt 215 E1
Isparta *Town* Turkey 145 D7
Israel *Country* S.W. Asia 18 E6, 147 E9
Istanbul *Town* Turkey 145 C5
Itaipú Dam Paraguay 71 K4
Italy *Country* Europe 18 C5, 103 E7
Ivano-Frankivs'k *Town* Ukraine 118 C6
Ivory Coast *Country* W. Africa 18 B8, 221 G11
Izabal, Lake Guatemala 44 C9
Izhersk *Town* Russian Federation 138 E7

Izmir *Town* Turkey 145 A7
Izmit *Town* Turkey 145 C5

J

Jabalpur *Town* India 167 G7
Jackson *Town* Mississippi, USA 37 C10
Jacksonville *Town* Florida, USA 37 F11
Jacques Cartier, Mt. Quebec, Canada 29 I5
Jaipur *Town* India 167 E5
Jakarta *Town* Java, Indonesia 196 F11
Jalandhar *Town* India 167 E3
Jamaica *Country* Caribbean Sea 18 V7, 46 K9
Jambi *Town* Sumatra, Indonesia 196 D9
Jan Mayen *Island* Norway 18 B2, 267 F9
Japan *Country* E. Asia 18 L6, 185
Japan, Sea of E. Asia 10 L5, 133 M9, 139 S11, 185 G7, 265 B3
Japanese Alps *Mountain range* Japan 185 G9
Jarris *Island* Pacific Ocean 19 Q9
Java *Island* Indonesia 133 K16, 196 G12
Java Sea Indonesia 10 J9, 196 F11
Jayapura *Town* Irian Jaya, Indonesia 197 T9
Jaz Murian *Salt Lake* Iran 153 J8
Jedda *Town* Saudi Arabia 153 B8
Jefferson City *Town* Missouri, USA 35 K7
Jember *Town* Java, Indonesia 196 I12
Jerez de la Frontera *Town* Spain 100 D8
Jericho *Town* Israel 147 E8
Jersey *Island/Dependent territory* UK 87 I13
Jerusalem *Town* Israel 147 E8
Jilin *Town* China 175 P5
Jinan *Town* China 175 N9
Jingdezhen *Town* China 175 N11
Jingmen *Town* China 175 M11
Jodhpur *Town* India 167 D5
Johannesburg *Town* South Africa 247 H9
John Day *River* Oregon/Washington, USA 33 H6
Johnston Atoll *Dependent territory* Polynesia, Pacific Ocean 19 P8, 255 M3, 265 F4
Johor Baharu *Town* Malaysia 189 G16
Jönköping *Town* Sweden 82 G10
Jordan *Country* S.W. Asia 18 E6, 147 G8
Jordan *River* S.W. Asia 147 E7
Juan Fernández, Islas *Island group* Pacific Ocean 11 U12, 19 V12, 265 K8
Juliaca *Town* Peru 59 E10
Juneau *Town* Alaska, USA 33 E3
Jura *Mountain range* Switzerland/France 97 I5, 106 B8
Jutland *Peninsula* Denmark 78 F8, 82 E11

K

K'ut'aisi *Town* Georgia 119 O12
Kabalebo Reservoir Surinam 59 J3
Kabul *Town* Afghanistan 161 G9
Kabwe *Town* Zambia 239 E13
Kaduna *Town* Nigeria 221 M10
Kafue Flats *Region* Zambia 239 C13
Kagoshima *Town* Japan 185 C12
Kahramanmaras *Town* Turkey 145 G8
Kaikoura *Town* New Zealand 262 E8
Kalahari Desert Botswana 10 D11, 205 G12, 247 F8
Kalemie *Town* Zaire 232 K12

Kalgoorlie *Town* Western Australia, Australia 258 E10
Kaliningrad *Town* Russian Federation 109 D8
Kamchatka Peninsula Russian Federation 10 M4, 133 P6, 139 T6
Kampala *Town* Uganda 239 G5
Kâmpóng Cham *Town* Cambodia 189 H10
Kananga *Town* Zaire 232 I12
Kandahar *Town* Afghanistan 161 E10
Kandi *Town* Benin 221 K10
Kano *Town* Nigeria 221 N9
Kanpur *Town* India 167 G5
Kansas *State* USA 35 H7
Kansas City *Town* Kansas, USA 35 J7
Kao-hsiung *Town* Taiwan 175 P14
Kapuas *River* Borneo, Indonesia 196 G9
Kara Kum *Desert* Kazakhstan 10 F5, 132 F9, 161 J4
Kara Sea Russian Federation 10 G2, 79 O3, 133 G2, 138 H4
Kara *Town* Togo 221 J10
Karachi *Town* Pakistan 167 B5, 203 F2
Karaganda *Town* Kazakhstan 161 H3
Karaj *Town* Iran 153 G4
Karakoram Mts. Central Asia 133 G10, 174 A8
Karakum Canal Turkmenistan 161 E8
Karbala *Town* Iraq 153 E5
Kariba Dam Zambia/Zimbabwe 239 E14
Karlsruhe *Town* Germany 95 F10
Karpathos *Island* Greece 131 K12
Karshi *Town* Uzbekistan 161 F7
Kashmir *Region* India/Pakistan 167 F2
Kathmandu *Town* Nepal 167 I5
Katowice *Town* Poland 113 H7
Kattegat *Channel* Denmark/Sweden 82 F10
Kauai *Island* Hawaii, USA 33 G14, 255 O2
Kaunas *Town* Lithuania 109 G8
Kawasaki *Town* Japan 185 H9
Kayseri *Town* Turkey 145 G7
Kazakh Uplands *Region* Kazakhstan 133 G7, 161 H3
Kazakhstan *Country* Central Asia 18 G4, 161 F4
Kazan' *Town* Russian Federation 138 E7
Kefallonia *Island* Greece 131 B7
Kelang *Town* Malaysia 189 E15
Kemerovo *Town* Russian Federation 139 J9
Kemijoki *River* Finland 82 J5, K4
Kendari *Town* Celebes, Indonesia 196 L10
Kénitra *Town* Morocco 208 G3
Kentucky *State* USA 37 E7
Kenya *Country* Africa 18 E9, 239 J4
Kenya, Mt. Kenya 239 J5
Kerguelen *Island group* Indian Ocean 18 G13, 203 G11
Kermadec Islands Polynesia, Pacific Ocean 19 O11, 255 L12, 265 E7
Kerman *Town* Iran 153 I7
Kerulen *River* Mongolia/China 175 L5
Khabarovsk *Town* Russian Federation 139 R10
Kharkiv *Town* Ukraine 119 J5
Khartoum *Town* Sudan 215 E7
Kherson *Town* Ukraine 119 H8
Khmel'nyts'kyy *Town* Ukraine 118 D5
Khon Kaen *Town* Thailand 189 G8
Khujand *Town* Tajikistan 161 G7
Khulna *Town* Bangladesh 167 J7
Khyber Pass *Mountain pass* Afghanistan/Pakistan 161 G9
Kiel *Town* Germany 95 G2
Kiel Canal Germany 95 G2
Kiev *Town* Ukraine 118 F5

Kigali *Town* Rwanda 239 F6
Kigoma *Town* Tanzania 239 E8
Kikwit *Town* Zaire 232 G12
Kilimanjaro, Mt. Tanzania 205 I9, 239 J6
Kimberley *Town* South Africa 247 G10
Kimberley Plateau *Region* Western Australia, Australia 254 C9, 259 F5
Kingman Reef *Dependent territory* Polynesia, Pacific Ocean 19 P8, 265 F5
Kingston *Town* Jamaica 45 L9
Kingston *Town* St Vincent and the Grenadines 45 V14
Kingston upon Hull *Town* UK 87 K8
Kinshasa *Town* Zaire 232 F12
Kirghiz Steppe *Region* Kazakhstan 10 F4, 132 D7, 161 D3
Kiribati *Country* Micronesia/Polynesia, Pacific Ocean 19 P9, 265 F6
Kirkuk *Town* Iraq 153 E4
Kirov *Town* Russian Federation 138 E6
Kirovohrad *Town* Ukraine 118 G7
Kisangani *Town* Zaire 232 I10
Kismaayo *Town* Somalia 215 I12
Kisumu *Town* Kenya 239 H5
Kitwe *Town* Zambia 239 E12
Kitzbühel *Town* Austria 106 G7
Kizil Irmak *River* Turkey 145 F5, G6
Kjølen Mts Norway/Sweden 78 G5, 82 G5
Klagenfurt *Town* Austria 106 I8
Klaipeda *Town* Lithuania 109 E7
Klerksdorp *Town* South Africa 247 G9
Klyuchevsk *Volcano* Russian Federation 139 T5
Knossos *Ancient site* Crete 131 H12
Knoxville *Town* Tennessee, USA 37 E8
Knud Rasmussen Land *Region* Greenland 21 O2, 267 E7
Kobe *Town* Japan 185 F10
Kodiak Island Alaska, USA 20 E7, 33 C3
Kola Peninsula Russian Federation 78 J5, 138 F3
Kolyma Range *Mountain range* Russian Federation 133 P5, 139 S5
Konya *Town* Turkey 145 E7
Koryak Range *Mountain range* Russian Federation 133 Q5, 139 T3
Kos *Island* Greece 131 K9
Kosciusko, Mt. Queensland, Australia 259 K11
Kosovo *Province* Serbia, Yugoslavia 123 I9
Kosovska Mitrovica *Town* Serbia, Yugoslavia 123 I9
Kota Baharu *Town* Malaysia 189 F13
Kota Kinabalu *Town* Borneo, Malaysia 196 J6
Kota *Town* India 167 E6
Kowloon *Town* Hong Kong 175 N14
Kragujevac *Town* Serbia, Yugoslavia 123 I7
Kraljevo *Town* Serbia, Yugoslavia 123 I7
Kramators'k *Town* Ukraine 119 K6
Krasnodar *Town* Russian Federation 138 A7
Krasnovodsk *Town* Turkmenistan 161 B6
Krasnoyarsk *Town* Russian Federation 139 K9
Krefeld *Town* Germany 95 D6
Kremenchuk *Town* Ukraine 119 H6
Krusevac *Town* Serbia, Yugoslavia 123 J7
Kryvyy Rih *Town* Ukraine 119 H7
Kuala Lumpur *Town* Malaysia 189 F15
Kuala Terengganu *Town* Malaysia 189 F14
Kuantan *Town* Malaysia 189 F15
Kuching *Town* Borneo, Malaysia 196 G8
Kujawy *Region* Poland 113 G4
Kumamoto *Town* Japan 185 C12

Kumanovo *Town* Macedonia 123 J10
Kumasi *Town* Ghana 221 I12
Kunlun Mts. China 10 H6, 133 H9, 174 D9
Kunming *Town* China 175 J14
Kupang *Town* Timor, Indonesia 196 M13
Kurile Islands *Disputed territory* E. Asia 10 M5, 133 O8, 139 U9, 185 K1, 265 C2
Kütahya *Town* Turkey 145 C6
Kuwait *Country* S.W. Asia 18 F6, 153 F6
Kuwait City *Town* Kuwait 153 F6, 203 E1
Kwajalein Atoll Marshall Islands, Pacific Ocean 265 D5
Kyoto *Town* Japan 185 F10
Kyrgyzstan *Country* Central Asia 18 G5, 161 H6
Kythira *Island* Greece 131 E11
Kyushu *Island* Japan 133 M10, 185 C11

L

L'viv *Town* Ukraine 118 B5
La Paz *Town* Bolivia 59 F10
La Plata *Town* Argentina 71 J8
La Serena *Town* Chile 71 F7
Labrador *Region* Newfoundland, Canada 29 I3
Labrador Sea Canada/Greenland 11 W3, 21 P6, 29 H2, 77 E3
Laccadive Islands Indian Ocean 203 G3
Laccadive Sea Indian Ocean 10 G8
Ladoga, Lake Russian Federation 10 E3, 78 J7
Lagao dos Patos *Lagoon* Brazil 67 G12
Lagos *Town* Nigeria 221 K12
Lahore *Town* Pakistan 167 E3
Lake District *Region* UK 78 D8, 87 I7
Lakshadweep *Island group* Indian Ocean 18 G8, 132 E13
Lambert Glacier Antarctica 269 I4
Lanai *Island* Hawaii, USA 33 G14
Land's End *Cape* UK 87 G12
Lansing *Town* Michigan, USA 37 E4
Lanzhou *Town* China 175 J9
Laos *Country* S.W. Asia 18 I7, 189 F6
Lapland *Region* N. Europe 78 H4, 82 I4
Laptev Sea Arctic Ocean 10 K1, 133 L2, 139 M4, 267 I4
Laredo *Town* Texas, USA 35 H13
Larisa *Town* Greece 131 D5
Larnaca *Town* Cyprus 145 E10
Larsen Ice Shelf Antarctica 269 B3
Las Vegas *Town* Nevada, USA 33 I11
Latvia *Country* E. Europe 18 D4, 109 G6
Lausanne *Town* Switzerland 106 B9
Laval *Town* Québec, Canada 29 H7
Le Havre *Town* France 97 E2
Le Mans *Town* France 97 E4
Lebanon *Country* S.W. Asia 18 E6, 147 F5
Leeds *Town* UK 87 J8
Leeward Islands Caribbean Sea 45 U10
Lefkada *Island* Greece 131 B6
Legaspi *Town* Philippines 196 L3
Leicester *Town* UK 87 J10
Leiden *Town* Netherlands 91 H6
Leipzig *Town* Germany 95 I6
Leiria *Town* Portugal 100 B5
Lelystad *Town* Netherlands 91 I5
Lena *River* Russian Federation 10 K2, 133 K5, L4, 139 N6, N8
León *Town* Nicaragua 44 D11
Léon *Town* Mexico 39 F7
Leskovac *Town* Serbia, Yugoslavia 123 K8
Lesotho *Country* Southern Africa 18 D11, 247 H10

Lesser Antilles *Island group* Caribbean Sea 11 W8, 41 G3, 45 R14, T12
Lesser Khingan Mts. N.E. Asia 175 O3
Lesvos *Island* Greece 131 I5
Leuuwarden *Town* Netherlands 91 J4
Levin *Town* New Zealand 262 F6
Lexington *Town* Kentucky, USA 37 E7
Lhasa *Town* China 175 F12
Liberia *Country* W. Africa 18 B8, 221 E12
Libreville *Town* Gabon 232 D10
Libya *Country* N. Africa 18 D6, 209 Q6
Libyan Desert Egypt/Libya/Sudan 10 D6, 205 G3, 209 T7, 215 C3
Liechtenstein *Country* Europe 18 C5, 106 E7
Liège *Town* Belgium 91 I10
Liepaja *Town* Latvia 109 E6
Ligurian Sea Italy 103 C6
Likasi *Town* Zaire 232 J14
Lille *Town* France 97 F1
Lillehammer *Town* Norway 82 F8
Lilongwe *Town* Malawi 239 H13
Lima *Town* Peru 59 C8, 265 L6
Limassol *Town* Cyprus 145 E10
Limoges *Town* France 97 E6
Limpopo *River* Southern Africa 205 I12, 247 I8
Lincoln Sea Arctic Ocean 21 O1
Lincoln *Town* Nebraska, USA 35 I6
Line Islands Kiribati, Pacific Ocean 11 P8, 255 O6, 265 F5
Linz *Town* Austria 106 I5
Lisbon *Town* Portugal 100 B6
Lithuania *Country* E. Europe 18 D4, 109 F7
Little Rock *Town* Arkansas, USA 35 K9
Liverpool *Town* UK 87 I9
Ljubljana *Town* Slovenia 123 B3
Llanos *Region* Colombia/Venezuela 11 V8
Locarno *Town* Switzerland 106 D9
Lódz *Town* Poland 113 H5
Lofoten *Island group* Norway 78 G4, 82 G3
Logan, Mt. Yukon Territory, Canada 27 A9
Logroño *Town* Spain 100 G2
Loire *River* France 78 D10, 97 D5, H6
Lombardy *Region* Italy 103 D4
Lombok *Island* Indonesia 196 J12
Lomé *Town* Togo 221 J12
Lomond, Loch *Lake* UK 87 H5
London *Town* Ontario, Canada 29 F6
London *Town* UK 87 K11
Londonderry *Town* UK 87 G6
Long Beach *Town* California, USA 33 H12
Long Island New York, USA 37 I5
Long Xuyen *Town* Vietnam 189 H11
Longyearbyen *Town* Svalbard 267 G8
Lop Nur *Lake* China 175 F8
Lord Howe Island *Dependent territory* Pacific Ocean 19 N11, 265 D8
Los Angeles *Town* California, USA 33 H12
Los Ángeles *Town* Chile 71 F10
Louang Phrabang *Town* Laos 189 F6
Louise, Lake Alberta, Canada 27 E13
Louisiana *State* USA 35 K11
Louisville *Town* Kentucky, USA 37 D7
Lowell *Town* Massachusetts, USA 37 J4
Loyalty Islands Pacific Ocean 11 N10
Luanda *Town* Angola 247 B2
Luanshya *Town* Zambia 239 E12
Lubbock *Town* Texas, USA 35 G10
Lübeck *Town* Germany 95 H3
Lubin *Town* Poland 113 K6
Lubumbashi *Town* Zaire 232 J14
Lucena *Town* Philippines 196 L3

Lucerne *Town* Switzerland 106 C8
Lucknow *Town* India 167 G5
Ludhiana *Town* India 167 E3
Lugano *Town* Switzerland 106 D9
Luhans'k *Town* Ukraine 119 L6
Lundy *Island* UK 87 H11
Luoyang *Town* China 175 L10
Lusaka *Town* Zambia 239 E13
Luts'k *Town* Ukraine 118 C4
Luxembourg *Country* Europe 18 C4, 91 J12
Luxembourg *Town* Luxembourg 91 J13
Luxor *Town* Egypt 215 E3
Luzon *Island* Philippines 133 L12, 196 L2
Lyon *Town* France 97 H6

M

Maastricht *Town* Netherlands 91 I10
Macao *Dependent territory* S.E. Asia 18 J7, 175 N14
Macao *Town* Macao 175 N14
Macdonnell Ranges *Mountain range* Northern Territory, Australia 254 D10, 259 G7
Macedonia *Country* S.E. Europe 18 D5, 123 J11
Maceió *Town* Brazil 67 L6
Machala *Town* Ecuador 59 B6
Machu Picchu *Ancient site* Peru 59 E9
Mackenzie *River* Northwest Territories, Canada 11 S3, 21 H5, 27 D9
Mackenzie Mts. Northwest Territories, Canada 20 G5, 27 C9
Macon *Town* Georgia, USA 37 E10
Macquarie Island *Dependent territory* Pacific Ocean 265 D9
Madagascar *Country* Indian Ocean 10 F11, 18 F11, 203 D7, 205 K12
Madeira *Island* Atlantic Ocean 10 A6, 18 A6, 77 H5, 205 A2
Madgeburg *Town* Germany 95 I5
Madison *Town* Wisconsin, USA 37 C4
Madras *Town* India 167 F11
Madre de Dios *River* Bolivia/Peru 59 F8
Madrid *Town* Spain 100 F4
Madurai *Town* India 167 F12
Magellan, Strait of *Channel* Chile 41 G16, 71 H16
Maggiore, Lake Italy/Switzerland 103 C3, 106 D9
Mahajanga *Town* Madagascar 203 D7
Mahalapye *Town* Botswana 247 G8
Mahé *Island* Seychelles 203 E6, 205 L9
Mahilyow *Town* Belorussia 109 K9
Maine *State* USA 37 K3
Mainz *Town* Germany 95 F8
Majorca *Island* Balearic Islands, Spain 100 L5
Makiyivka *Town* Ukraine 119 K7
Malabar Coast India 167 D11
Malabo *Town* Equatorial Guinea 232 C9
Malacca, Strait of S.E. Asia 203 I4
Málaga *Town* Spain 100 E8
Malang *Town* Java, Indonesia 196 H12
Malatya *Town* Turkey 145 H7
Malawi *Country* Africa 18 E10, 239 H13
Malaysia *Country* S.E. Asia 189 F15, 196 G7
Maldive Ridge Indian Ocean 203 G5
Maldives *Country* Indian Ocean 10 G8, 18 H9, 203 G4
Male *Town* Maldives 203 G5
Mali *Country* W. Africa 221 H6
Malmö *Town* Sweden 82 F11
Malta *Country* Europe 18 C6, 103 H15
Mammoth Caves Kentucky, USA 37 D7

Man, Isle of *Dependent territory* UK 87 H7
Manado *Town* Celebes, Indonesia 196 M8
Managua *Town* Nicaragua 44 E11
Manama *Town* Bahrain 153 F8
Manaus *Town* Brazil 67 E4
Manchester *Town* New Hampshire, USA 37 J4
Manchester *Town* UK 87 J9
Manchuria *Region* China 175 P5
Manchurian Plain *Region* China 10 K5, 133 L8
Mandalay *Town* Burma 189 C4
Manila *Town* Philippines 196 K3, 265 A5
Manisa *Town* Turkey 145 B7
Manitoba *Province* Canada 27 H11
Manizales *Town* Colombia 59 D3
Mannheim *Town* Germany 95 F9
Maputo *Town* Mozambique 247 I9
Mar del Plata *Town* Argentina 71 K9
Maracaibo *Town* Venezuela 59 E1
Maracaibo, Lake Venezuela 41 F3, 59 E1
Marañón *River* Peru 41 E6, 59 D6
Marathon *Ancient site* Greece 131 F7
Marbella *Town* Spain 100 E8
Mariana Trench Pacific Ocean 10 L8, 265 C4
Mariber *Town* Slovenia 123 D2
Marie Byrd Land *Region* Antarctica 269 D6
Maritsa *River* Bulgaria 127 I12
Mariupol' *Town* Ukraine 119 K8
Marka *Town* Somalia 215 I11
Marmara, Sea of Turkey 145 B5
Maroua *Town* Cameroon 232 F6
Marquesas Islands French Polynesia, Pacific Ocean 11 Q9, 255 R7, 265 H6
Marrakesh *Town* Morocco 208 G4
Marseille *Town* France 97 I9
Marshall Islands *Country* Micronesia, Pacific Ocean 11 N8, 19 N8, 255 J3, 265 D5
Martinique *Dependent territory* Caribbean Sea 45 V13
Maryland *State* USA 37 H7
Masai Steppe *Region* Tanzania 239 I7
Maseru *Town* Lesotho 247 H10
Mashhad *Town* Iran 153 J4
Massachusetts *State* USA 37 J5
Massif Central *Region* France 78 E11, 97 G7
Masterton *Town* New Zealand 262 F7
Matadi *Town* Zaire 232 E12
Matanzas *Town* Cuba 44 J5
Mato Grosso, Plateau of Brazil 11 W10, 41 H8, 67 F6
Maturín *Town* Venezuela 59 H1
Maui *Island* Hawaii, USA 33 G14
Mauritania *Country* W. Africa 18 B7, 220 D6
Mauritius *Country* Indian Ocean 18 F10, 203 E7, 205 L12
Mayagüez *Town* Puerto Rico 45 R10
Mayotte *Dependent territory* 18 E10, 203 D7, 205 J10
Mazar-e-Sharif *Town* Afghanistan 161 F8
Mazyr *Town* Belorussia 109 J11
Mbabane *Town* Swaziland 247 I9
Mbandaka *Town* Zaire 232 G10
Mbeya *Town* Tanzania 239 H10
Mbuji-Mayi *Town* Zaire 232 I12
McKinley, Mt. *see* Denali
McMurdo *Research station* Antarctica 269 F8
Mead, Lake Arizona/Nevada, USA 33 J11
Mecca *Town* Saudi Arabia 153 B8
Medan *Town* Sumatra, Indonesia 196 B7

Medellín *Town* Colombia 59 D2
Medina *Town* Saudi Arabia 15 C7
Mediterranean Sea 10 C5, 77 J5, 78 G13, 103 F14, 131 H13
Meerut *Town* India 167 F4
Meknès *Town* Morocco 208 H3
Mekong *River* Asia 10 J7, 133 J12, 175 G11, I15, 189 E5, F6, H8
Melaka *Town* Malaysia 189 F16
Melanesia *Region* Pacific Ocean 255 I7, 265 D6
Melbourne *Town* Victoria, Australia 259 K12
Melilla *Spanish enclave* Morocco 209 I2
Melville Island Northwest Territories, Canada 11 TI, 21 I3, 27 F5, 267 D4
Memphis *Town* Tennessee, USA 37 C8
Mendoza *Town* Argentina 71 G7
Mérida *Town* Mexico 39 K7
Mérida *Town* Spain 100 D6
Mérida *Town* Venezuela 59 E2
Mersin *Town* Turkey 145 F8
Mesa *Town* Arizona, USA 33 K12
Meseta *Region* Spain 78 D12
Messina *Town* Italy 103 I12
Mestre *Town* Italy 103 F4
Meuse *River* W. Europe 78 E9, 91 H11, J8, 97 H2
Mexicali *Town* Mexico 39 A1
Mexico *Country* N. America 19 T7, 39 E5
Mexico City *Town* Mexico 39 G8
Mexico, Gulf of 11 U7, 21 L11, 39 I7
Miami *Town* Florida, USA 37 G13
Michigan *State* USA 37 E3
Michigan, Lake USA 21 L9, 37 D4
Micronesia, Federated States of *Country* Pacific Ocean 18 L8, 255 I5, 265 C5
Mid-Atlantic Ridge Atlantic Ocean 77 F5, F7, H10
Mid-Indian Ridge Atlantic Ocean 203 G8
Mid-Pacific Seamounts Pacific Ocean 265 D4
Middelburg *Town* Netherlands 91 F8
Midway Island *Dependent territory* Polynesia, Pacific Ocean 11 O6, 19 O6, 265 E4
Milan *Town* Italy 103 C3
Milford Sound *Town* New Zealand 255 I15, 262 B10
Milwaukee *Town* Wisconsin, USA 35 D4
Minbu *Town* Burma 189 B5
Mindanao *Island* Philippines 133 L14, 196 L5
Mindoro *Island* Philippines 196 K3
Minneapolis *Town* Minnesota, USA 35 J4
Minnesota *State* USA 35 J2
Minorca *Island* Balearic Islands, Spain 100 L5
Minsk *Town* Belorussia 109 I9
Mississippi *River* USA 11 U6, 21 L9, 35 K4, K10, 37 B3, B9
Mississippi *State* USA 37 C10
Missouri *River* USA 10 U5, 21 J8, 35 F2, I5, K7
Missouri *State* USA 35 K8
Mitchell, Mt. Tennessee, USA 37 E8
Mitumba Mts. Zaire 232 J12
Mobile *Town* Alabama, USA 37 C11
Mogadishu *Town* Somalia 215 J11
Mojave Desert California, USA 33 H11
Moldavia *Country* E. Europe 18 D5, 118 E7
Moluccas *Island group* Indonesia 10 K9, 197 N9
Mombasa *Town* Kenya 239 K7
Monaco *Country* Europe 97 J8
Mongolia *Country* E. Asia 18 I5, 175 I5
Monrovia *Town* Liberia 220 D12

Mons *Town* Belgium 91 G10
Mont Blanc *Mountain* France 78 E11, 97 J6
Montana *State* USA 35 D2
Monte Albán *Ancient site* Mexico 39 H9
Montenegro *Republic* Yugoslavia 123 G8
Montería *Town* Colombia 59 D1
Monterrey *Town* Mexico 39 G5
Montevideo *Town* Uruguay 71 K8
Montgomery *Town* Alabama, USA 37 D10
Montpelier *Town* Vermont, USA 37 J4
Montpellier *Town* France 97 H9
Montreal *Town* Québec, Canada 29 H7
Monywa *Town* Burma 189 C4
Morar, Loch *Reservoir* UK 87 H4
Moravia *Region* Czech Republic 113 F8
Morocco *Country* N.W. Africa 18 B6, 208 G3
Moroni *Town* Comoros 203 D6
Moscow *Town* Russian Federation 138 C5
Mosel (Moselle) *River* W. Europe 91 K13, 95 E8, 97 I3
Mosquito Coast Panama 41 D2
Mostar *Town* Bosnia and Herzegovina 123 F8
Mosul *Town* Iraq 153 E3
Moulmein *Town* Burma 189 D7
Mozambique *Country* Southern Africa 18 E10, 247 J6
Mozambique Channel Madagascar/ Mozambique 10 E10, 205 J12
Muang Phitsanulok *Town* Thailand 189 E7
Muchinga Mts. Zambia 239 F12
Mufulira *Town* Zambia 239 E12
Mulhacén *Mountain* Spain 100 F8
Multan *Town* Pakistan 167 D4
Munich *Town* Germany 95 I11
Münitz *Lake* Germany 95 J3
Münster *Town* Germany 95 E5
Murcia *Town* Spain 100 H7
Murmansk *Town* Russian Federation 138 F3
Murray *River* New South Wales/South Australia, Australia 10 L12, 254 F13, 259 I10
Mururoa Atoll *Island* French Polynesia, Pacific Ocean 255 R10, 265 G7
Musala *Mountain* Bulgaria 127 F12
Muscarene Islands Indian Ocean 10 F10, 203 F8
Muscat *Town* Oman 153 I9
Mwanza *Town* Tanzania 239 G6
Mycenae *Ancient site* Greece 131 E8
Mykolayiv *Town* Ukraine 118 F8
Mykonos *Island* Greece 131 H8
Mysore *Town* India 167 E11

N

N'djamena *Town* Chad 232 F6
Naberezhnyye Chelny *Town* Russian Federation 138 E7
Nacala *Town* Mozambique 247 L5
Naga *Town* Philippines 196 L3
Nagasaki *Town* Japan 185 B12
Nagorno Karabakh *Region* Azerbaijan 119 R14
Nagoya *Town* Japan 185 G9
Nagpur *Town* India 167 F7
Nairobi *Town* Kenya 239 I6
Nakhon Ratchasima *Town* Thailand 189 F8
Nakhon Sawan *Town* Thailand 189 E8
Nakhon Si Thammarat *Town* Thailand 189 E12

Nakuru *Town* Kenya 239 I5
Nam Dinh *Town* Vietnam 189 H5
Namib Desert *Namibia* 10 C10, 205 F12, 247 C7
Namibia *Country* Southern Africa 18 D11, 247 D7
Namp'o *Town* North Korea 175 P7
Nampula *Town* Mozambique 247 L5
Namur *Town* Belgium 91 H10
Nanchang *Town* China 175 N12
Nancy *Town* France 97 I3
Nanjing *Town* China 175 O10
Nanning *Town* China 175 L14
Nantes *Town* France 97 C5
Napier *Town* New Zealand 262 G5
Naples *Town* Italy 103 G9
Nashville *Town* Tennessee, USA 37 D8
Nasik *Town* India 167 D8
Nassau *Town* Bahamas 45 M4
Nasser, Lake Egypt 215 E4
Natal *Region* South Africa 247 I9
Natal *Town* Brazil 67 L5
Nauru *Country* Micronesia, Pacific Ocean 19 N9, 255 J6, 265 D6
Navoi *Town* Uzbekistan 161 F7
Naxos *Island* Greece 131 I9
Nazareth *Town* Israel 147 E7
Nazca *Ancient site* Peru 59 D9
Ndola *Town* Zambia 239 E12
Neagh, Lough *Lake* UK 87 G7
Nebraska *State* USA 35 H5
Negev Desert Israel 147 E10
Neiva *Town* Colombia 59 D4
Nelson *Town* New Zealand 262 E7
Nepal *Country* S. Asia 18 H6, 167 H5
Ness, Loch *Lake* UK 87 I4
Netherlands *Country* Europe 18 C4, 91 I7
Nevada *State* USA 33 I9
New Brunswick *Province* Canada 29 I6
New Caledonia *Dependent territory* Melanesia, Pacific Ocean 19 N11, 255 I9, 265 D7
New Delhi *Town* India 167 F4
New Guinea *Island* Indonesia/Papua New Guinea 10 L9, 133 N15, 254 E7, 265 B6
New Hampshire *State* USA 37 K4
New Jersey *State* USA 37 I6
New Mexico *State* USA 35 E9
New Orleans *Town* Louisiana, USA 35 L12
New Plymouth *Town* New Zealand 262 F5
New Siberian Islands Russian Federation 10 L1, 133 N2, 139 O3, 267 H3
New South Wales *State* Australia 259 K10
New York *State* USA 37 I4
New York *Town* New York, USA 37 I6
New Zealand *Country* Australasia 11 N12, 19 N12, 262 E8
Newark *Town* New Jersey, USA 37 I6
Newcastle *Town* New South Wales, Australia 259 L10
Newcastle upon Tyne *Town* UK 87 J7
Newfoundland *Island* Canada 10 X4, 21 P8, 29 K4
Newfoundland *Province* Canada 29 J3
Newfoundland Basin Atlantic Ocean 77 F5
Nha Trang *Town* Vietnam 189 J10
Niagara Falls *Waterfall* Canada/USA 21 M9, 29 G9, 37 G4
Niamey *Town* Niger 221 K8
Nicaragua *Country* Central America 19 U8, 44 F11
Nicaragua, Lake Nicaragua 41 D3, 44 E12

Nice *Town* France 97 J8
Nicobar Islands Indian Ocean 10 H8, 18 H8, 133 I13, 203 I4
Nicosia *Town* Cyprus 145 E9
Niger *Country* W. Africa 18 C7, 221 O7
Niger *River* W. Africa 10 B8, 205 C5, E6, 221 E9, G8, K9, Mll
Niger Delta *River mouth* Nigeria 205 E7, 221 L13
Nigeria *Country* W. Africa 18 C8, 221 M10
Niihau *Island* Pacific Ocean 33 F14
Nijmegen *Town* Netherlands 91 J7
Nile *River* N.E. Africa 10 E7, 205 H3, I5, 215 E3, E5
Ninety East Ridge Indian Ocean 203 H7
Ningbo *Town* China 175 P11
Nis *Town* Serbia, Yugoslavia 123 K8
Niue *Dependent territory* Polynesia, Pacific Ocean 19 P10 265 F7
Nizhniy Novgorod *Town* Russian Federation 138 D6
Nkongsamba *Town* Cameroon 232 D8
Nome *Town* Alaska, USA 33 B2
Nord *Research station* Greenland 267 F7
Norfolk Island *Dependent territory* Pacific Ocean 19 N11, 255 J11, 265 D7
Norfolk *Town* Virginia, USA 37 H8
Normandy *Region* France 97 D3
North Albanian Alps *Mountain range* Albania/Yugoslavia 123 H9
North America *Continent* 11 T4, 20–21
North American Basin Atlantic Ocean 77 D5
North Cape Norway 78 H4, 82 J1
North Carolina *State* USA 37 G8
North Dakota *State* USA 35 G2
North European Plain Europe 78 G9
North Frisian Islands Denmark/ Germany 95 F1
North Island New Zealand 255 J13, 262 F5
North Korea *Country* E. Asia 18 K5, 175 P6
North Pole Arctic Ocean 267 F5
North Sea Atlantic Ocean 10 C4, 77 I3, 78 E8, 91 F7
North-Eastern Atlantic Basin Atlantic Ocean 77 H4
Northampton *Town* UK 87 K10
Northern Dvina *see* Dvina
Northern Ireland *Region* UK 87 G7
Northern Mariana Islands *Dependent territory* Micronesia, Pacific Ocean 10 L8, 18 L7, 254 F3, 265 C4
Northern Territory *Territory* Australia 259 G6
Northwest Territories *Province* Canada 27 F8
Norway *Country* Europe 18 C3, 82 G6
Norwegian Sea Atlantic Ocean 10 C3, 78 E5, 82 F5
Norwich *Town* UK 87 L10
Nottingham *Town* UK 87 J9
Nouakchott *Town* Mauritania 220 B6
Nova Scotia *Province* Canada 29 J6
Novaya Zemlya *Island group* Russian Federation 10 F2, 79 N2, 138 H3, 267 I7
Novgorod *Town* Russian Federation 138 C4
Novi Sad *Town* Serbia, Yugoslavia 123 H5
Novokuznetsk *Town* Russian Federation 139 J10
Novosibirsk *Town* Russian Federation 139 I9
Nubian Desert Sudan 205 I4, 215 E5
Nukus *Town* Uzbekistan 161 D6
Nullarbor Plain *Region* Western

Australia, Australia 256 F10
Nuremberg *Town* Germany 95 H9
Nuuk *see* Godthåb
Nyasa, Lake Southern Africa 10 E10, 205 I10, 239 H11, 247 J4

O

Oahu *Island* Pacific Ocean 33 G14, 255 O2
Oakland *Town* California, USA 33 G10
Oaxaca *Town* Mexico 39 H9
Ob' *River* Russian Federation 10 G3, 132 F4, 133 G6, 138 H6, 139 I8
Oban *Town* UK 87 H5
Odense *Town* Denmark 82 E11
Oder *River* Germany 78 G9, 95 K4
Odesa *Town* Ukraine 118 F8
Odra *River* Central Europe 113 D4, F6
Ogbomosho *Town* Nigeria 221 L11
Ohio *River* USA 37 C7, F6
Ohio *State* USA 37 F6
Okavango *River* Southern Africa 205 H12, 247 D3
Okavango Delta Botswana 247 F6
Okayama *Town* Japan 185 E10
Okhotsk, Sea of Japan/Russian Federation 10 L4, 133 O6, 139 S7, 185 J1, 265 C2
Okinawa *Island* Japan 185 A16
Oklahoma *State* USA 35 I9
Oklahoma City *Town* Oklahoma, USA 35 I9
Öland *Island* Sweden 82 H11
Olduvai Gorge Tanzania 239 I7
Oloy Range *Mountain range* Russian Federation 133 Q4, 139 R4
Olympia *Ancient site* Greece 131 C8
Olympia *Town* Washington, USA 33 F5
Olympus, Mt. Greece 131 D4
Omaha *Town* Nebraska, USA 35 I6
Oman *Country* S.W. Asia 18 F7, 153 G11
Oman, Gulf of Arabia/Iran 10 G7, 132 E11, 203 F2
Omdurman *Town* Sudan 215 E7
Omsk *Town* Russian Federation 138 H9
Onega, Lake Russian Federation 10 E3, 78 K6, 138 E4
Onitsha *Town* Nigeria 221 M12
Ontario, Lake Canada/USA 21 M9, 29 G8, 37 G4
Ontario *Province* Canada 29 D6
Oodaaq Island Arctic Ocean 267 F7
Oradea *Town* Romania 127 E5
Oran *Town* Algeria 209 J2
Orange River Southern Africa 10 D11, 205 G13, 247 E10, G10
Ore Mountains Czech Republic/ Germany 95 J10, 113 C6
Oregon *State* USA 33 G6
Örebro *Town* Sweden 82 G9
Orenburg *Town* Russian Federation 138 E8
Orinoco *River* Venezuela 41 G4, 59 H2, F3, G3
Orizaba *see* Citlaltépetl
Orkneys *Island group* UK 78 D7, 87 J2
Orlando *Town* Florida, USA 37 F12
Orléans *Town* France 97 F4
Orsha *Town* Russian Federation 109 K8
Orumiyeh *Town* Iran 153 F3
Oruro *Town* Bolivia 59 F10
Osaka *Town* Japan 185 F10
Osh *Town* Kyrgyzstan 161 H7
Oshogbo *Town* Nigeria 221 L11
Osijek *Town* Croatia 123 G4
Oslo *Town* Norway 82 F8
Osmaniye *Town* Turkey 145 G8

Osorno *Town* Chile 71 F11
Ostend *Town* Belgium 91 E9
Ottawa *River* Ontario/Quebec, Canada 29 F7
Ottawa *Town* Ontario, Canada 29 G8
Ouagadougou *Town* Burkina 221 I9
Oued Chelif *River* Algeria 209 K2
Oujda *Town* Morocco 209 I3
Oulu *Town* Finland 82 J5
Outer Hebrides *Island group* UK 78 C7, 87 G3
Oviedo *Town* Spain 100 D1
Oxford *Town* UK 87 J10
Oxnard *Town* California, USA 33 H12

P

Pa-an *Town* Burma 189 D7
Pacific Ocean 11 Q7, 255 L3, 265 H4
Padang *Town* Sumatra, Indonesia 196 C9
Padua *Town* Italy 103 E4
Pagan *Ancient site* Burma 189 C5
Painted Desert Arizona, USA 33 K11
Pakambaru *Town* Sumatra, Indonesia 196 C9
Pakistan *Country* S. Asia 18 G6, 167 B4
Pakokku *Town* Burma 189 C5
Pakxé *Town* Laos 189 H9
Palau *Country* Micronesia, Pacific Ocean 18 L8, 254 D5, 265 B5
Palembang *Town* Sumatra, Indonesia 196 E10
Palenque *Ancient site* Mexico 39 J9
Palermo *Town* Italy 103 G12
Palmerston North *Town* New Zealand 262 F6
Palmyra Atoll *Dependent territory* Polynesia, Pacific Ocean 19 P8, 255 N5, 265 F5
Palu *Town* Celebes, Indonesia 196 K9
Pamir *River* Afghanistan/Tajikistan 161 H8
Pamirs *Mountain range* Tajikistan 133 G9, 161 H8
Pampas *Region* Argentina 11 W12, 41 G13, 71 H9
Pamplona *Town* Spain 100 H2
Panama *Country* Central America 19 V8, 44 G15
Panama Canal Panama 41 E3, 44 H15
Panama City *Town* Panama 44 I15, 77 C7, 265 L5
Panama, Isthmus of Panama 41 D4
Pancevo *Town* Serbia, Yugoslavia 123 J5
Panevezys *Town* Lithuania 109 G7
Pantelleria *Island* Italy 103 E14
Papua New Guinea *Country* Australasia 18 M9, 259 L2
Paraguay *Country* S. America 19 W11, 71 I3
Paraguay *River* S. America 41 H9, 71 J4
Paramaribo *Town* Surinam 59 K3
Paraná *River* Argentina/Paraguay/ Brazil 11 W11, 41 H11, 67 G9, 71 J5, J7
Paranaiba *River* Brazil 41 I9
Paris *Town* France 97 F3
Parma *Town* Italy 103 D5
Parry Islands Northwest Territories, Canada 21 K3, 27 F4
Pasto *Town* Colombia 59 C4
Patagonia *Region* Argentina 11 V13, 41 F14, 71 H13
Patna *Town* India 167 H6
Patrai *Town* Greece 131 C7
Peary Land *Region* Greenland 21 R1, 267 E7
Pec *Town* Serbia, Yugoslavia 123 I9

Pegu *Town* Burma 189 C7
Peipus, Lake Estonia/Russian Federation 109 I4
Pelagie Islands Italy 103 F15
Pelée, Mt. *Volcano* Martinique 41 H2
Peloponnese *Island group* Greece 131 D8
Pematangsiantar *Town* Sumatra, Indonesia 196 B8
Pennines *Mountain range* UK 87 J7
Pennsylvania *State* USA 37 G5
Penza *Town* Russian Federation 138 C7
Penzance *Town* UK 87 G12
Peoria *Town* Illinois, USA 37 C6
Perm' *Town* Russian Federation 138 F7
Persian Gulf Saudi Arabia/Iran 132 D11, 153 F7, 203 E2
Perth *Town* UK 87 I5
Perth *Town* Western Australia, Australia 258 C10
Peru *Country* S. America 19 V10, 59 C6
Perugia *Town* Italy 103 F7
Peshawar *Town* Pakistan 167 D2
Petah-Tiqwa *Town* Israel 147 E7
Petra *Ancient site* Jordan 147 E10
Philadelphia *Town* Pennsylvania, USA 37 I6
Philippine Sea Philippines 10 K7, 196 L2, 254 C5, 265 B4
Philippines *Country* S.E. Asia 10 K8, 18 K8, 196 K5
Phnom Penh *Town* Cambodia 189 H11
Phoenix Islands Kiribati, Pacific Ocean 11 P9, 255 L6, 265 E6
Phoenix *Town* Arizona, USA 33 J12
Phuket *Town* Thailand 189 D12
Piatra-Neamt *Town* Romania 127 I5
Pico da Neblina *Mountain* Brazil 67 C3
Picton *Town* New Zealand 262 E7
Pierre *Town* South Dakota, USA 35 H4
Pietermaritzburg *Town* South Africa 247 H10
Pietersburg *Town* South Africa 247 H8
Pinar del Rio *Town* Cuba 44 H5
Pinatubo, Mt. *Volcano* Philippines 196 K2
Pindus Mountains Greece 131 C5
Pingxiang *Town* China 175 M12
Pinsk *Town* Belorussia 109 H11
Piraeus *Town* Greece 131 F8
Pisa *Town* Italy 103 D6
Pitcairn Islands *Dependent territory* Polynesia, Pacific Ocean 19 S11, 255 T11, 265 H7
Pitesti *Town* Romania 127 G8
Pittsburgh *Town* Pennsylvania, USA 37 G6
Piura *Town* Peru 59 B6
Plata, Rio de la *River* Argentina/ Uruguay 41 H12, 71 J8
Pleven *Town* Bulgaria 127 G10
Ploiesti *Town* Romania 127 I8
Plovdiv *Town* Bulgaria 127 G12
Plymouth *Town* UK 87 H12
Po *River* Italy 78 F11, 103 B4, E4
Podgorica *Town* Montenegro, Yugoslavia 123 H9
Podlasie *Region* Poland 113 K4
Pointe-Noire *Town* Congo 232 E12
Poitiers *Town* France 97 E6
Poland *Country* Central Europe 18 D4, 113 H4
Poltava *Town* Ukraine 119 I6
Polynesia *Region* Pacific Ocean 255 N9, 265 F7
Pomerania *Region* Germany/Poland 113 E2
Ponce *Town* Puerto Rico 45 S10
Pontchartrain, Lake Louisiana, USA 35 L12

Pontianak *Town* Borneo, Indonesia 196 G9
Pontic Mountains Turkey 145 G5
Poopó, Lake Bolivia 41 G9, 59 F11
Popayán *Town* Colombia 59 C4
Popocatépetl *Volcano* Mexico 39 G8
Port Elizabeth *Town* South Africa 247 G11
Port Harcourt *Town* Nigeria 221 M13
Port Hedland *Town* Western Australia, Australia 258 C7
Port Louis *Town* Mauritius 203 E7
Port Moresby *Town* Papua New Guinea 259 K3
Port of Spain *Town* Trinidad & Tobago 45 U16
Port Said *Town* Egypt 203 C1, 215 E1
Port Sudan *Town* Sudan 215 F5
Port-au-Prince *Town* Haiti 45 O9
Port-Gentil *Town* Gabon 232 D10
Portland *Town* Oregon, USA 33 F5
Porto *Town* Portugal 100 B3
Pôrto Alegre *Town* Brazil 67 G12
Porto-Novo *Town* Benin 221 K12
Portoviejo *Town* Ecuador 59 B5
Portsmouth *Town* UK 87 J12
Portugal *Country* Europe 18 B5, 100 B6
Posadas *Town* Argentina 71 K5
Potosí *Town* Bolivia 59 G11
Potsdam *Town* Germany 95 J5
Poznán *Town* Poland 113 F4
Prague *Town* Czech Republic 113 D7
Praia *Town* Cape Verde 77 G6
Pravets *Town* Bulgaria 127 G11
Prespa, Lake Greece/Albania/ Macedonia 123 J12, 131 C2
Preston *Town* UK 87 I8
Pretoria *Town* South Africa 247 H8
Prijedor *Town* Bosnia and Herzegovina 123 E5
Prince Edward Island *Province* Canada 29 J6
Prince Edward Islands Indian Ocean 10 E13, 18 E13, 203 E10
Pristina *Town* Serbia, Yugoslavia 123 J9
Prizren *Town* Serbia, Yugoslavia 123 I10
Prome *Town* Burma 189 C6
Provence *Region* France 97 I9
Providence *Town* Rhode Island, USA 37 J5
Pucallpa *Town* Peru 59 D7
Puebla *Town* Mexico 39 H8
Puerto Barrios *Town* Guatemala 44 D9
Puerto Montt *Town* Chile 71 F11
Puerto Natales *Town* Chile 71 G15
Puerto Rico *Dependent territory* Caribbean Sea 45 S10
Puerto Rico Trench Atlantic Ocean 77 D6
Puerto Santa Cruz *Town* Argentina 71 H14
Puncak Jaya *Mountain* Irian Jaya, Indonesia 197 R10
Pune *Town* India 167 D8
Punjab *Region* India 167 E3
Punta Arenas *Town* Chile 71 H15
Pusan *Town* South Korea 175 Q8
Putorana Mts. Russian Federation 139 L5
Pyinmana *Town* Burma 189 C6
Pyongyang *Town* North Korea 175 P7
Pyrenees *Mountain range* S.W. Europe 78 D11, 97 E10, 100 I2

Q

Qatar *Country* S.W. Asia 18 F7, 153 G8
Qazvin *Town* Iran 153 G4

Qena *Town* Egypt 215 E3
Qingdao *Town* China 175 O9
Qinghai Hu *Lake* China 175 H9
Qiqihar *Town* China 175 O4
Qolleh-ye-Damavand *Mountain* Iran 153 H4
Qom *Town* Iran 153 G4
Qornet es Saouda *Mountain* Lebanon 147 F5
Quang Ngai *Town* Vietnam 189 J8
Québec *Province* Canada 29 G6
Québec *Town* Québec, Canada 29 H7
Queen Charlotte Island British Columbia, Canada 20 G7, 27 A12
Queen Elizabeth Islands Northwest Territories, Canada 21 L2, 27 G4, 267 D5
Queen Maud Land *Region* Antarctica 269 F2
Queensland *State* Australia 259 J7
Queenstown *Town* New Zealand 262 B10
Querétaro *Town* Mexico 39 G7
Quezaltenango *Town* Guatemala 44 B9
Qui Nhon *Town* Vietnam 189 J9
Quito *Town* Ecuador 59 C5

R

Rabat *Town* Morocco 208 G3
Rach Gia *Town* Vietnam 189 H11
Rajkot *Town* India 167 C7
Rajshahi *Town* Bangladesh 167 J6
Raleigh *Town* North Carolina, USA 37 G8
Ramlat As Sab'Atayn *Desert* region Saudi Arabia/Yemen 153 D11
Râmnia Vâlcea *Town* Romania 127 G8
Rancagua *Town* Chile 71 F8
Ranchi *Town* India 167 I7
Rangoon *Town* Burma 189 C7
Rangpur *Town* Bangladesh 167 J6
Ras Dashen, Mt. Ethiopia 215 G7
Rasht *Town* Iran 153 G3
Rat Buri *Town* Thailand 189 E9
Ravenna *Town* Italy 103 F5
Rawalpindi *Town* Pakistan 167 D2
Razim *Lake* Romania 127 L8
Reading *Town* UK 87 J11
Recife *Town* Brazil 67 L5
Red River USA 21 K10, 35 H9
Red Sea 10 E7, 132 B11, 153 A7, 203 D2, 205 J4, 215 F3
Red Volta *River* W. Africa 221 I9
Regina *Town* Saskatchewan, Canada 27 G14
Reni *Town* Ukraine 118 E9
Rennes *Town* France 97 C4
Reno *Town* Nevada, USA 33 H9
Resistencia *Town* Argentina 71 J5
Resita *Town* Romania 127 D7
Resolute *Town* Northwest Territories, Canada 27 C5, 267 C5
Réunion *Dependent territory* Indian Ocean 18 F11, 203 E7, 205 L12
Revillagigedo Is. *Island group* Mexico 19 S7, 265 I4
Reykjavik *Town* Iceland 77 G3, 267 D10
Rheims *Town* France 97 G3
Rhine *River* W. Europe 10 C4, 78 E9, 91 J7, 95 D6, E10, 97 J3, 106 E7
Rhineland *Region* Germany 95 D8
Rhode Island *State* USA 37 J5
Rhodes *Island* Greece 131 L11
Rhodope Mts. Bulgaria/Greece 78 H11, 127 F12
Rhône *River* Switzerland/France 97 H8, 106 C9

Richmond *Town* Virginia, USA 37 H7
Riga *Town* Latvia 109 G6
Rijeka *Town* Croatia 123 B4
Rimini *Town* Italy 103 F5
Rio Cuarte *Town* Argentina 71 H7
Rio de Janeiro *Town* Brazil 67 I10
Rio Grande *River* Mexico/USA 11 T6, 21 J11, 35 F11, 39 G4
Rio Grande de Santiago *River* Mexico 39 E7
Riobamba *Town* Ecuador 59 C5
Rivadavia *Town* Argentina 41 G10, 71 H12
Rivne *Town* Ukraine 118 D4
Riyadh *Town* Saudi Arabia 153 E8
Rochester *Town* Minnesota, USA 35 K4
Rochester *Town* New York, USA 37 H4
Rockall *Island* UK, Atlantic Ocean 77 H3
Rockford *Town* Illinois, USA 37 C5
Rocky Mountains N. America 11 S4, 21 I7, 27 C11, 33 H5, 35 D6
Romania *Country* E. Europe 18 D5, 127 G6
Rome *Town* Italy 103, F8
Ronne Ice Shelf Antarctica 269 D4
Rosario *Town* Argentina 71 I7
Roseau *Town* Dominica 45 V13
Ross Ice Shelf Antarctica 269 E7
Ross Sea Antarctica 269 E8
Rostock *Town* Germany 95 I2
Rostov-na-Donu *Town* Russian Federation 138 B7
Rotorua *Town* New Zealand 255 K13, 262 G4
Rotterdam *Town* Netherlands 91 H7
Rouen *Town* France 97 E2
Rub 'al Khali (Empty Quarter) *Desert region* Saudi Arabia 10 F7, 132 C12, 153 E10
Rudolf, Lake *see* Turkana, Lake
Ruhr *River* Germany 95 F6
Ruse *Town* Bulgaria 127 I10
Russian Federation *Country* E. Europe/ N. Asia 18 D4, I3, 109 E8, 138–139
Ruwenzori Mts. Uganda/Zaire 205 H8, 239 E5
Rwanda *Country* Africa 18 D9, 239 F6
Ryazan *Town* Russian Federation 138 C6
Ryukyu Islands E. Asia 10 K7, 185 C15

S

Saarbrücken *Town* Germany 95 D9
Sabac *Town* Serbia Yugoslavia 123 H6
Sabah *Region* Borneo, Malaysia 196 J7
Sacramento *Town* California, USA 33 G9
Safi *Town* Morocco 208 F3
Sagaing *Town* Burma 189 C4
Sahara Desert N. Africa 10 C7, 205 D4, 209 M8, 221 H5
Sahel *Region* W. Africa 205 D6, 221 I7, 232 G5
Saimaa *Lake* Finland 10 D3, 78 I6, 82 K8
St Étienne *Town* France 97 H7
St George's *Town* Grenada 45 U15
St George's Channel Ireland/UK 87 G10
St Helena *Dependent territory* Atlantic Ocean 10 B10, 77 I9, 18 B10
St John's *Town* Newfoundland, Canada 29 L4
St Johns *Town* Antigua & Barbuda 45 V11
St Kitts and Nevis *Country* West Indies 19 V7, 45 U11
St Lawrence *River* Canada 21 N8, 29 H6

St Lawrence Seaway *Canal* Ontario, Canada 29 G8
St Lawrence, Gulf of Canada 21 O8, 29 I5
St Louis *Town* Missouri, USA 35 L7
St Lucia *Country* Caribbean Sea 19 W8, 45 V14
St Malo *Town* France 97 C3
St Paul *Island* Indian Ocean 18 H12, 203 G9
St Paul *Town* Minnesota, USA 35 K4
St Petersburg *Town* Florida, USA 37 F12
St Petersburg *Town* Russian Federation 138 D4
St Pierre and Miquelon *Dependent territory* 19 W5, 29 K5
St Pierre *Town* St. Pierre and Miquelon 29 K5
St Vincent and the Grenadines *Country* Caribbean Sea 18 V8, 45 V14
Sakhalin *Island* Russian Federation 133 N7, 139 S8
Salamanca *Town* Spain 100 D4
Salem *Town* Washington, USA 33 F6
Salisbury *Town* UK 87 J11
Salt Lake City *Town* Utah, USA 33 K8
Salta *Town* Argentina 71 G4
Salvador *Town* Brazil 67 K7
Salween *River* Burma/China 175 G11, H14, 189 D5
Salzburg *Town* Austria 106 H6
Samara *Town* Russian Federation 138 D7
Samarinda *Town* Borneo, Indonesia 196 J9
Samarkand *Town* Uzbekistan 161 F7
Samoa *Island* Pacific Ocean 255 M8
Samos *Island* Greece 131 J8
Samothraki *Island* Greece 131 I3
Samsun *Town* Turkey 145 G5
San Agustin *Ancient site* Colombia 59 C4
San Ambrosio Isla *Island* Chile 19 V11, 265 K7
San Antonio *Town* Texas, USA 35 I12
San Bernardino *Town* California, USA 33 H12
San Cristóbal *Town* Venezuela 59 E2
San Diego *Town* California, USA 33 H12
San Felix Isla *Island* Chile 19 V11, 265 K7
San Francisco *Town* California, USA 21 H10, 33 F10, 265 I3
San Jose *Town* California, USA 33 G10
San José *Town* Costa Rica 44 F13
San Juan *River* Utah, USA 33 K10
San Juan *Town* Argentina 71 G7
San Juan *Town* Peru 59 D10
San Juan *Town* Puerto Rico 45 S10
San Luis Potosí *Town* Mexico 39 F6
San Marino *Country* Europe 18 C5, 103 F6
San Miguel de Tucumán *Town* Argentina 71 H5
San Miguel *Town* El Salvador 44 D10
San Pedro Sula *Town* Honduras 44 D9
San Remo *Town* Italy 103 B6
San Salvador *Town* El Salvador 44 C10
San Salvador de Jujuy *Town* Argentina 71 G4
San Sebastián *Town* Spain 100 G1
San'a *Town* Yemen 153 C11
Sanandaj *Town* Iran 153 F4
Sandoway *Town* Burma 189 B6
Sankt Gallen *Town* Switzerland 106 D7
Sankt Pölten *Town* Austria 106 J5
Sanliurfa *Town* Turkey 145 I8
Santa Ana *Town* California, USA 33 H12
Santa Ana *Town* El Salvador 44 C10
Santa Clara *Town* Cuba 45 K6

Santa Cruz *Town* Bolivia 59 G10
Santa Fe *Town* Argentina 71 I7
Santa Fe *Town* New Mexico, USA 35 E9
Santa Marta *Town* Colombia 59 D1
Santander *Town* Spain 100 F1
Santiago *Town* Chile 71 F8, 265 L8
Santiago *Town* Dominican Republic 45 P9
Santiago *Town* Spain 100 B2
Santiago de Cuba *Town* Cuba 45 M8
Santiago del Estero *Town* Argentina 71 H5
Santo Domingo *Town* Dominican Republic 45 P10
São Luís *Town* Brazil 67 I4
São Paulo *Town* Brazil 67 I10
São Francisco *River* Brazil 11 X10, 41 K7, 67 I7
São Tomé *Town* São Tomé and Príncipe 232 C10
São Tomé and Príncipe *Country* Central Africa 18 C9, 232 C10
Sapporo *Town* Japan 185 H3
Sarajevo *Town* Bosnia and Herzegovina 123 G7
Saratov *Town* Russian Federation 138 C7
Sarawak Chamber *Cave* Borneo, Indonesia 196 I7
Sarawak *Region* Borneo, Malaysia 196 H8
Sardinia *Island* Italy 78 F12, 103 C10
Sargasso Sea Atlantic Ocean 77 E6
Sarh *Town* Chad 232 G7
Sari *Town* Iran 153 H4
Sarmiento *Town* Argentina 41 F14
Saskatchewan *Province* Canada 27 F12
Saskatoon *Town* Saskatchewan, Canada 27 F13
Satu Mare *Town* Romania 127 E4
Saudi Arabia *Country* S.W. Asia 18 E7, 153 D8
Sava *River* S.E. Europe 78 G11, 123 C3, E5, H5
Savannah *Town* Georgia, USA 37 F10
Savannakhét *Town* Laos 189 H8
Scandinavia *Region* N. Europe 82
Schwerin *Town* Germany 95 H3
Scilly, Isles of UK 87 F12
Scotia Sea Atlantic Ocean 77 E12, 59 C9, 269 C2
Scotland *Region* UK 87 I5
Scott Base *Research station* Antarctica 269 F8
Scutari, Lake Yugoslavia/Albania 123 H10
Seattle *Town* Washington, USA 33 G4
Seikan Tunnel *Undersea rail tunnel* Japan 185 H4
Seine *River* France 78 D10, 97 F3, G3
Selvas *Region* Brazil 41 G7
Semarang *Town* Java, Indonesia 196 G12
Semnan *Town* Iran 153 H4
Sendai *Town* Japan 185 I7
Senegal *Country* W. Africa 18 A8, 220 C8
Seoul *Town* South Korea 175 Q8
Serbia *Republic* Yugoslavia 123 I6
Seremban *Town* Malaysia 189 F15
Serengeti Plain *Region* Tanzania 205 I9
Sétif *Town* Algeria 209 L2
Sevan *Lake* Armenia 119 Q14
Sevastopol' *Town* Ukraine 117 H10
Severn *River* UK 87 I10
Severnaya Zemlya *Island group* Russian Federation 10 I1, 139 L2, 267 H5
Seville *Town* Spain 78 C13, 100 D7
Seward Peninsula Alaska, USA 20 C5
Seychelles *Country* Indian Ocean 10 F9, 18 F9, 203 E6, 205 K9

Sfax *Town* Tunisia 209 N3
Shackleton Ice Shelf Antarctica 269 J6
Shamiyah Desert Syria 147 I5
Shandong Peninsula China 175 O8
Shanghai *Town* China 175 P10, 265 A3
Shannon *River* Ireland 87 F8
Shaoxing *Town* China 175 O11
Shaoyang *Town* China 175 M12
Sheffield *Town* UK 87 J9
Shenyang *Town* China 175 O6
's-Hertogenbosch *Town* Netherlands 91 I7
Shetlands *Island group* UK 78 D7, 87 K1
Shijiazhuang *Town* China 175 M8
Shikoku *Island* Japan 185 D11
Shinano *River* Japan 185 G8
Shiraz *Town* Iran 153 G6
Shkhara *Mountain* Georgia 119 O12
Sholapur *Town* India 167 E9
Shreveport *Town* Louisiana, USA 35 J10
Shumen *Town* Bulgaria 127 J10
Siauliai *Town* Lithuania 109 F7
Siberia *Region* Russian Federation 10 J3, 133 K5, 139 M7
Sibiu *Town* Romania 127 G7
Sicily *Island* Italy 78 G13, 103 G13
Sidi Bel Abbès *Town* Algeria 209 J2
Siena *Town* Italy 103 E6
Sierra Leone *Country* W. Africa 18 A8, 220 D10
Sierra Madre Del Sur *Mountain range* Mexico 39 G9
Sierra Madre Occidental *Mountain range* Mexico 21 J11, 39 D5
Sierra Madre Oriental *Mountain range* Mexico 11 T7, 21 J11, 39 F5
Sierra Nevada *Mountain range* California, USA 33 G9
Sierra Nevada *Mountain range* Spain 78 C12, 100 F8
Silesia *Region* Czech Republic/Poland 113 F6
Simferopol' *Town* Ukraine 119 I10
Simpson Desert Northern Territory/ South Australia, Australia 254 D11, 259 H8
Sinai Desert Egypt 147 C11, 215 E2
Sincelejo *Town* Colombia 59 D1
Sindh *Region* Pakistan 167 B5
Singapore *Country* S.E. Asia 18 J9, 189 G16
Sinuiju *Town* North Korea 175 P7
Sioux Falls *Town* South Dakota, USA 35 I4
Sistan, Lake Iran 153 J6
Sittwe *Town* Burma 189 A5
Sivas *Town* Turkey 145 G6
Skagerrak *Channel* Denmark/Norway 78 F7, 82 K10
Skiáthos *Island* Greece 131 F6
Skiros *Island* Greece 131 G6
Skopje *Town* Macedonia 123 J10
Skye *Island* UK 87 H4
Slavonski Brod *Town* Croatia 123 F5
Sliven *Town* Bulgaria 127 I11
Slovakia *Country* Central Europe 18 D4, 113 H9
Slovenia *Country* S.E. Europe 18 C5, 123 B3
Smederevo *Town* Serbia, Yugoslavia 123 J6
Smolensk *Town* Russian Federation 138 C5
Snake *River* Washington/Idaho, USA 21 I9, 33 H5
Society Islands French Polynesia, Pacific Ocean 11 P10, 255 P9, 265 G7
Socotra *Island* Yemen 133 E13, 203 E3
Sofia *Town* Bulgaria 127 F11

Sohâg *Town* Egypt 215 E3
Solomon Islands *Country* Pacific Ocean 10 M9, 19 N10, 255 J7, 265 D6
Solway Firth *Gulf* UK 87 I7
Somalia *Country* E. Africa 18 F8, 215 J10
Somme *River* France 97 F2
Songkhla *Town* Thailand 189 E13
Sonoran Desert Arizona, USA/Mexico 11 T6, 21 I10, 33 J12, 39 A1
Sosnowiec *Town* Poland 113 H7
South Africa *Country* Southern Africa 18 D11, 247 F9
South America *Continent* 11 W9, 41
South Australia *State* Australia 259 H9
South Bend *Town* Indiana, USA 37 D5
South Carolina *State* USA 37 F9
South China Sea 10 J7, 133 K13, 189 H12
South Dakota *State* USA 35 G4
South East Cape Tasmania 10 L13, 254 F15, 259 K13
South Georgia *Island group* Atlantic Ocean 77 G12
South Island New Zealand 255 J14, 262 B11
South Korea *Country* S.E. Asia 18 K6, 175 Q8
South Orkney Islands Pacific Ocean 77 F12, 269 B1
South Polar Plateau *Region* Antarctica 269 G5
South Pole Antarctica 269 F5
South Sandwich Islands *Dependent territory* Atlantic Ocean 77 G12
South Shetland Islands Atlantic Ocean 77 E12, 269 A1
Southampton *Town* UK 87 J11
Southeast Indian Ridge Indian Ocean 203 J10
Southend-on-Sea *Town* UK 87 K11
Southern Alps *Mountain range* New Zealand 255 J15, 262 C9
Southern Ocean 265 G10, 269 G1, F9
Southwest Indian Ridge Indian Ocean 203 E9
Soweto *Town* South Africa 247 H9
Spain *Country* Europe 18 B5, 100 E5
Spitsbergen *Island* Norway 267 G8
Split *Town* Croatia 123 D7
Spokane *Town* Washington, USA 33 H4
Sporades *Island group* Greece 131 F5
Springfield *Town* Illinois, USA 37 C6
Springfield *Town* Missouri, USA 35 K8
Srebrenica *Town* Bosnia and Herzegovina 123 H7
Sri Lanka *Country* S. Asia 10 H8, 18 H8, 133 G14, 167 F13
Srinagar *Town* India 167 E2
Stanley, Mt. Zaire 232 K11
Stanovoy Range *Mountain range* Russian Federation 133 K6, 139 N9
Stara Zagora *Town* Bulgaria 127 H12
Stavanger *Town* Norway 82 D9
Stewart Island *New Zealand* 255 J15, 262 B12
Stockholm *Town* Sweden 82 H9
Stockton *Town* California, USA 33 G10
Stoke-on-Trent *Town* UK 87 J9
Stonington Island Antarctica 269 B4
Strasbourg *Town* France 97 J3
Stratford-upon-Avon *Town* UK 87 J10
Stromboli *Volcano* Lipari Islands, Italy 103 H11
Stuttgart *Town* Germany 95 F10
Subotica *Town* Serbia, Yugoslavia 123 H3
Suceava *Town* Romania 127 I4
Sucre *Town* Bolivia 59 G11
Sudan *Country* N.E. Africa 18 D7, 215 D6
Sudd *Region* Sudan 215 D9

Sudeten Mountains Czech Republic/ Poland 113 F7
Suez *Town* Egypt 203 C1, 215 E1
Suez Canal Egypt 203 C1, 215 E1
Suez, Gulf of Egypt 147 C11, 215 E2
Sumatra *Island* Indonesia 10 I9, 133 J15, 196 C8
Sumbawa *Island* Indonesia 196 J12
Sumy *Town* Ukraine 119 I4
Sun City *Tourist resort* South Africa 247 G8
Superior, Lake Canada/USA 21 L8, 29 D8, 37 D2
Surabaya *Town* Java, Indonesia 196 H12
Surat *Town* India 167 D7
Surinam *Country* S. America 19 W8, 59 J3
Suzhou *Town* China 175 O11
Svalbard *Island group* Arctic Ocean 10 C1, 18 C1, 267 G7
Swabian Jura *Mountain range* Germany 95 F11
Swansea *Town* UK 87 H10
Swaziland *Country* Southern Africa 18 E11, 247 I9
Sweden *Country* Europe 18 C3, 82 G7
Switzerland *Country* Europe 18 C5, 106 D8
Sydney *Town* New South Wales, Australia 259 L10, 265 C8
Syracuse *Town* New York, USA 37 H4
Syria *Country* S.W. Asia 18 E6, 147 I4
Syrian Desert S.W. Asia 10 E6, 132 C10, 147 H6, 153 D5

T

Ta'if *Town* Saudi Arabia 153 B9
Ta'izz *Town* Yemen 153 C12
Table Mt. South Africa 247 E12
Tabora *Town* Tanzania 239 G8
Tabriz *Town* Iran 153 F3
Tacloban *Town* Philippines 196 L4
Tacna *Town* Peru 59 E10
Tacoma *Town* Washington, USA 33 F4
Taegu *Town* South Korea 175 Q8
Tagus *River* Spain/Portugal 78 C12, 100 C5, E5
Tahiti *Island* French Polynesia, Pacific Ocean 11 Q10, 255 P9, 265 G7
Tahoe, Lake California/Nevada, USA 33 G9
Tai'an *Town* China 175 N9
Taipei *Town* Taiwan 175 P13
Taiping *Town* Malaysia 189 E14
Taiwan *Country* E. Asia 18 K7, 133 L11, 175 P13, 265 A4
Taiyuan *Town* China 175 L8
Tajikistan *Country* Central Asia 18 GS, 161 G7
Tajumulco *Mountain* Guatemala 44 A8
Takla Makan *Desert* China 10 H5, 133 G9, 174 C8
Talca *Town* Chile 71 F9
Tallahassee *Town* Florida, USA 37 E11
Tallinn *Town* Estonia 109 H3
Tamale *Town* Ghana 221 I10
Tampa *Town* Florida, USA 37 F12
Tampere *Town* Finland 82 J8
Tana, Lake Ethiopia 215 G8
Tanami Desert Australia 254 D9
Tanga *Town* Tanzania 239 K8
Tanganyika, Lake Central Africa 10 E9, 205 I9, 232 K12, 239 F8
Tanggula Mts. China 175 F11
Tangier *Town* Morocco 208 H2
Tangshan *Town* China 175 N8
Tanjungkarang *Town* Sumatra,

Indonesia 196 E11
Tanta *Town* Egypt 215 D1
Tanzania *Country* Africa 18 E9, 239 H8
Taranto *Town* Italy 103 J9
Târgoviste *Town* Romania 127 H8
Târgu Mure *Town* Romania 127 G6
Tarragona *Town* Spain 100 J4
Tartu *Town* Estonia 109 I4
Tashkent *Town* Uzbekistan 161 G6
Tasman Sea Australia/New Zealand 10 M12, 255 I13, 262 D6, 265 D8
Tasmania *Island/State* Australia 254 F14, 259 K13
Tassili n'Ajjer *Mountain range* Algeria 205 E3, 209 M7
Tatar Strait Russian Federation 139 S9
Taunggyi *Town* Burma 189 D5
Taupo *Town* New Zealand 262 G5
Taupo, Lake New Zealand 262 G5
Tauranga *Town* New Zealand 262 G4
Taurus Mts. Turkey 10 E5, 145 E8
Tavoy *Town* Burma 189 D9
Taymyr Peninsula Russian Federation 133 I2, 139 K4, 267 I5
Tbilisi *Town* Georgia 119 P13
Te Anau, Lake New Zealand 262 B10
Tegucigalpa *Town* Honduras 44 D10
Tehran *Town* Iran 153 H4
Tel Aviv-Yafo *Town* Israel 147 E7
Tema *Town* Ghana 221 J12
Temuco *Town* Chile 71 F10
Tennessee *State* USA 37 D8
Tenochtitlán *see* Mexico City
Teotihuacán *Ancient site* Mexico 39 G8
Teresina *Town* Brazil 67 J4
Ternopil' *Town* Ukraine 118 C5
Tétovan *Town* Morocco 208 H2
Tetovo *Town* Macedonia 123 J10
Texas *State* USA 35 H11
Texcoco, Lake Mexico 39 G8
Thabana-Ntlenyana, Mt. Lesotho 247 H10
Thai Nguyen *Town* Vietnam 189 H5
Thailand *Country* S.E. Asia 18 I7, 189 F8
Thailand, Gulf of 10 I8, 189 E10
Thames *River* UK 78 D9, 87 J11
Thames *Town* New Zealand 262 G3
Thane *Town* India 167 D8
Thanh Hoa *Town* Vietnam 189 H6
Thar Desert India/Pakistan 10 G6, 133 G11, 167 C5
Tharthar, Lake Iraq 153 E4
Thasos *Island* Greece 131 G3
Thaton *Town* Burma 189 D7
The Hague *Town* Netherlands 91 G6
Thessaloniki *Town* Greece 131 E3
Thimphu *Town* Bhutan 167 J5
Thunder Bay *Town* Ontario, Canada 29 E7
Thuringian Forest *Region* Germany 95 H7
Tianjin *Town* China 175 N8
Tiber *River* Italy 103 F7
Tiberias, Lake Israel 149 E6
Tibesti *Mountain range* Chad/Libya 232 G3
Tibet, Plateau of Asia 10 H6, 133 H10
Tibetan Autonomous Region China 174 D10
Tien Shan *Mountain range* Kyrgyzstan/ China 10 H5, 133 H8, 161 I6, 174 C7
Tierra del Fuego *Island* Argentina/ Chile 41 F16, 71 H16
Tigris *River* S.W. Asia 132 C10, 145 I7, 153 E3
Tijuana *Town* Mexico 39 A1
Tikal *Ancient site* Guatemala 44 C7
Tilburg *Town* Netherlands 91 H8
Timaru *Town* New Zealand 262 D10
Timbuktu *Town* Mali 221 H7

Timisoara *Town* Romania 127 D7
Timor *Island* Indonesia 133 L16, 196 M12
Timor Sea Australia/Indonesia 10 K10, 197 N13, 254 C8
Tirana *Town* Albania 123 H11
Tisza *River* Hungary 78 H10
Titicaca, Lake Bolivia/Peru 11 W10, 41 F8, 59 F10
Toamasina *Town* Madagascar 203 E7
Toba *Volcanic Crater* Sumatra, Indonesia 196 B8
Togo *Country* W. Africa 18 C8, 221 J11
Tokelau *Dependent territory* Polynesia, Pacific Ocean 19 P9, 255 M7, 265 E6
Tokyo *Town* Japan 185 H9, 265 B3
Tol'yatti *Town* Russian Federation 138 D7
Toledo *Town* Ohio, USA 37 E5
Toledo *Town* Spain 100 F5
Tomsk *Town* Russian Federation 139 J9
Tonga *Country* Polynesia, Pacific Ocean 11 O10, 19 O10, 255 M9, 265 E7
Tongking, Gulf of China/Vietnam 175 L15
Tónlé Sap *Lake* Cambodia 189 G10
Topeka *Town* Kansas, USA 35 J7
Torkestan Mts. Afghanistan 161 F9
Toronto *Town* Ontario, Canada 29 F9
Torres Strait *Channel* Australia/Papua New Guinea 259 J3
Toulouse *Town* France 97 F9
Townsville *Town* Queensland, Australia 259 L6
Trabzon *Town* Turkey 145 I5
Transantarctic Mts. Antarctica 269 F6
Transvaal *Region* South Africa 247 H8
Transylvania *Region* Romania 127 F6
Trenton *Town* New Jersey, USA 37 I6
Trier *Town* Germany 95 D8
Trieste *Town* Italy 103 G3
Triglav *Mountain* Slovenia 123 A2
Trinidad and Tobago *Country* Caribbean Sea 19 W8, 45 U16
Trinidade *Island* Atlantic Ocean 19 Y10, 77 G9
Tripoli *Town* Lebanon 147 F4
Tripoli *Town* Libya 209 O4
Tristan Da Cunha *Dependent territory* Atlantic Ocean 10 A12, 18 B12, 77 H10
Trivandrum *Town* India 167 E12
Tromsø *Town* Norway 82 I2
Trondheim *Town* Norway 82 F6
Tropic of Cancer 11 Z7
Tropic of Capricorn 11 Y11
Troy *Ancient site* Turkey 145 A6
Trujillo *Town* Peru 59 C7
Tuamotu *Island group* French Polynesia, Pacific Ocean 11 Q10, 255 Q8
Tubuai Islands French Polynesia, Pacific Ocean 11 Q11, 255 P10
Tucson *Town* Arizona, USA 33 K13
Tula *Town* Russian Federation 138 C5
Tulsa *Town* Oklahoma, USA 35 I8
Tunis *Town* Tunisia 209 N2
Tunisia *Country* N. Africa 18 C6, 209 N3
Turin *Town* Italy 103 B4
Turkana, Lake Ethiopia/Kenya 205 J7, 215 F11, 239 I3
Turkey *Country* W. Asia 18 E5, 145 E6
Turkmenistan *Country* Central Asia 18 F5, 161 D7
Turks and Caicos Islands *Dependent territory* West Indies 45 P8
Turku *Town* Finland 82 I8
Tuscany *Region* Italy 103 D6
Tuvalu *Country* Pacific Ocean 11 N9, 19 O9, 255 L7, 265 E6
Tuzla *Town* Bosnia and Herzegovina

INDEX

PICTURE SOURCES

The publisher would like to thank the following for their kind permission to reproduce the photographs.

t = top, b = bottom, c = centre, l = left, r= right

Allsport: Shaun Botterill 253tr, 257bc, Clive Brunskill 96tr, 242bc, Adrian Murrell 56tr, Pascal Rondeao 28tr.

Ancient Art & Architecture collection: 181tr.

Andes Press Agency: Carlos Reynes Manzo 66cr.

Art Directors: 71cl.

Asia Images: John Molloy 188tc.

Bridgeman Art Library: By courtesy of the board of trustees of the V&A 155br.

British Antarctic Survey: R. Mulvaney 268c.

Camera Press: 64br, 154cl, 146tr, 168cr, Steve Benbow 199bc, Thierry Charlier 184c, David Rubinger 156tr.

J Allan Cash: 20bl, 75tr, 81tr, 96cla, 105br, 108clb, 108cr, 112ca, 124tr, 124cr, 144bl, 153br, 162bl, 195tl, 205clb, 219br, 220tc, 229bc, 230cr, 230br, 231c.

Lester Cheeseman: 171bl, 172cl.

Churches Ministry Among the Jews: 150cb.

Stephanie Colasanti: 103br, 104cra.

Bruce Coleman: 53tr, 184cr, 239tl, 268br, Thomas Buchholz 81bc, 83clb, R. Campbell 206cl, Rob P. Carr 20bc, Brian J. Coates 197tl, 254cl, Alain Compost 133br, Raimund Cramm 21br, Gerald Cubitt 248cr, 250tr, Peter Davey 243tr, Keith Gunnor 63bl, Udo Hirsch 64cr, Harold Lange 24br, 94cr, Luiz Claudio Marigo 40bl, 69br, John Murray 204clb, Dr. Norman Myers 46bl, 228c, Carl Roessler 258bl, Jan Taylor 258cla.

Collections: Liba Taylor 88tr.

Colorific: Linda Bartlett 36cl, 122tr, M. Clark 90tr, Matrix /Robert Caputo 237cb /Sarah Leen 19tl, Claus Meyer 68clb, Kay Muldoon 219tr, Francois Perri 234tr, /Black Star: Peter Turnley 121tr, 121br.

Comstock: John Bulmer 61tr, Georg Gerster 2tl, 223tr.

Michael Copsey: 36tr, 37bc.

Corbis-Bettmann / Reuter: 271tr; /UPI: 228tr.

James Davis Travel Photography: 50tr, 57cr, 81tl, 100cb, 101tr, 101crb, 105tr, 124crb, 132cl, 132br, 140tr, 158bl, 260c, 262tr; **Ecoscene:** Joel Creed 71cla.

Empics: Stellan Danielsson 48br.

Environmental Picture Library: Bob Edwards 141cla.

European Space Agency: 61bl.

Mary Evans Picture Library: 50cr, 65tr, 260 tr.

Eye Ubiquitous: David Cummings 101clb, 112cl, 138cb, 140br, Patrick Field 186cl, Steve Lindridge 91 bl, Steve Miller 70tr, Kevin Wilton 89cl.

Ffotograff: Charles Aithie 152tr, Patricia Aithie 159tr.

Martyn Foote: 256tr, 258ca, 258c, 260cl

Frederick Foster: 26cb.

Sir Norman Foster and Partners: Ian Lambot 179tr.

Gambian Experience Magazine: 224bc.

Greenpeace: Green 256br, Morgan 264br.

Sonia Halliday Photography: T.C. Rising 134tr, 144tr.

Robert Harding Picture Library: 22tc, 23cla, 26cr, 28cr, 33cl, 42cb, 49bl, 57tl, 60cr, 74bl, 81crb, 85bl, 89cb, 92c, 98cl, 99cb, 102bl, 104crb, 110crb, 123br, 128tr, 129tr, 132cb, 142cr, 144cr, 147bc, 154cr, 155tl, 155bl, 163bl, 165cb, 170tr, 172 cr, 174cl, 179br, 183bc, 185bc, 190tr, 190c, 195cb, 198tr, 198cl, 198bl, 203bc, 207clb, 208ca, 209tr, 220bc, 222tr, 223cra, 225c, 227clb, 230tr, 242tr, 245tr, 248bl, 249tr, 253bc, 267cb, 275bc, 279bl, 280bc, Felix. A, 219cr, J.R. Ashford 63tr, C. Bowman 73cl, Jeremy Bright 105ca, G. Corrigan 177br, Rob Cousins 23tc, Mula Eshet 276bl, Alain Evrard 191cb, 201cl, 201crb, Robert Francis 151clb, Odyssey, Chicago / Robert Frerck 23tr, Robert Frerck 38tr, K. Gillingham 51cl, Gavin Hellier 117cr, Wally Herbert 86tr, Paulo Koch 149bl, 176cr, David Lomax 22br, 275cra, C. Martin 95br, Duncan Maxwell 171tl, Robert McLeod 194tr, H.P. Merten 95bl, Louise Murray 129crb, Gary Norman 61ca, Roy Rainford 93tr, Geoff Renner 204tr, 246cb, Christopher Rennie 141cr, Riffet 233cb, John G. Ross 70br, Sassoon 121ca, E. Simanor 148bl, James Strachan 47c, Luca Invernizzi Tettoni 189br, 190br, 198cr, Adam Woolfitt 31cl, 62br, 76bl, 79tr, 79 br, 127bl, 129cl, 216tr, Earl Young 47 cr, 114crb.

Holt Studios International: 214tr, Mary Cherry 229cl, Inga Spence 32bc, 51br.

Jeremy Horner: 62cr, 62bl.

Hulton / Getty: /Reuter 252tr, 268bl.

Hutchison Library: 17br, 29clb, 52 cla, 58tl, 68bc, 157cr, 162cr, 164cl, 164bl, 165tr, 172tr, 210 bl, 214cl, 214cr, 217ca, 217cl, 226crb, 226bl, 228clb, 234cla, 236cr, 247br, 249bl, Robert Aberman 144cl, 250cr, Christina Dodwell 142tc, John G. Egan 138clb, Sarah Errington 17tl, 55tr, 235tr, 237bl, Andrew Evans 130bl, Robert Francis 73br, Norman Froggatt 113 bl, Réne-Nicolas Guidicelli 179ca, Maurice Harvey 227cr, 245cr, John Hatt 148tr, Jeremy Horner 62tl, Chris Johnson 229tr, R.Ian Lloyd 188bl, 191tr, M. Macintyre 201cr, Brian Moser 65br, 193bl, B. Régent 227tr, P.W.Rippon 155cl, Trevor Page 219cla, Christine Pemberton 178tl, Stephen Pern 43cr, 70bl, 156cl, 240tr, Bernard Régent 202bc, 236cla, Kerstin Rodgers 65bl, T. Souter 150br, Liba Taylor 116c, Isabella Tree 259cr, Anna Tully 48tr, 230clb, Philip Wolmuth 54bl, 55bl.

ICCE: Robert Carlson 50bl, Glyn Davies 197tr

The Image Bank: 93br, 111tr, 180bl, 194bl, Luis Casteneda 72bl, 274bl, Michael Coyne 259br, L.D. Gordon 39cb, Burton Mc Neely 32cr, Morrin E. Newman 36cr, Terje Rakke 83tr, J. Schmitt 38cr.

Images Colour Library: 98br, 106bl /AGE Fotostock: 101cr, 108tr.

Impact: Christophe Bluntzer 164tr, Mark Cator 114tr, Piers Cavendish 49cr, 76cr, 146bl /Clic Clap 45tc, Anthony Coleman 116bl, 120cb, Sergio Doranles 39bl, Alain Evrard 136bl, Pilar Fernandez 37crb, Alain Le Garsmeur 49c, 49tr,53cl, 114c, Robert Gibbs 42clb, Philip Gordon 182tr, 277bl, Mark Henley Back cover cb, 2cb, 107br, 137cl, 192br, 195cl, Erol Houssein 126bl, VISA / H. Hughes 74tr, Javed A. Jaffererji 136tr, Colin Jones 21bl, 51cb, 204cr, Alan Keohane 14bc, Geraint Lewis 112tr, M. Milivojevic 117cla, Guy Moberly 279tl, Moradabadi 137tc, 155cr, Vitaly Orlot 161br, Gary Parker 243bl, Caroline Penn 158tr, 213tr, 240cr, Christopher Pillitz 70cr, David Reed 225cr, 225tr, Ray Roberts 85tr, Jaqui Spector 279cr, James Willis 157trb.

International Coffee Organisation: 66cb.

Japan Information and Cultural Centre: 184tr.

John R. Jones: 159c̀b, 188cra, 189tr, 192cl, 193tl, 193cr.

Katz: Rea Bellavia 180tr, Boisseaux-Chical 223bl, Bruno Hadjih 72cr, Randy G. Taylor 53br.

Roger Kohn: 75cra; **Korean Tourist Office:** 183bl.

Magnum Photos: Bruno Barbey 236tr, Steve McCurry 99cl.

National Cotton Council: 36crb.

Nature Photographers: Andrew Cleave 266cla.

Network: Homer Sykes 154c.

New Zealand Tourist Board: 263tl.

NHPA: Hellio and Van Ingen 132tc.

Novosti: 162tr, 162crb.

Christine Osborne Pictures: 148bc.

Oxford Scientific Films: Johnny Johnson 26crb.

Panos: M. Adler 235crb, 235bl, Trygve Bolstad 166bl, 251tr, Katri Burri 217tr, Neil Cooper 169tr, 169bl, 218tr, Jean-Léo Dugast 135clb,191cl, Mark Mc Evoy 149c, Alain le Garsmeur 137bl, 173bl, 178bl, Ron Giling 200cr, 200br, 222crb, Jeremy Hartley 113br, 160tr, 207tr, 226tr, 224cr, Chris Johnson 251c, Rhodri Jones 119tc, Barbara Klass 169cr, Jon Levy 276br, N.Durrell McKenna 73bl, Heldur Netocny 272tc, Micheal J O'Brien 120tr, Trevor Page 163cr, Bruce Paton 231bl, 246bl, 251bl, Betty Press 207cr, 241tr, 241c, Dominic Sansoni 202tr, Paul Smith 47tr, 251cr, Jon Spaull 136bc, Sean Sprague 48bl, 66tc, 128bl, 143cb, 218cr, 234bl, 241crb, Chris Stowers 144ca, 168bc, 170br, Penny Tweedie 208bl, 210bc, 244c, 244cra, 260cr, Philip Wolmuth 281bl, 68c.

Performance Arts Library: Clive Barda 88cr.

Pictor International Ltd: 23bl, 24tr, 25cb, 36bl, 41clb, 54c, 56cr, 56br, 59cr, 67bl, 68tr, 74br, 76br, 81c, 84tr, 93bc, 114cb, 116br, 117tr, 122bl, 129c, 130cr, 135br, 137tr, 186tr, 186bl, 190cb, 206br, 207cr, 209tl, 210tr, 212crb, 227br, 238bl, 243cl, 264bl, 268tr.

Pictures Colour Library: 25br, 52tr, 52bl, 58br, 60tr, 168tr, 246cla.

Planet Earth Pictures: Andre Bartschi 43tl, Dave Lyons 78tc, Nigel Tucker 47br.

Popperfoto: 152cb/ EPA: 48cb.

Zev Radovan: 146br.

Railway Gazette: 248c.

Rex Features Ltd.: 31cl, 75cla, 94tr, 119bl, 122cr, 125bl, 125br, 126c, 183cr, 200c, 213cra, 213cl, 244bc, 247bc, 270bc, 273cr, Argas 182br, Evrard 201tc, David Frazier 54br, Basile Grigorie 141tr, Tom Haley 122br, 125tr, Sylvain Julienne 117cb, Charles Knight 270tr, Juhan Kuus 246tr, Laine 121cr, Laski 119cr, Anatoly Lolis 139bl, V. Miladinovic 137cr, Tim Rooke 252tr, S. Tazana 13clb, Today 140bl, 152br.

Royal Geographical Society: Chris Caldicott 223cl, Sitting Images /David Constantine 193cl, Ian McWilliam 168c.

Peter Saunders Photography: 156c, 157 br, 158cl, 243bc.

Science Photo Library: Gregory Dimijian 14cr, Simon Fraser 13tc, Martin Land 13br, Peter Menzel 17cr, Dr. David Miller 268cra, Micheal Morten 79cr, David Parker 13cr.

ILLUSTRATORS

ACKNOWLEDGEMENTS

Additional editorial assistance:
Bernadette Crowley, Christiane Gunzi, Terry Martin

Additional design assistance: Diane Clouting

Index and gazetteer: Lynn Bresler

Additional picture research: Giselle Harvey

Additional DTP assistance: Nicky Studdart

Film outputting: Brightside, London

**Dorling Kindersley would like to thank the following people and organizations
for their help in the production of this book.**

Action Aid; The Algerian Embassy, London; The Arab British Centre, London; The
Argentinian Embassy, London; The Australian High Commission, London; The Australian
Tourist Commission, London; BP Exploration, London; The Belguim Embassy, London;
The Brazilian Embassy, London; Bridgestone Corporation, Belgium; British Airways
Holidays, West Sussex; The British Consulate General, Rio De Janeiro; The British Embassy,
Argentina; The British Embassy, Philippines; The British Museum Education Service,
London; The Bulgarian Embassy, London; C. P. Rail System, Montreal, Canada; Chamber
of Mines of South Africa, Johannesburg, South Africa; China National Tourist
Administration, London; Coal World Magazine; The Coffee Museum, London; Cotton
Council International, London; The Council for the Advancement of Arab-British
Understanding, London; Cyprus Olive Products, Cyprus; The Cyprus Tourist Board,
London; The Danish Embassy, London; De Beers, London; The Embassy of Ecuador,
London; The Embassy of Jordan, London; The Embassy of Mexico, London; The Embassy
of the Republic of Estonia, London; The Embassy of the Republic of Yemen, London; The
Embassy of the Syrian Arab Republic, London; Farmers Weekly; The Financial Times,
London; The Finnish Embassy, London; The Football Association, London; Sir Norman
Foster and Partners, London; Fyffes Group Ireland Ltd; Joss Graham; I. Hennig and Co
Ltd, London; Hong Kong Government Office, London; The Indonesian Trade Centre,
London; Institute of Civil Engineers, London; International Cocoa Organisation, London;
International Coffee Organisation, London; International Cotton Advisory Committee,
Washington, USA; Israeli Government Tourist Board, London; The Jordan Information
Bureau, London; Kew Gardens, London; Kibbutz Representatives, London; The Latvian
Embassy, London; The Lithuanian Embassy, London; The Luxembourg Embassy, London;
The Macau Tourist Information Bureau, London; The Malaysian Rubber Research and
Development Board; Menelik Restaurant, London; The Ministry of Agriculture, Grenada;
The Ministry of Tourism, Mexico; The Moroccan Embassy, London; Moss and Co, Timber
Importers, London; The Museum of Mankind, London; The National Cotton Council of
America, Memphis, USA; Neal Street East, London; Northern Territory House, London;
The Royal Norweigan Embassy, London; Oxfam, Oxford; Pilsner Urquell, Czech Republic;
Portuguese Trade and Tourism Office, London; The Queensland Tourist and Travel
Corporation, London; Railway Gazette International; The Romanian Embassy, London;
The School of African and Oriental Studies, University of London; Science Museum
Library, London; The Swedish Embassy, London; The Swiss Embassy, London; The Taipei
Representative's Office, London; The Trade Delegation of the Russian Federation in the
United Kingdom; The Tunisian Embassy, London; The Turkish Information Office,
London; Marion Turnock; Joan Twelves; UNICEF, Kampala; United Nations High
Commissioner for Refugees, London; Valley of the Kings Restaurant, London;
Wine and Spirit Education Trust, London.